CONTENTS

HISTORY OF
AVIATION

This picture is half a century younger than a first glance might suggest, for it was taken in 1969 and shows a replica of the German Fokker E III monoplane built by Mr. Doug Bianchi for the film *Crooks and Coronets.* The original Fokker Eindecker, the first fighting aircraft to have a synchronised front-firing machine-gun, was the scourge of Allied airmen on the Western Front in 1915-16.

HISTORY OF
AVIATION

John W R Taylor and Kenneth Munson

NEW ENGLISH LIBRARY

**Previous page. The first Canadian Avro Arrow
CF-105 which made its maiden flight in 1958. The
design and development of this supersonic delta-
winged interceptor was the largest programme
ever undertaken by the Canadian aircraft industry**

Printed and bound in Italy, by Fratelli Spada, Ciampino, Rome.

S.B.N 450 02146 7

INTRODUCTION

Human flight is the supreme achievement of our twentieth century. There are rivals to that claim. Nuclear energy, radio, television, satellites, advances in medicine and in a dozen other sciences have all brought great changes in the lives of men and women; but the ability to fly is more than a material gain, crude though it is by comparison with the flight of birds.

The earliest records of human thought and experience cry out for 'the wings of a dove' to bring escape in times of despair. There is a freedom in the flight of a bird that no human experience can match. The men who first dreamed of flying, and jumped to their death from high places, vainly flapping their home-made feathered wings, sought a kind of flight that few have known, even today.

Instead of the wheeling, soaring, boundless freedom of a bird, our flying in the 'seventies amounts to squeezing ourselves, like specks of toothpaste, into a hermetically-sealed tube and then roaring headlong into the almost airless fringe of the atmosphere on inadequate wings, pumping out smoke and fumes from deafening engines, until we can make an equally precipitous descent at our destination. The air-conditioning, armchair seats, prefabricated meals, in-flight entertainment and smiles of the stewardesses help to make it bearable; but how far it is from the dreams of the pioneers.

What we have, of course, is air transportation rather than flying. It is a public service that may not be altogether delightful; but our world would be infinitely poorer without it. Air transportation, in its myriad forms, means that no two people in the world need be more than a day or two apart. It takes millions of ordinary people on holiday flights to extraordinary places each year, at a cost which is almost unbelievably small. It brings us letters from the other side of the globe within two days. In different, utilitarian forms, it saves our vital crops by protecting them from disease, our tempers by sorting out traffic jams from the air, and our lives by plucking us to safety from a shipwreck or whisking us quickly to the very doorway of a hospital in an emergency.

The aeroplane is not only a long metal tube containing hundreds of seats. It is a graceful sailplane, a helicopter, a tiny racer, a time-saver for busy businessmen, an ambulance with wings, a farm implement, a postman, a vehicle to take the most venturesome literally out of this world, into space. It has made warfare infinitely more terrifying and destructive. In doing so, paradoxically, it has made major war no longer practicable as an extension of politics.

All of this has happened within the span of man's own 'three score years and ten', for it is not yet seventy years since two American brothers made the first, hesitant, powered, almost controlled flights in a heavier-than-air aircraft. The length of their first undulating leap was much less than the wing span of a modern four-engined airliner, yet it was the most famous flight in history for it fulfilled the dreams of generations.

The story of man's attempts to fly go back so far that it is easy to forget that the whole story of its achievement, in practical terms, has been recorded within the lifetime of many now alive. Yet even this brief span presents unsolved, unsolvable questions for the historians.

On the day that this Introduction is being written, a copy of *Soviet Military Review* has arrived by post, claiming to tell the story of 'the flight of the first jet-propelled plane (which) opened a new stage in the development of aviation.' The date of its first flight is given as 'May 15 1942, when the Great Patriotic War was approaching its climax.' Yet the German Heinkel He 178 jet-plane had flown nearly three years earlier, on 27 August 1939. And what about Coanda's *turbo-propulseur* biplane of 1910? Was not that a jet? And didn't it fly?

We accept the December 1903 flights of the Wright brothers as being the first powered, controlled and sustained flights in history. Yet, earlier that same year, Karl Jatho had covered a greater distance in Germany than the first hop by Orville Wright. However one may feel about this, it cannot be denied that the American brothers were soon flying with confidence, to a degree that staggered and inspired other pioneers in every country. Theirs, truly, is the glory of being first—but every claim of that kind must be defined precisely if history is to have any meaning.

The Wrights were by no means first to leave the ground, even with confidence, in a heavier-than-air machine. Lilienthal had made some 2,500 flights in his beautiful gliders a decade earlier. The powered aeroplane of Felix du Temple had hopped, carrying a pilot, at Brest in 1873; and Sir George Cayley had floated his reluctant coachman across a Yorkshire valley in a glider twenty-one years before that.

For an earlier 'first' we must go back nearly two centuries, to 1783, when the Montgolfier brothers invented the hot-air balloon in France and first gave men the power to float on the wind. Or so it was thought until recently . . .

There had been suggestions of strange happenings in Lisbon at a much earlier date. One or two reference books even quoted contemporary documents seeming to suggest that a Brazilian-born priest named Bartolomeu de Gusmão had demonstrated some kind of flying device before King John V of Portugal in the year 1709.

The first parts of this book had already been written when one of Portugal's most eminent aviation historians was commissioned, with the co-operation of the British Petroleum Group, to make a thorough investigation of the experiments of Gusmão, by consulting the original documents. The result was one of the major recent discoveries in the history of flight, confirming that Gusmão, and not the Montgolfiers, had tested successfully the first model hot-air balloon. Here was a completely new starting point for the story of the practical conquest of the air, after the initial dreams and schemes of men like Roger Bacon in England and Leonardo da Vinci in Italy.

These two, more than any others, form the link between the 'birdmen' of antiquity and the first builders of balloons and gliders. Yet history may yet have great surprises in store for those who carry on the research.

Only since the end of the second World War has the true significance of Sir George Cayley's experiments been appreciated. Now Gusmão, too, receives in fuller measure the honour due to him, as does Karl Jatho. In contrast, the once-revered work of John Stringfellow is now regarded far less highly than that of his contemporary, William Henson. Claims once made for Richard Pearse of New Zealand have also been disputed, although no-one doubts that he was a gifted engineer who foreshadowed certain 'modern' STOL (short take-off and landing) techniques.

The truth about these pioneers was uncovered only by years of diligent research by people in many countries, based on what was already known and recorded. What may yet be discovered is beyond our imagining, though it is unlikely that we shall ever find a practical explanation for the legends concerning birdmen like King Bladud of Britain or the Greek heroes Daedalus and Icarus.

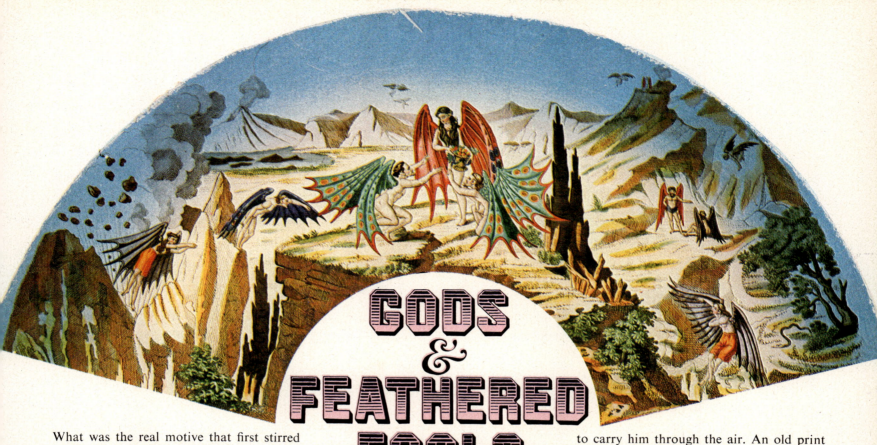

GODS & FEATHERED FOOLS

What was the real motive that first stirred man to dream of flying? Was it the desire for spiritual as well as physical elevation—to bring himself closer to the gods that he worshipped? Or was it simply envy—the oldest deadly sin of all—that made him strive to fly like the birds?

Even on the most mundane level it was natural that the sky should claim much of man's attention, for it was the source of the sunshine, wind and rain that governed his daily comfort and influenced the prosperity of his crops. Whatever the gods that he worshipped, they all dwelt "up there", for only from the heavens could they be all-seeing and direct the pattern of events upon the earth below. To the ancient Greek, it was perfectly natural to credit his gods with the power of flight—for how else could they descend from Mount Olympus? The Greek god Hermes, in particular, is always depicted wearing winged head-dress and sandals; while Swiatowid, a major god of the western Slav peoples, rode through the sky above his domains on a winged steed. Less successful was Phaethon, the son of Helios, the Greek sun-god, who tried to drive his father's fiery chariot across the skies. Unable to control the powerful horses, he is said to have flown so close to the earth that a part of it became scorched. So, says the legend, the Sahara desert was created.

This image of the winged object of worship repeats itself the world over, in the legends and folk stories of many nations; for man, unable to fly himself, regarded the ability to do so as proof of supernatural powers.

What, then, was he to make of the birds, which were essentially creatures of his own world yet also had the power of flight? The larger and more powerful birds of prey, like the eagle or the falcon, were frequently kept as pets by early kings and rulers, as symbols of their own power over their subjects. This led to interesting possibilities, and many centuries BC King Kai Kawus of Persia is said to have harnessed eagles to his throne

Top to bottom: Until he was able to fly himself, man endowed many of the beings of his supernatural and religious "other worlds" with the gift of wings.

Bladud, the British King who tried to fly. Father of Shakespeare's King Lear, he is said to have lived at the time of the prophet Elijah and to have ended his reign in a spectacular crash landing on the Temple of Apollo in what is now London

Model of one of Leonardo da Vinci's designs for a man-powered flapping-wing aircraft. The pilot was intended to operate the tail surfaces by moving his head, to which they were connected by a cable and head-band

to carry him through the air. An old print shows him clutching a bundle of arrows—giving him the dubious reputation of being the world's first-ever military pilot.

Oriental and Western folklore abounds with tales of magic carpets, witches on flying broomsticks, and other forms of aerial locomotion. A less common vehicle was the church door on which a priest from Cracow, in Poland, was reputed to have flown to Rome after entering into league with the Devil. In *A Thousand And One Nights*, one story tells how the sailor Sinbad escaped imprisonment on an island by tying himself to the leg of the great roc. This fabulous, gigantic bird of Oriental legend was said to feed its young upon elephants—an unwitting link, perhaps, with the "jumbo" transport aircraft of today! A much later tale, written in 1638 by Bishop Francis Godwin of Hereford, tells how his hero, Domingo Gonsales, trained a flock of geese to lift him to the Moon. The Polish nobleman and black magician Twardowski, riding on the back of a rooster, also reached the Moon—where, the story goes, he witnessed the successful landing of the first astronauts.

But man was not content for long to let birds do the work for him. Stories must have been handed down from the most primitive times of how the first birds of all, the pterodactyls, had evolved from earthbound, lizard-like creatures. When he reflected upon the great variety of birds that now inhabited the world, and how easy flying seemed to them, he must have felt that he, too, could learn to fly. True, he had not been born with wings, but he was by nature inventive. He was an artisan, and had already proved himself superior to all other living creatures. If he could build vehicles to transport himself over land and sea, it should not be difficult to construct artificially the means of flying. Thus appeared the first bird-men, both real and imaginary.

The best-known legend of all is that of Daedalus, the engineer who built the laby-

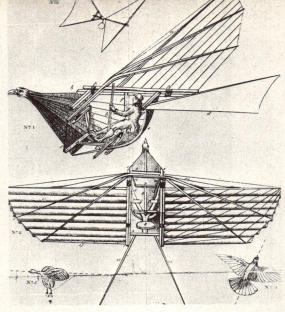

rinth on the island of Crete in which the Minotaur lived. With his son, Icarus, he was imprisoned by King Minos, but the captives escaped by making themselves wings of wax and feathers. With these Daedalus flew successfully all the way to Naples, but Icarus, excited by the thrill of the new experience of flying, let his youthful exuberance deafen him to his father's warning and flew too near to the sun, which melted the wax and sent the boy crashing to his death in the sea below.

Wayland the Smith, a wonder-worker of Norse mythology, was another early birdman. He made himself a winged garment of metal, with the aid of which he is said to have flown. Another with a reputation for wizardry was Bladud, ninth king of ancient Britain and father of Shakespeare's King Lear. Legend credits him with founding the city of Bath, where he is said to have created the hot springs by use of his magical powers. In the ninth century BC he made himself a set of wings with which, from the Temple

of Apollo in Trinavantum (London), he tried to fly over the city. But he, too, crashed and was killed. The 17th-century English poet John Taylor clearly felt that Bladud's attempt was ill-advised, declaring that: "On high the tempests have much power to wrecke; then best to bide beneath, and safest for the necke".

He was not the first—nor by any means the last—to voice such sentiments, but in spite of such discouragement history records many real as well as imaginary stories of would-be bird-men. G. B. Danti, an Italian scholar, tried to fly with home-made wings at Perugia in 1503, and was lucky to survive the attempt. Four years later John Damian, who planned to fly to France, instead "fell to the ground and brak his thee bane" (thigh bone) after jumping off the walls of Stirling Castle in Scotland. Miraculously, he survived, to attribute his failure to having used the feathers of chickens—which, he said, were "ground birds"—instead of eagle's feathers. Clearly he had never heard

of Count Twardowski!

Others who survived tower-jumping attempts included the English cleric Oliver of Malmesbury, whose feat is still remembered in the name of "The Flying Monk" inn there today. Another flying monk was Brother Cyprian, who is said to have glided down from the peak of a mountain in eastern Europe in 1780 using wings which he made himself. Several trips on home-made wings were also claimed for a Bohemian countryman named Fucík.

Among claims for successful flight which may well be true is that made for Hezarfen Celebi, a 17th-century Turk who is reputed to have launched himself from a tower in Galata, on the shores of the Bosphorus, and travelled several kilometres before landing safely in the market place at nearby Scutari. But on the whole, tower-jumping brought more deaths than disablements. Some six hundred years earlier a compatriot of Celebi, known only as "the Saracen of Constantinople", was certainly less fortunate in his

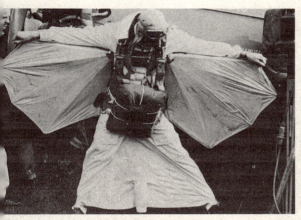

attempt. Instead of wings, he wore a voluminous stiffened cloak, but when one of its frames broke, the cloak collapsed, and he fell to the ground and was killed.

Not one of the early bird-men had realised —perhaps the truth was too unpalatable— that man's heavy, unstreamlined body is not built for the job of flying. His heart represents only 0.5 per cent of his total weight, whereas that of the golden eagle is over 8 per cent and that of the tiny hummingbird up to 22 per cent. Compared with man's normal heartbeat rate of 70 times a minute, even that of the sparrow throbs at a fantastic 800 times a minute in flight. These are essential features of a bird's high-revving engine, and a man would need a six-foot chest to hold all the muscles he would need to fly, even if his body had wings.

The limitations of human physiology in terms of the ability to fly were at last explained, in 1680, by the Italian Giovanni Borelli, whose *De Motu Animalium* went to some length to describe why man could never hope to sustain his own weight in the air without mechanical assistance. Even then the would-be bird-men were not entirely deterred, although their numbers did begin to diminish. In about 1742 the 62-year-old Marquis de Bacqueville tried to fly from the roof of a Paris hotel to the opposite bank of the river Seine, using four wing-like structures attached to his arms and legs. When halfway across, he fell into the river, striking a boat and breaking his leg.

Many flapping-wing designs appeared in later years. Two are credited to Titus Burattini, an Italian at the court of King Wladyslaw IV of Poland, and both are said to have lifted several feet off the ground. In 1784, a hundred years after Borelli's work appeared, a Frenchman named Gérard also designed a flapping-wing machine. It did not fly, but Gérard displayed remarkable foresight in giving it not only a "gunpowder motor" to flap the wings but a rudder for steering and a sprung landing gear. But by now the attention of the air-minded intelligentsia was focussed upon an alternative solution to the problem of flight—for, a year before Gérard's invention, the first successful ascents into the air had been made by an entirely different form of aerial locomotion —the hot-air balloon, the story of which begins on page 17.

We have mentioned only a few of the early would-be fliers. History is full of stories of men whose only successful flights were those of their own imaginations, and it would be easy for us, in this age of sophisticated technology, to scoff at their attempts as foolhardy efforts by ignorant men who knew no better. Yet many of them were among the most learned men of their times. Would we, with their knowledge, have fared any better? Would we even have had the courage to try? Do we forget that our own century has seen the exploits of latter-day bird-men like the American Clem Sohn or Frenchman Léo Valentin; and that our children still read with excitement the adventures of Batman who, after all, is only a present-day counterpart of Wayland the Smith or the flying Saracen. We watch displays by free-fall parachutists, who prove that with today's knowledge we can use thermal airstreams to help us glide through the air, within certain limits; and in the last decade several flights have been made in flimsy, paper-covered machines lifted into the air by human muscle-power with mechanical assistance—just as Borelli forecast several hundred years ago.

Kites

KITES HAVE PLAYED a long and honourable role in the history of technology. No plaything except the doll has had a longer period of unbroken popularity, and as a device for use by adults it has served a multitude of purposes over the centuries.

The origin of the kite is obscure, but it seems to have arisen in the Far East, probably in China. Although the first Chinese story of the invention of the kite tells of a wooden one built by Mo Tzu, for amusement only, the great majority of early Chinese accounts speak of kites as aids to warfare. In about 200 BC General Han Hsin used one to measure the distance to an enemy fortification; while in the 6th and 9th centuries AD kites were used for semaphore signals.

Marco Polo described a kite without really understanding what he was looking at, since kites were rare objects in mediaeval Europe and may have been totally unknown in Italy. Even if Marco Polo had known about kites, he might not have recognised the Chinese one, for what he saw was a giant square woven of withies, large enough to carry a man. Mariners used such kites to help them assess the chances of a successful voyage. If the manned kite flew straight, the omens were good; if it dipped to one side, putting the life of the flier in jeopardy, sailing on that day was unpropitious.

Kites of man-carrying proportions were, in fact, familiar in the east for centuries before the invention of the aeroplane. The Japanese have always been especially fond of building kites of immense size;

Top: One of the man-lifting kites designed by 'Colonel' S F Cody featured prominently in this portrait published by David Allen and Sons of Belfast in 1902. Cody went on to produce powered aircraft, in one of which he made the officially-recognised first flight in Britain on 16 October 1908. A copy of this poster-portrait fetched £65 at a London auction in 1971

Right: Lawrence Hargrave (left), perfector of the box-kite and greatest of Australia's early pioneers, measuring the lift of a kite with the aid of a spring balance in the 1890s

Below: Two Indian fighting kites. These kites, which may be flown without tails, can be made to manoeuvre very rapidly. Contests in which flyers attempt to sever one another's lines are popular throughout the east. A portion of the flying line near the kite is sharpened by passing it through a mixture of glue and powdered glass

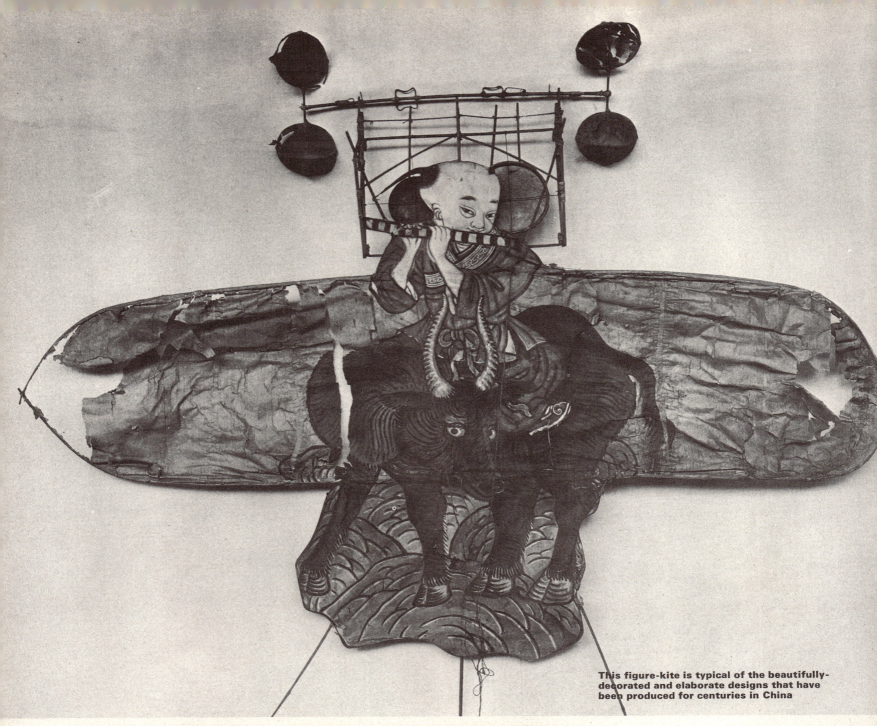

This figure-kite is typical of the beautifully-decorated and elaborate designs that have been produced for centuries in China

Left: A comparatively small figure-kite representing the Chinese phoenix

Below: S F Cody (right) at Farnborough with one of his early kites

Opposite page, top: Early 15th century pennon-kite. In 15th- and 16th-century Europe kites of this kind were flown by warriors on horseback

Centre: Expert users of the delta-shaped ski-kite have flown for hundreds of miles and risen more than 1,000 ft (305 m) into the air

Bottom: Drawing of a Japanese man-lifter of the 19th century

one, flown in 1906, weighed more than 6,000 lb (2,720 kg) and had a tail 480 ft (146 m) long. Man-carriers were used in the past for a great variety of purposes, including spying over enemy lines and landing soldiers in besieged cities.

Kites reached the west rather late, the first known European kite dating from 1326-27. This, like the early eastern kites, was apparently designed in the first place as an offensive weapon. It is shown, in a manuscript illustration, dropping a fire-bomb into enemy territory. Just as the eastern origins of the kite are shrouded in mystery, so it is not known at present how European kites began. They may possibly have been imported from the east, or they may have been quite independent inventions. Chinese kites, usually rectangular, with streamers for tails, seem to have spread into the Pacific and southeast Asian regions, but the European kites of the Middle Ages are significantly different in shape.

From the 14th to the 16th centuries European kites were elongated, pennon-shaped objects, built in the shape of dragons or serpents. They had rigid, rectangular heads, usually about 2 ft by 3 ft (60 by 90 cm) in size, with cloth tails of perhaps 15 ft (4.5 m) or more in length billowing out behind. These may have been free-flying developments of the dragon standard used by the cohorts of the Roman armies after the 2nd century AD, but this is far from certain. In any case the pennon-kites were never, so far as one can tell, of man-carrying size; and by the end of the 16th century European kites, now influenced by those brought back from the Indies by English, Dutch and Portuguese sailors, had dwindled to the proportions of the children's toy now familiar to everyone.

Despite this it is perhaps surprising that before the early 19th century no-one in Europe seriously contemplated using kites for man-carrying purposes. George Pocock, a Bristol school-teacher, made large arch-topped kites with which he pulled a horseless carriage across the countryside at speeds that astonished and sometimes frightened unprepared observers; with such kites he claims to have lifted his daughter Martha, later to become the mother of the great cricketer, W G Grace.

Even Pocock, however, did not think of kites as potential flying machines, and it was not until the end of the century that any serious study was made of their potentialities in this direction. Sir George Cayley used a kite for the wing of his delicate little glider of 1804, but it was the Australian Lawrence Hargrave who first took kites really seriously.

Hargrave made a multitude of kites before perfecting the simple and now familiar box-kite in 1893. Although during their early experiments the Wright brothers knew nothing of Hargrave and made no use of box-kite principles in their 'Flyers', Hargrave's design was incorporated, with modifications, into a great many early European aeroplanes and gliders, beginning with the Voisin-Archdeacon and Voisin-Blériot float-gliders of 1905.

The advent of the aeroplane by no means eclipsed the development of the kite, which continued to be used for a great variety of purposes. Ingenious systems for using kites in cases of shipwreck, many of them patented in the 19th century, were developed in sophisticated forms in the early decades of the 20th century. The box-kite was adopted by meteorologists as a comparatively cheap and effective way of raising instruments to heights of several miles. And during both World Wars kites were used from German U-boats as a means of raising men high enough to sight Allied shipping.

Two uses of kites in recent times deserve special mention. Even the Hargrave box-kite now looks clumsy and heavy beside the non-rigid or stickless kites which have been developed in America. One of these, the very fine Jalbert parafoil, takes the form of a cambered aerofoil, the upper and lower surfaces of which are of nylon cloth. The leading- and trailing-edges are open, and the kite is inflated by wind-pressure. (Vertical cloth members keep the surfaces flat.) This kite, which is of such remarkable efficiency that it can be made to fly almost vertically, has been used, among other things, for meteorological observations over mountain-tops.

An earlier design, still undergoing development, is the Rogallo flex-wing, which is fundamentally a delta-shaped parachute whose shroud lines are so adjusted as to keep the kite flying overhead. The Rogallo flex-wing has been used as the basis of a great many short-haul and STOL vehicles, and as a parachute-glider for dropping supplies.

Modern sophisticated toys have greatly lessened the popularity of kites among western children, but in contrast to this they have found increasing favour with adults. For example, kite-fishing, once known only in the Pacific and Indian Oceans, is now widely practised. The fisher flies a kite from which the baited line is suspended, thus enabling him both to fish in inaccessible places and to keep tell-tale human shadows away from the hook.

More popular still, of course, is the use of the kite in water-skiing. The towed gliders employed for this sport are usually rigid-framed developments of the Rogallo flex-wing. The daring feats of some of the fliers, and the occasional spectacular accidents, serve, more than any other use of the kite, to keep this age-old aeronautical object before the eyes of the public.

The enthusiasm of the amateur aircraft constructor for his home-built machine is well matched by the care which other enthusiasts lavish on re-creating exact replicas of historic aircraft. A modern reproduction of one of the earliest flying craft is this representation of the hot-air balloon made in the 18th century by Joseph and Etienne Montgolfier

Lighter than Air

Just as there were, in the earliest times, men who watched the birds and tried to emulate their flight, there were other dreamers who sought some magic substance that would enable them to defy gravity and soar into the sky. It is almost certain that this train of thought began far later than the desire to fit on a pair of wings. The birds were there for all to see, whereas the magic substance was only the product of man's imagination—and it required a more than usually perceptive imagination to see that such a natural phenomenon as the rising of smoke from a volcano or forest fire held the key to the problem of raising a solid body off the ground.

It is almost always dangerous to assert that any person was the first to achieve something. There is, however, good reason to believe that the Greek scientist Archimedes, in the third century BC, was the first to make a sound incursion into the theory of lighter-than-air flight, when he laid down his principle concerning the flotation of bodies in liquids and gases. Yet the next positively recorded piece of comment on flying does not appear until nearly 1,500 years later, in the writings of the Franciscan monk, Roger Bacon, who lived during the greater part of the 13th century. His major contribution to aviation history was to visualise something very much akin to the 20th-century aeroplane which he described in his *Secrets of Art and Nature* (*ca* 1250) as "Engines' for flying, a man sitting in the midst thereof, by turning onely about an Instrument, which moves artificiall Wings made to beat the Aire, much after the fashion of a Bird's flight." Bacon also had some ideas about a vessel to be kept aloft by "liquid fire" while it floated on the surface of the earth's atmosphere, and deserves credit for keeping the idea of flight by man rather more in the forefront of learned thinking than other visionaries managed to do.

In the 15th century, Leonardo da Vinci devised a variety of machines which had

Gusmão's *Passarola* must seem one of the strangest of all early projects, with its bird's head at the front, parachute sail on top and flapping wings at the sides. Yet there is good reason to believe that Gusmão was the first person to fly a lighter-than-air model, and that the *Passarola* was designed to make use of the theories proved in model form

great similarity to the powered aircraft of today, but it is worth noting, with some surprise, that this great thinker seems to have paid no attention to the possibility of lighter-than-air flight. Yet he must have known of ever-rising hot gases from Vesuvius, Etna and Stromboli which carried solid particles to great heights.

Another 200 years were to pass before the first faltering steps were taken to make a vehicle lighter than the air it displaced. These steps were only on paper, but at least they were logical, even if impracticable.

A Jesuit priest, Father Francesco de Lana-Terzi had made a study of work done on atmospheric pressure and vacuum conditions. He realised that a container full of air would weigh more than one from which the air had been evacuated to leave only a vacuum. De Lana (his second surname is seldom used) also reasoned that, if the materials of the container weighed less than the air needed to fill it, it would rise from the ground unless secured in some way. From this it was only a short step to conceiving a container so much lighter than the air it displaced that it might lift a weight in addition to itself.

De Lana designed a boat which was to be suspended from four spheres, each about 20 ft (6.10 m) in diameter. These spheres, which were to be made of copper foil so as to be of minimum weight, were to have the air completely evacuated, so that the whole device could rise and, presumably, lift one or more men with it. De Lana also gave his aerial boat a sail, failing to realise that a free balloon must travel with the wind anyway and cannot obtain any advantage from even the biggest spread of canvas.

By making the containers in the form of "perfect" spheres, de Lana believed they would be strong enough to withstand the immense air pressure to which they would be subjected from the outside. As any schoolboy today would know, the spheres would have collapsed with even a small pressure differential between the interior and exterior, but this reflects no discredit upon de Lana, for such aspects of elementary physics were quite unknown in his day.

Although impractical, de Lana's design was the forerunner of the lighter-than-air craft, and it is especially interesting to recall that when he finally acknowledged the physical limitations of his balloon-ship he pointed out that, in any case, God would never have allowed such a device to succeed because it had such immense capacity for destruction. He went on to describe, with uncanny foresight, how aerial ships could be used for military invasion and to destroy fortresses, fleets and cities. So, in 1670, just three hundred years ago, there was at least one man of learning who anticipated what flying might hold for the world and who, on paper anyway, was capable of designing a vehicle to do the job.

Even as late as the start of the 18th century, academic learning was confined largely to the church, and the next—and possibly the most important—pioneer was another Jesuit priest, Father Laurenço de Gusmão, who was born in Brazil in 1686.

He died in Europe when he was only 40, but during his short life produced some very original thinking.

In 1709, Gusmão obtained from the King of Portugal a patent for a flying machine—a somewhat exaggerated type of ornithopter (flapping-wing machine) called the *Passarola*. Such evidence as survives today suggests that it was built and may even have been tested. The full-size version could not have flown, but there is reason to suppose that Gusmão built a model, probably some sort of fixed-wing glider, that was demonstrated successfully. (Strictly speaking, this vessel has no place in a history of the balloon, but it has been included as evidence that Gusmão, who until recently was a victim of much malicious humour and contempt, did in fact have a wide and serious interest in the problems of flying.)

Indeed, the year 1709 was undoubtedly a busy one for Gusmão, for it is reliably recorded that on 8 August he gave a demonstration of a hot-air balloon before the king; and it is in this aspect of flying that his greatness lies.

There is no positive indication of what made Gusmão think in terms of hot air as a lifting agent, or of how long he had considered its possibilities. But he did so, and a contemporary report gives us a good description of the balloon and what happened during its demonstration:

"Gusmão's device consisted of a small bark in the form of a trough which was covered with a cloth of canvas. With various spirits, quintessences and other ingredients he put a light beneath it and let the said bark fly in the Salla das Embaixadas before His Majesty and many other persons. It rose to a small height against the wall and then came to earth and caught fire when the materials became jumbled together. In falling downwards it set fire to some hangings and everything against which it knocked."

The report concluded, with classic understatement, that "His Majesty was good enough not to take it ill."

Thus, 74 years before the Montgolfier brothers astounded the world with their public demonstrations of hot-air balloons (see page 20)—and nearly 2,000 years after Archimedes first set down the principle upon which lighter-than-air flight was to be founded—a relatively obscure Brazilian had proved that flight was possible, even if he did have to set part of a king's palace alight in doing so. Yet only in recent years has the true importance of Gusmão's work come to be fully understood and recognised.

One more major milestone before the Montgolfier era remains to be recorded. This was the contribution made by an English chemist, Henry Cavendish, who carried out experiments to determine the weight of hydrogen gas—then known as "inflammable air". In 1766 Cavendish reported to the Royal Society that hydrogen was considerably lighter than atmospheric air. The full importance of this discovery was to be fully recognised, and the knowledge given practical application, before the end of that century.

Above left: How could one make an object lighter than air? An alternative to de Lana's airless spheres was suggested by Cyrano de Bergerac. Noting that dew rose when the sun's rays fell upon it, he proposed to fill the bottom of his transparent spherical craft with dew so that it would take off automatically when the sun shone upon it. The result was clearly a fair-weather craft; but de Bergerac described it as a potential spacecraft for journeys to the moon

Left: Although de Lana's flying boat was impracticable, it represented the first definite design for a lighter-than-air craft. The boat was intended to be lifted by four thin copper spheres, made lighter-than-air by creating a vacuum inside them

Above: One of the more fantastic flying machines illustrated in the decade before the first balloon flights were made was this device powered by "electric globes". Apart from the fact that the two glass spheres were supposed to produce some unspecified electrical lifting force, the designer does not appear to have gone into much detail about his invention

Airborne – at last

In the first instalment of the hot-air balloon story(see page 17), references were made to the rather surprising failure of the intellectuals for 2,000 years to realise the implications of the volcanoes and forest fires that carried solid particles high into the air. Except for Gusmão, no-one even envisaged a practical application of such a phenomenon.

At long last a paper-maker named Joseph Montgolfier, ruminating in front of his fireplace, began to wonder why the smoke, sparks and more solid matter were steadily disappearing up the chimney. Was it possible, he wondered, to capture the "gas" that bore them and make it do useful work by lifting solid man-made objects? To satisfy his curiosity he made a bag of fine silk and lit a small fire under it. To his delight, and that of his landlady, it swelled up and rose to the ceiling. This happened at Avignon, in France, in November 1782.

Joseph wasted no time. Getting in touch with his brother, Etienne, who lived at Annonay, he suggested a test on a larger scale. This time, out of doors, the silk container rose to about 70 ft (21.5 m) before cooling and deflating.

A whole series of experiments then followed, with ever-larger "aerostatic machines" (as the brothers called their balloons). One of them, filled with "Montgolfier Gas", rose to around 1,000 ft (305 m) before descending nearly a mile away.

So far, the tests had been kept secret, but now the two men decided to give a public demonstration. They built a linen, paper-lined, envelope more than 100 ft (30.5 m) in diameter and, on 4 June 1783, in the presence of a large crowd, lit a fire under

it in the market place at Annonay. As it filled, it took the efforts of eight men to hold it down, and when it was released it rose to a height—supposedly measured scientifically—of 6,000 ft (1,830 m). Before coming down it travelled more than a mile.

The Montgolfier brothers informed the Académie des Sciences in Paris of their achievement, and were promptly invited to come to the capital and give a demonstration there. At the same time, the Académie took steps to raise funds for further research but, instead of handing over the money to the originators of lighter-than-air travel, they commissioned a young French physicist, Professor J. A. C. Charles, to continue the work. This choice was to have important consequences in France nearly a century later, but at the time it seemed a little unfair to the Montgolfiers. (Of Charles and his work, more will be said later. In fact, he demonstrated balloon flight in Paris *before* the Montgolfier brothers were ready, but it is more appropriate to complete their story of hot-air flight before moving over to the hydrogen operations of Charles.)

Etienne Montgolfier completed a much-decorated envelope almost 75 ft (22.8 m) high and showed it off to the Académie. It was highly successful, and resulted in a command to put on a show for King Louis XVI and Marie Antoinette at Versailles on 19 September 1783.

A new balloon—built in four days after the original one had been damaged by rain—was made ready for the great day, and the Montgolfiers decided to make the occasion still more impressive by sending aloft living creatures. They attached to the balloon a cage containing a sheep, a rooster and a

duck, and this menagerie, airborne for eight minutes, finally landed—with very small harm to its occupants—a mile and a half away.

Louis awarded the brothers the Order of St Michel and, from that time, all hot-air balloons became known as *montgolfieres*.

Clearly, once animals had flown safely, it became the turn of human beings to follow. A new balloon was built, much bigger and capable of lifting two men as well as its airborne fire to keep the envelope expanded. Louis XVI thought that a couple of criminals under sentence of death might be given the chance of freedom if they would volunteer to fly in the *montgolfiere*; but a certain Jean-François Pilâtre de Rozier, who had been a very active supporter of the whole project from the start, protested that the honour of being the first man to fly should not be given to a criminal. He won his argument and, on 15 October 1783, rose to a height of 85 ft (26 m) in a tethered balloon. By stoking the fire built into the balloon, he stayed aloft for nearly four and a half minutes.

After a series of such flights de Rozier and a passenger, the Marquis d'Arlandes, made a free flight on 21 November 1783. To the astonishment of all concerned, they stayed airborne for 25 minutes and finally landed on the opposite side of Paris.

Returning now to the work of Professor Charles, this physicist was quite sure that hot air was not the ideal medium to provide lift. He had studied the work of Henry Cavendish(see page 19) and felt certain that hydrogen "inflammable air" was the gas with which he should fill his envelope. He also knew—which the paper-maker Mont-

Left: First living creatures to fly under a balloon were a sheep, a duck and a cock. They travelled in a basket suspended beneath this Montgolfier hot-air balloon, which was launched at Versailles on 19 September 1783 before the French Royal Family, the court and 130,000 spectators

Below left: Pilâtre de Rozier and the Marquis d'Arlandes start the first aerial voyage in history, in a Montgolfier balloon on 21 November 1783. Their success in crossing Paris by air owed much to the Marquis' dexterity in putting out fires in the fabric envelope started by the burning brazier which supplied hot air to keep the balloon airborne

Below: One of the greatest photographers of all time, the Frenchman Nadar, shown in this contemporary caricature, pioneered the art of taking photographs from the air

Right: The hydrogen balloon invented by
J A C Charles was far more practical than the
original form of hot-air balloon. In this one,
on 1 December 1783, Charles and one of the
brothers Robert, who built it, made a flight of
more than two hours from the Tuileries
Gardens in Paris. After landing, Charles went
up again by himself, but was so alarmed when
the balloon shot up to over 9,000 ft (2,750 m)
that he never flew again

Below: One of the earliest practical uses for
balloons was for military reconnaissance.
This captive hydrogen balloon was sent up
by General Jourdan's French Army on
2 June 1794 to keep track of the enemy. By
robbing the enemy of an opportunity to make
surprise moves, balloons played a decisive
part in several battles of this era

MONTGOLFIER HOT-AIR BALLOON

Lifting agent: approx 77,700 cu ft (2,200 m³) of hot air, generated by burning straw inside the base of the balloon
Diameter: approx 49 ft (14.95 m)
Height: approx 75 ft (22.75 m)
Gross weight: approx 1,730 lb (785 kg)
Flight of 21 November 1783: of approx 25 minutes duration, covering a distance of 7½ miles (12 km) and reaching a height of over 3,280 ft (1,000 m)

The first public demonstration of a *montgolfière* was at Annonay on 4 June 1783. Details above apply to the balloon in which Jean-François Pilâtre de Rozier and his passenger, François Laurent, Marquis d'Arlandes, made the first human aerial voyage in history. The balloon, made of linen coated with alum to reduce the risk of combustion, took off from the garden of the Château de la Muette in Paris, landing at Butte-aux-Cailles some 25 minutes later.

golfier brothers did not—that two other brothers, by name A-N and M-N Robert, had produced a method of coating silk with rubber. This compound was as near to being gas-proof as anything then available, and with it Charles made an envelope some 13 ft (4.0 m) in diameter.

He had some difficulty in manufacturing the necessary 22,000 cu ft (620 m³) of hydrogen but, on 26 August 1783, he did fill the envelope and his balloon rose into the clouds—never to return. One of the spectators was the later US scientist-diplomat Benjamin Franklin, who, in reply to someone's query "Of what use is a balloon?" made the now-famous retort "Sir, of what use is a new-born baby?"

Charles, in company with M-N Robert, made the first human flight in a hydrogen-filled balloon from Paris on 1 December 1783, and, incidentally, improved markedly on the distance and time achieved by the Montgolfier flight.

The advent of the *charlière*, the name by which hydrogen-filled balloons became known, started a form of competition in flying which has been repeated in a variety of ways for the better part of two hundred years.

Both the hot-air and the hydrogen balloons of that era left much to be desired. They were liable to catch fire, they leaked and they were hard to control over their short periods of flight. But they did fly. Man's dream, dating back thousands of years, had at last achieved some degree of realisation. The future was no longer a dream it had become something which skill, design, imagination and hard work could convert into a practical means of transport.

If this seems to be a rather optimistic comment on the relatively crude work of these two groups of men it should be noted that, only two years later, a French engineer officer put on paper the design of an airship, which would be controllable in direction of flight. He was nearly a century ahead of practice, but already the balloons of the late 18th century had sown the seed of future air transport.

The Great Age of Balloons

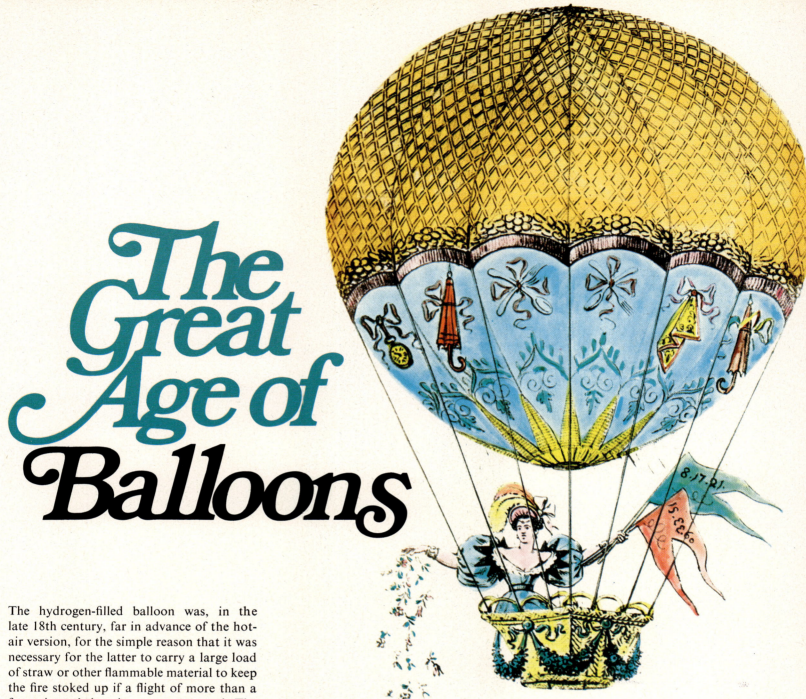

The hydrogen-filled balloon was, in the late 18th century, far in advance of the hot-air version, for the simple reason that it was necessary for the latter to carry a large load of straw or other flammable material to keep the fire stoked up if a flight of more than a few minutes' duration was attempted. The fire risk also was very great.

It was natural, therefore, that hydrogen should appeal more to the intrepid sportsmen of the time, and the ballooning craze caught on among the wealthy of France. What was surprising was the rapidity with which ever more ambitious ideas attracted the balloonists. It was little more than one year after the first balloon ascent that Jean-Pierre Blanchard and an American colleague, Dr John Jeffries, set off from Dover to fly over the English Channel. What is more, they succeeded, despite considerable difficulties resulting from loss of lift, which forced the aeronauts to dump every spare item to reduce weight—even to the extent of Blanchard throwing his trousers overboard!

In the meantime, captive balloons had already been used for observation purposes by the French Army, and other countries soon became interested. Ascents were made in England, Italy and Austria, and Blanchard gave demonstrations in Holland, Germany and Belgium. The first Englishman to make a balloon ascent, in 1784, was James Sadler. Pilâtre de Rozier, who had been the first human being to fly in a balloon (see page 20), tried the fatal combination of hot air and hydrogen, and crashed in flames to acquire another "first" in flying: the first

man to be killed in an aircraft accident after flight became practicable.

The first woman to fly was Madame Thible, who ascended in a *montgolfière* with the painter Fleurant. Their trip started at Lyons.

Another Englishman was destined to become one of the "aces" of the early period of flying. He was Charles Green, who made a notable flight from England to Germany. Early in the 19th century, he planned to attempt an Atlantic crossing by balloon in company with an American aeronaut, John Wise. Fortunately for them both, the enterprise stopped at the planning stage.

The rapid growth of ballooning as a sport, and the long flights made within only a few years of the first-ever ascent, have a modern parallel. Just as success after success was achieved by the balloonists in a very short period of time, so did space travel evolve in a dozen years from a lightweight unmanned satellite (Sputnik 1) to multiple journeys to the moon and the first successful landings there.

Perhaps there is a moral to be drawn from this. Man is clearly willing to devote time, money, even life itself, to press on to ever greater achievements in any form of

flying; whereas he shows himself, all too often, to be slow-moving in the advancement of other equally—if not more—important projects in the field of technology.

The period from 1783 to 1870 alone would require several books if one were to cover fully man's early achievements in lighter - than - air flying; for our purpose, let it suffice that in only 87 years ballooning reached a stage which resulted in the creation of what was, in effect, the world's first "airline". And that is one of the most exciting stories in flying history.

Late in 1870 the Prussian Army had surrounded Paris, cutting off all contact between the capital and the rest of France. In the city there were several balloons, the materials to make and inflate more, plus about half a dozen highly-trained balloonists. Governments are often slow to put unusual inventions to practical service, but this particular situation was so desperate that, on 23 September 1870, Jules Durouf ascended from the city and, sailing unharmed over the heads of the besieging troops, landed at Evreux in unoccupied France three hours later, carrying vital despatches.

So began the first "airline" in the world. Gaston Tissandier, perhaps the greatest of

The name "Garnerin" was among the most famous in the early days of ballooning. Andre-Jacques Garnerin made his name not only as an aeronaut but as the first person to make a successful parachute jump from a balloon, on 22 October 1797, over Paris. Both his wife and his niece Elisa (left) also became professional parachutists

Above left: Greatest of the early journeys made by balloon was the first aerial crossing of the English Channel by Blanchard and Jeffries in a hydrogen balloon on 7 January 1785. The balloon began losing height so rapidly at one stage that the aeronauts threw overboard everything on which they could lay hands to lighten it, including their trousers and a bottle of good brandy

Above right: First English balloonist was James Sadler of Oxford, who flew in a hot-air *montgolfière* on 4 October 1784. On 1 October 1812, at the age of 61, he attempted to fly the Irish Sea and is shown here leaving Dublin. He reached Anglesey safely but was unable to land quickly enough and was blown out to sea again, finally being rescued from the water 40 miles (65 km) from land

Right: An American balloonist named John Wise outflew even Charles Green, covering 1,120 miles (1,800 km) from St Louis to Henderson, New York, in 1859. Impressed, the *New York Daily Graphic* was persuaded later to finance a transatlantic attempt by Wise. He took off from New York in a huge balloon of 400,000 cu ft (11,325 m³) capacity in 1873, but crashed after covering only 41 miles (65 km)

all balloonists of the era, made a successful flight in spite of being fired on; Eugène Godard, who had made 800 ascents, was the next to go, and he was followed by another pioneer, Mangin. They all attracted attention from the muskets of the Germans and it was decided that future flights would have to be made at night.

There was another major problem. Once the balloon had landed safely, it and its pilot were lost to Paris, as this was strictly a one-way-only operation. Tissandier made several attempts to catch the right winds and get back, but even he was unable to do so. With only two or three qualified aeronauts left in the city, some new solution had to be adopted.

The remaining balloonists were fully capable of supervising the construction of balloons, and the manufacture of hydrogen was comparatively simple. Crews were another matter altogether.

One expedient was the conscription and training of a team of acrobats currently appearing at the Paris Hippodrome. These men were presumably happy enough on the high wire, but a balloon ascent at night, in sole charge of passengers and mail, was too much for them. No sooner were they airborne than they shinned down the trail rope and returned to terra firma, leaving the now-lightened balloon to shoot skywards with its unfortunate occupants.

The acrobat idea having failed, a more successful experiment was tried. In the city —for some reason not explained by the history books—was a large number of sailors of the French Navy. Disciplined, accustomed to the vagaries of the wind and trained to accept danger as part of their work, they made ideal balloon pilots and the airlift went merrily on.

Naturally, there were incidents. Wind forecasting was sketchy and unreliable: one balloon landed in Norway, after attracting hostile interest from a British naval ship in the North Sea! Another landed in Holland, and one or two were shot down by the Prussians; but the majority reached unoccupied France safely.

One sailor, named Prince, made a prophetic remark before ascending:

"I shall make an immense voyage; people will talk of my flight."

How right he was: blown out to sea, he was last seen in Cornwall, dropping his despatches at the Lizard as the wind carried him out over the Atlantic towards North America and oblivion.

The exact number of flights made during this operation is open to question, but the figure of 66 seems to be generally accepted. Nine tons of mail and 155 human beings were sent out of Paris, the cargoes including homing pigeons which occasionally flew back with messages. The last flight, on 28 January 1871, carried the sad news of the French capitulation.

It is fair to claim that this was an airline —with several differences. The first test flight of a new balloon became an operational flight over enemy territory—and often the captain was making not only his first solo flight, but his first flight of any kind!

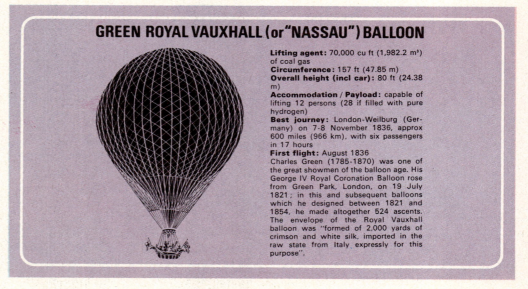

GREEN ROYAL VAUXHALL (or "NASSAU") BALLOON

Lifting agent: 70,000 cu ft (1,982.2 m³) of coal gas
Circumference: 157 ft (47.85 m)
Overall height (incl car): 80 ft (24.38 m)
Accommodation / Payload: capable of lifting 12 persons (28 if filled with pure hydrogen)
Best journey: London-Weilburg (Germany) on 7-8 November 1836, approx 600 miles (966 km), with six passengers in 17 hours
First flight: August 1836
Charles Green (1785-1870) was one of the great showmen of the balloon age. His George IV Royal Coronation Balloon rose from Green Park, London, on 19 July 1821; in this and subsequent balloons which he designed between 1821 and 1854, he made altogether 524 ascents. The envelope of the Royal Vauxhall balloon was "formed of 2,000 yards of crimson and white silk, imported in the raw state from Italy expressly for this purpose".

And the balloon could be used only once! It must have been a frightening experience for the crews and passengers of that epic airlift, especially since the average person, even a century ago, was far from being air-minded. Yet, with 57 of the flights (84 per cent) recorded as successful, the operation can only be described as a triumphant vindication for the supporters of flying.

Above: This mobile gun was built by the famous Prussian arms manufacturer Alfred Krupp in an attempt to shoot down the balloons leaving Paris in 1870/71. It was probably the first anti-aircraft gun in history

Above left: Green's balloon being prepared at the Mermaid Tavern, Hackney, for his 100th ascent on 14 May 1832

Left: Perhaps the most notable of all large-scale exploits by free balloons was the great airlift operated out of Paris during the Franco-Prussian War of 1870/71. This contemporary print shows the balloons being manufactured at the Gare d'Orleans

Right: A night ascent from the Gare du Nord during the Siege of Paris—based on a sketch sent out of the city by balloon post

DIRIGIBILITY

Almost all of the early designs for balloons showed them fitted with sails or oars, the designers believing, erroneously, that lighter-than-air craft could be directed on a pre-selected course. Many years passed before it was realised fully that the balloon became part of the wind, so that sails were useless. Oars, though theoretically capable of producing motion, were far too unwieldy if they were to have any effect at all.

So, while free ballooning became the sport of the rich in every civilised country in the world, the idea of a dirigible balloon was uppermost in the minds of those who visualised the air as a medium in which to travel. (There is still confusion about the word "dirigible": many people think it is an alternative to "rigid" or "non-rigid", which are words used to describe the basic types of airship structure. In fact it simply means "directable" or "steerable".)

To appreciate just how old is the concept of a dirigible airship or balloon, we must turn back in history to 1783. While J. A. C. Charles and the Mongolfier brothers were showing that balloon flight was possible, an officer of the French Corps of Engineers was hard at work producing a design for an airship which could make controlled flights. He submitted the design in 1784 to the Académie des Sciences, and very remarkable it was, embodying all the basic principles used in non-rigid airships more than a century later.

Such an airship retains its shape only because of the pressure of the gas inside it. When gas is released, to maintain the desired pressure differential according to the height at which the ship is flying, this gas is irreplaceable in flight. If the ship then descends the envelope takes up all manner of

strange shapes, becomes unmanageable and the craft may crash.

Meusnier overcame this problem by introducing an outer envelope, to be filled with air at more than atmospheric pressure. Much the same idea is used in non-rigids to this day, though the method is different. He chose the "cigar" shape, which came into common use many decades later, because it was aerodynamically more efficient. He included three two-bladed propellers, which he wanted to drive by what he called a "power engine". (Presumably he foresaw, vaguely, the eventual development of mechanical power units of some kind.) Lacking such an engine, he planned for the propellers to be operated by a crew of eighty men. This was perhaps not up to the standard of his other ideas, but the whole thing was a stroke of genius. He even drew up designs for a permanent hangar and a mobile shelter for use in the field—which showed how at least one Army officer was thinking in terms of aerial warfare two centuries ago.

For practical reasons the ship was never built, and Meusnier returned to his normal military activities; he was killed in action as a General some years later.

From 1800 onwards, interest in the dirigible balloon or airship grew apace. In England, two Swiss gunsmiths designed a fish-shaped airship in 1816 and, indeed, partially built it. Durs Egg was the designer and the ship, to be propelled by oars, rapidly became known as "Egg's Folly"

From 1816 to 1843 many other people put forward ideas, but nothing practicable emerged. Then an Englishman, Monck Mason, built a small airship and powered it with a clockwork engine driving a propeller. It flew, and is reputed to have reached a

Top: Typical of the larger non-rigid airships built before World War I was the Clement-Bayard VII, built in France for the Russian government. Powered by two 130-hp four-cylinder engines, it was 282 ft (86 m) long

Above: First successful airship was this 3-hp "steam balloon" in which Henri Giffard flew from Paris to Trappes at 6 mph in 1852. It was only partially controllable

Right: The unauthorised arrival of Zeppelin Z-4 on the French military parade ground at Luneville in early 1913 caused quite a sensation at a time when relations between Germany and France were near breaking point. Blown off course by the wind, the Z-4 was thoroughly inspected and photographed by French military authorities before being returned

Below right: Britain's first rigid airship, the R.1, built by Vickers for the Admiralty, being launched at Barrow-in-Furness on 22 May 1911. Its nickname of "Mayfly" proved all too appropriate. Whilst being removed from its floating shed on 24 September 1911, the R.1 was damaged beyond repair and never flew

speed of 5 mph (8 km/h). Of little practical use, Mason's airship nevertheless marked the turning point in the search for fully-controlled flight.

In the ensuing nine years a variety of experiments was made, but the world had to wait for another Frenchman, Henri Giffard, to build the first partially steerable airship. His steam-driven, cigar-shaped airship was 144.4 ft (44.0 m) long and about 39.4 ft (12.0 m) in diameter. The engine developed 3 hp and drove a three-blade propeller.

On 24 September 1852, Giffard took off from the Paris Hippodrome and flew, at about 5 mph (8 km/h) to Trappes, some 17 miles (28.0 km) away. At last man had made a semi-controlled flight under power.

The next major achievement came in 1860 when Etienne Lenoir invented the gas engine. It was not until 1872, however, that Paul Heinlein flew from Brünn an airship which was powered by a 5 hp engine using coal gas as the fuel. Neither his nor Giffard's flights were without their hazards, but they were important in pointing the way to safe, controlled flight. Even more important was the fact that all the material components necessary for complete success were by then in existence. Control surfaces were similar to those still used. Impregnated fabrics for the envelope, though inclined to leak, were available. Engines—though still requiring great development—were there; and man was beginning to understand the problems of flight and how to overcome them.

One of the most successful designs of this era was the *La France* of Renard and Krebs in 1884. Measuring 170 ft (51.8 m) in length, it was powered by a 9 hp electric motor. It reached a speed of 12 mph (19.3 km/h) and was completely manoeuvrable. It emphasised that at this stage France was still the leading country in flying research; but a big change was in sight.

On 8 July 1838, at Konstanz, a son, Ferdinand, had been born to Count Frederick von Zeppelin. Like all German aristocrats of that era, the young Zeppelin entered the Army in 1857. Thirty years later, as a lieutenant-general, he was disgraced for some undisclosed reason and was expected to disappear from the public eye. Far from it. No sooner was he out of the service than he turned his considerable talents to flying. With help from others, he started to design a rigid airship—i e one with a metallic framework to retain the shape and to contain a number of separate gasbags.

For seven years Zeppelin worked hard. A design was produced, but was turned down by the military commission to which it was submitted. Nothing daunted, he started again, formed a company and built a floating shed on Lake Konstanz. In it was built the first Zeppelin airship, the LZ.1. The dimensions are interesting and show how, from the start, Zeppelin considered that great size was important. LZ.1 was 420 ft (128.0 m) long, 38 ft 6 in (11.73 m) in diameter and had a gas capacity of 400,000 cu ft (11,327 m³). Power was supplied by

two 16 hp Daimler engines.

The first flight took place on 2 July 1900, and was successful only in that LZ.1 did not crash. Control—by rudder for lateral movement and by a shifting weight for vertical attitude—was almost non-existent, and the airship was lucky to get back to base in one piece.

For months it stayed in its shed while modifications were made, and on 17 October it flew again. Once more the flight left much to be desired, but LZ.1 again got back safely. One of the observers was a young, unknown journalist named Hugo Eckener. He was not impressed, and it is quite certain that he never dreamed then that one day he would be greatest of all Zeppelin captains.

Five years passed, and then the LZ.2 appeared. It was very similar to LZ.1, but for one major difference: its two engines developed 85 hp each. The first flight was a failure, nearly a disaster, and LZ.2 was towed ignominiously back to her floating hangar. But the worst was over.

In January 1906, LZ.2 emerged again. This time she flew well, and was easily controllable, reaching a height of 1,500 ft (457 m) and attaining a speed of 33 mph (53 km/h). Then an engine broke down, she was forced to land and was destroyed in the process.

This would have been enough for most people, but Zeppelin carried on. He brought Eckener into the business, and built another ship, the LZ.3, in a few months, the maiden

flight taking place on 9 October 1906. This time the flight was a complete success. The new Zeppelin flew 60 miles (97 km) in two hours and returned safely to base, repeating the performance the following day. Now the German government *had* to take an interest and, as later accounts will tell, Zeppelin airships became a force to be reckoned with in both military and civil aviation.

England was by this time showing a limited interest in airships for military purposes and E. T. Willows, originally a balloon maker, built tiny non-rigid airships from 1905 onwards. They were fairly successful, and one was handed over to the Royal Navy.

No story of those early days would be complete without mention of Alberto Santos-Dumont. Son of a wealthy Brazilian, he lived in Paris and became a flying enthusiast. Several airships were built to his designs, and with them he won numerous prizes, including the then enormous sum of 125,000 francs offered by Henri Deutsch de la Meurthe for a flight from St Cloud to the Eiffel Tower and back in less than 30 minutes. He also used an airship to take him on his local journeys, as people use their cars today. His airships appeared around the turn of the century; later, he became the first man to make a successful powered aeroplane flight in Europe, and lived to see aircraft used in war, and, commercially, as public transport vehicles.

In the late 19th and early 20th centuries a number of other names came to the fore in airship work. Among the best-known were those of Lebaudy, the Astra company, Clément-Bayard, Société Zodiac, and Parseval, all of whom built successful airships and built up an appreciable export trade. In the light of later developments it is only remarkable that the USA showed so little interest in the evolution of these craft.

Far left: This small airship, built by Ernest Willows, is shown under test at Farnborough before being handed over to the Admiralty in 1912. In all, Willows flew five airships, of which the last four had swivelling propellers which could be used to assist the craft to climb and descend. In No 2 Willows made the first airship flight across the English Channel

Above left: Santos-Dumont leaving Saint-Cloud at the start of the flight around the Eiffel Tower and back which gained him the Deutsche de la Meurthe prize of 125,000 francs on 19 October 1901. His little airship No 6 was powered by a 20-hp Buchet engine

Top: Not all non-rigid airships were small. The Clement-Bayard Adjudant Vincenot and Dupuy de Lôme of 1912 were each 290 ft (88 m) long and powered by two 130-hp engines

Middle: Before his success in airship No 6, Santos-Dumont had tried for the Deutsche de la Meurthe prize in No 5, shown here at Longchamps. He rounded the Eiffel Tower safely, but the wind then took charge and it seemed that he must be killed as the "gas-bag" exploded over the rooftops of Paris. He was, however, rescued by the fire brigade from the top of a six-storey building in the rue Henri Martin, as cheerful as ever

Above: The engine and streamlined car of Willows' 1912 airship

TWO GREAT DESIGNERS
Da Vinci & Cayley

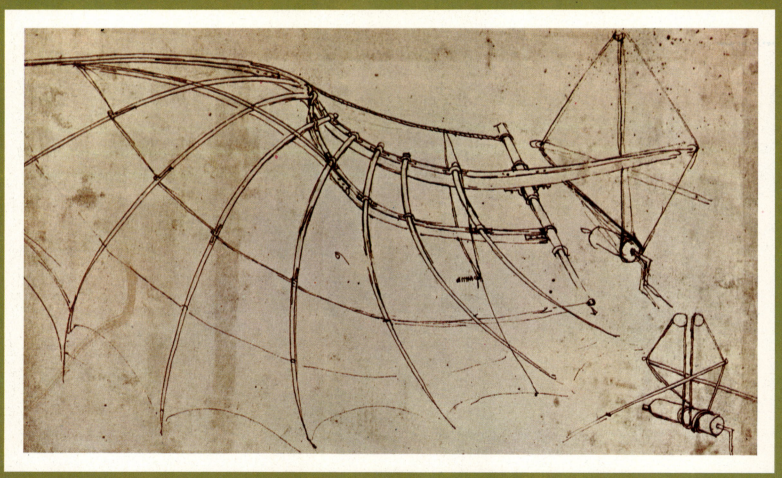

Above: After studying the delicate and intricate "mechanism" of a bird's wing, Leonardo da Vinci tried to reproduce it in wood and fabric. With no engine available, he devised a way of flapping the wings mechanically by connecting them to a continuous cable running around a hand-turned winch

Left: One of the most interesting and unique models in the Australian Qantas collection is of the triplane glider in which Sir George Cayley is said to have flown a small boy down hillsides in Yorkshire in 1849. Weakest feature of the design was its embodiment of ineffective flapping wings for propulsion

The name of Leonardo da Vinci lives in aeronautical history because this Italian genius was the inventor, or discoverer, of the parachute and helicopter. He also came near to inventing the propeller, or airscrew.

To say that Leonardo invented the parachute and helicopter does not imply that he made them work; but he showed them in his drawings, together with other remarkable aeronautical devices, including an ornithopter, or flapping-wing aircraft.

Born in 1452, this man of almost unbelievable attainments was the first to use scientific experience in investigating the problems of flight. With his profound knowledge of anatomy, so marvellously apparent in his paintings and 'cartoons', it is not surprising that his chief concern was with the means whereby a human being might imitate the birds and bats. This is regrettable, for in some of his later drawings he showed a fixed-wing glider which, together with the helicopter, might have proved far worthier of his attentions. To use his own

words, the wings of his ornithopter were intended to "row downwards and backwards", and he compared bird-flight with "swimming in the water". What he could not have realised was that a bird is not able to beat its wings purely backwards; and certainly the power of human muscles could never have lifted his flapping contraptions off the ground.

Leonardo did, in fact, propose an alternative means of providing power, involving a mechanism using a kind of bow-string which was to be rewound by the pilot in flight. He also proposed a machine having fixed wings, to the outer ends of which were attached flapping panels. Another of his designs showed a retractable undercarriage, and yet another a head-harness to work an elevator, causing the aircraft to climb or descend. This anticipated the harness developed later by Otto Lilienthal.

The parachute proposed by Leonardo was pyramid-shaped, and his helicopter had a helical, or spiral, screw.

It has been mentioned that Leonardo came near to inventing the propeller. This came about when he designed a device for turning a roasting-spit by revolving a shaft on which blades were mounted. Rotation was caused by hot air rising from the fire, and had he considered turning the blades by power, and thus caused them to move air instead of themselves being driven by heated air, he would have had a third aeronautical invention to his credit.

Although Leonardo intended that his designs should eventually be published and so, perhaps, inspire other men, they did not come to light until late in the 19th century, by which time the parachute and helicopter had been "reinvented". For many decades after the great Italian died, in 1519, little serious attention was paid to flying. In 1678, however, a French locksmith named Besnier gained publicity, if nothing more, with an attempt to fly with paddle-wings at Sablé. During 1709 Father Laurenço de Gusmão also seems to have built a model glider

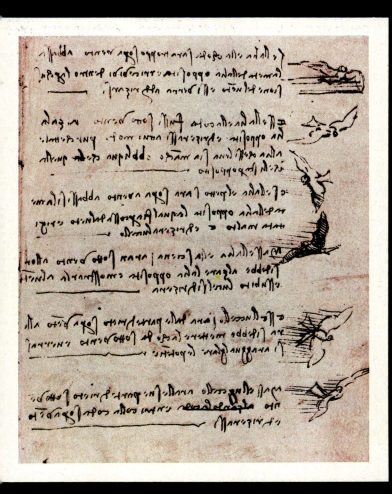

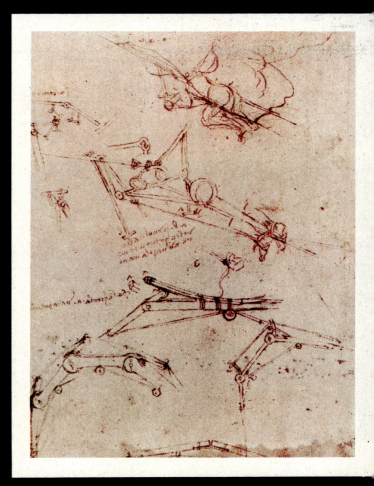

CAYLEY MAN-CARRYING GLIDER DESIGN (1852)

Surface area (main wing): 467 sq ft (43.4 m²)
Horizontal surface area (rudder): 48 sq ft (4.5 m²)
Design weight empty: approx 150 lb (68 kg)
Accommodation: Crew of 1
Details of this flying machine designed by Sir George Cayley (1773-1857) appeared in *Mechanics' Magazine* of 25 September 1852, and the silhouette reproduced here is based upon the somewhat simplified illustrations published on that occasion. In fact, as Cayley's text made clear, the wing was intended to have approx 8° of dihedral and to be set at an angle of incidence of about 5°. Cayley called the craft, which was meant to be released in the air from beneath a balloon, a "governable parachute"; though it was in reality a glider. Although never built, it incorporated all except one of the essential design features of a modern aeroplane.

Above left: This page from Leonardo's notebook describes and illustrates some of his observations of bird flight

Above: Leonardo's earliest design for a man-powered aircraft dates back to about 1485, when he was 33 years old. Realising the limitations of using only chest and arm muscles, he conceived it in such a way that the "pilot" lay prone and could use also his powerful leg muscles to flap the wings, via cables and pulleys

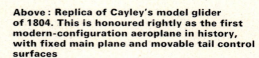

which he may actually have flown; and in 1772 a Canon Desfarges built an unsuccessful ornithopter.

There were other designers and experimenters, but none of great note until the time of Sir George Cayley (1773-1857). This Yorkshire baronet is now generally recognised as the originator of the aeroplane as we know it today, and Wilbur Wright said of him in 1909 that he "carried the science of flying to a point which it had never reached before and which it scarcely reached again during the last century".

Most of Cayley's work was done at Brompton Hall, near Scarborough. When he was twenty-three years old he made a model helicopter similar to that "reinvented" (Leonardo's designs still being unpublished) by the Frenchmen Launoy and Bienvenu in 1784. Within a few years, though without the research of others to guide him, except in relation to projectiles and windmills, he had formed his concept of the modern aeroplane. This is shown on a little silver disc, dated 1799 and now in the Science Museum, London. On one side of this disc Cayley has engraved his explanation of the forces acting on a wing and on the other side a sketch of a glider. The pilot is shown sitting in a boat-like fuselage beneath the fixed wing, operating a pair of paddle-like "flappers" for propulsion. The tail unit consists of a combined elevator and tailplane and a combined fin and rudder, arranged in the form of a cross. Had a propeller been shown instead of the flappers, the resemblance of this powered glider, or aeroplane, to an aeroplane of today would have been even more remarkable.

In about 1801 Cayley was studying bird propulsion and in 1804 was testing a model glider on a whirling arm. A little later he was firing finned projectiles over the sea at Scarborough, with an old artilleryman to spot the "fall of shot", and at about the same time was designing a "compound" type of aircraft having fixed wings attached to a wheeled car and carrying flappers at their tips. An understanding of this remarkable machine is not made easier by the fact that Sir George insisted on calling the wings "sails" and the flappers "wings".

In 1807 Cayley was at work on a hot-air engine, and another using gunpowder. About a year later he was concerned with a kind of "cyclogiro", or "paddle-wheel" aircraft, and in the same year designed an ornithopter, another form of glider, and special wheels and a form of tubular construction for aircraft. A year or so later still, he was studying fish in connection with what is today known as streamlining, and in the summer of 1809 built and flew the first successful full-size glider in history. This sometimes carried a man, and Sir George recorded that it would "frequently lift him

up, and convey him several yards together".

Research continued along several widely different lines, and 1843 saw the designing of Cayley's "convertiplane" (as it would be known today), with four helicopter screws for vertical lift and two propellers for forward propulsion.

During the remaining years of his life this great Englishman built model gliders of improved type; persistently, if misguidedly, pursued his ideas on flappers; successfully flew an improved helicopter model; and designed tandem-wing models and a rubber-powered machine. But he achieved far more, and in 1853 was able to relate how, "a few years ago" (actually 1849) he made a glider in which "a boy of about ten years of age was floated off the ground for several yards on descending a hill, and also for about the same space by some persons pulling the apparatus against a very slight breeze by a rope". Well might a correspondent of Cayley's declare: "Poor fellow. I dare say he feared the fate of some of our early aeronauts. . . . But excuse the freedom I take, for the bare idea of *flying*, you know, invariably gives rise to jokes".

There was one man, apparently, who did not regard flying as a joke, and that was the man—traditionally believed to have been Sir George's coachman—who was the occupant of a Cayley aeroplane (for flappers were fitted) when it was tested at Brompton Hall some time after June 1853. There are various accounts of this flight, which was made across a dale, but the most charming, and seemingly the truest, was given by Sir George's grand-daughter, Mrs Thompson, in later years:

"The coachman went in the machine and landed on the west side at about the same level. I think it came down in rather a shorter distance than expected. The coachman got himself clear, and when the watchers had got across he shouted 'Please, Sir George, I wish to give notice. I was hired to drive, and not to fly' (of course, in broad Yorkshire). That's all I recollect. The machine was put high away in a barn, and I used to sit and hide in it (from Governess) . . .".

Precise details of this remarkable experiment are absent, but clearly Sir George's aeroplane served one practical purpose at least. Among his papers is this note on the machine concerned:

	lb
August 25, 53. new flyer	
Car, and working handles and wheels, side masts upright	120
2 wings	17
Tail	5
Sails and yards	22½
	164½

One can only wonder, on seeing such non-aeronautical terms, if Sir George regarded his coachman as being skilled in seamanship!

Above: This model, in the Science Museum, London, is based on Cayley's 1843 design for what we should now call a convertiplane. The eight segments of each circular wing pivoted individually to form an eight-blade helicopter rotor for vertical take-off and landing. Two propellers were fitted for forward propulsion

Left: A far earlier proposal for a helicopter is shown in this drawing by Leonardo da Vinci. The word "helicopter" comes from the Greek *helix* (a screw) and *pteron* (a wing). Leonardo's design had a spiral wing which would literally screw itself upward into the air

FOR WANT OF A HORSE

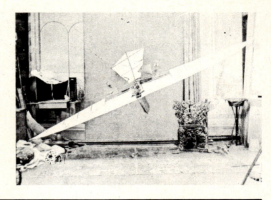

This page, top: When Henson became discouraged and emigrated to America, his colleague, John Stringfellow, built and tested this model in 1848. Spanning 10 ft (3.05 m), it was powered by a steam engine driving two pusher propellers. It succeeded only in gliding to the ground when launched from a wire. Like every experimenter in their century, Henson and Stringfellow lacked the lightweight power plant necessary to give their far-sighted designs a chance of success

Right: The mid-nineteenth century saw a sudden outburst of interest in helicopters. Enthusiasts in France even formed a society to promote their projects, of which the most fantastic was, perhaps, this 1863 design by Gabriel de La Landelle. It had much in common with the helicopter, *Albatross*, conceived twenty-three years later by Jules Verne for his story *Clipper of the Clouds*

SO FAR IN THIS HISTORY we have seen how the early dreams of flight were first realised by means of lighter-than-air craft, and how slow progress then began toward a practical and scientific understanding of the principles of heavier-than-air flight: what Sir George Cayley described as 'the art of flying, or aerial navigation as I have chosen to term it for the sake of giving a little more dignity to a subject bordering upon the ludicrous in public estimation'.

Cayley's words were apt enough. At the beginning of the 19th century, although balloon flight had been established for over fifteen years, the attitude of the vast majority of the general public. to the very idea of flight, powered or otherwise, was still one of ridicule and contempt. Fortunately for the future of aviation, a small band of enthusiasts still believed in the ultimate fulfilment of their dreams, and the published arguments of Cayley played an immense role in guiding them to success.

Probably his most notable disciple was William Samuel Henson, the Somerset engineer who in later years acknowledged Cayley as 'the father of aerial navigation'. It has been said of Henson that 'To him no mechanism was perfect. Each new device that he saw apparently challenged him to improve upon it. He would work intensively upon it for a while, then drop it—a new razor, an aeroplane, a breech-loading cannon, a method for waterproofing fabric, an ice machine, or a device for cleaning cisterns'. Such a variety of interests, one

might suppose, would mitigate against Henson's chances of success in any one field—though he had an excellent precedent, for Cayley himself pursued researches in many directions, ranging from artificial limbs to electrical apparatus and lifeboats.

When in his late thirties, Henson discussed his ideas for a flying machine with John Stringfellow, a philosopher and designer of light machinery for, among other things, the lace-making industry in which Henson worked. Because of Stringfellow's occupation, he was for a long time given the credit for designing the engine for Henson's aeroplane, but in fact the entire machine, including the engine, was Henson's own design. Stringfellow acted basically as the engineer-mechanic, from whom Henson ordered the engine in January 1842.

The design of the project—Henson's one and only aeroplane—was patented in 1843. Known as the Aerial Steam Carriage, it was never built in full-sized form; but it clearly owed much to Cayley's influence and, in all but two respects, had every ingredient required for a successful manned and powered flight. It deviated from Cayley's philosophy in being a monoplane—Cayley advocated triplane or multiplane lifting surfaces—and one has only to compare it with some of the successful European monoplanes of sixty years later, such as the Antoinette or the Taube, to appreciate how advanced a design it was.

The Ariel, as it later became known, had double-cambered wing surfaces to assist

lift, and horizontal and vertical movable rear surfaces designed to act as tailplane, elevator and rudder. Moreover, the wings, built up of strong spars and deep ribs covered with fabric, and braced with kingposts and wires, were as prophetic in their construction as in their configuration. The one ingredient which the design omitted was wing dihedral, though such an ardent follower of Cayley could hardly have failed to introduce this eventually.

The real problem faced by Henson, and all other pioneers for the next sixty years, was the lack of an engine which could produce sufficient power to propel an aeroplane without being so impossibly heavy as to prohibit any chance of success. With dihedral wings and a viable power plant, the Ariel must surely have flown. As matters turned out, it was to be another fifty years before the internal combustion petrol engine gave the first real hopes of a unit with a power/weight ratio capable of making powered flight possible. In the meantime, attention focussed chiefly upon engines driven by steam or hot air.

The full-size passenger-carrying Ariel was to have had a wing span of 150 ft (45.72 m), but at Stringfellow's suggestion a scale model was built first to test the soundness of the basic design. So, between 1844 and 1847, the two men built and tested a 20 ft (6.10 m) span scale prototype of the Steam Carriage, powered by a small steam engine driving two pusher propellers. At the final test, which took place at Chard, Somerset,

This engraving, showing Henson's Aerial Steam Carriage in imaginary flight over the Pyramids, produced ridicule rather than the hoped-for public support for the project. The design was, nonetheless, one of the great stepping stones between the theories of Cayley and the reality of flight in the twentieth century

in 1847, the model was launched down an inclined ramp, but the inadequate lift of the wings and the excessive weight of the engine succeeded only in pulling it earthward in what was euphemistically described as a 'powered glide'.

Both men, lacking funds of their own to launch their project, had by then become the victims of sharp businessmen. Their backers even managed to have a Bill promoted in Parliament for the formation of a public company, the Aerial Transit Company, to operate these large craft on services to the far parts of the globe. The publicity engendered by these suggestions, and accompanying pictures, was so lavish that it overcame its own purpose and succeeded only in heaping public ridicule upon the whole project.

Henson was so discouraged by the failure of the model tests that in the following year he emigrated to the United States. Although he remained in engineering, and retained his general interest in aeronautics, he took no part in further development of the Steam Carriage idea.

John Stringfellow continued to develop and adapt Henson's steam engine, and built a few more aeroplane models based upon Cayley's concept of triplane or multiplane lifting surfaces. But, although a first-class mechanic, Stringfellow did not have the inventive capacity of Henson, and none of his later models made a sustained free flight.

Thereafter, the emphasis in significant

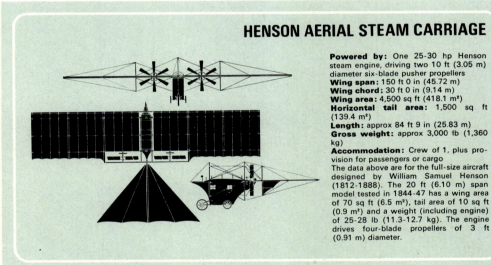

HENSON AERIAL STEAM CARRIAGE

Powered by: One 25-30 hp Henson steam engine, driving two 10 ft (3.05 m) diameter six-blade pusher propellers
Wing span: 150 ft 0 in (45.72 m)
Wing chord: 30 ft 0 in (9.14 m)
Wing area: 4,500 sq ft (418.1 m²)
Horizontal tail area: 1,500 sq ft (139.4 m²)
Length: approx 84 ft 9 in (25.83 m)
Gross weight: approx 3,000 lb (1,360 kg)
Accommodation: Crew of 1, plus provision for passengers or cargo
The data above are for the full-size aircraft designed by William Samuel Henson (1812-1888). The 20 ft (6.10 m) span model tested in 1844-47 has a wing area of 70 sq ft (6.5 m²), tail area of 10 sq ft (0.9 m²) and a weight (including engine) of 25-28 lb (11.3-12.7 kg). The engine drives four-blade propellers of 3 ft (0.91 m) diameter.

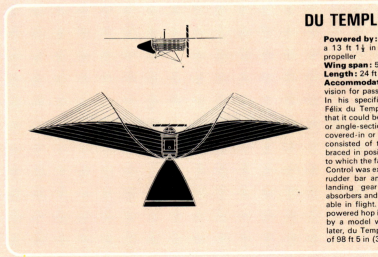

DU TEMPLE MONOPLANE

Powered by: One hot-air engine, driving a 13 ft 1½ in (4.00 m) diameter pusher propeller
Wing span: 55 ft 9 in (17.00 m)
Length: 24 ft 1 in (7.35 m)
Accommodation: Crew of 1, plus provision for passengers
In his specification for this aeroplane, Félix du Temple (1823-1890) suggested that it could be built of wood or of tubular or angle-section metal, the nacelle being covered-in or open as desired. The wings consisted of two cross-over main spars, braced in position by a network of cords, to which the fabric covering was attached. Control was exercised by a steering wheel, rudder bar and cables. The three-wheel landing gear was fitted with shock-absorbers and was designed to be retractable in flight. The aircraft, which made a powered hop in about 1874, was preceded by a model weighing 24.7 oz (700 gr); later, du Temple built a wing with a span of 98 ft 5 in (30 m).

Above : Although not particularly significant, Thomas Moy's big, tandem-wing 'Aerial Steamer' succeeded in lifting itself from the circular track around which it was tested, at the Crystal Palace, London, in 1875. It did not carry a man

This model, from the Qantas collection, depicts the aircraft, designed and built in France by Félix du Temple, which made the first-ever hop, carrying a man, at Brest in about 1874

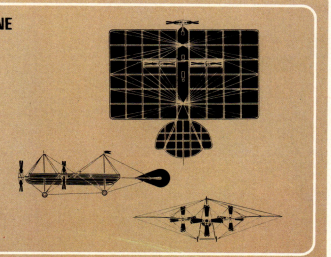

MOZHAISKI MONOPLANE

Powered by: One 20 hp steam engine, driving a 13 ft 1½ in (4.00 m) diameter four-blade tractor propeller and one 10 hp steam engine, driving two 11 ft 5⅜ in (3.50 m) diameter four-blade pusher propellers
Wing span: 74 ft 9½ in (22.80 m)
Wing chord: 46 ft 8 in (14.20 m)
Wing and horizontal tail area: 4,004 sq ft (372 m²)
Length: 75 ft 5½ in (23.00 m)
Width of fuselage: 4 ft 11 in (1.50 m)
Gross weight: 2,059 lb (934 kg)
Accommodation: Crew of 1, plus provision for passengers
A contemporary of du Temple, the Russian engineer Alexander Fedorovich Mozhaiski (1825-1890) designed this steam-engined monoplane which made a short powered hop in 1884, after running down a slope, with I N Golubev as pilot. It was preceded by tests with various models, of different sizes but similar basic configuration.

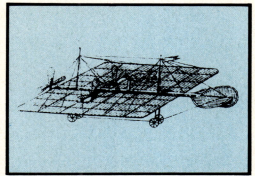

aeroplane development shifted to continental Europe, where in 1857-58 a French naval officer, Félix du Temple de la Croix, built an ingenious model monoplane that could take off under its own power—clockwork at first, later steam—hop for a short distance and land satisfactorily. Nearly twenty years later, du Temple followed this with a full-sized machine of similar design. It incorporated wing dihedral, a tailplane and rudder, a retractable undercarriage of sorts and a hot-air engine. In about 1874, with a young French sailor acting as pilot, it took off at Brest following a downhill run, and leapt a short distance into the air—the first powered man-carrying aeroplane to do so. Du Temple later fitted the aeroplane with a steam engine, but no record has been found of any tests with this power plant.

Another short powered hop, accomplished in similar manner, took place in Russia in 1884. After running down an inclined surface, a pilot named Golubev rose into the air in a large machine designed by Alexander Fedorovich Mozhaiski. The Mozhaiski aeroplane was also steam-powered, the two engines being of English manufacture with a combined output of some 30 hp, and followed successful demonstrations with models of similar configuration at least as early as 1876. A hop of 65-100 ft (20-30 m) was claimed for this machine, but the short distances covered by the du Temple and Mozhaiski aeroplanes, and the fact of their assisted take-offs, prohibits them from being regarded as proper

powered flights.

Nevertheless, the stage was almost ready for the achievement of the first true heavier-than-air powered flights of history. Cayley had established the necessary principles, and demonstrated their validity with unpowered flying craft; Henson had designed a capable craft that lacked only a suitable engine; and du Temple and Mozhaiski had come a little closer to achieving the goal with the engines available to them. One other major contribution should be mentioned: the work of another Englishman, Horatio Frederick Phillips, to whom goes the credit for establishing the foundation upon which all modern wing sections (aerofoils) are based.

Before the Wrights achieved success at Kitty Hawk in 1903, there were still other pioneers to come, some of whom would explore unprofitable avenues of research before finding the right path. But, essentially, all that was still needed was to master the art of control in the air, and to await and adapt the petrol engine to the requirements of powered flight. By the turn of the century, as the next two Parts of this history will show, the achievement of both goals was within reach.

This page, left: Stringfellow's triplane model of 1868 was no more successful than his earlier monoplane. It was, however, the first multi-winged design seen by the public and had a great influence in persuading later experimenters to adopt a biplane or triplane configuration

Above, top to bottom: This diagram of the structure of Henson's Aerial Steam Carriage, from *L'Illustration* magazine of 8 April 1843, shows well the ribs of its double-surfaced wings

Drawing of Mozhaiski's steam-powered aeroplane of 1884, which repeated du Temple's success by making a short hop-flight after gaining speed down a ramp

Model of the Henson Aerial Steam Carriage, with overwing stabilising fin, in the Musée de l'Air, Paris. Above it, left, is a model of the du Temple aircraft

C·ADER 1889

Ader, Maxim & Lilienthal

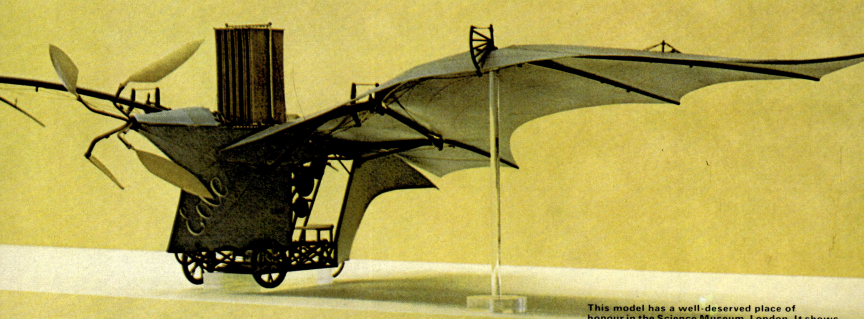

This model has a well-deserved place of honour in the Science Museum, London. It shows the bat-wing monoplane Eole, which became the first powered aeroplane to lift itself and a pilot from (presumably) level ground, on 9 October 1890. Piloted by its designer, Clément Ader, it hopped only some 50 m (164 ft) and lacked effective controls

Right: Otto Lilienthal (1848-96), greatest of the early pioneers of gliding

In the entire history of flying there is no more controversial figure than Clément Ader. Even today arguments persist concerning this Frenchman's achievements and their influence on aeronautical progress; but it is now generally admitted that Ader was the first man to leave level ground in a powered aeroplane. The arguments remaining are concerned largely with the difference between a true sustained flight and a 'running hop'.

Ader was an electrical engineer and inventor, and his name endures in history not only for his pioneering flight, or hop, which he claimed to have made in secret on 9 October 1890, but for his work in developing the telephone. The aircraft he used on the date given was called the *Eole*, and was the outcome of much earlier experiment, for Ader had publicly exhibited his first large model aeroplane in 1874. In appearance the *Eole* was like a bat, and it was powered by a steam engine which drove a tractor, or front-mounted, propeller. The wings were arranged to fold, as on modern naval machines used from aircraft carriers, but there were no controlling surfaces, and Ader himself mentioned 'insufficient stability' and 'the necessity for further study'.

A second machine, called by Ader the *Avion*, was never completed; but it gave the French their accepted name for an aeroplane. Its successor, the *Avion III*, was tested on two occasions late in 1897; but there is no real evidence to support the claims of Ader, made in later years, that this succeeded in becoming airborne. The most remarkable feature of this third machine was that it had two engines, driving two propellers.

Ader foresaw clearly the military uses of aeroplanes, and the French military authorities gave him financial assistance. When this was withdrawn, and Ader had spent his private fortune, work ceased. The *Eole* he destroyed, but the *Avion III* and its remarkable steam engines survive.

There were striking parallels between the work of Ader and that of Sir Hiram Stevens Maxim, a colourful American who, while resident in England, developed the renowned machine-gun bearing his name. In England, too, he built an amazing aeroplane.

Left and below: The huge biplane built by Sir Hiram Maxim, and tested at Baldwyn's Park, Kent, in 1894, lifted itself and its crew into the air—no mean feat for a machine that weighed over 3½ tons. Much of the credit goes to the two fine 180 hp steam engines which Sir Hiram designed especially for it. Each drove a propeller nearly 18 ft (5.49 m) in diameter.

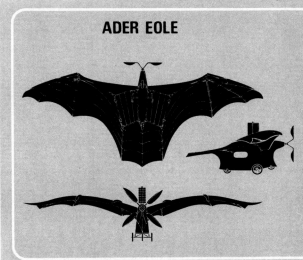

ADER EOLE

Powered by: One 20 hp Ader four-cylinder steam engine, driving a four-blade tractor propeller of approx 11 ft 6 in (3.50 m) diameter
Wing span: 45 ft 11 in (14.00 m)
Wing area: 301.4 sq ft (28.0 m²)
Length: 21 ft 4 in (6.50 m)
Weight empty: 498 lb (226 kg)
Gross weight: 652 lb (296 kg)
Accommodation: Crew of 1
The Eole was the first aeroplane designed by Clément Ader (1841-1925), and the first man-carrying aeroplane to take off under its own power, without other assistance, and make a short hop-flight. It did so on 9 October 1890, in the grounds of the Château Pereire at Armainvilliers, travelling about 164 ft (50 m) through the air at a height of some 8 in (20 cm) above the ground. Ader's later Avion III (1897) had a 52 ft 6 in (16.00 m) wing span, gross weight of about 882 lb (400 kg), and two 20 hp engines. It failed to fly.

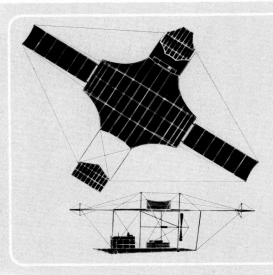

MAXIM 1894 BIPLANE

Powered by: Two 180 hp Maxim steam engines, each driving a 17 ft 10 in (5.44 m) diameter two-blade pusher propeller
Wing span: 104 ft 0 in (31.70 m)
Wing/elevator area (total): 4,000 sq ft (371.6 m²)
Length: approx 95 ft 0 in (28.96 m)
Gross weight: 8,000 lb (3,629 kg)
Accommodation: Crew of 4
Sir Hiram Stevens Maxim (1840-1916) began building this huge aeroplane in 1891, describing it as 'a flying machine that would lift itself from the ground'; he did not intend it to fly in the true sense. When tested in 1894, it ran along a railway track until, at a speed slightly above 42 mph (68 km/h), the wheels lifted clear of the track, fouled the guard rails placed to prevent a complete take-off, and the machine had to be brought to a halt. Maxim did not pursue its development further.

Extreme left, top: Lilienthal flying one of his very successful monoplane gliders, after taking off from an artificial hill near Berlin, in 1893 or 1894

Centre: Taken in October 1895, this photograph captures something of the lightness and elegance of Lilienthal's gliders. They were made of peeled willow wands, covered with waxed cotton cloth

Bottom: Percy Pilcher, who carried on the work of Lilienthal, in England, until he too was killed, in 1899

Above: A Lilienthal monoplane glider, showing how the fabric was attached under the cambered wing ribs and stitched around the spanwise willow wands

Left, top: Pilcher prepares to fly his most famous glider, the Hawk, from a hilltop. The small wheels made it much easier to move on the ground than Lilienthal's designs

Bottom: The Hawk airborne. Pilcher flew it up to 250 yards (230 m) and was about to fit a light oil engine to a later machine at the time of his death

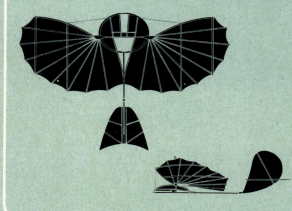

LILIENTHAL 1893 MONOPLANE GLIDER

Wing span: 22 ft 11½ in (7.00 m)
Wing area: 150.7 sq ft (14.0 m²)
Wing chord (max): 8 ft 2½ in (2.50 m)
Length: 16 ft 4¾ in (5.00 m)
Weight without pilot: 44 lb (20 kg)
Accommodation: Crew of 1
Otto Lilienthal (1848-1896) made approximately 2,500 successful glides in 1893-96, mostly in monoplane 'hang-gliders' of the type illustrated, in which he flew distances of up to 985 ft (300 m). Prior to this, Lilienthal had built two biplane gliders in 1891 and 1892. His philosophy was well summarised in his own words: 'To design a flying machine is nothing; to build it is not much; to test it is everything'.

Like Ader, Maxim was an electrical engineer, with a variety of inventions to his credit in other fields, and he, too, foresaw the value of the aeroplane in war, though he showed even less concern than the Frenchman with the problems of really practical flying. His first aim was merely to build a machine that would lift itself from the ground, and in 1889 he began to make models of wings and propellers which he tested on a whirling arm. Then he built an extraordinarily light steam engine, though he had also considered the merits of petrol. In the grounds of Baldwyns Park, Kent, which he had rented, he constructed an enormous biplane, propelled by two 180 hp steam engines, each of which drove a propeller 17 ft 10 in (5.44 m) in diameter. Including a crew of four this contraption weighed over 3½ tons. To limit the distance it could rise into the air, it was placed on a broad-gauge railway track having restraining guard-rails. During the third full-scale trial the machine actually lifted clear, but fouled the guard-rails and was brought to a stop. Apparently satisfied, Maxim then brought his experiments temporarily to a close. He was to build another aeroplane in 1910, though this was not successful.

Sir Hiram spent nearly £20,000 on his aeronautical experiments, and even though these contributed relatively little to the advancement of practical flying the man must be admired not only for his determination but for the brilliant engineering achievement represented by the very light steam engine he developed for his aero-

plane. Like the power plant of the *Avion III*, this exists today.

The work of Ader was more interesting than important; but the experiments of the German Otto Lilienthal were among the most important in aeronautical history, for they led directly to those of the Wright brothers. Although his most notable work was performed with fixed-wing gliders, Lilienthal remained mistakenly convinced that, when it arrived, the practical powered aeroplane would be an ornithopter, or wing-flapper. Some of his earliest experiments were, in fact, made with his brother Gustav on quite large ornithopters, but these were interrupted first by his service in the Franco-Prussian War and then by his profession of civil engineering.

In 1889 Otto Lilienthal published a book having the English title *Bird Flight as the Basis of Aviation*, wherein he studied the forms and anatomy of birds' wings and the application of data learned from them to the achievement of human flight. Some of his findings were later proved by the Wright brothers to be incorrect, but the book remains as one of the great classics of aeronautical literature.

In order to gain practical experience before returning to his work on ornithopters, Lilienthal built his first fixed-wing glider in 1891, and between that year and 1896 constructed five types of monoplane glider and two biplane types. His first means of launching was a spring-board, but this he soon abandoned in favour of hill-launching. Some of his tests were made from the Rhinower Hills, near Stöllen, but he also had constructed an artificial hill near Berlin.

Lilienthal supported himself in his gliders by his arms, so that after a running take-off his hips and legs dangled below the aircraft, allowing him to swing his body in any desired direction to achieve stability and control. After 1893 he was achieving glides of 300-750 ft (90-230 m), with remarkable ease of control. In 1895 he was developing a type of body harness to work a rear elevator. The purpose of this was to give better control in rising or descending by increasing the effect of the occupant swinging his body forwards or backwards and thus altering the centre of gravity. Lilienthal also tested a glider which had flapping wing-tips, driven by a small carbonic acid gas engine. This system could never have equalled in efficiency the new petrol engines and propellers which were soon to come into being; but the great German inventor/pilot was never to become aware of this, for he crashed in one of his gliders in the Rhinower Hills on 9 August 1896, and died in a Berlin clinic on the following day. His last words were 'Opfer mussen gebracht werden' ('Sacrifices must be made').

The name of Lilienthal stands as the greatest in the history of practical flying before the Wright brothers, to whose achievements, as already noted, his work led directly. The true value of his experiments became apparent only after his death. Not only were his writings carefully translated for the benefit of others, but, like the Wright brothers in later years, the great German pioneer recognised the value of photography in recording his experiments. People could see for themselves that, even without an engine, and using only the forces of the wind and gravity, a man could achieve successful flight. Perhaps the finest monuments to Lilienthal are the gliding clubs throughout the world which give such pleasant recreation to men and women at little cost.

Little known before Lilienthal's death was the practical help he had given to a young Englishman named Percy Pilcher, who paid him two visits. In 1893 Pilcher had been appointed assistant lecturer in Naval Architecture and Marine Engineering at Glasgow University, and it was there that he designed his first glider, the *Bat*. This was uncompleted at the time of his first visit to Lilienthal in 1895. On his second visit, in the following year, he made his first glides, under Lilienthal's tuition, and back again in Britain he tested and redesigned the *Bat* and built other gliders. In May 1899 he presided at a lecture given by the Australian Lawrence Hargrave on soaring kites, in the development of which Hargrave was pre-eminent. Pilcher then built a triplane glider embodying Hargrave's ideas, but before he could test this he crashed in the *Hawk* of his own design and died on 2 October 1899. Pilcher was the first Englishman to lose his life in a heavier-than-air flying machine.

Threshold of *Success*

Samuel Pierpont Langley, an American, had worked in his youth as a railway surveyor and civil engineer, and later became a famous astronomer. At the Smithsonian Institution during the 1880s he made many experiments with model wings on a whirling arm, and even tested stuffed birds in 'attempts to acquire the art of flight'. In 1891 he turned his attention to steam-driven model aeroplanes, of which the first four were failures; but in 1896 his No 5 and No 6 models flew successfully on many occasions, the longest flight measuring no less than 4,200 ft (1,280 m).

The successful models were made of metal and had two sets of wings, one behind the other. The wings each measured 14 ft (4.27 m) in span, and between them was the engine, driving two propellers amidships. The models were launched by catapult from a houseboat on the Potomac River.

After these tests Langley had intended to give up his aerial experiments, but in 1898 the President of the United States offered him government money if he would build a full-size aeroplane with a view to developing it for military purposes. This Langley undertook to do, and as a first step, in 1901,

built a quarter-size model powered with a small petrol engine. This was the first aeroplane to fly with an engine of that kind.

A full-size man-carrying machine was completed in 1903. This had a wing span of 48 ft (14.63 m) and was powered with a remarkably light and efficient petrol engine, made by Langley's assistant, C. M. Manly. Beyond doubt, Manly's engine was the true forerunner of the radial type of aero-engine which in later years was universally adopted, although he has seldom received the credit due to him.

It was Manly who was chosen to fly the *Aerodrome*, as Langley confusingly named the form of aeroplane he had designed. The full-size machine closely resembled his earlier models. But success was not to crown his brilliant efforts and those of his assistant, for in each of two trials over the Potomac in late 1903 the big *Aerodrome* fouled its launching mechanism and fell into the river. Manly was unhurt, but the government lost faith and the experiments ended. In later years the *Aerodrome* was flown as a seaplane, but it had by that time been extensively altered, and experts today are agreed that in its original form the

machine could not be regarded as a truly practical aeroplane.

Another American who, coincidentally, was a railway engineer as Langley had been, and who also made a notable contribution to the development of flying, was Octave Chanute. In 1894 a series of articles written by this engineer were reprinted as a book called *Progress in Flying Machines*, and it was this which stimulated the Wright brothers to begin their experiments. Though Chanute himself built successful gliders, it was as a collector and disseminator of information that his service to aviation may have been greatest.

In 1903 Chanute gave a lecture in France which had a profound effect on developments in Europe; but 1903 was also the year in which a German, Karl Jatho, made a number of 'hops' in a powered aeroplane. Historians have hitherto ignored, or been ignorant of, these attempts, but it must now be recorded that on 18 August 1903 Jatho himself recorded having made an 'aerial leap' of about 60 ft (18.30 m). In November he claimed 'many small flights' up to about 200 ft (61 m) in length, during some of which his aeroplane rose to a height of

Left: The first four aeroplane models made by Samuel Pierpont Langley in America were unsuccessful, but in 1896 his No 5 model (shown here) and the later No 6 made several excellent flights, the longest covering 4,200 ft (1,280 m). These model 'Aerodromes', as Langley called them, had dihedral wings mounted in tandem and were powered by a steam engine driving two propellers amidships

Below: The Wright brothers made nearly a thousand glides on their third glider, built in the autumn of 1902. This picture shows it in its modified form, after they had fitted a single movable rear rudder in place of the original pair of fixed tail fins

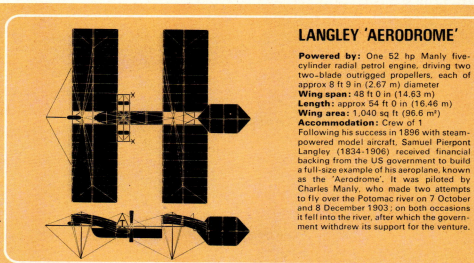

LANGLEY 'AERODROME'

Powered by: One 52 hp Manly five-cylinder radial petrol engine, driving two two-blade outrigged propellers, each of approx 8 ft 9 in (2.67 m) diameter
Wing span: 48 ft 0 in (14.63 m)
Length: approx 54 ft 0 in (16.46 m)
Wing area: 1,040 sq ft (96.6 m²)
Accommodation: Crew of 1
Following his success in 1896 with steam-powered model aircraft, Samuel Pierpont Langley (1834-1906) received financial backing from the US government to build a full-size example of his aeroplane, known as the 'Aerodrome'. It was piloted by Charles Manly, who made two attempts to fly over the Potomac river on 7 October and 8 December 1903; on both occasions it fell into the river, after which the government withdrew its support for the venture.

WRIGHT FLYER 1

Powered by: One 12 hp Wright four-cylinder water-cooled petrol engine, driving two pusher propellers, each of 8 ft 6 in (2.59 m) diameter
Wing span: 40 ft 4 in (12.29 m)
Length: 21 ft 1 in (6.43 m)
Wing area: 510 sq ft (47.4 m²)
Gross weight: approx 750 lb (340 kg)
Max speed: approx 30 mph (48 km/h) at ground level
Accommodation: Crew of 1
First flight: 17 December 1903
After several years of successful experimenting with biplane gliders, Orville and Wilbur Wright were ready in 1903 to build a powered aeroplane. Before this could fly, they had also to design and build the engine and propellers for it, since none of a suitable kind then existed. Their efforts were rewarded with success on 17 December 1903, when four flights were made, two by each of the brothers.

about 10 ft (3.05 m).

Though Jatho achieved more than Ader (see page 41), his work is quite overshadowed by that of the Wright brothers.

Wilbur and Orville Wright were the sons of a bishop and lived at Dayton, Ohio. The money and skills which they acquired as bicycle makers enabled them to begin their aeronautical work. Both brothers had been interested in flying since boyhood, but it was Wilbur who took the first practical step by writing to the Smithsonian Institution asking for a list of books and articles on the subject. Among those suggested was Chanute's *Progress in Flying Machines*.

By August 1899 Orville was as keen to fly as Wilbur, and in that month the two young men completed their first aircraft, a biplane kite. A feature of this kite was the use of warping, or twisting, of the wings to achieve lateral stability, or sideways balance, and in 1900 Wilbur wrote to Chanute concerning this and other matters, thereby opening a long, close and rewarding friendship.

The wing-warping features was used also in the brothers' first glider, built in 1900 and transported for tests to the lonely Kill Devil Hills sand-dunes, near Kitty Hawk, on the North Carolina coast. Generally resembling the kite, the glider had wings of 17 ft (5.18 m) span. The pilot lay prone, with the objects of making him comfortable, making landing safer and lessening resistance to the air. Though a number of piloted flights were made, the glider was flown mostly as a kite. From these flights the brothers learned

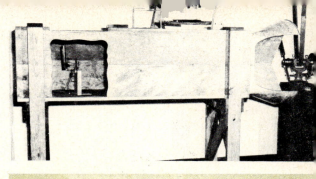

much, and Bishop Wright's 'boys' went home to Dayton not only pleased but more determined than ever to make powered flights.

The No 2 glider, built in 1901, was another biplane, though larger. The method of launching it was for one brother to grasp one wing and one of the Kitty Hawk 'locals' the other, and then dash forward hopefully. Troubles were encountered with the shape of wing employed, and although successful glides were made and the machine was controlled in stiff winds, the brothers returned to Dayton far less pleased than formerly. They made up their minds to rely in future entirely upon their own investigations instead of those of Otto Lilienthal, and this led to an amazingly thorough research programme, including the testing of model wings in a wind-tunnel. The outcome of these tests was a far greater confidence in their future success, and the No 3 glider, built in August and September 1902, had made nearly a thousand glides by the end of October. It was clear that the glider as it then stood needed only to be copied, altered a little and given an engine to produce a really practical aeroplane.

Being good businessmen as well as pioneers, the brothers took the precaution of applying for a patent for their design, and this was eventually granted in 1906. Meanwhile it remained to build the most historic aeroplane of all time, plus an engine and propellers to take it into the air. The engine was not only designed by, but partly constructed by, the brothers themselves. It

had four cylinders, was water-cooled, gave about 12 hp and weighed, complete with accessories, water and fuel, just over 200 lb (91 kg). No published data on propeller design being available, the Wrights did their own basic research in this difficult field.

The first powered machine was called the *Flyer*, and it was built during the summer of 1903. Making the now-familiar journey to Kitty Hawk, the brothers found the camp they had established there in bad repair and the No 3 glider damaged. This they mended for practice flights, but various difficulties with the *Flyer* delayed its readiness to fly until 12 December. Bad weather meant a further two-day delay, but on 14 December the *Flyer* was carried to the rail from which it was to be launched. Friends from the nearby Kill Devil Life Saving Station stood by as witnesses. The brothers tossed a coin to decide who should fly first, and Wilbur won. But Wilbur was not to be the first pilot, for when launched he pulled up the nose too high, the *Flyer* stalled, or lost lift, and ploughed into the sand.

The damage having been repaired, it was now Orville's turn to try; and on the morning of 17 December 1903, Orville Wright became the first man to achieve sustained, controlled flight in an aeroplane. This historic flight was of twelve seconds duration and covered about 120 ft (36.58 m). Of three flights which followed on the same day, one was of 852 ft (260 m) and lasted for 59 seconds. Lilienthal and Pilcher had not died in vain.

Left: Wilbur Wright, lying prone across the lower wing of the *Flyer I* after the first attempted take-off on 14 December 1903. This did not succeed, and the first flight of the *Flyer* was made three days later, with Orville Wright as pilot

Above, top to bottom: Replica of the wind tunnel designed by the Wright brothers and used in 1902. Inside the tunnel was a delicate balance on which they suspended scale model wings of different designs to test their aerodynamic properties in a 25-35 mph (40-56 km/h) airflow created by the fan on the right of the picture

The full-size Langley 'Aerodrome' of 1903, mounted on its launching platform above a houseboat on the Potomac River

Launching of the 14 ft (4.27 m) span Langley No 5 model 'Aerodrome' at Quantico, Virginia, in 1896

THE WRIGHT BROTHERS

CONSOLIDATE THEIR SUCCESS

Below: Replica of the 1909 Wright Military Flyer, in the USAF Museum at Wright Patterson Base, Ohio

Far left, above: Famous car, famous occupants. An early Rolls-Royce in which are seated (left to right) Horace Short, the Hon. Charles Rolls (who flew Short-built Wright biplanes), Orville Wright, Griffith Brewer and Wilbur Wright

Far left, below: Wilbur Wright's first pupil in Europe was the Comte de Lambert, here piloting a Wright *Flyer*

Left: Two-seat *Flyer* in front of the hangar at Hunaudières racecourse near Le Mans in August 1908. It was from this field that Wilbur Wright amazed European aviators by his exhibitions of skilful flying, the like of which they had never seen before

THE WRIGHT BROTHERS

CONSOLIDATE THEIR SUCCESS

After making the first successful heavier-than-air powered flight at the Kill Devil Hills, Kitty Hawk, on 17 December 1903, Wilbur and Orville Wright returned home to Dayton well satisfied, even though their precious *Flyer* had been wrecked beyond repair by a gust of wind after its fourth flight. Incredibly, the world at large did not learn of their historic exploit. Only garbled accounts were printed in the newspapers, and readers considered the trials unsuccessful, as were all the other attempts being made to fly at that time.

Back in Dayton the two brothers designed a second *Flyer*, with a new engine. It was finished in May 1904, and tested from a large field called Huffman Prairie, eight miles to the east of Dayton. A total of 105 flights were made, the longest lasting over 5 minutes and covering 2¾ miles (4.4 km). A problem experienced was the Flyer's tendency not to respond to control movements during a tight turn, so that it stalled and went out of control.

During the winter the brothers built *Flyer* No III. This also was tested from the Huffman Prairie, nearly fifty flights being made during the season. To solve the problem of stalling on turns, the control cables used for warping the wings and moving the rudder were separated. This permitted any desired degree of wing warp or rudder movement, either together or independently. Thus modified, the *Flyer* III was fully manoeuvrable, able to bank, turn and make circuits and figures-of-eight with ease. Its longest flight, with Wilbur at the controls, on 5 October 1905, lasted 38 minutes and covered over 24 miles (38.6 km).

A surprising feature of these trials was the continued lack of serious attention by the press. Reporters were invited to witness the first trials, but bad weather and engine troubles prevented flights, and they departed, convinced it was all a waste of time. The result was that, while the world at large remained ignorant of the flights, local farmers became so used to the sound of a *Flyer* passing overhead that they did not even bother to look up—at a time when some authorities were still asserting that mechanical flight was impossible!

One result of this lack of publicity was

that pioneering work in Europe tended to develop along its own, and in some ways more promising, lines. The Wright *Flyers* were deliberately designed to be inherently unstable, and the pilot had to control them continually. There was no automatic weathercock-like stability, such as would have been given by a fixed fin or tailplane behind the wings. This was in marked contrast to the ideas of earlier pioneers such as Cayley, Pénaud and Lilienthal, and of most of the pioneers who followed the Wrights.

But the *Flyer* III was a practicable machine and the Wrights were certain that 'the age of the flying machine had come at last.' Convinced that it had possibilities for military reconnaissance, they offered their design to the US Army. They were told that the authorities would not take any action 'until a machine is produced which by actual operation is shown to be able to produce horizontal flight and to carry an operator'! Not unnaturally, the Wrights, who had been flying for three years, were flabbergasted.

Negotiations with the British government proved equally disappointing. The Wrights wanted a guarantee that if their machine behaved according to the terms of the offer it would definitely be purchased; if it didn't, the government need not buy. But the authorities wanted to be allowed to inspect the machine closely, and witness its performance, without any obligation to buy if it was successful.

Disheartened and thwarted by such intransigence, the Wrights decided to stop all flying, to prevent commercial or military spying on their activities. For the next two and a half years, from October 1905 to May 1908, they neither flew nor allowed anyone to inspect their precious *Flyers*, which they continued to build. In May 1907 Wilbur took a new and carefully crated *Flyer* to Europe, to negotiate for manufacture under licence. But months went by without any results and, finally, disheartened, he returned, leaving the crated *Flyer* at Le Havre.

However, things changed rapidly in 1908. In February the US War Department at last agreed to witness an official test, and in March an agreement was reached for Wright aircraft to be built in France.

After refreshing himself with practice on the 'old' 1905 *Flyer* III, Wilbur returned to France, collected the *Flyer* he had left at Le Havre and assembled it at a racecourse at Hunaudières, about five miles south of Le Mans. The first public demonstrations were made on 8 August, and in the succeeding days further flights were made, followed by another hundred from the nearby Camp d'Auvours military ground.

This time the flights hit the headlines of the world, and there was no limit to the praise. Not only did the *Flyer* break every existing record for aeroplanes, but it demonstrated that the Wrights had developed an aeroplane which could climb, bank, turn, execute smooth circuits and figures-of-eight. Both the aircraft and the flying technique were far in advance of anything else in Europe at that time.

The machine used for this French début was a two-seat *Flyer*, the first of about

seven built between 1907 and 1909. It had a wing span of around 40 ft (12.19 m), a 30 hp four-cylinder engine driving twin pusher propellers, weighed 800 lb (363 kg) empty and flew at 35-40 mph (56-64 km/h). Although normally launched by the derrick-and-falling-weight technique, invented by the Wrights, it could also take off unassisted.

Meanwhile, Orville was achieving similar success at the US Army trials at Fort Myer. Of three aircraft ordered from different designers, his *Flyer* was the only one delivered, and in it he made ten flights, including four of more than an hour's duration, before crashing and killing his passenger.

The impact of the Wrights' demonstrations is not easy to assess. European aviators quickly realised that the *Flyer* was the culmination of prodigious effort and a carefully-planned series of logical experiments. In Europe not a single pioneer had attempted anything remotely like it. For five years, European aviators had groped blindly from failure to partial success, until by the beginning of 1908 they had reached the stage when, with luck, they could keep their aircraft airborne for one-and-a-half minutes, a few feet off the ground.

Wilbur's skilful demonstration had shown convincingly the vital importance of proper lateral control, and most of Europe's pioneers began to fit rudimentary ailerons or adopt wing-warping. After this, their efforts advanced much more rapidly, as will be seen in Part 11.

To their credit, European pioneers did not adopt the policy of deliberate instability. In the end even the Wright brothers had to admit the superiority of inherent stability. The first basic change to their efficient but tricky-to-master control system was the addition of a fixed tailplane behind the rear double rudder. Soon afterwards this was converted into an elevator, working in conjunction with the front elevator.

These *Flyers* were followed by the Wright Model B, on which the distinctive front elevator was at last abandoned, leading the newly-established *Jane's All the World's Aircraft* to record, picturesquely, that a 'headless' Wright had been produced. This Model B also embodied a wheeled undercarriage, another feature which, surprisingly, the Wrights took a long time to adopt.

The last Wright aircraft to appear was the Model L of 1915, a single-seat military scout powered by a 70 hp six-cylinder Wright engine.

It was a neat-looking biplane, with ailerons on both sets of wings; but it was not as good as its competitors. To Wilbur and Orville Wright, however, goes the lasting honour, not only of inventing the first powered aeroplane capable of sustained and controlled flight, but of setting their fellow aviators in Europe on the road to similar success. The progress in European aviation in the short time between Wilbur Wright's visit in 1908 and the first great air meeting at Reims a year later was truly remarkable, and was directly attributable to the Wrights' influence.

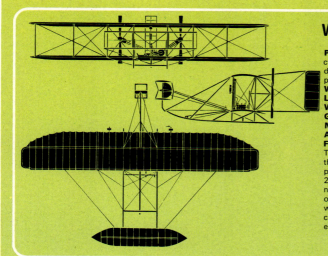

WRIGHT FLYER III

Powered by: One 15-21 hp Wright four-cylinder water-cooled in-line engine, driving two 8 ft 6 in (2.59 m) diameter pusher propellers
Wing span: 40 ft 6 in (12.34 m)
Length: 28 ft 0 in (8.53 m)
Wing area: 503 sq ft (46.73 m²)
Gross weight: approx 855 lb (388 kg)
Max speed: approx 35 mph (56 km/h)
Accommodation: Crew of 1
First flight: 23 June 1905

The *Flyer* III was the machine regarded by the Wrights themselves as their first fully practical powered aeroplane. Between 23 June and 16 October 1905 it made nearly 50 flights, some of which were well over half an hour in duration. Above all, it was a fully controllable aircraft, which could bank, turn and perform figure-of-eight manoeuvres easily.

Top left, below: The Wright flying ground at Dayton, Ohio, in 1911

Bottom left, below: Orville Wright about to start the Baby Wright machine. An earlier version, the Baby Grand racer built for the 1910 Gordon Bennett competition, was the first Wright design to embody a wheeled landing gear from the outset

Left, below: A Wright glider of 1911 in flight at Kitty Hawk, North Carolina. The sandbag hanging from the forward pole was used to adjust the aircraft's centre of gravity

Bottom: Powered by a 60 hp Wright engine, the Wright Model C-H of 1913 was intended as a commercial hydroplane

ALBERTO SANTOS-DUMON

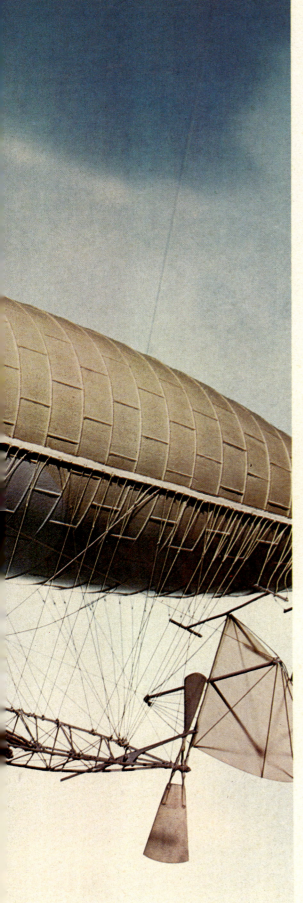

'At 11 am all was ready. The basket rocked prettily beneath the balloon, which a mild, fresh breeze was caressing. Impatient to be off, I stood in my corner of the narrow wicker basket with a bag of ballast in my hand. In the other corner M. Machuron gave the word: "Let go, all!"

'Suddenly the wind ceased. The air seemed motionless around us. We were off, going at the speed of the air current in which we now lived and moved. Indeed, for us there was no more wind; and this is the first great fact of all in spherical ballooning. Infinitely gentle is this unfelt movement forward and upward. The illusion is complete: it seems not to be the balloon that moves, but the earth that sinks down and away.'

Any man who could write so vividly and observantly about his first ascent in a balloon was clearly an enthusiast, and Alberto Santos-Dumont, who wrote those lines, was not only an enthusiast himself but one whose exploits aroused the interest of others. News of his romantic adventures, and especially of his hair-raising escapes from disaster, was awaited throughout the world with the kind of eagerness that is aroused today by international film stars and footballers. Alberto had 'personality', as well as being a great pioneer of aviation, and the force of that personality was expressed by a writer in 1904 thus:

'Nature made Santos-Dumont a very small, slim, slight man, weighing hardly more than one hundred pounds, but very active and muscular. The first time I ever saw him, in the Crystal Palace, London, where he was setting up one of his airships in a huge gallery, I thought him at first glance to be some boy, a possible spectator, who was interested in flying machines. His face, bare and shaven, looked youthful; he wore a narrow-brimmed straw hat and was dressed in the height of fashion. . . . A moment later he had his coat off and was showing his men how to put up the great fan-like rudder of the ship which loomed above us like some enormous rugby football, and then one saw the power that was in him. Brazilian by nationality, he has a dark face, large dark eyes, an alertness of step and an energetic way of talking. His boyhood was spent on his father's coffee plantation in Brazil; his later years mostly in Paris,

though he has been a frequent visitor to England and America. He speaks Spanish, French, and English with equal fluency. One finds him most unpretentious, modest, speaking freely of his inventions. . . .'

As a child Santos-Dumont had been inspired by the stories of Jules Verne, and from his tenth year he was driving railway engines on his father's plantation. During his schooling in Paris he familiarised himself with all aspects of ballooning and made his first ascent, as earlier described, in 1897. He enjoyed the experience so much that he had a balloon made for himself. Excitement quickly came his way. After one ascent from Nice he made a crash-landing which he once recalled in these words:

'I was dragged through the small trees and yielding shrubbery, my face a mass of cuts and bruises, my clothes torn from my back, in pain and strain, fearing the worst, and able to do nothing to save myself. Just as I had given myself up for lost the guide-rope wound itself round a tree and held. I was precipitated from the basket and fell unconscious. When I came to I had to walk some distance until I met some peasants. They helped me back to Nice, where I went to bed, and had the doctor sew me up.'

Trees were to loom very large in the life of the young Brazilian. In 1898 his first steerable airship came to grief in a line of them. Two days later, on descent, the repaired envelope began to crumple in the middle, but some boys siezed the guide-rope and dragged the airship against the wind, checking the descent. The second airship was dashed against trees and wrecked. The third lost its rudder and was damaged. To save weight in the fourth, Alberto sat on a bicycle saddle. The fifth had further tree-trouble, and Alberto was found in the branches, where he had lunch sent up to him. He was next discovered by firemen hanging in space above a courtyard of the Trocadero Hotel.

On one occasion the dashing Brazilian travelled by air down the Champs-Elysées and stopped at his house for a cup of coffee, and Parisians could often tell when he was visiting his club — from the airship tied up outside. All this *before* he began the second part of his flying career, as a European contemporary of the Wright brothers in heavier-than-air machines!

Below: the tail-first 14*bis* in which Santos-Dumont made the first successful powered flights in Europe in 1906

Right: Historic gathering at Mussel Manor, early home of the (later Royal) Aero Club. From left to right, standing, are Oswald, Horace and Eustace Short, Frank McClean, Griffith Brewer, Frank Hedges Butler and Dr Lockyer; seated, J T C Moore-Brabazon, Wilbur and Orville Wright, and Charles Rolls

Right, centre: the Blériot VIII of 1908, predecessor of the monoplane in which this famous Frenchman flew the Channel in the following year

Right, below: The Voisin-Archdeacon float glider of 1905, one of the Voisins' first aeroplanes and the first real application of Hargrave's boxkite configuration to a full-size aircraft

Far right, above: On the Voisin-Farman I biplane Henry Farman made, on 13 January 1908, the first officially-observed one-kilometre circular flight in Europe

Far right, below: The Gold Bug, first aeroplane built independently by American Glenn Curtiss, appeared in the Spring of 1909. From it he developed his famous Golden Flyer, which at Reims later that year proved itself one of the two fastest aircraft in the world

AFTER THE WRIGHTS

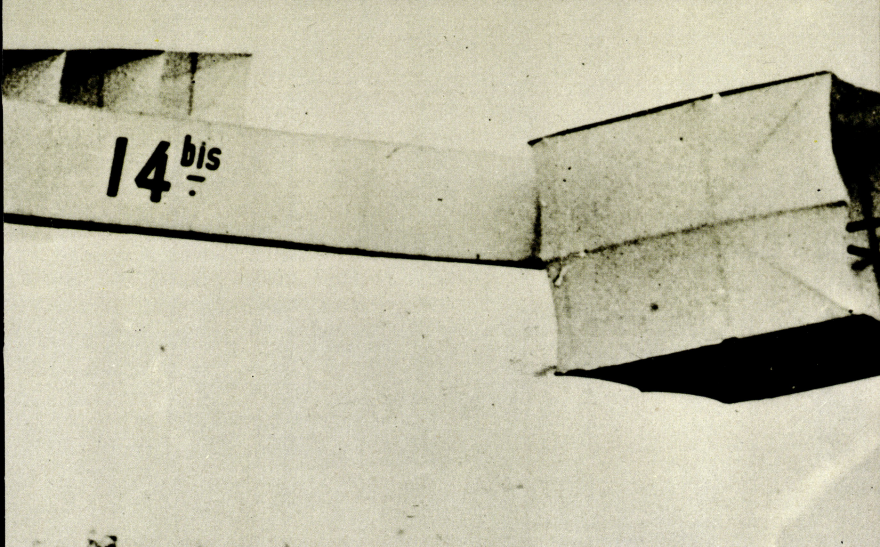

14 bis

Inspired by the work of the German Otto Lilienthal, described on page 43, Captain Ferber of the French Army began building gliders in 1899. These were unsuccessful at first, though one completed in 1904 was notable for Ferber's efforts to obtain stability, or self-righting power. In 1905 he built a powered aircraft which, although it could not sustain itself in level flight, made a successful 'power glide'; in the same year another Frenchman, Gabriel Voisin, made flights from the River Seine in a bi-plane glider towed behind a motor boat. In England, also during 1905, the American S F Cody flew a glider at Farnborough.

The first officially-observed powered flight in Europe was made by Alberto Santos-Dumont on 23 October 1906, in a large tail-first box-kite biplane, which he called the 14*bis* because it had first been tested slung from his No 14 airship. In the following month this same aircraft flew 722 ft (220 m) in 21 seconds. Earlier in 1906 the Hungarian Trajan Vuia who, like Santos-Dumont, lived in Paris, had achieved short hops in a little bat-winged monoplane with a carbonic acid gas engine.

During 1907 some famous names were established in aviation history. The first of these, Louis Blériot, had earlier been associated with Gabriel Voisin and his gliders, but Blériot decided to abandon the biplane type and built a tail-first monoplane, with which he achieved hops. He then turned to a machine of tandem-wing layout, which crashed as the earlier one had done,

and toward the end of 1907 built and flew an aircraft which foreshadowed remarkably the modern form of tractor monoplane. This, too, crashed and was abandoned; but Blériot and his later monoplanes were to make history.

A second great name to emerge in 1907 was that of Henry Farman, who bought a Voisin biplane in September. The name of Voisin is itself a famous one, though it still provokes controversy. What cannot be denied is that the brothers Gabriel and Charles Voisin established the classic type of 'pusher' biplane, with engine and propeller at the rear, and that theirs was the first company in the world to build aeroplanes for other people to fly.

The Voisin biplane acquired by Henry Farman was the third of the brothers' construction, and Farman made numerous alterations to it. By the end of 1907 he had managed to fly a circuit and to cover a distance of 3,380 ft (1,030 m).

Santos-Dumont was still busy, if not entirely successful, throughout 1907. After building a new biplane, which failed to fly, and a combination of aeroplane and airship, which was destroyed on the ground, he turned his attention to a monoplane, and by November was testing a tiny machine, with a wing span of only about 16½ ft (5.0 m), which he called his No 19. This was the first of the famous Demoiselles, of which more will be said later.

From a romantic Brazilian working in Paris, attention must now be turned to a

Above left: Unbelievable though it may seem, this incredible 'flying runner bean frame'—the Phillips multiplane of 1907—made a flight of about 500 ft (152 m) at Streatham in the first half of that year

Left: While a member of the Aerial Experiment Association, Glenn Curtiss designed and flew his first aeroplane, the June Bug. On Independence Day 1908 he won a magazine prize for the first officially-recorded flight of one kilometre to be made in the USA

Above: a two-seat version of the Wright Model B at the Wrights' premises at Sim's Field, Dayton, Ohio in mid-1911

Right, top: Englishman J W Dunne built a series of arrow-shaped swept-wing tail-less biplanes in his attempt to achieve a perfectly stable aeroplane. This one, the D.5, could fly straight and level without attention to the controls

Right, centre: This strange floatplane, with its tandem elliptical wings, was built for Louis Blériot by the Voisin factory in 1906, but it never flew

Right, below: Another Voisin design was this curious canard (tail-first) biplane, produced in 1911. It was later flown as a floatplane and ordered by the French Navy. This model of the original landplane is displayed in the Musée de l'Air in Paris

Far right: The upper picture shows the biplane model which in 1907 won A V Roe a *Daily Mail* prize of £75. He used the money to build his first full-size aeroplane, also a biplane; then, in 1909, he built his first triplane. At first this had an engine of only 6 hp; later, with a 9 hp engine, it flew for about half a mile (800 m), but was eventually damaged in the crash shown in the lower picture

little-known Englishman working in the London suburb of Streatham. This man was Horatio Phillips, and his name has figured far too little in aeronautical history. It goes on record here because there is good reason to believe that in 1907 Phillips flew an aircraft, which can best be described as resembling a row of Venetian blinds, for a distance of about 500 ft (152 m). This English engineer had taken out a patent as early as 1884 for a wing section, or profile, which helped to determine the design of modern wing forms, and he had built earlier 'Venetian blind' aircraft using his narrow-chord wings in 1893 and 1904.

Henry Farman began the year 1908 well by winning the *Grand Prix d'Aviation* for a circuit of nearly a mile. The date was 13 January, and he was airborne for about 1½ minutes. On 29 May, Farman made the first passenger-carrying flight in Europe, his companion being Ernest Archdeacon, who had done much to encourage the growth of European flying. Following tests made in February with a monoplane of his own design, known as the Gastambide-Mengin, Léon Levavasseur developed later in the year his famous Antoinette; and Blériot too was experimenting with new monoplanes. In England, S F Cody completed his biplane British Army Aeroplane No 1, and A V Roe built a biplane along the lines of a model which had gained him a prize in 1907; while he waited for an engine, the aeroplane was towed into the air at Brooklands by a motor car.

An especially remarkable machine of 1908 was the swept-wing tail-less Dunne D4, which made some good hops in Scotland during July. In America the Aerial Experiment Association, founded by Dr Alexander Graham Bell (the telephone inventor), Glenn Curtiss and others, built its first biplane, the Red Wing. This was designed by Lieut T Selfridge who, in September 1908, became the first man to be killed in an aeroplane (a Wright biplane flown by Orville). The Red Wing was followed by the White Wing (designer F W Baldwin), the June Bug (Glenn Curtiss) and the Silver Dart (J A D McCurdy). These aeroplanes led to the fine Curtiss Golden Flyer of 1909, but the crown of the year 1908 came with the first public flights by the Wright brothers in August and September—Wilbur in France, and Orville at home in the USA. Wilbur recorded: 'The newspapers and the French aviators nearly went wild with excitement'. And well they might: such flying had never been seen before.

The name of Santos-Dumont now enters the story yet again, for in March 1909 the dauntless little Brazilian flew an improved version of his No 19 of 1907. The name Demoiselle, which was given to this remarkable little monoplane, meant dragonfly, and the name was a good one; with its wing span of only 18 ft (5.5 m) and its ability to fly at about 60 mph (97 km/h) the tiny machine was to be seen buzzing around like an insect in the hands of sportsmen pilots. The main framework was formed by three bamboo poles (No 19 had only one!) and the pilot sat on a sheet of canvas stretched under the wing between the two lower poles. The engine was mounted on the wing, and the entire tail was movable on a ball-and-socket joint to provide control.

Although it was not a great success technically, being difficult to fly, the Demoiselle is an important aeroplane in history for two reasons. First, it was the original 'light aeroplane', and thus was the forerunner of such world-renowned machines as the de Havilland Moth and Piper Cub. Secondly, it was the first-ever 'home-built' aircraft, for Santos-Dumont announced that he was not seeking a patent for his design and that it was freely available to all.

The following year, 1909, was a golden one for aviation, for apart from the standard type of Demoiselle all the great French designers previously named built improved versions of their aircraft and put up some remarkable performances. The Blériot, Antoinette and Curtiss developments will be described in later Parts; for the present it is necessary to mention only Voisin, Farman and Roe. The standard Voisin biplane of 1909 weighed 1,323 lb (600 kg) and was offered in England at a price of £780, complete with 50 hp ENV engine. Among the engines offered with the considerably heavier Henry Farman was the famous 50 hp Gnome, a rotary engine remarkable for its lightness. The persevering A V Roe, however, had to make the best of a 9 hp JAP motor-cycle engine in the famous triplane which he flew in July. One of his assistants summarised the average programme of flying as 'Two weeks' work, a 50-yards hop, a crash and more work'.

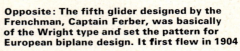

Opposite: The fifth glider designed by the Frenchman, Captain Ferber, was basically of the Wright type and set the pattern for European biplane design. It first flew in 1904

Left: the original 1909 Roe triplane is one of the star attractions of the Aeronautical Collection in the Science Museum, London

Left, below: The Antoinette IV and V established the classic pattern of the attractive monoplanes produced by Léon Levavasseur from 1908 onwards. This is the Antoinette V, seen with triangular ailerons but without the rudder originally placed between the fins

Below: The little No 19 designed by Alberto Santos-Dumont and first flown in November 1907. It was the prototype of the successful little ultra-light Demoiselle series

Bottom: The artist-turned-engineer Léon Levavasseur was the designer of the Antoinette aero-engines which successfully powered many of the early European aeroplanes. He began his career as an aircraft designer with this monoplane, built for M Jules Gastambide, whose daughter Antoinette gave the company its name

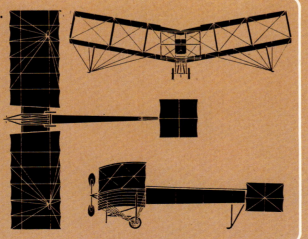

SANTOS-DUMONT 14 bis.

Powered by: One 50 hp Antoinette eight-cylinder water-cooled Vee-type engine, driving a two-blade pusher propeller of 8 ft 2½ in (2.50 m) diameter
Wing Span: 36 ft 9 in (11.20 m)
Length: 31 ft 10 in (9.70 m)
Wing area: 559.7 sq ft (52.00 m²)
Gross weight: 661 lb (300 kg)
Speed: approx 25 mph (40 km/h)
Accommodation: Crew of 1
First flight: 13 September 1906 (with 24 hp Antoinette engine)
On its first flight, the 14bis covered about 23 ft (7 m) before landing heavily and being damaged. It was repaired and fitted with a 50 hp engine for the October-November 1906 flights, and an octagonal aileron was fitted in each of the outboard wing 'boxes'. Their controls were connected to a body harness worn by the pilot, who leaned to left or right to keep the aeroplane on an even keel.

The only example of a genuine Blériot
Type XI monoplane still flying regularly
anywhere in the world is this one, owned by
the Shuttleworth Trust. Powered by a
25 hp three-cylinder Anzani engine, it is
similar to the aircraft in which Louis Blériot
made the first aeroplane flight across
the English Channel on 25 July 1909. Other
airworthy Blériots are replicas with
modern engines

Names to Remember

IN THE DEVELOPMENT of any new field of human endeavour there are always men of worth who remain in the background, neither seeking acclaim nor receiving it; and this is certainly true of aviation. Precisely what motivated the dedicated tower-jumpers, whose exploits were chronicled early in *History of Aviation,* we shall never know; but among their successors were little-known experimenters whose names we should know, names which must be honoured in any history of aviation for their resolute approach to the age-old problem of flight.

Numbered among these men was a French sea-captain, J M Le Bris, who was at work on the problem between 1856 and 1868. Basing his ideas on that most wonderful of natural fliers the albatross, which he had studied on his voyages to South America, he built a glider. During 1857 he had this mounted on a cart, driven along a road, and released when speed had been gained. Thus launched, he made a short glide, but on a second attempt he crashed and broke a leg. In 1868 he tested a second machine, prudently launching it for most of its glides

Top: The Danes still claim often that J C H Ellehammer was first to fly a powered aeroplane in Europe. This photograph was taken during his experiments on Lindholm Island in 1906

Above: Roger Bacon (1214-92), the British Franciscan monk who wrote of hollow globes of copper filled with 'aetherial air' which would float in the atmosphere, and flying machines in which men could sit and propel themselves by mechanical means

with ballast in place of a pilot. This also crashed, but a surviving photograph, in which it is seen mounted on the launching cart, shows its remarkable bird-like form. Certainly its constructor must go on record as a pioneer of flying.

Another such Frenchman was Charles Renard, who, in 1871, flew successfully a model glider having several superimposed wings and pendulum-operated 'winglets' to maintain stability. A third Frenchman whose name must endure was L P Mouillard, who, in addition to writing a classic book *L'Empire de l'Air*, built six gliders, the first in 1856 and the last in 1896. None of these was successful, but even the Wright brothers were to benefit from the researches recorded in Mouillard's book.

Another aeronautical classic is a paper entitled *Aerial Locomotion*, read by an Englishman, F H Wenham, at the first meeting of the Aeronautical Society in 1866. Among Wenham's discoveries was the wing of high aspect ratio—that is, one long in span but narrow in chord (distance from leading-edge to trailing-edge). Together with a man named John Browning,

Wenham also built the first wind tunnel, a research tool which was to influence the development of the aeroplane very greatly.

A tragic figure, in that he committed suicide at the age of 30, was the Frenchman Alphonse Pénaud, who in 1870 began to experiment with rubber-driven models. A compatriot, Pierre Jullien, had used the same source of power in 1858, but Pénaud's contribution to aircraft development went very much further. Not only did he make model helicopters with contra-rotating rotors but, in 1871, introduced his 'planophore', an undisputed ancestor of the modern aeroplane. This was a rubber-driven model monoplane with which, by careful arrangement of the wing and·tail surfaces, he achieved stability of an order never before attained. In the following year he was experimenting with flapping wings, but his most remarkable design, for which he was granted a patent, was for a monoplane amphibian. This was never built, but it incorporated such 'modern' features as an enclosed cockpit, control column, and retractable undercarriage with shock-absorbers.

Other ingenious Frenchmen were Victor Tatin, who used compressed air to drive his model monoplane, and G Trouvé, who flapped the wings of his ornithopter —probably the first machine of the type to become airborne—by the automatic firing of blank revolver cartridges.

Two Englishmen whose work in the last century must go on record were Thomas Moy and F W Brearey. At the Crystal Palace in 1875 Moy tested his 'Aerial Steamer', the motive power of which its name conveyed, and which managed to lift itself clear of its circular track. Moy also experimented with what he called 'water flying'. He made a boat with three 'planes' attached beneath it which, while under tow, was raised 'quite out of the water'. He may thus be considered to have invented the hydrofoil craft while experimenting in aeronautics.

Brearey, whose interest in flying stemmed from his father's friendship with Sir George Cayley, was appointed honorary secretary to the Aeronautical Society on its establishment in 1866 and held this post until his death thirty years later. Apart from advancing aeronautics in this capacity he made what has been called an 'undulator', comprising a pole with two pieces of cloth attached. These had rigid members at the front and were raised and lowered to impart a wave-like motion, producing both lift and thrust.

Within the British Empire, during the reigns of Queen Victoria and King Edward VII, a man was at work thousands of miles away from the main centres of aeronautical activity in Europe and America. This man was Lawrence Hargrave, who was born in England but

emigrated to Australia. He did much exploring, but from 1884 onwards devoted himself to the study of flight. Probably his most significant achievement was the invention of a type of box-kite, with which his name became associated, and upon which some of the earliest aeroplanes, built by Santos-Dumont and the Voisin brothers, were based. He made flapping-wing devices and a type of rotary engine which foreshadowed the famous Gnome. Hargrave also built what he called his 'steam catamaran', a true ancestor of the great flying-boats of later years, of which he remarked with admirable philosophy: 'My new apparatus is merely a steamer if it does not lift out of the water, and a flying machine if it does'.

A citizen of the British Empire who does not qualify for admission to the band of pioneers now being honoured, but an utterance by whom must nevertheless go on record as indicative of the kind of discouragement these men had to undergo, was the great physicist Lord Kelvin. As late as December 1896 this eminent gentleman declared : 'I have not the smallest molecule of faith in aerial navigation other than ballooning, or expectation of good results from any of the trials we hear of'.

One man who was far from discouraged by such opinions was Ferdinand Ferber,

a captain in the French army. While serving as an instructor at an artillery school Ferber read of the experiments of Otto Lilienthal, and late in 1899 he himself constructed the first of a series of gliders. He became friendly with Octave Chanute, who was in turn a friend of the Wright brothers, and passed from the influence of Lilienthal to gliders 'du type de Wright'. With these he obtained poor results, but in 1903 tested one such machine, having twin propellers, on a whirling arm. This too was a failure, but in 1904 Ferber made modifications to a basic Wright glider, incorporating a fixed tailplane as well as a forward elevator, which constituted a major step in the development of the aeroplane. Now much encouraged, he tested in 1905 a slightly larger machine, with a 12-hp engine, having a tractor propeller. This could not sustain itself in flight, but made a shallow 'power glide' and must be acclaimed as a notable advance. Eventually Ferber joined the Antoinette company, and soon foretold the marine aircraft to come only a few years later by declaring of a hydroplane ('skimming' motor-boat) which he tested that 'fitted with aeroplanes and an aerial screw, it could be made to rise from the water'.

Ferber was possibly the greatest of the

Above: Louis Blériot is remembered mainly as the pioneer who made the first aeroplane flight from France to Britain in 1909, in a rather primitive monoplane. Within six years he progressed to this handsomely streamlined monocoque scout, but achieved little success with it

Left: J W Dunne's Vee-winged aeroplanes were built at Farnborough, with the object of evolving an inherently stable design for military reconnaissance. The D.4 was underpowered by its 21/23 hp R.E.P. engine when tested in Scotland in 1908. Later designs were far more successful; yet Dunne is better known as the author of books such as *An Experiment with Time*

ESNAULT–PELTERIE R.E.P. 2 bis

Powered by: One 30 hp R.E.P. seven-cylinder air-cooled semi-radial engine, driving a four-blade propeller
Wing span: 28 ft 2¼ in (8.60 m)
Length: approx 22 ft 6¾ in (6.85 m)
Height: approx 8 ft 2¼ in (2.50 m)
Wing area: 169.5 sq ft (15.75 m²)
Gross weight: 772 lb (350 kg)
Speed: approx 50 mph (80 km/h)
Accommodation: Crew of 1
First flight: 15 February 1909

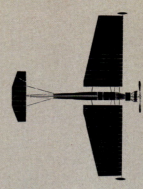

One of the few early pioneers to persevere with the monoplane, Robert Esnault-Pelterie applied to his work the benefits of a sound technical education; had he been more discriminating in some of the lines of research which he pursued his contribution to early aviation would undoubtedly have been greater. Even so, he was the first to apply aileron control to a full-sized aeroplane (a glider, in 1904), the first to use hydraulic wheel brakes, the first to develop an aircraft seat belt; he also designed the engines that powered his early aircraft. The R.E.P.2bis represented the culmination of development of his first powered aircraft, and in May 1909 it made its best flight, travelling some 5 miles (8 km). Before the end of the first World War, however, Esnault-Pelterie had transferred his interest to an even more exciting field: that of rocket propulsion and the prospect of space travel.

ELLEHAMMER SEMI-BIPLANE

Powered by: One 20 hp Ellehammer three-cylinder air-cooled radial engine, driving a four-blade propeller
Wing span: 30 ft 11¾ in (9.35 m)
Length: 20 ft 4 in (6.20 m)
Height: 10 ft 8¼ in (3.26 m)
Wing area: 398.3 sq ft (37.00 m²)
Gross weight: approx 397 lb (180 kg)
Speed: 35 mph (57 km/h)
Accommodation: Crew of 1
First flight: 16 August 1906

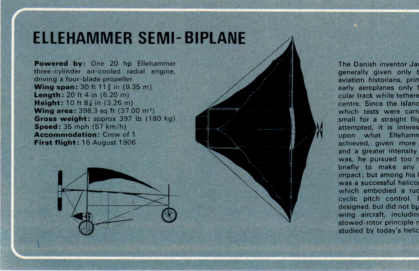

The Danish inventor Jacob Ellehammer is generally given only brief attention by aviation historians, primarily because his early aeroplanes only flew round a circular track while tethered to a mast in the centre. Since the island of Lindholm, on which tests were carried out, was too small for a straight flight to have been attempted, it is interesting to speculate upon what Ellehammer might have achieved, given more suitable facilities and a greater intensity of purpose. As it was, he pursued too many projects too briefly to make any lasting historical impact; but among his later achievements was a successful helicopter, built in 1912, which embodied a rudimentary form of cyclic pitch control. In the 1930s he designed, but did not build, other rotating-wing aircraft, including one using the stowed-rotor principle now actively being studied by today's helicopter designers.

VUIA No1 MONOPLANE

Powered by: One 20 hp modified Serpollet carbonic acid gas engine, driving a 7 ft 2¼ in (2.20 m) diameter two-blade propeller
Wing span: 22 ft 11½ in (7.00 m)
Length: 10 ft 6 in (3.20 m)
Wing area: 204.5 sq ft (19.00 m²)
Gross weight: approx 531 lb (241 kg)
Accommodation: Crew of 1
First flight: 18 March 1906

One of the first Europeans to make a powered flight in his own aeroplane, Traian Vuia is claimed as Romania's first aviator, although at the time of his early flights he was resident in Paris and his birthplace was then a part of the Austro-Hungarian empire. His first aeroplane, built with the assistance of Frenchman Victor Tatin, travelled no more than 78¾ ft (24 m) on its longest hop-flight, but had several novel features, including a variable-incidence wing and an undercarriage with pneumatic tyres. Later Vuia aircraft, although more conventional for their time and (in the case of the No 2 design) fitted with a more reliable engine, did not achieve flights of any great length compared with others of their day.

'lesser greats', but his name must be associated with those of two other Frenchmen who were active in the early years of this century. These were Robert Esnault-Pelterie and Leon Levavasseur. Esnault-Pelterie built both gliders and, later, successful aeroplanes known by his initials R.E.P. Levavasseur, who is remembered chiefly for the graceful Antoinette monoplanes, built and tested a powered aeroplane as early as 1903. Though itself a failure it helped to establish its designer on the road to success.

It must not be supposed that aviation developed solely in the USA, France and the British Empire, and acknowledgement must also be made to a German, Karl Jatho, who made 'hops' as early as 1903; a Dane, J C H Ellehammer, who was experimenting in 1904, and later achieved hops; a Hungarian domiciled in Paris, Traian Vuia, who made hops of his own in 1906; and an American domiciled in England, Samuel Franklin Cody, who began to experiment with man-carrying kites in 1899 and built his first powered aeroplane in 1908.

Cody was distantly related to the famous 'Buffalo Bill', and was likewise a born showman; but by no means all the pioneers of flight received, or even sought, the plaudits of the crowd.

The name of a pioneer designer named Howard can be found among those who took part in the *Daily Mail's* model aeroplane competition of 1907, which launched A V Roe on his great career. Towards the end of his life, Mr Howard was still experimenting with this little rubber-powered 'Flying Seagull', one of the most beautiful and natural flying machines ever perfected

Ferdinand Ferber at the controls of his 1907 aeroplane. Seldom mentioned in flying histories, Ferber was, perhaps, the greatest of the 'lesser greats'

THE PIONEERING HELICOPTER YEAR

AS NOTED ON another page, much of the early work on helicopters was obscure, and never properly recorded, and this was even more apparent in the early years of this century than it is today. There is evidence of it in the heart-cry of an engineer who sat down during 1911 to write what he called *A Plea for the Direct Lifter,* meaning the helicopter. Sixty years later his opening remarks lift this present article directly off the ground. They run as follows :

'Although at the present time a certain amount of attention is being given by thoughtful people to the possibilities of the direct lift flying machine, investigators who have the temerity to follow this line of research are receiving exactly the same measure of ridicule which was meted out, only four short years ago, to those enthusiasts who were experimenting with the power kite. It is natural that we should be moved to wonder and admiration at the marvellous success of the aeroplane, for even those of us who all along believed in the possibility of mechanical flight have been somewhat taken by surprise. Already, however, the novelty is beginning to wear off,'—this in 1911 !—'and in a little while we shall begin to realise the rather obvious limitations of the aeroplane.'

This clear-thinking, if somewhat impatient, gentleman went on :

'The information available on the subject of vertical lift experiments is exceedingly

fragmentary. Sufficient evidence exists, however, to show that the whole subject is of intense interest to all who have the real welfare of aeronautics at heart. The pity of it is that there should be such a great number of cranks in the field. These optimistic and apparently harmless gentlemen do not assist the movement. They mix up ideas which have at least a basis of theoretical possibility with those which, like perpetual motion schemes, are obviously unmechanical and useless from their very inception. The engineering mind revolts at their weird conceptions, and the suspicious capitalist is scared from assisting more reasonable experiments.

'The one pre-eminent advantage of direct lift machines when they reach the practical stage will be their ability to hover. In addition to this they will be able to rise from any sort of ground and from confined spaces. From a military point of view, it is at once apparent that, for the purpose of taking observations, a machine which can retain its position for any considerable period must be more serviceable than one which can only remain even *near* that spot by careering madly round in circles at forty miles an hour. Moreover, the possibilities of successful bomb dropping, which are a little doubtful at present, may be realised with the first successful direct lifter.'

With the frightening prospect of aero-

planes foredoomed to career madly round at 40 mph (64 km/h), and of helicopters hovering to drop their bombs, we may for the present take our leave of this enthusiast by quoting a final paragraph :

'M Paul Cornu, an engineer of Lisieux,' he assured his readers, 'was the first man to rise from the ground in a free helicopter carrying its own source of power. M Cornu's machine flew not once, but many times, and had it not been that his experiments were conducted at the period when aeroplanes were just beginning to astonish the public, and the Wright brothers were making their first sensational flights at Le Mans, the attention of the entire aeronautical world would have been arrested by his success. The pity of it is that, after such remarkably good results had been obtained, M Cornu should have been compelled to suspend his further researches on account of the great expense.'

In spite of this *Plea for the Direct Lifter,* the name of Paul Cornu continued to be an obscure one in the aeronautical history books, and it is good to have an opportunity to bring this engineer of Normandy into a brighter light.

Using an old Buchet engine which gave no more than 2 hp, M Cornu constructed during 1906 a working model of a helicopter which weighed 28 lb (12.7 kg) and lifted 35 lb (15.9 kg), the engine weight having been reduced from 31 lb (14.1 kg)

Opposite page: First helicopter to make a free flight carrying a man was this tandem-rotor machine built by Paul Cornu

Below: This Breguet-Richet Gyroplane No 1 had lifted itself from the ground, carrying a pilot, even earlier than the Cornu helicopter; but it was held steady by four assistants

Bottom: Close-up of one of the big eight-blade biplane rotors of the Gyroplane No 1. To the right is the centrally-mounted 45 hp Antoinette engine

Right: One that didn't work was this 'steerable airship', the *Bremen 1*, built by Carl Zenker between August 1873 and March 1900. Eight rotors and two propellers were intended to enable it to cover a kilometre in two minutes

to only 15 lb (6.8 kg). The two rotors were mounted side by side, and their framework, like that of the rest of the model, was of steel tubing. The drive from the engine was provided by a belt running over pulleys, a system which was to prove a great handicap to a full-scale machine which was finished in August 1907 and in which M Cornu made his first historic ascent (about 1 foot; 0.3 m) on 13 November of the same year. Happily it is possible to describe this helicopter in some detail.

The two rotors, which measured 19 ft 8¼ in (6.00 m) in diameter, were mounted one behind the other on outriggers. The length of the driving belt was some 66 ft (20 m), and ball bearings were used throughout the driving mechanism. Each rotor had two blades, made up of steel tubing and covered with rubber-proofed silk, and was built up on a large steel pulley which carried the driving belt. The angle of incidence of the blades, or angle at which they 'attacked' the air, was adjustable. Propulsion and steering were both achieved by means of two planes, or deflecting surfaces, carried on supports projecting out from the axes of the rotors. The air thrown down by the rotors reacted on these planes to provide horizontal propulsion, and the angle at which they were set determined speed and direction.

The backbone of the helicopter was a single, large-diameter steel tube, resembling an open letter V as seen from the side. This was braced by wire cables, attached to six secondary structures, and the pilot's seat and engine were mounted at the centre of the V. To each side of the centre portion was a pair of independently-mounted wheels, arranged in tandem.

The engine was a 24-hp water-cooled Antoinette, the water being carried in a tank ahead of the engine and the petrol in a tank behind the pilot. Above the engine was an oil tank, and under the pilot's seat were accumulators and the ignition coil.

Incessant trouble with the belt drive and the unreliability of the engine were among the many difficulties which beset M Cornu. Before the expense of his researches proved too great, he had started to build a machine of different design, somewhat resembling that which had been tested by his compatriot Louis Breguet in association with Professor Richet, and which had actually lifted a man from the ground as early as 29 September 1907. This is not generally accepted as the first manned helicopter flight, however, because the craft was manually stabilised. More explicitly, four men prevented it from capsizing by propping it up with poles, one under each of the four massive four-blade rotors. Although these men did not assist in lifting the machine they certainly enabled it to stay in the air.

The Breguet-Richet helicopter was called by its constructors a 'gyroplane', and the author of *A Plea for the Direct Lifter* recorded of it: 'The machine, weighing with its driver about 1,273 lb (577 kg) was tested at Douai. It showed itself capable of rising from the ground many times. On one occasion the machine rose rather suddenly, travelled forwards a hundred yards or more, and landed in a beetroot field, damaging itself considerably. M Breguet subsequently suspended his gyroplane experiments on account of the more immediate success to be obtained with the aeroplane, and he has since produced one of the most efficient aeroplanes in the world. It is to be hoped, however, that he will eventually find time to resume his vertical lift experiments.'

M Breguet did indeed continue his vertical lift experiments, and in 1935 produced the Breguet-Dorand *Gyroplane Laboratoire*, with contra-rotating co-axial rotors. Implicit in the name 'Gyroplane' was his continuing faith over the years, but *Laboratoire* suggested, quite correctly, that the helicopter had as yet to be perfected. When eventually it took its place alongside the aeroplane it made the efforts of Cornu and Breguet—and even that of the 'optimistic and apparently harmless gentlemen'—seem well worthwhile.

A fitting tribute to Mikhail Mil, one of the world's greatest helicopter designers, who died early in 1970, the V-12 is more than twice as big and four times as heavy as the largest helicopter built outside the USSR. Its four 6,500 shp Soloviev D-25VF engines and 114 ft 10 in (35 m) diameter twin rotors enabled it to lift a record 88,636 lb (40,204.5 kg) payload to a height of 7,398 ft (2,255 m) in 1969

Trials, Troubles and Triplanes

Above: One of the treasures of the Shuttleworth Collection at Old Warden, Bedfordshire, is this replica of the Roe IV Triplane, built for the *Magnificent Men* film and still flown regularly

Below: The Type D biplane of 1911 was the first step along the design path that led to the immortal Avro 504. It retained many features of the earlier triplanes, with the same kind of triangular girder fuselage. This was the fourth Type D with a 45 hp Green engine

Centre right: Removing A V Roe's 1907/8 biplane from its shed by the racing circuit at Brooklands. At this stage it had a 9-hp JAP engine

Bottom right: The Avro 504R Gosport, with 90-hp Avro Alpha engine, was an attempt to produce a low-powered version that would equal the performance of the RAF's 130-hp 504K. Refitted with a 504N undercarriage, G-EBPH landed successfully on the 3,118-ft (950 m) summit of Helvellyn on 22 December 1926

THERE IS A NOT-UNCOMMON belief, which has more than once been expressed in print, that A V Roe had something to do with the design of the Avro Lancaster bomber, which entered service during 1942. The fact is that he had parted from the famous company to which he gave his name as long before as 1929.

Certainly his achievements were such as to need no false associations to establish his place in aeronautical history; and they extend far enough back in time to have enabled him, in April 1912, to write an account of the earliest of them. That account bore the same title as the present article, and quotation from it enables this great British pioneer to begin his own story in his own words, thus:

'My first machine was a biplane, which was a familiar sight to some of the visitors to Brooklands in 1907-08. Though in appearance it somewhat differed from modern machines, it was in essentials of a fairly modern type, namely, Mr Cody's large biplane, only the forward plane was larger in proportion to the main planes. Experiments were made with the machine towed by cars, by means of a length of about a hundred feet of cable. The machine could be steered up and down all right, and the landings were quite good, but if it got sideways beyond a certain angle I could not get it back, try as I might. But if the cable was released I could land. Unfortunately inexperienced ''towers'', although warned of what would happen, would insist on hanging on, with a resulting smash.'

Those 'resulting smashes' were by no means the last that were to befall Alliot Verdon Roe, as he had been christened when he was born in Manchester on 26 April 1877 (though late in life he changed his name to Verdon-Roe).

A V Roe began his career as an apprentice at the Lancashire and Yorkshire Railway Locomotive Works, near his birthplace. He was a keen racing cyclist and won substantial prize money. After becoming a fitter at Portsmouth Dockyard and studying naval engineering in London he went to sea as an engineer, serving in that capacity from 1899 to 1902. For a period he was in the motor industry, and later, in America, undertook the detail design of a wholly unsuccessful helicopter, built to the ideas of a Mr Davidson. On his return to England he entered models of his own design for a competition organised by the *Daily Mail* at Alexandra Park, and one of these gained the highest award. Upon the design of that model he based the full-scale aeroplane he himself has described.

With an Antoinette engine installed in the same biplane, Roe claimed to have made some 'hops of fifty yards or so', though doubt has been cast on this.

Roe's own account of his 'troubles and trials' continued:

'The next machine was a triplane. It was built with the aid of a partner, but the combination was dissolved before it was finished. As a result it was put under the hammer at Friswell's, and the fuselage, wings, and wheelbase realised £5 10s, which I think was not such a bad price considering it was the first aeroplane auction. My second triplane was commenced shortly after this, and was taken to Lea Marshes, where it justified its existence by flying. The engine was a 9 hp twin-cylinder air-cooled JAP, with coil and accumulator ignition, which drove a four-bladed tractor screw with a V belt. Lightness was one of the principal qualities of the construction. The planes were covered with thin yellow butter paper, which was quite satisfactory in dry weather, but very apt to stretch and get soppy in the wet. . . .

'When the grass on the marshes was

long I was ordered off because, as it seemed, I was trespassing on somebody or other's grazing rights, and when it was short I was ordered not to interfere with the public playground.

'I had numerous smashes. One day I was addressed by a would-be suicide, a lady who had made up her mind to put an end to her financial troubles (she was an authoress) in the River Lea. When she saw the triplane, however, she begged me to let her take my place, as, though she was quite tired of life, she preferred, if possible, to end it in doing something useful.'

In October 1909 a flying meeting was held in Blackpool, and though Roe took two triplanes he failed to distinguish himself owing to engine trouble and dampened butter-paper. He then transferred his activities to Wembley, where he recalled being involved in 'a very great number of smashes'; but though his enthusiasm re-

Top to bottom:
This photograph emphasises the slimness of the fuselage of the Avro Type F. It was only 2 ft (0.61 m) wide but deep enough for the pilot to be totally enclosed. Lateral control in flight was by wing warping

The Avro 504 remained in service as a standard RAF trainer until 1933. Post-war variants, like this 504N, had radial engines instead of the original rotaries

When fitted with a dorsal fin and floats, the Lynx-engined 504 became the 504O. Export customers included the Naval Air Services of Brazil, Chile, Greece and Japan

mained unimpaired, money was short, and he was enabled to continue his experiments only with the assistance of his brother, H V Roe. By this time he had come to realise that he had been trying to fly with too little power, and proceeded to build two more triplanes with engines of 35 hp. While these were under construction he returned to Brooklands, now much changed and a centre of aerial activity.

From this base he set out with high hopes to another meeting at Blackpool—only to have his precious new machine destroyed in a fire caused by a spark from a locomotive. As dauntless as he was indestructible, he assembled another machine in three days and took it to Blackpool. 'I taxied forth,' he once said, 'two tyres burst in rapid succession, and I took off on the rims.' But he was able to add: 'Altogether I had three smashes at Blackpool,

The Avro 584 Avocet single-seat fleet fighter of 1927-28 had a Lynx radial engine of only 180 hp, which restricted its performance. It was, however, an interesting design, with constant-diameter metal-tube fuselage and Warren girder-braced wings which needed no rigging wires

Left: A V Roe (in shirtsleeves) returned to the triplane formula with the Avro 547A four-passenger cabin transport, which competed unsuccessfully in the Air Ministry Small Commercial Aeroplane Competition in 1920

Below: Another Avro design, the Model 621 Tutor, eventually replaced the veteran 504 in the early 'thirties. This one still flies at Old Warden

but they gave us a consolation prize of £75'.

Toward the end of 1910 Roe re-visited the USA to attend a flying meeting at Boston, taking with him a triplane he had built for the Harvard Aeronautical Society. On his return he continued experimenting at Brooklands while his brother superintended constructional work at Manchester. It was at this time that he built his first tractor biplane, forerunner of his masterpiece the Avro 504 and a Brooklands competition-winner. Of this biplane he said:

'The machine was afterwards bought by Commander Schwann, who fixed floats to it and used it as a hydro-aeroplane. This was the first machine of its type to fly, I believe.'

He was wrong; but it was one of the first seaplanes to fly in Britain.

The days of Roe's 'smashes' were now behind him, and some historic aircraft were taking shape in his mind and on his drawing board. For the Military Trials of 1912 he designed a biplane and a monoplane, both with fully enclosed cabin. These machines were not successful in the Trials, but this was to prove less important than the fact that early in 1912 the British government had ordered three Avro 500 biplanes, a type from which the 504 of 1913 was a direct development.

To state that the Avro 504 was the most famous aeroplane ever built would, perhaps, be dangerous; but none has ever rendered more valuable service in both war and peace, as recorded elsewhere in *History of Aviation*. Biplanes of this type were used in numerous versions for bombing, notably on the audacious Friedrichshafen raid of 21 November 1914; for fighting by day and night; for reconnaissance; and for numerous experiments, including catapult launching. But the 504's greatest fame lies in its adoption as a standard trainer, not only by the British flying services during the first World War but by numerous foreign air forces in later years. Of the 8,340 aircraft of this type constructed during 1914-18, a total of 3,696 were built by A V Roe & Co Ltd.

Among experimental machines turned out in the same period were the Pike and Manchester bombers and the Type 530 and Spider fighters; and before A V Roe left the company in 1929 (the year also of his knighthood) he had been associated not only with 504 developments but with such types as the massive Aldershot bomber, the Avocet and Avenger fighters and the Avian lightplane. Although the name of Roe lived on for many years, not only in that of the great Manchester company he had founded but in that of Saunders-Roe Ltd of Cowes (where he died on 4 January 1958), to flying men the world over an 'Avro' means one aeroplane only—the never-to-be-forgotten 504.

Right: Thanks to the skill of Avro apprentices who rebuilt it, and the Shuttleworth Trust which maintains it, this Avro 504K, with 110 hp Le Rhône engine, continues to demonstrate to thousands of people annually the qualities which enabled this great trainer to produce outstanding military pilots for both World Wars

Below: As this photograph of two RAF 504Ns illustrates, the spine-chilling cross-over that highlights performances of the Red Arrows aerobatic team is not new—although the old-timers flew at only 100 mph (161 km/h)

Opposite page, centre left: The Avro 561 Andover of 1924 was intended to replace D.H.10s as a 12-passenger transport or ambulance for six stretcher patients on the RAF's Cairo-Baghdad desert route. Only three were delivered, as the service was taken over by Imperial Airways

Bottom left: The Avro 604 Antelope was one of the most advanced two-seat day bombers of 1928, with a top speed of 173 mph (278 km/h), but was not ordered into production

Bottom right: The Avro 504M, with two passengers in a tiny cabin behind the pilot, was one of many post-war civil adaptations of the 504 trainer. The Japanese put into production a licence-built equivalent named the Aiba Tsubami IV, one of which was still giving good service in 1928

Failure and Triumph over the Channel

The two most glorious failures in the history of early peacetime flying were the attempt by Hubert Latham to fly the English Channel in 1909 and that by Harry Hawker and K Mackenzie-Grieve to fly the Atlantic about ten years later. On both occasions the aircraft came down on the water and remained afloat long enough to enable their occupants to be rescued, and both attempts were made to win a prize offered by the *Daily Mail*.

This British newspaper has always been to the fore in encouraging aviation, and as early as 1906 offered £10,000 for the first London–Manchester flight. The prize was won by Louis Paulhan in April 1910. Toward the end of 1908 the newspaper offered £1,000 to the first pilot to make a flight between England and France. Prominent among those who accepted the challenge was the dashing young Frenchman Hubert Latham, who had been educated in England. Latham's aircraft was an Antoinette IV, a monoplane developed from the Gastambide-Mengin referred to on page 58.

The Antoinette was a remarkable machine in many ways. Not only the structure, or airframe, but the engine also had been designed by Léon Levavasseur, and the name of the aircraft, its engine and the company which built them was conferred in honour of Mlle Antoinette Gastambide, daughter of the head of the firm. Antoinette engines had first been made for motor boats, and the fuselage of the monoplane was itself built like a boat, as inspection of a specimen at the Science Museum in London will confirm. This feature, together with the thick, buoyant wing, was to prove its value in dramatic circumstances.

Early on the morning of 19 July 1909, gunfire signalled to a French torpedo-boat, which had been detailed to accompany Latham, that the airman was leaving, and the Antoinette ran down a slope towards the cliff edge at Sangatte, near Calais. The 'wireless' flashed a message to Dover, where the firing of a maroon brought crowds into the streets and small craft streaming out of the harbour. The great cross-Channel contest had begun.

The rest of the story is taken up by Latham himself, at a point where the Antoinette had covered about 7 miles (11 km). The airman was preparing to take a photograph, and the engine was showing signs of failing, thus:

'Instantly I gave up any idea of photo-

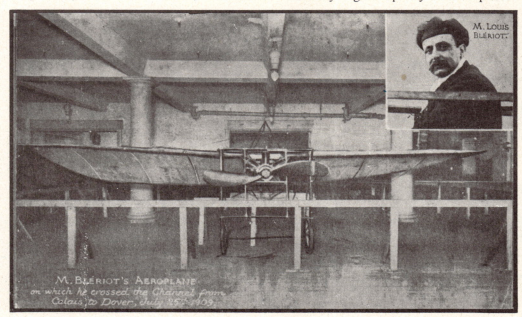

M. BLÉRIOT'S AEROPLANE on which he crossed the Channel from Calais to Dover, July 25th 1909.

M. LOUIS BLÉRIOT.

graphy. I examined all the electrical connections within my reach. I tried also to alter the carburisation and ignition of the engine. But it was all in vain; in a few seconds my engine had stopped entirely.

'At the moment my motive power was taken from me I estimate that I was about 1,000 feet up in the air. Thus, even though my first attempt at a Channel crossing failed, I think I can claim to have established a record for high flying in an aeroplane. Then I glided down to the surface of the water. . . . It seemed quite a long time before I struck the water. My speed at the moment of impact was about 45 miles an hour.

'The machine was under perfect control during this descent. Instead of diving into the sea at an angle I levelled it up and settled on the water in a horizontal position. I swung my feet up on to a cross-bar to prevent them getting wet. Then I took out my cigarette 'case, lit a cigarette, and waited.'

Latham did not have long to wait for rescue, and he was soon on his way to Paris to order a new Antoinette. Before this could be delivered to Sangatte, however, Louis Blériot was making preparations at nearby Les Baraques. For some days strong winds kept both airmen on the ground, and on the night of 24-25 July M Levavasseur, who was acting as Latham's manager, rose twice before dawn, returning to bed convinced that a start would not be possible for some time. Blériot, suffering from a burned foot, sustained in an aeroplane accident a few days before, rose at 2.30 am and went for a run in a motor car. The wind lessened, and at 4 am Blériot's monoplane was in the air for a test flight.

The tiny machine which was now on the brink of one of the most historic flights of all time had first appeared at a Paris exhibition in December 1908. Known as the Blériot XI, it was a tractor monoplane having a wing span of 25 ft 7 in (7.80 m). Its frail appearance was heightened by the fact that the rear part of the fuselage had no fabric covering, and thus disclosed to view was a curious cylindrical object. This was an air bag to help the little monoplane to float should it meet the fate of Latham's Antoinette. In the nose, driving a two-blade propeller made of walnut, was the 25-hp Anzani engine, with its three air-cooled cylinders arranged in the form of a fan. Prominent in the cockpit was an inverted cup-shaped fitting called the *cloche*, patented by Blériot in 1908. To this were attached four cables, two of which caused the outer portions of the wing to warp, or twist, making the machine bank from side to side. The other two cables operated the elevator at the tail, causing the aircraft to rise or descend. A vertical rudder at the tail was operated by a foot bar. These features may still be seen today, for the actual 'Cross-Channel Blériot', as the Blériot XI was soon to become known, is preserved at the Conservatoire des Arts et Métiers in Paris.

At 4.35 am on 25 July 1909, Blériot and his little monoplane rose into the air and flew out over the sand-dunes. An escorting

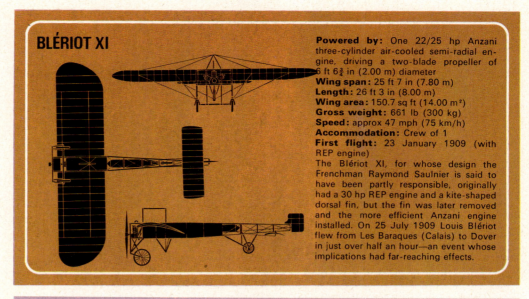

BLÉRIOT XI

Powered by: One 22/25 hp Anzani three-cylinder air-cooled semi-radial engine, driving a two-blade propeller of 6 ft 6¾ in (2.00 m) diameter
Wing span: 25 ft 7 in (7.80 m)
Length: 26 ft 3 in (8.00 m)
Wing area: 150.7 sq ft (14.00 m²)
Gross weight: 661 lb (300 kg)
Speed: approx 47 mph (75 km/h)
Accommodation: Crew of 1
First flight: 23 January 1909 (with REP engine)
The Blériot XI, for whose design the Frenchman Raymond Saulnier is said to have been partly responsible, originally had a 30 hp REP engine and a kite-shaped dorsal fin, but the fin was later removed and the more efficient Anzani engine installed. On 25 July 1909 Louis Blériot flew from Les Baraques (Calais) to Dover in just over half an hour—an event whose implications had far-reaching effects.

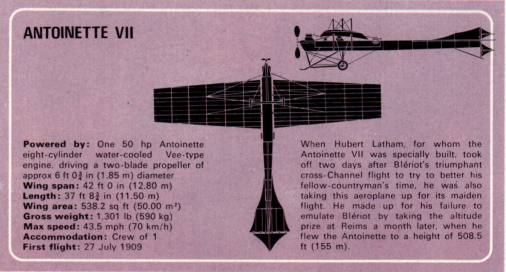

ANTOINETTE VII

Powered by: One 50 hp Antoinette eight-cylinder water-cooled Vee-type engine, driving a two-blade propeller of approx 6 ft 0¾ in (1.85 m) diameter
Wing span: 42 ft 0 in (12.80 m)
Length: 37 ft 8¾ in (11.50 m)
Wing area: 538.2 sq ft (50.00 m²)
Gross weight: 1,301 lb (590 kg)
Max speed: 43.5 mph (70 km/h)
Accommodation: Crew of 1
First flight: 27 July 1909

When Hubert Latham, for whom the Antoinette VII was specially built, took off two days after Blériot's triumphant cross-Channel flight to try to better his fellow-countryman's time, he was also taking this aeroplane up for its maiden flight. He made up for his failure to emulate Blériot by taking the altitude prize at Reims a month later, when he flew the Antoinette to a height of 508.5 ft (155 m).

destroyer was already at sea. The pilot later recounted what then occurred, thus:

'Ten minutes have gone. I have passed the destroyer, and I turn my head to see whether I am proceeding in the right direction. I am amazed. There is nothing to be seen, neither the torpedo-destroyer, nor France nor England. I am alone. I can see nothing at all. For ten minutes I am lost. It is a strange position, to be alone, unguided, without compass, in the air over the middle of the Channel. My hands and feet rest lightly on the levers. I let the aeroplane take its own course. And then, twenty minutes after I have left the French coast, I see the cliffs of Dover, the castle, and away to the west the spot where I had intended to land. What can I do? It is evident that the wind has taken me out of my course. . . . I press the lever with my foot and turn towards the west. Now indeed I am in difficulties, for the wind here by the cliffs is much stronger, and my speed is reduced as I fight against it. . . . I see an opening in the cliff. Although I am confident that I can continue for an hour and a half, that I might indeed return to Calais, I cannot resist the opportunity of making a landing on this green spot. . . . I enter the opening and find myself again over dry land. Avoiding the red buildings on my right, I attempt a landing, but the wind catches me. I stop my motor and the machine falls.'

But Louis Blériot was safely down, after a flight of which H G Wells said: '. . . in spite of our fleet this is no longer, from the

military point of view, an inaccessible island.'

Fifty years later, when a replica of the Blériot XI made a commemorative crossing, an experienced airline pilot looked at it and said: 'I wouldn't take that thing up for a solid gold clock.'

The gallant Latham made a second attempt on 27 July, in his brand-new Antoinette VII, but again came down in the water, this time cutting his face on broken goggles. It then remained for an aeroplane to make the first double crossing, and this was achieved, without an intermediate landing, on 2 June 1910. The aeroplane was a French-built Wright biplane and the pilot the popular English pioneer motorist and airman the Hon C S Rolls. Sad to relate, 'Charlie' Rolls was killed in an air crash at Bournemouth during the following month; but his name lives on, jointly with that of Sir Henry Royce.

BROTHERS IN AVIATION

Above and opposite page, top left:
Two Short Skyvan Srs 3M twin-turboprop light transports. The Skyvan above is in the camouflage of the Sultan of Muscat & Oman's Air Force; the other is a military demonstrator with nose weather radar. The name of their manufacturer—Short Brothers & Harland Ltd—perpetuates the early achievements of some of aviation's most celebrated brothers

It is common enough for several members of a family to perform their life's work in the family business, but less common for brothers to start the family business. At least, as a general rule this is true, but aviation has been the exception.

The first practical approach to human flight was unquestionably in 1783, when the first hot-air balloons were produced by the brothers Montgolfier, Etienne and Joseph. So started an interesting sequence.

Almost coincident with the Montgolfiers was the work of Professor Charles with hydrogen-filled balloons. This was only possible because of the process of coating fabric with rubber to make it gas-tight which had been developed by two brothers, Anne-Jean and Marie-Noël Robert.

Then follows a gap of nearly one hundred years, until the Paris Balloon Post came into operation. As described in an earlier part of this history, Gaston Tissandier was one of the leading figures in this event. But almost as important was his brother, Albert, who flew a balloon out of Paris and then co-operated with Gaston in determined attempts to fly back to the capital.

Airships do not seem to have made the same appeal to close relatives, and it is not until serious work on heavier-than-air craft began that the extraordinary pattern of brotherly collaboration came to full fruition. Wilbur and Orville Wright are names that everyone interested in flying already knows. It is worth pointing out, however, that they worked as a team, and so far as design goes it would be very difficult to say exactly who did what.

Contemporary with the Wrights were two other pairs of brothers. Frenchmen Charles and Gabriel Voisin built up a great reputation as designers and constructors of good aeroplanes in the first decade of the 20th century and were the first people to manufacture aeroplanes for others to fly. That remarkable man Alberto Santos-Dumont commissioned his first biplane (the 14 *bis*) to be built by Voisin Frères and was credited with making the first aeroplane flight in Europe in it.

Two other early pioneers, Henry and Maurice Farman, also worked as a team (with limited assistance from a third brother, Richard); but their French-built products achieved some degree of independence as well. Pilots of the first World

War will recall the marked difference between the Henry Farman and Maurice Farman machines. These two pairs of brothers, in France, were certainly among the most outstanding designers of the period.

One of the chief features of the Henry Farman aircraft flown at the 1909 Reims meeting was the revolutionary—in more senses than one—Gnome engine. This was

Above : This photograph, taken at Eastchurch in 1909, shows (left to right) Orville and Wilbur Wright with Horace Short and Griffith Brewer. The Shorts built six Wright biplanes under licence. Griffith Brewer was the first 'resident' Briton to fly as a passenger in an aeroplane, having been taken up by Wilbur Wright, in France, on 8 October 1908

Left : One of the Short-built Wright biplanes in flight

Below : To Charles (left) and Gabriel Voisin goes the distinction of being the first persons to manufacture aeroplanes for others to fly. After early experiments with gliders and powered aeroplanes, often in association with pioneers like Louis Blériot, they put a boxkite biplane of their own design into production at Billancourt for pilots such as Delagrange, Henry Farman and Moore-Brabazon. When the first World War began, in 1914, Voisin 'chickencoops' were among the first successful bombers; but the aircraft company did not survive long when peace returned, and Gabriel switched to the manufacture of motor cars in the 'twenties

Top left and above:

A V Roe with his first full-size aeroplane in the shed which he erected at Brooklands in 1908. Roe's claim to have flown in this aircraft, on 8 June that year, has created endless controversy to the present time

A V (later Sir Alliott Verdon) Roe, Britain's greatest pioneer of powered flying, in 1912

Above left and centre:

David Atcherley in the cockpit of the Gipsy Major-engined Comper Swift lightplane which he flew in the 1937 King's Cup Air Race. He was forced down with engine trouble on the sands at St Bees

Brother R L R Atcherley had had better luck in 1929, and is shown here receiving from Lord Thompson the King's Cup which he won in a dual-control Gloster Grebe

Left and bottom:

The original 'DH'—Sir Geoffrey de Havilland (third from left)—with members of his family at the 1937 King's Cup Race

Although produced officially by Hawker Siddeley Aviation, the HS 125 business jet was sold for many years as the DH 125 in the USA, where the initials 'DH' are still held in high esteem

designed by two brothers, Laurent and Louis Seguin, and set entirely new standards for aircraft power for nearly ten years. By modern standards the rotary engine was a thoroughly dangerous piece of equipment, but in 1909 its 50-hp output for a total engine weight of 175 lb (80 kg) was an engineering achievement without parallel.

In England an even more remarkable family business was being built up, which is famous to this day. This time three brothers, Eustace, Horace and Oswald Short, already established as makers of balloons, moved into the aeroplane business and created the first factory in Britain wholly devoted to building aeroplanes. They started by constructing six Wright biplanes under licence, but before long were designing their own types. By the time the first World War started the Short brothers were building floatplanes for the Royal Navy and, soon afterwards, turned out the first of the flying-boats for which they became world-famous.

In Britain there was another pair of Wright brothers, Howard and Warwick. Concerned more with selling aeroplanes than building them, they did, nevertheless, produce flyable aircraft and must take their place among the brethren of aviation.

More famous were the Roe brothers. Mr (later Sir) Alliott Verdon Roe first came to notice when he won a £75 prize with a biplane model at the *Daily Mail* model aeroplane competition in 1907.

After this he went on to build a full-size version in stables behind the surgery of his brother, Dr S Verdon Roe, in Putney, and then his famous 9-hp triplane (still to be seen in the Science Museum, London). The triplane originally had the legend 'Bulls Eye Avroplane' painted on its side, to record the fact that it was built with the help of H V Roe, the maker of Bulls Eye braces; but this is a case where only one brother's name has survived in aviation fame. A V Roe might—probably would—have succeeded without brotherly assistance, but there is no doubt that the encouragement given led to greatness just a little more easily.

In America there was another family, this time of two brothers and two sisters named Stinson. The aircraft they designed are still among the world's great aeroplanes and one of the sisters, Katherine, became one of the very early women to obtain a pilot's licence.

In those formative years before 1914 there were two other men who, behind the scenes, probably did more to advance aviation than any other ten men put together. They were the brothers Alfred and Harold Harmsworth, who later became, respectively, Lord Northcliffe and Lord Rothermere. Newspaper proprietors, they offered prizes of great cash value for aviation feats and, indeed, their principal paper, the *Daily Mail*, still does occasionally offer such inducements to aviation effort. Moore-Brabazon won £1,000 for the first

circular flight of one mile in Britain; Blériot a similar sum for his cross-Channel flight. Then followed £10,000 for London-Manchester, another £10,000 for the first Atlantic non-stop flight, and so on. Aviation owes much to these far-sighted brothers.

Among the aircraft which played a major part in the 1914-18 war in the air were the French Breguet, Morane, Nieuport and Caudron machines. All were used extensively in the French air force and, to a lesser degree, in the Royal Flying Corps; they were, respectively, the products of companies founded by Louis and Jacques Breguet, Léon and Robert Morane, Edouard and Charles Nieuport, and Gaston and René Caudron.

Sir Geoffrey de Havilland was the head of a famous family of aviation pioneers. His own brother was another of those who was not greatly in the public eye, but his sons all went into the business of building and flying aeroplanes. This is more a case of sons joining an established family business than founding one themselves, but they certainly should not be omitted from any account of aviation brethren.

On the operational side, Britain has had two very famous pairs of brothers. David F W Atcherley, who reached the rank of Air Vice-Marshal, had a distinguished career in the Royal Air Force and would undoubtedly have achieved even higher rank if he had not been lost while flying a Meteor over the Mediterranean in 1952. His brother, Air Marshal Sir Richard Atcherley, who died only recently, first made a name for himself as a member of Britain's Schneider Trophy team.

Also in the RAF were the brothers Salmond. Marshal of the Royal Air Force Sir John Salmond served in the RFC in the first World War and became Chief of the Air Staff in 1952. Sir Geoffrey Salmond also was appointed Chief of the Air Staff, but his comparatively early death prevented him from taking up the appointment. This is the unique example of two brothers each reaching the highest possible appointment in the same military force.

In the field of aircraft design the Miles brothers, Frederick and George, made their mark in the early 1930s and are still active in the business. They are best remembered for the excellent series of trainer aircraft used by the RAF during the last war.

It would be impossible to list all the brothers who have entered aviation as pioneers, but these few examples give some idea of how frequently such a family combination became a force to be reckoned with. It is also a fact that a great many of them lived to a considerable age, giving the lie to the general belief that anyone who went in for flying in its pioneer days had taken a one-way ticket to an early grave!

The First Air Shows

The popularity of various forms of entertainment—the theatre, the cinema, the circus—has waxed and waned over the years, but one form of spectacular show has continued to increase in its appeal in the sixty-odd years since the first one was held. This is the air show, display, pageant, call it what you will. Indeed, it might well be argued that there were shows long before the famous one at Reims in 1909, for balloon ascents from centres of entertainment like Vauxhall Gardens attracted huge crowds of sightseers as far back as the second half of the 19th century.

However, the present era certainly began with the Reims meeting in August 1909. The Wright brothers' flying had had little enough publicity at the beginning, but from 1906 other pioneers had been building, flying and crashing aeroplanes and after Wilbur Wright's visit in 1908 it was felt that a big get-together in France, then the home of European aviation, would not only have a considerable public appeal, but would make it possible for all the world's flying authorities to meet and discuss their problems and exchange ideas.

Reims was chosen as the locale for no very obvious reason except that the local authority was presumably very enthusiastic and helpful. Be that as it may, all the great flyers of the day converged on the city with their simple machines. So also did large numbers of wealthy sportsmen and women, together with crowds of the general public who went along for the thrill.

In addition to demonstration flights and elementary aerobatics, there were numerous races and an altitude contest. The latter was won by the unlucky Channel flyer Hubert Latham, who flew his new Antoinette VII monoplane to a height of 508.5 ft (155 m). The American, Glenn Curtiss, won the Gordon Bennett Trophy in his Golden Flyer biplane at an average speed of 47.09 mph (75.789 km/h). The fastest machine was the Blériot, powered by one of the first Gnome rotary engines. Flown by Louis Blériot himself, it reached 60 mph (97 km/h), but landed on fire when a fuel pipe broke.

The absolute cream of the aeronautical world assembled at Reims, and the discussions which took place after each day's flying between the Voisin brothers, Santos-Dumont, Farman, Delagrange, Blériot, Levavasseur, Paulhan and a number of others equally famous must have been fascinating to expert and layman alike. It can never be sufficiently regretted that the tape recorder had still to be invented. Even Tissandier, of Paris Balloon Post fame, was there.

England was still behind in the aviation race, but the concept of Reims caught on and some officials of the Blackpool Corporation, who went over to see the show, decided that their city should be the first to hold such a meeting in Britain. The meeting was held only one month later, but it was dogged by really bad weather. In his book *My fifty years in flying*, Harry Harper, the first-ever full-time aviation journalist, tells the story of a solitary onlooker, sitting in a stand throughout a morning of heavy rain, who asked a passing official: 'When is the interval?'

Nevertheless, the Blackpool meeting was not a failure. Latham, feeling that the spectators deserved something for their money, took up his Antoinette in winds gusting to gale force—something never done before—and gave a superb display of airmanship. This meeting was organised by the (now Royal) Aero Club, and at the same time another show was put on at Doncaster. There 'Colonel' Cody, Delagrange, Sommer and le Blon delighted the crowds. Incidentally, it was at Doncaster that Cody, always the showman, took his oath of allegiance to the King in the presence of a large crowd. The Stars and Stripes flying over his shed was lowered and the Union Jack raised as this American became a British citizen.

Static shows took place in both Paris and London. In 1908 there was an exhibition organised by a cycling club at the Grand Palais, but its importance was not very great.

In March 1909 the first of many Aero Shows was held at Olympia, London, organised by a consortium of the Society of Motor Manufacturers and Traders and the Aero Club. This attracted a lot of attention and was a great success. Later the same year an exhibition of *Locomotion Aérienne* was put on at the Grand Palais and this too was hailed as extremely interesting. Both the latter shows were very well attended and did much to introduce the general public to the concept of flying.

In the succeeding year three more flying shows took place in Britain, at Wolverhampton, Lanark and Bournemouth. It was at Bournemouth that the Hon C S Rolls, of Rolls-Royce fame, fell to his death following a structural failure of his Wright biplane. This was a grievous loss to British motoring and aviation.

MILANO CIRCUITO AEREO INTERNAZIONALE 24 SETT.re – 3 OTT.re 1910 PREMI L.300.000

Opposite page:

Extreme left: Ranked as eighth in a list of the ten best English pilots of 1910, L D L Gibbs is seen here at the controls of his clipped-wing Farman racer at Wolverhampton. He had first achieved fame by flying the tailless Dunne D.3 and D.4 aircraft at Blair Atholl, Scotland, in 1908

Top: The Fourth International Aero Show at Olympia, London, in 1913. Dominating the exhibits was the 175,000 cu ft (4,955 m³) British Army Airship *Delta,* built at Farnborough. Under its nose was a strange parachute-like helicopter, with 50 hp Gnome engine, designed by J R Porter. Far more practical were the aeroplanes, which included Geoffrey de Havilland's Farnborough-built B.E.2 *(bottom right of picture),* holder of the British height record of 10,560 ft (3,218 m), carrying two persons

Poster:
Artists captured daring flying displays in their colourful lithographic posters, this particular air show being in Milan

This page:
Centre: The large number of cars parked at the Harvard-Boston Aero Meet of 1911 indicates the interest in aviation that the American public was beginning to show by that time

Far left: Chief prize winner at the 1909 flying meeting at Blackpool was Henry Farman, who won £2,400 on a biplane of his own design

Left: Only three pilots were engaged for the first Irish aviation meeting on the Leopardstown race course in August 1910. The outstanding flight was made by Cecil Grace, who braved a strong and gusty wind to demonstrate his Farman biplane

Below left: Bleriot monoplanes at the Scottish International Flight Meeting at Lanark in August 1910. They won a high proportion of the prize money, which totalled £8,060, with speeds of up to 77.67 mph (125 km/h) over one kilometre, which was a world record, and a height record of 6,621 ft (2,018 m)

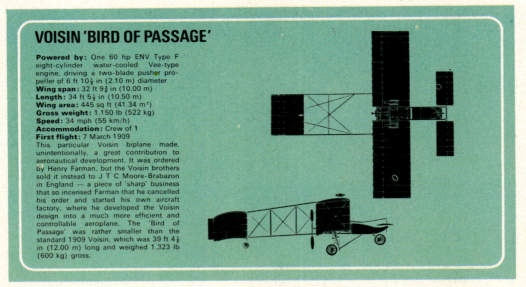

VOISIN 'BIRD OF PASSAGE'

Powered by: One 60 hp ENV Type F eight-cylinder water-cooled Vee-type engine, driving a two-blade propeller of 6 ft 10½ in (2.10 m) diameter
Wing span: 32 ft 9¾ in (10.00 m)
Length: 34 ft 5½ in (10.50 m)
Wing area: 445 sq ft (41.34 m²)
Gross weight: 1,150 lb (522 kg)
Speed: 34 mph (55 km/h)
Accommodation: Crew of 1
First flight: 7 March 1909
This particular Voisin biplane made, unintentionally, a great contribution to aeronautical development. It was ordered by Henry Farman, but the Voisin brothers sold it instead to J T C Moore-Brabazon in England — a piece of 'sharp' business that so incensed Farman that he cancelled his order and started his own aircraft factory, where he developed the Voisin design into a much more efficient and controllable aeroplane. The 'Bird of Passage' was rather smaller than the standard 1909 Voisin, which was 39 ft 4½ in (12.00 m) long and weighed 1,323 lb (600 kg) gross.

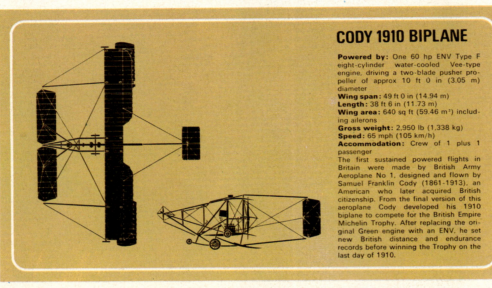

CODY 1910 BIPLANE

Powered by: One 60 hp ENV Type F eight-cylinder water-cooled Vee-type engine, driving a two-blade pusher propeller of approx 10 ft 0 in (3.05 m) diameter
Wing span: 49 ft 0 in (14.94 m)
Length: 38 ft 6 in (11.73 m)
Wing area: 640 sq ft (59.46 m²) including ailerons
Gross weight: 2,950 lb (1,338 kg)
Speed: 65 mph (105 km/h)
Accommodation: Crew of 1 plus 1 passenger
The first sustained powered flights in Britain were made by British Army Aeroplane No 1, designed and flown by Samuel Franklin Cody (1861-1913), an American who later acquired British citizenship. From the final version of this aeroplane Cody developed his 1910 biplane to compete for the British Empire Michelin Trophy. After replacing the original Green engine with an ENV, he set new British distance and endurance records before winning the Trophy on the last day of 1910.

By 1910 flying had become a popular sport for sightseers, and at any field where experimental flying went on large crowds would assemble whenever possible.

A small but most important show was put on by the *Daily Mail* at the Agricultural Hall, London, in March 1907. It was for model aircraft, capable of flying. Those approved at the static exhibition were taken to the grounds of the Alexandra Palace for flying trials, where they were watched by almost 7,000 people. The winner was the young A V (later Sir Alliott Verdon) Roe, who received the first prize of £75 for an elastic-driven biplane which flew extremely well. The money helped him considerably in the construction of his first full-size aeroplane and set the name Avro firmly in the records of aviation history.

Claude Grahame-White was not only a great airman, he was also a showman and astute in business. A rich man, he acquired a large tract of land at Hendon and turned it into an aerodrome; here he built aeroplanes, ran a most successful flying school and put on shows every weekend during the summer. He was regarded as a super-optimist when he formed the company, for suggesting that gate money for the shows would bring in £10,000 a year. In fact, his first year's operations netted £11,000.

A personal reminiscence is perhaps justified here. It was in 1912 that the author was taken, as a very small child, to Hendon one Saturday to see the races. As one gets older, childhood memories fade, but the

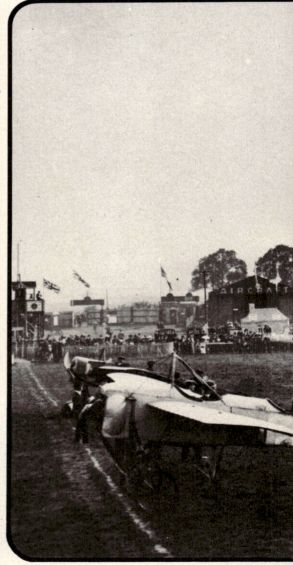

intrepid airmen flashing round the pylons at 60 mph (97 km/h) and the demonstrations of looping-the-loop remain as clear—perhaps even clearer—today than the first experience of supersonic flight or of crossing the Andes. One wonders how many others made aviation their business as a result of going to one of Grahame-White's Hendon epics.

Hendon was not, of course, the only centre at which the crowds were attracted to watch flying; but it was probably the best organised and certainly the only aerodrome at which frequent exhibitions were staged. It has remained to this day an aviation centre of vital importance. From civil flying it went over to military aviation in the first World War, became the site of the RAF displays in the inter-war years, was the base of a communications squadron later and is now the home of the RAF Museum. The cynics who decried Grahame-White—and there were many—were proved wrong time and time again. Fortunately he lived to be over 80, to see the manhood of the lusty infant he had helped to bring into the world.

A natural affinity existed between motor racing and aviation, both being among the most dangerous amusements that man could go in for, so it was natural that the Brooklands motor race track at Weybridge should become a centre for aviation. One of the most famous British designers, A V Roe, did some of his early flying there. His work and that of others attracted the enthusiasts

and, no doubt, added something to the income of the race track.

Prior to the first World War the Johannisthal airfield at Berlin was another popular centre for the crowds. There the most successful performer was the Dutchman Anthony Fokker, who was later to build the fighters that gave the RFC so many headaches over the Western Front and the great airliners which covered the world between the wars. Count Zeppelin, too, had made Germany very air-minded, and the many visitors to Johannisthal were enthusiastic for the various shows that were put on there.

America had its shows, too, though oddly enough the home of heavier-than-air powered flight was slow to become enthusiastic, a state of affairs difficult to understand now of the most air-minded country in the world.

Other countries, sometimes rather unexpected ones, also had their own early air displays. Soon after the Reims meeting one was held at Cairo. It was not especially remarkable, except in one respect. The 'Baroness' de La Roche, formerly a lady balloonist of some experience, made some of her first flights there as an aeroplane pilot. This lady, whose real name was Elise Deroche, had become the world's first woman pilot in October 1909, and in March 1910 became the first woman to hold a pilot's certificate. A story told of her at Cairo claims that she complained of 'these men drivers who got in her way': apparently

at least one of them admitted that he did! She died in 1919, in a crash when she was riding as a passenger in a new aeroplane on test.

No one can tell how much money has been attracted by air shows in the six decades since Reims, but from the immense crowds that go to the National Air Races in America, to Farnborough or Biggin Hill, to the air shows at Paris, Hanover, Turin and in Russia, the sum must run into uncountable millions. Truly, that little airfield in France really started something!

Far left: The Rumpler Taube exhibited at the Berlin Show in 1912 had the characteristic wing-tips and birdlike tail that were to become familiar two years later, in the early months of the first World War

Far left, below: Bleriot and Farman aircraft at the Midland Aero Club's meeting at Wolverhampton in 1910. In bad weather, the Hon C S Rolls won the speed contest in a Wright biplane. Claude Grahame-White came second on a Farman and also captured the duration prize by amassing 75 minutes in the air during the week

Left: In the first International Air Contest at Hendon in September 1913, the Hendon Trophy and prize money of £1,000 were won for Britain by Claude Grahame-White and Gustav Hamel, who finished first in three of the six events. Grahame-White's Maurice Farman is seen here flying over the two-seat Blériot of W L Brock (USA) and, behind, two Moranes

Above: First flying meeting of all was held at Reims in August 1909, when most of the world's leading pilots performed before a half a million people. The excitement as the biplanes of the time raced around pylons at around 40 mph is well reflected in this picture

Daily Mail
and Aviation

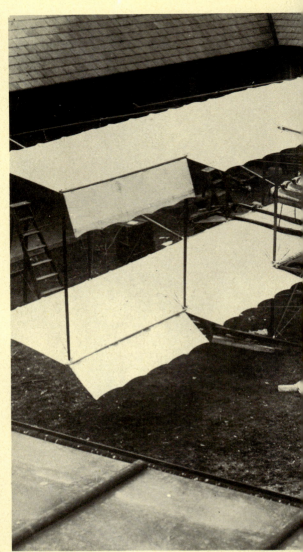

IT IS NOW COMMON PRACTICE for a newspaper to offer prizes or otherwise sponsor sporting achievement. At the beginning of the century, however, this, if not unknown, was remarkably unusual. To the *Daily Mail* newspaper must go the credit for establishing this kind of support for aviation.

Alfred Harmsworth, Viscount Northcliffe, as the paper's founder, was more than just chairman of the company. Although he was never a man to 'buy a dog and do the barking himself', he dictated policy and ensured that new developments which he considered worthwhile were not overlooked.

Always an enthusiast for scientific development, he became seriously interested in flying when Harry Harper approached him for backing in connection with a glider he (Harper) had designed. Northcliffe was sympathetic and, even though Harper's design was not a success, his approach had far-reaching effects for the whole world.

In 1906 Harry Harper became the world's first full-time newspaper air correspondent, and the *Daily Mail* broke new ground by employing such an apparently unnecessary—and expensive—journalist.

For a while Harper was just what he called himself, an air reporter. Then he put up an idea to Northcliffe that the *Daily Mail* should offer prizes for the best flying model aircraft. By comparison with later offers that first prize of £75 was remarkably modest, but at the final competition at the Alexandra Palace (North London), when it was won by an unknown young man called A V Roe, this small sum provided the real start to Sir Alliott Verdon Roe's career which resulted in a long series of great aeroplanes. The Avro 504, Anson, Lancaster, Shackleton and Vulcan, to name only a few, all owe their existence to that £75 awarded more than 60 years ago.

After this modest beginning the *Daily Mail*, run by Northcliffe and his brother Harold, who became the first Lord Rothermere, made a series of big prize offers. The first was £1,000 for the first circular one-mile (1.6 km) flight by a British pilot in a British-built aeroplane. That went to the holder of British Pilot's Licence No 1, J T C Moore-Brabazon, later Lord Brabazon of Tara and a great force in British aviation. Another £1,000 went to Louis Blériot for the first heavier-than-air flight

across the English Channel. Both these prizes were won in 1909.

Northcliffe provoked some sarcastic comment from his Fleet Street colleagues when he offered £10,000 for the first flight from London to Manchester in a period of less than 24 hours. A rival, Liberal, newspaper, derisively offered ten million pounds for the first flying machine of any kind to fly five miles from London and back to the departure point ! Ironically, many years later, this paper was absorbed by another of the same political persuasion which, in its turn, collapsed and was absorbed by the *Daily Mail*. Meanwhile,

Alfred Harmsworth, first Viscount Northcliffe and founder of the *Daily Mail*, whose patronage inspired many of the great flights of aviation's first two decades

attempts to win the prize resulted in a British pilot, Claude Grahame-White, making one of the first-ever night flights, but the great French pilot Louis Paulhan pipped him at the post.

In 1913, when the longest flight ever made was only a few hundred miles, the *Daily Mail* offered £10,000 for the first aeroplane flight, non-stop, between the British Isles and North America. The flight could be in either direction but must be completed in 72 hours. Once more Northcliffe was derided as a lunatic, but only six years later Sir John Alcock and Sir Arthur Whitten Brown won the money. A consolation award of £5,000 went to Hawker and Mackenzie-Grieve, for a

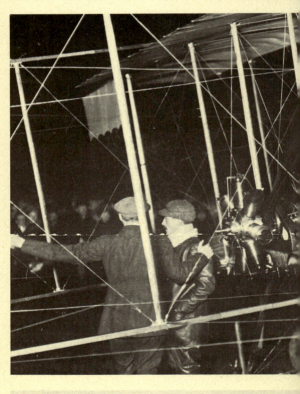

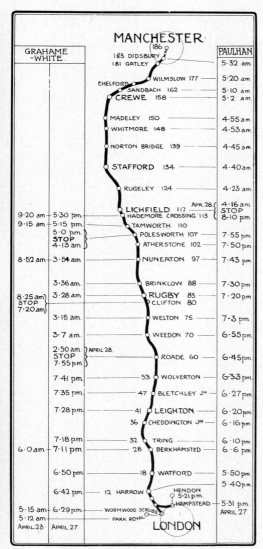

GRAHAME-WHITE		Location	PAULHAN
		MANCHESTER 186	
		183 DIDSBURY	
		181 GATLEY	5·32 am
		WILMSLOW 177	5·20 am
		CHELFORD	
		SANDBACH 162	5·10 am
		CREWE 158	5·2 am
		MADELEY 150	4·55 am
		WHITMORE 148	4·53 am
		NORTON BRIDGE 139	4·45 am
		STAFFORD 134	4·40 am
		RUGELEY 124	4·23 am
9·20 am	5·30 pm	LICHFIELD 117 — APR.28	4·16 am STOP 8·10 pm
9·15 am	5·15 pm	HADEMORE CROSSING 113	
	5·0 pm STOP 4·13 am	TAMWORTH 110	
		POLESWORTH 107	7·55 pm
		ATHERSTONE 102	7·50 pm
8·52 am	3·54 am	NUNEATON 97	7·43 pm
	3·36 am	BRINKLOW 88	7·30 pm
8·25 am STOP 7·20 am	3·28 am	RUGBY 83	7·20 pm
		CLIFTON 80	
	3·15 am	WELTON 75	7·3 pm
	3·7 am	WEEDON 70	6·55 pm
	2·50 am APRIL 28 STOP 7·55 pm	ROADE 60	6·45 pm
	7·41 pm	53 WOLVERTON	6·33 pm
	7·35 pm	47 BLETCHLEY Jn	6·27 pm
	7·28 pm	41 LEIGHTON	6·20 pm
		36 CHEDDINGTON JN	6·16 pm
	7·18 pm	32 TRING	6·10 pm
6·0 am	7·11 pm	28 BERKHAMSTED	6·6 pm
	6·50 pm	18 WATFORD	5·50 pm
	6·42 pm	12 HARROW	5·40 pm
		HENDON 5·21 pm	
		HAMPSTEAD	5·31 pm APRIL 27
5·15 am	6·29 pm	WORMWOOD SCRUBS	
5·12 am		PARK ROYAL	
APRIL 28	APRIL 27	LONDON	

Top left: Erecting the Henry Farman biplane flown by Claude Grahame-White in the London-Manchester air race of 1910

Top right: The times recorded on this diagram tell their own story of how Grahame-White's enforced landing at Roade, at nightfall, cost him the race despite a courageous take-off in darkness at 2.50 am

Centre left: Louis Paulhan preparing to take off from Lichfield on the last stages of his flight to Manchester. At this time, Grahame-White was still very much in the running as a result of his night flight, but was to be forced down again, by engine trouble, at Polesworth. The London-Manchester flight linked, symbolically, the two publishing centres of the *Daily Mail*

Left: Autographs on this menu of the banquet given in honour of Louis Paulhan are (top to bottom) those of Paulhan himself, Grahame-White, Mme Paulhan, Mrs and Miss Grahame-White, the Duke of Argyll (President of the Royal Aero Club) and Mr Marlowe, editor of the *Daily Mail*

Bottom centre: A crowd gathers around the Farman biplane of Louis Paulhan after his landing at Didsbury. The flight had been so demanding that he said he would not undertake it again for 'ten thousand times ten thousand pounds'

Left: This memorial near Dover Castle marks the spot where Louis Blériot ended the first cross-Channel flight in an aeroplane, to win another *Daily Mail* prize

Bottom left: The first *Daily Mail* prizes were awarded to winners of a model competition held at the Alexandra Palace, London, in 1907. One of the contestants was this Weiss Albatross glider. Typical of the designs of José Weiss, it was an attempt to produce inherent stability by the use of bird-like sweptback wings

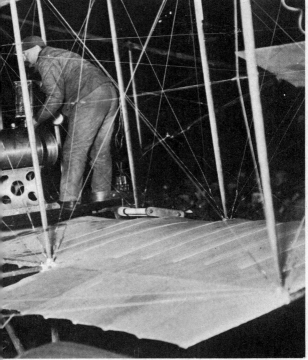

valiant effort which ended in the ocean half-way across.

Northcliffe died in 1922, and for some years his brother, Lord Rothermere, who became the principal proprietor of the *Daily Mail*, did not show such keen interest in aviation. This was not due to a change of policy but was simply because most of the dramatic flights had been made, usually by professional pilots with the backing of the aircraft industry. The era of the record-breaking flights in light aeroplanes was still to come.

In 1930, an unknown woman pilot named Amy Johnson left England on 5 May in a Gipsy Moth named *Jason*. Bound for Australia, she attracted no attention for the first few days. But when she got to Karachi in six days—thus establishing a new record—the press sat up and took a lot of notice. Not surprisingly, the *Daily Mail* was in the foreground, and when she reached Australia on 24 May the paper announced an award of £10,000 for her great effort.

The *Daily Mail* was the first newspaper to acquire its own aeroplane. Fitted with a darkroom and carrying a motorcycle, it speeded up news and picture-gathering. Today, aircraft are an automatic adjunct to news collection, but it was the *Daily Mail* that started it all.

Older readers will remember the general strike of 1926. What is not so well-known is that this actually started within the *Daily Mail* when printers stopped work rather than print an editorial entitled 'For King and Country'. Alone among British papers, the *Daily Mail* then had an office

in Paris where it printed a continental edition of the paper. London's *Daily Mails* were printed in Paris, flown to Croydon and other airfields near London, collected by fleets of cars and distributed to the newsagents only a few hours later than usual. This was the true beginning of bulk air freight, another *Daily Mail* 'first'.

Forgotten to-day is the fact that Lord Rothermere financed the design and construction of the prototype of the Bristol Blenheim bomber when he realised that Prime Minister Stanley Baldwin was not interested in the growing menace of Hitler. Such an action was—and still is—unique.

In conjunction with the Royal Aero Club, the *Daily Mail*, now under the

leadership of Esmond Harmsworth, second Lord Rothermere, has continued to stimulate aviation. In 1959, to commemorate Louis Blériot's cross-Channel flight 50 years earlier, the paper offered prizes for the fastest journey between the centre of London and the centre of Paris. Many thousands of pounds were involved and resulted in some remarkable efforts using cars, motorcycles, helicopters and jet aircraft. The winning time was less than one hour.

Then in 1969, to coincide with the 50th anniversary year of the Alcock and Brown flight, an even more outstanding contest was staged, for the fastest time between New York and London. Everything, from

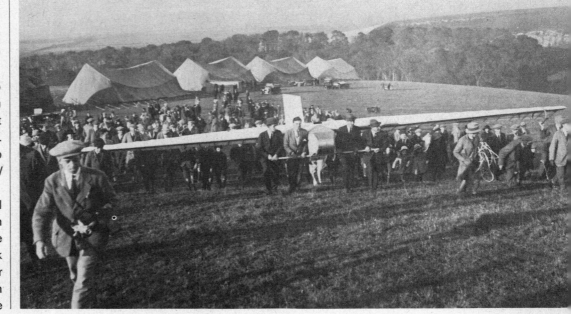

Carrying Raynham's glider to the top of Itford Hill, at the first British gliding competition organised by the *Daily Mail* in 1922

Above: *Geraldine*, **the D.H.61 acquired by the** *Daily Mail* **in August 1928. It carried a motorcycle on which photographers could speed to an assignment after landing. Negatives could be processed in a darkroom on board, and stories typed at a folding desk**

Right: Believing that the Air Ministry was not taking advantage of the capabilities of Britain's aircraft industry, Lord Rothermere ordered the Bristol 142 monoplane *Britain First* **as a four-passenger executive transport in 1935. When tested at Martlesham Heath, it proved to have a speed of 307 mph (494 km/h). As this was 100 mph (161 km/h) faster than the RAF's latest fighters, the Air Ministry quickly put the 142 into production as the Blenheim bomber**

supersonic jets, direct-lift jets, airliners, helicopters, cars, motorcycles and motor-boats, to bicycles, was pressed into service. In all, about £50,000 was given in prizes, and the Empire State Building was brought within about five hours of the London Post Office Tower. The use of the Harrier, taking off and landing in the city centres — by special permission, of course — brought the direct-lift airliner in sight at last.

Altogether, the *Daily Mail* has given considerably more than £100,000 in aviation prize money, and it would be difficult to estimate just how far this newspaper has brought aviation forward over a period of more than 60 years.

HENRY FARMAN III

Powered by: One 50 hp Gnome seven-cylinder rotary engine, driving an 8 ft 6½ in (2.60 m) diameter two-blade pusher propeller
Wing span: 32 ft 9¾ in (10.00 m)
Length: 39 ft 4¼ in (12.00 m)
Wing area: 430.56 sq ft (40.00 m²)
Gross weight: 1,213 lb (550 kg)
Max speed: 37 mph (60 km/h)
Accommodation: Crew of 1
First flight: 6 April 1909
Henry Farman's Type III biplane, which appeared in 1909, was a marked improvement over the Voisin boxkite aeroplane from which it was developed. At the famous Reims meeting that year it carried off the distance prize with a flight of 112 miles (180 km). In the *Daily Mail's* London-Manchester race of 1910, both competitors, Louis Paulhan and Claude Grahame-White, flew improved versions of the type illustrated which had slightly longer fuselages and an extension of the upper-wing span to 34 ft 1½ in (10.40 m).

Left: In 1959, to mark the 50th anniversary of Blériot's cross-Channel flight, the *Daily Mail* offered a prize for the fastest journey between London and Paris. This competitor alighted from an Alouette helicopter on to a platform built by Hungerford Bridge over the Thames

Below: On the 50th anniversary of Alcock and Brown's pioneer trans-Atlantic flight, in 1969, the *Daily Mail* organised yet another competition, for the fastest time between the centres of New York and London. Piloted by Squadron Leader Graham Williams, this Harrier V/STOL fighter is landing in a coalyard at St Pancras, London, to make possible a total time of 5 hr 59 min 58.52 sec between the tops of the Empire State Building and London's Post Office Tower

FIRST OF THE JETS

ROMANIA IS NOT AMONG those countries generally recognised as having pioneered in aeronautics, yet the achievements of her citizens were not only tangible but, in some respects, astonishing. The first name among them is that of Traian Vuia who, as early as 1906, was making brief hops in a monoplane of truly prophetic design, powered by a carbonic acid motor. These hops were made in France, where Vuia was head of a Romanian resistance group in both world wars.

Romanian also was Aurel Vlaicu who, although offered facilities to build his first aircraft in Germany, vowed to return to his own country, which he did in 1908. Such was the degree of success achieved by 1912 that Vlaicu gained first place at a big international flying meeting, though he was competing against Roland Garros, one of the greatest pilots of all time. For sheer technical ingenuity, however, one name stands above those of other Romanians, and very high indeed among those of all nations. This man is Henri Coanda, constructor of the world's first jet-propelled aircraft and still living in Paris in 1971.

Henri Coanda was born in Bucharest in 1887, the son of an army general who had graduated from the College of Mathematics in Paris and became subsequently a professor at the Military School of Engineering and Artillery in Bucharest. The young Coanda was himself educated to become an officer, and received his further education at Charlottenburg, Liège, Montefiore and Paris. In the French capital he attended the High School of Aeronautics, where he graduated in 1909 as the best pupil among the first intake. His aeronautical inclinations went back to even earlier days, for while still in Bucharest during 1905 he had built a mock-up of a rocket-propelled aircraft. Propulsion by jet reaction continued to occupy his thoughts, and at the Paris Salon of October 1910 he created a stir by exhibiting the jet-propelled aircraft already mentioned.

To state that this was the first aircraft in the world to have jet propulsion is not to imply that it was of the turbojet type, as developed in the 1930s and 1940s in Germany and Britain; but it certainly embodied what would today be termed a ducted fan. Operating within its duct, this fan drove plain air rearwards (not, be it noted, a fuel/air mixture) to provide propulsion, and was itself driven by a 50-hp Clerget engine. The entire installation is most nearly comparable with that of the Italian Caproni-Campini monoplane, first flown in 1940, though this embodied an afterburner for burning fuel in the tailpipe and thus increasing thrust.

Contemporarily the Coanda power unit was known as a *turbo-propulseur*, or turbine propeller, but although of strikingly modern appearance it could hardly have

Below: With its very clean lines and *turbo-propulseur* power plant, Coanda's remarkable 1910 biplane must be regarded as one of the great aeroplanes of history. Although it seems to have made only one brief flight, it was the forerunner of all the jets of today

Top: Henri Coanda built the world's first jet-propelled aeroplane in 1910, but is best remembered today for the designs he produced later for the British & Colonial (Bristol) company. The structural strength of his 1912 Bristol-Coanda monoplanes was tested in the then-standard manner, by loading the inverted wings with sand to show that they would not collapse

Centre left: When the Spaniards ordered five Bristol-Coanda B.R.7 two-seat biplanes in 1912, they insisted on the use of a 70 hp Renault engine of the kind fitted in their Maurice Farmans. The aircraft are remembered mainly for the fact that test pilot Collyns Pizey managed to land one of them with its carburettor on fire and leap out, with his passenger, before the biplane was burned out

Left: Coanda watching two of his monoplanes perform in the Military Aeroplane Competition at Larkhill in August 1912

delivered sufficient thrust for entirely successful flight, although a German technical journal declared: 'Coanda's experiments show that this method of propulsion is more efficient than the most advanced use of normal propellers'. As controversy has arisen concerning Coanda's first attempt at flight it is fitting to quote the Romanian inventor himself.

'It was', he has recalled, 'on 10 December 1910. I had no intention of flying on that day. My plan was to check the operation of the jet engine close to the ground, but the heat of the jet blast coming back at me was greater than I expected and I was worried in case I set the aircraft on fire. For this reason I concentrated on adjusting the jet and did not realise that the aircraft was rapidly gaining speed.

'Then I looked up and saw the walls of Paris approaching rapidly. There was no time to stop or turn round and I decided to try and fly instead. Unfortunately I had no experience of flying and was not used to the controls of this aircraft.

'The plane seemed to make a sudden steep climb and then landed with a bump.

First the left wing hit the ground and then the aircraft crumpled up. I was not strapped in and was fortunately thrown clear of the burning machine.'

This ill-fated, though historic, Coanda aeroplane of 1910 had features of distinction quite apart from its power plant. It was, for instance, of sesquiplane type, the lower of the two wings being much shorter in span than the upper one; and the wings themselves were covered not with the customary fabric but with plywood. Thereafter Coanda turned his attentions to more conventional designs, though even these possessed unusual features; the first, which was present at the Reims Concours Militaire during October 1911, had two Gnome engines driving a single propeller.

With his long black hair and somewhat theatrical air, Coanda created as much of a stir as did his inventions. This was especially noticeable when he came to England in 1912 to join the British & Colonial Aeroplane Company (later Bristol, and now part of the British Aircraft Corporation) as technical adviser. Among

his designs for this company was a fine-looking military monoplane. In a machine of this type, during September 1912, an officer of the newly-formed Royal Flying Corps, together with a passenger, was making a gliding descent near Oxford when the descent suddenly developed into a steep dive. The fabric of the starboard wing was torn off, the aircraft crashed, and both occupants were killed. Enquiry disclosed that a quick-release clip on one of the bracing wires had become detached; but, as the accident had been preceded by several others involving monoplanes, aircraft of this class were thereupon banned for British military pilots and technical progress was arrested as a result. Undismayed, Coanda developed his design into a biplane, and aircraft of this type were supplied to France, Italy, Germany and Coanda's homeland, Romania.

Coanda was not content merely to design military aeroplanes, and recognised that their full potential could be realised only when special equipment was developed for them. Accordingly he concerned himself with the means of sighting and launching bombs, and at the Paris Salon of 1913 again attracted attention, this time with a bomb sight of which a contemporary reporter wrote:

'In order to steer the machine over any desired spot two sights are mounted on top of the fuselage in front of the observer's seat. The rear sight can be moved sideways for a distance of about six inches. If the observer finds that steering a dead straight course for some prearranged landmark will not bring him over the desired point he can slightly alter the course by sliding the rear sight to one side or the other, so that although the pilot sees the landmark and the two sights in line, the machine is not actually heading straight for the landmark, but slightly to one side or the other. For use at night, when the pilot is unable to see the two sights, an electrical signalling system is employed, consisting of a series of push buttons in the observer's cockpit and a series of lamps in front of the pilot.'

This scheme was intended to operate jointly with a bomb-launching system wherein the projectiles were loaded into a cylinder like that of a revolver and were discharged by a piston.

Thus, not only did Coanda construct the first jet-propelled aircraft but he introduced what was certainly one of the first 'integrated weapon systems', to use current terminology. Nor did he overlook guns, for he designed for aircraft use a recoilless type of light construction.

To add that this same man was an accomplished performer on the cello and that he studied sculpture under Rodin, who described him as 'gifted and learned', might seem extravagant. Yet this was so.

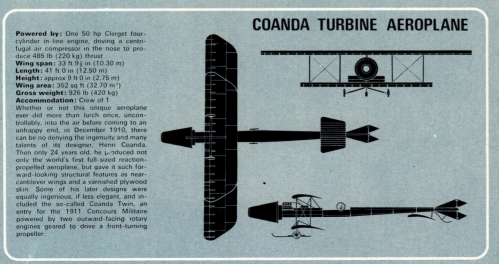

COANDA TURBINE AEROPLANE

Powered by: One 50 hp Clerget four-cylinder in-line engine, driving a centrifugal air compressor in the nose to produce 485 lb (220 kg) thrust
Wing span: 33 ft 9¼ in (10.30 m)
Length: 41 ft 0 in (12.50 m)
Height: approx 9 ft 0 in (2.75 m)
Wing area: 352 sq ft (32.70 m²)
Gross weight: 926 lb (420 kg)
Accommodation: Crew of 1
Whether or not this unique aeroplane ever did more than lurch once, uncontrollably, into the air before coming to an unhappy end, in December 1910, there can be no denying the ingenuity and many talents of its designer, Henri Coanda. Then only 24 years old, he produced not only the world's first full-sized reaction-propelled aeroplane, but gave it such forward-looking structural features as near-cantilever wings and a varnished plywood skin. Some of his later designs were equally ingenious, if less elegant, and included the so-called Coanda Twin, an entry for the 1911 Concours Militaire powered by two outward-facing rotary engines geared to drive a front-turning propeller.

Henri Fabre
Father of the Floatplane

Above, top: A rare action picture of the Fabre seaplane, with the 'lifting floats' almost clear of the water

Above, lower: One of the landplanes built for Louis Paulhan in 1911, with Fabre's unique lattice-girder spars

Right: Henri Fabre, the world's first seaplane pilot, by the pusher engine of his Hydro-aeroplane in 1911

Far right: Honoured today as the first powered aircraft to take off from water, Henri Fabre's strange machine was described in 1910 as being 'more hydroplane than aeroplane'

Henri Fabre was born in Marseilles, in 1882, into a family of shipowners and was destined, in due course, to enter the family business. In his youth he developed an interest in engineering as well as his inherited love of the sea. He obtained a science degree and began to specialise in hydrodynamics.

By the time he was 23 he had become an avid follower of the work of such aviation pioneers as the Voisin brothers and Blériot and, being in relatively comfortable circumstances financially, was able to give time and energy to research into aerodynamic problems.

For two years—from 1907 to 1909—he carried out a variety of experiments; some of them in the research ship *Essor*, where he investigated airflow over different surfaces; others on land, with a propeller-driven motor car. Perhaps his most important work was what would now be called pure research on immersed surfaces and floats.

Unlike some of the early—and usually unsuccessful—experimenters in the field of aviation, Fabre was working to a well-defined plan. In 1909 he decided that he had progressed far enough to apply his theoretical ideas to a practical flying machine. This was to be a seaplane, built on three floats, and having three Anzani engines coupled to a single propeller. Regrettably, it failed to fly; but this was not an uncommon experience in those days and Fabre followed this design with another later in the year.

His second aircraft was built at Martigues, near Marseilles, and, in March 1910, it flew. The construction of this machine was interesting, and bore several signs of Fabre's boat-building background. At the forward end it had twin rudders and two horizontal lifting surfaces, the upper one serving as an elevator. There was one float at the front and two under the monoplane wings, which were situated at the rear of the aircraft. The pilot's seat, more or less a saddle, was located fairly well forward on one of the two longitudinal beams which linked the wing assembly with the elevator unit. The engine, a 50 hp Gnome rotary, was rear-mounted and drove a pusher propeller. Fabre's *Hydravion* was, in fact, one of the first aircraft to be powered by this revolutionary new power plant.

Wing-warping was used instead of ailerons, a fairly common practice at the time, and control of the rudder-elevator assembly was by a form of tiller running horizontally back to the pilot. A spring balancing system was included to reduce the effort required to operate the stick.

The wing spars and the main fuselage beams were of a novel lattice-girder type of construction. The latter were boxed in, but the wing spars, being at right angles to the direction of flight, were left uncovered so that the air could flow freely through the lattice and reduce drag. The wings were covered with canvas, stretched over the ribs and attached to each rib end by a sprung hook. During storage or repair, by releasing the hooks, the canvas could be reefed up to the main spar like the sails of a boat.

All the framework was made of wood, and it is of especial interest that the floats were made of plywood and were relatively flexible, to meet the impact of running over water and the shock of landing. This must have been one of the earliest occasions —if not the very first—on which plywood was used as a main material in an aircraft. Also, the front float was steerable to assist control while manoeuvring on the water.

Henri Fabre's first flight was made from the harbour at La Mède, near Marseilles, on 28 March 1910, when he considered that the weather conditions (presumably a flat calm) were suitable. It is worth remembering that, although he had been an enthusiastic follower of the work of other designers, Fabre had never flown before, even as a passenger. On its first run, the *Hydravion* hydroplaned across the water at about 34 mph (55 km/h), but did not rise. On the second attempt, however, Fabre lifted his seaplane off the water and made a straight-line flight of some 1,640 ft (500 m) at about 37 mph (60 km/h), alighting safely as soon as he cut the power.

This was the first of four flights during the day, one of them including very gentle turns. In the afternoon he collected some official witnesses, in the shape of gendarmes and other government servants, and took off in their presence, again landing safely in the harbour of La Mède. On the following day, he covered a distance of about 3.75 miles (6 km).

Fabre was not a publicity-seeker, but he continued his flight experiments and soon came to the notice of Louis Paulhan

(winner of the *Daily Mail* prize for the London-Manchester flight in April 1910). In May of that year, Paulhan came to see a demonstration. Unfortunately, the aircraft was seriously damaged on landing and Paulhan lost interest in the floatplane; but he thought sufficiently highly of the basic design to ask Fabre to build a landplane with similar lattice-girder wing spars; two machines of this type were subsequently built and delivered to Britain.

The demonstration of the seaplane to Paulhan had finished with a descent at too high a speed. In Fabre's opinion the accident was caused by his aircraft having too much built-in stability and he set about rebuilding the machine so that it required more action—and skill—by the pilot to handle it. (Anthony Fokker made the same discovery in respect of his early machines.)

The principal modifications made to the original design were to double the area of the lower (fixed) forward lifting surface and to replace the aerofoil-shaped upper control surface with a flat one providing far less lift. The two small front rudders were removed, and the spring balance device eliminated, so that the pilot had some consciousness of the forces acting on the surface (in much the same way as artificial 'feel' is now incorporated in aircraft with powered controls).

The modified prototype was shown at the Aeronautical Exhibition in Paris in October 1910. Glenn Curtiss, who came over from the United States for the show, evidently spent a lot of time with Henri Fabre. There is no suggestion that Curtiss took any ideas from the Frenchman, but equally there is no doubt that he entertained a great respect for Fabre's work and was more than willing to learn from a fellow pioneer.

Fabre seems to have been plagued with trouble over the rudders and, after a further series of tests with them attached endplate-fashion to the fixed forward plane, he came to the conclusion that forward mounting was not the right arrangement. He moved the rudders to the rear, beneath the wings, and quickly achieved better control.

He tried to solve another directional problem by adding a retractable keel under the forward float, but this had the unfortunate result of causing the aircraft to turn over during a fast run. Following his modification to the air rudders, he removed this keel and, instead, fitted one behind each of the rear floats, making them independently retractable.

In March 1911, when an important motor-boat meeting was being held at Monaco, Fabre invited Jean Bécue, a pilot with far more experience than he had himself, to give a demonstration of the

modified *Hydravion*. The first flight was an outstanding success, but on the second Bécue made a bad mistake, landing too close inshore, in the surf. The machine was extensively damaged, and that was the end of Fabre's work in this direction. Though moderately well-off, he decided that the expense of continuing to develop the floatplane was too great, but did not by any means drop out of the aviation picture. Instead he concentrated on the design and manufacture of floats for other aircraft.

In 1911 he designed the floats for a Voisin biplane—another 'canard' design—which thus became the world's first amphibious aircraft; and he was responsible for all the floats used by the winning seaplanes at the Monaco Concours in 1913. His work in this field continued for many more years.

Unlike Glenn Curtiss, Fabre did not leave a great deal to posterity, but his parenthood of water-borne aircraft is undeniable.

In spite of the fact that—as older readers will recall—non-flying people in the pioneer days took it for granted that anyone going in for aviation was committing suicide, Fabre has lived on to a great age. Even in 1970, at the age of 88, he was still sailing his own boat—single-handed—in the bay at Marseilles.

Above: Wilhelm Kress' twin-hulled tandem triplane, tested in 1901, was the world's first powered marine aircraft. Unfortunately, as it began to lift from the water, Kress saw an obstruction ahead, slackened speed and tried to turn, and capsized

Left: First to fly—Henri Fabre's Hydro-aeroplane, seen here at Monaco in March 1911. Pilot Jean Bécue sat astride the fuselage beam

Top right: The first manned flight from water was made on 6 June 1905 by Gabriel Voisin, whose boxkite glider was towed off the Seine by a motor launch. His powered version, shown here, was less successful

Right: Initial tests of the seaplane designed jointly by Louis Blériot and the Voisin brothers, in 1906, were disastrous. Even when the forward ellipsoidal wing had been replaced by more normal boxkite wings, as illustrated, the machine failed to fly

Below: As Henri Fabre's Hydro-aeroplane was regarded in 1911 as being both motor boat and aircraft, it was entirely eligible for display in the Monte Carlo Motor Boat Exhibition of that year. It can be seen in the centre of this picture, surrounded by curious visitors

Wings over Water

There is a widespread belief that (to quote one standard reference work) 'in its earliest form the seaplane was merely an aeroplane to which was fastened the most elementary form of float chassis'. While this is generally true of the first really practical and successful seaplanes, the statement is misleading historically. The first aircraft to rise from water under its own power was exactly the opposite, being a highly specialised design which was as much a boat as an aeroplane, though it did not resemble either in any great degree.

Even this was preceded by a machine which, although it failed to fly, must go on record in this account of flying from water. The aircraft concerned was built in Austria by Wilhelm Kress, and was described in a letter from Octave Chanute to Wilbur Wright in 1903 as a 'flying boat'. In later years this term was used to describe a type of water-based aircraft, or seaplane, having a boat-like hull instead of floats. Chanute said of the Kress machine: 'It seems to me to possess some excellent points in construction, and that it may actually fly if a motor lighter than the present one can be obtained'. But this was not to be, for the craft capsized and was wrecked.

The first aircraft to rise from water was a glider of box-kite type, mounted on floats and towed from the River Seine by the racing motor-boat *La Rapiere* on 6 June 1905. The pilot was Gabriel Voisin. About two years later Wilbur and Orville Wright were experimenting with both floats and hydrofoil surfaces; but the distinction of having made the first powered flight from water belongs to Henri Fabre, a friend of the Voisin brothers. The date was 28 March 1910.

That Fabre's craft was indeed 'as much a boat as an aeroplane' is borne out by the fact that it was once considered as an entry for a motor-boat race at Monte Carlo, adjusted so that it could not rise altogether clear of the water. Hearing of this, a competitor said he was thinking of carrying a punt gun in case the 'long-legged monstrosity' looked like hopping over him! The description was not undeserved, for the three floats were carried on leg-like supports, one at the nose and two at the rear. These floats, of a type patented by Fabre, had a flat bottom and a curved upper surface, the intention being that they should provide a lifting force whether moving on the water or in the air.

Similar floats were fitted to a Voisin biplane, which flew tail-first like the Fabre machine, and which in August 1911 became the first aircraft to demonstrate amphibious qualities. The pilot, Maurice Colliex, took off on wheels from Issy aerodrome, alighted on the Seine, and made the return trip. In 1912 a Voisin tail-first biplane with Fabre floats became the first aeroplane to be carried by a French warship, the battleship *Foudre*.

After Fabre's first flight he persuaded his curious craft into the air on a number of occasions during 1910, and in modified form it reappeared at Monte Carlo in 1911, piloted by Jean Bécue. Its flying career then came to an abrupt end, as described in this contemporary account:

'The machine crossed the harbour in perfect style, skimming along the surface; nearing the harbour mouth, it rose up into the air to a height of about 30 yards, and soared along beautifully, greatly admired by thousands of spectators. As soon as it cleared the harbour, however, and encountered the full force of the wind outside, the machine became unmanageable, and to the horror of the onlookers was swept along at a terrific pace towards the rocks and stone walls below the terraces. Fortunately, the pilot, with great presence of mind, managed to throw himself clear of the machine into the sea, and was promptly picked up, none the worse for his startling experience.'

The historic Fabre monoplane, which, in spite of its strange appearance, was described by Gabriel Voisin as 'made like a masterpiece', was rebuilt many years after the 1911 crash and is preserved today in the French Musée de l'Air at Chalais-Meudon. In 1967 the Russian cosmonaut Yuri Gagarin dedicated a memorial at Martigues, the scene of its historic first flight.

Although 'water flight' was pioneered by the French, the greatest name in its early development was that of the American Glenn Curtiss. Late in 1908 Curtiss mounted his *June Bug* biplane on floats and called it the *Loon*, but was not successful in getting it off the water. He then developed another type of landplane; but when he made his famous Albany-New York flight he fitted under-wing floats, an air bag and a small hydrofoil. Clearly, his interest in seaplanes was very much alive. The next development respecting over-water flying, however, still concerned one of his landplanes.

During 1910 the US Navy was showing

FABRE HYDRAVION

Powered by: One 50 hp Gnome seven-cylinder rotary engine, driving a two-blade Chauvière pusher propeller of 8 ft 2½ in (2.50 m) diameter
Wing span: 45 ft 11 in (14.00 m)
Length: 27 ft 10¾ in (8.50 m)
Wing area: 183 sq ft (17.00 m²)
Gross weight: 1,047 lb (475 kg)
Speed: 55 mph (89 km/h)
Accommodation: Crew of 1
First flight: 28 March 1910
The 1910 *Hydravion* was Henri Fabre's second seaplane, his first design of 1909 (with three Anzani engines) having failed to fly. Before 28 March 1910 Fabre had never flown, even as a passenger, yet on his second attempt that day he flew the *Hydravion* for approx 1,640 ft (500 m). On the following day he made a flight of about 3.75 miles (6 km). He abandoned the aircraft after an accident in 1911, but for many years afterward was one of the leading European designers of floats for other water-borne aircraft.

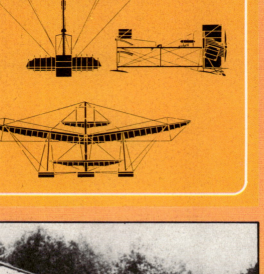

Above: Glenn Curtiss fitted floats to his famous *June Bug* and renamed it the *Loon*. It failed to fly when tested in 1908

Left: The Voisin brothers re-entered the marine aircraft scene in 1911, when they built several tail-first seaplanes fitted with Fabre floats. This example had four such floats. Another, flown by Maurice Colliex in August 1911, had three floats and four wheels and was the first successful amphibious aeroplane. It took off from Issy aerodrome and alighted on the Seine

Below left: By 1911 Glenn Curtiss was building small and highly efficient seaplanes, which quickly earned him a reputation as the greatest pioneer of flying from water. On 17 February that year, he paid a flying visit to the USS *Pennsylvania* in this seaplane, in San Diego Bay, and was hoisted on board the ship

Top centre: America's greatest pioneer after the Wrights, Glenn Curtiss first achieved fame by winning a trophy presented by the *Scientific American* magazine on 4 July 1908, with a flight of nearly a mile in his 40-hp *June Bug* biplane

Centre: The aircraft carrier was born on 14 November 1910 when Eugene Ely made a successful flight in a Curtiss biplane from a wooden platform built over the foredeck of the US cruiser *Birmingham* at Hampton Roads, Virginia. The aircraft dropped after leaving the platform and skimmed the water before gaining height and landing ashore

Top right: Eugene Ely completed his 'double' on 18 January 1911 by landing his Curtiss biplane on a specially-erected deck on the cruiser USS *Pennsylvania*. The aircraft was dragged to a stop by sandbags attached to the ends of ropes stretched across the deck so that they were picked up by hooks under the landing gear. Modern carrier arrester gear works on the same principle

Right: By the time of the 1912 Hydro-aeroplane Meeting at Monaco, seaplanes were becoming well established and entirely practical in Europe. Machines like the float-equipped Maurice Farman, which flew well with four passengers on board, could be compared with this diminutive Curtiss Triad, flown by Hugh Robinson

an interest in the aeroplane for scouting purposes, and the cruiser *Birmingham*, anchored at Hampton Roads, Virginia, was equipped with a sloping platform measuring 28ft x 83ft (8.53m x 25.30m). On 14 November 1910 a Curtiss pilot, Eugene Ely, flew a Curtiss pusher biplane of the *Golden Flyer* type from this platform and landed 2½ miles (4 km) away at Willoughby Spit. The aircraft carrier had been born. Two months later, on 18 January 1911, Ely put up an even more remarkable performance by taking off from the shore at San Francisco and landing on board the cruiser *Pennsylvania*. After a brief stay he flew ashore. For the 'landing on' an early form of arrester gear was used to bring the aircraft to a stop: cables were stretched across the deck, with a sandbag at each end, and these were engaged by a hook under the aircraft.

Within a few days of Ely's historic performance, on 26 January 1911, Glenn Curtiss succeeded in leaving the water in one of his biplanes, fitted with two floats set in tandem and a hydrofoil. During the following month a single 12-ft (3.66-m) float (pontoon in American terminology) was substituted, and thereafter the machine was altered extensively as Curtiss gained experience of water flying. On 17 February Curtiss continued Ely's demonstrations of ship-to-shore flying by taking off in his machine with the single large float, flying out to the *Pennsylvania*, and being hoisted on board.

Another remarkable development of 1911 was the launching of a Curtiss seaplane by a method which clearly presaged the modern catapult-launch from aircraft carriers. Invented by Lt T G Ellyson, this entailed supporting the aircraft on a thickly greased cable and balancing it by two other cables below the wings. At full throttle the aircraft rose swiftly into the air. Yet another prophetic event of 1911 was the 'air-sea rescue' by a Curtiss seaplane of a pilot who had forcibly ditched in Lake Michigan.

Curtiss seaplanes were acquired by several air forces and private pilots, and Curtiss lost no opportunity of extolling not only the value but the joy of water flying, describing it as 'something to arouse the jaded senses of the most blasé'. 'It fascinates, exhilarates, vivifies', he said. 'It is like a yacht with horizontal sails that support it on the breezes. To see it skim the water like a swooping gull and then rise into the air, circle and soar to great heights, and finally drop gracefully down upon the water again, furnishes a thrill and inspires a wonder that does not come with any other sport on earth.'

But the seaplane, whether in the form of the floatplane or the flying-boat—in the development of which Curtiss also played the principal part—was to find applications far beyond sport.

MISHAPS AT MONACO

Some early pioneers, like Langley in 1903, elected to make their attempts to fly over water because they considered it safer than trying to fly over land. These photos, taken at the 1913 Monaco Meeting, emphasise that water is by no means "soft" to land on! Fischer's Henry Farman (top) crumpled when a float strut broke, but was repaired in time to take part in the final event. Janoir wrecked his Deperdussin (centre) by misjudging his height when alighting. The tail of Prevost's Deperdussin (bottom) was snapped off by the landing impact. None of the occupants of these aircraft was hurt

Top left: One of the more interesting British marine aircraft of 1913 was the Radley-England Waterplane, designed and flown with great success by pioneer pilot E C Gordon England. Its three 50-hp Gnome rotary engines were geared to drive a single pusher propeller. Pilot and up to five passengers sat in the twin floats. This photograph shows early flotation tests on the River Arun

Left: Typical of the 1913 Curtiss flying-boats was this example, flown in France by Louis Paulhan. By enlarging the central float, as a boat-hull fuselage, Curtiss provided much more comfortable accommodation for pilot and passengers. Location of the 80-hp Curtiss engine under the top wing placed it near the centre of gravity and helped keep the propeller clear of spray during take-off

Below left: The Seabird floatplane was built during 1912 by the Lakes Flying Company, for use at their flying school at Lake Windermere. Powered by a 50-hp Gnome, it was originally a single-float two-seater. Later, it was modified to have two floats, as shown

The building of this splendid flying replica of a World War I Vickers 'Gunbus' was begun in 1965, and it flew for the first time just over a year later. Much of the construction work was carried out by members of the British Aircraft Corporation's Apprentice Training School at Weybridge, Surrey

The beautifully restored Sopwith Pup belonging to the Shuttleworth Collection at Old Warden Aerodrome in Bedfordshire, which has delighted thousands of spectators at flying displays at home and abroad. The Pup's design was classically simple, and its flying qualities have been called 'as near perfect as possible'

The Daring Ones

Left: Between watching stunts performed by the earliest aerobatic pilots, and exciting air races, visitors to Hendon aerodrome could make their first flights with famous men. Business was so good that Claude Grahame-White (at the controls) built the five-seat Aerobus—the 1913 counterpart of a 'jumbo jet'. His chief pilot, Louis Noel, used it to set up a world load-carrying record, by flying with nine passengers for nearly 20 minutes

Centre left: Adolphe Pégoud, whose aerobatic displays made him the idol of Paris and London, also demonstrated a device to dispense with the need for smooth, clear landing areas. It involved flying his Blériot monoplane under a cable stretched between two posts and then climbing slightly to engage a quick-release gear with a longitudinal cable under which the aircraft came to a stop. He also took off from the cable many times

Bottom left: A cap, turned back to front, was the traditional headgear of sporting pilots like Grahame-White. His passenger, Mrs Astley, seems more worried about her maxi-skirt than what would seem to be a totally inappropriate hat for flight in such an exposed position

Below: A visit to Hendon before the first world war was both a thrill and a social event. The well-to-do arrived by car and had tea on the lawn while watching the original magnificent men in their flying machines

Before the aeroplane provided a means of transporting people—and of killing them—it was used mainly to give them pleasure and thrills. A great flying meeting in the years before the first World War afforded not only spectacle, education and (for the venturesome few) aerial initiation, but gave employment to professional 'exhibition' pilots of several countries. These aerial showmen were the heroes of their time, and nowhere were their evolutions presented to better effect and received with warmer appreciation than at the London Aerodrome, Hendon. Steep banks, glides and dives were what the crowd loved, and flying in a wind of any strength filled them with astonishment. Also there was, of course, always the risk of an accident.

In June 1911 an observer of a Hendon demonstration organised by the Parliamentary Committee of Aerial Defence wrote: 'What was most striking was the magnificent trick-flying of Grahame-White on his old Farman. I must confess to feeling nervous myself when he wheeled his machine round, banking over at an angle of forty-five degrees at about 50 ft (15 m) over the heads of the majority of the two Parliamentary Front Benches, for I could imagine the wholesale smash there would be if the universal joint of his control lever broke—and such things have happened.'

Then, in 1913, the technical editor of *Flight* observed: 'Several accidents have resulted from the deliberate performance of tricks in the air, such as were at one time notorious in America, where several pilots have been killed in front of the spectators. Catering to the sensations of the crowd, these men would display the most amazing nerve in making steep dives followed by banked turns in which the wings would approach to a vertical position. On one occasion a machine actually turned turtle through over-banking, and the pilot was killed.'

What this writer evidently did not appreciate was that the most spectacular 'tricks in the air' were yet to come.

Early in 1913 a young man named Adolphe Pégoud joined the Blériot company, and quickly made his mark by parachuting from an old aircraft that had been condemned. He was thus the first pilot, though not the first man, to leave an aeroplane in flight, and his jump was a portent of the frequent 'baling out' by pilots in the great air battles of the second World War. But with Pégoud's name is associated another event, and one that can be linked directly with the dog-fights of the first World War, for on 2 September 1913 he flew upside down for the first time. This did not satisfy him, and on 21 September, in a specially strengthened Blériot monoplane, he succeeded in 'looping the loop', or flying his aircraft round in a vertical circle so that it was inverted at the top.

Pégoud also perfected other spectacular manoeuvres and was quickly in demand as an exhibition pilot, visiting Hendon and Brooklands in England and travelling also to Belgium, Italy, Romania, Russia and Holland. He was about to leave for the USA when war came and within a year he was killed as a pilot in the service of his country.

For many years it was generally believed that Pégoud was the first man to perform a loop, but historians now accept that this is not so and that the credit rightfully belongs to a Russian pilot named Peter Nikolaevich Nesterov. As a lieutenant in the Imperial Russian Air Service Nesterov looped a Nieuport Type IV monoplane on 20 August 1913. His superiors did not react enthusiastically, and for ten days he was under arrest, charged with endangering government property. Quickly, however, his feat received the recognition it deserved: he was promoted to staff captain and was awarded a medal by the Russian Royal Aero Club.

Sad to relate, this gallant Russian, like France's hero Pégoud, did not survive for long. On 26 August 1914, three Austrian aeroplanes, led by Lt Baron von Rosenthal, attacked the aerodrome near Sholkiv in Galicia, where Nesterov was stationed. The hangars were set on fire and Nesterov took off in an unarmed Morane Type M monoplane. With this he deliberately rammed the Baron's machine, and both men were killed.

It is pleasing to record that Nesterov's name now lives in history, not only as that of the first man to loop an aeroplane but as that of the town, renamed, that he gave his life to defend.

The Rotary Engine Revolution

During and after World War 2 aviation experienced a power plant revolution in which the gas turbine, in the forms of the jet and turboprop, began to replace the piston-engine which had previously been fitted to practically every powered aircraft. But few people can today remember an earlier revolution which, at the time, seemed every bit as important and exciting. This was the rotary engine revolution of 1908.

It was mainly the lack of a suitable engine that held back a successful powered flight until 1903. Admittedly Sir Hiram Maxim did build a most impressive giant biplane nine years earlier which, had it been freed from a hold-down rail, would certainly have flown on the power of two amazing steam engines; but practical aircraft had to wait for the availability of internal combustion engines in the first years of the 20th century. Even then these were not so much specialised aero-engines as developed and modified versions of motor-car engines.

To be an aviator in the first days of flying one had to be quite a character. One needed design skill as an engineer, because one had to be chief designer, chief stressman, weight-control engineer, chief aerodynamicist and chief production engineer all at once. One also needed skill as a pilot, in the role of chief test pilot; and a great deal of money, to pay for the whole project. When it came to an engine, few of the earliest pioneers of flying had the time, money and ability to design and build a new engine as well. The Wright brothers did build an almost new engine, but even this was based on a unit taken from a Pope-Toledo car; in any case their mechanic, Charles Taylor, was exceptionally skilled and they were all used to working far into the night. Most aviators just bought whatever was available.

Until 1908 the engines available were big and heavy. They were constructed of cast iron, steel forgings, blocks of brass and sheets of copper and weighed about 10 lb (4.5 kg) for each horsepower developed. They imposed a severe burden on the flimsy aircraft in which they were mounted, and the loads imparted to the slender airframe were increased considerably by the weight and thrust of the heavy wooden propeller, by the torque in the drive shaft and by irregular and intermittent firing of the big cylinders which sometimes shook the engine off its mountings or caused the aircraft itself to break up. However, there were two French brothers, Laurent and Gustav Seguin, who were certain that they could design a completely new engine, just for aircraft, that would be far better all round. In 1907 they decided to go ahead with the idea and build such an engine; they called it the Gnome, and

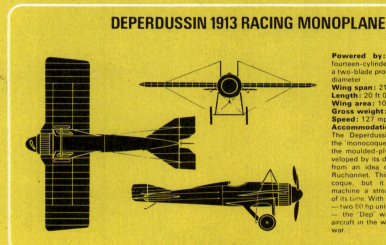

Opposite page: Rotary-engined Morane-Saulnier monoplanes were among the outstanding aeroplanes of the 1911-14 era, winning many races, setting an altitude record of 18,405 ft (5,610 m) and making the first crossing of the Mediterranean by air. This one had an 80 hp Le Rhône engine

Above: Early pioneers of streamlining were the designers of the French Deperdussin company. Their graceful monocoque racer of 1913 had a 160 hp Gnome rotary and was the first aeroplane to fly 200 km (124 miles) in an hour. It set a dozen world speed records

Left: Rotary engines currently displayed in the Shuttleworth Collection at Old Warden Aerodrome, Bedfordshire, England, include the 80 hp Le Rhône *(top left)* and the 50 hp Gnome installed in a 1912 Blackburn monoplane *(bottom left)*

before long every flying enthusiast was talking about it.

One of the main reasons for the great bulk and weight of previous aircraft engines was the need to provide a continuously-flowing water cooling system, complete with a big radiator and connecting pipes which tended to come apart or break. The Seguins decided to dispense with all of this and merely machine on to the cylinders cooling fins to dissipate the heat into the surrounding air. But they realised that something had to be done to keep the air flowing at high speed over the cylinders, even when the aircraft was at rest on the ground. Their answer was to reverse the usual arrangement, fixing the crankshaft to the aircraft and the engine to the propeller so that when the engine started up it spun round with the propeller, while the crankshaft stayed still. The Seguins considered that such an engine would never overheat, even if it had no water cooling.

To balance out the mass of the engine round the crankshaft the Seguins adopted a radial layout, in which the cylinders are arranged like the spokes of a wheel. An odd number of cylinders was chosen, seven at first, to even out the sequence of 'firing strokes'. This made the Gnome very smooth-running, and the whole engine behaved like a big flywheel to give a beautifully even drive to the propeller with minimum airframe vibration. A simple carburettor was designed, to produce a rich mixture which was fed to the central crankcase. From there it escaped through valves in the tops of the pistons into the combustion space in the cylinder. The piston valve shut to compress the mixture and the burnt gas then escaped through a single exhaust valve in the cylinder head.

The first Gnome of 1908 gave 70-80 horsepower, ran as sweetly as the proverbial sewing machine and weighed only 3 lb/hp (1.4 kg/hp). While other engine builders watched anxiously, the Gnome company went into production at rates that far outstripped them, and the Gnome was the most important engine in the first years of World War 1. New versions of it appeared. The Gnome Monosoupape (single-valve) overcame a fire risk (caused by sticking of the valves in the pistons) by omitting piston valves and using ordinary pistons in a special cylinder provided with fine holes near the bottom. Very rich mixture escaped from the crankcase through these holes until they were closed by the rising piston. Diluted by fresh air admitted through the exhaust valves, this mixture worked quite well and made for a safer engine; but industry found it difficult to make the cylinders to the accuracy needed of four-tenths of one-thousandth of an inch!

Another variation was the Le Rhône, using the more modern technique of inlet and exhaust valves in the cylinder head. Many thousands of these Gnome and Le Rhône rotaries, including versions made by Bentley, Clerget, BMW and other firms, served throughout World War 1 and for many years after. The main drawback to the rotary was its high fuel and oil consumption, plus the gyroscopic effect of the spinning engine, which caused tricky handling characteristics — so that the famous Sopwith Camel, for example, could turn to the left only sluggishly but flick to the right like lightning. Eventually, improved air-cooled cylinders made the stationary radial engine practical and the rotary obsolete. Today rotaries are seen and heard only in very rare screen epics or veteran aircraft gatherings. But in their time they had the world of aviation at their feet. The famous names of Gnome and Le Rhône later joined to form the Gnome-

Rhône company, which began by making Bristol Jupiter radial engines under licence and finally, after World War 2, was absorbed into the great French national engine company SNECMA. Within SNECMA today there are still a very few old hands who will look up from their work on the propulsion system of the Concorde to tell you about the 'rotary engine revolution' of over 60 years ago.

Above: Another famous type to be seen in the Shuttleworth Collection is the Sopwith Pup fighter of World War I, with an 80 hp Le Rhône engine. This aircraft is still able to display the aerobatic prowess which earned it countless combat victories

Above right: This 1911 Deperdussin monoplane, with 100 hp two-row Gnome, was fitted with extended wing roots

Right: Perhaps the most significant trainer of all time, the Avro 504 was fitted with a variety of engines during its two decades of service with the RAF. This example still flies regularly at Old Warden, with a 110 hp Le Rhône rotary engine

Far right: Most successful fighter of the 1914-18 War was the Sopwith Camel, which destroyed 1,294 enemy aircraft in air combat. Still flying in the USA is this 2F.1 naval version, built with both 130 hp Clerget and 150 hp Bentley BR1 rotary engines

Bottom: Another surviving Camel is this standard F.1 of the Royal Air Force Museum, Hendon. It has a 130 hp Clerget rotary engine

THE AIR MAIL BEGINS

When we look at some of the modern statistics of civil aviation—for example in 1969 the member airlines of the International Air Transport Association logged 2,413,000,000 tonne-kilometres of air mail carriage—it seems almost impossible to realise that there was ever a time when air mail did not exist. Yet, in fact, it is only just sixty years since the first letters were moved —officially—by air. (Some letters were, of course, carried in the pockets of individual pilots as a stunt before 1911 but, in England anyway, this would have constituted some sort of infringement of the rights of HM Post Office.)

The start of the carriage of mail by air was, remarkably enough, coincident with the demonstration of the first aircraft ever to be flown in India, indeed in Asia. Commander Sir Walter Windham, RN, had turned his interests to motor cars and aeroplanes and had a factory in the un-romantic purlieus of Clapham Junction, known best for its large railroad complex, then and now. He was invited by the Indian Government to bring some aeroplanes out to an exhibition to be held at Allahabad. He took no fewer than eight aircraft, six of them being similar to the then-popular Blériot monoplanes, with 35 hp air-cooled 3-cylinder Humber engines. The other two were Sommer-type biplanes fitted with 50 hp Gnome rotary engines.

The purpose of these aircraft was primar-ily to educate the Indian population about the extent to which aviation had developed by 1911. However, the event proved to have much more than academic value. Windham was approached by the clergyman in charge of Holy Trinity Church, Allahabad, to see if he could help to raise funds for a hostel planned by the church. It occurred to

Windham that if he could fly some mail from Allahabad across the river Ganges to Aligah, and put a special postmark on the letters before they went on by more prosaic means to their addresses, this might produce some very useful cash return.

The Post Master General of the United Provinces and the Director-General of the PO in India approved the idea and the special postmark was authorised. Less official was the appointment of the clergy-man as postmaster at the airfield (a parade ground in Allahabad) but bureaucracy turned a blind eye to Windham's usurping of the Royal Prerogative! A surcharge of 6 annas (about 2½ np sterling) was made and letters poured in from all over India.

On 20 February 1911, the first consign-ment was flown out by Mons Pequet, one of Windham's pilots. The occasion coincided with a religious festival and it was estimated that no fewer than one million Indians, who had come to the Ganges to wash away their sins, were observers of the event in addition to a rather more formal group consisting of the Governor, his wife, and many members of the Government Staff.

A number of flights were made by Pequet and the other pilot, Keith Davies. Enough money was made to build a hostel for Indian students, and it is of interest that by 1939 some of the covers flown during this experiment were selling for £25. Their value

Above: These stamps depict aircraft that helped to create world air mail services. The *Graf Zeppelin*, shown between Friedrichshafen and the Chicago Federal Building in 1933. More than a decade earlier, the US Air Mail Service had been established across the continent; when this was commemorated in 1968, the stamp showed a Curtiss 'Jenny' instead of one of the D.H.4s used for most of the flights. Italy's transatlantic formation flight of 1931, by Savoia-Marchetti flying-boats

Above: Hamel receives officially the first bag of letters for conveyance from Hendon to Windsor. In the centre is Captain Walter Windham, who organised both this service and the world's first air mail operation in India earlier in 1911

Opposite page, left: A 'late fee' letter is handed to a postman, on board a Valkyrie tail-first monoplane, during a rehearsal at Hendon for the 1911 Coronation mail service that was to start a few days later

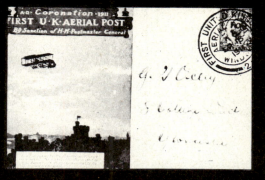

today must be many times that amount.

No sooner had Windham returned to England than he turned his attention to organising an air mail in the United Kingdom. The occasion he chose was the Coronation of King George V and he sought the co-operation of the General Post Office. This was not so simple as it had been in India; but the Post Master General, Sir Herbert Samuel, proved sympathetic and cut through some of the red tape which had hampered early negotiations.

The plan went through a variety of modifications; but it was finally agreed that no surcharge would be made—that would have needed an Act of Parliament—and that the Post Office would frank all envelopes and post cards with an official stamp reading '1st UK Aerial Post'. The cost of the operation would be met by the sale of specially printed envelopes and cards, which would be sent via special post boxes to Hendon Aerodrome, whence they would be flown to Windsor Great Park and then dispatched through normal Post Office channels to their destinations. All profits were to be given to the King Edward VII Hospital at Windsor.

King George, who had been a recipient of one of the first letters sent by air in India, gave his approval to the use of Windsor Great Park and the Grahame-White Company provided the aircraft and pilots, the team consisting of that great flyer, Gustav Hamel, Clement Greswell, Charles Hubert, a Frenchman, and E Driver, a South African.

In the meantime, however, another 'first' took place. For some reason, not very clear to most of us, air mail and air freight are treated as separate items. At the beginning of July 1911, one of the better-known pilots, Horatio Barber, who normally operated from the Valkyrie Flying School at Hendon, decided to attempt a cross-country flight from Shoreham (near Brighton) to Hendon, carrying a lady passenger. Whilst he was doing demonstration flights at Shoreham, he was approached by the General Electric Company to carry a carton of Osram lamps to Hove, a few miles away. This he did with considerable ease.

It was the first time freight had been carried by air, and it is worth adding that it was a strictly commercial operation. Mr Barber was paid £100 for his services. The aftermath of that flight was that he spent the money on the purchase of the Britannia Trophy which is awarded for the most meritorious performance by a British pilot every year. In its many decades of existence, the Trophy has been held by many very famous men and women.

The Coronation Air Mail preparations went ahead and the first flight, to be made by Gustav Hamel, was scheduled to leave Hendon for Windsor on 9 September 1911. The aircraft was a Blériot belonging to Greswell. A tremendous rush to deliver letters and cards took place at Hendon the previous evening, and during the Saturday when the inauguration was to take place a crowd of many thousands thronged the aerodrome and the surrounding area.

The weather was shocking, with winds gusting to more than 40 mph (64 km/h). In normal circumstances no pilot would have considered making a cross-country flight, but the occasion being one of great moment, Hamel took off, carrying one bag of mail, weighing 23 lb (approx 10 kg). He left the ground at 16.58 hrs and arrived at Windsor 10 minutes later, having averaged 105 mph (170 km/h). Conditions prevented landing at the prescribed spot but he came down fairly close, in the vicinity of the Royal Mausoleum at Frogmore, thus completing the first-ever delivery of air mail in Britain—indeed, in Europe.

Bad as the weather was, it did at least have the advantage that the wind added to Hamel's speed. Had it been in the opposite direction it is doubtful if even he could have completed the flight.

There was no flight on the Sunday, religious views being somewhat more effective than they became later; but on the Monday three flights were completed by Driver, Hamel and Greswell. There should have been four, but Hubert was unlucky enough to crash while making a circuit at Hendon preparatory to setting course for Windsor. The aircraft was written off and Hubert broke both legs, a most unhappy occurrence to mar one of the major events of early aviation history.

On the Tuesday four flights were made, Driver making two trips, and by the end of the third day a total of 20 bags of mail had been carried, weighing nearly a quarter of a ton (200 kg approx). In all the flying went on for ten days, involving 34 trips by the three remaining pilots.

A sum of £937 was raised for the hospital and was used to endow the 'Coronation Aerial Post Bed', an endowment which still operates though, regrettably, the buying power of the interest on the money today is very small indeed.

So began the air mail which we now take absolutely for granted.

The First Airlines

The early history of the Zeppelin airships—three out of the first four came to grief—hardly seemed to be a happy augury for the start of a commercial, passenger-carrying airline; but such was the unquenchable optimism of the now ageing Count Ferdinand von Zeppelin that by 1909 he was heavily involved in just such a project.

Supported by a member of the Collsman family (aluminium tycoons of the era) and by Hugo Eckener—later to become the overall head of the Zeppelin organisation and the world's greatest airship captain—the Count formed a company with the rather lengthy name of Deutsche Luftschiffahrts-Aktiengesellschaft, normally shortened to Delag. This company was intended to order airships, test their capabilities and put them into regular service. No small undertaking, it would seem; but some idea of the comparative ease with which such enterprises were launched 60 years ago is given by the fact that a capital equivalent to about £150,000 was found to be ample.

Various cities vied with each other to attract the airline. The local authorities of Frankfurt, Cologne, Dusseldorf, Baden-Baden, Munich, Leipzig, Dresden and Hamburg were among the first to provide funds for the building of hangars.

The first ship to be delivered to the line was the LZ.7, named, rather obviously, *Deutschland*. She completed her trials and was flown to Dusseldorf in June 1910 and, in the next two weeks, made six flights between Dusseldorf, Frankfurt and Baden-Baden, all carrying passengers. Then the Count's consistently bad luck came to the fore again when *Deutschland*, commanded by an ex-Army officer, crashed and was written off. Fortunately there were no casualties and a replacement, the LZ.6, as well as a second ship, named LZ.8 *Deutschland II*, began flying from Baden in March 1911.

The LZ.7's commander had been dismissed, as he was held responsible for the crash, and Collsman—who seems to have been almost as persuasive as the Count himself—prevailed upon Eckener to take his tests and

Opposite page, top: The Zeppelin *Viktoria Luise* of Delag, one of the airships used on the world's first passenger airline services, flying over Kiel harbour

Left: Two more Delag passenger Zeppelins, the LZ.6 and LZ.7 *Deutschland,* inside their shed at Friedrichshafen. The LZ.7 was the first airship used on regular services. After it was wrecked in a storm on 28 June 1910, with no casualties, it was replaced by the LZ.6

This page, top: The passenger cabin of the LZ.7 *Deutschland,* which carried 436 passengers in 24 flights with Delag in 1910. Powered by three 120 hp Daimler engines, it had a cruising speed of 37 mph (60 km/h)

Above: The LZ.10 *Schwaben* in a pastoral setting. This Zeppelin carried 3,622 passengers on 230 flights in 1911-12. It was powered by three 145 hp Maybach engines and cruised at 47 mph (75 km/h). Although burned out at Dusseldorf in June 1912, it offered the same high passenger safety standards as all Zeppelins. No passenger was ever killed in a commercial airship accident until 13 died in the *Hindenburg* in 1937. Non-rigid airships have not killed a single passenger in more than 60 years of flying, to the present day

command the ship personally. This was the turning point in Zeppelin history. The Count was a genius but not always practical; Collsman was a slick, though honest, businessman; but Eckener combined publicity knowhow and great business capacity with the ability to absorb technical facts and the much more important ability to apply them in practical ways. Eckener's lifetime was perhaps too recent yet to permit a true appreciation of his greatness; but future history will accord him the credit that he deserves.

Even Eckener was not free from trouble. Within a few months, a ship of which he was in command was damaged beyond repair while being 'walked out' of its hangar at Dusseldorf but, once again, no one was injured. In the event, this accident may have been fortunate, because it was the direct cause of the setting up of an embryo weather-forecasting service, an absolute necessity for all aviation but even more important for the bulky and slow-flying airships of 1911.

The next ship to enter service, the LZ.10 *Schwaben*, could reach 47 mph (75 km/h) and was thus able to operate in appreciably worse weather than her predecessors. In 1912, a sister ship, LZ.11 *Viktoria Luise*, put in an appearance. The two Zeppelins settled down to maintain regular operations until one day *Schwaben*, commanded by Captain Dorr, beat a heavy storm into Dusseldorf and only just managed to unload her passengers before being hit by a severe squall. She was damaged and next caught fire. The

uncanny freedom from personal injury continued however and, as in the theatre, 'the show went on'.

Hamburg was added next to the network and hangars were built at what later became Fuhlsbuttel Airport. Then came Potsdam, home of the German Emperor, Kaiser Wilhelm II. His Imperial Majesty had already shown considerable interest in Zeppelins when the Count took LZ.3 over Berlin in August 1909—even giving the Count a lift in his own car. But the Emperor never went so far as to risk his august person in one of the airships. His son and heir, Crown Prince Wilhelm—'Little Willie' to the irreverent British troops of the 1914-1918 War—showed a more adventurous spirit and seems to have set the seal of his approval on the new mode of transport.

Two more airships were added to the fleet by 1913. The *Hansa* (LZ.13) was first, followed by *Sachsen* (LZ.17). With *Viktoria Luise*, they kept up an extremely efficient service linking many of Germany's most important cities. *Sachsen* even went as far as Vienna, with Count Zeppelin and Hugo Eckener on board.

During the four years from 1910 until the start of war in 1914, Delag flew a total of 170,000 miles (273,600 km) and carried 35,000 passengers, entirely without injury—an almost incredible record in those early days, particularly when it is recalled how accident-prone the Zeppelins seemed to be.

Willingness to take an interest in anything new seems to be a rare attribute of government servants in any country, and those in

Germany were no exception to the rule. The Count had made effort after effort to persuade the armed forces to adopt the Zeppelin but, until 1913, his success had been minimal. Then, after Delag had operated so well for three years, the German General Staff invited Eckener to bring an airship to Gotha and take part in the military manoeuvres. *Hansa* was used and carried out successful 'bombing' operations with sandbags. A certain Colonel Ludendorff, later to become one of the country's great war leaders, said he was 'greatly impressed'.

This incident had a considerable bearing on the operations of the next twelve months. The German government, having at last been forced to remove its head from the sand, suddenly showed great enthusiasm for airships. Most flights included among their passengers (or, more correctly, supernumerary crew) an officer and several non-commissioned officers as airship trainees. As Eckener wrote in his book *My Zeppelins*, Delag became a sort of university of airship flight, and the majority of the Zeppelin crews who bombed Britain during the first World War received their early training while flying officially as passengers on a regular, scheduled air transport service. Thus was set a pattern which was followed again between the wars, when the German airline, Luft Hansa, was used as a training organisation for bomber pilots during the time when the Treaty of Versailles debarred Germany from possessing an air force. The general manager of Luft Hansa admitted this during a meeting with the writer in Ber-

Left: The LZ.13 *Hansa* which joined the Delag fleet in 1912. Seldom remembered today is that Delag resumed operations after World War I with the more advanced LZ.120 *Bodensee* and LZ.121. The former made 103 flights in 98 days in 1919, covering 32,300 miles (52,000 km) in 533 flying hours and carrying 2,380 passengers

Opposite page:
Left, top to bottom:
The control car of the *Hansa*

The German airship *Suchard*, built for an attempted crossing of the Atlantic from Tenerife to the USA in 1912. Its car consisted of a boat, which was intended to be detached and sailed to safety had the aircraft alighted in mid-ocean. Fortunately, perhaps, neither the airship nor the boat was ever put to the test

This model, in the Qantas collection, is of one of the two-seat Benoist flying-boats used on the first passenger-carrying aeroplane services between St Petersburg and Tampa, Florida

Right, upper photograph: Tony Jannus taxies out, before hundreds of spectators, on the first commercial service of the St Petersburg-Tampa Airboat Line on New Year's Day, 1914

Right, lower photograph: In-flight view of the little Benoist flying-boat en route to Tampa, with American flags and pennants streaming from its wing struts

lin in 1932, saying: 'We can afford to run uneconomic services to train our air force for the next war. How else could we train them?'

Looking back, there can be little doubt that Count Zeppelin was far more interested in getting his airships accepted for military duties than in flying passengers. This is understandable, for he had spent several decades reaching high rank in the Army and, like most German aristocrats of the period, his whole background was immersed in military tradition. Be that as it may, Count Zeppelin was also the father of civilian air transport.

It is a surprising thing that the United States of America, home of heavier-than-air flight, was so backward in developing it for commercial purposes. The Zeppelin services had been running for nearly four years when, on 1 January 1914, Tony Jannus, a well-known cross-country flyer, took off from Tampa, Florida, on a 22-mile overwater flight to St Petersburg, also in Florida, carrying one paying passenger in a Benoist flying-boat. Hardly different from a charter flight, one is tempted to say; but it was the start of a scheduled service, the first in the New World and forerunner of the close-mesh network of air routes that covers America today.

The line lasted only a few weeks and was, as might be expected, an economic failure. Nevertheless, it was the first-ever scheduled heavier-than-air passenger operation and, as such, is assured of its place in the history of aviation.

ZEPPELIN L.Z.8 DEUTSCHLAND II

Powered by: Three 115 hp Daimler-Mercedes four-cylinder water-cooled engines, one in each gondola and each driving a pair of outrigged three-blade metal propellers of 12 ft 0 in (3.66 m) diameter
Length: 485 ft 6¾ in (148.0 m)
Max diameter: 45 ft 11 in (14.0 m)
Volume: 529,720 cu ft (15,000 m³)
Gross weight: 36,375 lb (16,500 kg)
Speed: 35 mph (56 km/h)
First flight: 1911

The *Deutschland II* was one of the fleet of Zeppelin rigid airships with which, in 1910, the world's first-ever regular passenger services by air were operated. They had a rigid aluminium framework, divided into compartments each containing a drum-shaped gas 'balloon' and covered overall with a rubberised cotton fabric. After the outbreak of the first World War they were acquired and modified for military service.

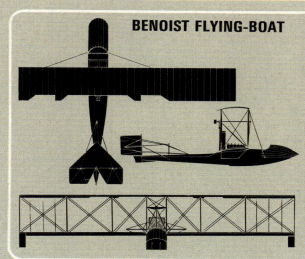

BENOIST FLYING-BOAT

Powered by: One 75 hp Roberts or 70 hp Sturtevant six-cylinder in-line engine, driving a two-blade pusher propeller of approx 7 ft 6 in (2.29 m) diameter
Wing span: 45 ft 0 in (13.72 m)
Length: 26 ft 0 in (7.92 m)
Wing area: approx 400 sq ft (37.16 m²)
Gross weight: approx 1,500 lb (680 kg)
Speed: approx 60-65 mph (97-105 km/h)
Accommodation: Crew of 1 and 1 passenger
First flight: 1913

To this small single-engined flying-boat goes the distinction of inaugurating, on 1 January 1914, the world's first scheduled passenger-carrying service by aeroplane. It seated a pilot and one passenger, who could travel the 22 miles (35.4 km) between Tampa and St Petersburg, Florida, for a fare of five dollars—more if the passenger weighed over 200 lb (90.7 kg). Two trips per day were made, but the operation was not an economic success and ended after only a few months.

Top left: When first flown the Sikorsky *Le Grand* had its four 100 hp Argus engines mounted in tandem pairs. Later, the rear engines were moved outboard to drive tractor propellers and so improve their efficiency

Top right: Igor Sikorsky (on right) with his crew in the nose of *Le Grand.* Taken after the engines had been re-arranged, this photograph shows also the searchlight mounted on the front of the fuselage

Above: Close-up of the rear, pusher, engine of the Short Triple Twin, first of the series of twin-engined aircraft built by Short Brothers in 1911-12. The front 50 hp Gnome drove two wing-mounted propellers through chains—a configuration reminiscent of the transmission on the original Wright biplanes

Left: The great Italian designer, Gianni Caproni, was a pioneer of big multi-engined aeroplanes. His first powered machine, the Ca 1 of 1910, had only a single 25 hp Miller engine; but its two wing-mounted propellers foreshadowed later three-engined designs that were to perform outstanding service as bombers in World War I

The World's First Multi-Engined Aircraft

There are two main reasons for fitting more than one engine to an aeroplane: to obtain greater power, and to increase the margin of safety in the event of engine failure. The earliest installations of twin engines, by Sir Hiram Maxim and Clément Ader, were made for the former of these reasons, but in 1911 the Short brothers in England were granted patents covering the installation of multiple engines which enabled them to claim in their advertisements: 'Shorts' twin engine system enables flights to be undertaken without fear of sudden descent due to engine stoppages'.

This represented a great advance in air safety, and the first aircraft built according to the Short patents was a remarkable one. The name 'Triple Twin' by which it eventually became known signified that it had three propellers and two engines. The first flight was made by Frank McClean, for whom the machine had been built, on 18 September 1911. It was followed by another flight, this time carrying the famous naval airman Commander C R Samson as a passenger, in the course of which each engine was throttled back in turn.

The two engines of the Triple Twin were of the French Gnome rotary type, in which the entire engine revolved. They were mounted in tandem, one at the front of the nacelle, or body, the other at the rear. Between the engines the two occupants sat side-by-side. The front engine drove two tractor, or pulling, propellers, attached to the bracing struts between the wings, while the rear engine directly drove a pusher propeller.

The tractor propellers were driven from their engine by chains.

Another notable feature of the Triple Twin was that, in addition to having two engines, it had two complete sets of flying controls, so that either of the occupants could fly it without changing seats. The control columns were rocked backward and forward for climbing or descending, and at the top of each column was a wheel which was turned to cause the machine to bank to right or left. The directional rudders were controlled from foot bars.

The Short brothers also built a similar aeroplane known as the Tandem Twin. On this the front engine was coupled directly to a single tractor propeller.

The next notable departure in the development of multi-engined aircraft stands to the credit of the great Russian designer/constructor/pilot Igor Sikorsky. Toward the end of 1911, at about the time when the Triple Twin was being tested, Sikorsky began to form his ideas of building a truly giant aircraft, and he gained financial support for the project in September 1912. The technical difficulties were many and great. The sheer size of the aircraft—its wing span was about 92 ft (28 m)—led Sikorsky to install no fewer than four engines, which he arranged in two tandem pairs, mounted on the lower wings. So impressive was this great aeroplane that although it was officially named *Russian Knight* it was generally called *Le Grand* ('The Great One'). Not the least remarkable feature was the enclosed cockpit, forward of the passengers' cabin. This

enclosing of the pilot, Sikorsky was warned, would render the aircraft impossible to fly, for the pilot would be unable to recognise fully or quickly enough any departure from normal flying attitude! In the ordinary aircraft of the period the pilot was more or less exposed to the airstream and so could quickly appreciate any change in its direction and force. This supposed difficulty was, of course, an imaginary one, but one problem that was very real concerned the form of landing gear required for such a large and heavy aeroplane. As no suitably large aircraft wheels were then in existence the undaunted designer decided to use no fewer

Above: This Coanda biplane of 1911 had two Gnome engines, mounted on each side of the nose and driving a single four-blade propeller through bevel gearing

Below: Most of the tri-motor Caproni bombers were biplanes, with two wing-mounted engines driving tractor propellers and a third, pusher, engine at the rear of the fuselage nacelle. In addition, several dozen huge triplanes, with a span of 98 ft 1¼ in (29.9 m), flew with the Italian and British services. Typical was the Ca 41 of 1917-18, recalled by this model in the Musée de l'Air, Paris

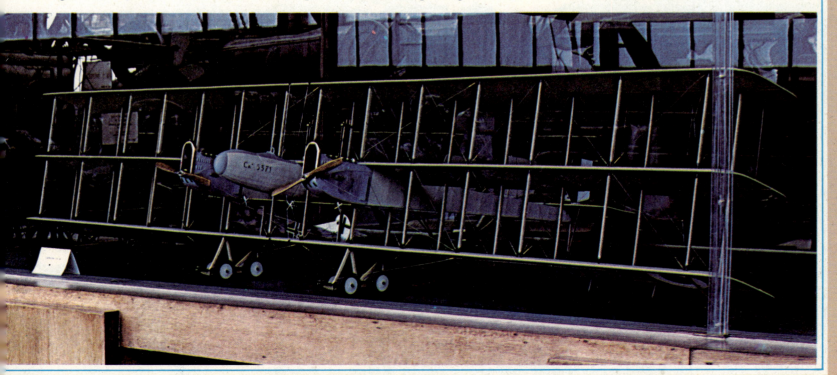

SHORT TRIPLE TWIN

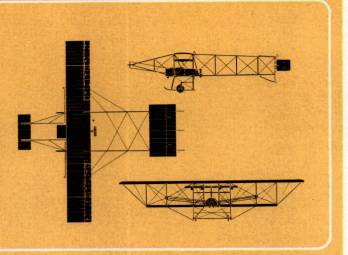

Powered by: Two 50 hp Gnome seven-cylinder rotary engines, driving one pusher and two tractor two-blade propellers, each of 8 ft 6 in (2.59 m) diameter
Wing span: 34 ft 0 in (10.36 m)
Length: 45 ft 0 in (13.72 m)
Wing area: 435 sq ft (40.41 m²)
Gross weight: 2,100 lb (952 kg)
Max speed: 55 mph (89 km/h)
Accommodation: Crew of 1 and 1 passenger
First flight: 18 September 1911

The Triple Twin, although preceded by such other multi-engined designs as the 1894 Maxim steam-powered aeroplane and Ader's *Avion III*, was the first practical aeroplane to be powered by more than one engine. It was built to the order of Francis McClean, and patents were granted to the Short brothers in 1911 regarding the installation of multiple engines in aircraft. The Tandem Twin had a similar power installation, but with each engine coupled directly to a single propeller, one at the front and one at the rear.

VICKERS F.B.5

Powered by: One 100 hp Gnome Monosoupape nine-cylinder rotary engine, driving a two-blade pusher propeller of approx 9 ft 6 in (2.90 m) diameter
Wing span: 36 ft 6 in (11.13 m)
Length: 27 ft 2 in (8.28 m)
Wing area: 382 sq ft (35.49 m²)
Gross weight: 2,050 lb (930 kg)
Max speed: 70 mph (113 km/h) at 5,000 ft (1,525 m)
Typical endurance: 4 hr
Accommodation: Crew of 2
Armament: One 0.303-in Lewis machine-gun in nose

First production version of what became known as the Vickers 'Gunbus' fighter, the F.B.5 was the outcome of development of the Vickers *Destroyer* biplane (E.F.B.1) first displayed at the Olympia Aero Show in February 1913. At that time no mechanism had been perfected to allow a machine-gun to fire forward past a front-mounted propeller without hitting it, and so the engine was installed at the rear, coupled to a pusher propeller.

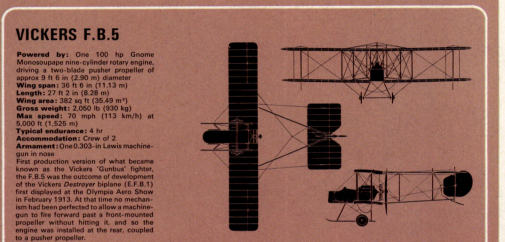

Left: Second Short multi-engined aircraft was the Tandem Twin, a conversion of Cecil Grace's single-engined S.27. Its two Gnome engines were mounted fore and aft of the cockpit, with direct drive to the propellers; hence it was often known as the *Gnome Sandwich*. Access was through a hole in the floor. Coupled with the slipstream, this made the cockpit so draughty that the Tandem Twin also acquired the nickname of *The Vacuum Cleaner* and was credited with the ability to 'pull the hairs out of a fur coat'

Below left: A Sikorsky *Ilya Mourometz* four-engined bomber of the Czar's Squadron of Flying Ships. Evolved from *Le Grand*, such bombers performed fine service in 1915-17

Above, top to bottom:
The huge Caproni Ca 60 flying-boat was powered by eight 400 hp Liberty engines (four tractor, four pusher) and was intended to carry 100 passengers. Its three sets of triplane wings spanned 100 ft (30 m). Too advanced for its time, it made only two short flights in 1921

Typical of the Caproni tri-motor bombers of World War I vintage, this machine was one of three built under licence in the USA. The war ended before production could get under way

The rear gunners on Caproni Ca 33 bombers stood on an open platform aft of the top wing, even during high-altitude flights over the Alps in Winter, and must be counted among the real heroes of World War I

Right: Perhaps the most famous of all early multi-engined aircraft was the twin-engined Vickers Vimy. Developed as a World War I bomber, it was too late for combat use and first captured the imagination of the public when flown across the Atlantic by Alcock and Brown in June 1919. This is a recently-built replica, photographed at the 1969 Paris Air Show

than sixteen wheels of an available type, grouping them in four pairs on each side of the aircraft. They were mounted together with massive skids, like the runners of a sleigh.

Superstition played no part in the make-up of Sikorsky or his workers, for the first flight of *Le Grand*, the world's first four-engined aeroplane, took place on 13 May 1913. The military airfield made available for the flight had been too busy all day and at about nine o'clock in the evening Sikorsky began to make arrangements instead for the test to be held on the next day. But the field was now free, and a Russian 'white night', in which it is never entirely dark, would give ample light for another hour. So, tired though he was, Sikorsky decided to take *Le Grand* into the air.

Ahead of the cockpit where he sat at the controls was an open balcony, and here a mechanic stood, to give the order to release the aircraft to men holding it back by the wings. Inside the main cabin was a third man, whose job was to move forward or aft if the machine proved tail-heavy or nose-heavy. For two minutes the pilot tested the four 100 hp Argus water-cooled engines, then signalled to the man in the nose. Released, the great biplane moved slowly forward. The tail (which also rested on a skid) came up, the controls became active as speed increased, and as he eased the control wheel back Sikorsky became aware that the shock from the wheels running along the ground had ceased. A four-engined aero-plane was in the air for the first time.

'The plane performed nicely', as its pilot later recorded. Evidently sensing this, the man on the balcony waved to the huge crowd which had gathered below. Then, to test the effect that a failing engine might have, the pilot eased back one of the throttles. *Le Grand* remained controllable.

About a mile from the field the great aero-plane turned in for the landing, an event described by the pilot as 'reasonably smooth'. When the machine had rolled to a stop the mechanic descended to inspect the undercarriage before taxying in; but, though everything was evidently in order, no taxying was possible, for the crowds had invaded the airfield and were moving towards *Le Grand*—'like a tide', as Sikorsky described it later. The three airmen stepped on to the balcony to wave and offer their thanks.

The Russian designer was now assured that in all essentials his theories concerning large multi-engined aeroplanes were correct. The principal defect on the first flight had been the poor take-off and rate of climb. As already mentioned, the four engines were arranged in two tandem pairs. The two front engines drove tractor propellers and the rear pair pusher propellers, which meant that the rear propellers were operating inefficiently in the slipstreams of those at the front. The engines and propellers were originally so arranged because Sikorsky was anxious to keep them as near as possible to the centre-line of the aircraft so that, in the event of an engine failure, the effect on controllability of the aircraft would be less than if the engines were mounted separately further out on the wings. However, so good was the controllability with 'asymmetric power' that Sikorsky decided after all to rearrange the engines so that all four propellers could work at their maximum efficiency. Accordingly he transferred the rear engines to positions on the lower wing outboard of the front pair, so that all four were individually mounted and drove tractor propellers. Even with this arrangement the rudders were effective enough to control the machine, not merely with one engine stopped but with both units on one side of the aircraft out of action.

Well might Igor Sikorsky declare in later years that the most important factor in the pioneering period of aviation was the creation of large four-engined aircraft.

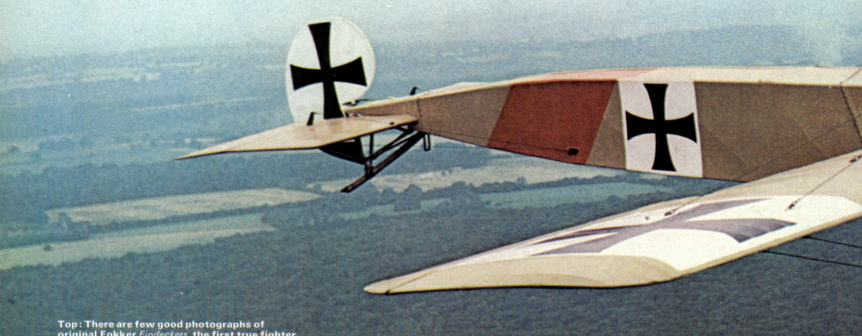

Top: There are few good photographs of original Fokker *Eindeckers*, the first true fighter aircraft. This beautiful E.III replica was built by Doug Bianchi for use in the film *Crooks and Coronets*

This page:
Centre: D.H.2 'pusher' fighters of No 32 Squadron, Royal Flying Corps, at a front-line airfield in France. The D.H.2 was one of the types which ended the so-called Fokker Scourge in 1916

Bottom: Typical of the aircraft with which the RFC entered World War I was this totally-unarmed Blériot monoplane, not very different from the machine in which Louis Blériot had made the first cross-Channel flight five years earlier. Pilots were ordered to ram any Zeppelin they sighted *en route* from England to France. In fact, the Blériots would probably have been unable to climb fast enough or high enough to make this possible

Opposite page:
Left, top to bottom: The Fokker D.VII, perhaps the best fighter of 1918. It was really a cantilever biplane; the interplane struts were added only to give the German pilots greater confidence in its sturdy structure

The Vickers F.B.5 Gunbus was the first British aircraft designed specifically to carry a machine-gun. The 'pusher' layout permitted this to be mounted on the nose of the crew nacelle

Like the Gunbus, the D.H.2 carried its machine-gun at the front of its nacelle. This was the best position until the perfection of an interrupter gear made it possible to fire bullets between spinning propeller blades

Right, top: The Bristol F.2B Fighter was outstanding as a two-seat combat aircraft. Its agility enabled the pilot to make full use of a synchronised forward-firing machine-gun, to supplement the efforts of the gunner in the rear cockpit

Right, bottom: Using a Hucks starter to start the engine of a Sopwith Snipe, Britain's counterpart to the Fokker D.VII. By engaging its engine-driven shaft with a spigot on the aircraft's propeller boss, the Hucks starter offered an easier, safer alternative to hand swinging the 'prop'

GENESIS OF AIR COMBAT

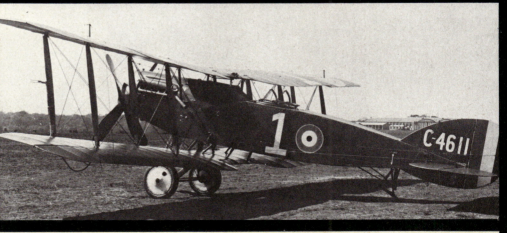

Although aviation in its broadest sense had already been used for military purposes for several decades before the Wright brothers' first aeroplane flights of 1903, it had in the main been confined to the use of free balloons for individual bombardment and tethered balloons for army reconnaissance. With the potential of controlled flight at the touch of a human hand, the military possibilities were recognised almost immediately.

Within a few years of its birth the aeroplane became the vehicle for experiments in gun and bomb carriage simultaneously in Great Britain, France, Germany and America. By 1911 several firing trials of machine-guns from aircraft pointed the path to one significant future for these frail structures; but, blinkered by centuries of inflexible ground strategy, the Army mind was capable of viewing the new means of locomotion only as an extension of the well-proven cavalry scout. With excusable finality, in view of the fragile nature of contemporary aircraft designs, most Army commanders regarded this new invention as a longer 'arm' of the infantry's primary requisite—reconnaissance. As such, the main characteristic sought in any military aeroplane was stability in flight, to provide a steady platform for the observer; any form of armament was considered unnecessary. Thus, at the outbreak of the European war in August 1914, few military aircraft were capable of carrying any form of bomb, while none was intended to carry a gun.

Despite these handicaps the first few weeks of the war saw attempts by a majority of pilots and observers to carry armament in their aircraft, albeit in most cases merely a Service rifle, pistol or private sporting gun. The concept of an aeroplane specifically designed for fighting was but dimly realised by a few individuals, with the result that in 1914 and early 1915 air units of the opposing air services were composed almost wholly of two-seat aircraft which were expected to fly in every role necessary for support of land operations. The few air casualties which occurred during the opening stages of the war were the outcome of sheer determination by individual crews; but on 1 April 1915 a new and deadly phase of air fighting was born. On that morning a lone French pilot, Roland Garros, took off in his Morane-Saulnier Type L monoplane on which he had fitted a crude device for air combat. After strapping a Hotchkiss machine-gun on the fuselage in front of his cockpit, firing forward along the line of flight, he had bolted steel wedges to the propeller in line with the gun barrel, to deflect any bullets that would otherwise strike the propeller blades. During his patrol Garros met a German Albatros observation two-seater and shot it down in flames.

Within a fortnight the Frenchman had claimed two more victims with his primitive and highly dangerous gun arrangement; but on 19 April he was forced to land behind the German lines after anti-aircraft fire had damaged his Morane. His gun device was salvaged from the partially-burned wreck of

This page, top to bottom:
No more than about 425 Fokker *Eindeckers* were built. Yet, because of their synchronised machine-guns, they almost shot the Allied air forces from the skies over France in 1915-16. The maximum take-off weight of the E.III version was 1,400 lb (635 kg)—about the same as the four air-to-air missiles carried as armament by some of its modern counterparts

An air mechanic handing photographic plates to the observer in an R.E.8 at an RFC aerodrome near Arras on 22 February 1918. Known affectionately as the 'Harry Tate', after a popular music hall artist of the time, the R.E.8 was the standard British photo-reconnaissance and artillery spotting aircraft in the last years of World War I

Bearing insignia typical of a machine flown by a German 'ace', this Albatros D.V scout belonged to Hauptmann Ritter von Schleich of Jasta 32, in 1917. Known as Germany's 'Black Knight', because he later flew an all-black D.Va, he was credited with 35 victories in air combat, and survived to become a leader of the new *Luftwaffe* in the 'thirties

Yet another of the fine replicas of World War I fighters built for use in films of the 'sixties was this Pfalz D.III. The genuine version was a contemporary of the Fokker D.VII and suffered unjustly from this, as German pilots were resentful when made to fly Pfalz D.IIIs and D.XIIs instead of the much-vaunted D.VII

Opposite page, top: This Fokker D.VII was photographed at Biggin Hill, England, in May 1919. Article IV of the Armistice Agreement signed by Germany had mentioned specifically that 'all machines of the D.VII type' were to be handed over to the Allies, the only time a specific aircraft type has ever been mentioned in such a document. Despite this, Anthony Fokker managed to smuggle about 120 more or less complete D.VIIs into his native Holland, where he re-started his business

Centre: Favourite mount of many of the British fighter pilots of World War I, the S.E.5a was a product of the Royal Aircraft Factory at Farnborough. Usual armament comprised a Lewis gun above the top wing, on a Foster mounting which enabled it to be slid down for reloading and for firing upward, and a forward-firing synchronised Vickers gun.

his aircraft and a copy was ordered immediately by the German high command for its own aircraft. Instead, three men of the Fokker aircraft company's staff produced a much-improved arrangement. They manufactured a mechanical interrupter gear which relied on the propeller itself to operate a machine-gun's firing mechanism, thus preventing the gun from firing when a blade aligned with the gun barrel. The gear was fitted to a Fokker M.5K monoplane scout and on 1 July 1915 Leutnant Kurt Wintgens used the new gun gear to destroy a French Morane. His victory was soon repeated by other Fokker pilots, including Oswald Boelcke, Max Immelmann and Max Mülzer. It was the start of what came to be called the 'Fokker Scourge', when the British and French flying services suffered rapidly increasing losses to the agile *Eindeckers*.

With no comparable gun gear immediately available, Allied designers were forced to compromise by producing aircraft with machine-guns mounted to fire outside the propeller arc on normal 'tractor' aircraft, as in the case of the French Nieuport scouts. A second answer to the problem was exemplified by the Vickers F.B.5 (the first British aircraft built specifically for fighting duties), de Havilland D.H.2 scout and the curiously efficient F.E.2b two-seater. All three of these were of the 'pusher' type, with both crew and machine-gun placed in front of the engine. Only the F.B.5s were in France in 1915, equipping No. 11 Squadron RFC, the first British unit formed for a fighting role. In February 1916, the D.H.2-equipped 24 Squadron arrived on the Western Front, commanded by Major Lanoe Hawker, VC, DSO, the RFC's first 'fighting' ace; and in the following month 25 Squadron (F.E.2bs) and 27 Squadron (Martinsyde G.100s) moved to France. Meanwhile, between the autumn of 1915 and early 1916 the Fokker scourge spread like a blight across the fighting areas above the Western Front. The almost defenceless Allied reconnaissance machines were no match for an armed Fokker scout, not least because their once-all-important stability robbed them of the ability to manoeuvre quickly when attacked.

Once the new fighters of British and French units got into their stride in the summer of 1916, the Fokker menace was soon abated and for a very brief period the Allies regained aerial supremacy. But their minor triumph was short-lived, for in late 1916 new fighting machines began to appear in German *Jagdstaffeln* (literally, Hunting Squadrons)—the Albatros D.I and D.II scouts and the Halberstadt D. series.

Of streamlined shape, with a plywood-skinned fuselage, the Albatros carried twin synchronised machine-guns firing through the propeller arc—an armament arrangement which was to become classic in most fighter aircraft for the remainder of the war and, indeed, for nearly twenty years after. Almost immediately the German Imperial Air Service regained its former air supremacy and it was not until the following spring that the Allies began receiving comparable aircraft types. Of these new designs,

Even after fighters became, generally, tractor-engined, Lewis-gunners still manned open gun positions in the nose of bombers like this Handley Page O/400 of September 1918

the most significant were the Bristol F.2B two-seat fighter, and the S.E.5 and Sopwith Camel scouts, all with synchronised machine-guns.

In many ways the Camel epitomised the World War I fighting machine. Armed with twin Vickers guns and powered by a rotary engine, it was a thoroughly unstable flying machine with the manoeuvrability of a will-o'-the-wisp, and so ideal for the lightning cut-and-thrust of 1917-18 air combat. Its highly unstable qualities, the antithesis of 1914 design ideals, made the little Sopwith one of the supreme dogfighters of the war, only equalled perhaps by the notorious Fokker Dr.I triplane scout which began to equip German units in late 1917.

During 1917 and 1918, fighter design showed an astonishing improvement over the fragile aircraft used on operations at the start of the conflict. Scouts were built and flown with four and even six machine-guns; while the French experimented with heavier-calibre shell guns of up to 37 mm from an early date. Primitive electrically-ignited rockets were employed with limited success, while on the German side experiments produced functional aerial cannon and even multi-barrel machine-guns—forerunners of the present-day weapons in international use.

In design, the 1918 scouts showed the influence of lessons learned in the hard school of combat experience over nearly four years of war. Engines, though still imperfect, were in the 150-185 hp range, giving speeds of over 100 mph (161 km/h) in normal flight. By that year Germany had produced her most successful fighting aeroplane of the war, the Fokker D.VII. With a basic structure of welded steel tubing, fabric covered, and capable of speeds in excess of 125 mph (201 km/h) at heights above 15,000 feet (4,570 m), the D.VII eventually equipped the bulk of *Jagdstaffeln* before the Armistice. Its nearest competitor in performance was a successor to the waspish Camel, the Sopwith Snipe, which was beginning to re-equip RAF units during the final weeks of hostilities.

With the cessation of fighting in November 1918, the impetus given to aircraft designers by the incessant demands of war was allowed to die away. It had been an heroic era which produced legendary names in military aviation history. Aircrews had fought and died two and three miles high over the muddied trenches, without benefit of oxygen, wireless communication, parachutes or heated cockpits. Tactics had been empirical, as were the ever-changing design requirements of the tiny aircraft in which such men had flown. But the tradition carved out by crews and aircraft proved to be a rock foundation for succeeding generations of men and machines.

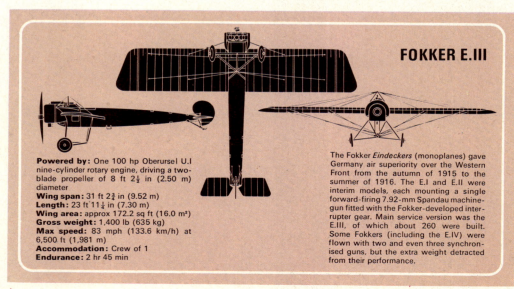

FOKKER E.III

Powered by: One 100 hp Oberursel U.I nine-cylinder rotary engine, driving a two-blade propeller of 8 ft 2½ in (2.50 m) diameter
Wing span: 31 ft 2¾ in (9.52 m)
Length: 23 ft 11½ in (7.30 m)
Wing area: approx 172.2 sq ft (16.0 m²)
Gross weight: 1,400 lb (635 kg)
Max speed: 83 mph (133.6 km/h) at 6,500 ft (1,981 m)
Accommodation: Crew of 1
Endurance: 2 hr 45 min

The Fokker *Eindeckers* (monoplanes) gave Germany air superiority over the Western Front from the autumn of 1915 to the summer of 1916. The E.I and E.II were interim models, each mounting a single forward-firing 7.92-mm Spandau machine-gun fitted with the Fokker-developed interrupter gear. Main service version was the E.III, of which about 260 were built. Some Fokkers (including the E.IV) were flown with two and even three synchronised guns, but the extra weight detracted from their performance.

Above: This Sopwith Pup is still flown regularly for the delight of visitors to the Shuttleworth Collection of historical aircraft at Old Warden aerodrome in Bedfordshire. It was built just after World War I as a Dove, civilian counterpart of the Pup. After an accident, it was converted into a Pup and still reminds both pilots and spectators why this type was regarded by many as the finest flying machine ever built

Extreme left: Known as 'The Eagle of Lille' Max Immelmann was the great exponent of the Fokker *Eindecker*. After claiming 15 victories in air combat, he was lost in action. German accounts attributed his death to a technical failure of his aircraft; the RFC claimed that he fell to the guns of Corporal Waller in an F.E.2b fighter

Centre, top: Judged by many to be the finest World War I aeroplane still flying in the USA, this Sopwith Snipe bears no visible scars of the Hollywood studio fire in which it was once severely damaged. Built in 1918, it still has its original 230-hp Bentley B.R.2 rotary engine.

Centre, bottom: The remains of Immelmann's Fokker monoplane, in which he died on 18 June 1916. It was stated officially that his interrupter gear had failed, causing the engine to 'run away' and break up the airframe after the propeller had been shot away. Immelmann's death symbolised the end of the Fokker's brief reign of supremacy

Left, top to bottom:
Hauptmann Ritter von Tutschek (27 victories) preparing to take off in his Fokker Dr.I triplane in March 1918. An aircraft of this type was the favourite mount of Germany's 'ace of aces', Manfred von Richthofen

Morane-Saulnier Type N scout of the Royal Flying Corps. One of many fine types acquired from French production, the Type N had steel deflector plates fitted to its propeller blades to kick aside any bullets from the machine-gun that would otherwise have hit them

Very few combat aircraft of Russian design served in World War I, except for Sikorsky's great Ilya Mourometz bombers. However, a few Sikorsky S-20s, like this one, reached front-line squadrons and are said to have been capable of 118 mph (190 km/h) on the power of a 110-hp Le Rhône engine

the start of air bombing

In 1670 Father Francesco de Lana-Terzi wrote a treatise on the feasibility of building an 'aerial ship'. Utterly convinced of such a possibility, the worthy cleric also foresaw clearly a military application for such a vehicle as a weapon of bombardment, being probably the first man to do so. It was to be two and a half centuries before his dire prophecy became reality.

The first known occasion of bombs being dropped from an aeroplane in war operations took place on 1 November 1911, during the Italo-Turkish conflict in Libya. On that date Second Lieutenant Guilio Gavotti of the Italian Air Flotilla threw four 4.4-lb (2-kg) 'Cipelli' grenades from his aircraft on to enemy troops at Taguira Oasis and Ain Zara. With eleven pilots flying a mixed collection of nine aircraft, Gavotti and his comrades exploited their air bombing technique to such good effect that a correspondent attached to the Turkish Army commented: 'This war has shown clearly that air navigation (*sic*) provides a terrible means of destruction. These new weapons are destined to revolutionise modern strategy and tactics'. His visionary remarks made little impact on contemporary military minds. Even the Wright brothers had optimistically proclaimed their invention as 'a certain means of ending war', while few nations considered the aeroplane as other than a passing fad, or at best a useful, if limited, adjunct to the armies.

The notion of utilising aeroplanes for bombing was by no means neglected entirely. In the USA as early as January 1910 serious trials of releasing a 'war load' were carried out, although the lethal load on the first occasion was merely three 2-lb (0.9 kg) sandbags. Almost exactly one year later the first test involving a live explosive bomb was completed with some success. In Britain, too, thought had been given to such employment of aircraft. By 1912 various experimental flights had begun to explore the possibilities of air bombing, notably by individual naval officers such as Charles Rumsey Samson and Robert Clark-Hall. Their experiences were largely ignored by both Admiralty and War Office, and on the outbreak of war with Germany in 1914 Britain's only stockpile of true aerial bombs comprised twenty-six 20-lb (9-kg) Hales bombs stored at Eastchurch on the Isle of Sheppey. All were intended to be released by hand, there being no such thing as a bomb carrier and very few aircraft capable of bearing a bomb load in Service use at that time.

France, with slightly superior foresight, had already decided that aerial bombardment was practical and began the war relatively well-equipped with several squadrons of Voisin 'pusher' bombers. Within a few weeks of hostilities beginning, these sturdy aircraft had carried out a series of short-range attacks against German targets behind the front lines. In Germany, too, the strategic possibilities of air power had been recognised early. With an airship fleet and a comparatively large aeroplane service, Germany already had plans for an aerial attack on England. Brain-child of an elderly Army Major, Wilhelm Siegert, this was to include the bombing of cities and industrial centres in south-east England and thus could be regarded as the true genesis of strategic air bombing.

Above, left: In the early days of the 1914-18 War, bombs were usually dropped by hand. This photograph shows an RNAS officer about to drop a bomb from the control car of an airship in this manner

Above, right: Loading a standard 112-lb (50-kg) bomb on the starboard wing rack of a D.H.4 of No 27 Squadron, RFC, in February 1918.

Opposite page:
Top left: This 230-lb (104-kg) bomb was also delivered by a D.H.4 of No 27 Squadron

Top right: At the outbreak of war, aeroplanes were still regarded by the armies of the world as novelties, useful only for reconnaissance. This unarmed Maurice Farman was typical of French military aircraft of the period

Centre right: This photograph of the unfortunate end of a Sopwith 1½-Strutter of No 5 Wing, RNAS, is interesting in that it shows clearly the 'bomb cell' in the fuselage, between the lower wings

Right: One of the North Sea class of non-rigid airships which put in fine service with the RNAS in World War 1

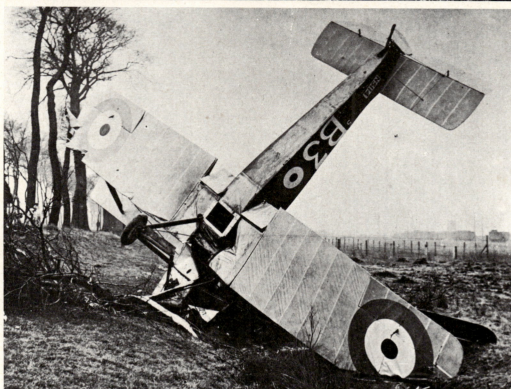

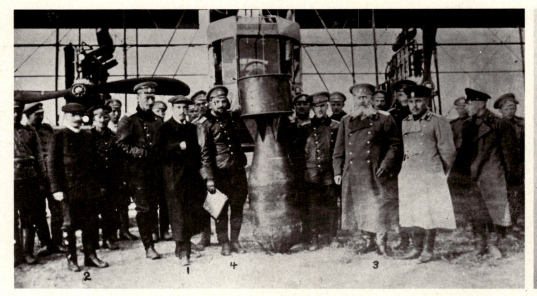

TUPOLEV TB-3

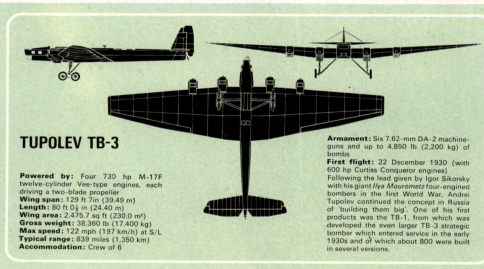

Powered by: Four 730 hp M-17F twelve-cylinder Vee-type engines, each driving a two-blade propeller
Wing span: 129 ft 7in (39.49 m)
Length: 80 ft 0½ in (24.40 m)
Wing area: 2,475.7 sq ft (230.0 m²)
Gross weight: 38,360 lb (17,400 kg)
Max speed: 122 mph (197 km/h) at S/L
Typical range: 839 miles (1,350 km)
Accommodation: Crew of 6

Armament: Six 7.62-mm DA-2 machine-guns and up to 4,850 lb (2,200 kg) of bombs
First flight: 22 December 1930 (with 600 hp Curtiss Conqueror engines)
Following the lead given by Igor Sikorsky with his giant *Ilya Mourometz* four-engined bombers in the first World War, Andrei Tupolev continued the concept in Russia of 'building them big'. One of his first products was the TB-1, from which was developed the even larger TB-3 strategic bomber which entered service in the early 1930s and of which about 800 were built in several versions.

CAPRONI Ca 5

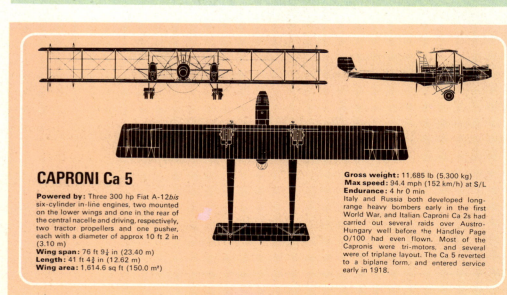

Powered by: Three 300 hp Fiat A-12*bis* six-cylinder in-line engines, two mounted on the lower wings and one in the rear of the central nacelle and driving, respectively, two tractor propellers and one pusher, each with a diameter of approx 10 ft 2 in (3.10 m)
Wing span: 76 ft 9¼ in (23.40 m)
Length: 41 ft 4⅜ in (12.62 m)
Wing area: 1,614.6 sq ft (150.0 m²)

Gross weight: 11,685 lb (5,300 kg)
Max speed: 94.4 mph (152 km/h) at S/L
Endurance: 4 hr 0 min
Italy and Russia both developed long-range heavy bombers early in the first World War, and Italian Caproni Ca 2s had carried out several raids over Austro-Hungary well before the Handley Page O/100 had even flown. Most of the Capronis were tri-motors, and several were of triplane layout. The Ca 5 reverted to a biplane form, and entered service early in 1918.

Top, left: Big bombers are nothing new in Russia. One of Igor Sikorsky's four-engined *Ilya Mourometz* bombers was used for tests with this 920-lb (417-kg) weapon. The figure 1 identifies Sikorsky; No 3 is General Michael Vladimirovich Shidlowsky, who commanded the 'Squadron of Flying Ships'

Top right: An *Ilya Mourometz* in flight. Of 73 built, about half were used at the front; only one was shot down over enemy territory

This page, centre: The IM-G3 version of the *Ilya Mourometz* had two 220-hp Renault inner engines and two 150-hp RBZ-6 outers. It had defensive gun positions in nose and tail, and a further machine-gun which could fire upward or downward from inside the fuselage. Bomb-load was 2,000 lb (907 kg)

Above: 'One night's rations'. Preparing 112-lb bombs for a night raid by No 149 Squadron, RAF, equipped with F.E.2bs, on 18 July 1918

Opposite page, top: Caproni's big Ca 42 three-engined triplane could carry up to 3,910 lb (1,775 kg) of bombs in the pannier on its bottom wing. Spanning nearly 100 ft (30 m), it had a maximum speed of 87 mph (140 km/h) and could fly for seven hours

Right: First used in February 1918, the 1,650 lb (748 kg) 'Minor' was the largest bomb dropped by British Handley Page O/400s. A 3,300-pounder, evolved for the four-engined HP V/1500, was never used operationally

The war soon accelerated progress in this field of operations. Within the first few months, individual pilots of the Royal Naval Air Service had undertaken bombing sorties against such targets as Zeppelin sheds and supply depots. The aircraft used were lightly loaded and woefully underpowered, but the morale value of their limited successes encouraged officialdom to regard the 'new' weapon seriously. Until late 1915, the use of bomb-carrying aircraft was still restricted mainly to tactical support of land operations; but before the year was out the Allied commanders had agreed to the formation of a unit for purely strategic operations. This unit, No 3 Wing RNAS, came into being by July 1916 equipped with Sopwith 1½-Strutter single-engined aircraft of limited range and light bomb load. The Wing's career was comparatively short, the aircraft being diverted to supply understrength RFC and RNAS squadrons along the Western Front by June 1917.

While able to lay claim to being the first strategic bomber unit, No 3 Wing RNAS was by no means the first formation created specifically for bombing operations. Apart from the French Voisin *escadrilles* already mentioned, Russia possessed a squadron of giant four-engined *Ilya Mourometz* aircraft, which made its first raid against a target in Poland on 15 February 1915; and in Italy Caproni three-engined bombers had flown their first long-range sorties on 20 August 1915.

Despite the hurried dispersal of No 3

Wing, the principle of strategic bombing was not abandoned by Britain, being reborn with the formation of the 41st Wing, Royal Flying Corps, in 1917. In addition to two squadrons equipped with F.E.2b and D.H.4 aircraft, the Wing employed a significant new design, the twin-engined Handley Page O/100. Conceived in 1914, this behemoth, with a wing span of 100 feet (30.48 m), was capable of lifting an 1,800-lb (816-kg) load over a range of at least 200 miles (322 km). With the improved O/400, it was the forerunner of several generations of British heavy bombers during the succeeding forty years. Beginning operations in October 1917, the Wing was strengthened by two additional squadrons in May 1918, by which time its title had become VIII Brigade, Royal Air Force. Primary targets were German cities, which were attacked by day and night, and in June 1918 VIII Brigade became the nucleus of a completely new formation, the Independent Force, RAF.

While the principle behind the creation of such a force was sound, its birth was due in no small measure to a simple, primitive desire for retaliation rather than any visionary concept of strategy. Due to the increasing number of bombing raids flown against Britain by the German Zeppelins (and, by 1917, Gotha bombers), British public opinion expressed a wish for vengeance. The Gotha raids began on 25 May 1917 and were undertaken by a group of four squadrons formed specially for the purpose of raiding the United Kingdom

This page:

Top: A Handley Page O/400 bomber of No 207 Squadron, RAF, flying over the Occupation Zone of Germany in May 1919

Left: This 1,650-pounder was dropped from an HP O/400 of No 207 Squadron on Le Cateau railway station during the night of 13/14 September 1918

Above: Powered by two 360 hp Rolls-Royce Eagle engines, the Handley Page O/400 had a top speed of 97.5 mph (157 km/h). About 400 were delivered to the British Services before the Armistice

Opposite page, top: Servicing an O/400 at Dunkirk in 1918. Its heavy defensive armament included twin guns in the nose and two more above the fuselage amidships. A fifth gun fired rearward and downward through the bottom of the fuselage

centre: One of the fine three-engined Caproni biplanes with which Italy pioneered long-range strategic bombing across the Alps in 1915-18

bottom: British bombs of 1914-18. From left to right: 16-lb (7.25-kg) incendiary, 65-lb (29.5-kg) high-explosive, 112-lb (50-kg) RL (Royal Laboratory), 100-lb (45-kg) RL and 230-lb (104-kg) RFC Mk 3. Those on the shelf at rear include 25-lb (11.3-kg) Coopers

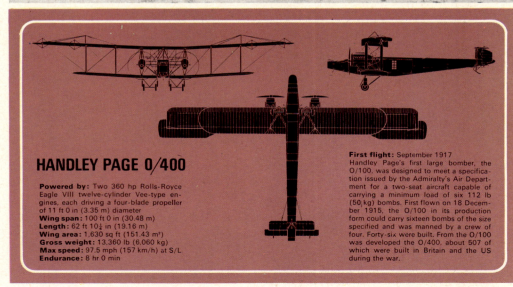

HANDLEY PAGE O/400

Powered by: Two 360 hp Rolls-Royce Eagle VIII twelve-cylinder Vee-type engines, each driving a four-blade propeller of 11 ft 0 in (3.35 m) diameter
Wing span: 100 ft 0 in (30.48 m)
Length: 62 ft 10½ in (19.16 m)
Wing area: 1,630 sq ft (151.43 m²)
Gross weight: 13,360 lb (6,060 kg)
Max speed: 97.5 mph (157 km/h) at S/L
Endurance: 8 hr 0 min

First flight: September 1917
Handley Page's first large bomber, the O/100, was designed to meet a specification issued by the Admiralty's Air Department for a two-seat aircraft capable of carrying a minimum load of six 112 lb (50 kg) bombs. First flown on 18 December 1915, the O/100 in its production form could carry sixteen bombs of the size specified and was manned by a crew of four. Forty-six were built. From the O/100 was developed the O/400, about 507 of which were built in Britain and the US during the war.

from bases in Belgium. In pursuance of the policy first propounded by Siegert in 1914, this group, titled *Kampfgeschwader Nr* 3 (the 'England Squadron') was equipped initially with twin-engined Gotha bombers capable of reaching most south-eastern counties of England, including London, with a useful bomb load. Later additional designs included the mammoth *Riesenflugzeug* or 'Giant' aircraft, and their depredations continued for almost exactly one year, until May 1918.

Within a month of the Gothas' final raid the Independent Force came into being under the command of Sir Hugh Trenchard. Initially it comprised units of the defunct VIII Brigade, but by September 1918 a further five squadrons had been added to its strength. The new Force's terms of reference included 'an extended and sustained bombing offensive against German munition industries'. In practical terms the IF's offensive produced a lowering of German civilian morale twenty times greater than the material damage accomplished. It was this latter effect, undoubtedly, which led to the formation of No 27 Group, RAF, a tiny collection of three new squadrons which were due to equip with Handley Page V/1500 bombers—four-engined developments of the well-proven O/400s. These 'Super-Handleys' were expected to reach and devastate Berlin, the German capital city, with loads of up to 3,400 lb (1,542 kg)—although it is open to speculation whether the V/1500s would have been capable of such sorties. The opportunity for practice never came, for the Armistice of November 1918 intervened.

The four years of war had seen bombing aircraft develop from frail 80-hp craft, whose pilots dispensed hand grenades and 20-lb (9-kg) bombs by hand, to giant aircraft spanning over 100 ft (30.48 m), twin- and four-engined and capable of transporting loads of up to nearly 4,000 lb (1,814 kg) weight over relatively long ranges with reasonable accuracy. And, most important, the first principles of strategic air policy had taken root in the more receptive military minds of all nations. Within two decades, the consequences were to bring devastating results.

HOW THE AEROPLANE WENT TO SEA

A mere decade after the Wright brothers had demonstrated, in their own words, 'that the age of the flying machine had come at last', the first World War gave an impetus to the development of the aeroplane which established its place firmly in the armouries of the nations. When the war started in 1914, however, the roles which could be played by the rudimentary machines of the period was far from clear. Whilst a handful of forward-thinking individuals grasped the significance of the aeroplane for military duties, to the majority it was still a novelty and little more than a frivolous toy.

Experiments often had to be conducted in the face of official apathy and public derision. The efforts to exploit the aeroplane as an adjunct to the operations of the Royal Navy were no exception. Interest in sea-flying had grown through the efforts of Fabre and Curtiss in 1910, and before the end of that year Ely in America had made the world's first take-off from a ship, the USS *Birmingham*. By 1911, it was becoming clear that the aeroplane might have a role for fleet reconnaissance and coastal patrol, and in the face of a somewhat reluctant Admiralty, Royal Navy aviators pressed ahead with experiments to see how ships and aeroplanes could work together.

Early in 1911, in America, Ely landed his Curtiss biplane on the *Pennsylvania*, which, like the *Birmingham* two months before, had a platform constructed for the purpose. During both flights, however, the ship was moored at the dockside. A similar take-off was made for the first time in Britain a year later, on 10 January 1912, by Lieut Charles Samson in a Short S.27 from a deck erected on HMS *Africa*. Thereafter, Samson played

a prominent role in developing the Royal Navy's flying branch. However, several years were to elapse before deck flying became a practical possibility.

In 1914, responsibility for the air defence of Great Britain was vested in the Royal Naval Air Service, adding to its duties of fleet reconnaissance and coastal patrol. Thus, the RNAS operated landplanes from land bases from the start of the war—and this provided the Service with experience in aerial defence which was later applied with good effect to its ship-based operations.

For coastal patrols, a mixture of landplanes and seaplanes was operated from shore bases such as that at Great Yarmouth. Guns and bombs were soon added to these aeroplanes—the majority were Short biplanes—making them the forerunners of today's shore-based maritime reconnaissance types such as the Nimrod, Orion and Atlantic.

Fleet reconnaissance, on the other hand, implied operation of the aircraft wherever ships of the fleet sailed. Samson's 1912 flight from the *Africa*, on a pontoon-equipped Short biplane, led to the introduction of seaplane carriers by the Royal Navy. Hastily converted merchantmen had wooden platforms erected over the bows, from which seaplanes could be launched (with the aid of a wheeled trolley) or could be lifted over the side to take off conventionally from the open sea. At the end of a mission, the seaplane would land alongside the carrier to be retrieved by crane.

Earliest of the ships so converted were the cross-Channel steamers *Empress*, *Engadine* and *Riviera*, each carrying four seaplanes, and the Cunarder *Campania*, which could carry ten seaplanes. Other conversions followed, including the cross-Channel *Manxman*, *Ben-My-Chree* and *Vindex*, plus the *Ark Royal*, a merchantman converted during construction.

On Christmas Day, 1914, a force of seven Short seaplanes from the *Empress*, *Engadine* and *Riviera* was launched from a position 12 miles (20 km) north of Heligoland to attack the German Zeppelin sheds at Cuxhaven. The raid was ineffective, due primarily to poor weather, but was the

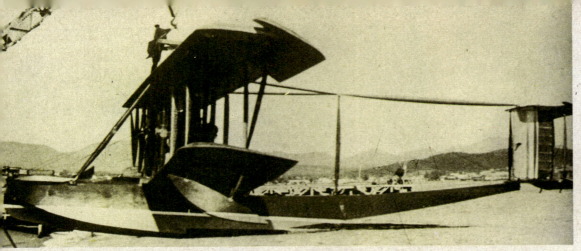

first demonstration of the way in which the range of offensive aircraft could be increased by operating them from ships. The deterrent value of this development was shown when the German Navy moved a number of its ships from the Channel ports to the Baltic, to avoid further attack.

Another demonstration of the growing importance of aeroplanes in naval operations came in 1915, in the Dardanelles campaign. Seaplanes from HMS *Ark Royal* began operating on 17 February 1915, spotting for the guns of the fleet. In August, the *Ben-My-Chree* arrived with two Short 184s, each able to carry a 14-inch (355 mm) torpedo. On 12 August a direct hit on a Turkish merchant vessel was claimed for a torpedo dropped by one of these aircraft.

Flying from the seaplane carriers, open water or coastal bases, seaplanes of the Royal Navy played a significant role throughout the war, and their evolution was matched by similar work in France and Germany. Meanwhile, the RNAS continued experiments to improve the technique of operating aircraft from ships, and this was to give Britain a clear lead by 1918 in the development of aircraft carriers in the modern sense of the term. The primary objective of the experiments was to permit the operation of wheeled aeroplanes from ships, which would not then have to heave-to in order to launch and recover their seaplanes.

An early experiment was made on 3 November 1915, when Flt Sub-Lt H F Towler took off in a Bristol Scout from the deck of the seaplane carrier *Vindex*, subsequently ditching alongside the ship with the aid of flotation bags. Further impetus was given to these developments by the growth of German Zeppelin operations, which could be combated only by fighters of considerably higher performance than the seaplanes in use by the RNAS. Early in 1917, both the *Campania* and *Manxman* were issued with Pup fighters, after Flt-Cdr F J Rutland had shown that this Sopwith biplane could be flown easily off the seaplane decks on these ships. By refining flying techniques, Rutland went on to demonstrate that the Pup could take off after a 15 ft (4.6 m) run at a speed of about 23 mph (37 km/h).

As a result of this development, a total of 22 British light cruisers, starting with HMS *Yarmouth*, were fitted with 20-ft (6.1-m) flying-off platforms and issued with fighters. On 21 August 1917, a Pup launched by the *Yarmouth* and flown by Flt Sub-Lt B A Smart intercepted and shot down the Zeppelin L.23. To overcome the objection that the ships had to turn into wind to launch their aircraft, Rutland evolved a technique for flying off platforms attached to the swivelling gun turrets of battle cruisers, which then adopted two fighters each as standard equipment.

An alternative scheme was evolved in 1918 by Charles Samson (by this time a Colonel) in which a fighter was towed on a 40 ft (12.2-m) barge behind destroyers or other warships. The barge had a rudimentary 'flight deck' from which the fighter could rise almost vertically when being towed at speed into wind. Using this technique, Flt Sub-Lt Stuart Culley was launched in a Sopwith Camel, towed behind the destroyer HMS *Redoubt*, off the Dutch coast on 11 August 1918 to intercept the Zeppelin L.53. This he did at the extreme ceiling of his aircraft, above 18,000 ft

This page, top left: When the French Navy needed more seaplanes desperately at the start of World War 1, a young engineer named Alphonse Tellier was engaged to design a suitable machine. This led, in 1917, to the production of 96 Tellier T.3 two-seat bomber flying-boats and 55 T.C.6s, armed with a 47-mm cannon. This later Tellier flying-boat had three 350-hp engines, and a 75-mm gun in the nose

Above: HMS *Furious* at the time when she had a completely clear flight deck. The smoke plume streaming back from the bows indicated when the ship was sailing dead into wind, so that flying off could begin

Top right: The serial number on the rudder of this prototype led to production models being known as Short 184s. One of them became the first aircraft ever to sink an enemy ship by torpedo, during the Dardanelles campaign. Another was the only aeroplane to take part in the naval Battle of Jutland

Opposite page, top right: America's first aircraft carrier, the USS *Langley,* was a converted collier. Her first squadron was equipped with Vought VE-7SF single-seat fighters. In one of these, Lt V C Griffin made the first-ever take-off from a US Navy carrier on 17 October 1922

Centre: The US Navy acquired a total of 22 Sopwith 1½-Strutters. Like the Royal Navy, it tried operating the type from a platform built over the gun turret of a warship

Bottom: HMS *Argus,* known in the Royal Navy as the 'flat iron' for obvious reasons, survived in combat use into World War 2. This photograph shows her operating with Seafires, off the North African coast, despite the fact that these fighters had a top speed three times as great as that of the fastest combat aircraft of 1918, when the ship was first commissioned

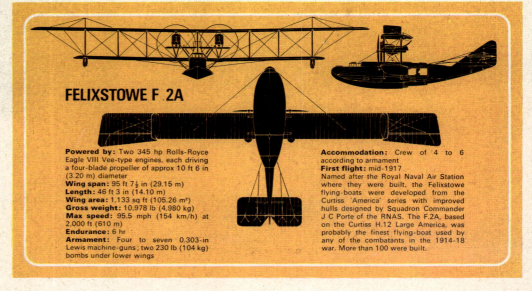

FELIXSTOWE F 2A

Powered by: Two 345 hp Rolls-Royce Eagle VIII Vee-type engines, each driving a four-blade propeller of approx 10 ft 6 in (3.20 m) diameter
Wing span: 95 ft 7½ in (29.15 m)
Length: 46 ft 3 in (14.10 m)
Wing area: 1,133 sq ft (105.26 m²)
Gross weight: 10,978 lb (4,980 kg)
Max speed: 95.5 mph (154 km/h) at 2,000 ft (610 m)
Endurance: 6 hr
Armament: Four to seven 0.303-in Lewis machine-guns; two 230 lb (104 kg) bombs under lower wings

Accommodation: Crew of 4 to 6 according to armament
First flight: mid-1917
Named after the Royal Naval Air Station where they were built, the Felixstowe flying-boats were developed from the Curtiss 'America' series with improved hulls designed by Squadron Commander J C Porte of the RNAS. The F.2A, based on the Curtiss H.12 Large America, was probably the finest flying-boat used by any of the combatants in the 1914-18 war. More than 100 were built.

(5,500 m); standing the Camel on its tail, he fired a short but fatal burst into the Zeppelin before stalling.

None of these techniques allowed the aircraft to land back on the ship which launched them, although provision was made for them to be ditched and hoisted back on board—provided the ship could be found at the end of the flight. The final stage, therefore, was to find a means of landing on deck. The first hair-raising experiments were made in August 1917 on board HMS *Furious*, a light battle cruiser converted during construction to carry seaplanes and wheeled aeroplanes, which were launched from a flying-off deck 228 ft (70 m) long ahead of the bridge structure.

Combining a ship speed of about 21 knots and a wind speed of 25 knots or more, the airflow over the flight deck could match the landing speed of the Sopwith Pup. Sqdn Cdr E H Dunning took advantage of this to show how the aircraft could be landed-on. Flying up alongside the *Furious*, he side-slipped in ahead of the bridge and virtually hovered over the deck while colleagues grabbed the aircraft as he cut the throttle. A successful landing—the first on board a warship under way—was made on 2 August 1917. Less than a week later Dunning was killed in a further attempt.

In March 1918, the final step towards the true aircraft carrier was taken with the provision of a landing deck on *Furious*, aft of the bridge structure. The eddies round this structure and the exhaust from the funnel made landing on this deck extremely hazardous, but all the ingredients of the true aircraft carrier had now been provided and the aeroplane was able to go to sea without losing its operational effectiveness.

SHORT 184

Powered by: One 260 hp Sunbeam Maori I, II or III Vee-type engine, driving a four-blade propeller of approx 10 ft 6 in (3.20 m) diameter
Wing span: 63 ft 6¼ in (19.36 m)
Length: 40 ft 7½ in (12.38 m)
Wing area: 688 sq ft (63.92 m²)
Gross weight: 5,363 lb (2,433 kg)
Max speed: 88.5 mph (142 km/h) at 2,000 ft (610 m)
Endurance: 2 hr 45 min
Armament: One 0.303-in Lewis machine-gun in rear cockpit; one 14-in torpedo or up to 520 lb (236 kg) of bombs under fuselage
Accommodation: Crew of 2

First flight: early 1915
The first torpedo launch from a British aeroplane took place from a 160 hp Short seaplane on 28 July 1914. As a result the Admiralty ordered an aircraft specially for this role, and this became known as the Short 184. In service, the weight of the torpedo made the aircraft difficult to fly, but from mid-1915 until the end of World War I the Short 184 served in nearly every theatre of war as a reconnaissance-bomber and anti-submarine patrol aircraft. About 900 were built, and a third of these were still in operation when the war ended.

AN INDUSTRY ARISES

Left: The J 1 was the earliest product of the Junkers factory in Germany, making its first flight on 12 December 1915. It was of all-metal construction, with even a covering of thin sheet iron which earned it the nickname of 'Tin Donkey'. Not for many more years were other companies to adopt all-metal structures

Below: Dolphin biplane fighters being assembled in a corner of the Sopwith factory at Kingston upon Thames in November 1917

Top right: As it was in the beginning. This photograph shows well the patient craftsmanship that went into aircraft of aviation's first decade, in this case the Short No 1 biplane of 1909. Mass production techniques, using less skilled labour, became essential under the demands of war

Right: To satisfy orders for thousands of fighters, Sopwith moved into a vast works at Ham, near Kingston. Wood for their airframes flowed in an endless stream from this sawmill

In August 1912 an event known as the Military Trials took place on Salisbury Plain in England. When the official requirements for the competing aircraft were published, one British constructor, who had then built only a handful of aeroplanes, declared: 'It is well that provision for auxiliary apparatus such as wireless, guns etc, has been left out.'

Two years later war came, and still no aircraft designed to carry armament were in service. Two years later still, the constructor who had expressed his satisfaction with the conditions of the Military Trials was preparing to deliver to the Royal Naval Air Service the first of forty twin-engined bombers of unprecedented deadliness. Another two years passed. The war ended, and the forty bombers had increased to about four hundred and fifty of the same general type.

The constructor concerned was Frederick Handley Page, bombers of whose manufacture continued to serve the RAF between the wars in unbroken succession and of whose four-engined Halifax of the second World War well over 6,000 were built.

These facts and figures serve not only to indicate the rapid growth of the military aeroplane in Britain, and the equal swiftness in the rise of British air power, but to illustrate also the true foundation of the nation's great aircraft industry during 1914-18.

The name of Handley Page is one of several which, although no longer present on the roll of British aircraft constructors, endure as household words. A few of the great names still remain current—Bristol, Fairey, Hawker, Rolls-Royce, Short, Westland—often in associations that would be unfamiliar to the founders of the companies that originally bore them.

Before tracing the growth of these and other great British aircraft companies during 1914-18, it is fitting to note the contribution made to Britain's war effort during that period by companies whose normal activities were quite outside the aircraft industry. How many Mini-drivers, for example, are aware that the Austin Motor Co (1914) Ltd not only made other people's aeroplanes but designed its own; that Sunbeam, Standard and Wolseley were among the firms closely involved in aircraft production? How many workers in industry know of the aeronautical contributions made by the Phoenix Dynamo Manufacturing Co, the Brush Electrical Engineering Co, Harland & Wolff and William Beardmore & Co?

How many boat-owners would believe that J Samuel White & Co and May, Harden & May were not without distinction as builders of aeroplanes, or that a contract for 500 Bristol Fighters was awarded to the Cunard Steamship Co? Disc jockeys would hardly credit, perhaps, that the Gramophone Co Ltd built a mighty bomber called the Kennedy Giant, nor farmers that fighters and trainers left the production lines of Messrs Ransomes, Sims & Jefferies. And one may marvel at the workmanship that must have been displayed by the D.H.9

bombers turned out by the venerable Waring & Gillow Ltd.

But whereas such companies as those named, together with the national aircraft factories established late in the war, were valuable sources for supplying the simple wooden-framed aircraft of the period, the heart of Britain's fast-emerging aircraft industry was a group of companies made up of Armstrong Whitworth, Avro, Blackburn, Boulton and Paul, Bristol, de Havilland, Fairey, Handley Page, Martinsyde, Parnall, Short, Sopwith, Supermarine, Vickers and Westland. From these organisations came not only aeroplanes in quantity but a succession of new designs and constructional techniques, to which the Royal Aircraft Factory at Farnborough made a very real, though often grudgingly acknowledged, contribution.

Rolls-Royce and Sunbeam were dominant among the designers and constructors of aero-engines, though the names of BHP (Beardmore-Halford-Pullinger), Bentley, Napier and ABC were prominent as the war approached its end. In the aero-engine field, as in that of aircraft, 'Farnborough' played its part. Both aeroplanes and aero-engines were purchased from abroad, but during the first twelve months of the war the average monthly delivery, from British and foreign sources combined, totalled only fifty. During the last twelve months the average deliveries were 2,700 a month, and at the Armistice the factory capacity in the United Kingdom alone was sufficient for 3,500 complete machines each month.

Aero-engines produced in Britain during the final twelve months of war delivered a total of eight million horsepower—a figure comparable with the total power of the engines built in the same period for the nation's ships.

Although at the war's end the vast majority of British aeroplanes were of biplane type, technical advances, both basic and in detail, were to be observed. Speed and rate of climb had benefited because less weight per horsepower was being carried. Wing sections, or profiles, were more efficient, and greater attention was being paid to reducing air resistance. Whereas in 1914 duplication of the main 'lift' wires had been considered more or less essential (in the event of one such wire being shot away), in 1918 the loads were taken by the 'incidence' wires, or those seen in side view. The main bracing wires in 1914 were of piano wire or stranded cable, but streamline wires of high-tensile steel were customary at the Armistice. For internal bracing, piano wire gave way to flattened rods with screwed ends for fitting.

The struts between the wings, which had originally been of solid spruce, were succeeded by laminated, or built-up, designs, because of the increasing size of aircraft and the scarcity of suitable wood. Steel tubes were sometimes used, especially for the undercarriage. The scarcity of silver spruce led to new forms of construction for the wing spars; splicing was tried, and laminated and box-type spars proved successful. Fabric covering was still general in 1918, but

partial plywood covering, as favoured by de Havilland, was also to be seen.

The true 'monocoque' fuselage, or one in which the skin bore most or all of the stresses, was little in evidence. Metal construction was tried, notably in connection with experimental versions of the Avro 504 trainer, for this type was absorbing about a third of the available wood supplies. Vickers experimented with duralumin, an aluminium alloy, and made the forward fuselage portion of their famous Vimy bomber of steel tubes. Monoplanes, notably the 130 mph (209 km/h) Bristol M.IC, had been produced, but in the development and use of the cantilever type of wing the Germans were far ahead.

With military aircraft today costing millions of pounds it may be worth noting that in 1918 the Sopwith Camel fighter, without engine, instruments or guns, cost £875 10s, and that the most expensive engines fitted added another £907 10s. The price tag on the bare airframe of the big Handley Page O/100 bomber was £6,000; its two Rolls-Royce Eagle engines cost a further £2,245.

After the Armistice Lord Weir of Eastwood, Secretary of State for Air in 1918-19, recalled: 'The provision of satisfactory timber was a continual difficulty. The textile problem became very grave when the supplies of Russian flax were cut off, and we were compelled to develop additional sources in Ireland and the Colonies. Acute difficulties were experienced in connection with the development of the chemicals required for dope manufacture. ('Dope' was used to treat the fabric covering.)

'At other times the supply of machineguns gave anxiety, while the development of synchronising gear for these guns necessitated very desperate measures. The production of ball bearings involved the provision of new facilities on a colossal scale and the demand for magnetos involved the building up of an entirely new industry; while the manufacture of the numerous classes of instruments, cameras, radiators and other fittings in each case produced a problem by itself. The solution of such problems constitutes an outstanding example of the enterprise, courage and ingenuity of British industry.'

What must never be forgotten, however, is the debt that the British aircraft industry, like that of the other early Allies, owed to its French counterpart. Only the French had a large and well-organised industry when the war started. As a result, every engine in the 73 aeroplanes taken to France and Belgium by the RFC and RNAS in August 1914 was of French manufacture, and 22 of the aircraft were wholly French. Subsequently, the British services continued to equip with French products while the home industry girded itself for massive achievements. Most of the great British fighter aircraft, such as the Pup, Camel and S.E.5, continued to utilise French power plants, and not until April 1918 did the British air services cease to fly aeroplanes built across the Channel.

To meet such requirements, the French industry built no fewer than 67,982 aircraft during the war years. Germany produced 47,637 and Italy about 20,000. The United States, home of the powered aeroplane, had fallen so far behind that its air forces had to rely on their allies for aircraft used in action in France. Only the Curtiss flyingboats, of home products, saw action on any scale. None the less, America built 15,000 aircraft during the 21 months of its participation in the war and these were to point the way to the greatest industry of all a quarter of a century later.

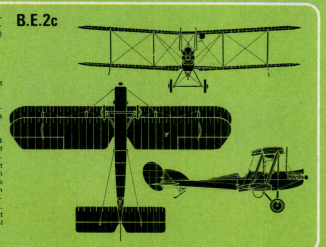

B.E.2c

Powered by: One 90 hp R.A.F. 1a eight-cylinder Vee-type engine, driving a four-blade propeller of 8 ft 10 in (2.69 m) diameter
Wing span: 37 ft 0 in (11.28 m)
Length: 27 ft 3 in (8.31 m)
Wing area: 371 sq ft (34.47 m²)
Gross weight: 2,142 lb (972 kg)
Max speed: 72 mph (116 km/h) at 6,500 ft (1,980 m)
Accommodation: Crew of 2
Armament: One 0.303 in Lewis machine-gun; up to 224 lb (102 kg) of bombs underwing
Endurance: 3 hr 15 min
First flight (B.E.2c): early summer 1914
One of the most striking early examples of the widespread mass-production of aircraft, the B.E.2 series was built by at least 22 British manufacturers, who between them completed well over 3,500 of these biplanes. Despite its unhappy reputation as 'Fokker fodder', the B.E.2c was considerably better in design than earlier B.E. types, due chiefly to the exhaustive test flying of the type by E T Busk of the Royal Aircraft Factory.

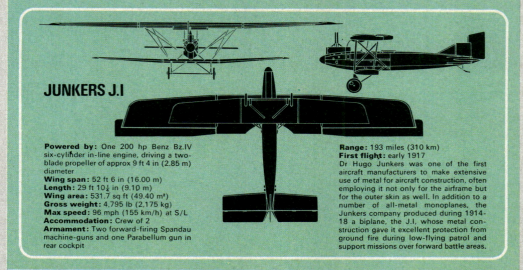

JUNKERS J.I

Powered by: One 200 hp Benz Bz.IV six-cylinder in-line engine, driving a two-blade propeller of approx 9 ft 4 in (2.85 m) diameter
Wing span: 52 ft 6 in (16.00 m)
Length: 29 ft 10½ in (9.10 m)
Wing area: 531.7 sq ft (49.40 m²)
Gross weight: 4,795 lb (2,175 kg)
Max speed: 96 mph (155 km/h) at S/L
Accommodation: Crew of 2
Armament: Two forward-firing Spandau machine-guns and one Parabellum gun in rear cockpit

Range: 193 miles (310 km)
First flight: early 1917
Dr Hugo Junkers was one of the first aircraft manufacturers to make extensive use of metal for aircraft construction, often employing it not only for the airframe but for the outer skin as well. In addition to a number of all-metal monoplanes, the Junkers company produced during 1914-18 a biplane, the J.I, whose metal construction gave it excellent protection from ground fire during low-flying patrol and support missions over forward battle areas.

Opposite page:
Top: British companies experimented with several monocoque and semi-monocoque designs, like this Sopwith Snark triplane. Production continued to be centred on simple fabric-covered wooden 'box' structures that could be built in huge quantities by relatively unskilled persons

Bottom: Very different from the wartime assembly lines was the Filton Erecting Hall of the British and Colonial (later Bristol) Aeroplane Company in early 1911. Its products were individually built, to a variety of designs. The aircraft in the foreground was designed by George Challenger and Archibald Low. First monoplane attempted by the company, it failed to fly

This page, top to bottom:
Women entered the aircraft industry in large numbers as more and more men were called up for the armed forces. These ladies are working on a Sopwith Salamander ground-attack fighter

Yet another contrast with the unhurried pre-war era is provided by this picture of work in progress on the very successful Prier monoplanes built at Filton in 1911

Women cutting fabric and stitching it on control surfaces at Sopwith's Ham works in 1918

Although the wartime urgency no longer applied when this photograph was taken at Ham in December 1918, the rows of aero-engines awaiting installation gives an idea of the extent to which the industry had grown in a few years

Birthplace of the 'Fokker Scourge'. The rapid production of several hundred monoplanes armed with synchronised machine-guns enabled Germany to almost shoot the Allied air forces from the skies over France in 1915-16

THE *Beginning* OF THE *Airlines*

The airlines of the world now carry hundreds of millions of passengers a year. Scheduled air services span the world, and at most major airports airliners have to queue to take off and be stacked while awaiting their turn to land. With this volume of air transport now commonplace, it is hard for many to realise that—if one excepts the early Zeppelin services of Delag and the brief activities of the St Petersburg-Tampa Airboat Line—it is only just over 50 years ago that regular scheduled air transport came into being.

The year when it all began was 1919, when the foundations of British, French and German air transport were laid and when Switzerland pioneered a military air mail and a short-lived passenger service.

British air transport developed from the far-sightedness of George Holt Thomas, who founded Aircraft Transport and Travel as early as 5 October 1916, and from the requirements for military air services following the ending of the war.

Cross-Channel air services were begun in December 1918 when the Royal Air Force provided transport between London and Paris for members of HM Government attending the Peace Conference, and regular London-Paris passenger and mail services were started by No 1 (Communication) Squadron, RAF, on 10 January 1919. These services continued until September 1919, by which time 749 flights had been made with 91 per cent regularity, and 934 passengers and 1,008 bags of mail had been carried. Some of the men taking part in these operations were destined to play an important role in developing commercial air transport, and a few of the aircraft passed to the first British civil airlines.

In February 1919 a Folkestone-Ghent parcel service began. This was to carry urgently-needed food and clothing to areas of Belgium which were suffering acute shortage. The service was flown by military D.H.9s with RAF pilots, but responsibility for the organisation was in the hands of Aircraft Transport and Travel and the company's name appeared on stickers on the aircraft.

Civil flying in Britain was allowed from 1 May 1919, and a number of special transport flights took place on that and subsequent days, but no regular services resulted. Then, on 24 May, Avro Civil Aviation Service began operation of the first United Kingdom domestic air service when it started a daily Manchester-Southport-Blackpool service using Avro 504 and 536 single-engined biplanes. This operation continued, unsubsidised, for 18 weeks and completed 194 of the 222 flights that were scheduled.

A most important date in British air transport history is 25 August 1919, for on that day regular daily scheduled international commercial air services began. Again, the operator was Aircraft Transport and Travel, and the route was that between London and Paris. The scheduled departure time from Hounslow Aerodrome, near the present Heathrow, and from Le Bourget was 12.30—which was to remain a basic and popular take-off time for British services over the route until shortly before the second World War.

On the great day the de Havilland 16 K-130, flown by Major Cyril Patteson and carrying four passengers, was airborne from Hounslow at 12.40, while a D.H.9, flown by Lieut J McMullin and carrying parcels, took off from Le Bourget at 12.30. Their flight times were respectively 2 hr 25 min and 2 hr 10 min. On that same day Lieut E H Lawford, with one passenger and goods, had left Hounslow for Paris at 09.05 in the D.H.4A G-EAJC, a flight whose purpose has never been explained although it has frequently, but wrongly, been described as the first of AT and T's scheduled services. One explanation is that it may have been a 'positioning' flight for the later service.

On 25 August 1919, Handley Page Transport flew an O/7 twin-engined aircraft to Paris; but that company's regular London-Paris services did not begin until 2 September, the pilot of the first scheduled flight being Lieut-Col W Sholto Douglas—later

Above: This seven-passenger Handley Page O/400 was typical of the converted bombers used on early airline services between Britain and the Continent in 1919-20

Below: Designed as a genuine six-passenger airliner immediately after the first World War, the German Sablatnig P III remained in service for many years. This is one of nine or ten acquired by Deutsche Luft Hansa when it began operations in 1926

Bottom: One of the first Sablatnigs used for passenger-carrying, this P I was evolved from the N I two-seat night bomber. As in most airliners of the period, the pilot sat in the open, but the four passengers had an enclosed, heated and lighted cabin.

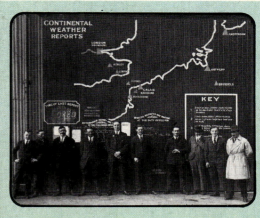

Left: French counterpart to the D.H.4A was the Breguet 14T2 Salon, with enclosed cabin for two or three passengers. Based on the wartime Breguet 14 reconnaissance-bomber, this one was used by Cie des Messageries Aeriennes, a predecessor of Air France

Top right: This chart at Hounslow represented one of the first attempts to provide the airlines with a meteorological service

Left: This converted AEG J.II marked a real step forward in passenger amenities, having not only an enclosed two-seat cabin in the former gunner's position but a large door and step for more elegant entry

Below: In aviation's first decade mail and freight—particularly newspapers—were often the most profitable and regular payloads. The aircraft is an LVG C.VI of Deutsche Luft-Reederei

Lord Douglas of Kirtleside and chairman of British European Airways. By the end of September, Handley Page Transport had opened a thrice-weekly London-Brussels service and on 11 October introduced the first airline meals—lunch baskets costing 3 shillings.

The third pioneer British airline made its appearance on 13 October 1919, when the shipowners S Instone and Company began a private air service between Cardiff and Paris, via London. This was intended to carry company staff and documents, but in February 1920 the operation became a public service between London and Paris. At the end of 1921, what had been the company's Aerial Transport Department became The Instone Air Line.

AT and T ceased operation in December 1920, to be succeeded by The Daimler Airway in 1922; and Daimler, Instone and Handley Page Transport became three of the four constituents of Imperial Airways in 1924. Imperial Airways, with the later British Airways, became BOAC, and thus the present corporation can trace its ancestry directly back to the very beginning of commercial air transport.

North Sea Aerial Navigation Company and British Aerial Transport both operated a few scheduled services in 1919, but these soon ceased and played no real part in the development of British air transport.

France claims to have begun Paris-London air services on 8 February 1919, when a twin-engined Farman Goliath flew from Paris to Kenley; but this was a special flight with eleven military passengers and thus was neither commercial nor regular and does not qualify as a service. But Farman Line did begin a weekly Paris-Brussels service at the end of March 1919 and Cie des Messageries Aériennes (CMA) opened a Paris-Lille goods service in April 1919.

Working eventually in pool with Handley Page Transport, CMA began Paris-London services on 16 September 1919, using single-engined Breguet 14s, and three days later the first French-operated London-Paris service was flown.

Immediately after the first World War, Latécoère began development of what was to become the famous French air service across the South Atlantic to South America. Proving flights began at the end of 1918; an experimental mail service had been established between Toulouse and Rabat and Casablanca by July 1919, and regular operation as far as Casablanca began in 1920. By June 1925, operations were undertaken as far as Dakar. These and other pioneer French air transport operations were to be consolidated in Air France, which was founded in October 1933.

In Germany, the first air services were operated in February 1919 when Deutsche Luft-Reederei began regular operation between Berlin and Weimar, using mostly A.E.G. and L.V.G. single-engined biplanes. In the following month the Junkers company started a Dessau-Weimar service with a modified J 10 all-metal monoplane (believed to have been the first air service ever operated by an all-metal aeroplane).

Hamburg and Berlin were connected by air services that March, and numerous German domestic air services were inaugurated during 1919, including that by Rumpler-Luftverkehr over the Augsburg-Munich-Nuremberg-Leipzig-Berlin route. Eventual mergers of the surviving companies led, in 1926, to the founding of Deutsche Luft Hansa, predecessor of the present Lufthansa.

The original Berlin-Weimar service of February 1919 can almost certainly be claimed as the world's first sustained daily passenger air service, while AT and T's London-Paris operation was the first sustained daily international service.

In Switzerland, on 8 January 1919, an experimental military mail service was opened between Zürich and Berne, with Haefeli DH-3 biplanes. The service was extended to Lausanne on 1 February. Public mail was carried from 5 May and passengers from June, but the service was closed at the end of October and not re-opened.

SNETA, the predecessor of Sabena, and KLM were both founded during 1919, but neither organisation undertook any operations during that year.

During 1919, in the United States the first sectors of the transcontinental air mail service were opened by the US Post Office, and Eddie Hubbard began an experimental mail service between Seattle and Vancouver; but it was to be several years before any United States company established sustained passenger air services.

The Junkers F.13 was one of the first specially-designed airliners and was notable for its all-metal cantilever monoplane construction in an age of wooden biplanes. With a comfortably-furnished cabin for four passengers, it remained in production from 1919 to 1932, a total of 322 being built

This airliner conversion of the Blackburn Kangaroo bomber was used on a scheduled service between Hounslow, Leeds and Amsterdam in 1919. Seven passengers travelled in the main cabin, with an eighth in solitary confinement in the nose

Centre: About six passengers were carried in the cabin of this converted Friedrichshafen G.IIIa bomber, which was powered by two 260 hp Mercedes D.IVa engines

Above: Predecessor of the commercial flying-boat was this three-passenger cabin version of the Friedrichshafen FF 49 seaplane. Its operator was Luft-Fahrzeug GmbH, and this company was responsible for the conversion

Below: Before the airlines began operation, the first sustained international passenger services had been flown by the Royal Air Force. Using converted bombers like this D.H.4A, No 2 Communications Squadron carried 934 passengers and 1,008 bags of mail between London and Paris in January–September 1919, mainly in connection with the Peace Conference at Versailles

FRIEDRICHSHAFEN FF49

Powered by: One 220 hp Benz Bz.IV six-cylinder in-line engine, driving a two-blade propeller of approx 9 ft 10 in (3.00 m) diameter
Wing span: 55 ft 9¼ in (17.00 m)
Length: 38 ft 2⅜ in (11.65 m)
Wing area: 766 sq ft (71.16 m²)
Gross weight: approx 4,718 lb (2,140 kg)
Cruising speed: approx 84 mph (135 km/h)
Max endurance: 6 hr
Accommodation: Crew of 1 and 3 passengers
First flight: May 1917

The Friedrichshafen FF49 was produced originally as a two-seat seaplane for patrol and reconnaissance duties with the German Naval Air Service in 1917-18. About 260 were built, and when the war was over several were modified to carry three or five passengers in an enclosed cabin behind the pilot's open cockpit. They were operated on some of the first regular airline services to be flown in Germany after the war.

DE HAVILLAND D.H.4A

Powered by: One 350 hp Rolls-Royce Eagle VIII twelve-cylinder. Vee-type engine, driving a four-blade propeller of 9 ft 0 in (2.74 m) diameter
Wing span: 42 ft 4⅝ in (12.92 m)
Length: 30 ft 6 in (9.30 m)
Wing area: 434 sq ft (40.32 m²)
Gross weight: 3,720 lb (1,687 kg)
Max speed: 121 mph (195 km/h)
Accommodation: Crew of 1 and 2 passengers
First flight: 1919

The D.H.4, designed in 1916 as a day bomber by Capt Geoffrey de Havilland, saw widespread service with the RFC, RNAS and RAF during the second half of the first World War. After the Armistice a small number were modified to have an enclosed two-passenger cabin in the rear fuselage, and to one of these aircraft went the distinction of inaugurating, on 25 August 1919, the first regular scheduled commercial air service from Britain.

THE FIRST OF
THE MANY

The routes followed by the Curtiss NC-4 flying-boat, Sopwith Atlantic, Alcock and Brown's Vimy and the airship R.34 during their pioneer trans-Atlantic flights in 1919

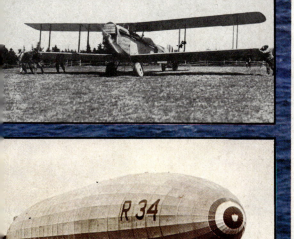

Below: The Curtiss NC-4, first aircraft to cross the Atlantic, in May 1919. Too late for use in World War 1, the NC flying-boats were each powered by four 400 hp Liberty engines, spanned 126 ft (38.4 m) and carried a crew of six in military trim

The first World War marked the breakthrough for aviation. Before 1914, aeroplanes were trial-and-error contraptions with poor reliability, but by 1918 they could be designed to meet a performance specification and made reliable enough for regular and continuous operation.

So it is not surprising that the more adventurous pioneers realised that, with the war over, it was now possible to fly anywhere. The years 1919 and 1920 were particularly noteworthy for great international first flights—across the Atlantic, down to Australia, and to South Africa.

The North Atlantic was the big lure, linking the Old World with the New. The *Daily Mail* newspaper had offered, as early

as 1913, a £10,000 prize for the first direct crossing of the North Atlantic, and this was revived when hostilities ended. Attention focussed on Newfoundland, where no fewer than 12 different aircraft were preparing simultaneously to attempt the first crossing to Europe. Bad weather delayed them all; but eventually, early in May 1919, a Sopwith Atlantic with Harry Hawker and Lt Cdr Mackenzie Grieve as crew, took off. They were not heard of for a week and were presumed dead. In fact, they had been forced down by overheating of their engine and had been picked up by a ship with no radio. A Martinsyde made its attempt on the same day as the Sopwith, but crashed on take-off.

The next to try were three American Navy-Curtiss flying-boats which departed from Trepassey Bay, Newfoundland, on 16 May. Two ended in the water, but the NC-4 flew on to Lisbon and Plymouth, having taken 15 days for the complete journey. Though this was the first air crossing from America to Europe, it was not strictly via the North Atlantic and it was not a direct (ie, non-stop) flight.

There were no more attempts until 14 June, when a Vickers Vimy piloted by Captain John Alcock and navigated by Lieutenant Arthur Whitten Brown left St John's, Newfoundland, and turned east across the Atlantic. Heavily loaded with fuel, the Vimy climbed slowly. It crossed the Newfoundland coast at 4.28 pm GMT at 1,200 ft (366 m). Much of the subsequent journey was either between cloud layers or seeking cloud-free altitudes. This made it difficult to fix the aircraft's position with accuracy, and it was not until after midnight that Brown was able to locate stars to confirm where the Vimy was.

After they had been in the air for nearly 11 hours they suddenly and unexpectedly ran into a thick bank of cloud. With no external visual references, Alcock was unable to orientate himself. From the rudimentary instruments it was not possible to regain control and the Vimy stalled and went into a spin, falling fast towards the invisible sea. Abruptly, below 500 ft (152 m), the cloud ended and they saw the sea, appearing to stand up alongside them because of the angle at which the aircraft was tilted. Only then was Alcock able to resume control and get the Vimy back on an even keel.

An hour later they met snow, hail and sleet. From time to time Brown had to climb out of the cockpit on to the top of the fuselage to wipe ice from the dial of the vital petrol flow gauge. There was, as he remarked later, scarcely any danger so long as Alcock kept the machine level.

At 8.15 am, while eating their sandwich breakfast at a height of 250 ft (76 m) above the waves, they passed over two tiny isles. Ten minutes later they crossed the Irish coast; the wireless masts at Clifden loomed ahead, giving them a clue to their location.

The clouds were still very low and there was a danger of running into hills if they flew on across Ireland in those conditions, so Alcock decided to land. The field he chose turned out to be a bog, and the aircraft tipped on to its nose at the end of its landing run, though with no injury to the two men and with little structural damage.

They landed at 8.40 am after being in the air for 16 hr 27 min, at an average speed of just over 121 mph (195 km/h) over 1,890 miles (3,032 km).

They were taken to London for a hero's welcome, receiving the £10,000 *Daily Mail* prize from Winston Churchill and later being knighted by King George V. Their Vimy is now housed in the Science Museum in London.

It was five years before another aeroplane crossed the North Atlantic, but there was one more crossing of the ocean by air in that same year—by the airship R34, which completed a two-way Atlantic flight just over a fortnight after Alcock and Brown.

The R34's design was based on that of the German L33 class of airships, one of which had been captured by the British in 1916. Two machines were built, R33 and R34, the latter being laid down in December 1917 and completed in March 1919.

She started her trans-Atlantic journey only four months later, departing from East Fortune, Scotland, in the early hours

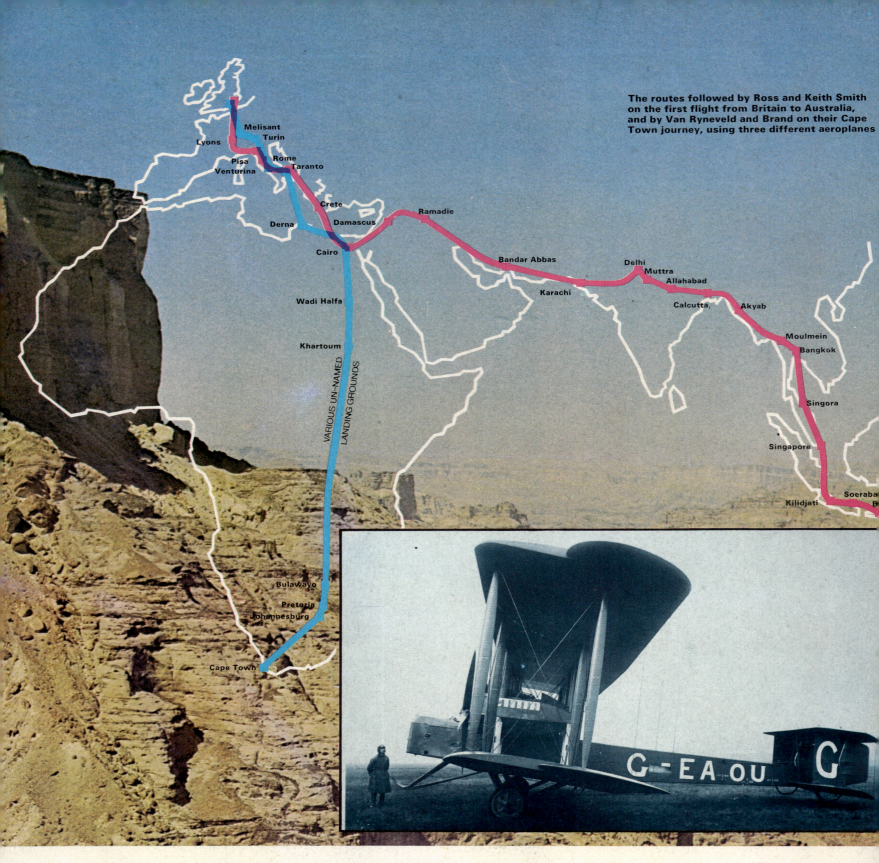

The routes followed by Ross and Keith Smith on the first flight from Britain to Australia, and by Van Ryneveld and Brand on their Cape Town journey, using three different aeroplanes

of 2 July 1919. Her crew of 30, headed by Major G H Scott, with their supplies and fuel, gave her a weight just one ton short of her all-up lift of 60 tons. After four and a half days (108 hours) she landed at Roosevelt Field, Mineola, Long Island, one of her officers parachuting to the ground before mooring in order to direct the ground party. R34 left for England on 10 July and landed at Pulham, Norfolk, 75 hours later, on 13 July.

The prize for the first crossing of the Atlantic by air was matched by a £10,000 contest sponsored by the Australian Government for the first flight from England to Australia, to be completed within a period of 30 days. Six teams entered, and within a space of 10 weeks all had started the 11,130-mile (17,912-km) journey. Only two completed the course, the prize being won by the first of these, brothers Ross and

Keith Smith in a Vickers Vimy, accompanied by two mechanics, J M Bennett and W H Shiers. They had left England on 12 November.

Ross, the younger of the two brothers, had a notable war record and had done his service with the Australian Flying Corps. Keith, who acted as co-pilot and navigator, had been with the Royal Flying Corps in Europe. The mechanics were both Australian servicemen.

The flight was remarkable for the amount of bad weather encountered. Across the Mediterranean, through the Middle East, and in south-east Asia, storms battered the Vimy day after day. The planned daily mileage of 600 (966 km) was brought down to 400 (644 km) and even to below 300 (483 km) on some days. In some places the Vimy was bogged down, in others it scraped over tree-tops as it struggled to

climb out of inadequate airfields; but it battled on and finally reached Darwin 28 days after it started from Hounslow Heath —and just 52 hours inside the time limit. It landed at Fanny Bay, Darwin on 10 December 1919.

Ross had said originally that he would fly to his home town of Adelaide, and although the Vimy was beginning to show the effects of its hammering by major defects requiring extensive repairs, he was determined to press on. Although the journey across the Australian continent was marred by a succession of breakdowns, Ross and Keith Smith were finally greeted by their parents at Adelaide on 23 March. On the way they set the record of the first flight from Melbourne (where they had been presented with their £10,000 cheque) to Adelaide.

At their journey's end, the Vimy was

VICKERS VIMY

Powered by: Two 360 hp Rolls-Royce Eagle VIII twelve-cylinder Vee-type engines, each driving a four-blade propeller of 10 ft 6 in (3.20 m) diameter
Wing span: 68 ft 0 in (20.73 m)
Length: 43 ft 6½ in (13.27 m)
Wing area: 1,330 sq ft (123.56 m²)
Gross weight (bomber): 12,500 lb (5,670 kg)
Max speed: 103 mph (166 km/h) at S/L
Max range (bomber): 1,880 miles (3,025 km); (trans-Atlantic Vimy): 2,440 miles (3,927 km)
Accommodation: Crew of 2
First flight (bomber): 30 November 1917
The Vimy flown by Alcock and Brown from St John's, Newfoundland, to Clifden, Co Galway, on 14/15 June 1919 was modified from a standard production machine, stripped of its military equipment and carrying 865 Imp gallons (3,932 litres) of fuel instead of the normal 516 gallons (2,346 litres). It completed the 1,890-mile (3,032-km) non-stop trip, despite appalling weather and icing difficulties, in 16 hr 27 min.

NAVY-CURTISS NC-4

Powered by: Four 400 hp Liberty 12 twelve-cylinder Vee-type engines (two mounted back-to-back in central nacelle and two singly), each driving a two-blade wooden propeller
Wing span: 126 ft 0 in (38.40 m)
Length: 68 ft 3½ in (20.85 m)
Wing area: 2,380 sq ft (221.11 m²)
Gross weight: 28,500 lb (12,925 kg)
Max speed: 91 mph (146 km/h)
Accommodation: Crew of 5
First flight: 30 April 1919

Four NC (Navy-Curtiss) flying-boats were built, as the result of collaboration between Glenn Curtiss and the US Navy, originally for the purpose of attacking enemy U-boats from the air. The first aircraft (NC-1) did not fly until October 1918, and so the type was too late for war service, but the fourth (NC-4) made aviation history by completing a four-stage crossing of the North Atlantic from Newfoundland to Plymouth between 16-31 May 1919.

Ross Smith with the Vimy used for the flight to Australia. Its registration was said, with grim humour, to stand for 'God 'elp All Of Us'

handed over to the nation; it is now on permanent display at Adelaide airport. Both brothers were knighted for their endeavours, but Ross Smith was killed in 1922, while piloting a Vickers amphibian in which he proposed to attempt a round-the-world flight.

The air link between London and the Cape—UK to South Africa—was another that had long challenged aviators. Many attempts had been made, and significant parts of the route had been flown, though an end-to-end journey was still to be accomplished.

In December 1919 the British Air Ministry announced that surveys had been completed by the RAF and a string of airfields established on the African route; it was now open to aviators. Less than a month later a Vickers Vimy, similar to those flown by Alcock and Brown and by Ross and Keith Smith, set out from England for the Cape. Piloted by Captains S Cockerell and F C Broome, with Dr Chalmers Mitchell, Secretary of the Zoological Society, it got as far as Tabora in Tanganyika before crashing, fortunately without injury to its occupants.

The South African Government had agreed to sponsor the attempt of two South African pilots, Lt Col Pierre van Ryneveld and Sqn Ldr Quintin Brand. They set out from Brooklands aerodrome on 4 February 1920 in yet another Vickers Vimy, named *Silver Queen*. Despite a fierce battle with the weather in an 11-hour crossing of the Mediterranean, the flight was more or less without incident until they reached Wadi Halfa, where an emergency landing in darkness ended with the aircraft as a complete write-off. The South African Government was no more daunted than the pilots; *Silver Queen II* was procured, and the journey was resumed 11 days later.

But *Silver Queen II* was no luckier than her predecessor and crashed 4,000 miles (6,440 km) further on at Bulawayo, Southern Rhodesia. Again coming to the rescue, the South African Government hastily provided a D.H.9 from surplus war stores, named it *Voortrekker*, and had it flown to Bulawayo and handed over to the two determined pilots. The journey was resumed on 17 March, and the airmen were greeted by enthusiastic crowds at Wynberg aerodrome, Cape Town, three days later.

Their flight of 45 days marked the end of the sense of isolation that had hung over the Europeans of South Africa. Even so,

it was 11 more years before scheduled airline services could link South Africa with Europe, such were the difficulties to be overcome on the 7,000-mile (11,265-km) route. Van Ryneveld and Brand, like Alcock and Brown and the Smith brothers before them, were knighted for their heroic flight, and received £5,000 from their government.

OPENING UP

Although today United States airlines carry about half of all the world's air passengers, apart from those of the Soviet Union and China, in the early days of air transport the United States lagged far behind Europe. Britain, France, Germany, the Netherlands and Scandinavia all had well-developed airline operations soon after the ending of the 1914-18 war.

As already described in *History of Aviation*, the British company Aircraft Transport and Travel operated the first sustained daily international scheduled services, which began over the London-Paris route on 25 August 1919; soon after this, French airlines and Handley Page Transport were working the same route.

AT and T opened services to Amsterdam, in conjunction with KLM, in May 1920, but at the end of the year it ceased all operations because of financial difficulties. Handley Page Transport and Instone continued to struggle against subsidised foreign competition, but they too had to suspend operations early in 1921 until granted a temporary subsidy. In April 1922 Daimler Airway began London-Paris services, and by March 1924 the three surviving British airlines operating services to the Continent had a route system serving Paris, Brussels, Cologne, Amsterdam, Berlin, Basle and Zürich. British Marine Air Navigation was operating a flying-boat service between Southampton and Guernsey.

Because of the uneconomic aircraft, poor traffic, bad weather and flying restricted mainly to daylight, among other things, the pioneer airlines suffered severe financial difficulties. Various forms of government subsidy were tried, but eventually it was decided to merge the four companies into a subsidised national airline and this came into being on 31 March 1924 as Imperial Airways. The new airline took over most of the former European routes, excluding that to Berlin, but its main task was the establishment of trunk services linking the United Kingdom with British territories overseas.

Priority was given to the opening of a route between England and India, but it was not until 1929 that this was achieved, although a survey flight between London and Delhi was made by an Imperial Airways de Havilland Hercules in December 1926-January 1927.

The first stage in developing what are now BOAC's round-the-world routes was the opening, on 7 January 1927, of a service between Basra and Cairo via Baghdad and

Gaza, and this service provided a connection with P & O mail ships linking Port Said and Marseilles. The first eastbound service left Cairo on 12 January.

Although this was the first part of Britain's overseas trunk air route system to be worked by a commercial operator, it actually took over the Cairo-Baghdad sector from the Royal Air Force which had flown the famous 'Desert Air Mail' since June 1921.

In 1929 the Cairo-Baghdad-Basra route was extended at each end to provide a through service between London and Karachi, although passengers had to travel by train over the Basle-Genoa sector. By December 1934 the entire route to Australia was opened for mail, with passengers being carried from April 1935. Second priority was given to the African route, which was opened in stages from February 1931, with Cape Town being served from January 1932.

It is of interest to recall that at the time these trunk routes were being pioneered it was by no means certain whether the aeroplane or the airship would become established as the principal long-haul air transport vehicle; but the issue was settled when the airship R101 crashed and was destroyed on its first flight to India in 1930.

During the 1920s an extensive network of European air routes was established, and two of these may, in the context of the period, be regarded as trunk routes. In France, Compagnie Franco-Roumaine de Navigation Aérienne (later succeeded by CIDNA) was founded in 1920; by October that year it had established services between Paris and Prague. Warsaw was reached by April 1921, Budapest by May 1922, Belgrade and Bucharest in September of that year, and Constantinople (now Istanbul) in the following month. Night services were operated over some sectors as early as 1923. The other trunk route was that opened in May 1922 by the joint Soviet-German airline Deruluft, between Königsberg and

Moscow via Kowno and Smolensk.

Most of the European services were operated only in daylight, and many were suspended during the winter. Although a few multi-engined aircraft were employed, the majority were single-engined and most had accommodation for fewer than a dozen passengers. Navigational aids were sparse, but regularity was surprisingly high due to exceptional standards of airmanship. Forced landings were frequent, but low landing speeds and short ground runs ensured that most such events were no more than incidents.

Another overseas venture by a European airline in the early 1920s was the establishment of flying-boat services in the Belgian Congo by SNETA. These were the first air services in Equatorial Africa. They began in July 1920, with operations between Léopoldville (Kinshasa) and N'Gombé, and by July 1921 covered the entire Congo River route between Léopoldville and Stanleyville. Although the Congo River services ceased in June 1922, SNETA's successor, Sabena, was to develop a large Congo network and link it with Europe.

It was also in the 1920s that the foundations were laid for the present great system of Australian air services. In December 1921 West Australia Airways began a Geraldton-

THE AIRWAYS

Aircraft Transport & Travel took good care of passengers who flew in its D.H.9Bs in 1919-20. They were provided with thick coats, helmets, goggles and gloves to keep out the cold in the open cockpit. Life-jackets, and a hot water bottle in really cold weather, completed a kit that must have presented problems when ladies climbed a wooden step-ladder and squeezed into the cramped fuselage

Opposite page, left: One of the three six-passenger Supermarine Sea Eagle amphibians operated on the Woolston-Cherbourg and Channel Islands services of the British Marine Air Navigation Co in 1923-24. When this company was merged into Imperial Airways, two of the Sea Eagles were taken over and used by Britain's new 'flag carrier'

Right, top to bottom:
The Dutch airline KLM began operations by chartering D.H.9Bs from A T & T for a London-Amsterdam service. By 1926, it was flying locally-built Fokker F.VII monoplanes like this, with a special compartment for baggage between the engine and the passenger cabin

The pioneer Belgian airline SNETA helped to form a company named Ligne Aérienne du Roi Albert (LARA) to operate a service between Kinshasa and Stanleyville in the Congo, in 1920-22. Using three-seat Levy Lepen flying-boats, LARA carried 95 passengers and 4,000 lb (2,000 kg) of mail before the operation was suspended

Forced landings were frequent in the early years of airline flying, leading to scenes such as this. G-EALX was a seven-passenger Handley Page O/400, built as a bomber and converted for use on the Continental services of Handley Page Air Transport

An inscription on the side reminded passengers in the Instone Air Line D.H.4A G-EAMU that it had won the first King's Cup Air Race on 8-9 September 1922, at a speed of 123 mph (198 km/h)

Before it was given this immaculate livery as G-EAAE, this O/400 was used for Handley Page Air Transport's first service, on 4 May 1919. The pilot was Lt Col W F Sholto Douglas (later Lord Douglas of Kirtleside, Chairman of BEA). Ten passengers were carried from Cricklewood, London, to Manchester

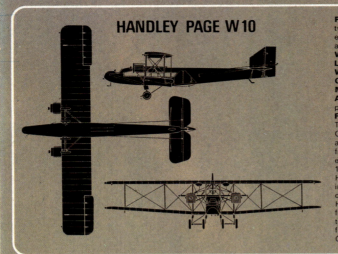

HANDLEY PAGE W 10

Powered by: Two 450 hp Napier Lion twelve-cylinder water-cooled engines, each driving a four-blade propeller of approx 10 ft 6 in (3.20 m) diameter
Wing span: 75 ft 0 in (22.86 m)
Length: 59 ft 4 in (18.08 m)
Wing area: 1,456 sq ft (135.26 m²)
Gross weight: 13,780 lb (6,250 kg)
Max speed: 112 mph (180 km/h) at S/L
Accommodation: Crew of 2 and 14 passengers
First flight: 10 February 1926
To replace the converted O/100 and O/400 bombers used for its early post-war airline services, Handley Page produced its first specialised transport, the twin-engined W 8, which entered service in 1921. Later versions, the W 8e and W 8f Hamilton, had a third engine in the nose to improve their safety and reliability. This concept was developed via the W 9a Hampstead of 1925; but the W 10, built for Imperial Airways a year later, reverted to a twin-engined layout—to its detriment, for two of the four built crashed in the Channel following engine failure.

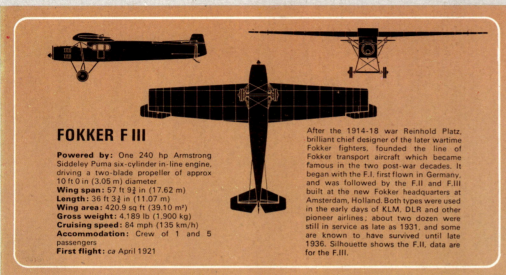

FOKKER F III

Powered by: One 240 hp Armstrong Siddeley Puma six-cylinder in-line engine, driving a two-blade propeller of approx 10 ft 0 in (3.05 m) diameter
Wing span: 57 ft 9¾ in (17.62 m)
Length: 36 ft 3¼ in (11.07 m)
Wing area: 420.9 sq ft (39.10 m²)
Gross weight: 4,189 lb (1,900 kg)
Cruising speed: 84 mph (135 km/h)
Accommodation: Crew of 1 and 5 passengers
First flight: ca April 1921

After the 1914-18 war Reinhold Platz, brilliant chief designer of the later wartime Fokker fighters, founded the line of Fokker transport aircraft which became famous in the two post-war decades. It began with the F.I, first flown in Germany, and was followed by the F.II and F.III built at the new Fokker headquarters at Amsterdam, Holland. Both types were used in the early days of KLM, DLR and other pioneer airlines; about two dozen were still in service as late as 1931, and some are known to have survived until late 1936. Silhouette shows the F.II, data are for the F.III.

Derby mail service and in November 1922 QANTAS began passenger services between Charleville and Cloncurry. Both companies used war-surplus single-engined biplanes.

In South America, the first short-lived airline was established in French Guiana in 1919; but one of great importance was SCADTA, in Colombia, which was founded in 1919 and began operations with a fleet of Junkers F 13 seaplanes in 1921. This company, which became Avianca, enables the present airline to make the justified claim that it is the oldest in the Americas.

In the United States the main consideration was given to carriage of mail, rather than passengers, by air, and the primary aim was the creation of a transcontinental mail service with all initial operations actually undertaken by the Post Office.

On 15 May 1918, a Washington-Philadelphia-New York mail service was begun and this continued, as an isolated operation, until the end of May 1921. Exactly a year after the inauguration of the Washington-New York service, the first sector of the transcontinental route was

opened, between Chicago and Cleveland, and on 1 July 1919 this was extended to New York. The short sector between San Francisco and Sacramento was opened on 31 July 1919, and the Chicago-Omaha portion came into being on 15 May 1920. The transcontinental air mail route was completed with the opening of the Omaha-Sacramento sector on 8 September 1920, but because flying was restricted to daylight some sections were worked by train. The US Post Office also opened, in 1920, two short-lived spur mail routes, Chicago-St Louis and Chicago-Minneapolis/St Paul.

In February 1921 experimental day and night flights were made over the entire transcontinental route, with the San Francisco-New York journey taking 33 hr 20 min. In order to speed up the service a lighted airway was installed between Chicago and Cheyenne in 1923, and on 1 July 1924 regular night flying was introduced over the entire route.

The Post Office used a wide assortment of aircraft, but most of the work was undertaken by US-built D.H.4 single-engined open-cockpit biplanes.

In 1926 private airlines began to operate mail services under contract to the Post Office and at least 11 routes were being flown by the end of the year, with passengers being carried on some of them. Then in 1927 Boeing Air Transport was awarded the mail contract for the San Francisco-Salt Lake City-Omaha-Chicago route, which was worked from 1 July 1927 with Boeing 40s and carried some passengers. At that time the Chicago-New York sector mails were taken by train, but from 1 September 1927 National Air Transport worked the Chicago-New York sector and the coast-to-coast time was cut to 32 hr.

From those first commercial mail services of 1926 and 1927 evolved some of today's largest airlines, including United Air Lines (as the successor to Boeing Air Transport and others), TWA, Western Airlines and Northwest Orient Airlines. In addition, the modern Boeing family of jet airliners stems from the early experience gained by Boeing in designing aircraft for the mail routes and the operation of those pioneer biplanes.

WINGS OVER

Dividing the Old World from the New, the Atlantic Ocean has always been a barrier to trade between Europe and the Americas, and the commercial importance of an aerial link was realised long before it became a practical possibility. A flurry of activity in 1919 proved that the Atlantic could be conquered, but many years were to pass before it was tamed; the pioneer flights of Read (first crossing), Alcock and Brown (first non-stop crossing) and Scott (first crossings by airship) were a far cry from commercial operations which could offer the required degree of reliability with an economic payload.

During the 'twenties and 'thirties, many ingenious solutions were advanced to the problem of crossing 2,000 miles (3,220 km) of water, frequently in adverse wind and weather and with inadequate navigational aids. The route across the South Atlantic was a little easier than that farther north. From Dakar, in Senegal, to Natal, in Brazil, the distance was just under 1,900 miles (3,050 km), the weather was usually good and, in an emergency, the island of Fernando de Noronha, 300 miles (480 km) off the Brazilian coast, could be used for refuelling. The enterprise of French and German pioneers led to the establishment of air routes across the South Atlantic within a decade of the first Atlantic crossings—but not before the North Atlantic had witnessed another epic flight which, in public acclaim, outdid even the achievement of Alcock and Brown.

The first Atlantic crossings had, not unnaturally, been concerned with little more than getting an aeroplane and its crew across the shortest distance of water separating Europe and America. It was not long, however, before attention was turned to linking centres of population further inland, and as early as 1920 a prize of $25,000 had been offered for the first non-stop flight between Paris and New York (in either direction).

The first attempt to cross the Atlantic from east to west, against the prevailing westerly winds, was made in 1924, when three Douglas Cruisers left Brough, in Yorkshire, and two succeeded in reaching Labrador in stages, with lengthy intervening stops. Further attempts in each direction during 1927 took the lives of the Americans Davis and Wooster, the Frenchmen Nungesser and Coli, and two crew members of the Frenchman Fonck. Then, with little prior publicity, the young American Charles Lindbergh arrived in Paris on 21 May 1927, at the end of a 33½-hour, 3,610-mile (5,810-km) flight from New York. His was the first non-stop solo flight, and the longest trans-

HE ATLANTIC

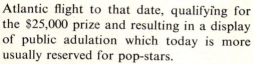

Atlantic flight to that date, qualifying for the $25,000 prize and resulting in a display of public adulation which today is more usually reserved for pop-stars.

Lindbergh, 25 years of age and a pilot by profession, had a natural flair for flying and above-average ability as a navigator. He needed both in good measure through the long watches of the moonless night over the Atlantic, as he battled through icing levels, unknown winds and poor visibility. His flight not only demonstrated great personal skill and courage, but also vindicated his faith in the single 237 hp Wright Whirlwind engine which powered the specially-built Ryan NYP (New York-Paris) monoplane *Spirit of St Louis*. Apart from the engine and rudimentary cockpit, from which the only forward view could be obtained through a periscope, the NYP was little more than a flying fuel tank, containing 450 US gallons (1,705 litres) in the fuselage and wings.

Like most other Atlantic fliers of the period, Lindbergh made his take-off with the aeroplane loaded to a weight far above normal; the ability of the aeroplane to leave the ground at this weight in the length of runway available was unknown until the start of the flight. After a hazardous but successful take-off, Lindbergh flew north from Long Island to cross Newfoundland before setting course eastwards. His land-fall, 28 hours after take-off, was only three miles (5 km) off course over the Irish coast, and the remainder of the flight, across the tip of Cornwall and on to Cherbourg and Paris, was uneventful.

Less than a year after Lindbergh, the Germans Köhl and von Hünefeld, to-gether with Fitzmaurice, an Irish Army Air Corps pilot, made the first non-stop crossing of the North Atlantic in the reverse direc-tion. Their aircraft was a Junkers W 33L. Other attempts in this period, however,

Top: Replica of Charles Lindbergh's *Spirit of St Louis,* **produced by conversion of a Ryan Brougham. In its original form, the Brougham was a four-seat cabin transport evolved from the trans-Atlantic NYP monoplane**

Bottom left: Charles Lindbergh with his wife, Anne, in 1930. They flew together on several of the airline surveys that Lindbergh made on behalf of Pan American. Best remembered of these surveys were flights made in a Lockheed Sirius in 1931-33, covering the North Pacific, North Atlantic and South Atlantic routes

Bottom centre: Those who saw the fuselage of the *Spirit of St Louis* **being towed from the Ryan Airlines factory, behind T Claude Ryan's open roadster, to the company's flying field could have had little idea that this was to become one of the most celebrated aeroplanes in history**

Bottom right: With Paris still 3,610 miles (5,810 km) and 33½ hours away, Charles Lindbergh takes off from Roosevelt Field, New York, on 20 May 1927

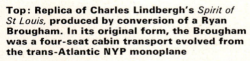

RYAN NYP 'SPIRIT OF ST. LOUIS'

Powered by: One 237 hp Wright J-5C Whirlwind nine-cylinder radial engine, driving a two-blade propeller
Wing span: 46 ft 0 in (14.02 m)
Length: 27 ft 8 in (8.43 m)
Wing area: 319 sq ft (29.64 m²)
Gross weight: 5,250 lb (2,381 kg)
Max speed: 124 mph (200 km/h) with trans-Atlantic fuel
Range: 4,650 miles (7,483 km)
Accommodation: Crew of 1
First flight: 28 April 1927

Charles Lindbergh's 33½-hour flight from New York to Paris was the 13th crossing of the Atlantic by air, and the fifth non-stop crossing; but it was the first between two great cities and the first to be achieved by a solo flier, and won for Lindbergh the $25,000 prize offered by New York hotelier Raymond Orteig. A fortnight later, the Bellanca Columbia which Lindbergh had first hoped to fly, piloted by Clarence D Chamberlin, also crossed the Atlantic successfully and flew 300 miles (483 km) further than Lindbergh, into Germany.

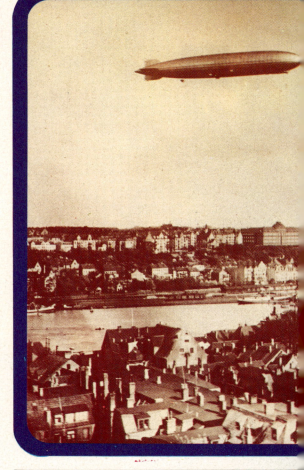

LZ 127 'GRAF ZEPPELIN'

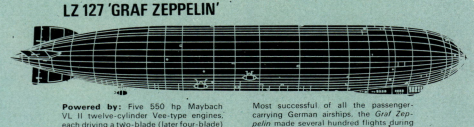

Powered by: Five 550 hp Maybach VL II twelve-cylinder Vee-type engines, each driving a two-blade (later four-blade) propeller
Total gas capacity: 3,708,040 cu ft (105,000 m³), including fuel gas
Length: 776 ft 3 in (236.6 m)
Max diameter: 100 ft 0 in (30.5 m)
Cruising speed: 71.5 mph (115 km/h)
Max endurance: 118 hours with payload of 29,568 lb (13,411 kg)
Accommodation: Crew of 45-50 and 20 passengers
First flight: 18 September 1928

Most successful of all the passenger-carrying German airships, the *Graf Zeppelin* made several hundred flights during the 1930s, of which well over 100 were across the South Atlantic between Friedrichshafen and Pernambuco. A typical year was 1935, when she made 82 trips carrying 1,429 passengers and 14 tons of mail and freight, and covering some 222,016 miles (357,300 km) in more than 3,500 flying hours. Instead of petrol, the *Graf Zeppelin's* engines burned a fuel gas called *Blaugas*, which accounted for about one-third of her total gas capacity; the main gas-bags were filled with hydrogen.

FAIREY III D

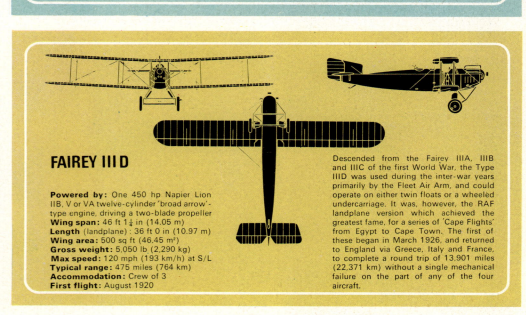

Powered by: One 450 hp Napier Lion IIB, V or VA twelve-cylinder 'broad arrow'-type engine, driving a two-blade propeller
Wing span: 46 ft 1½ in (14.05 m)
Length (landplane): 36 ft 0 in (10.97 m)
Wing area: 500 sq ft (46.45 m²)
Gross weight: 5,050 lb (2,290 kg)
Max speed: 120 mph (193 km/h) at S/L
Typical range: 475 miles (764 km)
Accommodation: Crew of 3
First flight: August 1920

Descended from the Fairey IIIA, IIIB and IIIC of the first World War, the Type IIID was used during the inter-war years primarily by the Fleet Air Arm, and could operate on either twin floats or a wheeled undercarriage. It was, however, the RAF landplane version which achieved the greatest fame, for a series of 'Cape Flights' from Egypt to Cape Town. The first of these began in March 1926, and returned to England via Greece, Italy and France, to complete a round trip of 13,901 miles (22,371 km) without a single mechanical failure on the part of any of the four aircraft.

776¼-ft (236.6-m) long mammoth was fitted out like a luxury hotel for 20 passengers, with all the comforts and amenities needed for lengthy aerial cruises. The first of many significant flights by the *Graf Zeppelin* began on 11 October 1928, when the airship successfully crossed the North Atlantic from Friedrichshafen to Lakehurst, New Jersey, returning at the end of the month.

In March 1932, the *Graf Zeppelin* was put into service by the Luftschiffbau Zeppelin across the South Atlantic, from Friedrichshafen to Recife and eventually to Rio de Janeiro. This company, in association with Deutsche Luft Hansa, formed the airline DZR (Deutsche Zeppelin Reederei) to continue the services from March 1935. By May 1937, about 140 Atlantic crossings had been made without incident; but the service was then discontinued after the Zeppelin *Hindenburg* burst into flames upon arrival in America, with the loss of 35 lives.

Although not part of the present story, it is interesting to record that the *Graf Zeppelin* was brought out of retirement in 1939 and made two secret reconnaissance flights across the North Sea and up the east coast of England to try to monitor transmissions from British radars. The airship and its helium-filled sister, the LZ 130 *Graf Zeppelin II*, were eventually scrapped in their hangars at Friedrichshafen in March 1940, bringing to an end four decades of Zeppelin activities in Germany.

Soon after the *Graf Zeppelin* went into service on the South Atlantic, another German airline, DLH (Deutsche Luft Hansa), began experiments with depot ships which would enhance the reliability of a commercial service between Europe and South America. This technique used, in the first instance, a Dornier Wal twin-engined flying-boat and the depot ship *Westfalen*, equipped with a catapult to launch the Wal and a derrick to lift it on board. A regular trans-Atlantic mail service was inaugurated by DLH in 1934 and continued, together with the Air France service, right up to the outbreak of war in 1939. Neither service carried passengers, however, this being the prerogative of the Zeppelins.

Similarly, on the North Atlantic the carriage of mail was the principal preoccupation of those airlines which had aspirations to the route prior to the second World War. Progress here lagged several years behind experience on the South Atlantic, but German initiative did reduce the elapsed time for carrying mail between Europe and America by about 36 hours, by using aircraft launched by catapult from the ocean liners *Bremen* and *Europa* between 1929 and 1936.

were less successful, claiming the lives of the Princess Lowenstein-Wertheim and her English crewmen Minchin and Hamilton, and Captain Hinchcliffe and his companion, Elsie Mackay.

Although the number of attempts increased steadily from this time on, crossing the North Atlantic by aeroplane was to remain a hazardous venture until 1937, when the first experimental commercial services were flown by Lufthansa, Imperial Airways and Pan American. Over the South Atlantic progress was more rapid, thanks to the efforts of the French airline Aéropostale. By 1930, Aéropostale was operating a route from Paris to Dakar and a network of routes in South America, and since 1928 had provided a sea link between Dakar and Natal for mail. In May 1930, the famous French aviator Jean Mermoz flew a Latécoère 28 seaplane over the westbound route in 19½ hours. This reduced the total time from France to the River Plate to four days, and encouraged the development in France of more suitable multi-engined aircraft to carry mail on this route.

One such was the three-engined Couzinet 70 *Arc-en-Ciel*, which Mermoz flew from St Louis, Senegal, to Natal in January 1933 in only 4½ hours. The plans suffered a temporary setback when Aéropostale went bankrupt. Eventually, Air France took over the project and, early in 1936, opened a through route for mail by air from France to Santiago in Chile, across the South Atlantic; but the Atlantic did not give up easily, and less than a year after the service began Mermoz himself disappeared while flying the Latécoère 300 *Croix du Sud* on the route, in December 1936.

Meanwhile, German efforts to bridge the Atlantic had been following two different concepts—one depending on the use of depot ships to refuel and service seaplanes and the other using the airships of the Zeppelin company. Thanks to the initiative and determination of Count Ferdinand von Zeppelin, Germany had built a series of airships between 1900 and 1936 which made their own particular contribution to aviation history, unmatched by the achievements of any other nation.

The most significant of all these craft was LZ 127, launched in 1928 and named *Graf Zeppelin*. The gondola of this five-engined,

Opposite page, left: Cutaway drawing of the *Spirit of St Louis,* showing the large tanks for 450 US gallons (1,705 litres) of fuel that filled the fuselage forward of the cockpit and the inner part of each wing. The pilot had no view directly forward, except by periscope

Above: Most successful passenger airship of all time, the *Graf Zeppelin,* flying over Flensburg, the birthplace of her equally famous skipper, Hugo Eckener. In just under nine years, this great craft made 590 flights, including 144 ocean crossings, carried 13,100 passengers and travelled 1,053,395 miles (1,695,272 km) in 17,178 flying hours

Left: A corner of the lounge of the *Graf Zeppelin.* Even the modern 'Jumbo jet' cannot rival its standard of spacious luxury

Top: Heinkel He 12 postal seaplane on its catapult on board the liner *Bremen.* The aircraft was launched operationally for the first time during the *Bremen*'s maiden voyage, on 22 July 1929, while the ship was still 250 miles (400 km) from New York. Eight flights that year showed that such a scheme could speed up trans-Atlantic mail delivery. As a result, the improved He 58 seaplane was built for a similar catapult mail service from the liner *Europa.* Both aircraft were replaced in 1932 by Junkers Ju 46 seaplanes, which maintained the operation until 1936

First over the Poles

Polar exploration has always been a magnet to attract the venturesome. What is seldom realised is that one of the earliest serious attempts to reach the North Pole *was by air*. Salomon August Andrée, Chief Engineer of the Swedish Patent Office, accompanied by Nils Strindberg and Knut Fraenkel, ascended in a balloon from Danes Island, Spitzbergen, at 1.50 pm on 11 July 1897—prepared for a 30-day drift across the Arctic which should have taken them over the Pole.

It was an optimistic attempt and, not altogether surprisingly, ended in disaster. Three days after lift-off they descended at 82° 55′ north, 29° 52′ east and abandoned the balloon. Thirty-three years passed before their subsequent fate was known. Then a ship called at White Island, near Spitzbergen, on 6 August 1930 and found the bodies of Andrée and Strindberg, together with their diaries which told a terrible tale of their experiences.

Meanwhile, men on foot had reached both Poles by 1911, but the urge to fly there remained. Roald Amundsen, who had beaten Captain Scott to the South Pole by a few weeks, made several attempts to reach the North Pole by aeroplane, but failed by less than three degrees (180 miles; 290 km) in 1925 and lost one of his two

aircraft in the process. He was accompanied by Lincoln Ellsworth, his American backer, and by two famous airmen, Hjalmar Riiser-Larsen and Oskar Omdal. No sooner was Amundsen back from this abortive, and expensive, effort than he decided to try again, this time by airship. With its longer range and greater comfort, such a craft seemed to offer a better chance of success. Ellsworth was able to offer considerable financial help; so Riiser-Larsen (later to be one of the founders of Polar commercial flight with his Scandinavian confrère, Bernt Balchen) went to Italy to negotiate the use of a semi-rigid airship, the N.1, built by Colonel (now General) Umberto Nobile.

The financial arrangement amounted to something like a charter of the airship on reasonable terms. But Mussolini introduced a sting in the tail of the contract, by insisting that at least five members of the crew must be Italian, with Nobile in command. Airship-wise this was a good thing, but the Italians knew nothing of the Arctic and would clearly be more of a liability in certain circumstances. However, that was the condition and Riiser-Larsen had to accept it. In passing, it is worth mentioning that the N.1 was offered on outright sale for $75,000, then worth about £15,000, not much more than the price of a 1971 Rolls-Royce!

Above: Flagship of Byrd's 1929 Antarctic expedition was the Ford Trimotor *Floyd Bennett*. Piloted by Bernt Balchen, it flew over the Pole— but only after the crew had thrown overboard everything that was not tied down, including even their emergency supplies
Right: Rear Admiral Richard Evelyn Byrd, USN, noted explorer and first to fly over both the North and South Poles
Far right: The prototype Fokker F.VII/3m *Josephine Ford* (later fitted with skis) in which Byrd made the first flight over the North Pole, piloted by Floyd Bennett, on 9 May 1926

A base was built at Kings Bay, Spitzbergen, and on 7 May 1926 the *Norge*, as the N.1 had been christened by Mrs Riiser-Larsen at a ceremony in Rome, arrived at Spitzbergen. She had flown 5,000 miles (8,000 km) in 103 airborne hours.

In the meantime, Lieutenant Commander Richard E Byrd, USN, had arrived at Kings Bay with his three-engined Fokker, the *Josephine Ford*, with which he hoped to be the first to reach the North Pole, the idea being to take off on skis instead of floats or wheels. He hit a lot of trouble and Amundsen, with his usual generosity, told Bernt Balchen, one of his own staff, to offer his services to Byrd. Balchen was a leading authority on aircraft skis, and this began an association which was to last many years.

Byrd, whose pilot was Floyd Bennett, had rather grandiose ideas about the flights

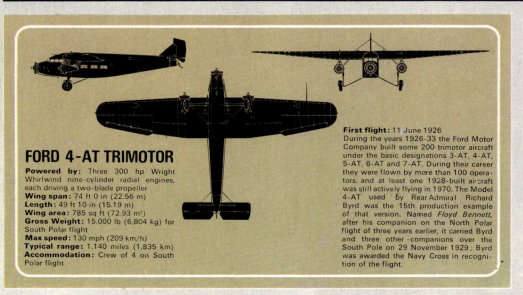

FORD 4-AT TRIMOTOR

Powered by: Three 300 hp Wright Whirlwind nine-cylinder radial engines, each driving a two-blade propeller
Wing span: 74 ft 0 in (22.56 m)
Length: 49 ft 10 in (15.19 m)
Wing area: 785 sq ft (72.93 m²)
Gross Weight: 15,000 lb (6,804 kg) for South Polar flight
Max speed: 130 mph (209 km/h)
Typical range: 1,140 miles (1,835 km)
Accommodation: Crew of 4 on South Polar flight

First flight: 11 June 1926
During the years 1926-33 the Ford Motor Company built some 200 trimotor aircraft under the basic designations 3-AT, 4-AT, 5-AT, 6-AT and 7-AT. During their career they were flown by more than 100 operators, and at least one 1928-built aircraft was still actively flying in 1970. The Model 4-AT used by Rear Admiral Richard Byrd was the 15th production example of that version. Named *Floyd Bennett*, after his companion on the North Polar flight of three years earlier, it carried Byrd and three other companions over the South Pole on 29 November 1929; Byrd was awarded the Navy Cross in recognition of the flight.

the *Josephine Ford* would make, and had several accidents. These necessitated a drastic scaling down of the take-off load and resulted in a plan simply to fly to the Pole and back, with no additional objectives thrown in. Thus, while Nobile and Amundsen were waiting for certain ground work to be completed—and the right weather— Byrd took off at 1.0 am on 9 May 1926 and set course for the Pole.

An hour before the estimated time of arrival at the Pole, an oil leak showed up in one of the engines but, being beyond any reasonable hope of rescue, they decided to go on, and reached the Pole at 9.02 am. For about a quarter of an hour they circled the pinpoint, taking numerous observations to confirm their position, and then turned back to Kings Bay, which they reached at 4.30 pm, having flown 1,600 miles (2,575 km). America was thus able to claim credit for the first successful attempts to reach the North Pole on foot (Peary, 1909) and by air. Beaten at the post, Amundsen, Nobile and Ellsworth were waiting with warm congratulations when Byrd and Bennett arrived back.

Two days later, on 11 May 1926, the *Norge* took off and arrived over the Pole

at 1.30 am Spitzbergen time. Flags of the three nations involved were dropped, and the flight then continued until they landed at Teller in Alaska, having been airborne for three and a half days. Though deprived of making the first flight over the North Pole, Amundsen and his companions did make the first flight right across the Arctic. Amundsen also became the first man to visit both the North and South Poles.

No sooner was he back in the United States than Byrd set plans in motion to fly to the South Pole. This was a tougher problem than his just-completed Arctic flight, for no habitation existed within more than a thousand miles (1,600 km) of the South Pole. Thus a vast base had to be set up in Antarctica; indeed, a two-year polar exploration had to be mounted. In the meantime, Byrd, Balchen, Acosta and Noville made a dramatic transatlantic flight in 1927—soon after the Lindbergh epic—and Balchen became a permanent associate of Byrd. Floyd Bennett had died of pneumonia.

Two ships and 60 men made up the Antarctic expedition, and four aircraft were taken along, including a Ford Trimotor named *Floyd Bennett*. A base was set up in

the Bay of Whales, close to Amundsen's old headquarters at Framheim, just after Christmas 1928, and was named Little America. 'Local' flying was carried on for as long as the season permitted and then the aircraft were bedded down as the expedition faced its long winter in the Antarctic darkness.

The Trimotor was intended for the Polar flight, but could not lift its equipment, a crew of four and enough fuel to make the return trip non-stop. So a refuelling base was laid down by Byrd, Dean Smith, Harold June and Ashley McKinley, by flying the *Floyd Bennett* to a point 440 miles (708 km) south of Little America. This was to be used during the return from the Pole.

On 28 November 1929, the Trimotor took off from Little America just before 4.0 pm. Take-off weight was 15,000 lb (approx 6,800 kg) and the crew consisted of Balchen, pilot; Byrd, navigator; June, radio; and McKinley, survey. They carried material to be dropped to a survey party at an advance base.

The drop completed, they approached the Queen Maud Range and found that they could not gain sufficient height to fly past the mountains. A difficult decision was taken.

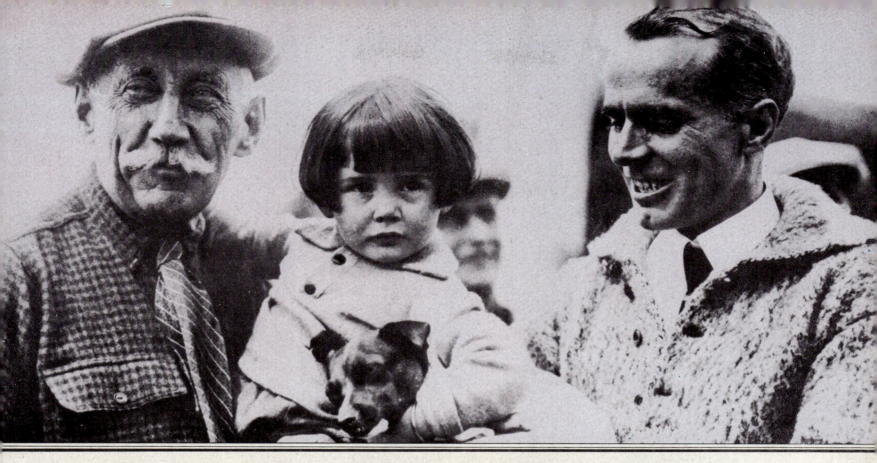

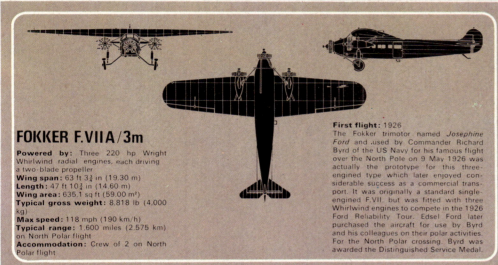

FOKKER F.VIIA/3m

Powered by: Three 220 hp Wright
Whirlwind radial engines, each driving
a two-blade propeller
Wing span: 63 ft 3¾ in (19.30 m)
Length: 47 ft 10¾ in (14.60 m)
Wing area: 635.1 sq ft (59.00 m²)
Typical gross weight: 8,818 lb (4,000
kg)
Max speed: 118 mph (190 km/h)
Typical range: 1,600 miles (2,575 km)
on North Polar flight
Accommodation: Crew of 2 on North
Polar flight

First flight: 1926
The Fokker trimotor named *Josephine
Ford* and used by Commander Richard
Byrd of the US Navy for his famous flight
over the North Pole on 9 May 1926 was
actually the prototype for this three-
engined type which later enjoyed considerable success as a commercial transport. It was originally a standard single-
engined F.VII but was fitted with three
Whirlwind engines to compete in the 1926
Ford Reliability Tour. Edsel Ford later
purchased the aircraft for use by Byrd
and his colleagues on their polar activities.
For the North Polar crossing, Byrd was
awarded the Distinguished Service Medal.

and food was dropped overboard—food
which might have made the difference between life and death had anything gone
wrong. It didn't. The first aeroplane ever to
fly over the South Polar plateau, the *Floyd
Bennett*, reached the Pole just under ten hours
after leaving Little America. An American
flag, weighted with a stone from Floyd
Bennett's grave, was dropped and Byrd
became the first man to reach both Poles by
air.

To describe any Antarctic flight as uneventful may sound ridiculous, but the
return trip merited that description. The
refuelling stop was made successfully and
the aircraft landed back at Little America
after a 19-hour absence in which history was
made.

Since then it has become routine to go
to the South Pole, and paying passengers
cross the North Polar regions in airliners
almost every day. This has happened in
little more than 40 years—another example
of the speed with which aviation continues
to develop.

As a postscript, it should be added that
Nobile later flew again to the North Pole, in
the airship *Italia*, and crashed. Amundsen
lost his life in a rescue attempt.

The ill-fated airship *Italia* on its mooring mast at
Kings Bay in May 1928

In the late 1960s the Fokker-designed F.27
Friendship eclipsed even the record of the
Vickers Viscount to become the world's
biggest-selling turboprop airliner, and in
1971 it was still in production, 13 years
after the first Friendship was delivered to
an airline. Basic accommodation is for 40
passengers or a comparable cargo load,
though up to 52 persons can be carried if a
high-density seating layout is installed

Fokker

THE FLYING DUTCHMAN

Above: A typical Fokker Spin (Spider) built and flown before the first World War. The inset photograph shows Anthony Fokker

Left: Four basic types of flying-boat were designed and built by the Fokker company in the 'twenties, all with a duralumin hull and wooden wings. Only one manufactured in any numbers was the B.IVa amphibian, a six-passenger aircraft powered by a 525-hp Pratt & Whitney Hornet engine

Below: The F.27 Friendship, powered by two Rolls-Royce Dart turboprops, is the aircraft with which Fokker re-entered the transport market after the second World War. By early 1971, a total of 568 had been sold to 125 customers in 48 countries

JAVA IS NOT the likeliest spot on earth to have associations with one of the greatest names in the history of aeronautics, yet it was in this island that Anthony Herman Gerard Fokker was born on 6 April 1890. That this name can truly be numbered among the great ones, notwithstanding what will later be said concerning its bearer's fame as an aircraft designer, is beyond all dispute. It is a name, moreover, which is perpetuated to this day in association with the Friendship and Fellowship airliners and with other fields of aeronautical activity.

The son of a wealthy Dutch coffee planter, 'Tony' Fokker, as he was to become known in many nations of the world, was educated in Holland before transferring his aeronautical activities to Germany. He had seen his first aeroplane in Brussels during 1908, and after Wilbur Wright's visit to France in that same year his interest in flying began to take a practical form in the making of paper and celluloid models. During a course of aeronautical instruction in Germany he participated in the design of full-scale aeroplanes, and he made his first 'hop' of about a hundred yards in a monoplane which he had built in collaboration with Franz von Daum.

The precise extent of his contribution to this and other early aircraft with which he was associated is difficult to assess, for his own account of his career did not always accord with fact. That he became a very skilful pilot has never been in doubt, though the granting to him of a patent covering the basic design of the *Spin* (Spider) monoplane of 1911, generally accepted as the first Fokker aeroplane, is not in itself real evidence of his technical ability. Indeed, only a few years ago Mr A R Weyl, who had an intimate knowledge of German aeronautics, flatly declared that the Fokker Spiders, of which some 25 were built, were designed by an eminent engineer named Jacob Goedecker. He went, in fact, much further, by contending that Goedecker supplied all these aircraft ready for assembly in Fokker's workshop at Johannisthal, Berlin, until 1913; that among the craftsmen employed by Fokker at Schwerin was Reinhold Platz, who became the 'unaided' designer not only of the world-famous Fokker Dr.I triplane and D.VII biplane fighters, but of the universally employed transport monoplanes bearing the same name; and, furthermore, that the deadly Fokker E.I/E.III monoplanes which precipitated the 'Fokker scourge' of 1915/16 were merely modifications of a French Morane-Saulnier design, associating Platz with these aircraft also.

Against these remarks, the good faith of which can hardly be in question, must be set the comments of one of Fokker's compatriots who pointed out that it was nothing unusual for an aircraft constructor to be assisted in larger or smaller measure by a technical team, headed by his chief designer. 'Fokker', he said, 'with much of his time taken up by many of the business affairs a manufacturer has to attend to, though he later delegated much to others, could not be expected to stand a full working day behind one of his firm's drawing boards. This is true of all aircraft constructors, who may have been Jacks of all trades at the start of their careers, but who had to call in technical assistance when their business grew.'

One other fact concerning Fokker is quite beyond dispute: that the story of his life and achievements does not find an end in any argument concerning the design of aeroplanes, for he was active in so many other fields. He was, above all, a man of the world, although he neither drank nor smoked; and when he said or did something people took notice. As a test pilot, for example, he could not only call attention to defects but could propose a remedy also. He once said 'No-one has yet found as many flaws in an aeroplane

FOKKER SPIN (SPIDER)

Powered by: One 50 hp Argus four-cylinder in-line engine, driving a two-blade propeller
Wing span: 36 ft 1 in (11.00 m)
Length: 25 ft 5 in (7.75 m)
Wing area: 236.81 sq ft (22.00 m²)
Gross weight: 882 lb (400 kg)
Max speed: 56 mph (90 km/h)
Accommodation: Crew of 1
First flight: August 1911
Anthony Fokker's first 'Spider', built in Germany in association with Jacob Goedecker, was based upon experience gained with two earlier monoplanes built in 1910-11. In 1912 Fokker formed his own company at Johannisthal, near Berlin, where improved versions of the *Spin* were put into production. The initial version, to which the data apply, was the A-1912; the later B-1912 had a 100 hp engine, and a few others were fitted with 70 hp Renaults. Whatever the truth regarding Fokker's ability as a designer, his undoubted skill as a flier contributed much to the pilot appeal of the fighters that he produced for the German Air Force in 1914-18.

FOKKER D.VII

Powered by: One 160 hp Mercedes D.III six-cylinder in-line engine, driving a two-blade propeller
Wing span: 29 ft 2¼ in (8.90 m)
Length: 22 ft 9¾ in (6.95 m)
Wing area: 220.66 sq ft (20.50 m²)
Gross weight: 1,984 lb (900 kg)
Max speed: 117 mph (189 km/h) at 3,280 ft (1,000 m)
Endurance: 1 hr 30 min
Accommodation: Crew of 1
First flight: January 1918
Indisputably one of the best fighters to appear during the first World War, the Fokker D.VII competed with 30 other aircraft (including six Fokker types) in fighter trials in Germany at the beginning of 1918. It outclassed every other competitor and was immediately ordered into large-scale production, the first examples reaching von Richthofen's squadron at the Front in April 1918. About 1,000 were built before the war ended, and production was continued in Holland after the Armistice, when more than 100 were smuggled out of Germany to prevent their seizure by the Allies.

of mine as I could find myself.' As a demonstration pilot also he excelled. When the Russian government organised a competition with a view to ordering aircraft in numbers, he climbed in a Spider to 1,500 ft (460 m) and made spectacular turns in a spiral glide. Although, like other competitors, he is said to have done as much bribing of officials as he could afford, no orders resulted on this occasion.

Fokker had talents also as a flying instructor, and by the end of 1912 was running a flourishing flying school. As a business man he was no less competent, and even before the first World War was employing as an agent in England one Felix Schulz, described by Fokker not merely as a German spy but a British one also. This mystery man has been linked with the 'acquiring' of drawings of an unknown British seaplane, and certainly before war came Fokker had been experimenting with a flying-boat and a float-plane. Fokker himself is said to have been caught making an unauthorised inspection of a Morane-Saulnier monoplane, and, as already noted, the Fokker monoplane fighters of 1915/16 were based on a design by this French company. Far from being slavish copies, however, they displayed unusual features, notably a fuselage of welded steel tubes which continued to characterise Fokker aeroplanes for many years to come.

Perhaps Fokker's greatest fame rests on his introduction in these fighters of a fixed, forward-firing machine-gun, so controlled as to allow the bullets to pass between the blades of the revolving propeller and aimed by the pilot pointing the aircraft bodily at the target. This innovation, which contributed far more greatly to the 'Fokker scourge' than the performance of the fighters concerned, was the outcome of the capture by the Germans of a French fighter flown by the great Roland Garros; but, whereas the French machine was fitted with plates on the propeller blades to deflect impinging bullets, the Fokker system gave positive control over the gun. Again it must be recorded that Fokker was not personally responsible, the credit apparently being due to his collaborator Heinrich Luebbe.

The Fokker D.VII of 1918 is regarded by many authorities as the finest fighter of the first World War, and was accorded the distinction of being mentioned by name in the Armistice Agreement. This aircraft provides a further insight into Fokker's character, for instead of handing over to the Allies 'all machines of the D.VII type' as required, he secreted airframes, engines and components, and smuggled into Holland about 120 more or less complete examples. Factory equipment was likewise spirited away, and from this nucleus there grew the Fokker factories which remain so active and successful to this day.

In peacetime the irrepressible Dutchman allied the welded steel-tube fuselage with a cantilever wooden wing to provide an entire family of transport aeroplanes which were adopted or imitated the world over. Fokker transports were the choice not only of the airlines but of many record-breakers also; but when the Douglas company in America (where Fokker had himself been active in the aircraft business) introduced the incomparable DC-2 the shrewd, perceptive Dutchman secured a business agreement which affords a final and personal glimpse of one of the most remarkable characters in the history of flying.

The story was obtained by the present writer one morning at Croydon Airport when Anthony Fokker was awaiting passage to Amsterdam. Introductory remarks on one's own part were deluged instantly by a eulogy of the new Douglas which left little doubt that Fokker in person was its designer. In mid-deluge he happened to glance over his shoulder, and, spotting the distinctive form of the Short *Scylla* of Imperial Airways—a creation which its most ardent admirers could hardly call elegant—demanded in shocked American 'What's *that*?'. Advised that it was Britain's latest airliner, he spun round in disgust to snap 'Well, you should be . . . well ashamed of it.'

Not only had he conveyed the impression, intentionally or not, that the DC-2 was *his* airliner but that this writer bore a personal guilt for the offending *Scylla*!

As may be judged, he was a great character as well as a great man, and the world of flying was far less lively after he died in 1939.

Top: After 30 years of service, this F.VIIa was flown by a veteran KLM crew from Copenhagen to Amsterdam in 1955 for display in the then-projected Dutch National Air Museum at Schiphol Airport. Built originally for Balair, it has been repainted to represent H-NACT, the first F.VIIa supplied to KLM

Left, top to bottom:
The F.XX *Zilvermeeuw* (Silver Gull) of 1933 was the only one of its type built. It introduced refinements such as an elliptical fuselage and retractable undercarriage, and carried 12 passengers

The C.VII-W of 1928 was a two-seat reconnaissance and training seaplane, of which 30 were built. Power plant was a 225-hp Armstrong Siddeley Lynx

A post-war side-by-side trainer, the S.11 Instructor, was built in the Netherlands, Italy and Brazil for the air forces of all three countries. It was powered by a 190-hp Lycoming engine

the airlines grow up

Above: History was in the making as this Swallow biplane, piloted by Leon Cuddeback, prepared for take-off at Pasco, Washington, on 6 April 1926, for the inaugural flight of Varney Air Lines. The flight from Pasco to Elko, Nevada, via Boise, Idaho, marked the beginning of post-war commercial air transportation in the USA. Varney later became a part of United Air Lines

Opposite page, top: The airliners built by Junkers in Germany in the 'twenties were cantilever monoplanes, with the added attraction of all-metal construction. The corrugated skin of this F 13 of Luft Hansa was almost a Junkers trademark

Bottom: This floatplane version of the Junkers F 13 was used for the first passenger flight of the Swedish operator AB Aerotransport, from Stockholm to Helsinki, in 1924

Right: The remarkable STOL (short take-off and landing) characteristics of the 'giant' airliners of the 'thirties are made clear by this picture of a four-engined H.P.42 of Imperial Airways on the small, grass airfield at Le Touquet, France

Below: This Fokker F.VIIa of KLM is typical of the modern-looking cantilever monoplanes which this Dutch manufacturer produced in the biplane era of the mid-twenties. Powered by a 400-hp Gnome-Rhône Jupiter engine, it carried two pilots and eight passengers

ENORMOUS CHANGES in air transport took place between the two World Wars, although development was not consistent throughout the world.

The first air services were operated mostly by surplus wartime aircraft, with varying degrees of modification to suit them for commercial operation. These modifications frequently meant only that guns and bomb racks were removed; but in some cases simple enclosed cabins were fitted, and a few types such as the Handley Page O/400 bomber made passable (if noisy) transport aeroplanes.

The pilots and ground staff were recruited almost entirely from the military flying services, and training for the job was virtually unknown. Old wartime hangars and wooden huts served as terminal build-

ings. Most of the early aircraft used on the pioneering air services were not equipped with radio, there was no air traffic control system, and goose-neck oil flares and a wind stocking were about the only landing aids.

However, the work of the earliest air transport pioneers should not be belittled. They did a magnificent job and laid the foundations for the present system of world-wide air services; but they were often short of money and experience, had to work with unsuitable aircraft, and to fight Government and public apathy and disbelief in air transport.

Europe was the principal pioneering air transport area and all the major European countries established airlines very soon after the first World War. Some early airlines were concerned mainly with domestic or very limited regional services; some set out to establish extensive European networks; and others such as Imperial Airways in Britain, KLM in the Netherlands, French and Belgian and, later, Italian airlines were involved in creating air communication between the home countries and their overseas territories.

Most of the air services were confined to daylight operation and many routes were closed down for the winter months. Navi-

gation consisted chiefly of a pilot's knowledge of the route and ability to map-read. Some routes were laid down, mostly following roads, railways or prominent geographical features, and to assist pilots the names of towns were often painted in large letters on railway station roofs.

Britain began very early to instal two-way radio in its aircraft, and soon developed a primitive system of air traffic control and radio direction-finding. The comparatively small amount of traffic kept collision risk to a low level, but in 1922 a French Farman Goliath and a British D.H.18 met each other head-on over northern France in bad weather when both pilots were following a road but each flying on the same side of it.

The early system of direction-finding consisted of three ground stations taking bearings on the radio transmission of an aircraft and then laying these off on a map with weighted strings—the weights being known as 'mice'. The strings did not all intersect at the same point, but formed a small triangle within which was the aircraft's position. The system was accurate to a couple of miles and was adequate for low-density traffic and low-speed aircraft; it remained in operation at Croydon up to the start of the 1939-45 War.

The primitive radio and direction-finding aids, combined with pilots' experience, enabled the airlines to achieve a surprisingly high standard of regularity, but these methods would not have worked with heavy traffic and were insufficient to provide safe bad-weather landings on a large scale. Landings were made in fog, but only because some pilots (the outstanding example being R H McIntosh) were exceptionally good at lining up on a glimpsed landmark and then making a timed approach.

In the early 1920s there were a number of urgent requirements for safe and economic airline operation. Most airlines were in need of reliable economic aeroplanes capable of making money—or at least capable of operation without making large losses. A major source of trouble was the water-cooled engine, with its heavy radiator and temperamental plumbing. Forced landings, which were frequent, were generally caused by engine trouble or bad weather.

Junkers in Germany and Fokker in the Netherlands both embarked on the design of small transport aeroplanes, the F 13 with all-metal structure and the F.II and F.III with wooden wings and steel-tube fuselage with fabric covering. These types each led to a series of developed aircraft, including the Fokker F.VII series, and played a major part in the development of air transport in many parts of the world. But the big breakthrough came with the introduction of a reasonably reliable air-cooled engine, one of the first and most successful of which was the Bristol Jupiter. It was when manufacturers began to produce multi-engined aircraft with air-cooled powerplants that the airlines got their first real chance of reliable and less costly operation.

The short days of the long European winter forced the airlines to find ways of operating at night. This led in turn to

lighted airways with 'lighthouses' at intervals along the routes, and to the development of airport lighting with location beacons, boundary lights, obstruction lights and floodlights (and, in some cases, sunken lights) to provide landing guidance at night and in poor visibility. In Germany and Scandinavia lighting brought about the operation of night mail services.

Gradually the air transport scene changed from a kind of civil version of wartime flying into a professional public transport system with safe, reliable, comfortable aeroplanes flown by uniformed crews and operating to and from more advanced aerodromes with permanent terminal buildings, radio and lighting.

But the progress was uneven. In some parts of Europe lack of land aerodromes forced the airlines to operate with flying-boats and seaplanes, and terminal facilities were unable to keep in step with land airport development.

The average speed of the early transport aeroplanes was around 100 mph (161 km/h), and the 200 mph (322 km/h) airliner had only just gone into limited service when the second World War started. The low speed meant that comparatively short journeys took a long time. The London – Paris schedule was more than 2 hr and a flight across Europe took an entire day or longer. It was therefore necessary to make aircraft as comfortable as possible by reducing engine noise in the cabin, by heating cabins and providing meal service.

As early as October 1919 Handley Page Transport introduced lunch baskets on its services and in 1922 Daimler Airway began carrying cabin boys. In the mid-1920s Imperial Airways and the French Air Union introduced stewards and provided first a buffet service and then full meals. In-flight service reached its pre-war peak on Imperial Airways' four-engined Handley Page 42s, introduced in 1931, and Short Scylla and Syrinx in 1934. Full-course lunches and dinners were served in cabins which were comfortably furnished and quieter because the engines were in or between the wings and well away from the fuselage. Most earlier, and many later, airliners had nose-mounted engines which were noisy and caused considerable vibration.

A few attempts were made, mainly in France and Germany, to equip aircraft with sleeping berths, but no evidence has been found to suggest that sleeper services were regularly operated in Europe. In most pre-1939 airliners smoking was not allowed and at least one passenger was fined because he insisted on doing so.

All airports gradually developed in size and had terminal buildings with booking halls, waiting rooms and Customs; almost all had grass landing areas. In the 1930s paved runways began to appear, with Amsterdam, Stockholm, Oslo and Helsinki being among the first in Europe. Surfaced runways were also introduced in the United States.

Paved runways became necessary as aircraft increased in weight, but to some

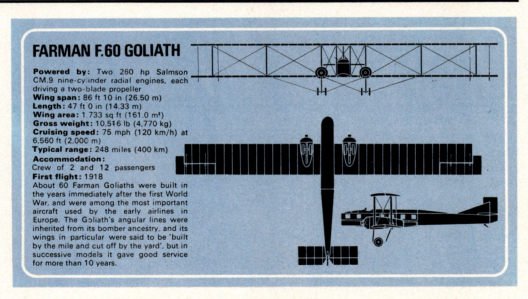

Top left: Sir Alan Cobham in the open cockpit of the Jaguar-engined D.H.50J which he used for several of his pioneering flights for Imperial Airways in the mid 'twenties. This picture shows also the hatchway through which photographer B W G Emmott recorded highlights of the surveys

Left: The D.H.34s of Daimler Hire introduced new standards of comfort and convenience when they entered service in 1922. Passengers sat in a roomy, enclosed cabin, with a steward to serve refreshments, and there was a separate compartment to the rear for baggage

Above: First monoplanes to serve Imperial Airways were eight Armstrong Whitworth A.W.15 Atalantas, built in 1931-32. Each was designed to carry nine passengers and a heavy load of mail and freight on the airline's Nairobi-Cape Town and Karachi-Singapore routes. This picture shows *Andromeda* refuelling at Moshi, Tanganyika, with Mount Kilimanjaro in the background

Right: Another great Armstrong Whitworth airliner of the between-wars period was the three-engined Argosy, seen here in front of Croydon's famous control tower. Argosies operated Imperial Airways' lunchtime 'Silver Wing' service to Paris—the world's first 'named' airline service

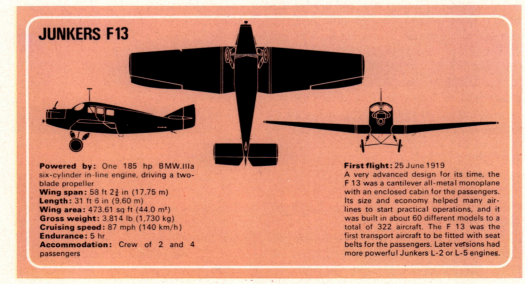

FARMAN F.60 GOLIATH

Powered by: Two 260 hp Salmson CM.9 nine-cylinder radial engines, each driving a two-blade propeller
Wing span: 86 ft 10 in (26.50 m)
Length: 47 ft 0 in (14.33 m)
Wing area: 1,733 sq ft (161.0 m²)
Gross weight: 10,516 lb (4,770 kg)
Cruising speed: 75 mph (120 km/h) at 6,560 ft (2,000 m)
Typical range: 248 miles (400 km)
Accommodation: Crew of 2 and 12 passengers
First flight: 1918
About 60 Farman Goliaths were built in the years immediately after the first World War, and were among the most important aircraft used by the early airlines in Europe. The Goliath's angular lines were inherited from its bomber ancestry, and its wings in particular were said to be 'built by the mile and cut off by the yard', but in successive models it gave good service for more than 10 years.

JUNKERS F 13

Powered by: One 185 hp BMW.IIIa six-cylinder in-line engine, driving a two-blade propeller
Wing span: 58 ft 2¼ in (17.75 m)
Length: 31 ft 6 in (9.60 m)
Wing area: 473.61 sq ft (44.0 m²)
Gross weight: 3,814 lb (1,730 kg)
Cruising speed: 87 mph (140 km/h)
Endurance: 5 hr
Accommodation: Crew of 2 and 4 passengers
First flight: 25 June 1919
A very advanced design for its time, the F 13 was a cantilever all-metal monoplane with an enclosed cabin for the passengers. Its size and economy helped many airlines to start practical operations, and it was built in about 60 different models to a total of 322 aircraft. The F 13 was the first transport aircraft to be fitted with seat belts for the passengers. Later versions had more powerful Junkers L-2 or L-5 engines.

extent they impaired bad weather operations; in poor visibility it was easier to land on a large expanse of grass than align with a narrow runway.

A feature of the 1920s and 1930s which has now disappeared was the emergency landing ground. These were spaced out along the routes and were frequently used by aircraft suffering engine trouble, running into poor visibility or getting low on fuel after meeting strong headwinds. One aircraft flying from London to Paris is reported to have made about fourteen intermediate landings, while others in the 1920s took more than 4 hr to complete the 200-mile (322-km) journey because of the headwinds they encountered and their low cruising speed. It has even been related that a London – Paris service Argosy was once overtaken by a train. It must be remembered that a 90 mph (145 km/h) aeroplane flying into a 60 mph (97 km/h) gale has a ground speed of only 30 mph (48 km/h); with an endurance of 4 hr such an aircraft would have to land for fuel about every 100 miles (161 km).

In spite of all the problems of unsuitable aircraft, primitive navigational aids and poor airports, the airlines of Europe built up a comprehensive network of reliable and reasonably comfortable services.

Imperial Airways, KLM, Sabena and a number of French airlines had to develop long-distance services over a variety of terrains and through a wide range of climates. These operations involved passengers in several days of travel with

numerous night stops—some at forts in the desert or rest houses constructed by the airlines. In many cases the airlines had to provide their own aerodromes, laid down in the deserts or cut out of the bush. Conditions were often primitive and for many years the long-distance services operated under conditions akin to those in Europe in the early 1920s.

It must be remembered that all these early air services were worked by unpressurised aircraft. This meant cruising at modest altitudes and thereby suffering the worst of European weather and, on Eastern and African routes, the severe turbulence of the tropics. It was the pressurised cabin which made the biggest contribution to passenger comfort. Another factor affecting operation was the short range of the aircraft used—averaging about 500-600 miles (805-966 km)—and this was the reason for remote aerodromes having to be established in desert and jungle regions; the aircraft simply could not fly the long stages between developed areas of habitation.

By the early 1930s the modern stressed-skin all-metal multi-engined monoplane transport was beginning to appear and these types, with retractable undercarriages, flaps, variable-pitch airscrews, automatic pilots and blind-flying instruments, were to revolutionise air transport and make it acceptable as a normal means of transport ranking with rail, road and sea. In the same period de-icing and anti-icing equipment began to become standard.

Air transport had become widespread, reasonably safe and, in some cases, economic, but weather remained a major obstacle to regularity. A means of landing in poor visibility, or when the cloud base was low, was urgently required. Germany gave much thought to the problem and eventually in the 1930s the Lorenz system of following a beam down to the airport came into limited use. This was in due course developed into the present universally used ILS (Instrument Landing System) which has now been coupled to the automatic pilot so that automatic landing is possible.

Although not adopted in Europe before the war, by the 1930s the United States had developed a navigational system whereby aircraft flew from radio beacon to radio beacon along the paths of beams which formed an airway. This in turn led to the present system of radio beacons which are the standard navigational aid.

The airlines of the 1920s and 1930s thus developed from primitive organisations with unsuitable aircraft and few outside aids to a highly complex transport system which was ready in 1945 to take advantage of all the aeronautical progress of the war. But without the trial-and-error efforts of the pioneer airlines we would not have the present great system of air routes which have, in many areas, become the primary means of transport. Over the North Atlantic, for instance, air passengers outnumber sea passengers by several million a year.

The piston-engine has given way to the gas-turbine; the primitive radio has developed into the inertial navigation system; the grass aerodrome has progressed to the vast airport with concrete runways, ILS and sophisticated lighting systems; and the steward and buffet have been replaced by a whole team of cabin staff, full galley service and a range of in-flight entertainment including films.

The present-day passenger sitting watching a film at 40,000 ft (12,200 m) in a warm, pressurised cabin and travelling at 600 mph (966 km/h) can hardly imagine the conditions under which the early passengers flew, for air transport's development has transformed him from a participant into a mere spectator. Progress has both good and bad aspects—but flying will never be the exhilarating experience that it was 40 years ago.

Above: The Fairey IIID seaplane *Santa Cruz* in which Captains Sacadura Cabral and Gago Coutinho completed their first crossing of the South Atlantic in 1922. The photograph was taken in 1928 on the island of Taipa, the air station of Macao on the coast of South China, commanded by Lieut José Cabral

Left: First aeroplane to cross the North American continent non-stop was this Fokker T.2 monoplane of the US Army Air Service, which flew from New York to San Diego in May 1923

Below: Pilots on the 2,520-mile (4,055-km), 26 hr 50 min transcontinental flight were Lts John A Macready and Oakley G Kelly

OVER OCEANS AND CONTINENTS

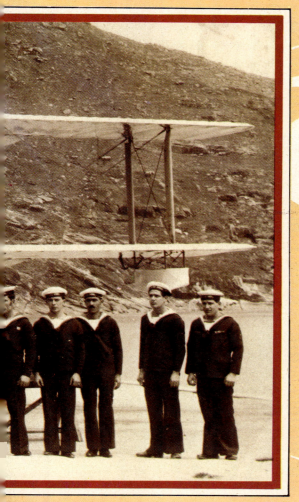

FROM 1920 TO 1930 was a period of tremendous advance in long-distance aviation, with individual pilots as front-page news. Aircraft builders, engine makers, oil companies, and others, all contributed invaluable assistance to these glamorous figures; but, in the final analysis, it was the man—or woman—in the cockpit who did the job and took the risks, of which there were a multiplicity.

Vickers Vimy aircraft had flown from England to Australia and South Africa, and from North America to Britain. These flights set the pace, but the use of such relatively large aircraft was out of the question for most private adventurers.

The South Atlantic was first flown in 1922. On 13 March, Captains Gago Coutinho and Sacadura Cabral of the Portuguese Navy took off from Lisbon in a Fairey IIIC floatplane, flew to Las Palmas, then on to the Cape Verde Islands and Porto Praia. Bad weather caused long delays at the stopping points, and it was not until 18 April that they set off for the true ocean crossing. Their destination was Fernando de Noronha, some 200 miles (320 km) from the Brazilian coast. They failed to reach it, and made a forced landing at St Paul's Rock, seriously damaging the aircraft.

A Portuguese cruiser was standing by, and the airmen remained on board until a second Fairey floatplane arrived at St Paul's Rock to allow them to continue their flight. This, in turn, was wrecked at Fernando de Noronha and they eventually arrived in Brazil on 16 June in a third seaplane. Now both the North and South Atlantic had been flown by heavier-than-air craft.

In the following year the first non-stop coast-to-coast flight across North America

was made. Lieutenants O G Kelly and J A Macready, flying an Army Fokker T.2 powered by a Liberty engine, flew from New York to Rockwell Field, San Diego, on 2-3 May, in 26 hours, 50 minutes and 3 seconds (The inclusion of seconds in the record time was a sign of the increase in the speed of travel; previously, accuracy to a minute was good enough).

The first round-the-world flight took place in 1924. Four Douglas World Cruisers, with interchangeable wheel and float landing gears, started from Seattle on 6 April and flew west via the Aleutians, Japan, India, Europe, Iceland, Greenland and the USA. Only two of the aircraft completed the trip, on 28 September, but there were no human casualties. Elapsed time for the 27,534 miles (44,312 km) was 175 days, which included 15 days, 11 hours and 7 minutes flying time (no question of seconds in this log!). The flight was sponsored by the US Army and the successful crews were Captain Lowell H Smith and Lieut Leslie P Arnold in the *Chicago*, and Lieuts Erick H Nelson and John Harding in the *New Orleans*.

In the same year a man whose name was later to become a household word, Alan Cobham, accompanied by the British Director of Civil Aviation, Sir Sefton Brancker, left London for Rangoon on 20 November in a D.H.50 powered by a 230 hp Siddeley Puma engine. They completed the 17,000-mile (27,360-km) round trip and arrived back in London on 18 March 1925. This was one of many flights made by Alan (later Sir Alan) Cobham which blazed the trail for the Empire services of Imperial Airways.

Though not in strict chronological order, it is interesting to continue the Cobham

saga. Almost exactly one year after starting his Rangoon trip, Cobham, accompanied this time by A B Elliott and B W G Emmott, a photographer, took off from London in the D.H.50, re-engined with a 385 hp Jaguar, and flew (via Egypt and East Africa) to Cape Town and then back to London, arriving home on 13 March 1926. Three months after that, on 30 June, he took off again in the same aircraft, now fitted out as a floatplane, to fly to Melbourne. On 29 August he started back and landed on the Thames outside the Houses of Parliament at 2.0 pm on 1 October. He had given his ETA a long time before arrival and it caused astonishment that even a pilot of Cobham's ability could fly 13,000 miles (20,900 km) across the world and land on schedule. Seconds again! It was after this trip that Cobham was knighted. Unfortunately, his engineer, Elliott, has been killed by a stray bullet from a Bedouin rifle while the D.H.50 was in flight over the desert between Baghdad and Basra on 5 July.

The year 1927 saw the first non-stop crossing of the South Atlantic. In a Breguet XIX (600 hp Hispano-Suiza engine) Captain Dieudonné Costes and Lt Cdr Joseph Le Brix flew, on 14 October, from St Louis, Senegal, to Natal, Brazil, a distance of 2,125 miles (3,420 km) in 19 hours 50 minutes. This flight, completely uneventful, was part of a six-month round-the-world trip.

The first light aeroplane flight from England to India started at Stag Lane, near London, on 15 November 1927, only six weeks after a de Havilland Moth, flown by Flt Lt R R Bentley, had arrived at Cape Town at the end of the first light aeroplane

flight to South Africa from London. Again it was in two D.H. Moths, powered by Cirrus engines, that T Nevil Stack and B M Leete reached Karachi (it was in India in those days) on 8 January 1928.

These flights were not in themselves wildly dramatic and, in terms of elapsed time, compared unfavourably with surface transport. They were, however, tremendously important in that they were the forerunners of the great record-breaking dashes that people like Bert Hinkler, Jim Mollison and Amy Johnson were to make in the next few years. They were also remarkable for the standard of navigation that they demanded. The light aircraft of that era had almost no instruments and any student pilot of the 'twenties will remember, vividly, how easy it was to lose one's home aerodrome after about two minutes' flying. Yet these people managed to find their way across oceans and continents, sometimes with the aid of maps which were sketchy at best. Often no maps existed and dead reckoning—with no knowledge of wind

speed and direction—was the sole means of navigation. Yet they got there.

The year 1928 saw the start of the competition to get to distant places in the fastest time. Squadron Leader H J L (Bert) Hinkler, in an Avro Avian, flew from Britain to Australia between 7 and 22 February. Just 15 days to Australia: now the ship was hopelessly outclassed, and by a lone pilot in a tiny aircraft.

While Hinkler was on his way, Lady Heath, also in an Avian, flew out of South Africa en route to London (Croydon), starting on 12 February and arriving on 17 May. This was not fast, but it was the first-ever flight over that route by a woman, and one who was certainly not a great navigator by training.

The tempo increased rapidly. While Lady Heath was coming north, Lady Bailey flew a D.H. Moth from Britain to South Africa, *and back* later. The outward flight started on 9 March and she landed at Cape Town on 30 April. The return flight, via the West

African route, took from 21 September to 16 January 1929.

Most of the vital routes had been flown by early 1928—except the Pacific. This was soon remedied. On 31 May that year Captain (later Sir) Charles Kingsford Smith, with Charles Ulm, a fellow Australian, and two Americans, Harry Lyon and Jim Warner, took off from San Francisco in a three-engined Fokker, the *Southern Cross*. Twenty-seven hours later they landed at Honolulu after a flight of 2,408 miles (3,875 km). The next stage to Fiji, 3,150 miles (5,070 km) in length, took $34\frac{1}{2}$ hours. Then, after a rest, they flew on to Brisbane, which they reached on 10 June. The Pacific, too, had yielded to the aeroplane, and the navigational skill required to find pinpoints like Fiji was of no mean order.

The nineteen-twenties closed with Byrd's flight over the South Pole (described earlier in *History of Aviation*). Thus this decade saw the entire world criss-crossed by flight.

Opposite page, top: *Chicago,* one of the Douglas World Cruisers used for the first round-the-world flight by crews of the US Army Air Service in 1924

Far left: The pioneer flights of the 'twenties were made possible by the fuel companies, which established fuelling stations at frequent, remote points along all the major routes. Shown here with a Shell fueller at Calcutta is the Fokker C.IV biplane in which Major Zanni of the Argentine Flying Corps made an unsuccessful attempt to fly round the world in 1924. He left Amsterdam on 26 July and abandoned the flight at Tokyo on 11 October

Left: The World Cruisers used interchangeable wheel and float landing gears for different stages of their long flight

This page, top: Minus wings and tyres, Sir Alan Cobham's D.H.50J is paraded in triumph through London after its trailblazing flight to Australia and back in 1926

Right: Two years earlier, powered by a Puma engine, the same D.H.50 had been used by Cobham for a survey flight to India. He is seen here, garlanded on arrival, with Sir Sefton Brancker, also garlanded, on his left, and his mechanic, A B Elliott, on his right

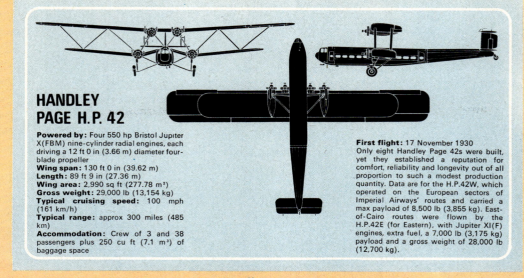

HANDLEY PAGE H.P. 42

Powered by: Four 550 hp Bristol Jupiter X(FBM) nine-cylinder radial engines, each driving a 12 ft 0 in (3.66 m) diameter four-blade propeller
Wing span: 130 ft 0 in (39.62 m)
Length: 89 ft 9 in (27.36 m)
Wing area: 2,990 sq ft (277.78 m²)
Gross weight: 29,000 lb (13,154 kg)
Typical cruising speed: 100 mph (161 km/h)
Typical range: approx 300 miles (485 km)
Accommodation: Crew of 3 and 38 passengers plus 250 cu ft (7.1 m³) of baggage space

First flight: 17 November 1930
Only eight Handley Page 42s were built, yet they established a reputation for comfort, reliability and longevity out of all proportion to such a modest production quantity. Data are for the H.P.42W, which operated on the European sectors of Imperial Airways' routes and carried a max payload of 8,500 lb (3,855 kg). East-of-Cairo routes were flown by the H.P.42E (for Eastern), with Jupiter XI(F) engines, extra fuel, a 7,000 lb (3,175 kg) payload and a gross weight of 28,000 lb (12,700 kg).

Top: The Westland Wapiti epitomises the 'general purpose' type of aircraft used for air control. To keep costs to a minimum it used as many existing D.H.9A components as possible including, originally, complete 'Ninak' wings

Left: The Vickers Victoria was a 22-passenger troop transport based on the Virginia bomber. Eight Victorias of No 70 Squadron spearheaded the famous airlift from Kabul, which evacuated 586 civilians, including King Inyatullah of Afghanistan and his family, during the rebellion of 1928-29

Bottom left: Powered like the Victoria Mk VI with Pegasus engines, the Valentia could be distinguished by its tail-wheel which replaced the tail-skid of the earlier type. It served for ten years from 1934, in the Middle East and India

Above: Workhorse of the air control squadrons was the D.H.9A. After extremely effective daylight bombing of German targets in the last few months of the first World War, this two-seater fought the Bolsheviks in Russia and dissident tribesmen everywhere from Aden and Iraq to the North-West Frontier of India

Centre right: The city of Mosul, in Iraq, was just one of the places kept in a state of relative peace by the air control squadrons. By maintaining the deterrent threat of bombing trouble-makers, aircraft like this Wapiti avoided the bloodshed on both sides that had always seemed inevitable when land forces were used

Bottom right: First of the famous series of Caproni 'colonial' bombers produced for the Italian Air Force in the inter-war years was the Ca 73. Layout was unusual, as the upper wing had a smaller span than the lower one, and the two 400 hp Lorraine engines were slung between them in a tandem 'power egg'

Far right: The Sopwith Snipe single-seat fighter was another combat aircraft of first World War vintage which was employed for many years on air control duties. These Snipes of No 1 Squadron were photographed near Baghdad in 1926

Air Control

AS EARLY AS 1911-12, during the Italo-Turkish War in Tripolitania, the aeroplane had demonstrated its potential for bombing, reconnaissance and leaflet-dropping. Thus it was first applied as an instrument of colonial warfare, an application which was to be emphasised to the point of exercising primary, and even absolute, air control in later years. The story of how this came about relates firstly to the RAF, and the philosophy behind such operations was once set out by an officer of that Service in these terms:

'Air control is the use of aircraft as the primary arm to support the political administration of an undeveloped country for the purpose of creating or restoring law and order. Aircraft usually act in co-operation with land forces, which fill some ancillary, but, nevertheless, important role—the securing, for instance, of the base for police purposes, or the pushing home of advantages gained by the air arm. Mountain, desert, marsh and swamp offer no obstruction to aircraft, which, ignoring such barriers, can penetrate to the source of trouble—right to the leader's fortress—within a few hours of its discovery. Against this arm uncivilised people are almost helpless, for they have practically no means of retaliation. Much of the effectiveness of air control depends, however, on good intelligence, which gives an intimate knowledge of the habits, mentality and pulse of the people, and enables pressure to be applied and confined at the centre of unrest. . . . Air operations are planned not to spread death and suffering, but to wear down the tribesman's morale, dislocate his normal life and thus make his existence wretched and intolerable.'

These plainly enunciated principles were carried into effect frequently in the years between the wars—years when RAF overseas operations were considerably more extensive than is commonly supposed, although it was seldom necessary to send

home-based squadrons abroad to supplement those already there. Another point which is not, perhaps, widely enough appreciated is that almost every RAF officer and man with more than five years in uniform served at least once with an overseas command. Air operations were mounted not only against the tribesmen of the North-west Frontier of India, but in Afghanistan, China, Egypt, the Sudan, Somaliland, Iraq, Palestine, Transjordania and Asia Minor. In 1922 the small military forces in Iraq were placed under the command of the Air Officer Commanding-in-Chief, Air Vice-Marshal Sir John Salmond, and the RAF assumed responsibility for the military and air control of the country. Later all other British military forces were withdrawn, and the RAF continued to exercise its responsibilities assisted by the Iraq Army and Assyrian Levies.

Notwithstanding the earlier pronouncement that, against the aeroplane, uncivilised peoples were 'almost helpless', they quickly learned the effectiveness of well-directed rifle fire, as attested by this letter written in 1928 by an RAF officer engaged in the Wahabi War:

'Now for the Shaiba news and the war with ed Dowish. This show is really nasty. He runs a gang of 2,500 well-trained raiders, all very good shots. So far he has shot down three people with direct hits in the radiator. Sqn Ldr Vincent was the first, and *he* got away with it. Jackson was the next. He was hit in the radiator and came down in the middle of them. Tried to scrap them with his revolver, but was killed —one in the head and the other in the heart. He was found later, stripped, but not mutilated. Next young Kellett was shot down in the same way, but landed over a ridge out of sight. He got away with both locks and bolts out of his guns, and collected all his ammunition before they appeared. . . . Our people dare not fly below 3,000 feet now, as they are shot up at once.

Two Vickers went with four 500-pounders, and nine 9As with Coopers. The photographs were good, and they show that one 500-pounder got a lot of sixty. They bombed the fort with the big stuff and all ran out and met the Coopers outside. . . .'

Such could be the perils, and potential destructiveness, of air control.

From the foregoing it will have been gathered that a standard type of aircraft used for air control was the de Havilland D.H.9A, from the basic design of which a successor, the Westland Wapiti, was developed. These were robust single-engined two-seat biplanes which, as adapted for operations overseas, accumulated a remarkable series of excrescences, such as a spare wheel, desert rations, a water skin or containers for beer bottles, and picketing gear. Jointly with their external armament this gained for them the reputation of carrying 'everything except the kitchen sink'.

It was not, however, in 'policing' operations alone that the RAF can be considered to have exercised air control. One unwarlike, though none the less significant, achievement was the establishment of an air mail service between Cairo and Baghdad—an instance of policemen turned postmen. Furthermore, the 'showing-the-flag' cruises, notably that of 27,000 miles (43,450 km) to Australia and back by Supermarine Southampton flying-boats, served notice that the RAF policemen had long arms. That they offered real protection to British citizens in foreign lands was evident when families were evacuated from Kabul in Vickers Victoria troop-carriers, over 10,000 ft (3,050 m) mountains during one of the most severe winters on record.

Although the D.H.9A and Wapiti merited their official classification as 'general-purpose' aircraft they were essentially bombers, descended from the D.H.4 of 1916. Aircraft even better qualified to share their 'GP' classification were the Italian Caproni monoplanes, developed specially for colonial operations. In being high-wing, strut-braced monoplanes they contrasted sharply with the British biplanes, and a capacious fuselage with enclosed cabin enabled them to serve not only as bombers and reconnaissance aircraft but as transports also. Of these the tri-motor Ca 101 entered service shortly before the Italian campaign against Abyssinia, in the course of which it served not only for attack but in maintaining supplies. Also employed in the same campaign was a similar aircraft having only a single engine and designated Ca 111; later still came the Ca 133, which reverted to the three-engined formula. This last-named type was used to transport Italian paratroops in the invasion of Albania, and its relatively roomy fuselage may have suggested its nicknames of *Caprona* (she-goat) and *Vacca* (cow). These appellations seem somewhat invidious, having regard to the fact that the British biplanes could exhibit quite bovine characteristics (especially when carrying objects underneath) yet have commonly been styled 'workhorses'.

For operations in the French colonies, Breguet single-engined biplanes were generally employed, though experimental examples of a new class known as *type coloniale* were built. One of these, three-engined like the Ca 101 and 133, had the sides of the fuselage entirely cut away, the top then forming a sort of canopy for the rear gunner. Thus protected from colonial suns, he could doubtless have made his contribution to air control with a degree of comfort beyond the dreams of the crews who did the pioneering—with everything except the kitchen sink.

Left: The spare wheel carried by this D.H.9A of No 30 Squadron was typical of the appendages which tended to sprout on air control machines. It was not unusual to see a goatskin of water dangling from the cockpit

Top: The D.H.10, less well-known than most de Havilland designs, was just too late to see action in the first World War. This D.H.10 of 216 Squadron helped to establish the Cairo-Baghdad mail service across the desert in 1921

Above: The Vickers Vincent, with 660 hp Pegasus engine, was the type which finally replaced the Wapiti and Fairey IIIF in 1934. Operated entirely overseas, in the Middle East, Africa and India, the Vincent was in action in Iraq as late as 1941

Centre right: The Hawker Hart two-seat day bomber was one of the family of combat aircraft with which the company's great chief designer, Sydney Camm, made his mark in the 'thirties. When it entered service in 1930, RAF fighter squadrons tried in vain to catch it

Bottom right: Best-remembered RAF floatplane of the air control era was the Fairey IIID, with 450 hp Napier Lion engine

DE HAVILLAND D.H.9A

Powered by: One 400 hp Liberty twelve-cylinder Vee-type engine, driving a two-blade propeller
Wing span: 45 ft 11½ in (14.00 m)
Length: 30 ft 3 in (9.22 m)
Wing area: 488 sq ft (45.34 m²)
Gross weight: 4,645 lb (2,107 kg)
Max speed: 123 mph (198 km/h) at sea level
Endurance: 5 hr 15 min
Accommodation: Crew of 2
First flight: early 1918

Descended from Geoffrey de Havilland's D.H.4 day bomber of 1916, via the D.H.9, the D.H.9A or 'Ninak' combined the airframe of the latter (with slightly increased wing area) with a more reliable engine. Four RAF squadrons had been equipped before the Armistice in 1918, and after the war the D.H.9A served with 12 home squadrons and 9 overseas, nearly 2,500 being built by a dozen British companies and remaining in RAF service until the early 1930s.

CAPRONI Ca 111

Powered by: One 970 hp Isotta-Fraschini Asso 750 RC eighteen-cylinder W-type engine, driving a four-blade propeller
Wing span: 64 ft 6⅞ in (19.68 m)
Length: 50 ft 2¼ in (15.30 m)
Wing area: 664.13 sq ft (61.70 m²)
Gross weight: 11,795 lb (5,350 kg)
Max speed: 186 mph (300 km/h)
Range: 1,245 miles (2,000 km)
Accommodation: Crew of 3/4

The Ca 111 was typical of the range of 'colonial' aeroplanes of the early 1930s which, in Italy, were almost the exclusive prerogative of the Caproni company. They derived from the Ca 97 and were built to a basic formula allowing them to be powered by one, two or three engines. Although ordered ostensibly for reconnaissance, they carried three or four machine-guns and a small load of bombs, and were used extensively during the Italian campaigns in Africa during the 1930s. Caproni continued the concept later in the decade with a series of twin-engined monoplanes for similar duties, beginning with the Ca 309 Ghibli (Desert Wind) of 1936.

Winner over 103 other designs in a light
aircraft competition held in 1953 by the
Royal Aero Club of Great Britain, the
Airtourer was designed and originally
produced in Australia. The 170 built by
Victa Ltd have been followed by many
others manufactured by Aero Engine
Services Ltd, a New Zealand company
which currently produces this highly-
attractive and fully-aerobatic two-seat
aeroplane for civil and military customers
in several parts of the world

Left: Sir Charles Kingsford Smith's 'old bus', the Fokker F.VIIB/3m *Southern Cross*, is preserved today in a specially built display room at Brisbane's Eagle Farm Airport, where it ended its most famous flight

Above: The *Southern Cross* in flight

Below: 'Smithy' by the tail of the Lockheed Altair *Lady Southern Cross* in which he made the first west-to-east flight across the Pacific with Sir Gordon Taylor

CHARLES KINGSFORD SMITH

PIONEER AIRMEN were all ahead of their time, because they were so often facing the unknown. One of the greatest, who faced a barrage of unknowns, was Australia's Sir Charles Kingsford Smith, who set out in the late 1920s to prove that long hops across sea and land were not only safe and reliable but could become an economic proposition.

At one stage he held 11 world aviation records, but throughout a hectic life he was modest, meticulous to detail in pre-flight preparation and always in command in the air—often in the most appalling weather, for meteorology was still in its infancy.

His epic 1928 trans-Pacific flight in his 'old bus', the *Southern Cross,* was perhaps the most glamorous of all his great flights; but there were many others just as daring and often requiring even greater skill—like the time in mid-1935 when he limped back 650 miles (1,045 km) across the Tasman Sea to Sydney at 500 ft (150 m) with his co-pilot, Sir Gordon Taylor, transferring oil manually from the dead starboard engine to the port motor, which was thirsty for oil and threatening to stop due to low pressure. Sir Gordon Taylor was awarded the George Cross, but Kingsford Smith's flying contributed to their safe return.

'Smithy', as he was universally known, was no daredevil airman who gambled all to achieve his goal. He was a devoted, almost simple man, in love with machines and flying, and set on one goal—to prove the ability of the aeroplane to be an asset to man.

His World War 1 exploits taught him much and brought him many friends. He had learned to fly the hard way, rising through the ranks from a motorised despatch rider to a commission in the Royal Flying Corps and the Military Cross on his uniform.

In 1919 the young Kingsford Smith, then in England, saw first the Atlantic conquered and then England linked with

Australia. He had hoped to enter the latter competition himself, but youth and inexperience had disqualified him. Dismayed at this, he sailed for Hollywood, to tackle instead the dangerous assignment of stunt flying in films. Back in Australia by 1921, he experienced his first civil flying in the country areas of New South Wales, and then for two hard years in the rugged north of Western Australia. Time between flights was not wasted, for it was during this spell of outback flying that he dreamed of conquering the Pacific.

This was a goal that most people con-

sidered impossible, and sponsorship proved his greatest hurdle. Fortunately another wartime Australian flier, Charles Ulm, shared his enthusiasm. They became a great, almost inseparable pair—Kingsford Smith a 'born' flier, full of courage, nervous energy and a passion for thoroughness when preparing an aircraft for flight; while Ulm became the organiser and business brain.

In 1927 the pair established a round-Australia record of 10 days and 6 hours. Then they set off for America to undertake the conquest of the Pacific. Their 7,000-mile (11,265-km) flight some 18 months later in the three-engined Fokker *Southern Cross* (bought, minus motors and instruments, from the Australian-born polar explorer Sir Hubert Wilkins) succeeded because they modified the aircraft for long-distance flying and used the most modern radio and navigation aids then available. The backing of a rich Californian, Captain Allen Hancock, gave them the foundation they needed to begin the epic flight.

On reaching Australia, 'Smithy' and his three-man crew (the navigator and radio operator were Americans) were acclaimed heroes. Despite all the glory, financial rewards, and the honorary rank of Squadron Leader awarded him by the Royal Australian Air Force, his greatest satisfaction was the proof that such a flight was not only possible but could point the way to a regular link between his country and the USA.

Success had come the hard way, but 'Smithy' was determined that it would never be his master. Each record-setting flight which followed showed more than the last what a great airman he was. Incidents were few: his greatest enemy was always the weather. When the *Southern Cross* flew non-stop from Australia to New Zealand and back, the weather was so bad on the eastbound leg

Top: The *Southern Star,* one of the Avro Tens (licence-built Fokker F.VIIB/3ms) operated by Australian National Airways, the airline founded in 1929 by Kingsford Smith and Charles Ulm

Above: Unloading at London's Croydon Airport the Christmas mail from New Zealand and Australia delivered by Kingsford Smith in *Southern Star* on 16 December 1931. 'Smithy' had saved the situation by flying long forced stages after the *Southern Sun,* in which the mail left Australia, had been badly damaged in a take-off accident at Alor Star in Malaya

Above right: Another picture of the *Southern Cross.* After its pioneer trans-Pacific flight, this great aircraft was first across the Tasman Sea and then first to fly around the world with a crossing of the equator en route

Below: 'Smithy' in the helmet, leather coat and goggles that were the hallmark of a professional pilot in the open-cockpit era of the 'twenties and early 'thirties

that he had to have new propellers fitted before he could leave Christchurch. When the New Zealand Government gave him £2,000, he commented with typical frankness: 'We did not fly here to win 2,000 quid; we flew here to link two hitherto unlinked outposts of Empire'.

This trans-Tasman flight taught Kingsford Smith and his ever-present co-pilot Charles Ulm that a commercial air service between the two countries could be opened once more powerful and reliable aero-engines had been developed. In the meantime the two airmen formed, in December 1928, Australian National Airways Ltd. They flew to England in the *Southern Cross* and placed orders for four Avro Ten monoplanes. Then, while Ulm returned to Australia to establish their

civil airline, Kingsford Smith planned two more ventures—an east-west crossing of the Atlantic in the *Southern Cross* and a solo flight from England to Australia.

After a stint in Australia to help Ulm on the airline venture, he returned to Holland where the *Southern Cross* was being overhauled by the Fokker company. With KLM co-pilot Evert Van Dyke, he then left Portmarnock beach in Southern Ireland hoping to fly non-stop to New York. Wind and weather were against him, and the aircraft landed in Harbour Grace, Newfoundland, after 31½ hours' flying; but New York still gave him its traditional ticker-tape welcome. By flying on to Oakland, California, he became the first man to fly round the world with a crossing of the Equator en route.

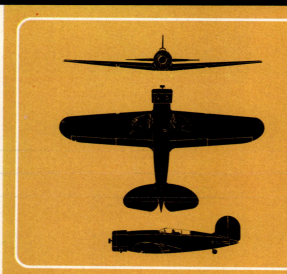

LOCKHEED ALTAIR 8D

Powered by: One 450 hp Pratt & Whitney R-1340-SE Wasp nine-cylinder radial engine, driving a 9 ft 0 in (2.74 m) diameter two-blade propeller
Wing span: 42 ft 9¼ in (13.04 m)
Length: 27 ft 1 in (8.25 m)
Wing area: 294.1 sq ft (27.32 m²)
Gross weight: 4,600 lb (2,086 kg)
Max speed: 227 mph (365 km/h)
Accommodation: Crew of 2
First flight: 1930 (as Sirius); 1934 (as Altair)
During 1929-32 Lockheed built a series of 25 elegant single-engined monoplanes with the names Explorer, Sirius and Altair. Five Sirius were later converted into Altairs, and it was one of these, known as an Altair 8D, in which Charles Kingsford Smith and P G Taylor made their epic trans-Pacific flight from Brisbane to San Francisco in October-November 1934. Longest single stage of the journey was the 3,150 miles (5,070 km) from Fiji to Honolulu.

Left: Sir Gordon Taylor demonstrates how he performed the feat that made him an Australian national hero. When the starboard engine of *Southern Cross* stopped over the Tasman Sea and the port engine began to give trouble through oil shortage, he transferred oil manually from the 'dead' engine by clambering along the support struts between the cockpit and engines

Right: One of the last 'outdoor' photographs of *Southern Cross* shows it with a DC-6 of British Commonwealth Pacific Airlines which followed, after World War 2, the trail it had pioneered between Australia and the USA

The *Southern Cross* came to rest, temporarily, in the care of Captain Hancock, who had helped so much in the early days with the South Pacific flight.

The ensuing years brought many records 'Smithy's' way, mainly in small single-engined aircraft. In the *Southern Cross Junior,* an Avro biplane, he flew from England to Australia in less than 10 days. His comment on reaching Darwin was: 'This shows there is really nothing in these long air trips beyond the reach of the ordinary pilot'. Kingsford Smith was now 34; his airline was established, and all was going well. The *Southern Cross* was shipped from California to join the company fleet, but then disaster struck when one of ANA's passenger aircraft, the *Southern Cloud,* was lost in the Snowy Mountains between Sydney and Melbourne, where it was not found until 27 years later.

Undaunted by the loss of money and prestige, he again launched into the international aviation field, this time with a series of remarkable mail flights, often linking with those of Imperial Airways between London and Australia. Record followed record, and in 1932 he was knighted for his services to aviation. In October 1933 he flew from England to Australia in seven days to establish yet another record. Then, while attempting a further record flight, he disappeared off the coast of Burma. The mystery was not solved until 1937, when a wheel of his Lockheed Altair was recovered from the Andaman sea off Burma.

Sir Charles Kingsford Smith, in 18 crowded years of flying, blazed trails far beyond the wildest dreams of many. He is remembered today in many countries, but in none so much as his own Australia. His original 'old bus' is maintained in a museum at Brisbane's airport—where it landed on that morning in 1928 after his conquest of the Pacific. Sydney, which has always claimed him as its own, named its international airport after him. The new Australian $20 note carries his portrait, as have many stamps issued by the Australian Post Office over the years. Such honour is justified. Sir Charles Kingsford Smith was a perfectionist, who sought the impossible and achieved his goal through a host of qualities that made him a truly great Australian.

At 07.00 hours on Sunday, 7 December 1941, the majority of US Navy and Air Corps personnel based in Hawaii were still very much at ease; a fairly normal state for any Service units in times of peace. Ratings and privates that had been on overnight duty yawned and waited impatiently for their reliefs: ahead lay tropical-island Sunday—a day of sun and peace.

Only in the experimental radar post at Opana was there the slightest suggestion that this might be a Sunday with a difference. There, on the screen, two large and mysterious blips appeared, and at about 07.10 hours were reported to the duty officer at Fort Shafter. 'Nothing to worry about', he said, 'it's either some B-17s we are expecting or naval aircraft on an exercise.'

Just 45 minutes later, all hell broke loose as the first wave of Japanese fighters streaked across Bellows, Hickam and Wheeler Fields and the Marine Air Station at Ewa Town, their task to eliminate the defences of Pearl Harbor. Almost simultaneously, torpedo-bombers and other bombers strafed the US Navy's Pacific Fleet, lying at anchor off Ford Island.

When the attackers withdrew, 1 hour and 45 minutes later, they left behind a shambles of wrecked aircraft and military installations, wreathed in smoke and flames; more than 2,000 dead; and the wreckage of the Pacific Fleet. In that short period of time Japan, seizing the initiative and using only air power, had gained domination of the Pacific.

What, you may ask, has this to do with General 'Billy' Mitchell, who died on 19 February 1936?

The connection is that Mitchell predicted just this event almost six years before it occurred. In his book *The Wild Blue Yonder,* Emile Gauvreau recorded carefully the words of Mitchell's comments on what he considered to be the greatest threat to the United States. It concluded: . . . Hawaii is swarming with Japanese spies. As I have said before, that's where the blow will be struck—on a fine, quiet Sunday morning.'

Those responsible for the defence of the USA did not believe him. In 1906, before the US Army owned even a single aeroplane, Mitchell had said: 'Conflicts, no doubt, will be carried out in the future in the air . . .'. Authority had ignored him then. In 1925, in his own book *Winged Defence,* he wrote: 'In the future, campaigns across the seas will be carried on from land base to land base under the protection of aircraft.' Again, no-one heeded his words—except, perhaps, the Japanese.

In fact, Mitchell's reward for his outspoken condemnation of the US Navy and War Departments resulted in court-martial and disgrace. He had become a nuisance to authority, a vitriolic agitator against what he believed to be the shortsightedness of the War Department. What, then, were the facts that led to this sad termination of the career of a devoted Air Corps officer?

Born in Nice, France, in 1879, son of a US senator, William E Mitchell began his Army service as a private, enlisting at the outbreak of the Spanish-American War. Soon commissioned, he served with the Signal Corps in Cuba, the Philippines and Alaska before his first keen interest in aviation was aroused.

During the period 1907-14 he studied deeply the strategy of war and in 1915 was asked to prepare a report on the needs of Army aviation. So well did he tackle this job that his report was reproduced in pamphlet form and given wide distribution. Overnight, Major 'Billy' Mitchell—not yet a pilot—became the United States' exponent of air power.

Too old at 36 and too high in rank to be given pilot training by the Army, he learned to fly at his own expense. When the USA entered World War I, Mitchell was one of five US Army aviation officers in Europe, and lost no time in gaining permission to visit the front. He managed to spend ten days there and, on his own initiative and with French assistance, drafted a plan for an American air force in France.

One of his proposals was for a large

Left: Seen in flight over Washington, the Martin MB-1 bomber was evolved for the US Army in 1918 in an attempt to better the performance of the Handley Page O/400, then bring produced under licence in America

Above: The MB-2, developed from the MB-1, was the bomber used by 'Billy' Mitchell for his attacks on old battleships at sea in 1921-23. Two 420-hp Liberty engines gave it a top speed of 99 mph (160 km/h). A 2,000 lb (907 kg) bomb-load could be carried and range was 400 miles (640 km)

Right: 'Billy' Mitchell (on right), wearing the leather coat, helmet and goggles that were essential for flight in the open-cockpit military aircraft of the early post-war years

ATOR AGITATOR

strategic air component. It was not authorised, but this shows clearly his advanced understanding of the use of air power. In the closing months of the war, Mitchell was able to give at least one great demonstration of its potential.

For nearly four years the Germans had held a salient which penetrated deeply into the French lines at St-Mihiel. Before a general advance could be made on this front it was essential that the enemy strongpoint be wiped out. Mitchell concentrated no fewer than 1,483 aircraft along an eighty-mile (130-km) front, camouflaged cleverly from the enemy. When he was able to deploy this armada, on 14 September 1918, numerical superiority in the air enabled him to maintain the initiative. War-weary troops, foot-slogging it through the mud and misery below, were so heartened to see for the first time a defensive umbrella of their own aircraft that, within days, the Allies were advancing everywhere along the line.

When war in Europe ended, Mitchell remained with the Army of Occupation. On his return to America, in 1919, he was staggered to discover that the mighty Army Air Service of 1918 had been almost liquidated; by the following year it was but 5 per cent of its wartime strength.

Most difficult post-war problem was to resolve the future deployment of the Air Service. Those who had thought deeply

concerning the potential of air power were convinced that it would dominate any future war—a conclusion that was directly opposed to Naval thinking.

Foremost of the air power 'radicals' was Mitchell, audacious, outspoken and ready to employ any medium to gain an audience for his views. When his suggestion of tests to prove that battleships were impotent when confronted by bombers was opposed by the Navy, he focussed public attention on the Army-Navy conflict by means of the National press.

When, finally, the tests were carried out during July 1921, Martin bombers sank three ex-German warships anchored in Chesapeake Bay, including the 'unsinkable' battleship Ostfriesland. When the exercise was repeated in 1923, two obsolete US battleships shared the same fate. Here was proof, if any was needed, that the days of naval power were numbered, said Mitchell and his supporters. The Navy, on the other hand, was not slow to argue that the result might have been very different had Mitchell's bombers attacked battleships able to retaliate and take evasive action, instead of stationary, unmanned, unprotected hulks.

Naval opinion, prestige and power, backed by Congress, were the winners. Mitchell was the disappointed loser and continued his air power campaign at any and every opportunity, becoming in the

process an embarrassment even to higher-ranking officers in his own Service.

Impatience and outspoken comment led to his downfall: after the loss of the Navy dirigible Shenandoah in 1925, he publicly accused the high command of the Army and Navy of being guilty of 'incompetency, criminal negligence and almost treasonable administration of the National Defense.' The inevitable court-martial, which Mitchell had hoped to use as a platform to expound his air power theories, found him guilty and suspended him from the air force for five years. Rather than suffer this disgrace, he resigned his commission.

For ten more years he campaigned and crusaded, wrote scathing articles, books and letters to the press. He lectured the length and breadth of America, arguing that air power, properly conceived and deployed, could, alone, bring about an enemy's defeat. Only one thing could stop him. The ceaseless campaigning for what he believed to be right—the creation of a mighty air arm as the sword and shield of his own beloved country—proved a tremendous strain, and he died of a heart attack early in 1936.

How ironical that it took the tragedy of Pearl Harbor and the subsequent American bomber offensive to vindicate his foresight and beliefs, and that ten years after his death Congress awarded him posthumously the Medal of Honour.

THE BARNSTORMERS

THE DEBT OWED by aviation to the aerial showmen, the clowns and thrill-providers, the 'barnstormers', the exponents of the 'one-night stand' and the providers of 'five-bob flips' is greater than is generally acknowledged, even though some of these practitioners occasionally brought their profession into disrepute. In a purely technical sense the great meeting at Reims in August 1909 was the biggest stimulus that flying had experienced up to that time; but it also provided a public spectacle which led to near-hysteria and to the staging of other great meetings on the Continent, in Britain and in the USA. Eminent among these were the displays at the London Aerodrome, Hendon, arranged by Claude Grahame-White and his associates. 'G-W' had learned to fly in France, and had already distinguished himself in his famous duel with Louis Paulhan in the London-Manchester race of 1910. His name was also famous in the USA, where he had created a sensation by landing on Executive Avenue (now Pennsylvania Avenue) in front of the White House to call on President Taft.

Grahame-White was a born showman, and on his return from America he established the aerodrome already mentioned. From 1911 until war came in 1914 he promoted frequent meetings for the entertainment and edification of the public, who sometimes numbered over 50,000. But he achieved far more than this by appraising members of Parliament of the military potential of flying and by his crusading call of 'Wake Up, England!', associated with a seaplane flight round Britain in 1912. A Grahame-White advertisement of that year announced: 'Racing every Saturday and Holiday (weather permitting). Special Exhibition Flights every Thursday, Saturday and Sunday afternoon by well-known Aviators. Admission to enclosures 6d, 1s and 2s 6d. Passenger flights from £2 2s.' Fixtures listed included 'Illuminated Night Flying Display (7.30 pm)' and 'Naval and Military Day'. This same advertisement carried the footnote: 'All Naval, Military and Territorial Officers joining our school will be entitled to a special reduction off our usual terms.'

Fittingly, the Hendon aerodrome, so beloved of Londoners, became the venue for the ever-memorable RAF Displays of the 1920s and 30s. Showmanship, it became evident, was not the prerogative of the free-lance civilians: and, indeed, it achieved new levels of perfection when

governed by the discipline (sometimes disguised as clowning) of Service flying.

Shortly after the Reims meeting Louis Blériot showed how lucrative exhibition flying could be by receiving the equivalent of \$4,000 for five days' flying in Berlin, and while the American Glenn Curtiss was concluding his resounding success at Reims one of his pupils, Charles F Willard, was giving his first public display at Toronto, Canada.

Willard is acknowledged as the first of the legendary American 'barnstormers', a name deriving from the itinerant players whose theatre was any convenient barn. In January 1910 Willard astonished the crowd at the first US flying 'meet' by the accuracy of his spot-landings. This event took place at Dominguez Field, Los Angeles, and was under the management of the air-minded actor Dick Ferris. Other great names on the bill were Louis Paulhan, Glenn Curtiss, Charles Hamilton, Roy Knabenshue and Lincoln Beachey—the last two with airships! Dick Ferris's wife, actress Florence Stone, was persuaded to ascend with Paulhan, who won nearly \$20,000 in prizes.

Later in 1910 both Glenn Curtiss and the Wright brothers were training pilots for exhibition flying, and in September the British pilots Claude Grahame-White, A V Roe and T O M Sopwith themselves went barnstorming with marked success at the Harvard-Boston Meet, where American pilots included Curtiss, Willard, Ralph Johnstone, Walter Brookins, Earl Ovington and Clifford B Harmon. The Belmont Park Meet of the following month was a society occasion: barnstorming, on the grand scale at least, was now respectable, though some lesser freelances were little better than charlatans.

Perhaps the most popular of the American exhibition pilots was Lincoln Beachey, who is said to have held his audiences in contempt, declaring: 'They only come to see me die'. And die he did, while performing at the San Francisco Exposition of 1915.

Before 1914 aerobatics in the modern sense were unknown, and pilots had their individual methods of thrilling the crowd by flying dangerously, or apparently so. Beachey believed in doing things in style: he picked up handkerchiefs with a wing-tip, flew under the Falls Bridge at Niagara, and, disguised as 'The Mysterious Woman Aviatrix', played a joke on his rival Blanche Stuart Scott, the first woman trained by

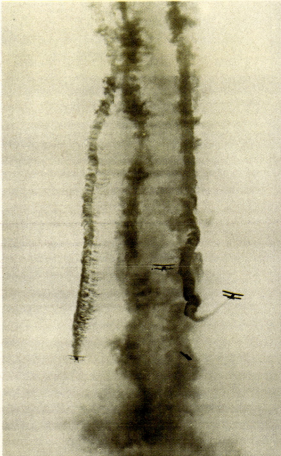

Top: Variants of the Avro 504 were the most celebrated of all British barnstorming aircraft in the 'twenties and early 'thirties. Some, like the Avro 536, were modified to carry as many as four passengers, in side-by-side pairs, in the rear cockpit

Centre: Smoke-trailing aerobatics are nothing new, as is proved by this photograph of three Grebe single-seat fighters at the 1930 Foyal Air Force Display. These annual pageants did much to keep alive public interest in the RAF during the lean inter-war years

Bottom: During its first three months with Air Alan Cobham's National Aviation Day barnstormers, the prototype Airspeed Ferry carried about 36,000 passengers, ten at a time. Turnrounds were often made in less than half a minute; refuelling took 90 seconds

Below: Pioneer of barnstorming was the Avro Transport Company, which operated these float-equipped 504Ks from the slipway at Bowness where the Lakes Flying Company had offered joyrides in the Avro-built Water Bird eight years earlier, in 1911. Chief pilot was Howard Pixton, who had given Britain her first Schneider Trophy victory in a Sopwith Tabloid seaplane in 1914

Bottom: To demonstrate the 'high speed' of aeroplanes in a dramatic manner in 1915, American pilots often staged races against the fastest cars of the time. The resulting thrills are evident in this picture of De Lloyd Thompson's 90-hp Gyro-Duplex Day biplane just leading the famous racing motorist Barney Oldfield

Curtiss. A real bandwaggon advertised 'The Moissant Flyers', team stars Mathilde Moissant and Harriet Quimby. Like many others of her profession, Miss Quimby was killed before the eyes of her public.

One great individualist was Glenn Martin, later to be associated with big bombers and flying-boats. He flew for the growing Hollywood film industry, performing such stunts as dropping a baseball into a catcher's mitt and hunting coyotes from the air. He demonstrated the advertising value of the aeroplane by showering Los Angeles with leaflets, though he also took care to demonstrate more useful applications, such as delivering mail and newspapers, taking films, and tracking escaped convicts.

But the golden age of the barnstormers had not as yet arrived. This came about only when war-surplus aircraft were offered at knock-down prices after the 1918 Armistice. Pilots and mechanics were likewise surplus. Teams of these men swarmed, as it has been said, 'like locusts across the American countryside'. Passenger flights, usually in Curtiss 'Jennies', were offered at $12.50 for ten or fifteen minutes, though the fee soon dropped to under $3. 'Jennies' served also for the staging of 'hair-raising' dogfights and 'death-defying' feats, among which wing-walking, 'riding' the tail and dangling from the undercarriage were among the more spectacular. By using rope ladders or by interlocking wings the stunt men would change from one aircraft to another; but their careers were brief, and a growing accident rate, sometimes linked with poor maintenance, had severely reduced their numbers by 1923. Gradually the fabulous barnstormers became air-taxi operators.

One of their stunts, however, had foreshadowed a tremendous development in aeronautics, for in July 1921 Earl May demonstrated mid-air refuelling by changing aircraft with a can of gasoline strapped to his back.

In Europe, and especially in Britain, war-surplus aircraft similarly provided the public with their *baptême de l'air* or 'first flip', though the spine-chilling stunts were mainly American. Opposite number of the 'Jenny' in Britain was the Avro 504, variously adapted for passenger-carrying. 'Joy-ride' Avros were familiar round British resorts until the early 1930s, but as they aged so business waned.

One pilot who started giving joyrides in 1919 was Alan (now Sir Alan) Cobham. Notwithstanding his historic flights across the Empire he retained his interest in giving the public a show, and from April to October in the years 1932 to 1936 his Air Display 'circuses' put on well over 12,000 performances and carried nearly a million passengers. With their conclusion the barn doors finally closed.

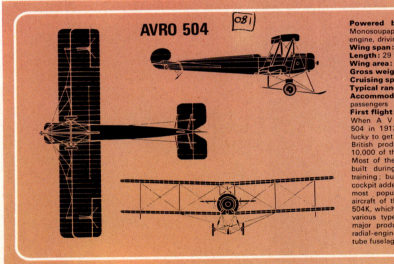

AVRO 504

Powered by: One 100 hp Gnome Monosoupape seven-cylinder rotary engine, driving a two-blade propeller
Wing span: 36 ft 0 in (10.97 m)
Length: 29 ft 5 in (8.97 m)
Wing area: 330 sq ft (30.66 m²)
Gross weight: 1,829 lb (830 kg)
Cruising speed: 75 mph (121 km/h)
Typical range: 225 miles (362 km)
Accommodation: Crew of 1 and 2 passengers
First flight: July 1913
When A V Roe designed the original 504 in 1913, he thought he would be lucky to get an order for six; by the time British production ended in 1932, over 10,000 of these biplanes had been built. Most of them were originally 2-seaters, built during the first World War for training; but after the war, with a third cockpit added, the 504 became one of the most popular 'circus' and joy-riding aircraft of the 1920s. Data apply to the 504K, which had a universal mounting for various types of rotary engine. The last major production model was the Lynx radial-engined 504N, which had a steel-tube fuselage; 598 were built.

Top: What the well-dressed American barnstorming pilot wore in the 'twenties

Centre: Standard mount of US joyriders was the Curtiss 'Jenny', America's counterpart of the Avro 504. This was one of the slightly different N-8s, as used in the Mexican expedition of 1915-16

Above: Star performer at the Cobham displays was Geoffrey Tyson, whose tricks included picking up a handkerchief on the wingtip of his Tiger Moth. To celebrate the 25th anniversary of Blériot's first Channel flight, in 1934, he flew his Tiger inverted across the same stretch of water

Left: G-EBSG was one of five Avro 504Ks operated successively by South Wales Airways from a hillside hangar at Wenvoe. Refuelling was done with standard motor fuel from the local garage

Above: No picture taken in the years immediately after the first World War conveys the barnstorming spirit better than this photograph of a 504K performing a loop. This war-proven Avro trainer was ideally suited to give the public its first taste of flying, and is still remembered as one of the great aeroplanes of all time

Left: Marine counterpart of the picture at the bottom of page 521, this photograph shows Raymond Morris, the manager of the Curtiss Company in California, matching one of his flying-boats against a 90-hp speedboat in 1915

lightest of

THE WORLD'S FIRST real light aeroplane, and the first 'home-built' also, was Santos-Dumont's Demoiselle, developed from the venturesome little Brazilian's 'No 19' of 1907. This was not a great success, for it was difficult to fly; yet such was the lure of the air that sportsman-pilots purchased Blériot monoplanes, Farman biplanes and similar types, or even built machines themselves. They then began to use them for cross-country flying, and it was not unknown for these daring young men to drop in on friends for tea, leaving their spidery craft on the lawn, for many of the aeroplanes of those times possessed true STOL (short take-off and landing) qualities. There were attempts to enclose the cockpits for greater comfort and better streamlining, and some constructors made special efforts in the directions of cheapness and simplicity; but when war came in 1914 there was a general piling-on of engine power for the highest possible military performance, and though it was still not unknown for a pilot to drop in for tea he did so in the knowledge that tea-times ahead might be few.

The Armistice of 1918 found people weary of war and often weary too of aeroplanes; but the benefits of air transport for both public and private purposes were clearly too great for total neglect, and little sporting and touring aeroplanes came into being alongside the first airliners. The Sopwith company brought out the Dove, a two-seat development of their little Pup, considered by experts to be the most delightful of all fighters to fly; but times were hard, flying tuition expensive, and very few Doves appeared. Strictly speaking, the Dove was not the first Sopwith light aeroplane, for during the war the company had built two types of 'runabout' for their famous test pilot Harry Hawker.

Seeking simplicity and cheapness, the Blackburn company produced a little monoplane which they called the Sidecar, because the two occupants were seated side-by-side; but the greatest distinction this achieved was that of being exhibited at Harrods. The Sidecar had an engine of only 40 hp, as had the Bristol Babe, likewise built in 1919, while the Avro Baby of the same year flew on only 35 hp. One Baby flew to Australia and another to Russia, but only eight were

the light

G-EBME

Opposite page:
Top left: One of the first post-war attempts to produce an economical private-owner type, the Sopwith Dove was evolved from the famous Pup fighter

Centre left: This fearsome-looking machine was, in fact, a gentle, 70 mph (112 km/h) BAC Drone, powered by a 23 hp Douglas Sprite motorcycle engine. Built in the early 'thirties, it represented an attempt to bring powered flying within the reach of a wide cross-section of the public

Top right: Despite its diminutive size, the Avro Baby was used for many great flights in the years immediately following the first World War. The prototype, shown here, had a 35 hp Green engine dating from 1911; its total flying life was only two minutes, as it spun into Hamble foreshore from 300 ft (91 m) when the engine was accidentally switched off soon after its first take-off

Bottom: This Cygnet of 1924 is remembered not only as the winner of the Light Plane Competition at Lympne two years later but as the first Hawker design by the great Sir Sydney Camm. It was rebuilt after World War 2 and this photograph was taken in 1949

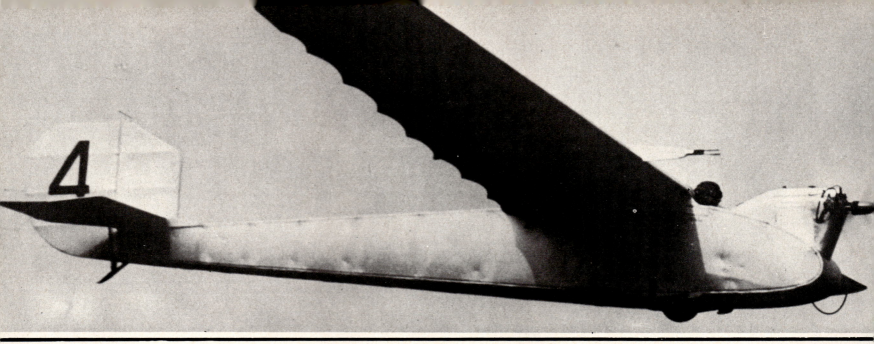

built. Other light aeroplanes of 1919 were the Grahame-White Bantam, Boulton & Paul P.9 and Central Centaur IV, having engines of 80, 90 and 100 hp respectively. Certainly among the best private-owner aeroplanes of the period was the Austin Whippet, though the same could hardly be said of the BAT Crow — an attempt to revive the Demoiselle formula of Santos-Dumont.

In 1922 the Bristol company produced their Taxiplane, an excellent 100-hp three-seater designed with the private owner much in mind; but though a technical success this proved a commercial failure. A more significant event of the same year was the *Daily Mail* Gliding Competition at Itford Hill, for this aroused great interest in engineless flight and led to a new class of British light aeroplane, generally described as powered gliders. Using engines of extremely low power to sustain them in the air, machines of this class were already being developed in Germany and France, and the work of British designers in the same field was stimulated in April 1923 by the offer of £500 in prize money by the Duke of Sutherland. This was quickly followed by an offer of £1,000 from the *Daily Mail*, which, not without some justification, had come to regard flying competitions as its own preserve.

The contests which resulted were held during the week beginning 8 October 1923 at Lympne aerodrome, Kent, and were known as 'The Motor Glider Competitions', though some people argued that this was a misnomer as a glider with an engine was an aeroplane. But the name did serve to stress that the £1,500 was to be awarded for low fuel consumption, though donors came forward with prizes for other qualities.

Included among the 27 entries, four of which were French or Belgian, were two remarkable monoplanes of a type built by the English Electric Company to the order of the Air Ministry and known as the Wren. This type had been designed before the competition rules were made public and was powered with an ABC motorcycle engine of 398 cc capacity. Quickly the Wren proved itself capable of level flight using a mere 3½ hp, although its loaded weight was 420 lb (190.5 kg). Features of

the Wren were a cantilever wing and wheels which protruded through slots in the fuselage bottom. Other types designed before the rules were known were the Gnosspelius Gull, a birdlike monoplane with a central engine driving two propellers, and the ANEC, another monoplane, in which the pilot sat below the wing and looked out through a window above him and cut-outs in the sides.

A particularly pretty monoplane was Captain Geoffrey de Havilland's D.H.53 Humming Bird, and a particularly ingenious one was the Parnall Pixie, with its two sets of wings, one for economy and one for speed. The pioneer A V Roe entered his Type 560, a monoplane of extremely 'clean' appearance, and another Avro, the Type 558 biplane, was designed by Mr Roy Chadwick — a far cry from his mighty Lancaster bomber of later years. The smallest entry of all was the Gloster Gannet, the biplane wings of which spanned a mere 18 ft (5.5 m). Viget was the name of a biplane from Vickers, and the famous composite name of Martinsyde was echoed by that of Mr George Handasyde, who designed a monoplane along the lines of his earlier glider. Captain W H Sayers, who during the war had designed the tiny Grain Kitten fighter (span 18 ft = 5.5 m, weight loaded 491 lb = 223 kg), had three monoplanes built by Handley Page. Hurricane was the name of a monoplane from the Aero Club of the Royal Aircraft Establishment, Farnborough. Its pilot was Flt Lt P W S Bulman, who, twelve years later, was to take a more famous Hurricane on its maiden flight.

Astonishing performances were put up by some of these little aeroplanes. One of the Wrens achieved a consumption figure of 85.9 miles (138.2 km) to a gallon of petrol, and for one of the two ANECs which competed a figure of 87.5 miles (140.8 km) per gallon was recorded. Although the meeting was marred by a fatal accident to one of the foreign contestants it was a lively affair, and among its sequels was a flight by Mr A J (now Sir Alan) Cobham to Brussels in a D.H.53; but although the manufacturers publicised the fact that the cost of fuel and oil had been no more than 7s 6d they had already made up their minds that a faster, more powerful machine would be required

Top: The English Electric Wren flew more than 85 miles (137 km) on one gallon of petrol at the 1923 Lympne competition

Above: Like the British Gnosspelius Gull, the American Gallaudet Chummy Flyabout had two pusher propellers, driven by a pair of Indian motorcycle engines mounted forward of the very 'chummy' tandem two-seat cockpit

Opposite page:

Top: Designed personally by A V Roe, the Avro 560 distinguished itself in the 1923 Lympne trials by completing 80 laps of the 12½ mile (20 km) circuit without a forced landing. Its pilot was H J (Bert) Hinkler, famous later for his record long-distance flights

Centre left: Although the Westland Woodpigeon I achieved little success at Lympne, it came second in the 1924 Grosvenor Trophy race. Its 32 hp Bristol Cherub engine was so low powered that the grass had to be cut with a hand mower before it would take off for its first flight

Centre right: A unique feature of the Parnall Pixie IIIA two-seater was that it had a detachable upper wing and could be flown in either monoplane or biplane form

Bottom: The Supermarine Sparrow was a 1924 ultra-light two-seater designed by R J Mitchell, who is better remembered for his later products such as the Schneider Trophy-winning S.6B and Spitfire

ENGLISH ELECTRIC WREN

Powered by: One 398 cc (3.5 hp) ABC motorcycle engine, driving a 3 ft 6 in (1.07 m) diameter two-blade propeller
Wing span: 37 ft 0 in (11.28 m)
Length: 24 ft 3 in (7.39 m)
Gross weight: 420 lb (190.5 kg)
Max speed: 50 mph (80.5 km/h)
Typical range: 75 miles (121 km) at 41 mph (66 km/h)
Accommodation: Crew of 1
First flight: 1923

Two examples were built of the English Electric Wren, designed early in 1923 by W O Manning. The one flown in the Lympne Light Aeroplane Trials by Sqn Ldr Maurice Wright of the RAF took second place in the mileage competition for a £1,000 *Daily Mail* prize by flying for 85.9 miles (138.2 km) on one gallon (4.5 litres) of fuel. In 1957 parts of this aircraft were used to restore to flying condition another Wren, which was handed over during that year to the Shuttleworth Trust.

by private owners.

Clearly, a two-seater was needed, not only so that a passenger could be carried but for instructional purposes also, and in 1924 the Air Council and other donors put up prize money for two-seater competitions which were duly held at Lympne during the autumn. The emphasis on fuel economy was no longer dominant, but, as before, the competing light aeroplanes (for such they were called), were of both monoplane and biplane types. From Bristol came two Brownie monoplanes, one with wooden, one with metal wings; from Westland, who were playing safe, the Woodpigeon biplane and the Widgeon monoplane; from Blackburn the Bluebird biplane, with side-by-side seats. Avro and Vickers sent developments of the Type 558 and Viget, named respectively the Avis and Vagabond; and Parnall went one better than their interchangeable-wing scheme of the previous year by producing a version of the Pixie which could be flown either as a monoplane or a biplane. Mr Sydney Camm of the Hawker company (later Sir Sydney) was responsible for the design of the Cygnet biplane, a masterpiece of weight-saving, as a surviving example bears witness. Remarkable for those times was the Short Satellite, which was of all-metal construction. The Supermarine Sparrow was a biplane, but Mr W S Shackleton's winning Beardmore Wee Bee was a monoplane.

Clearly the limit of 1,100 cc engine capacity imposed by the rules was inadequate, and for contests in 1925 it was stipulated merely that the engine used should not weigh more than 170 lb (77 kg).

However, 1925 was the year of the Moth . . . which is another story.

THE REAL BEGINNING of flying clubs as we know them today was in 1901—and the idea came from a woman. Her suggestion, to form the Aero Club of the United Kingdom, was made during a flight in a balloon, piloted by Stanley Spencer, from the Crystal Palace on 24 September 1901.

Frank Hedges Butler, his daughter Vera and the Hon C S Rolls were the passengers in the balloon. Immediately after landing, they hurried to Somerset House to register the name of the club, which became effective on 29 October 1901.

The Aero Club had a chequered history but did tremendous work to promote the growth of flying in Britain—a fact which was acknowledged on 15 February 1910 when it received permission to use the prefix 'Royal' in its name. By that time it had more than 1,000 members.

Important as the Royal Aero Club was—and is—it was open only to the wealthy. This was not due to snobbishness—a fault encountered rarely among flying people—but because flying was an expensive business which only the well-to-do could afford.

After the first World War, however, there were thousands who had learned to fly as military airmen, and many of them wanted to continue doing so in civilian life. Money was still the problem. There were almost unlimited quantities of ex-military aircraft on sale, at absurdly low prices, but they were costly to run and to maintain, and so it was still only the well-off who could fly. A few flying clubs had, it is true, come into being; but no real progress was being made towards bringing private flying within the financial reach of the average person.

Then, following the *Daily Mail*'s offer of a £1,000 prize in a competition for powered gliders, interest in a 'light' aeroplane began to grow. Simultaneously, Major-General Sir Sefton Brancker, Director General of Civil Aviation at the Air Ministry, was giving close attention to the idea of financial support for flying clubs. This far-sighted man not only wanted the 'man in the street' to become air-minded; he also foresaw that any future war would demand even greater effort in the air and that a nucleus of trained pilots would be invaluable. His influence went far to persuade the Air Ministry to offer a grant to those flying clubs with real potential for training private pilots.

On 1 September 1924, the Ministry announced a scheme of assistance to light aeroplane clubs, with the Royal Aero Club as a guiding body. Ten clubs were to be given £2,000 each, provided they produced a similar sum themselves and insured their equipment. Additionally, a subsidy of £500 a year was to be paid to each of them for two years; and, on top of that, £10 was to be paid by the Ministry for each flying certificate obtained, up to an initial total of 50 members per club.

Such sums may sound modest by today's standards, but a reasonably good light aeroplane could be bought at that time for

THE START OF THE FLYING CLUB MOVEMENT

£800; any competent pupil could go solo after eight hours' dual instruction, and could obtain his licence after three hours' solo flying and a not-too-difficult examination. With tuition costing no more than £5 an hour, the assistance was clearly an important step forward.

One of the main requirements was for a better club aircraft. The Ministry considered that such an aeroplane should have an engine weighing not more than 170 lb (77 kg), but the only type which really met the specification was the de Havilland Moth, which first flew in February 1925 and used a Cirrus engine weighing 270 lb (122 kg). By April 1925 Brancker managed to get the Ministry to approve purchase of the Moth out of the grant of £10,000 for certain of the approved clubs.

The London Aero Club, an offshoot of the Royal Aero Club, was one of those formed in 1925 and, after only two months' operation, reported that 200 flying hours had been logged. Many of its members had flown solo, and one had obtained a pilot's licence—clear evidence that once flying was brought down to a reasonable cost there would be no lack of potential club members.

The de Havilland Moth was an easy-to-handle biplane with a landing speed of around 45 mph (72 km/h) and was fitted with dual controls, the instructor occupying the front seat. Fuel consumption was only a few gallons an hour, and maintenance was simple. It had few, if any, vices and a more sophisticated version, the Tiger Moth, later became one of the principal *ab initio* trainers of the RAF in the second World War. Many of them, indeed, are still in club use today.

Left: The aeroplane which started it all—the prototype D.H.60 Moth, first flown by Geoffrey de Havilland on 22 February 1925

Opposite page, bottom: The Miles Hawk was conceived in 1932 as a monoplane successor to the Moth. This was the first of 55 production machines, which cost between £395 and £450 each

Top right: Eighth Moth to be completed, in August 1925, G-EBLV still flies regularly. It is owned by Hawker Siddeley Aviation

Right: The ANEC IV Missel Thrush, built for the 1926 *Daily Mail* light aeroplane competition, was an attempt to produce a low-cost two-seater with an engine of only 35 hp

Below: G-AAGV, a Simmonds Spartan, was fairly unusual in having a two-seat front cockpit. Powered by a 95 hp Cirrus III engine, it was used for joyriding

Bottom left: Unstaggered wings distinguished the Avro Club Cadet. This was one of three used by the Airwork School at Heston

Bottom right: The three-seat Desoutter monoplane began life in 1929 as a licence-built version of the Dutch Koolhoven F.K.41. A total of 41 were built, in various forms

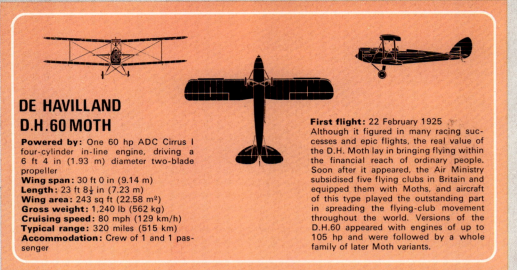

DE HAVILLAND D.H.60 MOTH

Powered by: One 60 hp ADC Cirrus I four-cylinder in-line engine, driving a 6 ft 4 in (1.93 m) diameter two-blade propeller
Wing span: 30 ft 0 in (9.14 m)
Length: 23 ft 8½ in (7.23 m)
Wing area: 243 sq ft (22.58 m²)
Gross weight: 1,240 lb (562 kg)
Cruising speed: 80 mph (129 km/h)
Typical range: 320 miles (515 km)
Accommodation: Crew of 1 and 1 passenger

First flight: 22 February 1925
Although it figured in many racing successes and epic flights, the real value of the D.H. Moth lay in bringing flying within the financial reach of ordinary people. Soon after it appeared, the Air Ministry subsidised five flying clubs in Britain and equipped them with Moths, and aircraft of this type played the outstanding part in spreading the flying-club movement throughout the world. Versions of the D.H.60 appeared with engines of up to 105 hp and were followed by a whole family of later Moth variants.

When a further Light Aeroplane Competition was organised for 1926, other manufacturers took an active interest in the potential market. The Avro Avian and Blackburn Bluebird, in particular, offered some competition to de Havilland; but, although both types made some outstanding record flights a little later, the Moth remained the outstanding club aeroplane.

One early highlight in the Moth's career was its winning of the 1926 King's Cup race. Flown by Captain Hubert Broad, a Cirrus Mark I Moth completed the course of 1,464 miles (2,356 km) at an average speed of 90.5 mph (145.6 km/h). This annual event, though usually won by experienced pilots, proved beyond question that the light aeroplane was no mere toy, and that members of aero clubs who learnt to fly such aircraft really were learning, not playing.

By 1927 an Association of Flying Clubs was formed, affiliated to the Royal Aero Club. Ten clubs made up the initial list, covering England from Hampshire to Northumberland.

Although it might appear that the flying club movement was by now quite successful, this was only partially true. Not all clubs were well managed, and some were still only centres for the wealthy. True, their flying fees were comparable with others, but the cost of their social activities put them beyond the pockets of many potential members. Unfortunately, most clubs, even with their subsidies, found it hard to keep going unless they had a profitable social side.

Nevertheless the clubs expanded, even if those members who could not afford to 'buy a few bricks for a control tower' (then the hallmark of a thriving airfield) moved over to other clubs where the social quarters were still in an ex-Army hut. It would be unfair to claim that the real flying only took place at these 'poor-relation' clubs, but it is true to say that their members joined primarily to fly rather than to indulge in social activities.

When war broke out in 1939 there were about 5,000 British pilots either qualified or in training. A high proportion of the male pilots joined the RAF Volunteer Reserve, giving yeoman service by flying bomber, fighter, coastal and transport aircraft and so bringing Sir Sefton Brancker's original dream to fruition.

This brief account would be incomplete without reference also to the women who learned to fly in the pleasant pre-war conditions. Nearly all the qualified pilots who were fit and of a suitable age group joined the Air Transport Auxiliary, which played an invaluable wartime role by ferrying aircraft from manufacturers to squadrons. Three famous names among the many were Amy Johnson—who died on this duty —Pauline Gower and Joan Hughes. Many

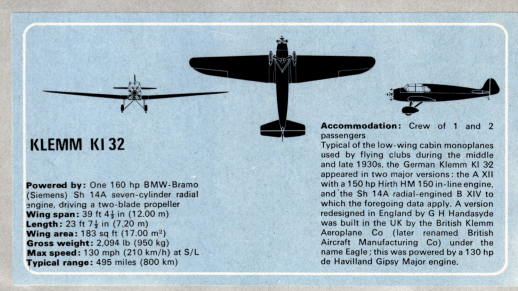

KLEMM KI 32

Powered by: One 160 hp BMW-Bramo (Siemens) Sh 14A seven-cylinder radial engine, driving a two-blade propeller
Wing span: 39 ft 4½ in (12.00 m)
Length: 23 ft 7½ in (7.20 m)
Wing area: 183 sq ft (17.00 m²)
Gross weight: 2,094 lb (950 kg)
Max speed: 130 mph (210 km/h) at S/L
Typical range: 495 miles (800 km)

Accommodation: Crew of 1 and 2 passengers
Typical of the low-wing cabin monoplanes used by flying clubs during the middle and late 1930s, the German Klemm Kl 32 appeared in two major versions: the A XII with a 150 hp Hirth HM 150 in-line engine, and the Sh 14A radial-engined B XIV to which the foregoing data apply. A version redesigned in England by G H Handasyde was built in the UK by the British Klemm Aeroplane Co (later renamed British Aircraft Manufacturing Co) under the name Eagle; this was powered by a 130 hp de Havilland Gipsy Major engine.

men, unfit for military service or past combat age, also joined the ATA, and men and women alike contributed an incalculable service to the war effort. Whether or not those officials at the Air Ministry in the mid-1920s foresaw how valuable their work was to be, those who survive have every reason to feel that their activities in support of the aero clubs earned a rich reward.

GEOFFREY DE HAVILLAND

GEOFFREY DE HAVILLAND, one of the most famous and best-loved of British aviation pioneers, was born the son of a clergyman in 1883. His remarkable career extended from the days of the Wright *Flyer* to the entry into service of the Comet 1, the world's first jet airliner; and he was one of that select band of pioneers who designed and built not only an aeroplane but its engine as well, and then learned to fly on it.

'DH', as he was almost universally known, was interested in engineering from boyhood, and in 1908, in association with a friend named Frank Hearle, he built his first aeroplane. This curious machine, with a long fuselage extending fore and aft of the wings, ailerons, an elevator in front and rudder at the back, crashed on its first attempt to take off.

Using the same engine, DH built another machine. This flew well, and on it he taught himself to fly. Recognising the skill of DH and Hearle, the government offered the two young men posts in the Royal Aircraft Factory, later to become the Royal Aircraft Establishment, at Farnborough. Here DH designed the B.E. (Blériot Experimental) No 1, the first of a series of tractor biplanes that were to become one of the mainstays of Britain's air effort in the early stages of the first World War.

In 1912 he was also mainly responsible for the B.S.1, the first fast single-seat scout of history and the ancestor of every scout and fighter which has followed. This handsome little aeroplane had a finely - streamlined monocoque fuselage which contributed to its top speed of 92 mph (148 km/h).

In 1914, seeking more scope, he joined the Aircraft Manufacturing Co at Hendon as designer and test pilot. Meanwhile, he had been commissioned in the RFC, but his true brilliance was at the drawing

board, and he was soon back at Hendon, to design in steady succession the D.H.1, 2, 4, 5, 6 and 9. The D.H.4 was one of the great combat aircraft of the 1914-18 war. It was considered by many to be the finest day bomber of its time, and was one of the very few foreign aircraft to have been built in America, where it made possible that country's original air mail service.

In 1920 de Havilland formed his own company, at Stag Lane, in North London. Almost immediately his character, a rare mixture of reserve, defiance and technical genius, impressed itself on the company and on its people. He always insisted, with genuine sincerity, that the de Havilland company was a team, not a man. He picked good young men, offered them his own example and, wisely, gave them their heads. He had the rare gift of delegating complete responsibility, perceiving the limitations of an older generation before they did—and before many of his contemporaries did—as aeronautical technology advanced into the age of the specialist. His own technical influence and judgment came to be sought rather than exerted.

The result was a remarkable dynasty of aeroplanes. Each proudly bore the prefix 'D.H.', and more than half of the 50-odd D.H. designs that flew in the half-century after 1915 were outstanding either for their usefulness or for the advanced nature of their design.

In 1925 the Moth appeared. This was a light but robust, cheap and easy-to-fly two-seat biplane, powered by a 60 hp Cirrus engine produced by the Aircraft Disposal Company. Offering powered flying for pleasure to men and women of modest means, it became the backbone of private flying in half the countries of the world. It was the most successful light aeroplane in history, and helped to establish the

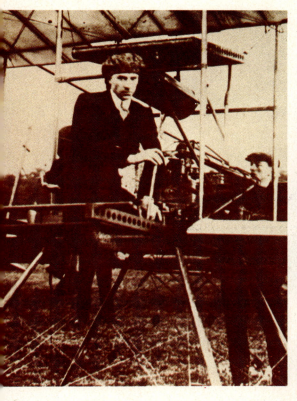

"De Havilland" Army Aeroplane.

MAYS, ALDERSHOT, 2156.
13.

Above: 'D.H.' at the controls of his Biplane No 2, which made its first flight of $\frac{1}{4}$ mile (400 m) on 10 September 1910. Sold to the government for £400, it was flown subsequently to Farnborough, where 'D.H.' developed his talents as both a designer and test pilot

Top right: The first successful D.H. design, Biplane No 2, at Farnborough in 1913. It was re-designated F.E.1 (Farman Experimental), as its layout was similar to that of the famous Farman biplanes built in France

Right: The B.E.1 (Blériot Experimental) was the aeroplane which first established Geoffrey de Havilland's reputation at Farnborough. It was used for some of the earliest wireless experiments in 1911 and continued in use until 1915

Below: A famous de Havilland type of the 'twenties, the D.H.66 Hercules was used on the first stages of Imperial Airways' Empire air routes in the Middle East. After a spell of joyriding in Australia in 1932, this one continued in airline service in New Guinea until the early days of the war with Japan

This page, top: The D.H.60 Moth is the aeroplane with which the name of Geoffrey de Havilland is linked for ever. The fourth production Gipsy Moth, G-AAAH, was a single-seater built for a high-speed flight to Kisumu and back by W L Hope in September 1928—an exploit which inspired a long series of great flights in these 100 hp lightplanes

Centre: One of the few military prototypes built by de Havilland between the World Wars was the D.H.72 bomber—a huge three-engined biplane spanning 95 ft (28.95 m). It is shown here with the ultra-light Gloster Gannet at Brockworth

Left: One of the D.H.9As supplied to the Australian Air Force as 'Imperial Gift' machines in 1920. They were not uncrated and put into service until 1925

Opposite page, top: In both World Wars the name of de Havilland was associated with wooden bombers fast enough to outfly the best enemy opposition. The World War 2 type was the Mosquito, which served in a variety of other forms for fighter, photo reconnaissance, attack and training duties

Bottom: The D.H.108 tailless research aircraft was built to provide data for both the Comet jetliner and the Sea Vixen fighter. 'D.H's' son, Geoffrey, was killed in the second prototype in 1946, flying faster than anyone else had ever travelled up to that time

de Havilland company. In various and subsequent versions it remained a basic aircraft for private flying and service training for more than thirty years.

In 1933 came the D.H.84 Dragon, the first of a new concept in small, compact, transport aircraft. From this developed the twin-engined D.H.89 Rapide and four-engined D.H.86 Express. In turn these feeder-liners were replaced, after the 1939-45 war, by the Dove and Heron. These were the last aircraft to embody the distinctive curved fins by which every DH aeroplane was immediately recognisable since the earliest days. These fins became as much the 'badge' of de Havilland as the famous hat he invariably wore.

During the 1939-45 war DH contributed as greatly to the British effort as he had done in the earlier conflict. This time, however, the effort came in one outstanding type, rather than with a succession of designs.

The aircraft was, of course, the Mosquito, a rare union of excellence and elegance which represented the realisation of an ideal—an unarmed bomber that would depend for its defence upon sheer performance. It was constructed of wood, a non-strategic material which also permitted the mobilisation of a wide range of factories which otherwise would not have contributed so effectively to the war effort. The Mosquito's versatility was such that it saw widespread service not only as a bomber, but for photographic reconnaissance, long-range day fighting, night fighting and ground attack duties. It excelled at each.

After the war the de Havilland company pioneered the commercial jet age with the Comet. This, the world's first jet airliner, was powered initially by de Havilland Ghost engines, and had a simplicity of form rarely equalled and not yet surpassed. The Comet was followed by the last aircraft to be identified by Sir Geoffrey's initials, the three-engined D.H.121 Trident airliner and the D.H.125, a small twin-jet business aircraft. At the start of the 'seventies, both were in widespread service throughout the world.

Technological advances and the accompanying trend towards nationalisation saw the de Havilland company taken into the Hawker Siddeley organisation in 1961. Even then, at the age of 78, DH continued to take an active interest in the affairs of the enterprise he had founded. This interest continued up to the time of his death in May 1965.

Today, the name de Havilland has gone from the public eye in Britain. But it continues overseas, in Australia as the Hawker de Havilland company and in Canada, where fine aeroplanes with DH designations continue to do honour to a great British aviation pioneer.

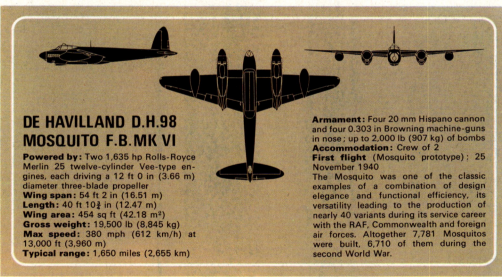

DE HAVILLAND D.H.98 MOSQUITO F.B.MK VI

Powered by: Two 1,635 hp Rolls-Royce Merlin 25 twelve-cylinder Vee-type engines, each driving a 12 ft 0 in (3.66 m) diameter three-blade propeller
Wing span: 54 ft 2 in (16.51 m)
Length: 40 ft 10¾ in (12.47 m)
Wing area: 454 sq ft (42.18 m²)
Gross weight: 19,500 lb (8,845 kg)
Max speed: 380 mph (612 km/h) at 13,000 ft (3,960 m)
Typical range: 1,650 miles (2,655 km)

Armament: Four 20 mm Hispano cannon and four 0.303 in Browning machine-guns in nose; up to 2,000 lb (907 kg) of bombs
Accommodation: Crew of 2
First flight (Mosquito prototype): 25 November 1940
The Mosquito was one of the classic examples of a combination of design elegance and functional efficiency, its versatility leading to the production of nearly 40 variants during its service career with the RAF, Commonwealth and foreign air forces. Altogether 7,781 Mosquitos were built, 6,710 of them during the second World War.

IT ALL BEGAN on Labor Day 1929. Labor Day is peculiarly American, and the air races carried out each year on this day during the 1930s were peculiarly American too. In 1929 a young Georgian named Doug Davis successfully flung his howling red-and-black Mystery ship around the pylons at Cleveland, Ohio, to humiliate even the hottest military fighters. Indeed, thinking he had cut inside a pylon on the third lap, Davis recircled it not once but *twice*. The crowd fell silent as he relapped the entire field to win the first Charles E Thompson sponsored race and launch a decade of civilian-dominated spectacle not duplicated before or since.

As the 1930s opened, fame and glory—and cold cash—beckoned from the air race circuit to a world despondent from the dust-bowl of the depression. Men cast rationality to the slipstream that whipped their squinting, watering eyes, eyes set on one goal—to win. These were the penniless itinerants who worked secretly in bare sheds and hangar corners, building 'class' into their mechanical progeny, stuffing in more horsepower, clipping off more wing, tightening, patching, doping. These grimy-fingernailed 'grease monkeys' sleeked their steeds more by eye than science. They drove engines to the point of destruction, their safety margins were based on guesswork, and often proved woefully low. Many race pilots died at their trade, but this only added 'edge' to the glamour. Wing flutter remained an exotic mystery. Tails would hammer unaccountably in tight turns. A single aircraft would reappear year after year, each time further disguised, converted, transmuted, sporting different shapes, colours, a bigger engine, often with little regard—or time—for proper balancing or stress analysis.

But every one of them had the makings of a winner to the eager Roman-holiday crowds that squeezed by the dozen-thousands on to creaking grandstands to watch them perform, straining for a glimpse of the coloured wings splashed near the base of checkerboard pylons.

The two big-time races were those for the Thompson Trophy, a closed-course pylon affair first run in 1929, and the Bendix Trophy, a long, cross-country Derby begun in 1931. Scores of lesser races appeared and ebbed away over the years, races classed by cubic-inch displacement, donated by patrons eager for publicity. But whatever its prestige, the race itself was everything. Men sold their souls to be close to where the race action was. The motive was not altruistically to straighten out aerodynamic question marks. Man had made the broad jump from 200 to 300 mph (322 to 483 km/h) during the previous decade, and the backyard race pilots of the 1930s were more modifiers than innovators. Rather was it a

★★★★★★★★★★★★★★★★★★★★★★
AIR RACES

gathering of virile moths around a candle-flame, all gambling on how much abuse their wings could tolerate, knowing full well some would get scorched.

Biplanes still dominated the races in 1930 and 1931. 'Speed' Holman gunned the snarling Pratt & Whitney Wasp in Matty Laird's black-and-gold *Solution* to win the 1930 Thompson after Marine Capt Arthur Page in his blue Navy monoplane racer crashed, overcome by carbon monoxide. Then, in 1931, the year Holman was killed, the perennial, ubiquitous 'Jimmy' Doolittle flew the updated *Super Solution* (called in those days the 'Skyways Buzzard') coast-to-coast in 11 hr 16 min 10 sec (with fuel stops) to capture the first trophy given by Vincent Bendix.

But the biplane era was fast waning, and the next breed of racers to dominate the 1930s—indeed, the breed that, more than any other, so completely characterises the era—were the Gee Bees. These were fat 'Flying Silos', and Gee Bee (G.B.) referred to the five Granville Brothers of Springfield, Massachusetts. Zantford ('Granny') Granville was the eldest, a persevering mechanic who built seven muscle racers in an abandoned dance pavilion. The Gee Bee racers were 'wild SOBs'—all seven crashed —but each mysteriously enjoyed 'Granny's built-in tail-wind' despite having bodies shaped like barrels to match the four-foot (1.2 m) diameter of their engines. The experts told Granny 'you'll never build a 300 mph airplane around a radial engine, and you know it.' But NACA had devised a new engine cowling that was far superior to the old 'horse-collar' type, and Granville thought he'd try.

Granny's 'Silos' won two Thompson races, in 1931 and 1932, the latter at the hands of the Gee Bee's only undisputed master, Jimmy Doolittle—who also, on 3 September 1932, drove one at 296.287 mph (476.741 km/h) for a landplane speed record. But Lowell Bayles, Russell Boardman, Cecil Allen, Florence Klingensmith and Francisco Sarabia were all killed in violent Gee Bee crashes; and 'Granny' himself was killed in 1934, at about the time the lustre tarnished and the firm went bankrupt.

While Gee Bee's flamboyant story became a part of American folk-lore a contemporary brand of racers, almost forgotten today, was earning far more prize money. These were the three aircraft with the 'barn-door wings' built by Jimmy Wedell, the one-eyed son of a Texas bartender. Jimmy was known as the 'Air Hobo', and his only drawings were reputedly chalk outlines on the hangar floor; but, backed by New Orleans dandy Harry Palmerson Williams, he was able to build aeroplanes aesthetically beautiful which remained gritty, consistent top money winners until 1936. His scarlet number 44 ('hot as a .44

Above: A new era in American air racing began in 1929 when the Travel Air 'Mystery' aircraft took part in the National Air Races for the first time. Its name resulted from the fact that the original 400-hp Model R was flown from the Wichita factory to Cleveland Airport, centre of the races, hangared immediately and covered with canvas screens until race time. With a top speed of 235 mph (378 km/h) it was 70 mph (112 km/h) faster than the Army's standard fighters of the time. A Mystery won the main event in 1929. This one, piloted by James Haizlip, came second in the 1930 Thompson Trophy Race

Opposite page, centre: One of the few British aircraft seen at the National Air Races, this Miles Sparrowhawk was built as G-ADWW for the 1936 King's Cup Race and then sold in America

Bottom: Colonel Roscoe Turner and the Wedell-Williams which he flew to third place in both the Bendix and Thompson races in 1932. Aircraft of this type filled the first three places in the Bendix that year, Turner clocking 266.674 mph (429.171 km/h) in the 3km Shell speed dash

This page, left, top to bottom:
One of the cleanest aircraft ever built, the Crosby CR-4 of 1939 spanned only 16 ft (4.88 m). It recorded 263 mph (423 km/h) on only 350 hp in the qualifying event

Another big name of the late 'thirties was Keith Rider, whose R-3 came second in the Thompson in 1936, 1937 and 1938. This was his R-5, known also as the Marcoux-Bromberg *Jackrabbit*

The Rider R-4 *Firecracker* in which Tony LeVier took two first places, and one third, at the 1938 Oakland International Air Races and then won the 1938 Greve Trophy. Engine was a 544 hp Menasco

and twice as fast') hit 305.33 mph (491.38 km/h) on its landplane speed record flight of 4 September 1933, and scored firsts and seconds in both Thompson and Bendix races until 1934 when Doug Davis, trying to duplicate his 1929 win, high-speed-stalled it on a pylon turn and was killed. That year Jimmy Wedell was killed as well.

The great Roscoe Turner, resplendent in his robin's-egg-blue uniform and whip-cord breeches, and with his waxed, spiked moustache and live lion cub mascot, earned the first of his three remarkable Thompson victories in a colourful, Hornet-powered Wedell-Williams racer the same year. 'Go-grease' Benny Howard, chief engineering pilot for United Air Lines, was the hero of the pulp-reading model-builders as the man who fashioned the DGA series of racers. DGA stood for 'Damned Good Airplane', which the earliest had to be. Built for bootleggers, they 'hauled a helluva lot of whisky!' The early Menasco-powered DGA racers were more

popularly known as *Pete, Mike* and *Ike;* they were typical of dozens of similar, medium-powered racers that flourished during the 1930s. Then came, in 1935, the great DGA-6 *Mr Mulligan*, in appearance a staid anomaly, a *four-seat* strut-braced high-wing nose-thumber at the tiny, rakish speedsters. It cruised at 238 mph (383 km/h) to win the 1935 Bendix—but only just. Benny left his flaps down by mistake across the country and came within 23 seconds of losing the race. Harold Neuman flew it to victory in the Thompson; *Mr Mulligan* cracked up in the following year, injuring Benny, but the design survived to become a commercial success.

During the mid-1930s wealthy oil heir and movie magnate Howard Hughes was near the peak of his influence. He decided to dabble in air racing, and for 18 months held secret sessions with his designer Dick Palmer while, hidden from view, his sleek, blue-and-silver H-1 racer took form

frame by frame. In the incredibly advanced H-1, on 13 September 1935, Hughes rocketed to a landplane speed record of 352.388 mph (567.026 km/h), and on 17 January 1937, he sliced from Los Angeles to New York in an astonishing 7 hr 28 min 10 sec, doubling the speed of the recent Bendix winner Louise Thaden. Some petty criticism of Hughes' 'unfair advantage' restrained him from entering his sure winner in the National Air Races. Today it still exists, concealed in humidity-controlled secret storage!

The object of additional criticism in 1936 was the government-funded, laboratory-built French Caudron C.460 which flashed into Los Angeles and in a 246.261 mph (396.318 km/h) blue blur whined away with the Thompson Trophy, piloted by Lindbergh's close friend Michel Detroyat. Fresh from its 314.2 mph (505.6 km/h) 1934 landplane speed record and 1935 victory in the 1,243-mile (2,000-km) Coupe Suzanne Deutsch de la Meurthe,

GEE BEE R-1 SUPER SPORTSTER

Powered by: One 800 hp Pratt & Whitney Wasp nine-cylinder radial engine, driving a two-blade propeller
Wing span: 25 ft 0 in (7.62 m)
Length: 17 ft 9 in (5.41 m)
Empty weight: 1,840 lb (835 kg)
Gross weight: 3,075 lb (1,395 kg)
Max speed: 296.287 mph (476.741 km/h) on 3 September 1932
Accommodation: Crew of 1
First flight: 13 August 1932
Two Super Sportsters were built. The R-1, which set the speed record shown above, won the 1932 Thompson Trophy race two days later, flown by 'Jimmy' Doolittle. The R-2 (silhouette) had a 550 hp Wasp Junior engine and extra fuel. Both were entered for the 1933 Bendix Trophy contest, R-1 with a 900 hp Hornet engine, its Wasp engine being transferred to R-2; but R-2 withdrew after the crash which destroyed the R-1, and itself crashed later the same year. The salvaged R-1 fuselage and R-2's engine and wings were combined in a new aircraft for the 1935 Bendix race. When this, too, crashed the era of the Gee Bee racers came to an end.

the Caudron easily outclassed the competition, even though its Renault-Bengali 488-cu in (8,000 cc) in-line engine had less than half the capacity of the over-boosted Wasp radial that powered the second-place Keith Rider R-3. Nevertheless, the Yankee message was clear, and state-supported foreign competition never returned to the National Air Races.

A twin-row R-1830 Wasp of 1,050 hp also powered the last—and most successful—Thompson racer, the LTR (Laird-Turner Racer) 'Meteor', which was completed just in time for the 1937 events. Made of wood and fabric, with a fixed landing gear, the LTR to the casual observer might be indistinguishable from Doug Davis's Beech-built Travel Air Mystery ship of 1929. In ten years the wires had disappeared, but the lines were much the same. The horsepower, however, had tripled, making the LTR 30 per cent faster through the air. Roscoe Turner raced the

LTR for three years, winning the final two pre-war Thompsons in 1938 (at his best speed, 283.419 mph; 456.119 km/h) and 1939. Roscoe could have won the 1937 race as well, but thinking he had cut a pylon, he recircled, lost the lead, and finished third. In any event his 1939 victory brought plane-builder Matty Laird full circle for the decade.

In retrospect the performance gains made in the National Air Races during the 1930s were the result, not of great advances in design, but primarily of durability perfected in the engine laboratories of Pratt & Whitney. The makeshift, garage-hatched pylon-dusters were ill-equipped to plumb the subtle mysteries of compressibility, laminar flow and a host of other aerodynamic problems. Indeed, the factory-built Seversky pursuits appearing—and winning—in the races at the decade's end began to reverse the military neglect apparent ten years earlier. By 1939 civil

pilots were bewildered over the breakdown of their old, dependable axiom that more power guaranteed more speed. One quickly lost count of the myriad 'class races' in which the same familiar, lower-powered ships continued to repeat in tiresome fashion more columns of decimal-point gibberish to add to the long lists of race statistics—but provided nothing else really new. The National Air Races turned into a razzle-dazzle circus of stunting, parachute-jumping, and grandstand prices, and by 1939 few still cared.

Yet there will always be those who would relive those dilated moments just before the Thompson's start: the engines wind up, hats sail away in the dusty maelstrom, a dozen trembling racers wing-to-wing await the starter's flag, all 'rarin' to go'—'1,200 horses in your lap and a feather on your tail', as Roscoe Turner said, all for headlines and prize money.

Bottom left: Last of the great pre-war races, the 1939 Thompson, was won by Roscoe Turner. After recircling a missed pylon, he overtook the field in his 1,050 hp Laird-Turner LTR; then retired from racing

Right, top to bottom:
Extreme example of the National Air Race minimum-airframe/maximum-engine concept was the Gee Bee Super Sportster. Although successful when flown by pilots like 'Jimmy' Doolittle, both Super Sportsters eventually crashed, killing their pilots

One of the most famous racers of all time, Steve Wittman's *Bonzo* was clocked at 325 mph (523 km/h) on a 485 hp Curtiss D-12 engine. Post-war he won the 1949, 1950 and 1952 Continental Trophy races

R-6 *Eightball,* last of the Keith Rider racers and the only all-wooden one, finished third in the 1938 Greve contest

Below: After coming second in three successive Thompsons, Earl Ortman flew the Keith Rider R-3 to third place in 1939

Bottom: Drawing on US air racing experience, the organisers of the Irish Sweepstakes entered this Bellanca monoplane, the *Irish Swoop*, for the 1934 MacRobertson Race to Australia. It failed to meet weight/runway regulations and could not compete

Flying Aircraft Carriers

THE WHOLE HISTORY of fighter aircraft development is one of an unending conflict between the demand for higher speeds and improved manoeuvrability (requiring low wing loadings) and the need for greater range and bigger armament loads (implying high wing loadings). As weights have increased, so have take-off and landing runs, and the need to keep these distances within acceptable limits imposes continuous restraints on designers.

Consequently, many schemes have been established over the years for assisting heavily-loaded fighters into the air, or for extending their range without adding to the internal fuel capacity. One group of schemes can be categorised as 'parasite fighters', which all have in common the use of a 'mother ship' to carry the fighters aloft, although the purpose for doing so has varied.

Some of the earliest experiments with parasites were little more than stunts, or were part of the plethora of 'suck-it-and-see' experiments in the first decade of flying which made up in ingenuity for what they lacked in realism. By 1918, all three major airship powers—Britain, Germany and America—had conducted experiments in which aircraft were carried aloft and then released. The German experiment comprised an Albatros D.III launched from the L35 rigid airship, while the RFC used a Camel from the rigid R23. In America, a Curtiss JN-4 of the Army Air Service was dropped from the Navy C-1 blimp.

Britain returned briefly to the airship-carrier idea in 1925, when R33 was modified to incorporate a trapeze which would allow aircraft to be retrieved in flight, as well as launched. This had been a major omission in the 1918 trials, severely limiting the operational usefulness of the idea. The R33 trials made use of two suitably-modified D.H.53 monoplanes, and the first attempts to fly on and off were made on 15 October 1925. Further launching trials were made with two Gloster Grebes late in 1926, but these aircraft were not modified to link up with the trapeze at the end of their flight. The whole of the R33 parasite programme was conducted in a desultory manner and was ended in December 1926, since which time there have been no further experiments involving airborne aircraft carriers in Britain.

The R33 experiments had been suggested to the RAF by the interest being shown in trapeze-equipped airships in America. As early as 1921, Army Air Service officers had been attracted by the possibility of developing a means of operating aircraft both from and to semi-rigid airships, and Lawrence Sperry (son of the inventor of the gyro-compass) obtained a contract to develop equipment to make this possible. A practicable system was evolved by the end of 1924, and on 13 December in that year the first attempt was made to complete an aerial link-up between a hook-equipped Sperry Messenger biplane and the Army blimp R-3.

The first attempt failed when the Messen-ger was caught in the turbulent flow around the blimp and was thrown against the trapeze bar on which it was supposed to hook. The propeller was shattered and the Army pilot, First Lt Clyde V Finter, had to make an emergency landing (exactly the same thing happened a year later when Sqdn Ldr Rolls de Haga Haig made the first attempt to hook the D.H.53 on to R33). Finter persevered and on 15 December made a successful hook-up after several attempts. As with the RAF, however, US Army interest in trapeze-rigged airships soon waned and it was left to the US Navy to exploit the idea more fully in subsequent years.

In October 1928, the Navy signed contracts with the Goodyear-Zeppelin Corporation for two new rigid airships, to be built in the US essentially to German design. In the event, they were the Navy's last rigid airships, named *Akron* and *Macon*, but when ordered it was hoped they would be the first of a large force capable of playing an important role scouting ahead of the Fleet. To increase their scouting capability, the airships were designed from the start to carry aeroplanes.

To prepare for the coming airships, the Navy began trapeze flying in 1929, with the necessary equipment mounted on the *Los Angeles* (built for the US as war reparations by the Zeppelin company in Germany) and on a Vought VO-1 biplane. The first hook-ons were made on 3 July 1929 by Lt A W Gorton, who found the same difficulties

Opposite page: These two Gloster Grebe single-seat fighters were launched successfully from the airship R.33, flying at 2,000 ft (610 m), in 1926

Top: One of the hooked Curtiss F9C-2 Sparrowhawks which were operated very successfully from the US Naval airship *Macon* until she was lost in 1935

Above: Photographed a moment after release from the airship R.23, this World War 1 Sopwith Camel fighter was piloted by Lieut R E Keys, DFC, of No 212 Squadron

Above right: This photograph of a Sparrowhawk approaching the *Macon's* trapeze shows how the little fighters were dwarfed by the airship's 785 ft (239.3 m) bulk

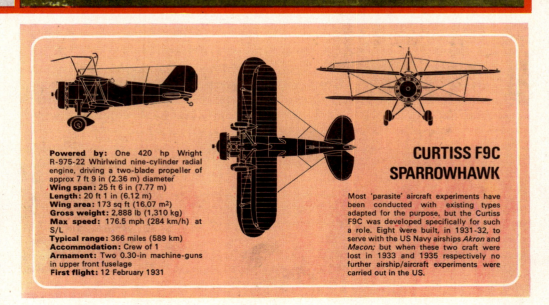

Powered by: One 420 hp Wright R-975-22 Whirlwind nine-cylinder radial engine, driving a two-blade propeller of approx 7 ft 9 in (2.36 m) diameter
Wing span: 25 ft 6 in (7.77 m)
Length: 20 ft 1 in (6.12 m)
Wing area: 173 sq ft (16.07 m²)
Gross weight: 2,888 lb (1,310 kg)
Max speed: 176.5 mph (284 km/h) at S/L
Typical range: 366 miles (589 km)
Accommodation: Crew of 1
Armament: Two 0.30-in machine-guns in upper front fuselage
First flight: 12 February 1931

CURTISS F9C SPARROWHAWK

Most 'parasite' aircraft experiments have been conducted with existing types adapted for the purpose, but the Curtiss F9C was developed specifically for such a role. Eight were built, in 1931-32, to serve with the US Navy airships *Akron* and *Macon*; but when these two craft were lost in 1933 and 1935 respectively no further airship/aircraft experiments were carried out in the US.

which had been experienced by Finter and de Haga Haig but persisted in the development of suitable flying techniques. Within eight weeks, three pilots had made hook-ons without further difficulty and the Navy declared that the trials were a success.

For the *Akron*, which made her first flight on 23 September 1931, a special aircraft had to be delivered, to fit the T-shaped opening through which access was gained to the hangar inside the airship. This limited the size to a span of 30 ft (9.14 m) and length of 24 ft (7.32 m). With funds low, the Navy decided in 1930 not to develop a new lightweight scout of the type really needed by the *Akron* but to adapt, instead, a Curtiss fighter already under development, the XF9C-1 Sparrowhawk. For training, six Consolidated N2Y-1 biplanes were fitted with the sky-hook equipment, and the XF9C-1 prototype was similarly fitted, for trials aboard the *Los Angeles*, while seven more Sparrowhawks were put into production.

Trapeze operations aboard the *Akron* did not begin until mid-1932, and extended training exercises occupied the final quarter of that year. Although the F9C-1s were single-seat fighters, they operated from *Akron* as scouts, their purpose being to extend the range of search. The technique evolved by the *Akron* and the crews of the unique HTA (Heavier-Than-Air) Unit which was formed to operate the Sparrowhawks was for two fighters to take station, one each side of the airship, providing a visual scan over an area 100 miles (160 km) wide. With refinements, and improved radio to allow the aircraft to remain in contact with the airship, it was foreseen that the width of search could be increased to 200 miles (320 km).

Problems were many, as might be expected. Navigation had to be precise, but the overriding concern was that mechanical failure of the trapeze, or a 'hang-up' by one of the aircraft, might make it impossible for aircraft already launched to return to the airship. The need for duplication of the trapeze was thus soon recognised, but was never implemented, for the Navy was still operating on a shoe-string when *Akron* was lost in the Atlantic on 3 April 1933.

The first flight of the second 'heavier-than-air' carrier, the *Macon*, was made only two weeks later, on 21 April. Fortuitously, none of the aircraft were aboard *Akron* when she crashed, so the HTA squadron was able to continue its work almost without interruption. The operational techniques were refined, although there was still only one trapeze, and by mid-1934 confidence in the whole scheme was such that it was customary for the undercarriages to be removed from the Sparrowhawks as soon as they were flown aboard the *Macon* for manoeuvres over the sea. However, Navy interest in the whole concept was fast waning by this time and it is unlikely that much more would have been achieved even if the *Macon* had not been lost in the Pacific on 12 February 1935. Four of the F9C-2s went down with her and, so far as is known, no other airships since that date have been

McDONNELL XF-85 GOBLIN

Powered by: One 3,000 lb (1,361 kg) st Westinghouse J34-WE-7 turbojet engine
Wing span: 21 ft 1¼ in (6.44 m)
Length: 14 ft 10½ in (4.53 m)
Wing area: 90 sq ft (8.36 m²)
Gross weight: 4,550 lb (2,064 kg)
Max attained speed: 362 mph (583 km/h)
Endurance: approx 30 min
Accommodation: Crew of 1
Armament: Four 0.50-in machine-guns in nose
First flight: 23 August 1948
Conceived during the second World War, two examples were built of the XF-85, one of which is still preserved in the USAF Museum. Only 5 ft 4¾ in (1.64 m) wide and 10 ft 8 in (3.25 m) high with the wings folded, it was intended as a 'parasite' defensive fighter to be carried in the bomb-bay of the Convair B-36. Tests were disappointing, the aircraft falling well below its intended maximum speed of 664 mph (1,068 km/h), and further development was cancelled when long-range versions of more conventional fighters became available.

used for aircraft hook-ons.

A rather different line in parasite fighters had been pursued meanwhile in Russia, where the idea of using 'mother aircraft' to extend the range of fighters had originated in 1931. Russia had had a lead in the development of outsize bombing aircraft ever since the giant Ilya Mourometz biplanes had been designed by Igor Sikorsky. Thus, aircraft were available which were large and powerful enough to carry aloft two or more fighters mounted above or below the wings.

In the earliest trials, I-5 biplane fighters were carried by TB-1 bombers, but greater success was achieved after the I-16 monoplane became available in 1935. For the first I-16 trials, a TB-3 was fitted with tubular-steel frames to carry an I-16 beneath each wing outboard of the engines. The aircraft were attached on the ground, after which the I-16s' undercarriages were retracted. This combination was tested with considerable success, and encouraged a much more ambitious scheme, first tested on 20 November 1935, in which the two I-16s were carried under the wings, two I-5 biplanes were

carried *above* the wings and a trapeze was fitted to allow a fifth fighter to 'hook-on' under the fuselage after the combination was airborne.

To take off, this unwieldy contraption needed the power of the four fighters as well as the bomber itself, but the operation was completed successfully with a hook-on and then a simultaneous launch by all five fighters. It is scarcely surprising that this scheme did not proceed very far, but in 1937–38 further work was done with a developed TB-3 and two improved I-16s, each modified to carry two 550 lb (250 kg) bombs in a dive-bombing role. After successful trials, this combination reached operational status with several units of the Soviet Air Force for a short time. At least one sortie was made during the second World War, when two of these combination aircraft launched an attack on a bridge across the Danube in August 1941.

In the Russian experiment, it was not intended that the fighters should rejoin their mother ship after launching, but such a capability was an essential part of the

Opposite page: Fastest of the Bell X-1 series of supersonic research aircraft, the 1,650 mph (2,655 km/h) X-1A is prepared for hoisting under the belly of the B-29 'mother-ship' from which it was launched in the air. This technique conserved its rocket fuel for the brief high-speed phase of each flight

Top: Locked on its trapeze, a Republic F-84F Thunderstreak is hoisted into the bomb-bay of a GRB-36 bomber during the USAF's FICON (Fighter-In-CONvair) experiments

Above: One of the ugliest aeroplanes ever flown, the McDonnell XF-85 Goblin was built to stow into the bomb-bay of a B-36 as a means of defence for this USAF strategic bomber

Right: Another research aircraft that was air-launched from a Superfortress bomber was the Bell X-2 rocket-plane, which flew faster and higher than any previous piloted aeroplane in 1956. It reached 2,148 mph (3,457 km/h) and an altitude of 126,200 ft (38,466 m)

parasite fighter scheme evolved by the USAAF in 1942. The object this time was to provide a built-in defensive fighter for the global bombers then beginning to appear on the drawing boards of American designers. Elements of both the US Navy and the Soviet schemes were incorporated in the USAAF's ideas, which were for a fighter with no conventional landing capability. The pilot would be carried in the mother bomber, entering the fighter only in preparation for launching, and the fighter had to be small enough to fit right inside the bomber, in order not to compromise the latter's performance.

To meet this unusual requirement, McDonnell Aircraft Company designed the diminutive XF-85 Goblin, a little jet-powered fighter with upward-folding wings (for stowage in the bomb-bay) and a fine array of tail fins in all directions to meet the limitations on overall width.

A prototype development programme was started by the USAAF with a view to adopting the Goblin as standard equipment in the mighty B-36 bombers, which would have had a retractable trapeze in their bomb-bays. Two XF-85 prototypes were built, and a Boeing B-29B was fitted with a trapeze for experimental hook-ups. The trials were made in August 1948-March 1949, with conspicuous lack of success. Only three hook-ons were achieved, and on several occasions an emergency landing had to be made on the steel skid provided under the fuselage for the purpose. In view of the difficulties experienced by highly-skilled test pilots, it was clear that the concept was impractical for squadron use and the project was cancelled in 1949.

However, there remained a body of opinion in the USAAF which favoured the provision of a fighter escort for reconnaissance versions of the B-36, which were stripped of some of their armament to accommodate cameras and electronic equipment. Consequently, a new programme was initiated to permit the RB-36s to carry, beneath their bomb-bay, a Republic RF-84F Thunderflash fighter. Once again, a retractable trapeze was used, in order to swing the aircraft well clear of the fuselage for launch and hook-on.

Trials were made successfully in May 1953, and about a dozen B-36s were then converted as carriers, while one squadron of RF-84F reconnaissance fighters was modified to have sky-hooks for operation to and from the carriers. By this time, the concept had changed once again, the emphasis now being upon extending the range of the parasite aircraft rather than defending the carriers. Little operational flying was done with the FICON (Fighter-In-Convair) aircraft, however, and the last of the parasites passed out of service by the end of the 1950s.

Left: This tiny biplane was the first of two aircraft built by the Sopwith company for Professor Low's 'A T' missile experiments in the first World War. Aerials for radio control can be seen wound around the outer wings and rear fuselage

Opposite page, top to bottom:
This model of the US Army Air Service's guided missile can be seen in the USAF Museum. Known as the Kettering Bug, the 'aerial torpedo' weighed 560 lb (254 kg) and was intended to carry 180 lb (82 kg) of explosive 40 miles (64 km) at 55 mph (88 km/h). Tests were terminated with the end of the first World War

US Navy counterpart of the Bug was this autopilot-controlled aircraft tested by the Sperry Gyroscope Company

Six 'ATs' of this type were built at Farnborough in 1917, for testing by Low. Use of a fixed elevator, as a prelude to radio control, caused the first three aircraft to crash soon after launch. Others were tested with a four-wheel undercarriage, and on skids, instead of the two-wheel type shown

As an outcome of earlier work on pilotless missiles, the British Services began to use full-size aircraft as pilotless targets for anti-aircraft gunners in the 'thirties. Last type designed specifically for this purpose was the Airspeed Queen Wasp which, like the others, could be flight tested and ferried as a normal piloted aeroplane

The First Doodlebugs

GUIDED MISSILES have a longer history than is generally supposed. Experiments with small pilotless aircraft were under way in the United States and Britain as early as 1915—just 12 years after man first flew.

The first known American effort was a 600-lb (272 kg) 'aerial torpedo' biplane, built by the Sperry and Delco companies. Powered by a 40-hp Ford engine, the machine took off from a four-wheeled carriage which ran on two rails laid out on a grass field. Once airborne its direction was controlled by a simple gyroscope device and its altitude by an aneroid barometer.

The launch crew were supposed to estimate the distance to the target and assess wind drift before release, then point the Bug in the right direction and set its engine to run for the appropriate time. Hopefully, the plane arrived over its target with a 300-lb (136-kg) bomb load, the engine cut out and an associated mechanism pulled a series of bolts which jettisoned the wings!

Although no great accuracy could be claimed for the missile, it flew successfully in 1915 before US Navy observers at Long Island.

The first really significant experiments in guided weapons, however, were made in England by a team led by Professor A M Low, a former President of the British

Below: Last aircraft wholly designed and constructed at the RAE, Farnborough, Larynx (long-range gun with Lynx engine) was tested successfully in 1927-29. Twelve were built, and one Larynx, catapult-launched from HMS Stronghold, made a long flight off the coast of Somerset, Devon and Cornwall. It was intended to carry a 250 lb (113 kg) warhead 300 miles (480 km)

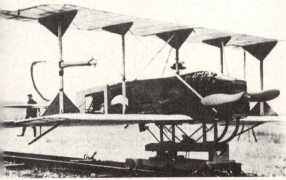

Interplanetary Society. The idea appears to have originated with Generals Caddell and Pitcher in 1914 and was taken up by Sir David Henderson, Director-General of Military Aeronautics. The work, which proceeded under great secrecy, was coded 'A T' to give the impression that it concerned merely an Aerial Target. In fact, the aim was to develop a small pilotless aeroplane which could be steered over a surface target by radio to drop bombs.

Experiments began at Brooklands, Surrey, and then moved to Feltham in Middlesex, where—after many trials and tribulations—radio apparatus was put together to control a small high-wing monoplane built by Geoffrey de Havilland. It had a wing span of 22 ft (6.7 m), a four-wheeled undercarriage, and was powered by a 35-hp engine designed by Granville Bradshaw.

Flight trials got under way at the Royal Flying Corps' training school at Upavon in March 1917; but to Low's dismay the engine failed during take-off and the aircraft 'flopped ungracefully into the mud'. It managed to become airborne on the next attempt, and actually flew under

control for a short time; then, after executing a loop, the engine stalled and it bore down on its creator, crashing almost at his feet.

Though work on the A T project ended, Low's enthusiasm for radio-controlled aircraft never waned, and after a period the Royal Aircraft Establishment was encouraged to begin experiments, by which time more money was available for basic research.

The Larynx monoplane developed by RAE in 1927 was ramp-launched from the deck of HMS *Stronghold* and flew at 200 mph (322 km/h). It was designed to carry a 250-lb (113-kg) bomb load 300 miles (480 km).

Further advances in pilotless aircraft followed rapidly, though by now offensive applications had given way to the growing requirement (no longer a 'cover story') for aerial targets. The Queen Bee and Queen Wasp of the late 'thirties and early 'forties were full-size pilotless aircraft. Flown both as landplanes and seaplanes, in the latter form they were catapult-launched and capable of landing alongside their parent ship and being winched back on board.

KETTERING 'BUG'

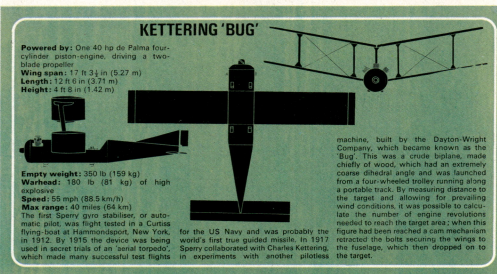

Powered by: One 40 hp de Palma four-cylinder piston-engine, driving a two-blade propeller
Wing span: 17 ft 3½ in (5.27 m)
Length: 12 ft 6 in (3.71 m)
Height: 4 ft 8 in (1.42 m)

Empty weight: 350 lb (159 kg)
Warhead: 180 lb (81 kg) of high explosive
Speed: 55 mph (88.5 km/h)
Max range: 40 miles (64 km)
The first Sperry gyro stabiliser, or automatic pilot, was flight tested in a Curtiss flying-boat at Hammondsport, New York, in 1912. By 1915 the device was being used in secret trials of an 'aerial torpedo', which made many successful test flights for the US Navy and was probably the world's first true guided missile. In 1917 Sperry collaborated with Charles Kettering, in experiments with another pilotless machine, built by the Dayton-Wright Company, which became known as the 'Bug'. This was a crude biplane, made chiefly of wood, which had an extremely coarse dihedral angle and was launched from a four-wheeled trolley running along a portable track. By measuring distance to the target and allowing for prevailing wind conditions, it was possible to calculate the number of engine revolutions needed to reach the target area; when this figure had been reached a cam mechanism retracted the bolts securing the wings to the fuselage, which then dropped on to the target.

Top: A total of 420 Queen Bee radio-controlled pilotless versions of the Tiger Moth were produced in 1934-43. They were used primarily as targets for naval gunners, but were operated also by the army. This shows a Queen Bee being controlled from the panel in the foreground

Below: Predecessor of the Queen Bee and Queen Wasp, the Fairey Queen was produced at the RAE by fitting radio control to a Fairey IIIF floatplane and increasing the wing dihedral to improve stability. The first two conversions crashed soon after launch from HMS *Valiant*. The third flew well, surviving more than two hours' concentrated gunfire by the Home Fleet in the Mediterranean in January 1933

Less known is Russian work with pilotless aircraft carried out between the wars by a group under Sergei P Korolyev, later to achieve fame as the designer of Soviet space vehicles.

In 1935-36 Korolyev was working secretly on Project 212, a scheme for a small ramp-launched flying bomb designed to fly 50 km (31 miles) with a 30-kg (66-lb) warhead. Only 3.2 m (10 ft 6 in) long, with a wing span of 3 m (9 ft 10 in), the tiny monoplane was eventually test-flown in 1939. It was boosted into flight on a rocket-propelled carriage along an inclined twin-rail ramp.

The ORM-65 engine in the tail, fuelled by kerosene and nitric acid, had a thrust which could be varied between 49 and 177 kg (108 and 390 lb). A much-improved design, the 212A flying bomb, was on the drawing board but never reached the flight test stage.

IN 1917, WHEN MAJOR POWERS were concentrating their every resource to turn the tide of war in Europe, French munitions and aircraft manufacturer Pierre Latécoère —like Holt Thomas in Britain—was already turning his thoughts to more peaceful uses of the aeroplane that could be realised when the war ended. He looked towards Morocco, considering it the first stepping-stone of a route to South America, and believing that aircraft would one day be able to provide fast and safe travel to this far country, where French prestige stood at a high level. It then took almost two months to receive a reply to a letter posted from Paris to Buenos Aires: Latécoère estimated that air mail could provide a reply within a single week, offering considerable scope for an operator with initiative.

Thus it was that, in 1919, at Montaudran airfield, near Toulouse, the Lignes Aériennes Latécoère became established. The men who came to fly the aircraft of this pioneer service were recently demobilised, happy to face any task, however menial, if only they could avoid withdrawal from the exciting 'drug' called aviation that was coursing in their veins. Their enthusiasm did much to ensure the success of the new company, but it was the airline's manager, Didier Daurat, who welded them into a disciplined team, to whom the delivery of the mail became almost a sacred mission.

To this brotherhood, the unwieldy title Lignes Aériennes Latécoère became abbreviated simply—and proudly—to 'the Line'.

It was to the Line, late in 1926, that a young man called Antoine de Saint-Exupéry applied for employment as a pilot and, in due course, came face to face with the perceptive Didier Daurat. Saint-Ex, as he soon became known, assured Daurat that, above all else, he wanted to fly. 'You must do as the others', growled the manager, 'take your place in the line'. This meant accepting gracefully the chores of early aviation, working in cold hangars, lessons in meteorology and navigation, cleaning aircraft, helping mechanics.

Daurat believed that this commitment into a communal life, sharing the hard work and daily tasks, was an essential part of apprenticeship to the Line. For Saint-Ex, a spoilt child of the aristocracy, it offered a real challenge. In his earlier experience of aviation, in the French Air Force, he had been feather-bedded by commissioned rank, and required only to learn how best to handle his aircraft. Non-commissioned ranks performed the menial tasks.

In course of time came his call to carry the mails. In a book that became an aviation classic, *Wind, Sand and Stars,* Saint Exupéry told of his pride, fears and thoughts after Daurat had given him his instructions. How, with a sense of in-

BROTHERS OF THE LINE

Right: One of the last photographs ever taken of Antoine de Saint-Exupéry showed him in the cockpit of the P-38 Lightning fighter in which he disappeared on 31 July 1944, when the liberation of France had begun

Below: Two photographs of Latécoère 28 floatplanes. These aircraft will always be associated with Jean Mermoz, whose most famous flights, across the South Atlantic, were made at their controls. Only Saint-Exupéry could have recorded the magic of those mail flights, and the never-to-be-forgotten moment when Mermoz had to fly his Laté 28 between huge black waterspouts like the pillars of some primordial temple

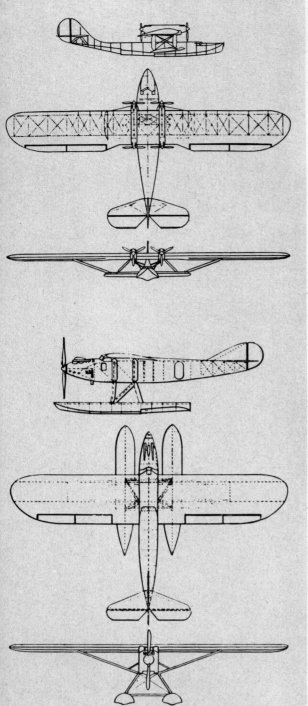

Above, top to bottom: The Latécoère 300 flying-boat *Croix du Sud*, in which Jean Mermoz disappeared on 7 December 1936. Powered by four 750 hp Hispano-Suiza engines, it spanned 145 ft (44.20 m) and had a take-off weight of 50,700 lb (23,000 kg). Maximum range was 2,980 miles (4,800 km) at 130 mph (210 km/h)

The Latécoère 28 seaplane, as flown by Jean Mermoz, was powered by a single 750 hp Hispano-Suiza engine and was able to fly 3,290 miles (5,295 km) non-stop. Wing span was 63 ft 1¾ in (19.25 m), maximum take-off weight 12,550 lb (5,690 kg) and maximum speed 147 mph (237 km/h)

F-AIEI (c/n 608) was a typical Laté 17 used on the mail routes of Lignes Aériennes Latécoère. The airframe was silver-doped with red cabin section

adequacy, he sought the experienced Guillaumet to provide the signposts of personal knowledge that no text book can hold. Guillaumet was to become his closest friend, one of the true pioneers of aviation, whose escape from a forced-landing in the Andes is an epic of personal triumph, described graphically by the pen of Saint-Exupéry. But on that night in 1926, the inexperienced pilot sat alongside Guillaumet' . . . And there, bent over in the lamplight, shoulder-to-shoulder with the veteran, I felt a sort of schoolboy peace.'

The demands of the Line soon provided self-confidence, exemplified by his initiative when sent to take charge of the company's refuelling station at Cape Juby on the Rio de Oro coast, one of ten similar points on the Casablanca-Dakar route.

When, in July 1928, brother pilots Riguelle and Dumesnil force-landed in the desert some 18 miles south of Juby, he exercised considerable ingenuity to recover their aircraft. Within two days he had organised a caravan of horses, donkeys and camels to carry men and supplies, and constructed a four-wheeled cart, made up from timber and aircraft wheels and hauled by a single camel, to carry the replacement engine and lifting tackle.

When this expedition arrived at the aircraft it was to discover that hostile tribes-men who frequented the area had stolen everything useful and that a flailing con-necting rod had severed the wing struts. This meant fetching a wing assembly from Juby—a two-day task—and while this was being done a strip some 25 by 300 ft (7.5 by 91.5 m) was levelled in the desert from which the repaired aeroplane would be able to take off.

Saint-Exupéry received news that a band of armed tribesmen was likely to attack them and so, when the wing assembly was received, every effort was made to com-plete the repairs as quickly as possible. The work progressed, under the 'guard' of six armed Moors, who exchanged rifle fire several times with the raiders, successfully preventing any serious attack. Finally, with the repairs more or less completed, Saint-

Left: The *Croix du Sud*, despite its tragic end, remains one of the most famous aircraft in the history of French commercial flying. It shared with the Couzinet 70 monoplane *Arc-en-Ciel* the hazardous Dakar-Natal sector of Air France's mail route to South America from the beginning of 1934

Below: The Latécoère 300 flying-boat was first flown in this form, as F-AKCU. It sank near Marseilles in late 1931, was salvaged and rebuilt as F-AKGF, the *Croix du Sud*

Bottom: Jean Mermoz logged 8,200 flying hours, including 23 trans-Atlantic mail flights in an age when it was still a headline-making achievement to complete even a single crossing

Ex, with his mechanic Marchal aboard, flew the aircraft back to Juby.

Without personal knowledge of any man it is difficult to attempt any balanced judgment of his capabilities. In the case of Saint-Exupéry the task is even greater, for his was a complex character. He appears to have been an average pilot of those early pioneering days, for biographers, while admitting his skill and daring, cannot forget that he was also absent-minded and unpredictable. He had a personality that could charm the birds from the trees and yet, in a moment, would flare with a temper that hurt those around him. Of one thing there is no doubt: he was a gifted writer, and aviation literature has been enriched by his almost-poetic contributions.

At Juby, Saint-Ex met many brothers of the Line—men like Guillaumet, Lécrivain, Riguelle, Joly and Mermoz who, for the sake of their chosen task—the carriage of mail—accepted the hazards of the desert. Not without trepidation, perhaps, for many of their comrades, forced down by the frailty of their craft, had been captured by the Moors. Some had been tortured, others assassinated. The best they could hope for was some degree of maltreatment before being ransomed.

Jean Mermoz had suffered the latter experience after being forced down on his fourth desert flight in May 1926. Exhausted by a trek across the burning sands, he fell asleep, awaking to find himself the prisoner of a band of tribesmen. More astute than most, they negotiated a ransom of 50,000 francs before releasing him. Thus, Mermoz lived on to gain fame as a pilot.

Pierre Latécoère, it will be recalled, had envisaged a mail service that would link France with South America. It was a dream far in advance of any aircraft that could make it reality. But there was no reason why the South American end of the route should not be developed, pending aircraft that would, one day, make crossing of the South Atlantic routine.

Late in 1927 Jean Mermoz embarked for Rio where, on the orders of Didier Daurat, he was to blaze the new air mail routes. Daurat excelled at sizing up a man: his choice of Mermoz for this particular task could not have been bettered, for the latter was an adventurous pilot, disciplined only by Daurat and allegiance to the Line. He lost little time in accepting this new challenge to his ability as a pilot: by October 1929, aided by other brothers of the Line, the most difficult routes had been surveyed and established. He had overcome distance and the impenetrable tropical forests, skimming triumphantly over them to Asunción in Paraguay and even as far as Corumba in Bolivia. Together with his mechanic, Collenot, he had climbed the inhospitable heights of the Andes, crossing over into Chile. He was then but six

months away from his greatest adventure.

The French contributed an outstanding achievement to early aviation by creating a route which extended from France, through West Africa, over the South Atlantic, and skirting the east coast of South America before crossing the Andes to terminate at Santiago in Chile. The first section, Toulouse-Montaudran to Dakar, was established by 1925; in 1927 the South American section, Natal to Buenos Aires, was opened. By the following year mail was being carried along the entire route, with fast ships linking Dakar and Natal. By then Lignes Aériennes Latécoère had given way to its successor, Cie Générale Aéropostale; subsidiaries of this company, Cia Aeropostal Brasileira and Cia Aeroposta Argentina, completed the South American routes.

On 12 May 1930 a Latécoère 28 float-plane, F-AJNQ *Comte de la Vaulx*, lifted off the water at St Louis, Senegal, carrying about 285 lb (130 kg) of mail. Mermoz was at the controls, accompanied by L Gimié and J Dabry as crew. The flight was not without incident, and Saint-Ex tells of the moment when the aircraft came out of the clouds into a fantastic scene. Ahead lay huge black waterspouts, almost like pillars of a temple, reaching up and supporting the clouds above. It was night, and a full moon sent beams of sylvan light between the almost immobile pillars. Mermoz, fascinated by the sight and experience, flew '. . . through these corridors of moon-light towards the exit from the temple'. When the floatplane touched down at Natal, 21 hours after take-off, Pierre Latécoère's dream had become reality.

Jean Mermoz is remembered especially for his South Atlantic flights, and on 16 January 1933, flying a Couzinet 70 land-plane, F-AMBV, named *Arc-en-Ciel*, he completed the St Louis-Natal crossing in 14 hr 27 min. By 1936 he had made 23 trans-Atlantic flights and then, on 7 December 1936, flying the Latécoère 300 flying-boat *Croix du Sud*, four hours out from Dakar, he radioed that he was cutting an engine. No other word came from him, and despite extensive air and sea searches no trace of the flying-boat or its crew was ever found.

Antoine de Saint-Exupéry was also to be lost without trace, on 31 July 1944, while flying a P-38 Lightning on a high-altitude wartime reconnaissance flight to the east of Lyons.

It is, perhaps, trite to suggest that both, given the choice, would have elected to end their lives travelling the corridors of the sky which they had known for so many years during the formative period of air transportation. What is certain is that these two brothers of the Line have assured themselves of a never-to-be-forgotten place in the history of aviation.

The Triumphant Thirties

THE ATLANTIC WAS conquered by the aeroplane in 1919 and the Pacific during the 1920s. In the third decade of the century also, aeroplanes flew round the world and over the North and South Poles. Yet with the coming of the 1930s much remained to be accomplished, especially in the way of trail-blazing the great air routes of the future, demonstrating the aeroplane's growing versatility, proving navigational techniques and, quite unashamedly, exploiting the courage and endurance of pilots in the name of record-breaking and publicity. Not least among these pilots were several women.

Governments played a part in probing and shrinking the globe by sending long-range aircraft on spectacular missions, the most impressive of which were the massive formation flights headed by the Italian General Balbo. Airships and the great Do X flying-boat made contributions of their own; but it was the achievements of a few individuals, some of them hardly more than amateurs, which kept the world agog in the decade now reviewed. While most of the flights concerned were notable for distance covered, there was one in which the attainment of very high altitude was the decisive factor. This was the first flight over Mount Everest (29,141 ft; 8,882 m) by the Marquess of Clydesdale and others in April 1933. The aircraft used in this historic aerial expedition were two specially-prepared Westland biplanes, originally designed for military duties and powered with highly-supercharged Bristol Pegasus engines.

As a long-distance pilot, fame came almost overnight to 26-year-old Hull-born typist Amy Johnson, whose first aerial experience had been a 'five-bob flip'. In her de Havilland Moth *Jason*, now preserved in the Science Museum, London, she left Croydon on 5 May 1930 and reached Australia on the 24th of the same month. On returning to England she toured the country lecturing, and in January 1931 tried unsuccessfully to fly to Japan via Russia. Her project eventually succeeded in July/August of the same year when, in her Puss Moth *Jason II*, she flew to Tokyo by way of Moscow.

In August 1932 Miss Johnson married James Mollison who, in 1931, had flown his own Moth from Australia to England in just under nine days, and who, in the month of his marriage, had crossed 2,600 miles (4,185 km) over the Atlantic in 30 hours. This was

the first Atlantic flight by a light aeroplane—the same little Puss Moth which had earlier carried Mollison from England to Cape Town. Later in the year Amy Mollison decisively bettered her husband's time to the Cape, using a more powerful Puss Moth.

But the Mollisons had hardly begun. Again using a Puss Moth, 'Jim' flew from England to Brazil in February 1933, thus making the first east-west solo crossing of the South Atlantic. The first west-east solo crossing had been made in an aircraft of the same type by H J ('Bert') Hinkler in November 1931. Together, in a twin-engined de Havilland Dragon, the Mollisons made an east-west Atlantic crossing in July 1933, both sustaining injuries in a crash-landing just short of New York City; and, though

unsuccessful in the England-Australia race of 1934, their Comet racer established an England-India record of 22 hours.

Another woman who achieved distinction for the British Empire was Jean Batten, who in 1934 became the first of her sex to make the England-Australia-England double journey. Francis Chichester, whose earlier exploits are referred to elsewhere in *History of Aviation*, continued to display his navigational skill by making the first solo seaplane flight between New Zealand and Japan in 1931 and by flying from Australia to London by way of Peking in 1936.

An eminent name in the period under review was that of the Australian Sir Charles Kingsford Smith, who in June 1930 flew his three-engined Fokker monoplane *Southern Cross* from Ireland to Newfoundland. His intended 'farewell' flight in the Lockheed Altair *Lady Southern Cross*, in which he had

Top: General Italo Balbo, the dashing Italian Air Minister, who led two huge mass flights of Savoia-Marchetti flying-boats over the South and North Atlantic in 1931 and 1933 respectively

Centre: Six of the S.55s used for Balbo's first formation flight. Neither exploit was completed without loss of life, but they gave a remarkable demonstration of the growing reliability and possibilities of aviation

Above: The Couzinet 70 *Arc-en-Ciel*, built for the trans-Atlantic section of Aéropostale's route from France to South America. The top of the rear fuselage was tapered and upswept to form a rather unique tail-fin

made the first flight from Australia to America, proved a farewell in the most tragic sense, for, together with his navigator J T Pethybridge, the great 'Smithy' disappeared off the coast of Burma in 1933.

The Mollisons were not the only husband-and-wife team active in the 1930s. With his incomparable trans-Atlantic solo flight already some four years behind him, and having in the meantime made extensive flights to Central America and the Caribbean, Charles Lindbergh flew to the Orient in 1931 accompanied by his authoress wife Anne Morrow Lindbergh. In 1933 the couple made a 30,000-mile (48,280-km) flight round the Atlantic, charting and inspecting possible new routes for airlines. As technical adviser to Pan American Airways, Charles Lindbergh assisted not only in route development but in technical matters also. Igor Sikorsky has written, concerning the design of the S-40 Flying Clipper: 'I returned to the factory and gave orders to continue the design along the lines suggested by Colonel Lindbergh.'

The greatest of all the American long-distance pilots of the 1930s, however, was Wiley Post. The name of this one-time barnstormer will always be associated with the Lockheed Vega high-wing monoplane, which can certainly be accorded a corresponding status among long-distance aeroplanes; and the most famous Vega of all was the *Winnie Mae*. This aeroplane was acquired in 1930 by Oklahoma City oil magnate F C Hall, in whose daughter's honour

it was named. Post was hired as Mr Hall's personal pilot, but instead of making business trips the Vega was prepared for one of the most exciting flights of all time— a high-speed dash round the world.

With Harold Gatty as navigator, Post lifted the *Winnie Mae* from Roosevelt Field, New York City, early on the morning of 23 June 1931. Eight days 15 hr 51 min later he set the Vega down on the same field, having beaten dramatically the previous record time of 21 days set up by the airship *Graf Zeppelin*. Stops had been made in England, Germany and Siberia, where the Vega was 'weathered in' for 14 hours before returning to America by way of Alaska and Canada.

This magnificent flight was not only a great technical achievement but one demanding extraordinary fortitude, for in covering its route of nearly 15,500 miles (24,945 km) the Vega had spent over 106 hours in the air, and as its occupants both had a full-time job to do there was no chance of sleep except at stops.

In 1933 the record remained unbroken; but Post decided that the time had arrived to better it, and on 15 July of that year he set out once again in the *Winnie Mae*, this time unaccompanied, though with the aircraft now fitted with an automatic pilot and a radio direction-finder. With these aids he succeeded in trimming his time by nearly a full day, and to other achievements recorded on the Vega's sleek wooden fuselage was added: 'Around the World. 7 days 18 hrs 19 min.'

Even now this great aeroplane had not given its all to the advancement of flying, for it was adapted for high-altitude development work, with Post rigged out in a pressure suit which, in conjunction with the eye-patch he wore and the features which proclaimed his Indian blood, gave him an appearance which was, to say the least, singular.

Sad to record, this great American pilot was killed, together with his friend, philosopher/humorist/air enthusiast Will Rogers, in an air crash during 1935. Happily the *Winnie Mae* survives, and may be seen and admired today in the National Air and Space Museum, Washington.

A Lockheed Vega was also used by Amelia Earhart, the greatest American air-woman of the 'thirties and the greatest of all women pilots, for a solo Atlantic crossing from Newfoundland to Ireland in May

Top: D-2053 *Groenland-Wal* was one of the Dornier Wal flying-boats used for pioneer journeys across the North Atlantic by Wolfgang von Gronau

Above: One of the great moments in flying history was captured in this photograph of the Houston-Westland (P.V.3) biplane approaching Mount Everest for the first flight over the highest point on Earth, on 3 April 1933

Top left: Second of the Westland biplanes which flew over Everest on that day was the modified P.V.6/Wallace prototype. Like the P.V.3, it was fitted for the occasion with a highly-supercharged Bristol Pegasus I.S.3 engine and an enclosed rear cabin. The pilots sat in open cockpits at nearly 30,000 ft (9,145 m)

Left: The Percival Gull used by Jean Batten for her fine solo flights from England to South America in 1935 and to her homeland, New Zealand, in 1936. The aircraft can still be seen in the Shuttleworth Collection at Old Warden in Bedfordshire

Below: Charles Lindbergh with his wife Anne and the Lockheed Sirius in which they made a trans-Pacific goodwill flight and a 30,000-mile (48,280-km) tour to Europe and South America

1932. Previously she had become the first woman to fly across the Atlantic, though only as a passenger, when she accompanied Wilbur Stultz and Louis Gordon in their Fokker seaplane during 1928. In 1935 Miss Earhart became the first person to fly solo from Hawaii to California and from Mexico City to New Jersey. Aspiring to fly round the world, she set out in 1937 with navigator Fred Noonan in a twin-engined Lockheed Electra. In New Guinea she discovered that her radio was faulty, but nevertheless continued out across the Pacific. After a Coast Guard cutter had received some radio messages distorted by static Amelia Earhart was never heard of again.

As the 'thirties neared their end, so record-breaking and transoceanic flights became less sensational. What the lone adventurers could do the adapted bombers, the big flying-boats, the airliners and the specially-built contenders could do better. Two American flights remain to be mentioned, however, as illustrating contrasting approaches to such ventures. In one instance the pilot, Douglas ('Wrong Way') Corrigan, declared on landing his Curtiss Robin in Ireland during 1938 'I guess I made a mistake', assuring the incredulous natives that on taking off from New York City he had intended to fly to California. The fact was

that a few days before the flight Corrigan, who had worked as a mechanic on Lindbergh's *Spirit of St Louis*, had asked the US Department of Commerce to sanction the venture, and had been refused permission because of the age and condition of his aircraft.

There was no such subterfuge respecting a remarkable performance by millionaire Howard Hughes, likewise in 1938. Hughes, who in the previous year had flown his H-1 high-speed monoplane from Los Angeles to New York in 7 hr 28 min 25 sec, setting a new transcontinental record, equipped a twin-engined Lockheed with the latest navigational aids and flew round the world in 3 days 19 hr 14 min. He never departed from his planned schedule by more than a few minutes, and although the flight is now but little remembered, perhaps because of the intervention of the war, it was much acclaimed in America, Hughes and his four-man crew heading a triumphal parade led by New York's Mayor La Guardia, himself a pilot during the first World War.

It would be far from just if this account left an impression that all the great flights of the 1930s were accomplished by pilots of the British Empire or the USA. The first round-the-world trip by a flying-boat was a German achievement, the aircraft being a twin-

engined Dornier Wal and the crew Wolfgang von Gronau, Gert von Roth, Fritz Albrecht and Franz Hack. This flight, which spanned 111 days, was made in 1932. In August 1930 von Gronau had commanded a Wal which had made the first east-west Atlantic crossing by a flying-boat and, again using a Wal, this same German pilot later headed a flight from Germany to New York and another from Sylt Island to Montreal, in both instances by way of Greenland.

Outstanding French pilots whose names were linked in the records of long-distance flights were D Costes and M Belonte who, in 1930, flew from Paris to New York in a Breguet XIX biplane, and P Codos and M Rossi who, in 1933, flew a Blériot 110 monoplane from New York to Rayak, in Syria. The name of Jean Mermoz was associated particularly with flights across the South Atlantic, using at first a Latécoère flying-boat and later a Couzinet landplane.

As already intimated, the airliners themselves were beginning to make pioneering flights, a notable example being the voyage of a Sikorsky S-42 flying-boat, commanded by Capt Edwin C Musick, from San Francisco to Hawaii and New Zealand in 1937. The days of the great lone trail-blazers were drawing to a close.

Top left: First of the great women long-distance pilots of the 'thirties was Amy Johnson, who earned the kind of adulation now reserved for pop stars by flying her little Moth *Jason* solo from England to Australia

Bottom left: *The Heart's Content,* the de Havilland Puss Moth in which Amy Johnson's husband, Jim Mollison, flew the North Atlantic, from Ireland to New Brunswick, at petrol and oil cost of £11 1s 3d in August 1932

Above: *Jason* is exhibited today among other famous aircraft of flying history in the Science Museum, South Kensington, London

Below: J9479 was the first of two Fairey Long-range Monoplanes built for an attempt on the World distance record. It was unsuccessful; but the second machine (K1991), flown by Sqn Ldr O R Gayford and Flt Lt G E Nicholetts, broke the record by covering 5,309 miles (8,544 km) non-stop from Cranwell to Walvis Bay, South Africa, on 6-8 February 1933

Top: Another of the famous aircraft of the 'thirties which can still be seen in the Shuttleworth Collection is G-ACSS, the de Havilland D.H.88 Comet *Grosvenor House* which won the 1934 MacRobertson Air Race from Mildenhall, England, to Melbourne, Australia. Its crew, C W A Scott and Tom Campbell Black, brought Australia within three days' flying time of England for the first time

Above left: Lockheed's five-seat, 450-hp Vega, named after the brightest star in the heavens, made many great flights. None were more spectacular than the two round-the-world dashes by Wiley Post in the *Winnie Mae*, which could jettison its undercarriage to increase speed

Above: Wiley Post lost an eye while working as an oil driller. This did not prevent his learning to fly and becoming one of the most famous pilots of his time. Like many of his contemporaries, he began by wing-walking and parachuting in the barnstorming days. He is shown here with the pioneer pressure suit which he wore for high-altitude research in the *Winnie Mae*

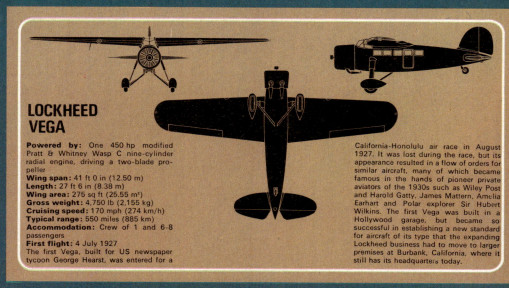

LOCKHEED VEGA

Powered by: One 450 hp modified Pratt & Whitney Wasp C nine-cylinder radial engine, driving a two-blade propeller
Wing span: 41 ft 0 in (12.50 m)
Length: 27 ft 6 in (8.38 m)
Wing area: 275 sq ft (25.55 m²)
Gross weight: 4,750 lb (2,155 kg)
Cruising speed: 170 mph (274 km/h)
Typical range: 550 miles (885 km)
Accommodation: Crew of 1 and 6-8 passengers
First flight: 4 July 1927
The first Vega, built for US newspaper tycoon George Hearst, was entered for a

California-Honolulu air race in August 1927. It was lost during the race, but its appearance resulted in a flow of orders for similar aircraft, many of which became famous in the hands of pioneer private aviators of the 1930s such as Wiley Post and Harold Gatty, James Mattern, Amelia Earhart and Polar explorer Sir Hubert Wilkins. The first Vega was built in a Hollywood garage, but became so successful in establishing a new standard for aircraft of its type that the expanding Lockheed business had to move to larger premises at Burbank, California, where it still has its headquarters today.

the Wings Rotate

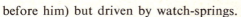
G-AAUA

THE HELICOPTER IS something for which the Greeks did not have a word, though the name is derived from their *helix* (spiral) and *pteron* (wing). Nevertheless, it is remarkable that this form of aircraft, which proved so difficult to perfect, should have been among the earliest to engage the attentions of the two great figures in the dawn of flight, Leonardo da Vinci and Sir George Cayley. The explanation is simple. For ages man had wished not merely to fly but to be able to lift himself vertically from the earth and set himself down again without forward run; and this is exactly what a helicopter, with the power-driven rotor or rotors which stamp it as a member of the 'rotary-wing' family of aircraft, now enables him to do.

As noted in connection with Cayley, his first helicopter model was based on a 1784 design by the Frenchmen Launoy and Bienvenu. It was a simple form of vertical-lift device which, in turn, had been based on

an early Chinese idea, consisting of two screws, one at each end of a shaft and rotated in opposite directions by means of a bowstring.

In 1828 an Italian named Vittorio Sarti designed another contra-rotating device, and at about the same time an Englishman named Mayer actually built a man-powered helicopter. Having regard to the problems of man-powered flight outlined elsewhere in *History of Aviation*, it is hardly surprising that this failed to leave the ground. Better success attended the efforts of W H Phillips who, in 1842, caused a model helicopter to ascend by rotating the blades by jets of gas which issued from the tips. This was a forerunner of the helicopter with jet-driven rotor, developed, though relatively little used, in modern times. A year or so later another Englishman, named Bourne, experimented successfully with small helicopter devices composed of feathers stuck in corks (as Cayley and the French had done

before him) but driven by watch-springs.

More helicopter proposals were put forward in the late 1850s and 1860s. An Englishman named Henry Bright had further ideas about man-powered possibilities; the Frenchman Gabriel de La Landelle showed during 1863 designs for a veritable airliner; and in the same year his fellow-countryman, the Vicomte de Ponton d'Amécourt, built another unsuccessful steam-driven model. He achieved far better results with clockwork-driven models. When the spring of one of these ran down, the little craft descended by parachute.

A name of more eminence in aeronautics (one, indeed, which has been ranked with that of Cayley) is Alphonse Pénaud, who had several inventions to his credit including the development, during 1870, of a twisted-rubber motor. This he successfully applied to helicopter models. An American, J B Ward, designed in 1876 a craft which has been classified by modern authorities both

as a helicopter and as an air-cushion vehicle. However, since it never left the ground, the point may be considered an academic one.

Among the forms of motive power proposed by the persevering helicopterists of the 1870s were gunpowder, a gas turbine, and compressed air; but the greatest success was achieved by the Italian Enrico Forlanini (later to design airships and hydrofoil boats) using steam-driven models. Little in the way of helicopter development ensued until 1907, and the remarkable events of that year, involving Cornu and Breguet, are chronicled on earlier pages.

A man whose work has come into prominence only in recent years, and this only because the 'turbine machine', or 'gyroparachute', which he invented in 1908 has been regarded as a form of air-cushion vehicle, is J Robertson Porter. In his book *The Helicopter Flying-Machine*, published in London during 1911, he said: 'The turbine machine is a late arrival, and but little experimental work has been carried out on it. It may be described as an improved form of helicopter, the air being drawn from above and being driven downward with similar effect; but instead of being driven directly downward it is turned in its course by means of the deflecting surfaces through an angle of 90 degrees twice.' With its 'annular jet' and 'flexible skirt' this remarkable craft, which was never perfected, certainly resembled a hovercraft more than a modern helicopter.

It was at this period that the greatest name in the history of helicopter development first entered the story, for it was during 1909 that the Russian Igor Sikorsky built his first machine of this class. In common with many earlier designs, and resembling likewise the successful Soviet Kamov helicopters of today, this had contra-rotating rotors, with the object of cancelling out torque—the twisting of the aircraft round its axis in the opposite direction to rotation of the rotor. But this first Sikorsky helicopter never left the ground, and a second which followed in 1910 lifted nothing but itself. Sikorsky thereupon transferred his interests to fixed-wing aircraft until the 1930s.

While it is true that the young Sikorsky had insufficient knowledge of the principles of rotary-wing flight, he was handicapped also by lack of power. It was not, in fact, until the coming of highly-efficient petrol engines that the helicopter had any real prospect of success. Sikorsky had a mere 25 hp at his disposal, though in 1908 Wilbur R Kimball had experimented in the USA with a helicopter having a 40-hp engine.

Much of the early work on helicopters was done in obscurity or secrecy and was never properly recorded, and it is thus not always easy to accord full credit where it was deserved. Modern helicopters are largely dependent on the principle of cyclic pitch control, and it is important to note that this was first suggested by the Italian G A Crocco in 1906 and was first demonstrated in 1912

by Jacob Ellehammer, a Dane whose contributions to the development of fixed-wing and rotary-wing aircraft are sometimes insufficiently acknowledged.

Although Louis Breguet was at work in France during the 1914-18 war there was little progress in that period on a broad front. The 1920s saw renewed activity, and one name prominent in this connection was that of the Marquis de Pescara, an Argentinian who built a number of helicopters in France and Spain. Pescara used not only cyclic pitch control but provided also for autorotation. On 18 April 1924 one of his helicopters established a world record by flying nearly half a mile.

Almost without exception the early heli-

CIERVA C.8L

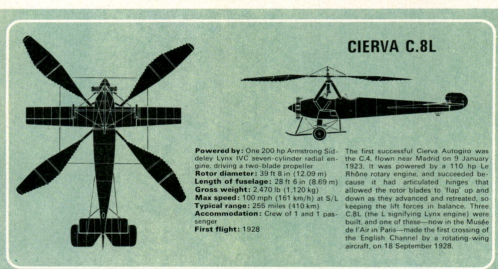

Powered by: One 200 hp Armstrong Siddeley Lynx IVC seven-cylinder radial engine, driving a two-blade propeller
Rotor diameter: 39 ft 8 in (12.09 m)
Length of fuselage: 28 ft 6 in (8.69 m)
Gross weight: 2,470 lb (1,120 kg)
Max speed: 100 mph (161 km/h) at S/L
Typical range: 255 miles (410 km)
Accommodation: Crew of 1 and 1 passenger
First flight: 1928

The first successful Cierva Autogiro was the C.4, flown near Madrid on 9 January 1923. It was powered by a 110 hp Le Rhône rotary engine, and succeeded because it had articulated hinges that allowed the rotor blades to 'flap' up and down as they advanced and retreated, so keeping the lift forces in balance. Three C.8L (the L signifying Lynx engine) were built, and one of these—now in the Musée de l'Air in Paris—made the first crossing of the English Channel by a rotating-wing aircraft, on 18 September 1928.

FOCKE-ACHGELIS Fw 61

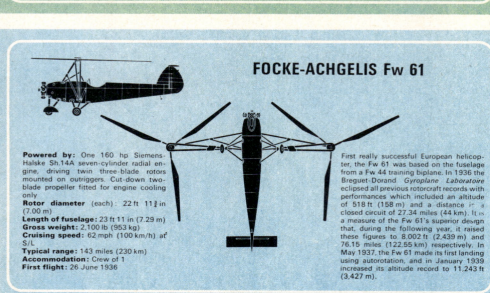

Powered by: One 160 hp Siemens-Halske Sh.14A seven-cylinder radial engine, driving twin three-blade rotors mounted on outriggers. Cut-down two-blade propeller fitted for engine cooling only
Rotor diameter (each): 22 ft 11¾ in (7.00 m)
Length of fuselage: 23 ft 11 in (7.29 m)
Gross weight: 2,100 lb (953 kg)
Cruising speed: 62 mph (100 km/h) at S/L
Typical range: 143 miles (230 km)
Accommodation: Crew of 1
First flight: 26 June 1936

First really successful European helicopter, the Fw 61 was based on the fuselage from a Fw 44 training biplane. In 1936 the Breguet-Dorand *Gyroplane Laboratoire* eclipsed all previous rotorcraft records with performances which included an altitude of 518 ft (158 m) and a distance in a closed circuit of 27.34 miles (44 km). It is a measure of the Fw 61's superior design that, during the following year, it raised these figures to 8,002 ft (2,439 m) and 76.15 miles (122.55 km) respectively. In May 1937, the Fw 61 made its first landing using autorotation, and in January 1939 increased its altitude record to 11,243 ft (3,427 m).

copters were grotesque or comical in appearance, or exhibited some remarkable feature. The Isacco 'helicogyre' developed in France in 1926 was certainly no exception: small engines driving propellers were fitted at the tips of the rotor blades.

On 25 October 1933 Nicolas Florine, a Russian-born engineer who became a Belgian subject and was financed by the Belgian National Fund for Scientific Research, established an endurance record by remaining in the air for just under 10 minutes; but progress continued to be slow, and by the end of 1934 the records for height and distance respectively were only 57 ft (17.4 m) and 1,184 yd (1,083 m).

Problems of control were dominant among those which persisted into the 1930s and which afflicted Louis Breguet's otherwise successful *Gyroplane Laboratoire* of 1935. The first really controllable helicopter was the German Focke-Achgelis Fw 61, which put up some remarkable performances between 1937 and 1939. The two rotors of this single-seater were carried on outriggers and were driven by an engine mounted in the nose; and the full technical significance of the design is conveyed by comparing its record-breaking figures for endurance and height with those in the foregoing paragraph. These figures were, respectively, 1 hr 20 min and 11,243 ft (3,427 m). Controllability was demonstrated when the famous German airwoman Hanna Reitsch flew the machine inside the Deutschland Halle in Berlin. Now remembered as the world's first woman helicopter pilot, she held the machine stationary, made 360-degree turns, and flew backwards, forwards and sideways.

The Germans were not quick to exploit their success, and their Fa 223, the first helicopter to go into production, did not fly until 1940. This was a quite ambitious transport machine, but was never employed operationally.

Successful though the Fw 61 undoubtedly was, it was not the forerunner of a great line of essentially similar helicopters having immediate and varied practical applications for civil and military use and continuing and multiplying until the present day. This distinction belongs to the Vought-Sikorsky VS-300, first tested in November 1939.

Igor Sikorsky, whose experiments of 1909-10 have already been noted, had never lost interest in helicopters, and in 1931 he applied for a patent which, he has said, 'included nearly all major features of the VS-300.' One especially important feature was the 'penny-farthing' arrangement, which meant that there was a single main rotor and a small anti-torque rotor, spinning in a vertical plane, at the tail. Such a scheme had been developed in the Netherlands during the late 1920s by A G von Baumhauer.

The helicopter's great bugbear of poor controllability continued to beset the VS-300 and extensive alterations had to be made. With two horizontal rotors in addition to its other two it was flown successfully in May 1940, and almost exactly a year later, after further development, it surpassed the German record by remaining aloft for 1 hr 32 min 36 sec.

From the VS-300, which was placed in the Edison Museum, Dearborn, Michigan, in 1943, was developed the R-4, more than 400 of which served in China, Burma, India, the Pacific, Europe and Alaska in the second World War and afterwards.

Even now, the story of early rotary-wing development is far from complete, for it remains to explain how aircraft of this class, though not true helicopters, were rendering valuable service well before the German and American successes. The calendar is now turned back to 1920 and the scene to Spain, with a young engineer named Juan de la Cierva at work on a form of aircraft having the fuselage and engine of an ordinary aeroplane but utilising, instead of fixed wings, a rotor mounted above the fuselage. The most important difference between the 'Autogiro', as Cierva called his invention, and the helicopter was that the rotor was not driven by the engine but rotated itself as the aircraft was drawn along by its

propeller: that is to say, it was autorotating. Extremely short take-off and landing runs were possible, and a forced landing in the event of engine failure was a far safer procedure than with fixed wings; but the Autogiro could not move sideways or hover in still air like a helicopter.

Although the first aircraft of the type was a complete failure, and the second and third proved unstable, Cierva achieved success in 1922/23 by adopting flapping hinges for the rotor blades. At the invitation of the British Air Ministry he demonstrated his C.6A machine, which used components of the Avro 504K trainer, at Farnborough during 1925, and by 1928 Autogiros were being built under licence in England and the USA. By January 1930 The Cierva Autogiro Co Ltd, of London, was advertising the 'C.19 Mark II. A two-seater light 'plane of wood and metal construction with Armstrong Siddeley Genet Major 100 hp engine. Top speed 95 mph (153 km/h), take-off run 30 yards (27.4 m), landing run none. Range 300 miles (483 km) at 70 mph (113

km/h)'. On the later C.30 type the engine could be geared to the rotor to 'pre-spin' it; the gear was then disengaged immediately before take-off, the length of which was thus further reduced. This technique was known as the 'jump-start', and gave the Autogiro an even closer kinship with the helicopter.

Although the Autogiro enjoyed only a limited success, it stimulated development of the true helicopter, especially by demonstrating the merits of flapping hinges for the blades, and aircraft of this type continue to be built and flown today.

The name of Cierva is thus an honoured one in rotary-wing history; but that of Sikorsky is honoured above all others.

SIKORSKY

It was on 25 May 1889 that Zinaida Sikorsky, wife of Professor Ivan Sikorsky, gave birth to a son, Igor Ivanovitch, in the ancient Russian city of Kiev. Unlike some destined to achieve fame, Igor was fortunate in that his parents were not only in a comfortable position in life; they were also people of high intellectual standing, the Professor being one of the great doctors of Russia while Zinaida was also a doctor, a very rare distinction for a woman in those days.

Relationship between Igor and his father was both happy and scientifically rewarding, but it is due to his mother that Igor's interests turned, almost in infancy, to aviation. Among her earliest teaching of her son were stories of Leonardo da Vinci and his ideas for a helicopter, and by the time Igor was twelve he had built a model rotary-wing aircraft which, powered by rubber bands, *actually flew*. Famous

men have often reminisced about how much they owed to their mothers. Igor Sikorsky is one of the few who can claim that his life's work stemmed directly from his mother's teaching.

His interest in flying was intense. The Wright Brothers became all-important to young Igor but, at that time, his heart was set on the helicopter. In 1908 he left school and, armed with money for aviation study and the purchase of an engine, went to Paris. The money came from Igor's sister Olga, who ran a school for retarded children.

In Paris he met many of the pioneers, all of whom were enthusiasts for fixed-wing aircraft and gravely doubtful of the helicopter. He learnt much and returned to Kiev to build his first helicopter, in which he installed his Anzani engine acquired in Paris.

To put it briefly, his attempts at helicopter

flight failed; he never got off the ground. Profiting by what he had learned in Paris he turned his attention to fixed-wing aircraft and built the S-1. Let it suffice to say that it did not fly. He tried again. The S-2 had a more powerful engine. It did fly —just. A few days later it crashed after a 49-second flight. The S-3 was only a little better. All this was costing money which even the Sikorsky family could provide only with some sacrifice. But with their encouragement he went on and built the S-4 and S-5. One year after his first hop in S-2, Sikorsky had in the air an aeroplane which really flew.

He won prizes, streamlined his aircraft, carried passengers and, in 1912, was appointed as Designer and Chief Engineer of the aircraft section of the Society of Russia Baltic Railroad Car Factories. He went on to greater success with small aeroplanes, and then came *Le Grand*. The

24

Right: This was Igor Sikorsky's second helicopter. Built in 1910, it was no more successful than number one; so he concentrated on fixed-wing aircraft for nearly thirty years before returning to his first love and becoming the greatest of all helicopter pioneers

Below: Igor Sikorsky at the controls of his S-2 biplane in 1910. Its first twelve-second hop was also the first time its designer had flown

Left: Sikorsky's second four-engined aeroplane, the *Ilya Mourometz*, had a promenade deck above the rear fuselage on which intrepid passengers could take a stroll in flight

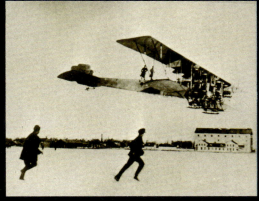

first four-engined aeroplane in the world, it had a cabin, even a washroom, and once carried 16 passengers. It was the forerunner of the—then—huge four-engined *Ilya Mourometz* bombers, which were used most effectively by the Imperial Russian Army in the 1914-1918 War.

Right: The aircraft which first identified the design genius of Igor Sikorsky—*Le Grand*, the world's earliest successful four-engined aeroplane

Colour: All Igor Sikorsky's early hopes for the helicopter are fulfilled by the big CH-54A (Sikorsky Model S-64) Skycrane. It consists of little more than a backbone structure, carrying a crew cab at the front, power plant and main rotor amidships, and anti-torque/control rotor at the tail. Between its stalky main undercarriage legs, it carries interchangeable Universal Military Pods which can be used to transport 45 combat-ready troops or 24 stretchers, or can be fitted out as field hospitals, communications centres or command posts

This was the highlight of Sikorsky's career in his native country. Came the revolution in 1917 and he, like many other educated Russians, decided to go to the USA. He had made what was then a fortune of about £100,000 but he left Europe, with little more than £100 and the clothes he stood up in.

His early life in New York was tragic. Speaking little English it was hard to get a job, especially as aviation was almost dead in America at that time. For several years he almost starved and then his determination took charge. He formed a small company with other Russian emigrés and started to build the S-29-A, a twin-engined passenger and freight carrier. With a capital of around $800 and some promises he had a rough time; but the aircraft progressed and he managed to get his daughter Tania, and his sisters Olga and Helen, with the latter's children Dmitri Viner and Galena Viner, over to the USA. His parents and wife were dead by then.

Rachmaninoff, the famous composer, gave $5,000 and the S-29-A was completed. The engines were old and weary, some of the airframe parts from junkyards and Woolworths, the tyres so bad

Top left: The suffix letter "A" in the designation of the S-29-A transport signified that it had been built in America. Built in the open on a farm, because Sikorsky could not afford a factory, by men who often worked without pay, it made many successful passenger, freight and publicity flights before crashing to destruction in the film *Hell's Angels*

Top right: With Igor Sikorsky at the controls, the VS-300 helicopter lifts itself a few inches off the ground on its first flight, on 14 September 1939. From this aircraft have evolved all the "single-rotor" helicopters of today

Above right: The skeleton of the S-29-A and the entire force of men who built it. Most, like Sikorsky, were Russian emigrés

Right: Sikorsky helicopters are used to retrieve America's astronauts from the ocean after their flights into earth orbit and to the moon. This photograph shows one of the Apollo 12 astronauts being hauled up into the cabin of a Coast Guard HH-52A (S-62) during pre-flight practice in getting out of the spacecraft at sea

that they sometimes burst while the aircraft stood still on them. On 4 May 1924 a take-off was attempted—with too many of the loyal workers who had built her on board, because Igor had not the heart to refuse them. She flew and she crashed, without serious injury.

But Sikorsky would not give up. More money was raised and the S-29-A was re-born. She was a great aeroplane and established Sikorsky, for the second time, as a great designer. The S-29-A finished its career by being converted to simulate a Gotha bomber and crashed while making the film 'Hells Angels'.

More types followed, all good ones, including the magnificent series of flying-boats which allowed Pan American to open up first the Caribbean and, later, the Pacific. That story is too long to tell here. There were troubles, but it was mainly a tale of success.

All this time the helicopter bug was biting Sikorsky. His first love was never forgotten. Whenever time allowed he worked on designs and, with better engines and materials plus immense aero-nautical knowledge, a shape emerged which he was convinced would fly. On 14 September 1939 the VS-300 (Sikorsky always kept the letter 'S' in the designations of his aircraft types), flown by its designer, lifted a few inches off the ground in controlled flight. The practical helicopter had arrived and its greatest enthusiast was its creator.

Details of the work done by the ever-improving series of helicopters bearing Igor Sikorsky's name are well known and will be covered later in this work.

What of the man? A brilliant engineer, designer and pilot, his determination has been apparent throughout his whole life. Yet he was—and is—one of the gentlest people one could ever hope to meet. He is retired now, though still acting as a consultant to his company; but all those lucky enough to meet him are impressed by his profound knowledge and his willingness to pass it on. He is unassuming,

kind, dignified—in fact, the perfect gentle-man'.

An example of his modest demeanour occurred when I had the honour of flying in his company in an S-51 helicopter giving a demonstration in Toronto University football ground in 1948. The aircraft was flown by his chief test pilot Dmitri (Jimmy) Viner, Igor's nephew. After a fantastic performance, flown entirely between the goal posts, we were mobbed by questioners but Sikorsky faded quietly away. Not for him the limelight.

The world owes a lot to this man—and to Zinaida Sikorsky for setting him on the right road.

Above: An early post-war portrait of Igor Sikorsky, at the time when he headed the world's leading helicopter design team

Above left: Sikorsky Aircraft senior executives received first-hand evidence that their chief had lost none of his youthful daring when Igor Sikorsky (at right) invited them to join him for a trip at 1,500 ft (450 m) altitude on an open platform under the first Skycrane

SIKORSKY S-64 SKYCRANE

Powered by: Two 4,500 shp Pratt & Whitney JFTD12-4A turboshaft engines.
Rotor diameter: 72 ft 0 in (21.95 m).
Length: 70 ft 3 in (21.41 m).
Gross weight: 42,000 lb (19,050 kg).
Max. speed: 127 mph (204 km/h) at sea level.
Accommodation/Payload: Crew of 2 or 3 + up to 90 persons or 17,500 lb (7,937 kg) of cargo in detachable pods, or up to 22,400 lb (10,160 kg) of slung cargo.
Max. range: 253 miles (407 km).
First flight: 9 May 1962.
The S-64 is a "flying crane" helicopter, consisting of a basic skeletal airframe to which can be attached large freight containers or "people pods" for short-haul transportation. In addition to its use by civil operators on a variety of duties, it is also used by the US Army, by whom it is designated CH-54.

SIKORSKY LE GRAND

Powered by: Four 100 hp Argus four-cylinder in-line piston-engines.
Wing span: 91 ft 10¼ in (28.00 m).
Length: 62 ft 4 in (19.00 m).
Gross weight: approx. 9,039 lb (4,100 kg).
Max. speed: approx. 59 mph (95 km/h) at 3,280 ft (1,000 m).
Accommodation: Crew of 2 + 8 passengers.
Typical endurance: 1 hr 45 min.
First flight: 13 May 1913.
The world's first four-engined aeroplane, the Le Grand was built in about six months, and featured such advanced items as a fully-enclosed cabin (with un-breakable glass windows) and dual controls for the crew. It was dismantled in the Autumn of 1913 after having made more than fifty successful flights.

LARGE AIRCRAFT
Between the Wars

Above: When completed in the summer of 1929, the Dornier Do X flying-boat was the largest aeroplane in existence. During flight trials on 21 October it flew with 169 people on board, made up of 10 crew, 150 passengers and nine stowaways

Right: The nose of G-AAGX, first of the H.P.42s, was so high off the ground, and the flight deck so far forward of the rest of the aircraft, that a structure was fitted temporarily forward of the windscreen to provide an 'orientation' reference for the pilots

Opposite page, top: Like the H.P. V/1500, the Tarrant Tabor triplane was intended to bomb Berlin from bases in Britain. The only example built was assembled in the balloon shed at Farnborough, from which it had to be extracted sideways on small trucks running on rails. When the upper pair of its six 450-hp Napier Lion engines were opened up during the first attempted take-off, on 26 May 1919, the Tabor upended on to its nose, fatally injuring its two pilots

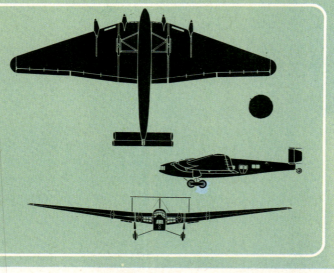

JUNKERS G 38

Powered by: Four 750 hp Junkers Jumo 204 diesel engines, each driving a four-blade propeller
Wing span: 144 ft 4½ in (44.00 m)
Length: 76 ft 1½ in (23.20 m)
Wing area: 3,229.2 sq ft (300.0 m²)
Gross weight: 52,910 lb (24,000 kg)
Cruising speed: 128 mph (208 km/h)
Accommodation: Crew of 7 and 34 passengers
First flight: 6 November 1929
As well as pioneering the use of metal construction and cantilever wings, Dr Hugo Junkers was a firm believer in a 'flying wing' type of aircraft which could carry most of its fuel and payload within the wing structure. The nearest he came to realising this objective was with the G 38, in which six of the 34 passengers were seated in the wing centre-section and could look out of windows in the leading-edge. Only two G 38s were built, but these operated with Deutsche Luft Hansa for several years; one crashed in 1936, and the other was destroyed by RAF bombers during 1940.

FOR THE NEW GENERATION of big-capacity, wide-body commercial transports which have recently made their debut, publicists have coined the term 'jumbo', making use of an adjective much over-worked by American advertising men to describe something larger than normal.

But had 'jumbo' been an 'in' word in the 1930s it might well have had an aeronautical application then, instead of having to wait for the present-day Boeing 747. For when the world's aircraft industries were struggling to throw off the last traces of adolescence, the 1930s produced a crop of outsize aircraft designs. Although not particularly colossal by today's standards, a number of them represented radical strides forward in the state of the aeronautical

designer's art.

Perhaps the best-known example was the Dornier Do X, a giant of a flying-boat which, having made its first flight on 25 July 1929, made the majority of its headline-hitting flights during the early 'thirties.

The Do X's claims to fame were many. At the time of its maiden flight it was easily the largest aeroplane in the world. It appeared when German airship development was at its zenith and in some respects, such as passenger facilities and comfort, could rival the Zeppelins. One observer of the time was less impressed by the fact that on 21 October 1929 the Do X carried a record 169 passengers aloft on its three decks, for a one-hour flight, than by the provision of a dining-room-cum-dancing-salon which was

nearly 60 ft (18.3 m) long!

Mistakenly, the 'X' in the aircraft's designation is often taken as a Roman numeral meaning that it had 10 engines, but in fact the flying-boat had 12 engines, mounted back-to-back in six nacelles, each with one tractor and one pusher propeller. Rather the 'X' was meant to signify 'unknown quantity', for that is what an aircraft of its size certainly was at that time.

Aesthetically the Do X was unglamorous, the flying-boat hull being flat and slab-sided and the massive wing of 157 ft 5 in (48.0 m) span being braced to sponsons attached alongside the hull. The engines were mounted on struts high over the wing to keep them clear of spray.

First trials of the Do X were made from

Friedrichshafen, on Lake Constance, with 550 hp Siemens (Bristol) Jupiter radial engines installed, but these were subsequently replaced by 600 hp Curtiss Conqueror liquid-cooled power plants with which it could attain 134 mph (216 km/h).

In true airship-type style, Dornier built into the design a means for the engines to be inspected and serviced while the aircraft was in flight. This was accomplished by means of a trolley system which ran along within the wing so that regular maintenance could be performed on the power plants and their complex individual electrical and other systems.

An epic flight made by the Do X involved a flight from Lake Constance to New York, where it arrived on 5 August 1931—having set out on 2 November the previous year—after a journey packed with incident. The flight was made in stages by way of Amsterdam, Calshot, Lisbon and the Canary Islands, storm and fire damage sustained en route all contributing to make the trip hazardous and frustrating.

The huge fuel load for the trans-Atlantic crossing contributed to a take-off weight of 55 tons. For this reason, and to take advantage of 'surface effect' (as Lindbergh had done), parts of the flight were made at low level. The flight to New York was the first of three such crossings, and the aircraft also flew down to the Caribbean and South America. Two more examples of the Do X were built for use in Italy and these differed primarily in having 600 hp Fiat engines which gave a normal range of 1,750 miles (2,815 km).

A contemporary of Dr Claude Dornier, who was responsible for the Do X design, was Professor Hugo Junkers, whose four-engined G 38 commercial transport, produced in 1930-32, also had pretensions to great size.

For its day the G 38 possessed many advanced features, not least of which was a patented Junkers slotted flap which extended the entire length of the wing trailing-edge. It also had several novel features which must have contributed to passenger appeal, including two seats in the extreme nose position—the totally-enclosed cockpit was above the wing leading-edge—plus a further three on each side of the fuselage in the wing leading-edge, complete with glazed panels.

The main passenger accommodation was divided between two decks, and at the tail end there was a separate smoke room. In all, the G 38 carried 34 passengers plus a crew of seven.

The four 750 hp Junkers Jumo 204 six-cylinder engines could, like those of the Do X, be inspected in flight. In terms of size, the span of the G 38 approached closely that of the Dornier flying-boat, and its maximum take-off weight was almost as great. For an aircraft of such bulk the G 38 had the very creditable cruising speed of 128 mph (208 km/h).

By and large, British aircraft manufacturers of the 1930s did not attempt to emulate their German counterparts by producing quite such outsize designs, although there were one or two notable exceptions. One was the Inflexible, built by William Beardmore and Sons, a Glasgow engineering and shipbuilding firm which had embarked on aircraft manufacture during the first World War.

Beardmore withdrew temporarily from aviation in 1921-24, but a revival of interest led to development of designs originated by the German Rohrbach company and the Inflexible was a result of this work. When it flew on 5 March 1928, the Inflexible was said to be the largest all-metal landplane then in flight test. A tri-motor design, powered by 650 hp Rolls-Royce Condor II engines, it was unusual in that the main structure was entirely of duralumin (apart

ANT-20 'MAXIM GORKI'

Powered by: Eight 900 hp M-34FRN twelve-cylinder Vee-type engines, three in each wing and two mounted in tandem above the fuselage, and each driving a two-blade propeller of approx 14 ft 9 in (4.50 m) diameter

Wing span: 206 ft 8¼ in (63.00 m)
Length: 107 ft 11¼ in (32.90 m)
Wing area: 5,231.3 sq ft (486.0 m²)
Gross weight: 92,595 lb (42,000 kg)
Cruising speed: 137 mph (220 km/h)
Typical range: 745 miles (1,200 km)
Accommodation: Crew of 23 and up to 40 passengers
First flight: 19 May 1934

The ANT-20, designed by A N Tupolev and built by the TsAGI (Central Aero and Hydrodynamic Institute) in Moscow, can probably claim to be the largest aeroplane ever built for aerial advertising. Electrically-illuminated signs and slogans could be displayed under the wings, and inside the fuselage and wings were a printing press, wireless broadcasting station and cine equipment for disseminating propaganda leaflets, films shows etc. After only one year's flying the *Maxim Gorki* was destroyed on 18 May 1935 in a collision with another aircraft; but a developed version, the ANT-20*bis*, is believed to have served briefly as a conventional transport aircraft from 1940.

Top: In retrospect, it seems hard to believe that the lumbering Vickers Virginia biplane, with a maximum speed of only 108 mph (174 km/h), was still a standard RAF heavy bomber at the time of the rebirth of the *Luftwaffe* in the mid-thirties. It spanned 87 ft 8 in (26.72 m), had a loaded weight of 17,600 lb (7,983 kg) and carried 3,000 lb (1,360 kg) of bombs.

Left: Early Junkers projects for a flying-wing transport culminated in the bat-like G 38, which flew for the first time on 6 November 1929. D-APIS was the second of two that were used spasmodically by Luft Hansa. Two seats in the nose and three in the centre-section leading-edge of each wing gave some of the 34 passengers a unique view forward

from certain steel components), which contributed significantly to weight reduction. At maximum take-off weight the aircraft grossed only 37,000 lb (16,783 kg).

Even earlier than this the Italian Caproni company, already renowned for the very large bomber aircraft produced during the first World War, had evolved in 1919 an even more gigantic civil design, the Ca 60. It had nine wings—three triplane sets at front, centre and rear of its boat-hulled fuselage—and was powered by eight 400 hp water-cooled engines. Unfortunately the available engine power was insufficient to overcome the tremendous frontal drag created by the wings and their multitudinous bracing struts, and this 100-seat 'jumbo' of 50 years ago was a sorry failure.

Probably the best-known large British aircraft of the era was the Handley Page H.P.42, in airline service from 1931 to 1941, and one of the biggest biplanes ever produced. Eight of these four-engined transports were built for Imperial Airways, four of the *Heracles* class for use on European routes and four of the *Hannibal* class which were employed on services from Cairo to South Africa and India. They enjoyed a reputation for safety and reliability which was second to none and is still remembered with affection by *aficionados* of air transport to this day. By the outbreak of the second World War, *Heracles* itself had carried more than 100,000 passengers and flown more than 1,300,000 miles (2,092,100 km).

The H.P.42 enjoyed the distinction of being the first four-engined airliner to see service anywhere in the world. Two engines were mounted on the top wing and two on the bottom. The *Heracles* class aircraft seated 38 passengers in two cabins, while the *Hannibal* class carried more fuel and had increased toilet and galley facilities and accommodation for 24 passengers.

Like Germany, Britain had also been strong in flying-boat development, which led to the birth of the famous 'C' class or 'Empire' flying-boats. The most remarkable task that an Empire 'boat was ever called upon to perform was to be the lower half of the Mayo composite aircraft. The composite theory, the brain-child of Major R H Mayo, technical general manager of Imperial Airways, involved mounting a smaller, four-engined, twin-float seaplane on top of a 'C' class' boat, piggy-back fashion, using the latter's engine power and fuel to lift off the payload-carrying upper aircraft.

Once airborne, the two components separated; the launch aircraft returned to base while the upper half, loaded to a weight which would have precluded a take-off under its power alone, continued on its trans-Atlantic journey. The first actual separation of the composite—*Mercury* was the top part and *Maia* the lower—was made on 6 February 1938.

The Mayo composite was a giant of some distinction. Of no less stature, and certainly no less intriguing, was the ANT-20, which first flew in Russia in May 1934 and was given the name *Maxim Gorki*, which was painted prominently underneath the wings. The Russians hailed the aircraft as the largest landplane in the world, but it was destroyed in 1935 in a mid-air collision with heavy loss of life.

The *Maxim Gorki* was powered by eight engines—six on the wings plus a pair in tandem above the top of the fuselage. The aircraft was also something of a champion heavyweight: the credited fully-loaded weight was 92,595 lb (42,000 kg), much of which was undoubtedly attributable to its Kremlin-style aeronautical architecture!

Left: An Italian giant of 1929 was the Caproni Ca 90 P.B. bomber, which spanned 152 ft 9 in (46.58 m) and had a loaded weight of 66,000 lb (30,000 kg). Six 1,000-hp Isotta-Fraschini Asso-1000 engines gave it a top speed of 127 mph (205 km/h). Its 'inverted sesquiplane' design was a scale-up of that of the twin-engined Ca 73, a standard Italian Air Force bomber. The Ca 90 was the largest bomber design of its day

Bottom left: The six-engined ANT-20 *Maxim Gorki* flying over Red Square, Moscow, in formation with two fighters. Such an exploit led to its destruction, when it collided with another aeroplane that was supposedly escorting it

Bottom right: The ANT-20*bis* was built by public subscription after the loss of the *Maxim Gorki*. It was powered by six engines – three in each wing, had a span of 206 ft 8½ in (63 m), weighed 102,956 lb (46,700 kg) and carried 60-64 passengers

Handley Page

FREDERICK HANDLEY PAGE, born at Cheltenham on 15 November 1885, was to earn a place in the history of aviation as honoured as any man could hope to do. He was already a qualified electrical engineer when he built his first aircraft, the Bluebird, in 1909. It was not a success, but in 1910 he demonstrated an improved version, the 'Yellow Peril', so called from the colour its wings were painted.

Handley Page Limited was formed in 1909, and remained one of the leading companies in the British aircraft industry until 1970. Frederick Handley Page flew his early aircraft personally, but was never well known as a pilot: his fame came from aircraft design and manufacture. His first aircraft were monoplanes incorporating a marked sweepback of the leading-edge of a crescent-shape wing—a feature inspired by the gliders of the Austrian designer José Weiss which was to reappear in Handley Page designs in much later years.

'HP' did not emerge fully as a public figure until the first World War, when his large twin- and four-engined bombers brought a new concept of strategic air power. At the time the war ended in November 1918 his big four-engined V/1500s were being made ready to bomb Berlin from bases in England. When this became unnecessary, a V/1500 was taken instead to Newfoundland for an attempt on the *Daily Mail*'s £10,000 prize for an Atlantic crossing. Once Alcock and Brown's Vimy had made the crossing, there was no point in the Handley Page aircraft doing the same; instead, it was demonstrated in North America, where it created quite an impression.

During the next few years 'HP' built both civil and military aircraft. The 12-passenger W 8, derived from the O/400 twin-engined bomber, appeared in 1920 and went into service on the company's airline routes to the Continent.

Although Handley Page never took any great interest in light aircraft as such, his work made them—and larger machines—much safer. The Handley Page slot, first demonstrated on a modified D.H.9 air-

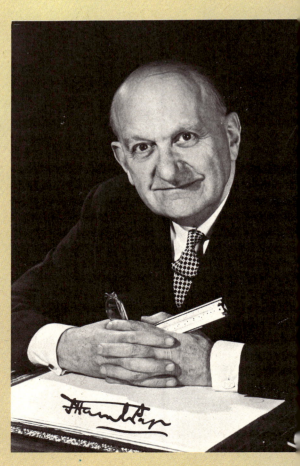

Top: The original Handley Page works, at Barking, in 1909. In front of the buildings is the unsuccessful 8-hp quadruplane built for G P Deverell Saul, an early seeker after inherent automatic stability

Centre: *Hannibal,* one of the eight H.P.42s which are, perhaps, the best remembered of all Handley Page products

Above: The turboprop Jetstream transport is the aircraft on which the Handley Page company pinned its hopes for survival into the 'seventies. It will go down in history as the last type to bear the company's name

Left: A characteristic portrait of Sir Frederick Handley Page, who remained, in every way, a leader of the British aerospace industry until his death on 21 April 1962

craft in 1920, was developed later into an automatic device which so improved the low-speed handling (and thereby the safety) of an aeroplane that the Air Ministry made it a compulsory feature for all RAF aircraft. The device created a marked delay in the onset of wing stall and also reduced the risk of spinning, an unpleasant and often dangerous manoeuvre, especially for an inexperienced pilot. 'HP' was also involved in the design of slotted ailerons and flaps to reduce landing and take-off speeds, and a combination of these features appeared in the H.P.39 Gugnunc, built in 1929 as a competitor in the Guggenheim Safe Aircraft Competition held in the USA.

One of Handley Page's finest aeroplanes was the H.P.42, an immense four-engined biplane which carried up to 38 passengers at a rather ponderous 100 mph (161 km/h) on the European and Eastern routes of Imperial Airways. Eight were built: they flew, collectively, over 10 million miles (16,093,400 km) and there was never a fatality in peacetime service. Their life

span lasted from 1930 (in service 1931) to after the start of the second World War. One of them, *Heracles,* carried over 100,000 passengers, nearly one-fifth of all the people carried by Imperial Airways in its 16 years of operation. The big bomber tradition was maintained between the wars by the Hinaidi, Hyderabad and Heyford.

Prior to the second World War, Handley Page Ltd was already producing the Hampden bomber, with the Halifax on the drawing board. The Hampden was used extensively in the early days of the war; later, while the Avro Lancaster acquired a greater share of the glamour, the Halifax played an immensely important part in the bomber offensive against Germany.

Sir Frederick was never content to remain a chairman in name only. His concentration on the day-to-day running of his firm became a tradition. After the war, with the inevitable run-down of the aircraft industry, he repeated his performance of converting bombers into airliners by turning the Halifax into the Halton; but such improvisations could not

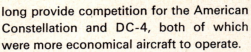

Right: 'H P' at the controls of the Bluebird. Powered by a 25-hp Advance engine, this first Handley Page design (excluding an early glider) made a few short hops on 26 May 1910

Lower right: Crescent-shaped wings, adopted for the mighty Handley Page Victor V-bombers of the 'fifties and 'sixties, were nothing new for this company's products. Its first really successful aeroplane, the 50-hp Gnome-powered H.P.5 of 1911, used such a wing-form to achieve a high degree of stability

Below: Britain's giant of the 1914-18 War, the Handley Page V/1500 four-engined bomber was just too late to undertake its designed task of attacking Berlin from bases in the UK. On short ranges it could carry thirty 250-lb (113-kg) bombs, and a 3,300-lb (1,500-kg) bomb was produced specially for use by V/1500 squadrons

long provide competition for the American Constellation and DC-4, both of which were more economical aircraft to operate.

A more realistic post-war transport was the Hermes. Anyone who flew long distances in this aircraft, operated by BOAC, soon came to the conclusion that there was little or nothing to rival it for passenger comfort and blessed the name of Handley Page for creating it. It had some severe early teething troubles, but developed into one of several useful stopgaps during BOAC's Comet-less years between 1954 and 1958. Later, on charter operations with a 50 per cent increase in passenger load, it was quite profitable if far less comfortable. Its military counterpart, the Hastings, served for many years with Transport Command of the RAF.

Sir Frederick—he was knighted in 1942—had an immense range of interests, most of which were in one field or another of aviation: President of the SBAC, Vice-President of the Air Registration Board, President of the Royal Aeronautical Society—these were only three of his many offices, and his distinctions filled half a column of 6-point type in the 'Who's Who of British Aviation.'

The jet age overtook Handley Page when his company was no longer one of the giants of world aviation. 'HP' never produced a jet airliner, but the company did prepare a design for a supersonic airliner, long before the Concorde began to be

Above: First aeroplane to utilise both Handley Page leading-edge slots and slotted ailerons was this monoplane conversion of a D.H.9A, known as the X4B

Above right: The style of furnishing and decoration embodied in the passenger cabins of the H.P.42 looks strange to modern eyes. It offered such comfort in the 'thirties that Imperial Airways carried more passengers to Europe from London in its H.P.42s than all other airlines combined

Right: No photograph could be more typical of its era than this shot of the H.P.42 *Helena* in front of Croydon Tower

Opposite page: The pride with which Imperial Airways regarded its H.P.42s is evident in this illustration from one of its publicity brochures of the 'thirties

226

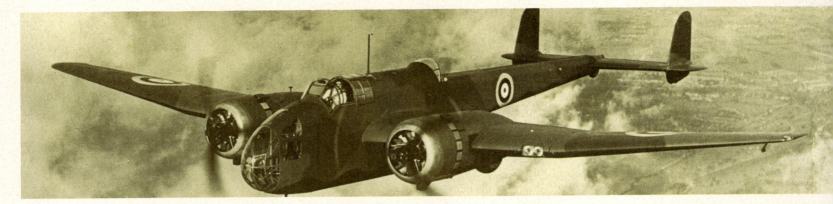

Top left: Known often as the 'flying suitcase' because of its pod-and-boom fuselage, the Handley Page Hampden was one of the RAF's standard bombers at the outbreak of the second World War

Far left: The Halifax, with the Lancaster, bore the brunt of Bomber Command's offensive in the second World War. This batch was built by The English Electric Company at Preston

Left: Some of the credit for the success of the Concorde supersonic airliner must go to the little H.P.115 research aircraft, which tested the handling characteristics of narrow-delta wings at low speeds long before the Concorde flew

Below: As well as being a vehicle for Britain's nuclear weapons, the Victor could carry no fewer than thirty-five 1,000-lb (454-kg) 'iron' bombs of the kind shown here

Below right: One of the best of the interim airliners acquired by BOAC, pending the switch to jet travel with the Comet, was the Handley Page Hermes

Bottom right: BEA used three turboprop Heralds for a time on its Scottish routes, for which their short take-off and landing runs made them particularly suitable

built. On the military side, there was the Victor bomber, which could carry nuclear weapons over tremendous distances at almost the speed of sound. Later, many Victors were converted into flight refuelling tankers, in which role they will continue to serve until the middle or late 1970s. Others are responsible for the RAF's vital strategic reconnaissance operations.

Handley Page did make one vitally important excursion into the realms of SST design. A special 'slim delta' research aircraft, the H.P.115, was built to test the slow-speed characteristics of such a wing, as part of the Concorde development programme. It was used in conjunction with the modified Fairey Delta 2, which explored the Mach 2 speed range with a similar wing.

The last major Handley Page venture was the Herald feeder-liner—a small aircraft this time, seating 38-56 passengers and having two turboprop engines; but although it attracted customers from most parts of the world it failed to achieve a large sales total.

When the drastic mergers within the British aviation industry came about during the late 1950s and early 1960s, Handley Page at first remained doggedly independent, as he had done all his life. Then, when he had after all made up his mind to accept an offer of amalgamation with another major British airframe manufacturer, cancellation of a large government contract caused the offer to be withdrawn and Handley Page Ltd had to survive this period of change as an independent company. Sadly, the survival was short-lived, for the company found it almost impossible to compete with the two large consortiums, Hawker Siddeley and British Aircraft Corporation. When its final product, the Jetstream, also failed to find the military and civil market that its design merited, this famous company—the first limited company incorporated in Great Britain for the purpose of manufacturing aeroplanes —succumbed to the inevitable and in March 1970 went into liquidation.

Sir Frederick himself had died on 21 April 1962, and thus—mercifully, perhaps —was spared the sight of the final collapse of the great company of which he remained chairman and managing director to the end of his life.

THE MODERN transport aeroplane may be said to have been born on 8 February 1933 when the prototype, all-grey, Boeing Model 247 twin-engined 10-passenger monoplane made its first test flight at Seattle in Washington State. The 247 was a low-wing cantilever monoplane with cleanly-cowled 550 hp Pratt & Whitney Wasp air-cooled radial engines. It had an all-metal structure, a single fin and rudder and retractable main undercarriage.

Before the advent of the Boeing 247 the world's air services had been operated by a wide assortment of aircraft, comprising biplanes and both high-wing and low-wing monoplanes. Many were built of wood and had fabric covering, although some had metal structures. The Fokker monoplanes had fabric-covered metal-framed fuselages and wooden cantilever wings, but their undercarriages were not retractable. The Junkers monoplanes were of all-metal construction but their load-bearing skins were corrugated and they, too, had non-retractable undercarriages. In the United States the Ford Tri-motors, although they did much to develop air transport, were of Fokker layout but Junkers-type construction.

Thus the Boeing 247 made a complete break with the past, representing a new breed of transport aeroplane with which the earlier types were unable to compete. It cruised at 155 mph (250 km/h), had a range of 485 miles (780 km) and a service ceiling of 18,400 ft (5,600 m).

Sixty Boeing 247s were ordered by United Air Lines while the type was in the mock-up stage. The first of the new aircraft entered service in March 1933 and when put on the US transcontinental route cut the journey time to just under 20 hr, compared with the previous 27 hr. It suffered certain shortcomings. These included the fact that the spars passed through the cabin, causing some obstruction, and that at high and hot aerodromes take-off performance was impaired by the fixed-pitch propellers.

To overcome the performance problem a new version, the Model 247D, was produced. This had controllable-pitch propellers, increased fuel capacity, more power at higher altitudes, and various other refinements which increased the cruising speed to 189 mph (304 km/h) and the range to 745 miles (1,200 km). Most of the original aircraft were brought up to 247D standard and a total of 75 of the 247 series was built.

TWA was anxious to acquire Boeing 247s, but Boeing was unable to deliver them quickly enough and the airline therefore issued a specification for a competitive aircraft—visualised originally as a three-engined type. Douglas decided to meet the TWA specification and designed the DC-1. This was of similar layout to the Boeing 247 but proved to have superior performance and, of great importance, had its spars beneath the floor to leave a completely unobstructed passenger cabin.

The DC-1 first flew on 1 July 1933, and

Above: Experience gained with the D.H.88 Comets, built in 1934 for the MacRobertson air race to Australia, inspired the D.H.91 Albatross, one of the cleanest and most beautiful aeroplanes of all time. Seven were built, including the prototypes, offering a vivid contrast with the 'built-in headwinds' of Imperial's H.P.42s, one of which appears in the background to this photograph

Top left: Using the moulded plywood construction first seen in their 1920 Model S-1 Sportsplane, Lockheed produced a series of very clean, fast monoplanes in the late 'twenties and early 'thirties. Typical was the six-seat Orion, with retractable undercarriage, which could fly at 225 mph (362 km/h) on only 420 hp

Top centre: One of the great aeroplanes of history, the Boeing 247 was the true ancestor of all modern monoplane airliners. This one, built in 1933, has been restored in its original United Air Lines insignia

MODERN AIRLINER

Above: One of British Airways' fleet of Lockheed 14s. This particular aircraft, the flagship, carried Prime Minister Neville Chamberlain to his meeting with Adolf Hitler which produced the infamous Munich Agreement of 1938

Top right: Three of Swissair's DC-2 fleet at Croydon Airport, London. Although later than the Boeing 247, the DC-2 was more successful and was evolved into the immortal DC-3

was delivered to TWA—making a record 13 hr 4 min Los Angeles-New York flight with mail in February 1934. TWA ordered 28 examples of a refined version known as the DC-2 and when this type, with accommodation for 14 passengers, entered service in July 1934 it was the world's most advanced passenger transport aeroplane. From its inception the DC-2 was fitted with variable-pitch propellers; these contributed significantly to its performance and gave it better single-engined characteristics than had been achieved previously by any twin-engined aeroplane.

In October 1934 a DC-2, operated by KLM, took part in the England-Australia air race. It won the handicap section and took only a few hours longer to reach Melbourne than did the specially-designed racing Comet which won the speed event. This success, combined with its outstanding performance in airline service in the United States, led to a number of foreign orders, and DC-2s eventually served many of the main US airlines and others in Europe, South America, Australia and China. About 220 were built, of which 160 were used in airline service. The DC-2 had 710 hp Wright Cyclone engines, cruised at 170 mph (274 km/h) and had a range of 1,190 miles (1,915 km).

It was followed by the most significant transport aeroplane ever built—the Douglas DC-3—which did more than any other type of aircraft to develop and establish a reliable system of worldwide airlines and

create the traffic which led to the production of modern four-engined airliners.

The DC-3 was an enlarged, direct development of the DC-2. It was designed to meet a requirement of American Airlines for a sleeper aircraft for use over the US transcontinental route. At the time American Airlines was using Curtiss Condor biplanes on sleeper services, but these proved unable to compete with Boeing 247s and Douglas DC-2s and it was obvious that a new aircraft had to be acquired if American Airlines was to attract its fair share of the traffic.

The fuselage of the DC-2 was too narrow to take sleeping berths but the new design, known as the DST (Douglas Sleeper Transport), could provide berths for 14 passengers. When used for daytime operation its greater width could accommodate 21 passengers—a 50 per cent increase in capacity compared with the DC-2 for only slightly increased unit and operating costs.

The prototype first flew on 17 December 1935, and both the DST (sleeper) and DC-3 (dayplane) were put into production. American Airlines began DC-3 operations, between New York and Chicago, in June 1936 and DST transcontinental operations in September of that year, to a 17¾-hr westbound and 16-hr eastbound schedule.

Initially DC-3s and DSTs had 1,000 hp Wright Cyclone engines, but the 1,200 hp Pratt & Whitney Twin Wasp was soon destined to become the main source of power for the DC-3 series.

231

By the time of the Japanese attack on Pearl Harbor, Douglas had built more than 800 DC-3s and about 450 of these, including 38 DSTs, had been delivered to airlines. During the war large-scale production of military DC-3s was undertaken, mainly of the C-47 and C-53 versions, and the Royal Air Force name for the type, Dakota, is that by which the DC-3 is now widely known. A considerable number of DC-3s was built under licence in the Soviet Union, at first as the PS-84 and later as the Lisunov Li-2; some were built in Japan, and commercial DC-3s were put back into production for a time after the end of the war. There is disagreement about the total number produced but it was about 11,000 and this means that there were far more DC-3s and DC-3 variants than any other type of transport aeroplane.

Even after the war the DC-3 remained the backbone of the US commercial air fleets and the type has been used by almost every major and very many minor airlines as well as most of the world's air forces.

The DC-3 has been used for almost every type of civil and military transport duty; it has served as a glider tug, one was actually converted to a glider, it has operated on skis, and one was a twin-float seaplane. Even in the Vietnam war it has been operated in an offensive role as a gunship.

Designed as a 21-seat aeroplane, the DC-3 has for years been operating with 28 seats and some have been equipped to carry 36 or more passengers.

One DC-3 is known to have achieved more than 84,000 hr flying and well over 800 are still in airline service in many parts of the world. In their original role the DC-3s were replaced by more modern types but the numerous efforts to produce a 'DC-3 replacement' have failed and 35 years after its first appearance there are air transport tasks which still only the DC-3 can perform. Typical present-day DC-3 cruising speed and range are 180 mph (290 km/h) and 1,500 miles (2,415 km).

Although they were of less importance than the Boeing 247 and Douglas DC-2 and DC-3, mention must be made of a Lockheed series of twin-engined airliners.

Lockheed had achieved considerable success with its Air Express and Vega high-wing and Orion low-wing single-engined monoplanes, some of which entered airline service—Orions being used by Varney in the United States and Swissair in Europe. Lockheed then decided to build a clean twin-engined all-metal low-wing monoplane, the L.10 Electra, which first flew in February 1934 and entered service in August 1934 with Northwest Airlines. The Electra was generally similar to the Boeing 247 and Douglas DC-2 but was considerably smaller and, unlike the other types, had twin fins and rudders. It had accommodation for only 10 passengers but was faster than the original Boeing 247s and the DC-2s. A total of 148 Electras was built; most had Pratt & Whitney Wasp Junior engines, and the type saw airline service in many parts of the world.

Successor to the Electra was the Lockheed 14, also known as the Super Electra. This was a slightly larger, refined version of the Electra and it incorporated a number of significant new features. These included Fowler area-increasing flaps, which allowed higher wing loadings while retaining a modest stalling speed, two-speed super-chargers and underfloor cargo holds. The Lockheed 14 first flew on 29 July 1937, and numbers went into airline service. British Airways had a fleet of Lockheed 14s and the type was used by airlines in several parts of the world.

Developed from the Lockheed 14, the 14-passenger L.18 Lodestar first flew on 21 September 1939. This type was powered by two 1,200 hp Wright R-1820 engines and entered service in March 1940, with Mid-Continent Airlines. More than 600 Lode-stars were built and these saw wide-scale airline and military service.

Total production of these Lockheeds was about 1,000 and they provided valuable experience which was incorporated in the four-engined Constellation and Super Constellation series.

The Boeing 247, the Douglas Commercials and, to a lesser extent, the Lockheed 'twins', set the pattern for the modern transport aeroplane when they introduced the clean cantilever low-wing design with smooth stressed-skin metal covering, retractable undercarriages, flaps, variable-pitch propellers, airframe de-icing, automatic pilots and full duplicated controls and flight instruments. The fleets of four-engined monoplanes which followed, including the turbojet types of today, all owe their existence to the 247 and the twin-engined Douglas types which brought new standards to air transport between 35 and 40 years ago.

BOEING MODEL 247

Powered by: Two 550 hp Pratt & Whitney R-1340-S1H1G Wasp nine-cylinder radial engines, each driving a 9 ft 8 in (2.95 m) diameter three-blade propeller
Wing span: 74 ft 0 in (22.56 m)
Length: 51 ft 7 in (15.72 m)
Wing area: 836.13 sq ft (167.90 m²)
Gross weight: 13,650 lb (6,192 kg)
Cruising speed: 189 mph (304 km/h) at 12,000 ft (3,658 m)
Typical range: 745 miles (1,200 km)
Accommodation: Crew of 2 and 10 passengers, plus 400 lb (181 kg) of mail
First flight: 8 February 1933

The great revolution in airliner design which heralded the end of the era of 'slow-but-sure' biplanes began with the Boeing Model 247, of which 75 examples were produced. Most of these were either built as, or converted to, Model 247D standard, with modified cockpit wind-screens, controllable-pitch propellers and other refinements; the data apply to this version. One specially-modified 247D, flown by Col Roscoe Turner and Clyde Pangborn, came second in the transport division of the 1934 MacRobertson race from London to Melbourne and third in the overall placings for speed.

Top left: The DC-1, first of the whole great family of Douglas Commercials, at Grand Central Air Terminal, Glendale, California. While still registered 'X' for experimental, the aircraft carried many passengers as guests of TWA on demonstration flights

Above: One of the original American Airlines fleet of DC-3s, with starboard-side passenger door, over Manhattan

Top right: A standard pre-war DC-3 of KLM, flying near Amsterdam with the starboard engine shut down

Centre right: Largest airliner built for Imperial Airways before the second World War, the Armstrong Whitworth Ensign was intended to carry 27 passengers on distant Empire routes, 40 in Europe. Underpowered with the original 850-hp Tiger engines, the type was re-engined with 950-hp Wright Cyclones

Bottom right: Predecessor of the Ensign, Armstrong Whitworth's Atalanta of 1931-32 was of plywood-covered steel construction, had four 340-hp Armstrong Siddeley Serval engines and carried only nine passengers, as mail and freight formed a high proportion of available payloads at that time

THE ERA OF AIRLINE FLYING-BOATS

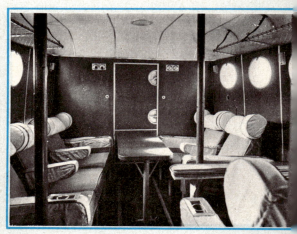

This page, top: The *America* flying-boat built by Glenn Curtiss for an attempted trans-Atlantic flight before the first World War. The pilot was to be John Porte. Later, as an RNAS officer, Porte ordered similar aircraft for maritime patrol duties around Britain. From them was evolved the whole family of Felixstowe 'F' boats

Centre: Largest flying-boats operated by Imperial Airways prior to introduction of the 'C' Class were three Short Kents, each powered by four 555 hp Bristol Jupiter engines and carrying 16 passengers

Left: *Canopus*, the first of the fleet of 'C' Class flying-boats used on the Empire routes of Imperial Airways from 1936 onward

Above: The cabins of the 'C' Class flying-boats may look spartan by modern standards. In 1936, they represented the height of comfort and luxury

Opposite page: When Imperial Airways began planning its Empire routes in the 'twenties, it was decided that the Mediterranean over-water sector could only be operated safely by flying-boat. This led to production of the 15-passenger Short S.8 Calcutta, the prototype of which was moored at Westminster for three days in August 1928, for inspection by Members of Parliament

IN THE THIRTEENTH CENTURY an English monk named Roger Bacon had envisaged the atmosphere as an invisible fluid, and believed that if an object could be made lighter than air it would float in this aerial ocean, just as a ship floats on water. Bacon's idea of a flying-boat appears to have been little more than a thin copper cylinder, filled with rarefied air.

Better-known is the design for an aerial ship by the Jesuit Father Francesco de Lana in 1670. This consisted of a vessel supported by four copper spheres which were to be emptied of air, and hence would rise. The basic principle was sound, but had it been possible to construct such globes they would, of course, have been crushed by atmospheric pressure.

The boat-shaped bodies of such early projects were chosen because boats had proved efficient for carrying passengers across the oceans of the Earth, rather than because the inventors foresaw their being operated from water. However, it was not long after the Wright brothers made their first flights in 1903 that aviators began to appreciate some of the advantages of flying from water.

Like the 1903 Wright *Flyer*, many of the frail aircraft of the time were damaged after their brief hops, through heavy landings on uneven ground. The self-levelling properties of water, it was argued, would certainly take care of the bumps; similarly, if an aircraft remained over water for the whole of its flight, the chances of a fatal crash would be lessened. Most of the resulting early aircraft designed to operate from water had floats instead of wheels and were thus 'floatplanes' or 'seaplanes' rather than flying-boats, which embody a boat-like fuselage.

In 1912 the American pioneer Glenn Curtiss replaced the pontoon of one of his seaplanes with a boat-shaped hull in which the pilot could sit instead of being perched in the open on the lower wing. It was not a very handsome machine; its engine developed only 60 hp and drove two propellers through a system of chains. But it was the world's first practical flying-boat, and from it descended an ambitious machine known as the *America*, designed to cross the Atlantic.

The first successful flying-boat built in Europe was Britain's Bat Boat. This was designed by T O M Sopwith, who wanted to combine the sport of yachting with the new thrill of flying. Its best-remembered exploit was winning the Mortimer Singer Prize for amphibious aircraft in July 1913, piloted by Harry Hawker, the fine Australian airman who later gave his name to one of Britain's greatest aircraft companies. For this competition the Bat Boat was fitted with retractable wheels, making it one of the earliest aeroplanes to embody this type of landing gear.

A major indication of the usefulness of flying-boats came with the Great War of 1914-18. John Porte, an Englishman, took Curtiss's *America* design, and the larger H.12, and evolved them into a superb series of 'boats. The first of these, the Felixstowe 1, or F.1, had a pronounced V-section floor, which gave it excellent take-off and landing

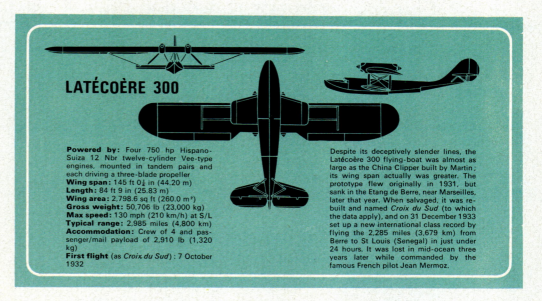

LATÉCOÈRE 300

Powered by: Four 750 hp Hispano-Suiza 12 Nbr twelve-cylinder Vee-type engines, mounted in tandem pairs and each driving a three-blade propeller
Wing span: 145 ft 0¼ in (44.20 m)
Length: 84 ft 9 in (25.83 m)
Wing area: 2,798.6 sq ft (260.0 m²)
Gross weight: 50,706 lb (23,000 kg)
Max speed: 130 mph (210 km/h) at S/L
Typical range: 2,985 miles (4,800 km)
Accommodation: Crew of 4 and passenger/mail payload of 2,910 lb (1,320 kg)
First flight (as *Croix du Sud*) : 7 October 1932

Despite its deceptively slender lines, the Latécoère 300 flying-boat was almost as large as the China Clipper built by Martin; its wing span actually was greater. The prototype flew originally in 1931, but sank in the Etang de Berre, near Marseilles, later that year. When salvaged, it was rebuilt and named *Croix du Sud* (to which the data apply), and on 31 December 1933 set up a new international class record by flying the 2,285 miles (3,679 km) from Berre to St Louis (Senegal) in just under 24 hours. It was lost in mid-ocean three years later while commanded by the famous French pilot Jean Mermoz.

Powered by: Four 830 hp Pratt & Whitney R-1830-S1A4G Twin Wasp fourteen-cylinder radial engines, each driving a three-blade propeller
Wing span: 130 ft 0 in (39.62 m)
Length: 90 ft 7½ in (27.62 m)
Wing area (incl sponsons) : 2,315 sq ft (215.07 m²)
Gross weight: 52,000 lb (23,587 kg)
Max cruising speed: 163 mph (262 km/h) at 7,000 ft (2,135 m)
Range: 3,200 miles (5,150 km)
Accommodation: Crew of 4 and 36-43 daytime passengers (18 in sleeper configuration)
First flight: 1936

MARTIN 130 CHINA CLIPPER

Size, speed and comfort were demanded by the airlines in the 1930s on behalf of their passengers. The Martin China Clipper flying-boat certainly offered two of these features, but its speed was not particularly high and over trans-oceanic ranges it could carry only 12 passengers. Even this remarkably low payload/weight ratio (by today's standards) was, however, an improvement over its contemporary, the smaller Sikorsky S-42. It went into service across the Pacific on 21 October 1936, with Pan American.

qualities. It revolutionised flying-boat design and gave Britain a lead in this type of aircraft which was maintained for nearly half a century.

From the F.1 there evolved the F.2, F.2A, F.3 and F.5 flying-boats. Unfortunately, this took time and it was not until 1917 that sufficient large flying-boats were available to take an effective role in the anti-U-boat and anti-Zeppelin war, by which time Britain's merchant fleet had suffered crippling losses. However, once the flying-boats really got going they proved to be among the most potent aerial weapons against the submarine.

After the war, flying-boats played a major part in pioneering civil air routes. In May 1919 the Atlantic was first conquered by a Curtiss flying-boat, which completed the long journey in stages via the Azores. Less spectacular, but nonetheless significant, was a 2,450-mile (3,940-km) tour of Scandinavia by an F.5 from Felixstowe, intended to demonstrate the commercial possibilities of flying-boats. It achieved its object, for the F.5 suffered no mishap of any kind during the twenty-seven days it was away. This was a remarkable record for that time, not least because the aircraft concerned was the first F.5 built.

The major advantage of flying-boats during this period was their ability to operate without the need for special landing grounds. *The Aeroplane* commented prophetically that the flying-boat should prove particularly attractive for civil use because: 'As aircraft grow larger the question of landing space will become more and more prominent. . . . The flying-boat can be increased in size to any limit commensurate with efficiency, and there will always be room in which to alight without laying waste land possessing other and greater uses'.

In 1926 Shorts launched their prototype Singapore, which introduced the technique of metal stressed-skin construction to flying-boats. This was thoroughly tested by Sir Alan Cobham, who used the Singapore for his famous 20,000-mile (32,185-km) survey flight round Africa in 1927. This survey was the climax to a whole series of flights made by Sir Alan to demonstrate how air transport could link every part of the British Empire more closely together.

The fact that the Singapore was independent of prepared landing grounds proved invaluable. The only mooring facility at most of the pre-arranged stopping places was a buoy; when, as sometimes happened, this broke adrift, the aircraft's own anchor was used.

From the Singapore there developed the three-engined Short Calcutta which, on one occasion, was moored on the Thames at Westminster as a luxury floating cocktail lounge for the benefit of Members of Parliament. Three Calcuttas went into service on the Mediterranean section of Imperial Airways' London to India service, and proved so satisfactory that Shorts were asked to design a slightly bigger flying-boat to supersede them. The result was the Short Kent, which could carry 16 passengers, 800 lb

(362 kg) of luggage and freight, and no less than 1½ tons of mail.

Though not so fast as contemporary landplanes of comparable size, they were popular with passengers because of their comfort and safety. Encouraged, Imperial Airways in 1935 ordered a new fleet of twenty-eight Short flying-boats, to be used exclusively on all their Empire routes. It was an unprecedented gamble as the order, which totalled nearly £2 million, was placed while the highly-advanced design was still on the drawing board.

The gamble paid off spectacularly. The prototype, *Canopus*, flew in July 1936, and the rest of the fleet of 'Empire Boats', as they were called, were launched at the rate of about two a month. Each was powered by four 910 hp Bristol Pegasus engines and accommodated twenty-four passengers with their luggage, plus two tons of mail and freight. Cruising at 164 mph (264 km/h), they had a range of 810 miles (1,300 km); their maximum speed of 200 mph (322 km/h) was as high as that of many fighters of their day. The first scheduled flight, from Alexandria to Brindisi, was made on 30 October 1936, only three months after the first flight of *Canopus*. On 5 March 1937 a new Imperial Airways flying-boat base at Hythe, near Southampton, was formally opened and from that date onwards Empire landplane services from the historic airport at Croydon ceased.

Although misfortunes were encountered —eight aircraft were lost during the first two years of operations—the 'Empire Boats' gave Britain a lead on the civil air routes of the world such as she had never known before and has not since regained. By 1938 seven services a week were being operated to Egypt, four to India, three to East Africa and two each to South Africa, Malaya and Australia.

These few years before the outbreak of war in September 1939 were the golden era for water-based aircraft. In Germany Dornier flying-boats, and Blohm und Voss floatplanes, performed valuable service. They were often catapulted from ships and made many experimental mail-carrying flights across the north and south Atlantic between 1937 and 1939.

America, too, produced a fine series of flying-boats. In 1934 there appeared the Martin Model 130 and Sikorsky S-42. These were followed, in 1938, by the first of the Boeing 314 'Clippers', which formed the proud flagships of the Pan American air fleet and maintained a regular trans-Atlantic air route during the second World War. A military adaptation of the Empire boat, known as the Sunderland, also served right through the war, and afterwards, proving as effective for convoy patrol and anti-U-boat duties as had the F 'boats of the first World War.

After the war the flying-boat never regained its pre-war eminence. The development of long-range land-based troop transports had given this class of aircraft a lead over its water-based contemporaries. In addition, the construction during the war of hundreds of concrete airstrips all over the

globe represented a capital investment which could not be ignored. Also relevant was the sad fact that, despite more than three-quarters of the surface of the Earth being water, many major cities, industrial complexes and holiday centres requiring air services are not close to a handy stretch of water suitable for flying-boat operations.

Perhaps the nearest the civil flying-boat came to post-war success was when the Saunders-Roe Princess took to the air on 22 August 1952. This majestic ten-turboprop giant was designed to carry 105 passengers in ocean-liner luxury at 385 mph (620 km/h) over trans-Atlantic ranges. Unfortunately the £5 million needed to complete the proposed fleet of seven was withheld by the government of the day when BOAC lost interest in marine aircraft. Even more unfortunate was the dog-in-the-manger attitude which prevented the three Princesses which were built from being put into service by private-venture operators who were keen and willing to do so.

Today only a handful of military flying-boats, such as Japan's Shin Meiwa PS-1 and Russia's Beriev M-12 maritime reconnaissance aircraft, remain in service to remind us of the pre-war heyday of these graceful ships of the sky.

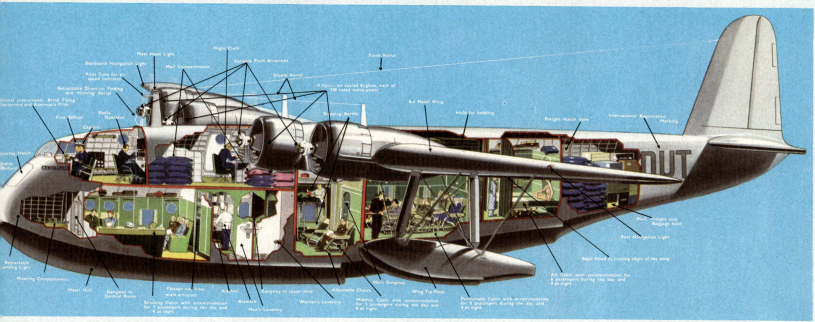

Masthead Light · Flight Clerk · Variable Pitch Airscrews · Fixed Aerial
Mail Compartments · Dipole Aerial
Starboard Navigation Light
Pitot Tube for air speed indicator
Retractable Direction Finding and 'Homing' Aerial · 4 Bristol air cooled Engines, each of 740 rated horse-power · All Metal Wing · Hold for bedding · Freight Hatch here · International Registration Marking
Blind Flying Instruments, Blind Flying Equipment and Automatic Pilot
First Officer · Radio Operator · Sleeping Berths
Captain
Mooring Hatch
Retractable Landing Light
Metal Hull · Gangway to Control Room · Kitchen · Gangway to upper deck · Women's Lavatory · Adjustable Chairs · Main Gangway · Wing Tip Float · Aft Cabin with accommodation for 6 passengers during the day and 4 at night · Mail, Freight and Baggage hold · Port Navigation Light · Flaps fitted to trailing edges of the wing
Mooring Compartment
Passage-way from main entrance · Steward · Man's Lavatory · Midship Cabin with accommodation for 3 passengers during the day and 4 at night · Promenade Cabin with accommodation for 8 passengers during the day and 4 at night
Smoking Cabin with accommodation for 7 passengers during the day and 4 at night

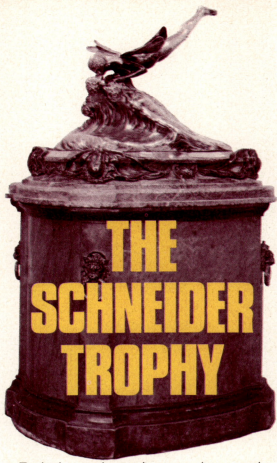

THE SCHNEIDER TROPHY

Tucked away in an alcove on the second-floor landing of the Royal Aero Club in Pall Mall is an imaginative piece of bronze and marble sculpture for the custody of which, back in the 1920s, governments strove and pilots died. This is the Schneider Trophy, presented to the Aéro Club de France in December 1912 by Jacques Schneider and won outright by Britain in 1931.

The trophy has been photographed from many angles, but like most works of art it can be properly appreciated only in the flesh. (And I say flesh advisedly, because the kiss that the nude winged figure representing speed is bestowing on the recumbent zephyr floating on a breaking wave is unmistakably sensual.)

Born near Paris on 25 January 1879, Jacques Schneider was a member of the well-known armaments family. He was trained as a mining engineer; but when aviation fever spread through France after the flying of Wilbur Wright at Le Mans in 1908, he turned his energies in the reverse direction. He gained his pilot's brevet in March 1911, qualified as a pilot of free balloons a fortnight later, and in 1913 broke the French altitude record in his balloon *Icare,* with a height of 33,074 ft (10,081 m). But he was also a keen racing motorist, and a serious accident on the Monte Carlo circuit restricted his personal career as an aviator.

After the accident Schneider devoted more and more of his time to organising aviation competitions, and he was soon struck by the neglect of the seaplane as opposed to the landplane. At the banquet following the Gordon Bennett Cup Race for landplanes, in 1912, he presented the Trophy which bears his name.

Schneider's conception of a special con-

Schneider Cup Machine

Top left: One of many problems facing early seaplane designers was to persuade their products to leave the water, especially if the surface was very calm. Hence the somewhat unusual planing bottom on the floats of this Nieuport monoplane which took part in the first contest for the Schneider Trophy in 1913

Far left: Reginald Mitchell's Supermarine Sea Lion appeared for the first time in the 1919 contest at Bournemouth. The day was so misty that its pilot landed to find his bearings, hit an object in the water and holed its hull when taking off again, and began to sink when he eventually gave up and alighted near Christchurch. The Sea Lion II gave Britain her second victory in 1922

Top: Howard Pixton resting on the lower wing of the Sopwith Tabloid in which he won the 1914 contest for the Schneider Trophy. Basically similar aircraft, on wheels, made the first successful bombing raids of World War I a few months later

Above: Jacques Schneider (second from right) congratulating Pixton after the 1914 contest at Monaco

Left: Interested in all forms of speed on water, Jacques Schneider is shown here at the wheel of his de Lambert-Tissandier "glisseur" prior to a 50 mph (80 km/h) demonstration run on the Nile early in 1914. On his left is Lord Kitchener. The craft's aeroplane propeller was driven by a 120 hp Salmson engine

test for seaplanes thus combined a vision of maritime aviation with a passion for speed. But the notion that the contest began as a searching test for seaplanes and degenerated into a speed contest pure and simple is false; it was a speed contest from the start, with seaworthiness a necessary but secondary consideration.

One word dominates the descriptions of the early hydro-aeroplane meetings: farce. Aeroplanes either failed to get off the water or crashed when they did. The earliest practical seaplanes were usually seaworthy, but they were cumbersome, and the successful racing seaplanes were mostly land-planes with floats substituted for wheels. It was such an aircraft, the streamlined Deperdussin monoplane, which won the first Schneider contest at Monaco in 1913.

Just as the Rheims meeting of 1909 coincided with the beginning of the practical aeroplane, so the Monaco meeting of 1913—and especially the first race for the Schneider Trophy—showed that the seaplane had arrived.

The victory of the Sopwith Tabloid in 1914 confirmed a trend and helped to establish the biplane form; but with seaplane development failing to keep pace with the wartime development of land-planes, the standard degenerated after the war. The revolution came in 1923 when the Americans, fielding a well-trained military team, outclassed their European rivals and carried off the Trophy. The American government had entered the racing field in earnest in 1921, when two pursuit-type biplanes were ordered from the Curtiss company and were entered subsequently for the Pulitzer race of that year; they came first and second, and similar machines took the first four places in 1922. Meanwhile the Gordon Bennett Cup had been won outright by France, and with the entry of the Americans in 1923 the Schneider Trophy became the blue riband of international air racing.

Reduction in head resistance, and such other design features as the streamlined cowling of engines, wing-surface radiators, metal propellers and low power/weight ratios, were among the many lessons emphasised by the American victory, plus the overriding importance of efficient organisation and thorough training. From a club competition they transformed the race into a military operation, and from this point on no nation could hope to win without generous government support.

Britain's entries at Baltimore in 1925 were a Supermarine S.4 monoplane designed by R J Mitchell and a Gloster biplane designed by H P Folland; both were lent back to the manufacturers by the government for the race—a half-hearted method of support that proved a costly failure. The S.4 crashed, the Gloster was comfortably beaten, and an Italian

entry, too, was left far behind. Had the Americans not abandoned the 1924 race for lack of a challenger they could now have taken permanent possession of the Trophy; but they were still well placed to complete the necessary three wins in five years. This indeed they were determined to do, as the contest had served its purpose for them in the research and development fields and the law of diminishing returns was beginning to operate.

Campaigning for a two-year gap between races, Britain prepared for 1927 and made no attempt to enter in 1926. Fortunately for her the Italians, inspired by Mussolini, took up the challenge, and basing their ideas on a combination of American, British and their own experience they produced in six months a distinctive monoplane, built by Aeronautica Macchi around a new Fiat engine. This aeroplane, the M.39, finally ended the supremacy of

the Curtiss biplane, though the margin was narrow enough to console devotees of the biplane form. With this defeat the American government, having changed the whole nature of the races by their entry in 1923, abandoned the contest to private enterprise; not surprisingly, no American entrant got to the starting line again.

In Britain, industrial and political opinion had moved the other way, international prestige having become closely associated with success in this kind of contest. The Treasury was finally persuaded of the advantages in research, development, training and trade that must accrue from a successful challenge, and the RAF was given the task of competing at Venice in 1927. An exhaustive research programme was chiefly responsible for the victory that followed, and Britain's superiority in airframe and engine design was maintained two years later on the Solent.

With this second victory, the British government felt that all the lessons they could afford to learn for the moment had been learnt, and like the Americans before them they were anxious to consolidate. Public opinion, however, demanded that an effort be made to secure the Trophy; and thanks to a £100,000 donation from Lady Houston and a change of heart by the government a satisfactory entry was made. When the challenging nations withdrew at a late hour, Britain did not hesitate simply to fly over the course for victory.

So much has been said and written about the development of the Spitfire from Mitchell's designs for these races, and of the Merlin and Griffon engines from the Rolls-Royce "sprint" engine, that the strictures of the time against the complete unsuitability of seaplane races for the development of service types are mostly forgotten; but for practical purposes the contest was far from ideal. Yet everyone closely connected with the races has testified to the enormous technological advances that were made race by race—advances that would otherwise have taken years to achieve—and to the exercise provided in co-operation with and within the aircraft industry. To this, so far as Britain was concerned, must be added the imponderables of prestige, air-mindedness, readiness, and self-confidence, and the knowledge that when the aircraft industry and the RAF put their minds together they made a formidable combination. The races provided a stimulus when a stimulus was needed; much of the effort was unproductive, but the remainder bore rich fruit.

SUPERMARINE S.4 and S.6B

Powered by: One 700 hp Napier Lion W-type piston-engine
Wing span: 30 ft 6 in (9.30 m)
Length: 27 ft 0 in (8.23 m)
Gross weight: 3,150 lb (1,429 kg)
Max speed: 239 mph (385 km/h) at S/L
Accommodation: Crew of 1
Range at full power: 320 miles (515 km)
First flight: 25 August 1925
The S.4, to which the above data apply, was the first of the family of British Supermarine Schneider Trophy seaplanes, from which were developed the S.5, S.6 and S.6B. The silhouette depicts the S.6B, which was fitted with a 2,300 hp Rolls-Royce "R" engine when it won the Trophy outright in 1931 at an average speed of 340.08 mph (547.29 km/h). Later, with the engine boosted to 2,550 hp, it set a new world seaplane speed record of 407.5 mph (655.81 km/h).

Above left: Jimmy Doolittle, one of the most colourful figures in US aviation, is seen here with the Curtiss R3C-2 seaplane in which he won the 1925 Schneider Trophy contest

Above top to bottom: Towing out one of the Supermarine S.5s which began the series of British victories, at Venice in 1927. The Curtiss aircraft had proved the value of streamlining; Supermarine now established the superiority of the monoplane

Two of Italy's beautiful Macchi M-67 seaplanes were unsuccessful challengers in the 1929 contest at Spithead. Neither completed the course, but the later Macchi MC-72 set up a speed record of 440.7 mph (709.2 km/h) in 1934, which has never been beaten

Supermarine's brilliant chief designer, R. J. Mitchell (left), whose seaplanes gained the Schneider Trophy outright for Britain, with Sir Henry Royce of Rolls-Royce

In the National Aeronautical Collection of the Science Museum in London, an example of the Spitfire fighter is displayed side by side with the Supermarine S.6B seaplane which inspired its design—one of the greatest vindications of the costly Schneider victories

Above right: Mitchell's graceful S.6B, the aircraft which won the last of the contests for the Schneider Trophy in 1931. Later, with its Rolls-Royce engine boosted to 2,600 hp, it raised the world air speed record above 400 mph (650 km/h) for the first time

THE FIRST BRITISH WINNER

The two races held for the Schneider Trophy before the outbreak of the first World War were no straight-up-and-down affairs just to find the fastest aeroplane; they were a pretty good test of an aircraft's staying power as well, requiring the completion of 28 laps of a 10-kilometre course —a total distance of 172.83 miles. In 1913, only one out of the nine competitors, and in 1914 two out of thirteen, even completed the course.

The Deperdussin monoplane, which won in 1913, did so at an official average speed of 45.75 mph (73.63 km/h). At first sight this might seem uncommonly slow for an aeroplane with a 160 hp engine and which in its landplane form had already flown at well over 100 mph (161 km/h) in other competitive events. The reason is that, at Monaco, its pilot, Maurice Prévost, crossed the finishing line in a manner apparently unacceptable to the judges, who insisted that he took off and flew the final lap again. For the statutory 28 laps, his actual average speed was in the region of 61 mph (98 km/h).

However, even this speed was beaten handsomely in the 1914 race by a British newcomer, the little Sopwith Tabloid biplane, whose winning speed of 86.78 mph (139.66 km/h) was more than 50 per cent faster than that of the Swiss FBA which finished second. Other pilots refused to compete after hearing of the time set up by Howard Pixton in the Tabloid. Pixton underlined his victory by going on to complete two extra laps of the course in order to set up a new world seaplane speed record of 92 mph (148 km/h).

The Tabloid was something of a radical design for its time, for "pusher" biplanes, rigged and braced with a maze of struts and wires, were still the predominant biplane form. The Tabloid, on the other hand, was essentially a simple design with the minimum amount of bracing and a tractor (front-turning) propeller. The name Tabloid was chosen to signify its small size—it weighed only 1,080 lb (490 kg) gross originally — and compact nature. This gained the aircraft some unexpected publicity, for, as Sir Thomas Sopwith later recalled:

"Tabloid was the registered trade name of a tablet marketed by Burroughs Wellcome, who took a dim view of our naming of the aeroplane, so we had to abandon the name—officially. But the name stuck and thereafter several small aeroplanes made by other firms were also nicknamed Tabloid, much to the indignation of Burroughs Wellcome, who could not do anything so long as the name was not official—except perhaps take their own Tabloids as sedatives."

Later in its career the Tabloid was to become one of the most successful early scout aeroplanes of the war years, gaining the distinction of being the first British aircraft to destroy a German airship during a raid on the Zeppelin sheds at Dusseldorf.

Quest for SPEED

The Boeing P-26 represented a halfway stage between the World War I and World War II concepts of fighter design, in that it retained an open cockpit, wire-braced wings and fixed undercarriage while switching to an all-metal monoplane layout. This one served with the Guatemalan Air Force until 1955, was returned subsequently to the US and now wears the 1935 insignia of the 34th Pursuit Squadron, US Army Air Corps

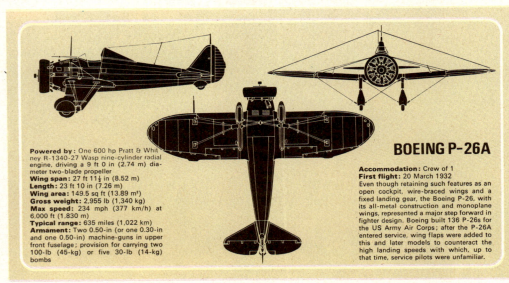

Powered by: One 600 hp Pratt & Whitney R-1340-27 Wasp nine-cylinder radial engine, driving a 9 ft 0 in (2.74 m) diameter two-blade propeller
Wing span: 27 ft 11½ in (8.52 m)
Length: 23 ft 10 in (7.26 m)
Wing area: 149.5 sq ft (13.89 m²)
Gross weight: 2,955 lb (1,340 kg)
Max speed: 234 mph (377 km/h) at 6,000 ft (1,830 m)
Typical range: 635 miles (1,022 km)
Armament: Two 0.50-in (or one 0.30-in and one 0.50-in) machine-guns in upper front fuselage; provision for carrying two 100-lb (45-kg) or five 30-lb (14-kg) bombs

BOEING P-26A

Accommodation: Crew of 1
First flight: 20 March 1932
Even though retaining such features as an open cockpit, wire-braced wings and a fixed landing gear, the Boeing P-26, with its all-metal construction and monoplane wings, represented a major step forward in fighter design. Boeing built 136 P-26s for the US Army Air Corps; after the P-26A entered service, wing flaps were added to this and later models to counteract the high landing speeds with which, up to that time, service pilots were unfamiliar.

Above: Two Gloster VI Golden Arrow seaplanes were built for the 1929 Schneider contest. They did not compete against the winning Supermarine S.6s, but one of them set up a speed record of 336 mph (541 km/h) on 9 September that year

Left: Smallest aircraft that could be built around a 240 hp Siddeley Puma engine, the Avro 539A was reserve British seaplane for the inconclusive 1919 Schneider contest. It spanned a mere 25 ft 6 in (7.77 m)

Opposite page, top to bottom:
The rapid progress made towards streamlining the still-standard biplane layout in the early 'twenties can be gauged by comparing this Gloster III, built for the 1925 Schneider Contest, with the Avro 539A. A 670 hp Napier Lion gave the Gloster III a speed of 225 mph (362 km/h)

One of the great pace-setters in aircraft design after the first World War was the Short Silver Streak of 1920, which pioneered the modern concept of all-metal (duralumin) monocoque construction. It was to be years before the Air Ministry took advantage of the leadership it offered

Experience gained in producing many of the greatest fighters of the first World War was used by Sopwith to design this 450-hp, 170 mph (274 km/h) seaplane for the 1919 Schneider Trophy contest. Fog caused its retirement

AIRCRAFT, REPRESENTING a technology that even today is still fairly new, have always developed at a rapid pace; but in the 21 years between the two World Wars aeroplanes progressed quite remarkably even for a new technology. Yet in the 1920s and 1930s there was very little money available, and even that was doled out sparingly by governments that were parsimonious almost to the point of folly. Nowhere was this more true than in the United States, where military aviators had to fight for every single dollar needed for new aircraft.

In this harsh environment, when few chief designers could expect to earn even £1,000 a year and complete aircraft development programmes had to be undertaken for not more than about £2,000 to £5,000, companies working on shoestring budgets transformed the design of aeroplanes. In 1919 most were creations of spruce, plywood, steel tube, wire and fabric, made up into strut-braced biplanes of the kind used in the first World War. By 1939 they were cantilever monoplanes with flush-riveted stressed skins of aluminium alloy, retractable undercarriages, powerful flaps fitted to the wings and geared and supercharged engines driving constant-speed propellers.

In the 1930s the biplane became obsolescent and the speedy monoplane brought a new level of high performance. Many writers, notably C G Grey, lamented what seemed to be a bad trend, in that aircraft were becoming heavier yet had smaller wings, and thus had to take off and land faster, despite the use of flaps. They were afraid that a wing loading of 30 lb/sq ft (146.5 kg/m²) and a landing speed of 60 mph (97 km/h) would be highly dangerous. Today, thanks to better airfields, we have wing loadings of 150 lb/sq ft (732.5 kg/m²) and landing speeds of over 180 mph (290 km/h). And the reason for it all can be summed up in one word: performance.

Between the wars there was little pressure at first to increase the speed of civil airliners; but the world's air forces have never ceased to want faster, higher-flying and generally superior aircraft, and this alone would have ensured that aircraft design could never sink into a state of stagnation. But there were other factors that exerted a powerful pull on designers to increase aircraft performance. Probably the greatest was the need to win races, and the greatest of these was the Schneider Trophy, donated by the French arms magnate Jacques Schneider originally for annual competition. As airfields were generally no better than ordinary fields they made very fast landplanes dangerous; but the sheltered water of harbours, estuaries and other inshore areas offered much greater room and made it a practical proposition to design very fast marine aircraft. Some of the early Schneider contestants were flying-boats, but all the later contestants were float seaplanes.

By 1923 the flying-boats had been driven from the scene by US Navy racers, principally a fine series of small biplanes by the Curtiss company, powered by Curtiss engines, which went round the tight triangular course at some 230 mph (370 km/h). These

in turn were defeated in 1926 by the Italian Macchi monoplanes, and from then onwards it was a duel between the Italians and the British. Until 1927 the British government had not spent a penny on air racing and, unlike the other entries, the British Schneider contestants had been private ventures. But in 1927 the RAF took part, and one of their bright blue and silver Supermarine S.5 seaplanes finished victorious, beating the red Macchis at a speed of over 281 mph (452 km/h). In 1929 the S.6, a much improved S.5, again won, at a speed of 329 mph (529.5 km/h); and the RAF completed the hat-trick by winning in 1931 with the S.6B at 340 mph (547 km/h). Britain thus had the Schneider Trophy for keeps.

The significance of the Supermarine seaplanes, designed by Reginald Mitchell, is told elsewhere in *History of Aviation*. Mitchell went on to design the Spitfire fighter and Rolls-Royce developed its Merlin engine. Without them the Allies would have been markedly weaker in the air in the second World War.

In the United States there was no such clear-cut link between air racing and combat aircraft, although the Thompson Trophy and other national races exerted a profound influence on high-speed design—in this case on landplanes, which was probably more useful. It was in these races that the superiority of the aerodynamically clean monoplane became complete, and by the early 1930s the winning US racers were little more than big engines with a tiny monoplane fixed behind them. One such was the Gee Bee Super Sportster which 'Jimmy' Doolittle—a former Schneider pilot and later a famous General—used to take the landplane speed record at 294 mph (473 km/h) in 1932. Boeing had by then produced a fighter, the Model 248 or P-26, along the same lines. The US Army Air Corps was thus one of the first air forces to use monoplane fighters. A little later a wealthy young man named Howard Hughes, today an eccentric billionaire with vast interests in airlines, aerospace and many other activities, besides owning most of Las Vegas, built a racer considerably more advanced in design and flew it at a remarkable 352 mph (566 km/h)—more than 100 mph (161 km/h) faster than anything in any air force in the world.

In Europe the French Coupe Deutsch de la Meurthe led annually to excellent racing landplanes with relatively small engines, because the handicapping formula penalised large engines. The Caudron company excelled in this race and their slim, small-winged wooden racers did remarkably well on tiny Renault engines which, like those of later Grand Prix cars, were highly supercharged to give high power from small cylinders. The C.460 of 1934 had an engine of only 8 litres capacity, but its 370 hp drove the C.460 to a landplane speed record at 314 mph (505 km/h). But by 1939 the new German Luftwaffe had taken the lead, both Heinkel and Messerschmitt fighters having been modified to reach speeds which in 1939 culminated in 464 mph (747 km/h) and then 481 mph (774 km/h). The latter figure, by

the special Bf 209 flown by Fritz Wendel, was almost 100 mph faster than any ordinary Bf 109 fighter until the Bf 109G of 1943, which by the end of the war was reaching 440 mph (708 km/h) with special power-boosting. But nobody beat Wendel's figure. After the war such aircraft as the Mustang, Bearcat and Corsair were hotted up in the US for racing, and the Spiteful, the successor to the Spitfire, was supposed to reach 494 mph (795 km/h) in full operational trim, but nobody succeeded in beating 481 mph under the carefully observed conditions needed for a ratified record until the late 1960s.

In 1934 the MacRobertson race from Mildenhall to Melbourne—a gruelling test of men and machines in an era when merely to cover such a distance at all was front-page news—led to decisive wins in the two sections of the race, the 'speed' section and the 'handicap' section. The speed rules simply said that the fastest contestant was the winner. The de Havilland Aircraft company set about designing a special machine intended to win. It had to be not only faster but also to have a longer range than its rivals. Eventually the D.H.88 Comet emerged, just in time to take part, looking as futuristic as a space rocket among the lumpy competitors around it. It had two 230 hp Gipsy Six engines and a streamlined body that was almost entirely full of fuel right back to the tiny cockpit in front of the tail which seated two people in tandem. A Comet flown by C W A Scott and T Campbell Black won in the amazing time of 71

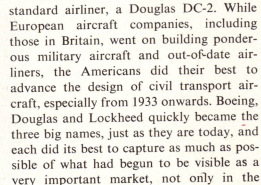

This page, above: Although the three Gloster IV seaplanes built for the 1927 Schneider contest were biplanes, their lines were hardly less beautiful than the Supermarine monoplanes. Fastest was the 875 hp Gloster IVB, with a top speed of 295 mph (475 km/h)—nearly twice as fast as most fighters of the time

Right: Although each of its engines developed only 230 hp, the D.H.88 Comet racer won the greatest-ever long-distance air race and pointed the way to the Mosquito of the second World War

Opposite page, top: Like the British Spitfire, Germany's Messerschmitt Bf 109 single-seat fighter heralded the switch to the modern concept of all-metal low-wing monoplane design, with enclosed cockpit and retractable landing gear. This Bf 109E was one of many exported to Switzerland

hours. And from this speedy wooden machine stemmed the de Havilland idea for a wooden bomber faster than any fighter, which led to the famous Mosquito of 1940.

Winner of the handicap section was a standard airliner, a Douglas DC-2. While European aircraft companies, including those in Britain, went on building ponderous military aircraft and out-of-date airliners, the Americans did their best to advance the design of civil transport aircraft, especially from 1933 onwards. Boeing, Douglas and Lockheed quickly became the three big names, just as they are today, and each did its best to capture as much as possible of what had begun to be visible as a very important market, not only in the United States but all over the world. The DC-2 of 1934 flew into second place in Melbourne, and easily won the handicap section of the race.

In Britain little was done to produce effective airliners to rival the DC-2 and DC-3. Bristol, however, had decided in 1934 to try to beat the fast US transports and built for Lord Rothermere, the newspaper owner, a machine called *Britain First*. As it could fly 1,000 miles (1,610 km) at an easy 280 mph (450 km/h) it was immune to interception by any RAF fighter, and the Air Ministry suddenly wondered—as Rothermere had intended—whether they might not be well advised to order a Bristol bomber

Below: The extent to which the Comet influenced design in the later 'thirties is evident in this photograph of the French Caudron C.641 Typhon high-speed mailplane

along the same lines. The result was not only the Blenheim bomber, which fired the first Allied shot in the second World War, but also the Beaufort torpedo carrier and the Beaufighter night fighter.

In 1938 Supermarine, encouraged by the Air Ministry, prepared a special Spitfire racer called the Speed Spitfire, but this had no chance of beating the 481 mph set by the Bf 209 and left no mark in the halls of fame. Another non-starter was the less well-known Napier-Heston Racer. In 1937 Napier had begun to develop a remarkable 24-cylinder engine called the Sabre, which in its initial form was rated at 2,200 hp, almost twice the power of a Merlin. Heston Aircraft built a single, very small racer to gain the world speed record with this engine. It was a beauty to look at, and was officially judged capable of 520 mph (837 km/h). Unfortunately the war stopped its development—but not until it had flown—and eventually brought about its destruction before anybody had seen just how fast a piston-engined aeroplane could fly.

In any case, in the summer of 1939 Flugkapitän Erich Warsitz had flown two small prototypes that made such an exercise pointless. They were the He 176, which had a rocket engine, and the He 178 which had a turbojet. The quest for speed was about to enter upon a new and even more challenging era.

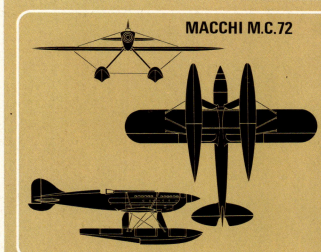

MACCHI M.C.72

Powered by: One 2,800 hp Fiat A.S.6 twenty-four-cylinder Vee-type engine (two twelve-cylinder A.S.5s mounted in tandem), driving two two-blade contra-rotating propellers
Wing span: 31 ft 1¼ in (9.48 m)
Length: 27 ft 3½ in (8.32 m)
Wing area: 161.46 sq ft (15.00 m²)
Gross weight: 6,409 lb (2,907 kg)
Max speed (world record): 440.681 mph (709.209 km/h) in October 1934
Accommodation: Crew of 1
First flight: 1931
The M.C. (Macchi-Castoldi) 72, whose world speed record for seaplanes stood unbeaten for nearly 30 years, was built to compete in the 1931 race for the Schneider Trophy. It was unable to do so due to development problems with its unusual engine installation, the tremendous torque from which drove the aircraft round in circles on the water and prevented it from taking off. The problem was solved eventually by using contra-rotating propellers to cancel out this effect, and the M.C.72's design was vindicated by successive speed records culminating in the figure recorded.

But for the war, the Heston racer, with Napier Sabre engine, might have proved itself the fastest piston-engined aircraft of all time. It is still regarded by many as representing the peak of achievement in powered flight before the advent of the jet engine

Improving the Breed

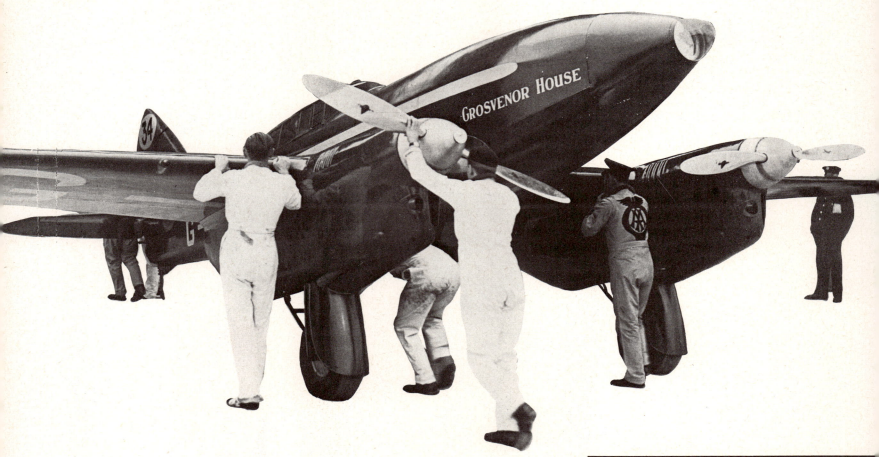

ALTHOUGH THE LAST great contest for the Schneider Trophy had been flown in 1931, the remaining years of the decade were to see new lustre added to the field of sporting flying by other sporting events; and just as the Supermarine Schneider racers had sired the Spitfire, so was technical progress clearly influenced by other machines specially designed for competitive purposes. Among these the twin-engined de Havilland Comet was pre-eminent, bearing as it did the same relationship to the incomparable Mosquito as did the Schneider Supermarines to the Spitfire.

The Comet was something altogether new. Not only was it fast, but it had a very long range into the bargain. A press release issued by the de Havilland Aircraft Co Ltd on 12 September 1934 set out essential facts, thus:

'The Comet is a twin-engined, two-seater, long-range, low-wing cantilever monoplane. Throughout its design the aim has been to produce an aeroplane which conforms in every respect to the conditions and regulations governing the MacRobertson Race from England to Australia and which will have the maximum chance of success, having regard to the route, the lengths of the "legs", the climatic and other conditions likely to be encountered. Purchasers have been guaranteed a top speed of 200 mph (322 km/h). Outstanding features are the remarkable cleanness of design, the exceptionally thin wing section attained by the use of "stressed skin" construction, the completely retracting undercarriage and the employment of controllable-pitch airscrews.

Three machines are being built and have been entered in the Race by Mr & Mrs J A Mollison, Mr A O Edwards (pilots Mr C W A Scott and Mr T Campbell Black) and Mr Bernard Rubin. Work on the building of the airframes and the special racing Gipsy Six engines commenced some three months ago. Day and night work has been necessary to ensure their completion in time for the event.'

The MacRobertson Race must rank as the greatest single sporting event in the history of flying. The prizes had been furnished by Sir William MacPherson Robertson, and the race was organised as part of the Melbourne centenary celebrations. In fact, it comprised two sections, or classes: a 'speed' race and a handicap event, both run concurrently. No pains were spared to make the contest safe as well as exciting. Competitors in both classes had to land at five main control points, namely Baghdad (2,530 miles; 4,072 km), Allahabad (5,372 miles; 8,645 km), Singapore (7,040 miles; 11,330 km) and Charleville (10,513 miles; 16,919 km), and there were intermediate check-points at Marseilles, Rome, Athens, Aleppo, Bushire, Alor Star, Batavia, Rambang (Sumatra), Koepang (Timor), Newcastle Waters, Cloncurry and Narromine. No 'freak' aircraft were admitted, or at least none having dangerous characteristics. All had to conform with requirements laid down by the International Commission on Aerial Navigation regarding take-off run, climb and strength. Every competing pilot had to give evidence of his competence. There was no limit on the number of crew,

Top: Everyone helped when competitors in the MacRobertson Race arrived at the newly-opened RAF station of Mildenhall, Suffolk, in October 1934. This AA man and the white-garbed students from the College of Aeronautical Engineering at Chelsea could not know that they were handling the aircraft that would win the race to Australia a few days later

Centre: The winning crew: C W A Scott and Tom Campbell Black, who brought Australia within three days of Britain for the first time

Bottom: G-ACSS, the D.H.88 which won the MacRobertson Race, is now part of the Shuttleworth Collection at Old Warden

and, with the exception of the pilot-in-charge, replacements were permitted en route. Provisions for at least three days were demanded, as well as lifebelts.

Many varieties of aircraft from thirteen countries were among the original 64 entries; but although only 20 of these were on the starting line at Mildenhall, Suffolk, at dawn on 20 October 1934, no-one present among the 60,000 spectators will ever forget the tension nor the thousands of cars which congested the roads. Once the starter's flag went down for the Mollisons, who had drawn 'first off', the world became abuzz with news as the field of aircraft, ranging from lightplanes to airliners, went streaming eastward.

First at Baghdad, after flying non-stop for 12 hr 40 min, were the Mollisons. They were followed by the other two Comets, a Douglas DC-2 airliner of KLM crewed by the Dutchmen Parmentier and Moll, and another American airliner—a Boeing 247D —having as pilots Col Roscoe Turner and Clyde Pangborn.

Luck did not long continue to favour the Mollisons and they retired with mechanical trouble, having flown to Karachi in the record time of 22 hr 13 min. In the second of the Comets, however, Scott and Campbell Black pressed on to complete the 11,300 miles (18,186 km) to the Flemington Racecourse, Melbourne. To these men— Scott already a seasoned record-breaker, Campbell Black a pioneer pilot in East Africa—went first prize for speed; but this was not gained without risk, as was later recalled by Sir Geoffrey de Havilland. Scott and Campbell Black were stuck at Darwin, Northern Australia, with trouble in one engine. Major Frank Halford, who had designed the Gipsy Six, somehow discovered that a London newspaper had a telephone line open to Australia, and got permission to use it. Sir Geoffrey related:

'He was soon talking to Scott and heard what the symptoms of the trouble were. It was obviously connected with oil pressure, and Halford realised that it might possibly be only a defective oil pressure gauge that was the cause. He told Scott to go ahead, forget the gauge and give the engine a rather easier time when in the air. Scott and Campbell Black arrived first at Melbourne and won the £10,000 prize. They had taken 70 hr 59 min to cover 11,300 miles —an outstanding feat of skill and endurance. Our gamble with the Comet Racer, and Halford's own gamble with the oil pressure trouble, had both come off.'

Second and third places in the speed race were taken by the Douglas and Boeing airliners already mentioned; but, as the prizes were so distributed that no contestant could receive awards in both the speed and handicap events, the second and third prizes went to Turner and Pangborn in the Boeing, and Cathcart-Jones and Waller, who were flying the third of the Comets. First and second prizes in the handicap race were gained by Parmentier and Moll in the DC-2, and J Melrose, a young Australian who flew solo in a Puss Moth.

Although the MacRobertson Race may be regarded as unique in scale it was not the only long-distance event of the 'thirties, for in 1936 Mr T W Schlesinger inaugurated a race to South Africa in connection with the Empire Exhibition at Johannesburg, offering a prize of £4,000 to the winner of the speed event together with handicap prizes. The route was optional, but aircraft had to fly over Belgrade for identification and a landing at Cairo was compulsory. The start was from Portsmouth on 29 September. Scott was flying a Percival Vega Gull, together with Giles Guthrie, later to become chairman of BOAC. Again Scott won—if only because the other eight machines failed to finish. Such were the hazards of long-distance air racing in the 'thirties.

If the hazards of this type of racing were largely natural ones, then those attending the great American races which flourished in the same period were in great measure man-made, that is, by the aircraft designers involved, for the custom-built aircraft concerned were intended primarily for speed. This meant that they had high wing loadings and high landing speeds, while the use of large-diameter radial engines, jointly with the positioning of the pilot, allowed only very restricted forward and downward view. If their pilots were unable to stick their necks out in a literal sense then they were

Above: Among the last six aircraft to leave Mildenhall were (left to right) the Miles Hawk Major of MacGregor and Walker which set new light aeroplane records to India and Australia; the British Klemm Eagle of Flt Lt Shaw, who retired at Bushire with a damaged undercarriage; the Airspeed Courier of D E and K G Stodart, who were placed fourth in the handicap race; and the Puss Moth of C J Melrose, youngest pilot in the contest, whose solo flight earned him third place and £1,000 in the handicap event

Left: Third in the speed contest was the Boeing 247D of Roscoe Turner and Clyde Pangborn, which reached Melbourne in 92 hr 55 min 38 sec and gained a £1,500 prize

Right: A week before the MacRobertson Race began, these 34 pilots were portrayed as probable starters. The 20 aircraft which left Mildenhall were crewed by Roscoe Turner (1), H Walker (2), J H Wright (3), Jensen (4), John Polando (6), G Shaw (7), J K L Baines (8), M MacGregor (9), K G Stodart (10), Amy Mollison (11), James Mollison (12), J D Hewett (13), Jacqueline Cochran (15), J J Moll (16), M Hansen (17), C W A Scott (18), T Campbell Black (19), J Woods (20), K D Parmentier (21), H D Gilman (23), H L Brook (24), K F H Waller (25), C J Melrose (26), Clyde Pangborn (28), T Neville Stack (29), C L Hill (30), C G Davies (31), C E Kay (32), S L Turner (33), O Cathcart Jones (34), D L Asjes, D C Bennett, G E Hemsworth, G J Geysendorfer, Miss E M Lay, R Parer, Wesley Smith and D E Stodart

Top left: The standard airline DC-2 of KLM, piloted by Parmentier and Moll, with two crew, three passengers and mail, staggered everyone by reaching Melbourne in 90 hr 13 min 36 sec, to finish second in the speed contest

Left: On the final stages across Australia, the DC-2 ran into heavy storms and became bogged during its landings. Although volunteers helped to drag it free, the unexpected delays cost it many hours

Above: When Wright and Polando arrived at Mildenhall in the Lambert Monocoupe, after flying up from Hamble in less than an hour, one expert commented 'There's a likely winner, perhaps of both races.' He added 'But it lands rather like a gliding brick'. In fact, Baby Ruth got no further than Calcutta

Left: The Caudron C 714 fighter was based on experience gained in the Coupe Deutsch de la Meurthe races in 1933-35. Top speed was 302 mph (486 km/h) although its Renault engine gave only 450 hp and it weighed a mere 3,826 lb (1,735 kg). This C 714 is in Finnish insignia

Below: C W A Scott (left) followed up his MacRobertson triumph by winning the 1936 air race from England to South Africa. His companion in the Vega Gull was Giles Guthrie and they were the only crew to finish

PERCIVAL VEGA GULL

Powered by: One 200 hp de Havilland Gipsy Six Series II six-cylinder in-line engine, driving a two-blade propeller
Wing span: 39 ft 6 in (12.04 m)
Length: 25 ft 6 in (7.77 m)
Wing area: 184 sq ft (17.09 m²)
Gross weight: 2,750 lb (1,247 kg)
Max speed: 170 mph (274 km/h)
Typical range: 620 miles (1,000 km)
Accommodation: Crew of 1 and 3 passengers
First flight: December 1935
Three months after winning the King's

Cup Air Race in 1936, the Vega Gull cabi monoplane headed for even greate triumph in October when it became th only competitor in the Schlesinger rac to complete the course from Portsmout to Johannesburg. Flown by C W A Sco of 'MacRobertson' fame and Giles Guthri (later chairman of BOAC), it complete the trip in a few minutes under 53 hour In subsequent years many other Vega Gul were used by private owners, trainir organisations and aerial taxi companie and from this type was developed the wa time Proctor.

certainly obliged to do so metaphorically! Yet there is a link between these machines, their brave, though by no means self-effacing pilots, and the MacRobertson Race. That link is the name of Roscoe Turner, already mentioned in connection with the Boeing 247D.

A one-time 'barnstormer', Roscoe Turner took up air racing in 1929. Not only did he establish numerous inter-city and transcontinental records but he shared with the great 'Jimmy' Doolittle the distinction of winning both the Thompson and the Bendix Trophy races. These were the two great American classics of the 1930s, the last of the Pulitzer races having been flown in 1926. The Thompson Trophy had first been offered for the Cleveland National Air Races of 1929 and the Bendix contest was established as a coast-to-coast race to terminate at the same event.

Roscoe Turner's Wedell-Williams monoplanes, so familiar in those great American races, were typical of their class, bullet-like, though less obese than the well-nigh incredible Gee Bee Super Sportster. They served not only for racing but as advertising media, and the degree of commercial success which attended their pilot is suggested by the fact that he still serves, as this is written, as

chairman of the board of Roscoe Turner Aeronautical Corporation and president of the Turner Aviation Corporation.

'Jimmy' Doolittle, who likewise happily survives, had won the Schneider Trophy for the USA in 1925, and in 1930 resigned his Army commission to become an executive of the Shell Oil Company. This did not prevent him from winning the Bendix Trophy in 1931 and the Thompson in 1932.

In the period under review American women pilots began to present some aggressive competition. Two Bendix Trophies were, in fact, awarded annually, one for the winner of the main Bendix contest and one for the winning lady pilot. In 1936 Louise Thaden flew away with both, and in the same year second place in both competitions went to Laura Ingals.

The first woman entrant for the Bendix was Jacqueline Cochrane: she flew in the 1935 event but was prevented by exhaustion from completing the course. This spurred her on to take first place in the women's division during 1937 and to win the main event in 1938. On this occasion she was competing with nine men, and, having flown from California to Ohio, continued on to the east coast to establish a transcontinental record of 10 hr 27 min 55 sec.

Although it could hardly be claimed that American competitive flying contributed to technical progress in the same degree as the Schneider and MacRobertson races, it may be noted that during 1938 Seversky aircraft, forerunners of the Republic Thunderbolt fighter of the approaching war, put up some notable performances in the hands of sporting pilots. In one machine of the type Jacqueline Cochrane set a new speed mark for women by attaining just over 292 mph (470 km/h), and a Seversky was used by Frank Fuller Jnr to fly from Vancouver, Canada, to Agua Caliente, Mexico, in 4 hr 54 min. Thus were the speed and range of the Thunderbolt portended.

One aspect of the Comet which has not yet been mentioned is that it showed what could be accomplished with relatively low power, for the two Gipsy Six R (racing) engines delivered only 230 hp each. But the Comet was not alone in demonstrating possibilities in this direction. For the Coupe Deutsch de la Meurthe races, held in France in the mid-1930s, the Caudron company built small machines, much along the lines of the Comet except that they were single-engined, and similarly powered with inverted in-line air-cooled engines of low frontal area. From these were developed three types of light fighter, one of which, the C.714, went into production. It displayed some excellent characteristics, but owing to its low power had a poor rate of climb. Certainly it showed how racing aircraft of the 1930s 'improved the breed'.

DE HAVILLAND D.H.88 COMET

Powered by: Two 230 hp de Havilland Gipsy Six R six-cylinder in-line engines, each driving a two-blade propeller
Wing span: 44 ft 0 in (13.41 m)
Length: 29 ft 0 in (8.84 m)
Wing area: 212.5 sq ft (19.74 m²)
Gross weight: 5,320 lb (2,413 kg)
Max speed: 237 mph (381 km/h)
Max range: 2,925 miles (4,707 km)
Accommodation: Crew of 2
First flight: 8 September 1934
In a gesture that no present-day manufacturer could hope to make, de Havilland

offered in 1933 to build a long-range racing aircraft to compete in the England-Australia 'MacRobertson' race in the following year, whether they made a profit from its sale or not. All they asked was for orders to be given nine months before the race started, and the first Comet flew only six weeks before the 'off'. But the effort was well worth it: Scott and Campbell Black's red-and-white Comet won the race, and Cathcart-Jones and Waller were placed fourth in another of the three which had competed.

A MONOPLANE AIRLINER having two fuselages, with passengers seated in the nose of each; having two engines also, the front one driving a tractor propeller and the rear one a pusher, with the pilots sitting between them; and one moreover having no fewer than four vertical tail assemblies, may be regarded as something quite out of the ordinary. Yet such was the Blériot 125 of 1930. True, the majority of airliners of the decade then beginning departed little from conventional design, and the most freakish aeroplanes were, not surprisingly, those built for research. But in every class, military and civil, there were types remarkable in outline or having uncommon features.

The tailless form continued to attract attention, as it had in the two previous decades, following the lead set in England by J W Dunne. The Pterodactyls of Prof G T R Hill, which similarly had sweptback wings to obviate stalling, continued in development, the most advanced example being the Pterodactyl V, a powerful two-seat fighter. The tailless arrangement was thought to be ideally suited to this class of fighter, giving the gunner at the rear an extremely wide field of fire with no intervening structure; but no orders were placed and the Pterodactyl was abandoned.

A tailless aircraft of different form, having no sweepback on the wing trailing-edge, was built in Germany by Dr Alexander Lippisch, and this was a precursor of the delta (triangular) form adopted for high-speed aircraft of more recent times. In the USA the Waterman Arrowplane was among the first tailless designs, but one of the earliest productions of the newly-formed Northrop company, which many years later was to build truly mammoth bombers of this general design, was an attempt at a 'flying wing'. Another aircraft which came near to the ideal of the true flying wing, and one which actually went into service, was the Junkers G 38 airliner, in which the engines were completely 'buried'. This was an astonishing realisation of ideas first put forward by Hugo Junkers in a patent of 1910. Highly experimental aircraft in the flying-wing class were the Arup, which somewhat resembled a ladybird, and the diamond-shaped Canova. These descriptions are no more extravagant than the aircraft themselves; and hardly less justifiable were the terms 'flying saucer' and 'flying umbrella', applied to a monoplane built at Miami University and having a circular wing perched above a conventional fuselage.

Far from conventional was the central body applied to the Burnelli monoplanes of the 1930s, for these transports embodied the lifting-fuselage principle first introduced in a biplane during 1922. They achieved no commercial success, and this was likewise denied the Makhonine 'extensible-wing' monoplane, in which the outer portions of the wing could be telescoped in and out of the inner portions, depending on whether high lift or high speed was desired.

Representing the class of aircraft somewhat curiously known as *canards*, and which had the remarkable distinction of flying tail-first, was the Focke-Wulf Ente of

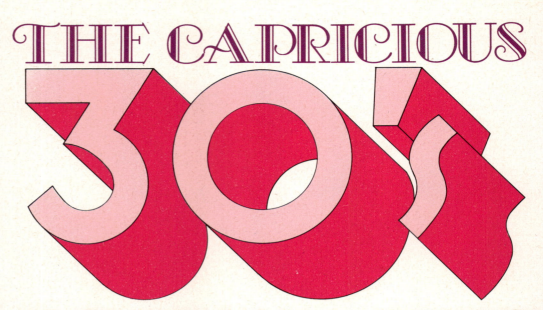

THE CAPRICIOUS 30's

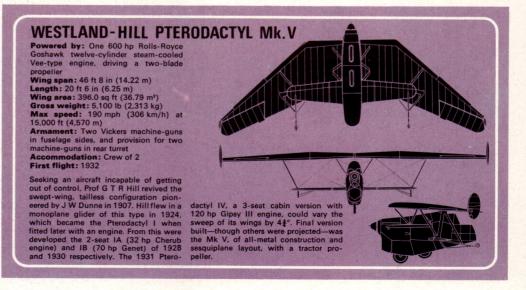

WESTLAND-HILL PTERODACTYL Mk.V

Powered by: One 600 hp Rolls-Royce Goshawk twelve-cylinder steam-cooled Vee-type engine, driving a two-blade propeller
Wing span: 46 ft 8 in (14.22 m)
Length: 20 ft 6 in (6.25 m)
Wing area: 396.0 sq ft (36.79 m²)
Gross weight: 5,100 lb (2,313 kg)
Max speed: 190 mph (306 km/h) at 15,000 ft (4,570 m)
Armament: Two Vickers machine-guns in fuselage sides, and provision for two machine-guns in rear turret
Accommodation: Crew of 2
First flight: 1932

Seeking an aircraft incapable of getting out of control, Prof G T R Hill revived the swept-wing, tailless configuration pioneered by J W Dunne in 1907. Hill flew in a monoplane glider of this type in 1924, which became the Pterodactyl I when fitted later with an engine. From this were developed the 2-seat IA (32 hp Cherub engine) and IB (70 hp Genet) of 1928 and 1930 respectively. The 1931 Ptero- dactyl IV, a 3-seat cabin version with 120 hp Gipsy III engine, could vary the sweep of its wings by 4¾°. Final version built—though others were projected—was the Mk V, of all-metal construction and sesquiplane layout, with a tractor pro- peller.

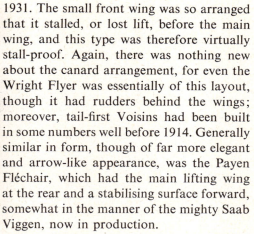

Left: The pod-and-boom fuselage of the Handley Page H.P.47 general-purpose military monoplane was intended to give the rear gunner the clearest possible field of fire

Top: Several tailless light aircraft were tested in the USA in the 'thirties. This side-by-side two-seater was designed by Thomas Hoff

Above: Second of the series of highly successful sweptwing tailless aircraft designed by Captain (later Professor) G T R Hill was this Pterodactyl, flown in the late 'twenties with a 32 hp Bristol Cherub engine

Below: Six passengers were carried in each fuselage boom of the Blériot 125, with the crew of two seated above the wing, between the engines

1931. The small front wing was so arranged that it stalled, or lost lift, before the main wing, and this type was therefore virtually stall-proof. Again, there was nothing new about the canard arrangement, for even the Wright Flyer was essentially of this layout, though it had rudders behind the wings; moreover, tail-first Voisins had been built in some numbers well before 1914. Generally similar in form, though of far more elegant and arrow-like appearance, was the Payen Fléchair, which had the main lifting wing at the rear and a stabilising surface forward, somewhat in the manner of the mighty Saab Viggen, now in production.

Even without considering rotary-wing designs (with the exception of the Buhl autogyro, which was unique in its pusher engine installation) it is possible to enumerate many other extraordinary machines of the 1930s. Among light aircraft, for instance, there was the Mignet Pou-du-Ciel, or Sky Louse, constructed privately by many enthusiasts after 1935. In this tiny aeroplane the high-set monoplane wing, which measured less than 20 ft (6.10 m) in span, was arranged to tilt up or down to give fore-and-aft control, while the large, lower-set tailplane (which could be regarded as a second wing) was fixed. The only movable tail surface was the rudder. Recurrent accidents with these simple little machines rendered the class almost, though not entirely, extinct.

Among more conventional light aeroplanes there were some distinctly unconventional engine installations. The Couzinet 100, for instance, seated only three people but had as many engines and looked in consequence like a baby airliner, the Booth single-seat flying-boat had a boat engine in the hull, driving the propeller through a shaft; the Heath Parasol used a converted Henderson motor-cycle engine; while the Pietenpol Aircamper was propelled by a converted Ford Model A car engine. (Conversely, aero-engines were installed in racing cars.)

Racing aeroplanes afforded astonishing contrasts in design, ranging from the extremely beautiful Macchi M.C.72 seaplane (which, nevertheless, had an entirely unconventional power plant, embodying two engines mounted one behind the other) to the dumpy Gee Bee landplanes. In the former it was evident that every attempt had been made to keep cross-sectional area to a minimum, with a view to reducing air resistance, or drag; while in the latter it appeared that the designer had chosen an engine having the greatest possible cross-section and had, as it were, attached a small aeroplane behind it. Whereas the engines of the Macchi racer were water-cooled, having cylinders in line, that installed in the Gee Bee was an air-cooled radial, with cylinders radiating out from the crankcase. This form of engine had been developed to a high pitch of efficiency in the USA, and although of large diameter it enabled the fuselage to be made approximately in the form of a teardrop—and a teardrop is by no means the least streamlined of forms. At the same time the radial engine was light and compact.

So short was the fuselage of the Gee Bee

Super Sportster that the pilot's enclosed cockpit was virtually part of the tail fin. What the occupant may have lacked in forward view he certainly made up for in courage; and even if the Super Sportster did resemble a dumpling, then the proof of this particular pudding was its speed record for landplanes of 296.287 mph (476.741 km/h), established in 1932.

Unorthodox among American racers because it appeared so orthodox was 'Benny' Howard's *Mr Mulligan*, which, except for the small area of its wing, resembled the high-wing strut-braced American executive aircraft of the 1930s. Although this aeroplane, like the Gee Bees, had a fixed undercarriage, the racer built by Capt Frank Hawks had not only retractable wheels but a retractable pilot as well. American competitive flying in the 1930s was not a field of activity which encouraged half-measures!

Among military types some curious shapes resulted from the efforts of designers to secure wide fields of fire. Mention has been made of the Pterodactyl V, which had nothing to hamper the gunner when firing astern or abeam. The nearest approach to this ideal with an aircraft having a tail was to carry the tail on the slenderest possible fuselage, or boom, and examples of this practice were the Handley Page H.P. 47 and certain Breguet types. With the increasing adoption of enclosed gun turrets French bombers began to assume the aspect of mediaeval citadels. 'Flying fortresses' they may not have been, but their sheer appearance was frightening enough.

Provision of amphibious capabilities likewise produced some startling results, especially in the Short Gurnard, the wheels of which were arranged to retract on each side of the central float, where they remained fully exposed. When taxying on land with wheels down this naval fighter presented a memorable duck-like spectacle.

For distinction of appearance some of the contenders for altitude and distance records rivalled even the Gee Bee racer. The former were characterised by great wing areas, for maximum lift in thin air. The Bristol Bulldog fighter, for instance, although able to climb to about 27,000 ft (8,230 m), became quite a different aircraft when fitted with special wings for a 40,000-ft (12,190-m) record attempt. This did not come to pass, but Bristol twice gained the record, once using a Pegasus-engined Vickers Vespa, which had a large wing area in any case, and on another occasion a special monoplane of their own design.

The long-range record-breakers were extremely graceful, having wings of very high aspect ratio (ratio of span to chord, or distance between leading- and trailing-edges). The best example was the Russian ANT-25, which, although single-engined (to keep fuel consumption and drag to a minimum), had a span of 111 ft 6 in (33.98 m)—nearly ten feet greater than that of the Lancaster four-engined bomber of the second World War.

Certainly the 1930s were not lacking in design variety, even without the 'cyclogyros', or aircraft having paddle-wheels instead of wings. These were closely investigated in Germany and America but never took the air. Perhaps this was just as well!

Opposite page, top: Principle of the Burnelli transport was the use of an aerofoil-shape main fuselage to increase lift and improve efficiency. These photographs show (left) the 15-seat British Burnelli OA-1, built in 1938 with 710 hp Perseus engines, and one of its US counterparts

Bottom: Intended for duty with the fleet, the Short Gurnard II prototype had main wheels which retracted upward on each side of its central float

This page, below: The Westland Dreadnought, designed by M Woyevodsky, a Russian engineer, was a flying-wing prototype which stalled and crashed on its maiden flight in May 1923

Top right: Resplendent in pearl and black glossy cellulose, this Bristol Bulldog IVA was a test-bed for the new Perseus IA sleeve-valve engine in 1934

Centre right: The prototype Bulldog I was fitted with high aspect-ratio wings, spanning 50 ft (15.25 m), for an attempt on the altitude record in 1927. Although it was expected to reach nearly 40,000 ft (12,190 m), the idea was dropped when Donati of Italy reached 38,800 ft (11,826 m)

Bottom: One of the later, improved versions of Henri Mignet's Pou-du-Ciel can still be seen in the Musée de l'Air in Paris. It reminds visitors of one of the most enterprising attempts to produce the sort of aeroplane that anyone could build and fly

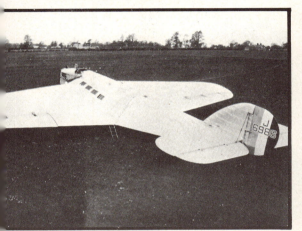

STRETCHING
THE RANGE

ON 1 JULY 1935, a tiny Curtiss Robin monoplane landed at Meridian, Mississippi, after remaining airborne for four weeks. Flown by two brothers, Al and Fred Key, the aircraft had taken off from Meridian on 4 June and had remained in close proximity to the airport for most of the 653 hours 34 minutes of the flight. During that time, 400 contacts were made between the Robin and a supply aircraft in order to transfer fuel, oil and food.

This flight was a dramatic, if somewhat impractical, demonstration of the possibilities for refuelling an aircraft in the air. No-one was likely to want to stay aloft for a month at a time for any purpose other than a stunt; but the expanding commercial application of the aeroplane during the 1930s created an interest in any means of increasing the non-stop range over which a useful payload could be carried. Refuelling in flight offered one such means.

Range, of course, was a function of the fuel capacity of the aircraft and the rate at which fuel was consumed by the engine(s). Fuel capacity, in turn, was limited by the maximum weight at which the aircraft could take off. Greater take-off weights required either more engine power (with comparably higher consumption), greater aerodynamic efficiency (limited by the 'state-of-the-art' at any given point in time) or longer take-off distances (limited by the lengths of runway available).

Today, improvements in the propulsive efficiency of modern jet engines, aerodynamic refinements and extended runways at most of the world's major airports have combined to allow the development of aircraft which have enough non-stop range for virtually all the commercial needs of modern airlines. But in the period up to the outbreak of war in 1939 and in the few years after its end, commercial requirements had stepped ahead of engineering achievement and alternative means of increasing range were tried. Then, as now, it was the non-stop trans-Atlantic air routes which represented the prime objective for new developments.

Flight refuelling, although the most promising of the various techniques tried in this period, was also the most difficult to perfect. It required the use of a 'tanker' aircraft with which the 'receiver' aircraft had to rendezvous; a connecting hose then had to be passed between the two aircraft while they flew in close formation for as long a period as was necessary for the fuel to be transferred. The possibilities were first demonstrated in 1923 in the USA, but it was not until 1936 that serious attention was given to adopting the technique for commercial use.

In 1936 a company named Flight Refuelling Ltd was founded in England to continue development of the refuelling system which had been patented by Flt Lt R L R Atcherley after watching demonstrations in America. With support from the Air Ministry, Flight Refuelling Ltd modified a series of large aircraft to demonstrate the receiver/tanker technique, including two Vickers Virginias, the Armstrong Whitworth A.W.23, the Handley Page H.P. 51, the Vickers B.19/27 and a Boulton Paul Overstrand.

The demonstrations with these aircraft showed that flight refuelling had reached the point where it could be considered seriously for commercial use. At this time, in 1938, Imperial Airways was committed to the use of flying-boats for a scheduled service carrying mail between Southampton and New York. After a series of demonstrations in which the A.W.23 tanker refuelled the Short C class flying-boat *Cambria*, Flight Refuelling Ltd received a contract to provide a refuelling service for the scheduled operation—the world's first use of the technique as routine.

The 'ejector' method which had now been developed by Flight Refuelling Ltd required the receiving aircraft to trail a weighted line. The tanker, flying slightly to one side and behind the receiver, fired a second line across the receiver's line, which became gripped in the pawls of a grapnel. The tanker then winched in the linked lines and attached a hose to the receiver's line, which

was then, in its turn, pulled back into the receiving aircraft until the hose was connected to a refuelling valve. Fuel was then transferred at an average rate of about 100 gallons (455 litres) per minute.

For normal operations, the C class 'boats were cleared to take off at 48,000 lb (21,772 kg) gross weight. Special clearance was obtained for operation at a flying weight of 53,000 lb (24,040 kg), so that about 5,000 lb (2,268 kg) more fuel could be taken on shortly after take-off for the Atlantic crossing. Two of the Short flying-boats, *Cabot* (G-AFCU) and *Caribou* (G-AFCV) were modified for the service, and the latter took off from Southampton on the first scheduled mail flight on 5 August 1939. A ground refuelling stop was made at Foynes (Shannon), and shortly after take-off from there *Caribou* was refuelled in the air from one of four Handley Page Harrow tankers that had been specially converted for the purpose. A similar refuelling was made off the Newfoundland coast after

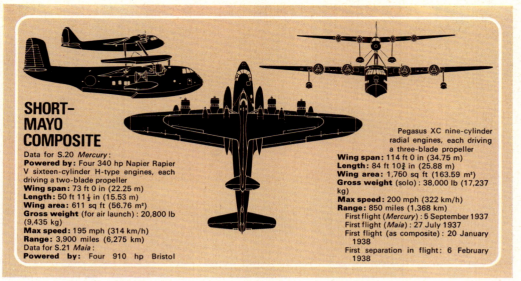

SHORT-MAYO COMPOSITE

Data for S.20 *Mercury*:
Powered by: Four 340 hp Napier Rapier V sixteen-cylinder H-type engines, each driving a two-blade propeller
Wing span: 73 ft 0 in (22.25 m)
Length: 50 ft 11½ in (15.53 m)
Wing area: 611 sq ft (56.76 m²)
Gross weight (for air launch): 20,800 lb (9,435 kg)
Max speed: 195 mph (314 km/h)
Range: 3,900 miles (6,275 km)
Data for S.21 *Maia*:
Powered by: Four 910 hp Bristol

Pegasus XC nine-cylinder radial engines, each driving a three-blade propeller
Wing span: 114 ft 0 in (34.75 m)
Length: 84 ft 10¾ in (25.88 m)
Wing area: 1,760 sq ft (163.59 m²)
Gross weight (solo): 38,000 lb (17,237 kg)
Max speed: 200 mph (322 km/h)
Range: 850 miles (1,368 km)
First flight (*Mercury*): 5 September 1937
First flight (*Maia*): 27 July 1937
First flight (as composite): 20 January 1938
First separation in flight: 6 February 1938

Opposite page, far left: The aircraft used for catapult mail flights from the German trans-Atlantic liner *Europa* in 1930-31 was this Heinkel He 58 seaplane

Left: America was not the only country in which first World War de Havilland bombers were used for flight refuelling experiments in the 'twenties. In Belgium, two airmen named Crooy and Groenen remained airborne for 60 hr 7 min 32 sec in a D.H.9

Bottom left: A BOAC Liberator 'receiver' photographed from a Lancastrian tanker during a night refuelling on the airline's non-stop Montreal-London service in the late 'forties

Bottom right: *Mercury*, the trans-Atlantic component of the Mayo Composite, being lowered into position on its launch aircraft, *Maia*

take-off from Botwood on the return flights.

The Imperial Airways trans-Atlantic mail service was doomed to be discontinued within a month, because of the outbreak of war, but 16 crossings were made and on all but one (when favourable winds made additional fuel unnecessary) successful refuellings were completed.

An interesting alternative to flight refuelling had also been studied by Imperial Airways for the North Atlantic operation, at the suggestion of Major Robert Mayo, Imperial Airways' Technical Adviser. The idea was for a 'mother' aircraft to take off with a smaller, heavily-loaded aeroplane on its back, to be launched when cruising height and speed were reached. Such 'pick-a-back' aircraft were not new in concept but had never been considered previously for commercial operation. Backed by the Air Ministry, Short Brothers proceeded to design a suitable pair of aircraft in 1935, the object being to produce an air-launched seaplane which would have sufficient range

to cross the North Atlantic after launch. Flight testing of the Short-Mayo Composite began early in 1938 and the first Atlantic crossing was made by *Mercury* on 21 July, non-stop to Montreal after launching off Shannon.

For various reasons, Imperial Airways never operated the Composite on a regular service, but the potential of the project was demonstrated in October 1938 when *Mercury* was launched by *Maia* near Dundee, Scotland, and completed a record-breaking flight for seaplanes of 5,997.5 miles (9,652 km) to the Orange River in South Africa, which stands to this day.

While Imperial Airways was looking towards a North Atlantic service, France and Germany were devoting their attention to the shorter South Atlantic route. With air routes established from Paris to Dakar in West Africa and also down the east coast of South America from Natal to Buenos Aires, the French company Aéropostale relied upon a ship for the sea crossing between Dakar and Natal for a mail service opened as early as 1928. After Air France took over the operation, aircraft were developed to open a through mail service in 1936.

The German line, Deutsche Luft Hansa, similarly used ships to carry mail between the Canary Islands and Fernando de Noronha from 1930 until 1932, when the first of the unique seaplane depot ships came into service, to provide refuelling services for a Dornier Wal flying-boat used for the trans-Atlantic sector of the journey. The technique required the flying-boat to land alongside the ship; it was then hoisted on board, serviced, refuelled and

launched by catapult. Accelerations of about 4½ g made the technique unsuitable for passenger-carrying, but the service was operated successfully right up to the outbreak of war in 1939 at a frequency of about two return flights a week.

The German operations in the South Atlantic were actually preceded by some experimental mail-carrying flights in the North Atlantic, also using catapult launches. The first such operations were by a Heinkel He 12 seaplane launched from the liner *Bremen* when still about 300 miles (482 km) away from New York on its maiden voyage. On the return, aircraft were similarly used to save about 36 hours in the time taken for mail to reach Germany via Cherbourg. The technique became standard on the *Bremen* and later on *Europa*, using a Heinkel He 58 and/or a Junkers Ju 48.

In September 1936, DLH began experiments across the North Atlantic based on the depot ship technique. Two Dornier Do 18 flying-boats flew a series of journeys from Berlin to New York, with a refuelling stop alongside the *Schwabenland* in mid-Atlantic. A year later, two Blohm und Voss Ha 139s made a series of 12 flights from the *Schwabenland* steaming off the Azores. No scheduled flights were possible, however, as Germany was unable to negotiate traffic rights with the USA.

Following the end of the war in 1945, the possibilities of flight refuelling were again investigated, using Lancaster and Lancastrian tankers and Lancaster and Liberator receivers. Trials were made over the English Channel (1946), the South Atlantic (1947) and the North Atlantic (1948) with few operational difficulties; but by this time aircraft with adequate range for trans-Atlantic operation were becoming available, and subsequent interest in flight refuelling concentrated on its military aspects.

COMFORT IN THE AIR

Top: Boeing Model 80, known as the 'Pioneer Pullman of the Air', was one of the first large transport aircraft adopted for airline use in the USA, in 1928. It carried 12 passengers and was followed by the 18-passenger Model 80-A which established a 27-hour coast-to-coast service across America

Above: These eight young ladies, all trained nurses, were the world's first airline stewardesses. At the prompting of Ellen Church (third from left) they were hired by Boeing Air Transport, a predecessor of United Air Lines, in 1930. Each had to be not older than twenty-five, with a weight of 115 lb (52 kg) or less, and not over 5ft 4in (1.62m) tall. Pay was $125 per month for 100 hours of flying

Left: Nelly Diener of Swissair was Europe's first air hostess. Aircraft in background is a Curtiss Condor, a type in which she flew

Opposite page, top: This photograph, taken in the mock-up of the Short 'C' Class flying-boat at Rochester in 1936, shows sleeping berths as fitted in the midships cabin of this Imperial Airways transport. Two berths were made up for passengers who wanted to rest or felt unwell, but sleeper services were not operated

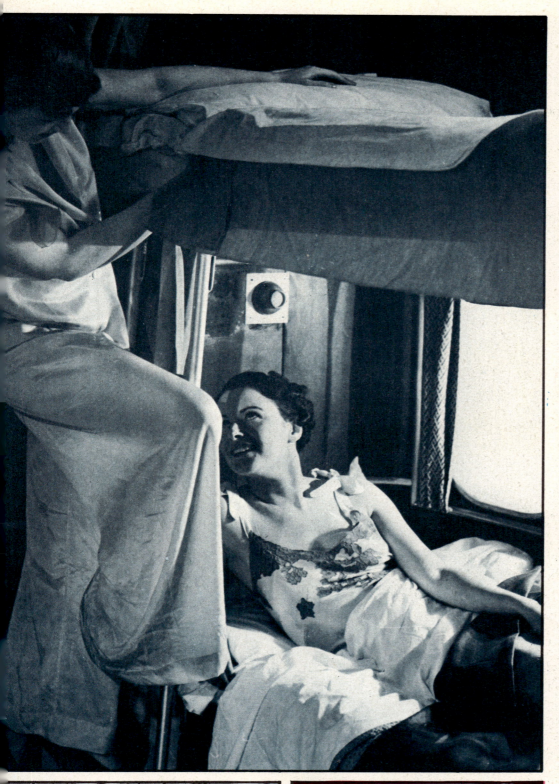

MANY OF THE FIRST air passengers flew in open cockpits and, as they were lent flying clothing by the airlines, it might truly be said that the airlines have always been concerned about passenger comfort.

The problems in the early days were primarily those of warmth and noise reduction. Warm air for cabin heating was soon provided by tapping the engine exhaust system, but the provision of quiet cabins took many years to achieve. The early aircraft had fabric cabin walls and their interior noise level was not very different from that on the outside. In three-engined types the centre engine was the cause of considerable noise and vibration. But as the aeroplane became more efficient it was possible to allow an increase in weight for soundproofing; at the same time soundproofing materials themselves improved.

Ventilation was not, initially, a problem because most aircraft had windows which could be slid open; some of the Junkers monoplanes even had windows which could be lowered on a strap, as in railway carriages. When speeds increased it was no longer possible to have opening windows, and fresh air vents were provided. This improved safety, for in one type of British aeroplane it had been possible to slide open the window and put one's hand into the propeller, while a danger to those on the ground beneath was emphasised in at least one type of French aircraft by notices in the cabin stating 'It is absolutely forbidden to throw anything out of the window'. So air vents had quite a few advantages.

In the 1920s and 1930s most aircraft cabins were virtually rectangular boxes with windows on each side, two rows of seats, a light luggage rack, possibly a bulkhead map, one or two instruments, and air-sickness bowls beneath the seats. Aft of the cabin there was normally a lavatory.

Seat design was not a fine art—for the most part weight-saving was the main consideration. Few aircraft had carpets and for many years the various Junkers types were about the only transports with seat belts.

A major step forward came in 1931 when Imperial Airways introduced the four-engined Handley Page Heracles and Hannibal biplanes. These each had two well-furnished cabins, with comfortable cushioned seats and fixed tables between each pair of facing seats. (It is possible that they were the first aircraft to have double seats on each side of the aisle.) Between the fore and aft cabins were two lavatories and a galley. On European routes, multi-course meals were served by two stewards. All four engines were mounted on the wings, with consequent reduction in noise and vibration although these were still at a high level by present-day standards. The cabins were fairly well heated.

These Handley Pages provided much higher standards than had been achieved previously, but were not the first aircraft to carry stewards. Meal service had been provided on some of the German Zeppelins before the first World War; cabin boys had been carried (without meal service) by the

Above: Developed from the Vimy bomber, as used for the first non-stop trans-Atlantic flight, the Vimy Commercial was a 10-passenger transport first flown on 13 April 1919. It had the typical lightweight wicker chairs of the period

Right: Although quite small, with accommodation for 12 to 17 passengers, de Havilland's first stressed-skin all-metal aircraft, the twin-engined Flamingo airliner of 1938, was surprisingly roomy. Reclining seats reflected the new emphasis being put on passenger comfort

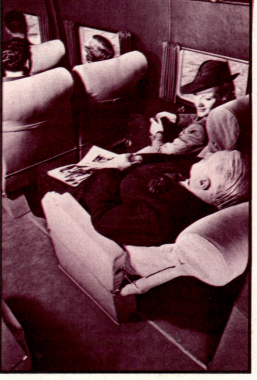

Daimler Airway in 1922; Imperial Airways had provided steward service on the Argosy *Silver Wing* London-Paris services from May 1927; and Air Union had introduced a restaurant service in about 1928 or 1929.

Stewardesses first became a feature of air transport in the United States when they started flying with Boeing Air Transport on 15 May 1930. Originally, they were all nurses and first served on the three-engined Boeing 80 biplanes flying the San Francisco-Salt Lake City-Chicago route. In Europe Swissair employed at least one stewardess; some flew with KLM and there is some evidence that girls flew on certain Luft Hansa routes, one of their duties being secretarial work for passengers.

In general, smoking was not allowed on aircraft prior to the second World War, but the Luft Hansa Heinkel He 111s of 1936 had a four-seat smoking cabin, while the Focke-Wulf Condors of 1938 had nine-seat smoking cabins and smoking was permitted in the forward cabins of Imperial Airways' Armstrong Whitworth Ensign landplanes and Short 'C' class flying-boats.

The 'C' class represented another big step forward in that they had four separate cabins, including one which incorporated a promenade deck on which passengers could stand and watch the view. Much attention was given to soundproofing, carpeting and lighting, and the seats, incorporating life-belts, could be reclined to a number of different angles. Normally these 'boats had two berths made up, although they were never operated as sleeper aircraft.

In the United States some use was made of sleeper aircraft. Curtiss Condor sleeper biplanes were operated on transcontinental services, and the famous Douglas DC-3 owes its existence to American Airlines' requirement for such an aircraft—the first DC-3 actually being designated DST or Douglas Sleeper Transport.

Britain, France and Germany, and possibly Italy, also fitted berths to aircraft and planned sleeper services; but so far as is known no sustained sleeper services were operated by these countries' airlines before the war.

The problems of providing adequate passenger comfort were probably greatest on the trunk route services which traversed widely-ranging terrain, in varying climates, on journeys taking a week or ten days. The difficulties were increased by the low cruising speeds of the aircraft employed, together with their very limited range and endurance, and the lack of night-flying facilities.

INTERIOR OF A HANDLEY PAGE TWIN ENGINE AEROPLANE

Opposite page, top left: The Handley Page H.P.42 'Hannibal' Class airliner *Hanno* at Sharjah in the Persian Gulf, with the fort/rest house in the background. The armed guard can be seen sitting on the ground beyond the barbed-wire defences. Above the flight deck is the British Civil Air Ensign, always flown on the ground

Top right: Part of the main (aft) cabin of a 'Hannibal'. The door leads to the galley, lavatories and forward cabin. The old Imperial Airways badge appears on the door

Bottom: Passengers in the spartan cabin of this early Handley Page airliner could follow their route between London and Paris on a ceiling chart supplied by BP, whose aviation spirit, it proclaimed, was used exclusively on Handley Page aeroplanes

This page, above left: The standard of cabin service offered by Imperial Airways in the mid-thirties is evident in this photograph taken in the galley of one of its Short *Scylla/Syrinx* four-engined landplanes

Above right: By August 1945 the second World War was nearly ended and passengers were beginning to look forward to a return of peacetime air travel. The caption to this photograph, taken inside a DC-3 of Australian National Airways, commented 'Light refreshments bring happy faces'

Below: The Fokker F.XXXVI of 1934 was designed to provide sleeper accommodation for 16 passengers on KLM's Far East route. In the event only one was built, and used in Europe, as KLM bought DC-2s instead

Below right: A completely new concept of passenger comfort was heralded by the 33-passenger Boeing Stratoliner of 1939. Based on the B-17C Flying Fortress bomber, it had a pressurised cabin and could fly above much of the bad weather that had been the primary cause of airsickness since the start of airline flying

Imperial Airways' African and Indian routes well illustrate the problems and the attempts at their solution. The aircraft used, such as the de Havilland Hercules and Short Calcutta land and flying-boat biplanes, had to touch down every 200-300 miles (320-480 km) for fuel and cruised at only 90-100 mph (145-160 km/h). It was considered in the late 1920s and early 1930s that passengers could be expected to fly only about 700-1,000 miles (1,125-1,600 km) a day. Even these stages meant spending 7 to 10 hours a day in the air, while three or four en route refuelling stops could add another 3 or 4 hours to the journey. Early starts were made, and the end of the day's flying was normally at last light.

Such stage restrictions meant that in many cases night stops had to be made in remote areas. This involved construction of rest houses with bedrooms, bathrooms and meal service; and, because of the state of the world at that time, in some places the rest houses had to be within forts with armed guards on duty. Examples were those at Rutbah Wells, in the desert between Damascus and Baghdad, and at Sharjah on the Oman Peninsula.

Much of the flying was extremely rough, because the aircraft were incapable of reaching altitudes at which the air was cool and stable over the deserts; and, of course, bad weather areas had to be penetrated rather than skirted, because of the limitations on endurance and cruising altitude.

The discomforts of travel over such routes could be overcome only gradually, as aircraft speed, range, ceiling and payloads increased.

One most important contribution to comfort was cabin pressurisation, which enabled transport aircraft to fly at greater altitudes, thus avoiding desert turbulence and much of the worst weather—although the long-cherished dream of over-the-weather flight was not achieved with the completeness claimed in early airline advertising. When the second World War started, numerous pressurised transports were in the design and development stage, but the only 'pre-war' pressurised airliner was the Boeing 307 Stratoliner, which was ordered by TWA and Pan American Airways and put into service in mid-1940.

The war brought back austerity in air transport and the next major developments had to await the introduction of turboprop and turbojet power in the 1950s, although there were some refinements such as the general introduction of pressurisation, higher cruising speeds and greater range in piston-engined aircraft.

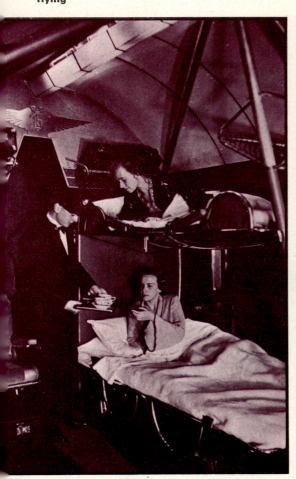

Rough & Ready

THE TERM 'RUGGED', as now commonly applied to an aeroplane, is an Americanism which describes not only a very robust type of machine but the kind of territory in which it may be called upon to operate; and certainly it was apt in both instances to the Canadian 'bush' flying of the 1930s.

In the Canadian wilderness during the late 1920s the aeroplane had proved its capabilities in exploring and developing new tracts of the world's second largest land mass—second only, that is, to the USSR, of which a similar story might be told; and the nature of the flying and the aircraft employed was mirrored in the characters of the pilots.

Among these men C H 'Punch' Dickins retains an almost legendary status. In the summer of 1928 this pilot took off from Baker Lake, a little west of Hudson's Bay, and headed out across uncharted regions of the Barren Lands. For much of his 800-odd mile (1,300-km) flight his eyes were scanning territory never before seen by civilised man. In the following year he set out northward from Edmonton, Alberta, for a 1,500-mile (2,400-km) trip along the Mackenzie River, this time carrying air mail. His northernmost alighting point was Aklavik, where the river joins the Arctic Ocean.

'Punch' Dickins was typical of his breed in resourcefulness as well as hardihood. Once, landing on ice-hard snow, he bent the tips of his metal propeller and broke an undercarriage strut. A dog-sled was despatched to the nearest settlement, and meanwhile Dickins and his mechanic set to work. An abandoned boat provided a length of piping to repair the strut, and a saw was the means of removing six inches (15 cm) of each propeller blade. This surgery got the men airborne once again, and they beat the dog-sled to the settlement by an hour. On another trip 'Punch' sustained a completely shattered propeller, which he replaced with one manufactured for him at a northern trading post. The materials were laminations of oak sleigh board; the glue was made from moose horns.

The aeroplanes which served in such rigorous conditions were so well fitted to their task that their essential characteristics are clearly evident today in two post-war types of aircraft—the de Havilland Canada Beaver and Otter—designed specifically to carry on their work. The types concerned in the 1930s were mainly of Fairchild, Bellanca, Fokker, Travel Air and Noorduyn design, and all were high-wing single-engined monoplanes. The high-wing arrangement gave not only stability, an essential quality in such exacting circumstances, but ease of loading and unloading also, for cargoes varied greatly in weight and shape. Clearance was also thus allowed for natural

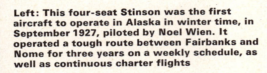

Above: Early Fairchild monoplanes were the mainstay of Canadian 'bush' operations for many years. Typical was this 1928 FC-2W2 used on Colonial Airways' passenger and mail routes between New York and Montreal

Top left: This eight-passenger American Airplane & Engine (Fairchild) Pilgrim of 1931 marked its retirement from regular airline service by posing with the prototype Boeing 707 jet-liner in the mid-fifties. It was operated by Alaska Airlines for 18 of its years on scheduled services

Left: This four-seat Stinson was the first aircraft to operate in Alaska in winter time, in September 1927, piloted by Noel Wien. It operated a tough route between Fairbanks and Nome for three years on a weekly schedule, as well as continuous charter flights

Below, left: One of the best-known Canadian 'bush' aircraft, the Noorduyn Norseman eight/ten-seater was first flown in 1935 and was put back in production by the Canadian Car & Foundry Company after the second World War

Bottom: Wien Alaska Airlines is still a famous name on the most exacting air routes in North America. Its founder, Noel Wien (left in photo), flew this party of prospectors 300 miles (482 km) from Fairbanks to Selby Lake in the Kobuk area in a Hamilton monoplane in March 1929

obstacles.

Being seated under the leading-edge of the wing, the pilot had a wide range of vision, a most essential quality when the flying conditions were sometimes among the worst in the world. The robust wheeled undercarriage was interchangeable with floats, for the lakes of Canada were natural bases; and skis extended further the scope of operations. As on the Beaver and Otter of today, the floats were commonly of Edo make, and the favoured engine was, as now, of Pratt & Whitney air-cooled radial type, sometimes with special provision for functioning in cold weather. Typical was the Bellanca Pacemaker, a six-seat aircraft measuring 50 ft 6 in (15.40 m) in span.

Displaying their national 'CF' registration letters, and perhaps the 'GR' and crown device proclaiming 'Royal Mail', such aeroplanes as these penetrated deeper and deeper into the continent, gradually superseding the dog teams of former years. The time of travel was reduced from days to hours, although cruising speeds were of the order of only 100 mph (160 km/h). Supplies —fresh vegetables and fruit not least among them—arrived with increasing regularity at the remotest points. Traders, hunters and trappers shared with doctors, 'Mounties' and missionaries the benefits of the new mode of transport.

Yet, although entire families and communities came to depend on the 'bushplane' for travel and sustenance, the pilots' battle with nature and the elements continued unabated. Emergency equipment would typically include a tent and a sleeping bag, an axe, firearms and ammunition, rations and a first-aid kit. Temperatures as low as −60 deg Fahrenheit (−51°C) could be encountered, and with only rudimentary navigational aids the sturdy monoplanes flew over inadequately or inaccurately charted territory in the face of swiftly changing weather, including fog, snowstorms and freezing rain.

As though these were not sufficient hazards to contend with, the aircraft compasses could be strongly influenced by the very mineral deposits which they were instrumental in helping to discover and exploit. Familiarity with the terrain was an absolute essential, and if ever pilots could be said to have flown 'by the seat of their pants' then the tough Canadians were certainly among them, especially as a phenomenon called a 'white-out' might suddenly be encountered at any time. This meant that the horizon would be blotted out by minute particles of ice formed in the air. As there were often no shadows, the contours of the ground below could not be judged with any certainty.

Particular hazards could attend a landing, especially in the far North where, in a freeze-up, a float undercarriage would be ruled out by ice; skis were likewise barred because the ice was too thin to bear the aircraft's weight.

By the late 1930s regular services were being flown on more than thirty routes, forming links with, for example, the Empire's northernmost radio station at Aklavik (68 deg N) and with points bearing

such evocative names as Fort Norman and Fort Rae, Goldfields, Coppermine, Dawson and Great Bear Lake. Operators like Canadian Airways, United Air Transport, General Airways, Mackenzie Air Service, Starrat Airways and Transportation, Dominion Skyways, M and C Aviation, and Wings Ltd served areas hundreds of thousands of square miles in extent, carrying not only the men who were opening up the great and challenging Dominion but freight as widely assorted as mining machinery, medical supplies and furs, in addition to mail.

No longer was it necessary for the fur traders to stockpile their wares until the coming of spring, nor for prospectors to stake their claims only after harrowing overland journeys. The fishing industry benefited likewise. In 1938 it was reported: 'Seal spotting by aircraft to assist fishing fleets is one of the more recent branches of north-western air activity. One firm, anxious lest its considerable air-transports of fish from the north should reduce the supply to extinction, sent 1,100 speckled trout to be dropped in lakes whose stocks were rapidly declining.'

As in Canada, so in the vast outback of Australia—a continent then having a total population less than that of Greater London—where the bushplane served outlying settlements never reached by railway. The first of the 'Flying Doctor' services, now world-famous as an example of how the aeroplane can serve humanitarian causes,

had begun in 1928. Soon the portable two-way radios, supplied with pedal-driven generators to remote homesteads, were tapping out in Morse their pleas for aid.

As the larger operators, such as QANTAS, developed their services along the trunk routes, other companies, like WASP, Ansett Airways, Victoria and Interstate Airways, and Southern Air Lines and Freighters, linked the capital cities with distant points in the interior. As befitted its name, Guinea Airways ran services not only between Adelaide and Darwin, following roughly the line of the historic Overland Telegraph, but also in the mandated territory of New Guinea. Here exploration and prospecting, allied with the air-lifting of stores and mining machinery, were vital factors in developing a densely forested terrain, peopled by primitive tribes. By 1934 four companies were using twenty-one aeroplanes for transport between the goldfields and coastal points. Here, as elsewhere, prosperity followed the bushplanes.

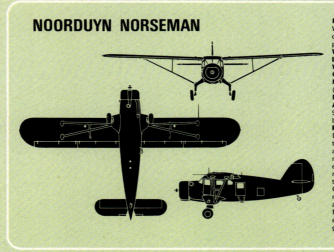

NOORDUYN NORSEMAN

Powered by: One 600 hp Pratt & Whitney R-1340-S3H1 Wasp nine-cylinder radial engine, driving a two-blade propeller
Wing span: 51 ft 8 in (15.75 m)
Length: 31 ft 9 in (9.68 m)
Wing area: 325 sq ft (30.2 m²)
Gross weight: 7,400 lb (3,357 kg)
Max cruising speed: 148 mph (237 km/h) at 5,000 ft (1,525 m)
Max range: 1,150 miles (1,840 km)
Accommodation: Crew of 1 and up to 9 passengers and 595 lb (270 kg) of baggage and freight
First flight: 1935
Designed by a Canadian, R B C Noorduyn, the Norseman was the only one of his aircraft to be built in quantity; but in more than 35 years of operation it has established a reputation as one of the most outstanding utility aircraft of its time. In 1946 the Canadian Car & Foundry Co continued manufacture of an improved model, the Norseman V, and the data apply to the landplane version of this. All Norseman aircraft can be fitted with interchangeable wheel, ski or float landing gear.

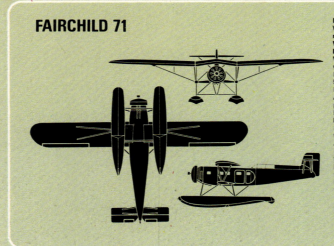

FAIRCHILD 71

Powered by: One 420 hp Pratt & Whitney R-1340-1 Wasp nine-cylinder radial engine, driving a two-blade propeller
Wing span: 50 ft 0 in (15.24 m)
Length: 32 ft 10 in (10.00 m)
Wing area: 335 sq ft (31.12 m²)
Gross weight: 5,500 lb (2,495 kg)
Max speed: 129 mph (208 km/h) at 5,000 ft (1,525 m)
Range: 900 miles (1,450 km)
Accommodation: Crew of 1 and 6 passengers, or equivalent mail or freight load
First flight: 1929
Known today as a leading aircraft manufacturer in the USA, Fairchild originated as a Canadian company with its works at Longueuil, near Montreal, and was noted for a range of aircraft types which contributed to the start of 'bush' flying in Canada. Typical was the Model 71, which had foldable wings and an interchangeable wheel, float or ski landing gear, and was used by the US Services as well as by private operators. The silhouette depicts an improved, closed-cockpit version, the Super 71; the data apply to the Model 71-C.

FLYING DOCTOR

IN 1928 an injured or seriously ill person living in the British Isles could be brought to a doctor—or a doctor to him—in minutes or hours or, in even the most remote places, in a day. In the same year, in Australia's outback—an area larger than Western Europe where there were no railways or stagecoaches—there *were* no doctors or nurses and the only way a patient could receive medical attention was by taking a slow, painful journey by cart, buggy or motor car across trackless country. The exception was in north-western Queensland, where isolated settlers were served by a doctor who flew to them from a newly-established base at Cloncurry. With the practicability of using aircraft in a land of open spaces and good flying weather, the

inception of a full-scale flying doctor service was inevitable.

A pioneer was needed, of course, to get it all started—someone with drive and dedicated purpose; someone, too, who lived and worked in the outback, who understood the medical problems associated with living and bringing up children in those millions of remote square miles. Such a man was John Flynn, born and bred on the Victorian goldfields, who became a minister of the Free Church of Scotland's Smith-of-Dunesk Mission of South Australia—a Mission founded on money left for its cause by a mother whose son had perished in the arid centre of Australia.

Flynn's job was not simply to maintain religious interest, but to relieve the isolation of station homestead families, regardless of creed, and to offer basic medical services—such as pulling teeth and lancing boils. He sometimes used camels, and later a remarkable Dodge tourer, to visit people of the inland, making journeys of hundreds of miles—a wandering link between settlers and civilisation.

There is virtually no end to the outback.

DHA-3 DROVER

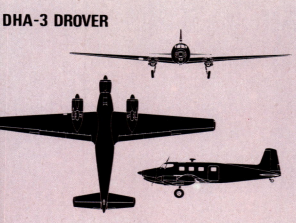

Powered by: Three 180 hp Lycoming O-360-A1A four-cylinder horizontally-opposed engines, each driving a two-blade propeller
Wing span: 57 ft 0 in (17.37 m)
Length: 36 ft 6 in (11.12 m)
Wing area: 325 sq ft (30.19 m²)
Gross weight: 6,500 lb (2,948 kg)
Max cruising speed: 140 mph (225 km/h) at 5,000 ft (1,525 m)
Max range: 900 miles (1,450 km)
Accommodation: Crew of 1 or 2, and 2 stretchers with 2 medical attendants, 9 passengers or 1,500 lb (680 kg) of cargo
First flight: 23 January 1948
First aircraft to be designed by the Australian branch of de Havilland, the Drover bush transport was based broadly on the D.H.104 Dove, though it had a three-engined configuration for increased safety while flying over 'outback' areas and more utilitarian lines than its British predecessor. Originally the Drover was powered by 145 hp D.H. Gipsy Major 10 Mk 2 engines, but all Flying Doctor aircraft were converted to Drover 3s in 1960 with Lycomings. Data apply to the latter version, which flew for the first time in May 1960.

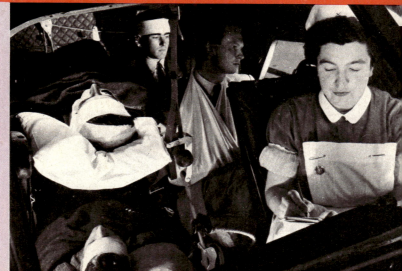

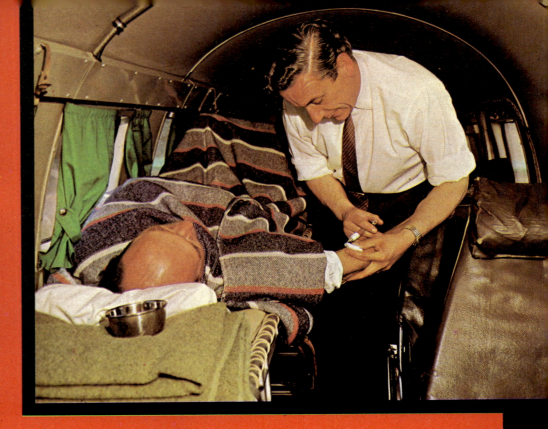

DE HAVILLAND D.H.50

Powered by: One 230 hp Siddeley Puma six-cylinder in-line engine, driving a two-blade propeller
Wing span: 42 ft 9 in (13.03 m)
Length: 29 ft 9 in (9.07 m)
Wing area: 434 sq ft (40.32 m²)
Gross weight: 4,200 lb (1,905 kg)
Max speed: 112 mph (180 km/h)
Range: 380 miles (612 km)
Accommodation: Crew of 1 and 4 passengers
First flight: August 1923
Although built in only small numbers, the D.H.50 has at least two strong claims to a place in the history of aviation. In 1925-26 one of these aircraft, refitted with a 385 hp Jaguar radial engine, was used by Sir Alan Cobham for his famous survey flights to Cape Town and Australia on behalf of Imperial Airways; another, sold to QANTAS in 1924, later became the first aeroplane to be used for the Australian Flying Doctor Service.

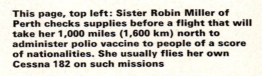

This page, top left: Sister Robin Miller of Perth checks supplies before a flight that will take her 1,000 miles (1,600 km) north to administer polio vaccine to people of a score of nationalities. She usually flies her own Cessna 182 on such missions

Above: Mr Alfred Traegar tests his latest type of outback radio receiver. Equipment of this type has created a network throughout Australia which helps bring medical aid to the remotest door

Below: This Beechcraft Queen Air of the NSW Ambulance Transport Service can carry four stretcher patients, four walking patients and special medical equipment

Top right: There is plenty of room inside the cabin of the Drover for a doctor to attend to his patients in flight

Right: The lead set by John Flynn has been followed by other dedicated people all over the world. This photograph shows medical staff hurrying to an An-2 ambulance aircraft to answer an urgent call for help in Russia

Opposite page: In Scotland, BEA's ambulance aircraft land on the firm beach on the Island of Barra. The aircraft is a Rapide, which gave fine service until replaced by Herons

On large sheep and cattle stations there is usually a second homestead, the remote 'outback station'; beyond are 'outback paddocks', and further on, usually in the direction of desert country, is what bushmen call 'the outback'. The 'inland' was the general area of the centre: to the west the desert country was practically uninhabitable; but to the north, into Northern Territory, and to the east, into western Queensland and the north-west corner of New South Wales, cattle stations and some sheep stations were well established when John Flynn, in 1911, began his bushman's life of 'dropping in' after camel or buggy rides that took days, sometimes weeks, from homestead to mining camp or lonely boundary rider's shack.

Seeing the plight of these people when illness or injury struck them, hundreds of miles from medical care, encouraged in Flynn and the Missions a determination to establish nursing homes wherever possible and whenever finance allowed. In 1912 he made a survey for the Home Mission directors, travelling from the railhead at Oodnadatta to Alice Springs, Pine Creek, Burketown, Camooweal, Cloncurry, Birdsville, Innamincka and Broken Hill—a journey of thousands of miles across the inland. As a result of his report other travelling ministers were employed to serve the Australian Inland Mission, and nursing homes were planned.

Flynn and others saw the possibilities of aircraft as early as 1912. He was particularly encouraged by an Australian Flying Corps pilot, Clifford Peel, who had been a medical student and was killed later while flying in France in 1918. It was evident even in those days that the use of aircraft was feasible, but there was not much point in having an aeroplane standing by if messages to get it flying were to take days or weeks to be delivered to its base. There

was little hope that the government would string telegraph wires all over the inland; so the AIM dreamers examined the possibilities of that other turn-of-the-century invention, wireless. But this was still in its infancy, expensive, complicated and bulky: they would have to wait until some genius produced a set that could be operated by amateurs in country where there was no electric power.

Meanwhile, in 1920, the Queensland And Northern Territory Aerial Service Limited (QANTAS) began operating, carrying mail, passengers and goods, providing the new era with regular, accident-free flights. In 1922 an Aerial Medical Services Fund was launched to 'stimulate local endeavour in making medical aid available to Australia's isolated pioneers'—one of the efforts of many organisations and individuals to lay the foundations of a remarkable service which would fly out doctors in answer to a radio signal. There followed the financial backing of H V McKay, the aviation advice and assistance of the QANTAS founder, Hudson Fysh, and the radio know-how of Amalgamated Wireless, offered by T E Fisk.

Then a genius came on the scene: Alf Traeger, who improved on the large, crude wireless sets with which experiments had been made in the outback. In 1927 he developed the pedal generator. The following year he and Flynn set out in the Dodge to show the pedal sets to station people and instruct them in the use of Morse. In 1929 there were eight sets installed at various points in the Gulf country and western Queensland, with Cloncurry established as the home station; more nursing homes had been established and, two years earlier, a doctor had actually flown to a case.

Dr George Simpson had grown up on an outback cattle station and, because of his interest in the work of Flynn and other Inland ministers and priests, had become

medical adviser to the AIM. Visiting Cloncurry in June 1927, he heard that a miner at Mount Isa had broken his pelvis and QANTAS flew him out in a D.H.50 to bring the man to Cloncurry—a flight that persuaded an influential Mission sub committee to recommend the immediate formation of a flying doctor service. Applicants for the post of resident doctor were offered £1,000 for a trial year, and the same amount was accepted by QANTAS to provide a D.H.50 and a pilot for the doctor's use. A surgeon, K St Vincent Welch, was appointed, and on 15 May 1928 he started work as the world's first flying doctor. In the next twelve months Welch made 50 flights, saw 250 patients and logged 20,000 flying miles (32,200 km).

Despite the depression, the second World War and long droughts—which also dried up some of the financial backing—the Aerial Medical Services expanded: in 1936 mileage flown was 36,800 (59,220 km); the following year, when a second aircraft was based at Normantown, the figure rose to 47,600 (76,600 km). Fox Moths had been introduced in 1934, replacing the old D.H.50, and in that year wireless was also installed in one of the aircraft. In 1936 radio-telephones were introduced. As the service expanded into each state and a Federal Council was formed, the demand increased for more aircraft with the desirable characteristics of low landing speed, short take-off for use on station paddocks, and cabin space for stretcher and patient, doctor, nurse, a passenger and medical and wireless cabinets. de Havilland Dragons were the first twin-engined aircraft used in 1960 three-engined Drovers (a version of the Dove) went into service in NSW and Queensland; and the most useful single-engined aircraft has been the Cessna 182.

Some cattle and sheep stations have excellent landing fields, with permanent wind-socks; but sometimes an aircraft has to land on a strange paddock to pick up injured patients who cannot be moved. Then a fire is lit, so that the smoke indicates wind direction, and the pilot relies on a local estimation of ground surface. People living in the outback usually contribute annually to an ambulance fund, the rest coming from large Federal Government grants, trusts, bequests, gifts and donation (one grazier left £30,000 to the RFDS) to pay for this non-profit-making, public benefit organisation.

Today, the two largest areas of the Royal Flying Doctor Service (the 'Royal' prefix was granted by Queen Elizabeth in 1955) are the Broken Hill and Darwin branches each serving an area of over half a million square miles (1,295,000 km²). Miles flown annually by all the branches' aircraft exceed 500,000 (804,670 km), carrying more than 1,000 patients; the doctors usually make over 10,000 consultations and from 12 bases are in radio contact with some 1,300 outposts. Furthermore, the service founded by John Flynn has its modern counterparts all over the globe, often staffed by Christian missionaries but flourishing also in countries of the Communist *bloc*.

The end of two inter-war decades came when a Bristol Blenheim IV, like this, became the first RAF aeroplane to cross the German frontier on a wartime reconnaissance mission, on 3 September 1939

20 Years on

OPERATING FROM AN AIRFIELD at Chemy, France, on the night of 10/11 November 1918, a force of Handley Page O/400 bombers attacked the railway sidings and junction at Louvain. Many direct hits were claimed for the 112 112-lb (51-kg) bombs dropped by the squadron, and an ammunition train was hit, causing (in the words of the official communiqué) 'explosions and fires all over the sidings'.

Flying from the RAF base at Wattisham, Suffolk, a force of Bristol Blenheims attacked German warships near Wilhelmshafen on 4 September 1939. Using 500-lb (227-kg) bombs, they achieved hits on the pocket battleship *von Scheer*, but little other success.

These two events—the last operation by the Royal Air Force in the first World War and its first bombing raid in the second World War—provide a yardstick by which to measure some of the advances made in military aircraft development in the intervening 21 years.

The Handley Page O/400 of 1918 was Britain's standard heavy bomber of the first World War. A large biplane, with a span of 100 ft (30.5 m) on the upper wing, it was powered by two Rolls-Royce Eagles or alternative engines of 250-350 hp each. A crew of three was usually carried, there being an open cockpit seating two side-by-side and open gunners' cockpits in the extreme nose and in the fuselage behind the wings. The guns were mounted on Scarff rings which allowed them to be swivelled through a 360-degree arc, and another gun was mounted in the underside of the fuselage to fire downwards and aft.

The O/400 could carry sixteen 112-lb bombs inside the fuselage, the bomb-bay being covered by spring-loaded doors which opened under the weight of the bombs as they were released. Other combinations of larger bombs could be carried, up to a single example of the 1,650-lb (750-kg) bomb which was the largest used by the RAF in that war. Two more bombs could be carried on external racks under the fuse-

lage. With a gross weight of about 13,500 lb (6,125 kg), the O/400 could reach a speed, flat out, of nearly 100 mph (160 km/h) and had a range of about 600 miles (965 km). Construction was of wood, with fabric covering.

The Blenheim IV with which the RAF entered the second World War was, by contrast, a sleek, all-metal monoplane powered by two Bristol Mercury radial engines, each giving 920 hp. Carrying a crew of three, the Blenheim had a span of only 56 ft 4 in (17.17 m) but the gross weight was about the same as that of the O/400. Maximum speed was 262 mph (422 km/h) and range 1,800 miles (2,895 km). A 1,000-lb (454-kg) bomb load could be carried and defensive armament included a pair of guns in a dorsal turret.

Even the Blenheim was far from being the last word in bombers in 1939. The RAF already had the larger Wellington in service and the first of the real 'heavies', the Manchester and Stirling, were under development. In fighter design, even more dramatic progress could be demonstrated between the Fokkers and Sopwiths of the Kaiser's war and the Messerschmitts and Hawkers of Hitler's war. The joining of combat between the world's major powers in 1939 added even greater impetus to aircraft development, concentrating into the few years which followed at least as much progress as had been achieved in the two previous decades.

In times of peace, military budgets are frequently kept down to such levels that innovation appears to be thwarted. Nevertheless, it is the demands of military aviation which have consistently set the pace of aviation development, and even the years of uneasy peace between 1919 and 1939 failed to put a brake on this process.

The evolution of air power in those interwar decades followed two interdependent paths. One depended on the progress made by designers and engineers, making possible a steady advance in aircraft performance. Hand-in-hand with this progress was the growing awareness in the minds of military

Above: Taken from the rear gun position of a Virginia bomber approaching Weybridge, this photograph illustrates dramatically the revolution in design that divided such machines from the high-speed metal monoplanes of 1939. Weybridge housed, inside the famous Brooklands motor racing circuit, factories of both the Vickers and Hawker companies

Far left: Typical of the new warplanes of the late 'thirties, the Blenheim IV had a retractable undercarriage and a turret for its dorsal machine-gun. Top speed was 266 mph (428 km/h) compared with the Virginia's 108 mph (174 km/h)

Upper left: Slow and lumbering though they were, the RAF's Virginias were formidable heavy night bombers in their heyday, in the 'twenties, and made a brave sight in formation during exercises. The final, Mk.X version, while still fabric-covered, changed from wood to metal construction

Lower left: Last of the RAF's biplane heavy bombers was the Handley Page Heyford. To facilitate re-arming, its 1,660-2,660 lb bomb-load was stowed in the thickened centre-section of the bottom wing, which was close to the ground as a result of mounting the fuselage under the upper wing. A retractable under-fuselage 'dustbin' gun-turret helped to ensure all-round defence

Willy Messerschmitt's early Bf 109 fighter was one of the combat types tested by the *Luftwaffe* in Spain during the Civil War. Lessons learned were embodied in the improved Bf 109E version, shown here, which was to prove itself superior to all but the very best Allied fighters in 1940

Below: A further warning of the quality of the new *Luftwaffe* was given in 1937 when a Dornier Do 17 bomber outflew a French D.510 fighter—then considered the best in Europe—at a military aircraft competition in Zurich

Above right, top to bottom:
The Hawker biplanes of the 'thirties, such as this High Speed Fury, were fine aircraft. The magnitude of the re-equipment problem that faced the RAF is indicated by the fact that they outnumbered all other combat types in service at the time Hitler revealed the existence of the *Luftwaffe*—created in defiance of the Versailles Treaty and already switching to monoplane designs

The Boeing P-12F of 1932 was typical of the racy, radial-engined biplanes beloved of American military formations. Even when it was superseded by monoplanes, they still retained its armament of only two machine-guns, unchanged since the first World War

Another of the German types sent to Spain, the Heinkel He 111B twin-engined bomber could outfly all opposing fighters and needed no escort. This led to over-confidence when other He 111s had to face Spitfires and Hurricanes in the Battle of Britain a few years later

Although it never had an opportunity to prove itself in action in the 'thirties, the Martin B-10 was the aircraft which pointed the way to the whole new generation of clean metal monoplane bombers with retractable undercarriage

strategists of the role which could be played by air power.

The first World War had given only a glimpse of the possibilities. Bombing raids by both sides had little strategic or tactical effect on the outcome of ground battles; air-to-air fighting, while deadly in its purport, was an extension of the jousting by chivalrous knights of a former age rather than a significant aid to winning the war in the trenches below. The most important role of the aeroplane from 1914 to 1918 was reconnaissance—a means of extending the battlefield commander's line of sight over the horizon.

In a world still suffering the trauma of the 1914-18 War, the prophets of air power found scant support for their views in the years which followed. After General 'Billy' Mitchell showed that bombers could sink battleships, and thus usurp the traditional role of the Fleet, he was court-martialled, thus sharing the fate of heretics down the ages. But hide-bound generals and admirals

could do nothing to prevent aircraft designers dreaming their dreams and, here and there, putting their theories into practice.

Thus, in America, in Britain, in France, in Russia and, clandestinely, in Germany, were forged the tools which, in 1939-45, would provide the key to victory or defeat. All the ingredients were already there in the aeroplanes of 1918—it was only a question of how they were mixed, refined and improved.

The Bristol Blenheim, already mentioned for its early operational role in 1939, was one of the pace-setting aeroplanes of the inter-war decades. When its prototype, the Bristol 142 *Britain First*, was tested by the RAF in 1935, it was found to be a full 50 mph (80 km/h) faster (while carrying a full load) than the Gloster Gladiator fighter which the RAF had only recently put into service.

Significantly, the Bristol 142 design was a private venture, and not the outcome of an official requirement—although it was,

Blenheim Is in production at Filton, Bristol, in 1938. Britain's massive re-armament programme came almost too late. Fortunately, what the RAF lacked in quantity it made up in the quality of its new aircraft

Below: On the other side of the Atlantic, the Boeing Y1B-17, then a 'Flying Fortress' in name only, hinted at the great fleets of four-engined bombers that were to show unmistakably the war-winning potential of air power in the global conflict to come

of course, gladly adopted by the RAF once it had been demonstrated. Almost every major advance in military aircraft design has similarly resulted from the enterprise of designers and private companies who have been able to see possibilities beyond the stereotyped official view. This was true to a greater or lesser extent of such aeroplanes as the Hawker Hurricane, Supermarine Spitfire, Martin B-10/B-12 bombers, Boeing Flying Fortress and Avro Lancaster, among others.

The revolution in aircraft design in this period had many aspects. The end result was a series of aeroplanes which could fly faster and higher, go farther, carry a bigger load and operate under a variety of conditions by day or night. These advances were made possible by such innovations as monocoque light alloy structures, cantilever monoplane wings, retractable undercarriages, enclosed cockpits, powered gun turrets, wing flaps, variable-pitch propellers, engine superchargers, and a range of flying

and navigation aids including the autopilot. All these developments were forged in the inter-war period and had been adopted as standard features by 1939.

While aircraft design and performance thus followed a fairly clearly-defined upward curve, with military types at the head of the progression, the way in which these new types should be deployed was seen less clearly. The first World War ended, as already noted, with the aeroplane firmly established as a tool to aid armies and navies to fulfil their time-honoured, earth-bound roles. The concept of air power as a third, and perhaps the most important, force in a nation's armoury, were only slowly appreciated, largely because the peace-time activities of the world's air forces gave little opportunity for the potential of the new weapon to be displayed.

This explains the intense interest which was aroused by the air actions during the Spanish Civil War and the Italian attack on Abyssinia. The latter was strictly a one-sided affair, giving a frightening foretaste of the effectiveness of uninhibited bombing of civilian targets which reached its peak over Hiroshima and Nagasaki a decade later. But in Spain, with Nationalist and Republican forces both strong enough to purchase and operate modern combat aircraft, a microcosm of modern aerial warfare was on view.

Seeing in this conflict an opportunity to obtain vitally useful operational data on their new warplanes, most of the major

nations made aircraft available to the Spanish combatants, either openly or covertly. One result was that an extraordinary mixture of British, French, German, Italian, Russian and American types operated alongside or in opposition to each other. More significantly, however, pilots of some of these nations, and Germany in particular, gained combat experience in Spain which left them in no doubt that superiority in the air had become an essential prerequisite for success in a ground battle.

This was the undeniable consequence of the increased lethality with which designers had endowed their newest creations. How well Germany learned the lesson was shown by the *Blitzkrieg* attacks on her European neighbours in 1939-40.

Further refinements in aircraft design, accelerated by the urgency of the all-out war which followed, brought the military aeroplane to the pinnacle of its importance; but it was the groundwork laid in the two previous decades that made it all possible.

HENDON'S HEYDAY

ON A RECENT DISMAL winter afternoon the writer had a business engagement in Colindale Avenue, Hendon, north-west London. Though much development has taken place in recent times this thoroughfare does little to uplift the heart, and certainly not on a dreary winter day—until one glimpses at the eastern end the erstwhile London Aerodrome, latterly Royal Air Force Hendon and the scene of the never-to-be-forgotten RAF Pageants and Displays. Then the imagination and the spirits soar up and away across the years.

In the mind's eye it is nearing noon on a Saturday in summer. The press of people gathering to view the 1937 RAF Display is already great. Vendors of ice cream, and of wholly bogus programmes, do nothing to alleviate the crush; but entrance is gained at length, and the well-loved London Aerodrome, which still exhibits much of its early character, lies fully in view.

Imagination once again transforms the scene to an even earlier occasion, as the fabulous Frenchman Louis Paulhan departs in his Farman from a spot nearby on an April day in 1910 to wrest from Claude Grahame-White the *Daily Mail* prize for a London-Manchester flight. Then Grahame-White himself appears, gazing from a point near Hendon church, across the valley, upon the site of the flying ground he is deciding to establish. The delights and thrills of the flying meetings that ensued have already been recorded; we may now imagine ourselves there once again, at the RAF Display of 1937.

Near at hand, on entering, is the New Types Park, fraught with secrecy; away to the left the western enclosures, prices 5 shillings or 2 shillings. The 10-shilling enclosure, with boxes 1 to 248 flanking the Royal Enclosure, stretches off to the right; across the grass field, along the northern boundary, a train goes puffing and whistling through the heat haze of the railway. More enclosures line this boundary, and off to the northern end is the park for participating aircraft. Rising beyond this again is Mill Hill, with crowds assembling for a view of the imminent proceedings at no more cost than a sunburn.

This, then, is the Hendon dear to hundreds of thousands; so with a glossy official programme, procured for a shilling from a pink-cheeked aircraftman and resplendent in the cover reproduced opposite, we await events.

The preliminary events, which are lettered, begin at 12.15; the main, numbered ones at 3 pm. Event A is the Headquarters Race. In a field which includes Bristol Blenheim and Fairey Battle bombers, Gloster Gladiator fighters and a Super-

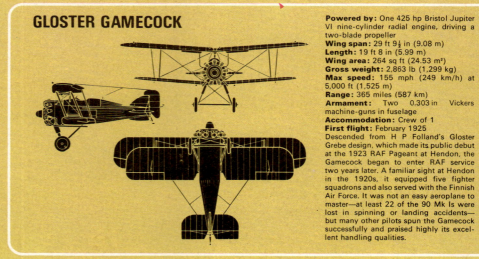

GLOSTER GAMECOCK

Powered by: One 425 hp Bristol Jupiter VI nine-cylinder radial engine, driving a two-blade propeller
Wing span: 29 ft 9½ in (9.08 m)
Length: 19 ft 8 in (5.99 m)
Wing area: 264 sq ft (24.53 m²)
Gross weight: 2,863 lb (1,299 kg)
Max speed: 155 mph (249 km/h) at 5,000 ft (1,525 m)
Range: 365 miles (587 km)
Armament: Two 0.303 in Vickers machine-guns in fuselage
Accommodation: Crew of 1
First flight: February 1925
Descended from H P Folland's Gloster Grebe design, which made its public debut at the 1923 RAF Pageant at Hendon, the Gamecock began to enter RAF service two years later. A familiar sight at Hendon in the 1920s, it equipped five fighter squadrons and also served with the Finnish Air Force. It was not an easy aeroplane to master—at least 22 of the 90 Mk Is were lost in spinning or landing accidents—but many other pilots spun the Gamecock successfully and praised highly its excellent handling qualities.

marine Walrus amphibian, the winner proves to be a Hawker Hart: average speed 164 mph (264 km/h).

'Individual Aerobatics' is the title of the next event, the programme listing the manoeuvres performed by a glinting Hawker Fury as a dive; upward roll—loop out—dive; half-roll off top of a loop; loop; aileron turn; rocket loop; stall turn; slow roll; climbing turn; slow roll (pausing inverted before rolling out); half roll; 45 degrees roll—change direction and dive; half upward roll—loop out; and finally, steep turn to right and left.

The day is a still one, and the absence of wind gives no benefit to contestants in the Landing Competition, involving Hawker two-seaters. The pilots, explains the programme, 'are required to land their aircraft, without the assistance of the engine, over a tape which is six feet (1.83 m) above the ground, between two hurdles'.

In a demonstration of air gunnery training, a Fairey Gordon streams a canvas sleeve target 300 yards (275 m) astern while six Gloster Gauntlets make passes, firing blank ammunition. The demonstration being completed, the target is released over the 'aerodrome', as the programme styles this romantic old airfield.

Eighty gallons (365 litres) a minute is the announced rate of 'Refuelling in the Air', now demonstrated by two bombers—an Overstrand and the Vickers B.19/27. The olive-green Vickers was rejected as a standard RAF type and is serving out its time at the Royal Aircraft Establishment.

Events F, G and H are, respectively, a dive-bombing competition, in which the victorious Hawker Hind achieves an average error of only 8.75 yards (8.0 m) with its four smoke-filled bombs; an 'air combat', with three Hawker Demons of the Auxiliary Air Force (not yet 'Royal') harassing an Overstrand bomber, which itself manoeuvres like a fighter; and a demonstration of army co-operation, with a squadron of the new Hawker Hectors dropping supply containers and picking up messages with their trailing hooks.

All this excitement—and the main events have yet to begin.

'Event 1, Mass Flight' proclaims the programme, 'A fly-past of 250 aircraft . . . The mass will fly across Hendon Aerodrome once only from north-west to south-east.'

'Mass' indeed is the word for this cavalcade of Britain's fast-growing might. Ansons, Harrows, Hinds, Gauntlets—a procession three-quarters of a mile (1.2 km) long and over half a mile (0.80 km) wide, steady at 130 mph (209 km/h). 'Undoubtedly the most impressive flying spectacle ever seen in this country', notes down a journalist, gazing aloft from the doorway of the Press Tent, oblivious for a minute of its hospitality.

And now for something a little more intimate, with some silly ass, addressed by his 'instructor' as Peabody, committing outrages on a Hart Trainer. Then 'Smoke', as the programme labels Event 3, involving five Gauntlets in evolutions with that substance. They even manage the Royal Cipher—the crown and 'GR'.

Above: Close formation flying by Gloster Gauntlets of No 19 Squadron, the first to equip with the type in May 1935. Fastest RAF fighters in service, Gauntlets took over from Bulldogs the traditional display of formation aerobatics at Hendon, using coloured smoke trails

Left: One of the new Blenheim bombers graced the front cover of the official programme for the last Royal Air Force Display at Hendon, in June 1937. Inside were proud advertisements by great companies like Bristol, Supermarine, Vickers, Handley Page and de Havilland, whose products were soon to fight and win a great war but whose very names would disappear later during industrial upheavals. An Austin Fourteen saloon car was advertised at £235, with no purchase tax. Imperial Airways proclaimed that their 'great new flying fleet' of Empire flying-boats had a top speed of nearly 200 mph (322 km/h). Event 12, the final Set Piece, timed for 5.5 pm, was headed 'England is at war with Blueland'. Within little more than two years Germany was to be Blueland and the bombs and bullets were to be real

ROYAL AIR FORCE DISPLAY

SAT. 26TH JUNE 1937

How Grahame-White would have loved it all.

No RAF Display is complete without the matronly old Vickers Virginia, and two of them come droning over 'to attack Hendon'. Gauntlets intercept; a 'Jinnie' falls, trailing smoke and parachutes. ('Virginia aircraft are used for parachute training on account of their suitability for this work' the programme advises us).

A turn of the page and we are warned: 'A noted big game shot accompanied by his tame dragon will demonstrate a typical day's shooting. The game are selected from a number of monsters said to be found in the stratosphere.'

Some excellent sport can be had with monster balloons, a shotgun and an old Farman biplane, but for sheer topsy-turveydom it would be difficult to surpass the ensuing 'Demonstration of inverted flying in formation by instructors from the Central Flying School'. If sound and fury are the required ingredients then Event 7, a low-flying attack by three squadrons of Hinds, provides them. Hawker biplanes, we note, dominate the entire programme, and four of the now-ageing, though ceaselessly fascinating, little Furies contribute an item the thrills of which are hardly conveyed by the mere title 'Formation Aerobatics'. The favoured formations are, in fact, 'diamond', 'line astern' and 'abreast'. Ageing or not, the Furies are mere chickens compared with the genuine, original Bristol Fighter, S.E.5a, Sopwith Triplane and L.V.G. which, together with the time-honoured 'Attack on Kite Balloons', take us back twenty years to grimmer times.

A shade mysteriously, for they were designed to intercept high-flying bombers,

Furies once again come on the scene. Is the programme compiler having a private joke with 'intercept'? 'A band of pirates having carried out a successful raid on a river steamer up-country is returning home with the loot. A fighter squadron is called out to intercept and to deal with the band. The squadron intercepts the pirates and carries out a low-flying attack upon them.'

Whether climbing at bombers or diving at pirates, the Fury thrills; and in any case how far can fantasy be removed from grim reality, for among the 'New and Experimental Types' listed as participating in Event 11 is an unnamed Blackburn fighter/dive-bomber. What no-one present knows is that, just over two years hence, one of these aircraft, by this time named Skua, is to become the first British aeroplane to shoot down an enemy machine in the second World War.

But, here at Hendon in 1937, war is finally represented, as always, by the Set Piece. In face of anti-aircraft fire and a section of the new Balloon Barrage, Vildebeests sweep in to torpedo the lock gates of a port. Whitleys, Wellesleys and Blenheims bomb; Hinds dive-bomb; Gladiators and Demons intercept. Seven squadrons of the Royal Air Force to give a grand finale to the grandest Display of the series.

A day to remember; and remember it we may, for this was to be the last of all the great Hendon events. The RAF was becoming increasingly preoccupied with the rearmament programme, and, with much faster aircraft in prospect, and demanding ever more sky space, the same intimacy of presentation could no longer be contemplated. But, before memory fades, we may recall some of the thrills of former years.

For many of these we have to thank Major Sandbags, with his heart-stopping bale-outs from his stricken kite balloon, the first drop having been made at the first Pageant, of 1920. (The term Display was adopted later to emphasise that the occasion had become no circus performance but the culmination of a year's training.)

There was, too, the shattering converging bombing by Fairey Flycatchers of the Fleet Air Arm, matched by the screaming low-level attacks by Fairey Foxes. Great flying-boats came booming in from the sea, and in 1930 that doomed leviathan the airship R101 rode serenely in the summer sky. Royalty attended often: HRH Prince Henry was present at the very first Pageant, and in 1925 King George V directed by wireless the manoeuvres of a squadron of Gloster Grebes. In 1920 the occasion was graced by 21-year-old Miss Sylvia Boyden, who dropped in by parachute, and the great Harry Hawker performed aerobatics in his Sopwith Swallow. Strange shapes appeared, an early Autogiro and the tailless Westland-Hill Pterodactyl among them. In 1927 two Avro 504s put on a display of 'crazy flying' which set a popular pattern for later years. On the same occasion Siskins manoeuvred to music and no fewer than four Schneider Trophy pilots—D'Arcy Greig, Stainforth, Atcherley and Waghorn—flew inverted in Genet Moths. Sometimes the events had a particular technical interest, as for instance in 1928, when Siskins, some with super-charged and some with unsupercharged engines, had a climbing race.

Never again will the like of those displays be seen, though something of the spirit and tradition that pervaded them will yet be preserved at Hendon—in the RAF Museum.

VICKERS VIRGINIA

Powered by: Two 580 hp Napier Lion VB twelve-cylinder W-type engines, each driving a two-blade propeller
Wing span: 87 ft 8 in (26.72 m)
Length: 62 ft 3 in (18.97 m)
Wing area: 2,178 sq ft (202.35 m²)
Gross weight: 17,600 lb (7,983 kg)
Max speed: 108 mph (174 km/h) at 5,000 ft (1,525 m)
Range: 985 miles (1,585 km)
Armament: One 0.303 in Lewis machine-gun in nose and one or two in tail; up to 3,000 lb (1,360 kg) of bombs
Accommodation: Crew of 4

First flight: 24 November 1922
Intended as a long-range successor to the famous Vickers Vimy, the Virginia served with RAF bomber squadrons for 14 inter-war years, and a few were still flying as late as 1941. Of 126 Virginias built, in various models, 50 were Mk Xs (to which the data apply) and 53 of the earlier machines were converted to the same standard. One early experiment, not adopted for Service aircraft, was the fitting of 'fighting tops'—nacelles attached to the upper wings to carry two forward-firing and two rearward-firing machine-guns.

Opposite page: The 1933 counterpart of today's 'Red Arrows' was this team of instructors from the Central Flying School in three of the Avro Tutor trainers that had recently replaced Avro 504s of 1914-18 War vintage

This page, top: Hawker biplanes dominated the RAF Displays of the 'thirties, when they outnumbered all other combat types in RAF service. These Harts belonged to No 57 (Bomber) Squadron

Above: Pilots of No 19 Squadron giving dramatic proof of the fact that when the RAF claimed to fly its Gauntlets in close formation it meant just that

Below left: Retired Virginia bombers were used for parachute training and displays. They took off with the trainees standing on platforms, clutching the outer wing bracing struts. At the opportune moment, each man pulled his ripcord and was dragged off by the opening canopy

Below: Regular participants in the parade of flying-boats at Hendon, from 1933 to 1936, were Saro Cloud amphibians

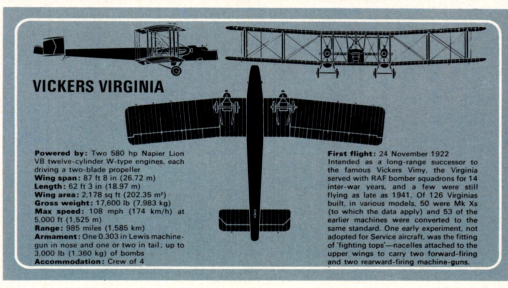

THE GROWTH IN AIRCRAFT ARMAMENT

THE FIRST GUN installed on an aeroplane appears to have been a very heavy one, even by modern standards. It was mounted on a Voisin biplane towards the end of 1910 but (mercifully, perhaps, for the crew) was never fired in the air. Nevertheless, a gun of 37-mm calibre was indeed fired from a Voisin before war came in 1914, and guns of this same bore were used fairly extensively by the French in action, mainly in free installations but also rigidly mounted on the Hispano-Suiza engines of Spad fighters, firing through the propeller shaft.

The favoured calibre for aircraft guns was, however, that of the common infantry rifle and machine-gun, and a Springfield '30-06' rifle was apparently the first firearm to be discharged in flight. The date was August 1910; the aircraft a Curtiss pusher biplane. Even before 1914 it was becoming clear that automatic weapons of similar calibre held the greatest promise for aerial use, and the first machine-gun fired in flight (from a Wright biplane in June 1912), was of the newly-invented Lewis drum-fed type. This American weapon was to prove the most successful of its kind used by the Allies in the coming war.

When the war began, no aircraft specifically designed to carry a gun was available to either side. Pistols, carbines, rifles and even shotguns were carried as personal weapons; somewhat later, rifles and Lewis guns were mounted (literally) in lash-up installations. The first truly historic development in air gunnery was the fitting of a

fixed machine-gun on one of Anthony Fokker's monoplanes, the firing mechanism being so synchronised with the engine as to allow the gun to fire between the revolving blades of the propeller. The classic type of fixed-gun fighter had thus arrived. Pilot, aeroplane and gun were now, as it were, all of a piece. Aim could be deadly, and deadly indeed was the 'Fokker scourge' of 1915-16.

With the development of synchronising gears in England, the belt-fed Vickers gun was adopted for fixed installations. Like the Fokker's LMG.08—the 'Spandau' beloved of fiction writers—it was based on the Maxim gun. Typical armament for a single-seat fighter as the war approached its end was twin, fixed, rifle-calibre machine-guns, mounted immediately ahead of the pilot so that he could attempt to clear stoppages in flight. Gun-heaters were developed to prevent the lubricating oil from freezing at high altitude, and ammunition belts composed of disintegrating metal links avoided the difficulty of disposing of the earlier continuous canvas belt. The gun-sights commonly fitted on Allied fighters were of the elementary ring-and-bead type and the Aldis tubular optical variety. This latter form of sight was not 'telescopic', as is commonly stated.

For free-gun installations many types of mounting were evolved, the most successful being that designed by Warrant Officer Scarff of the RNAS. This took the form of a rotating ring, encircling the gunner and carrying the gun (or sometimes twin

guns) on an arm, or bow, capable of elevation or depression.

For many years after the Armistice there were few developments of note in air gunnery. Economy dictated the using-up of war-surplus items, and, although a somewhat improved type of Vickers gun was adopted for the RAF, the standard fighter firepower in that Service remained virtually unchanged from the Sopwith Camel of 1917 to the Gloster Gauntlet of 1934. True, there was the much-publicised Gloster S.S.19 of 1931, with its two Vickers and four Lewis guns; but even this purely experimental installation had been anticipated by the Sopwith Snark of 1918.

Not until the mid-1930s were there any real advances in British fighter armament. During 1937 the first Gloster Gladiators entered service with four Browning guns, of the pattern adopted in succession to the Vickers; but a truly massive increase in firepower came about when no fewer than eight Brownings were specified for the Hurricane and Spitfire. This formidable battery was required by the Air Ministry because it was believed that a pilot would be able to hold his sight (by this time of the illuminated reflector type) 'on target' for a mere two seconds. Only eight Brownings, it was considered, could provide the required 'lethal dose'.

A size of gun favoured during the inter-war years in the USA and Italy was of about $\frac{1}{2}$-inch bore—what the Americans know as a 'fifty caliber'—and it was customary to

Opposite page, top: The Vickers Gunbus of 1915 was claimed to be the first aeroplane designed from the start to carry armament. As no-one had perfected a means of firing between the blades of a turning propeller, a front gun could be carried only by 'pusher' aircraft of this kind

Centre left: Machine-gun in the rear cockpit of a Blackburn Shark torpedo-spotter-reconnaissance aircraft of the mid-thirties

Centre right: Loading torpedoes on to a squadron of Vickers Vildebeest IVs of the RAF. Two Vildebeest squadrons were used in action against the Japanese invaders of Singapore as late as 1941

Bottom: One of the earliest 'big bombers', this 250 hp Short of the first World War could carry four 230 lb (104 kg) or eight 112 lb (51 kg) bombs and was armed with a single Lewis gun in the rear cockpit

This page, left: The 2,150 lb (975 kg) torpedo carried by the Hawker Horsley was the heaviest weapon of its kind fitted to any landplane when the type entered service in 1928

Below: Fitting a practice torpedo in place between the widely-splayed main undercarriage legs of a Horsley

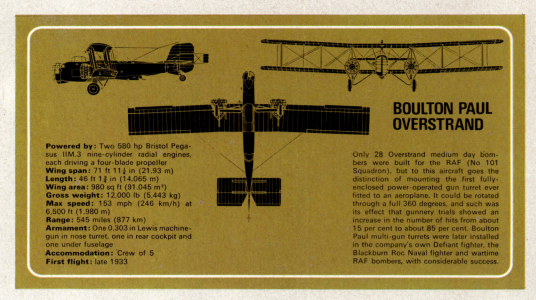

BOULTON PAUL OVERSTRAND

Powered by: Two 580 hp Bristol Pegasus IIM.3 nine-cylinder radial engines, each driving a four-blade propeller.
Wing span: 71 ft 11½ in (21.93 m)
Length: 46 ft 1¾ in (14.065 m)
Wing area: 980 sq ft (91.045 m²)
Gross weight: 12,000 lb (5,443 kg)
Max speed: 153 mph (246 km/h) at 6,500 ft (1,980 m)
Range: 545 miles (877 km)
Armament: One 0.303 in Lewis machine-gun in nose turret, one in rear cockpit and one under fuselage
Accommodation: Crew of 5
First flight: late 1933

Only 28 Overstrand medium day bombers were built for the RAF (No 101 Squadron), but to this aircraft goes the distinction of mounting the first fully-enclosed power-operated gun turret ever fitted to an aeroplane. It could be rotated through a full 360 degrees, and such was its effect that gunnery trials showed an increase in the number of hits from about 15 per cent to about 85 per cent. Boulton Paul multi-gun turrets were later installed in the company's own Defiant fighter, the Blackburn Roc Naval fighter and wartime RAF bombers, with considerable success.

mount a gun of this size alongside one of rifle calibre. In France and Germany, however, there was a growing conviction that a more desirable gun would be one of 20-mm calibre, capable of firing explosive ammunition. In the mid-1930s the French tried wing-mounted installations of a new type of 20-mm Hispano-Suiza gun, but found that the wings of fighters of the period were insufficiently stiff to give the desired accuracy of fire. So they continued to favour the engine-mounted installation, or *moteur canon*.

In 1936 a Dewoitine D.510 having such an installation was bought by the British Air Ministry, and later a licence was acquired to build the Hispano-Suiza gun in the United Kingdom. For many years thereafter the 'British-Hispano' was to be the principal weapon of British fighters, though it was not available in quantity for the Battle of Britain. The first British fighter designed specifically for the new gun was, in fact, the Westland Whirlwind; as an interceptor the type was unsuccessful, and the very dense concentration of fire afforded by four 20-mm guns grouped closely in the fuselage nose was employed mainly against ground targets.

When the German Air Force was newly re-created in the early 1930s its first fighters to enter service were biplanes with two rifle-calibre machine-guns; but as thoughts turned to monoplanes, and in particular to the Bf 109, so they turned likewise to 20-mm guns, and a Swiss Oerlikon gun of this calibre was adopted. This was a less hard-hitting gun than the Hispano-Suiza, but was very compact, and fitted well into the wing of the Bf 109. The standard armament of that fighter as used in the Battle of Britain was, in fact, two 20-mm guns in the wing and two of rifle calibre in the fuselage; but the assertion that this armament was 'proved in the Spanish Civil War' is erroneous, for when used in Spain the Bf 109 was armed only with rifle-calibre machine-guns.

One of the most remarkable innovations in the 1930s was the introduction of the power-driven gun turret, enabling the gunner to aim without effort and in comfort. Though the turret in the nose of Britain's Boulton Paul Overstrand bomber is generally hailed as revolutionary in this

respect, it must nevertheless be recorded that it was based on French ideas. This was less true of the Frazer-Nash turret installed later on the Hawker Demon two-seater fighter—a forerunner of the 'F-N' turrets familiar on British bombers of the second World War.

The earliest record of bomb-dropping from an aeroplane appears to be the following item in an American newspaper, dated January 1910: 'On Wednesday of last week M Paulhan carried Lt Beck of the US Artillery as passenger on his Henry Farman in order that experiments might be made in the dropping of dummy bombs'. The first live bomb was almost certainly dropped by Lt Myron S Crissy, US Army, in January 1911, and the first bombing raids in warfare were made by the Italians in November of the same year.

Most successful among the bombs developed in the ensuing months was that designed by the Englishman Frederick Marten Hale, who had earlier produced a rifle grenade of a type which was numbered among the heterogeneous collection of weapons pressed into aerial service on the outbreak of war. In British service the Hale's bombs, as they were known, were succeeded by numerous types designed at the Royal Laboratory, and bearing 'RL' designations.

Typical bombs in British service at the war's end were: HERL 250 lb Mk I; HERL 112 lb Mk III; HE Cooper 20 lb; 40 lb Phosphorous Mk I; Baby Incendiary 6½ oz; Thermalloy Incendiary, 34 lb; Bomb, HE 520 lb (Light Case). Generally speaking the HE (high-explosive) bombs were intended for the demolition of such targets as buildings and communications systems and for attacks on submarines, for which there were special adaptations. The Cooper bomb was the outstanding example of the fragmentation type, for use against personnel, and was carried by fighters as well as by bombers. Incendiary bombs, which in some early instances had been filled with petrol, were of several types; and there were special bombs for producing smoke. AP (armour-piercing) and 'SAP' (semi-armour-piercing) bombs were introduced for attacking warships.

One of the earliest practical bomb-sights was developed at the Central Flying School,

as were some of the earliest bomb-carriers; but the best-known sight, which served the RAF in the 1920s and 1930s, was the Wimperis course-setting sight, known in the Service as 'CSBS'. The earliest bombs were dropped by hand, and later by pulling a toggle; but in the 1930s electrical release came into general use. There were numerous types of stowage: if carried externally the bombs were generally horizontal; if internally, either horizontal or suspended vertically by the nose.

The gun and the bomb were quickly joined in the aeronautical armoury by the torpedo, of adapted naval type and bearing no relationship to the 'aerial torpedo' which existed only in popular imagination. The torpedo-dropping aeroplane was developed to its highest pitch in Great Britain. Following pioneering work by Naval officers and the Short and Sopwith companies, the Blackburn company was largely responsible not only for the design and production of suitable aircraft but for developing special methods of carrying, releasing and heating the torpedo, and adjusting it for depth of 'running' in the water. Notwithstanding assertions to the contrary, however, the Italians were the true pioneers of torpedo-dropping. General A Guidoni, one of the greatest names in Italian aeronautics, left record:

'I was ordered in 1912 to help Mr Pateras Pescara, who had suggested to the navy the building of a torpedo-plane. Mr Pescara was a lawyer. Had he been a technical man he would probably have been refused permission to try out his scheme. . . . With my faithful Farman I succeeded in dropping 170 lb (77 kg), so I concluded that with a machine of 6,000 lb (2,720 kg) total weight it would be possible to drop a small torpedo.' Having described the special seaplane he then built the general said: 'With this machine in February 1914 I succeeded in dropping a torpedo of 750 lb (340 kg); and perhaps this can be considered as the first torpedo launch.'

It can indeed be so considered.

Opposite page, top: First RAF bomber to have a power-operated gun turret was the Boulton Paul Overstrand

Bottom: The four-gun Nash and Thompson turret in the tail of the Armstrong Whitworth Whitley bomber. The guns were staggered to facilitate 'feeding' with the belts of ammunition

This page, left: Sir Kingsley Wood, Secretary of State for Air in 1939, tries his hand at firing the Vickers 'K' gun used by air observers. Rate of fire was 1,000-1,100 rounds a minute

Centre: A 2,000 lb (907 kg) bomb waiting to be stowed on board a Whitley of RAF Bomber Command in 1941

Bottom: First squadron to be equipped with Hawker Hurricanes in 1937, and hence the first to fly a modern eight-gun monoplane fighter, was No 111 of RAF Fighter Command

Zygmunt Pulawski
THE GREAT POLISH AIRCRAFT DESIGNER

DESTINED TO SHAPE ideas on Polish fighter aircraft for years to come, and to exercise a profound influence upon international fighter development in the early and middle 1930s, Zygmunt Pulawski was exceptional among the world's leading designers in achieving widespread recognition and acclaim in the space of only four years. By a cruel twist of fate, he died when he was twenty-nine years of age and only a debutant in the art of aircraft design; yet his achievements were already so great as to put him among the most outstanding of all Polish aviation engineers.

Son of a factory worker, Zygmunt Pulawski was born on 24 October 1901 in Lublin, where he left his gymnasium (secondary school) in 1919 to become an active member of the Polish Scouting movement. In 1920 he began advanced studies at the *Politechnika Warszawska* (Warsaw Technical University) and took part in the activities of the SL (Aviation Section of the University's Engineering Students' Circle). During his studies he gave private tuition to help his family, but still found time to evolve his first aviation projects and pursue intensive sporting activities, mainly swimming, rowing, skiing and mountaineering. In 1923-24 he de-

signed a glider, the S.L.3, for the second Polish glider contest, held in May-June 1925, but the machine, a simple and fragile structure weighing only 77 lb (35 kg), failed to achieve distinction. In 1924 he prepared a study for a two-seat army-support biplane for a combat aircraft design competition and his proposals, known as the 'Scout' and based upon a 450 hp Lorraine W-type engine, shared fourth place with Wojciechowski's 'Wujot' fighter when the results were declared in November 1925.

Pulawski graduated in 1925, and in view of his excellent academic progress and the promise shown by his imaginative 'Scout' project he was sent to the Breguet factory at Villacoublay, near Paris, to gain practical experience. After returning to Poland he completed his national service, during which he trained as a pilot and received his Polish Air Force 'wings'. In the autumn of 1927 he began work at the CWL company, which became the famous PZL concern at the beginning of the following year. An ambitious programme of aircraft design was undertaken by PZL, and Pulawski was entrusted with the task of developing a single-seat interceptor. The resulting study, designated P.1 and calling for construction entirely

of metal, reflected Pulawski's originality and brilliance of mind, and initiated the line of warplanes which were to place Poland in the forefront of international fighter development; progressively improved, they stayed in production until the second World War.

Pulawski selected a high-wing monoplane configuration and, in order to ensure the best possible view for the pilot, devised an ingenious gull-type arrangement which, subsequently patented, became widely known as the Polish or Pulawski wing. The inboard panels tapered sharply in chord and thickness towards the root, their thinnest sections sloping down to join the fuselage immediately behind the cylinder banks of the upright-Vee engine, thus eliminating the obstruction to vision imposed by the wing which was common to all other layouts.

Another unique feature of the P.1 was its use of an undercarriage of the so-called 'scissor' type, in which extension levers acted on oleo-pneumatic shock-absorbers placed on opposing sides inside the fuselage. This arrangement, also the subject of a PZL patent, combined considerable aerodynamic advantages with the protection of shock-absorbers from dust, low temperatures, etc.

The revolutionary P.1, powered by a 600 hp Hispano-Suiza Vee engine, made its first brief flight in August 1929, the first official flight taking place on 25 September. During early trials it recorded a maximum speed of 184.5 mph (297

Left to right: The PZL P.8/II, most formidable of the 'P' family, with a maximum speed of 217.5 mph (350 km/h)

Above: The PZL 12 (PZL-H) amphibian in which Zygmunt Pulawski lost his life

Below: A damaged P.24 of the Royal Hellenic Air Force captured by the Germans at the end of the Greek campaign. Such fighters played a vital part in the Greco-Italian War of 1940-41 and achieved notable successes against the Regia Aeronautica

Left to right: First fighter to display the revolutionary 'Pulawski wing' was the PZL P.1. This photograph shows the P.1/II second prototype in its original form, in the spring of 1930, with cream and red finish

Zygmunt Pulawski (left) and Col Jerzy Kossowski (centre) with the P.1/II, registered SP-ADO, which the latter flew in the International Fighter Contest at Bucharest in 1930

When it re-armed with aircraft of Pulawski design the Polish Air Force became the first in the world to convert entirely to all-metal monoplane fighters

Following the switch to radial engines, the P.7 was the first Pulawski type to go into quantity production for the Polish Air Force; 150 were delivered

km/h). The second, aerodynamically cleaner prototype, the P.1/II, achieved a considerable international success in the International Fighter Contest staged by the Romanian Air Force in Bucharest in June 1930 and proved superior on most counts to the best contemporary fighters.

At that time Poland was negotiating to obtain manufacturing rights for Bristol aero-engines, and Pulawski was instructed to adapt the basic design for radial power plants. This led to the P.6 and P.7, which employed new circular-section fuselages married to the wings, tail assembly and undercarriage of the P.1. The original Pulawski concept of the Vee-powered interceptor with a slim fuselage was still pursued in the form of the P.8, which appeared in the summer of 1931 and embodied a number of structural improvements aimed at reducing airframe weight. The second prototype, the P.8/II (which, fitted with a supercharged 500-800 hp Lorraine Petrel, represented the proposed P.9 production variant) was generally regarded as the most formidable of all the 'P' fighters, its maximum speed being 217.5 mph (350 km/h). The installation of a number of other high-powered liquid-cooled engines was investigated, and a study for the P.10 interceptor equipped with a Rolls-Royce Kestrel looked most promising. Unfortunately, in view of an official decision that Bristol power plants would be standardised in Poland, the Vee-engined fighter had to be abandoned in favour of its radial-powered counterpart.

Meanwhile two P.6 prototypes, each fitted with a low-altitude 450 hp Jupiter VIFH radial engine, and two P.7 prototypes with the high-altitude 485 hp Jupiter VIIF radial, were completed, the first P.6 flying in August and the first P.7 in October 1930. The P.7 was selected for quantity manufacture and a pre-production contract for ten was followed by further orders, bringing to 150 the total of P.7s delivered to the Polish Air Force. By the end of 1933, when rearmament with the P.7 was completed, the Polish first-line fighter force was the first in the world to be equipped entirely with all-metal monoplanes.

In 1930 Zygmunt Pulawski was requested to evolve a new development of his fighter design based upon the smaller-diameter, higher-powered Mercury radial, and this materialised as the P.11. Realising that the introduction of the wide circular-section fuselage and radial engine impaired visibility, he initiated studies for successive versions with a lowered engine and raised pilot's seat, these proposals leading eventually to the P.11c and P.24 series; but he was not to see his final fighter progeny. Passionately interested in light aircraft, Pulawski constructed a two-seat light amphibian for his own use. This machine, known initially as the P.Z.L.-H and later given an official designation, P.Z.L.12, crashed on its sixth flight and the life of Poland's most promising designer, who was piloting the aircraft, came to a tragic and untimely end.

Pulawski's ideas lived long after his death, inspiring new P.11 variants and the superior, cannon-armed P.24 interceptor.

The famous 'P' fighters, which combined revolutionary design features with an extremely advanced all-metal stressed-skin construction, and formed a link between strut-braced biplanes and fully-cantilever monoplanes, aroused tremendous international interest. Years ahead of their time, they were copied in a number of leading industrial countries of Europe and were purchased in substantial quantities by the air forces of Bulgaria, Greece, Romania and Turkey, being built under licence in the two latter states. A total of more than 750 PZL Pulawski-wing fighters were delivered to world air forces in the years 1932 to 1939, including 150 P.7s and 205 P.11s for the Polish Air Force; 56 P.24s (out of 60 ordered) for the Bulgarian Air Force; 36 P.24s for the Royal Hellenic Air Force; about 130 P.11s (including about 80 IAR-built) and 46 P.24s (including 40 IAR-built) for the Romanian Air Force; and about 140 P.24s (including about 100 Turkish-built) for the Turkish Air Force.

These large orders from abroad were perhaps the highest tribute to the genius of Pulawski, one of Poland's greatest aircraft designers, whose name will ever be associated with his pioneering work on fighter design in the inter-war years.

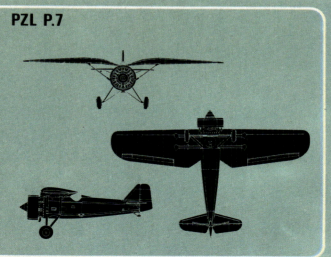

PZL P.7

Powered by: One 485 hp Polish-built Bristol Jupiter VIIF nine-cylinder radial engine, driving a two-blade propeller
Wing span: 33 ft 9½ in (10.30 m)
Length: 23 ft 6 in (7.16 m)
Wing area: 192.67 sq ft (17.90 m²)
Gross weight: 3,047 lb (1,382 kg)
Max speed: 200 mph (322 km/h) at 16,400 ft (5,000 m)
Range: 435 miles (700 km)
Accommodation: Crew of 1
Armament: Two 0.303 in Vickers machine-guns in forward fuselage
First flight: October 1930
First major production fighter to utilise the gull-wing concept developed by Zygmunt Pulawski, the P.7 entered service with the Polish Air Force at the end of 1932. It remained in service with the PAF, along with the later P.11, until the second World War, and large numbers of the developed P.24 were exported to neighbouring European countries. During 1933, all first-line squadrons of the PAF's four fighter Air Regiments were equipped with the P.7a, so becoming the first fighter force anywhere in the world to be equipped entirely with all-metal monoplanes.

Poland, the Phoney War and the Battle of France

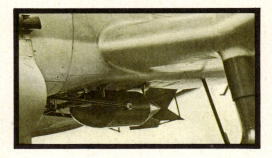

AT 04.30 HOURS on 1 September 1939 three Junkers Ju 87 dive-bombers from Germany's Stukageschwader 1 made an attack on Polish units around the bridge over the Vistula at Tczew; the second World War had begun.

The Poles had a total of just over 300 combat aircraft, comprising roughly equal numbers of fighters and bombers. Most of these, particularly the open-cockpit PZL machines which equipped the fighter units, were between three and seven years old and frankly obsolescent. Bad decisions at the highest level had left the Polish Air Force chronically weak in reserves, and had further dissipated the available forces by splitting them into 'penny packets' around the country, allocating fighter and bomber squadrons in ones and twos to the five Polish land armies. Only the Pursuit Brigade, based around Warsaw for defence of the capital, was in any condition to offer effective resistance; its five squadrons mustered some 50 machines, and were supported by an efficient warning and control system. The other units were spread so thinly that they could never enjoy even local superiority; when liaison and ground facilities broke down under the hammer blows of the Wehrmacht, these isolated groups could only make shift as best they could, and die—superbly.

The units of Kesselring's Luftflotte 1 and Löhr's Luftflotte 4 mustered an effective total of some 1,300 fighting aircraft, comprising 900 bombers and dive-bombers, 200 fighters committed to the offensive, and a further 200 fighters positioned to defend Germany against retaliation. The German estimates of Polish strength erred wildly, and the Luftwaffe was convinced it faced about 900 defending machines. Herein lay the seeds of the old myth that the Polish Air Force was bombed out of existence on the ground. Mobilisation sent the squadrons of the Lotnictwo Wojskowe from their peacetime bases to small combat airstrips which had largely eluded German reconnaissance. When the bases marked on their maps (and the carefully deployed dummy aircraft) had been left in cratered chaos, and when the Germans encountered only

some 150 fighters in the air, they assumed that the rest of those '900 aircraft' had been bombed to scrap. In fact the PZLs were almost exclusively destroyed in aerial combat between 1 and 16 September.

The bomber attacks on Polish airfields, factories, communications and troop concentrations which began on 1 September and continued—when the weather permitted—almost without cease for three weeks met with determined, but necessarily scattered, resistance. The thinly-spread Army Air Forces were hamstrung from the start, and made a really significant contribution only through their bombing attacks on advancing German troops; but the Pursuit Brigade showed by its success on 1 September what a Polish Air Force might have achieved if properly equipped and organised. Two major raids on Warsaw were turned back on that day; in the morning raid not a single bomb fell on the capital, in the afternoon only isolated flights penetrated the defences. Twelve raiding bombers were shot down (four others were destroyed by an Army Air Force squadron in the vicinity) for the loss of 10 PZLs destroyed and 24 damaged.

This success was not, sadly, to become the pattern for Polish defensive operations. The Army Air Forces were unable to offer serious resistance, although the courage with which the handfuls of fighters and bombers rose to contest the skies and to press home low-level raids on armoured columns was nothing less than suicidal. In individual spirit and determination the excellently - trained Polish aircrews were second to none in the world; but more than courage was needed when a thousand enemy aircraft invaded airspace defended by 150. Reduced to threes and fours, exhausted, without fuel, without ground handling and repair facilities, without replacements, bedevilled by conflicting orders, the squadrons bitterly conceded mile after mile.

By 16 September the 50 or so surviving Polish fighters were gathered near Lublin, and about 30 bombers were operating from fields in Volhynia. There was not enough fuel to get even a third of them into the air. The next day, in a long-planned move, Soviet Russia invaded eastern Poland and put paid to any last hope of establishing a defensive line. The surviving combat aircraft were flown into exile in Hungary and Romania by their crews, who now began a long and eventually doomed search for a way to save Poland by sacrificing themselves for the safety of foreign allies. The skies belonged to the Luftwaffe, and the ruthless use it made of that freedom should have warned the world that total war had begun in earnest.

The crucifixion of Poland had cost the Luftwaffe some 280 machines destroyed and a roughly similar number so badly damaged that they were eventually written off. The personnel casualties included 413 trained aircrew killed or missing. These losses lent weight to the orders which held the western front in stasis; to build up the strength of the squadrons would take time, and Luftwaffe units in the west were forbidden to seek combat. There were lessons to be digested; in particular, the effectiveness of obsolescent fighters, when flown with determination, had been greater than anticipated.

In the west the picture was one of hesitancy and indecision. Statesmen who had not yet faced the reality of war still hoped for a political settlement, and felt that their military obligations were fulfilled by maintaining a relatively peaceful status quo throughout the winter of 1939-40. German air activity over Britain was confined to isolated attacks of no real significance, on ports and shipping, and flights by single Dornier reconnaissance machines which played hide-and-seek with the RAF in the winter clouds. Two RAF formations—the Advanced Air Striking Force of Blenheim and Battle light bombers supported by Nos 1 and 73 Hurricane Squadrons, and Nos 85 and 87 Hurricane Squadrons supporting the Air Component in the extreme north-east of France—had been sent to the continent in September. French appeals for a larger contribution led to the despatch of two Gladiator squadrons to the Air Component in November. Air Marshal Dowding, commanding RAF Fighter Command, was even at this stage unwilling to weaken his Home Defence network by stripping it of any further Hurricanes.

The Allied fighter strength in France and the Low Countries in the spring of 1940 totalled perhaps 550 French types (of which the majority were obsolescent Morane-Saulnier MS.406 monoplanes, and only 36 were Dewoitine D.520s); some 40 Hurricanes and 20 Gladiators; and a few score Dutch and Belgian machines, of which not more than two dozen were of a quality even faintly comparable to current German equipment. When Hitler had secured his northern flank by occupying Norway and Denmark in April—a campaign involving a heroic but hopeless defence by pitifully weak Norwegian and RAF forces—he was free to concentrate on blitzkrieg in the west; and on 10 May 1940 the war stopped being a 'phoney' with shocking suddenness. The story is too well documented to repeat in detail here: the heavy and co-ordinated attacks on airfields, rail centres, aircraft factories and road bottlenecks; the constant strafing attacks by single- and twin-engined fighters; the surgical removal of strong-points and blocking positions by dive-bombers; the humiliating and exhausting retreat of the Allied squadrons from airfield to airfield, until only the sea lay behind them. In pure aviation terms there was no secret, no lesson to be learned—except that 1,000 modern fighters can beat 600 obsolescent ones.

The real lesson of German success in 1939 and the spring of 1940 was, in fact, that 'pure aviation' was secondary to the intelligent co-ordination of all arms—land, sea and air. Blitzkrieg was no magical formula by which defeat could be turned into victory, no secret technique by which the weaker could defeat the stronger. To succeed it required forces of comparable if not superior strength, and definitely superior equipment. It required an impetus to be built up through the elements of surprise, and maintained by tireless advance; its cumulative effect was everything, while each of its separate elements could have been defeated by the forces which opposed it, if dealt with in isolation. Long-range raids by medium bombers could be turned back or broken up; they were turned back at Warsaw, and they were later to be broken up over Kent.

Dive-bombers could not survive in skies defended by modern, co-ordinated fighter forces, well controlled and forewarned. Paratroop landings were necessarily of limited strength and lightly equipped, and could be isolated and engulfed by cool defenders before they could do serious harm—as in the early days of the battle for Crete. Strafing sweeps were harder to counter, but by themselves could not turn a determined defence into a rout. Yet the combination of all these types of operation, backed by strong ground forces advancing on unexpected axes and accompanied by their own mobile anti-aircraft batteries, proved overwhelming.

The defenders lacked a unifying command, a contingency plan, stable ground facilities and proven early warning networks; most of all they lacked the hardware. The attacker had been bending every sinew, for years on end, to build up large and well-trained forces equipped with the most modern equipment, and to shape those forces according to sound tactical principles. The defender had allowed his technology to starve and his tactical thinking to stagnate. Sheer technical brilliance is nothing unless the political will exists to back it, buy it, and consider how it may best be employed. It has been one of the great tragedies of our time that this will seems to grow lustily in the soil of dictatorships, and to wither and die in democracies.

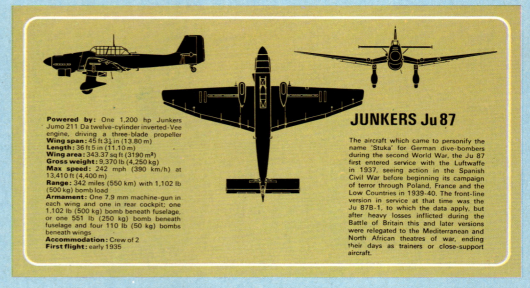

JUNKERS Ju 87

Powered by: One 1,200 hp Junkers Jumo 211 Da twelve-cylinder inverted-Vee engine, driving a three-blade propeller
Wing span: 45 ft 3¼ in (13.80 m)
Length: 36 ft 5 in (11.10 m)
Wing area: 343.37 sq ft (3190 m²)
Gross weight: 9,370 lb (4,250 kg)
Max speed: 242 mph (390 km/h) at 13,410 ft (4,400 m)
Range: 342 miles (550 km) with 1,102 lb (500 kg) bomb load
Armament: One 7.9 mm machine-gun in each wing and one in rear cockpit; one 1,102 lb (500 kg) bomb beneath fuselage, or one 551 lb (250 kg) bomb beneath fuselage and four 110 lb (50 kg) bombs beneath wings
Accommodation: Crew of 2
First flight: early 1935

The aircraft which came to personify the name 'Stuka' for German dive-bombers during the second World War, the Ju 87 first entered service with the Luftwaffe in 1937, seeing action in the Spanish Civil War before beginning its campaign of terror through Poland, France and the Low Countries in 1939-40. The front-line version in service at that time was the Ju 87B-1, to which the data apply, but after heavy losses inflicted during the Battle of Britain this and later versions were relegated to the Mediterranean and North African theatres of war, ending their days as trainers or close-support aircraft.

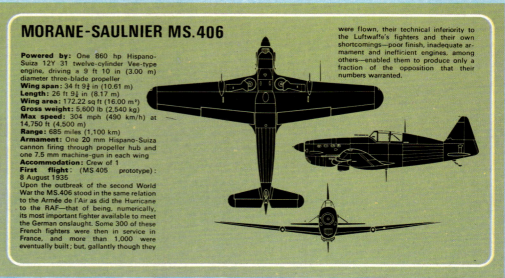

MORANE-SAULNIER MS.406

Powered by: One 860 hp Hispano-Suiza 12Y 31 twelve-cylinder Vee-type engine, driving a 9 ft 10 in (3.00 m) diameter three-blade propeller
Wing span: 34 ft 9¾ in (10.61 m)
Length: 26 ft 9½ in (8.17 m)
Wing area: 172.22 sq ft (16.00 m²)
Gross weight: 5,600 lb (2,540 kg)
Max speed: 304 mph (490 km/h) at 14,750 ft (4,500 m)
Range: 685 miles (1,100 km)
Armament: One 20 mm Hispano-Suiza cannon firing through propeller hub and one 7.5 mm machine-gun in each wing
Accommodation: Crew of 1
First flight: (MS 405 prototype): 8 August 1935

Upon the outbreak of the second World War the MS.406 stood in the same relation to the Armée de l'Air as did the Hurricane to the RAF—that of being, numerically, its most important fighter available to meet the German onslaught. Some 300 of these French fighters were then in service in France, and more than 1,000 were eventually built; but, gallantly though they were flown, their technical inferiority to the Luftwaffe's fighters and their own shortcomings—poor finish, inadequate armament and inefficient engines, among others—enabled them to produce only a fraction of the opposition that their numbers warranted.

Opposite page: Airmen of a Battle day-bomber unit of the RAF's Advanced Air Striking Force warm themselves by a fire in a truly Artic setting in France during the winter of the 'Phoney' war

This page, top left: The DC-2s and DC-3s of KLM proclaimed their nationality, and optimistic neutrality, in no uncertain manner in the autumn of 1939

Left: The Fairey Battles of the AASF were to pay dearly for their attempts to stem the German advance in May-June 1940. Excellent when first flown, they were outdated and almost defenceless by the outbreak of war

Above: A Morane-Saulnier MS.406 of one of the French squadrons that flew side-by-side with the AASF. Since nationalisation in the mid-thirties, the French aircraft industry had produced but a trickle of modern combat aircraft, though several fine designs had reached the prototype and pre-series stages

Below: By far the best of the French fighters in service in 1940 was the Dewoitine D.520, of which this example survives in the Musée de l'Air in Paris. Only 36 were operational at the time of the German blitzkrieg

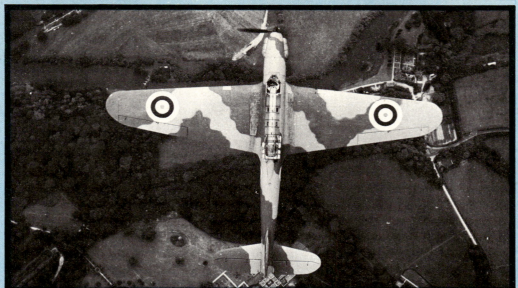

Battle of Scotland

IT IS NO EXAGGERATION to say that hundreds of books and thousands of articles have been written about the Battle of Britain (10 July–31 October 1940). So have a good few books and articles about the Battle of France in the months preceding the Battle of Britain, when a handful of RAF pilots fought alongside continental squadrons in a hopeless bid to halt the Luftwaffe. What students of aerial warfare have largely overlooked is the Battle of Scotland—the period from October 1939 to April 1940, before the Low Countries were overrun, when German aircraft, mostly Heinkel He 111s, approached Scotland on bombing and, more often, reconnaissance missions. The presence of warships in Scapa Flow and the Firth of Forth drew their attention. Additionally, merchantmen, trawlers, drifters and lightships were assailed.

The first (unexploded) German bombs found in the United Kingdom were recovered in the Shetland Isles in December 1939, having been dropped on 22 November when six German aircraft, flying a round trip of about 1,000 miles (1,600 km), attacked seaplanes at their moorings. The four bombs recovered weighed 110 lb (50 kg) apiece. Earlier, on 16 October, the Luftwaffe had made its first attempt to strike by air at the British Fleet in the Firth of Forth.

Winston Churchill in Vol I of *The Second World War: The Gathering Storm,* first published in 1948, said of this attack: 'Twelve or more machines in flights of two or three at a time . . . bombed our cruisers lying in the Firth . . . Twenty-five officers and sailors were killed or wounded; but four enemy bombers were brought down, three by our fighter squadrons and one by anti-aircraft fire . . . The following morning, the 17th, Scapa Flow was raided . . . Another enemy aircraft was shot down in flames . . .'

Two famous Scottish squadrons, fighting within sight of their families, grappled with the Luftwaffe on 16 October. They were Nos 602 (City of Glasgow) and 603 (City of Edinburgh) Auxiliary Squadrons, and they fought the first Fighter Command action of the war.

It was a section of 602 Squadron, patrolling the Firth of Forth over May Island between 10 and 11 am, that made the first sighting of enemy aircraft, possibly on reconnaissance. Bursts of fire from the guns of two of the Squadron's Spitfires broke up the enemy formation.

It was in the afternoon of 16 October, however, that the Germans made the first of the Firth of Forth raids, their targets being British naval units; and it was only by a matter of minutes that 602 lost to their friends and rivals of 603 the honour of bringing down the first enemy aircraft over these islands.

What happened was that one section of 602, patrolling over Dalkeith, engaged enemy aircraft. A dog-fight ensued, and one of the enemy aircraft crashed in the sea off Crail. Meanwhile 603 were in combat with other enemy aircraft, and a few minutes before 602's victory they brought down a Heinkel He 111 in the sea about four miles (6.4 km) south of Port Seton. The Air Officer Commanding-in-Chief, Fighter Command, Lord Dowding, sent them the following telegram: 'Well done. First blood to the Auxiliaries'.

Then, on 28 October 1939, the first enemy aircraft since the first World War was forced down on British soil. The victors were again the Edinburgh and Glasgow squadrons working as a pack.

Main credit for the victory—the fight took place on a Sunday and had the largest and best-dressed audience of any of the early air battles over the area—went to Flying Officer Archibald M'Kellar, DSO, DFC, of 602, of whom A B Austin in *Fighter Command,* published in 1941, said: 'He was the little Scots fighting man of the past, the Alan Breck build, with bonnet cocked against the world . . .' F G Nancarrow in *Glasgow's Fighter Squadron,* published in 1942, said of the forcing down by M'Kellar of this 1./KG26 Heinkel He 111 bomber: 'The German rear gunner, who had been fighting back, was suddenly silent . . . The big plane shuddered, lost height, climbed again to clear the roof of a farm house, and then slid on its belly up a sloping field. Once, almost as if it were trying to make the air again, the Heinkel soared, only to fall back mortally wounded. M'Kellar, triumphant, circled overhead'.

The Heinkel, which had its nose shattered, its back strained and its starboard tailplane wrenched off, was riddled with bullets. Two of the crew were dead, the pilot wounded, and the lucky observer unhurt but badly shaken. The exact spot was close to the Longyester-Humbie road near Kidlaw Farm, Gifford, East Lothian, in the Lammermuir Hills.

On 29 January 1940, the biggest bombing raid to date was made by German

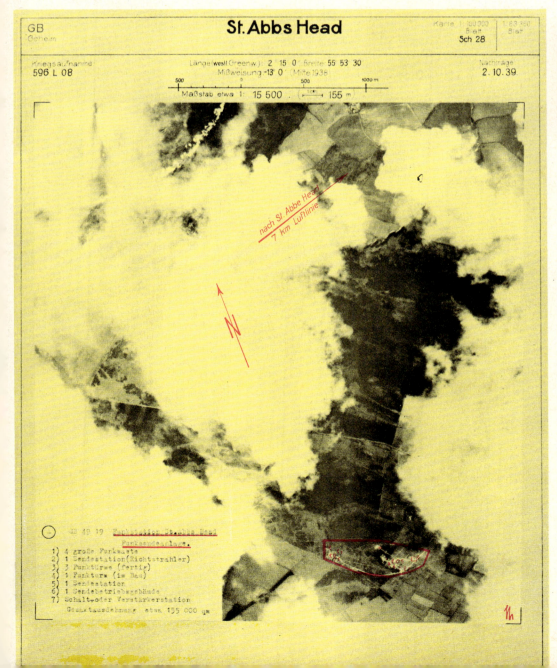

Opposite page: German vertical photograph of Leith docks, dated October 1939 and annotated with target data for Luftwaffe bomber formations. Similar photographs were taken over a high proportion of the potential target areas in the UK

This page, top and above: Two photographs of the Heinkel He 111 bomber forced down south of Edinburgh on 28 October 1939. This was the first enemy aircraft brought down on British soil in the second World War; bullet holes peppering the airframe bear testimony to the accurate shooting of the Auxiliary squadrons which intercepted it. Two of the four-man crew were killed, one badly injured.

Left: Dated 2 October 1939, this reconnaissance photograph shows the radar station at St Abb's Head. Had the enemy realised the important part that such installations were to play in the Battle of Britain, and concentrated his attacks on them, the course of history might have been changed

aircraft on north-east coastal shipping. Five separate attacks were launched involving, it was estimated, about 20 machines. Eight lightship men were killed.

It was near St Abbs Head, Berwickshire, on 22 February 1940, that an incident more typical of the first World War took place over lonely country. Squadron Leader Douglas Farquhar, DFC, of 602 Squadron, first sighted a reconnaissance He 111 off St Abbs Head and, on firing at it, took the first gun-camera pictures secured by Fighter Command for RAF records.

F G Nancarrow noted in *Glasgow's Fighter Squadron:* 'As Farquhar followed the side-slipping Heinkel down, he saw it had a good chance of landing safely some distance inland. He held his fire . . . The Heinkel landed, and Farquhar saw the crew climbing out. It then occurred to him that they would probably set fire to their machine . . . He decided to go down and prevent them doing so. But when the Spitfire landed alongside the Heinkel, its wheels bogged in marshy ground, and the fighter turned right over on its back. Farquhar, held by his shoulder straps, hung ingloriously upside down . . . The next thing of which he was aware was a pair of hands gripping him while others released his harness . . . His rescuers were the unwounded German aircrew who, having got out a comrade who had been hit in the legs, placed him some distance away and then fired the Heinkel so that its cameras were destroyed, leaving only the rear fuselage, tail, wings and engines.'

Then the squadron leader, having taken their revolvers, marched his prisoners to Lumsdaine Farm, Coldingham, near Eyemouth, where the wounded crew member was placed on the kitchen table and the others stood against the kitchen wall with their hands up. In 1966, when a survey was made of Scottish crash sites of the second World War, Mrs E M A Millican, who received the mixed party at her farm on 22 February 1940, produced a letter from Squadron Leader Farquhar, thanking her for her hospitality, and identification plates from the Heinkel, one of which showed that it was an He 111P (W Nr. 1594).

Of course, the Scottish squadrons—602 and 603—were not the only RAF units to engage German aircraft in the north during the period under review. Among others were Nos 43, 111 and 605 Squadrons. Airfields then in use included Castletown, Drem, Turnhouse and Wick.

On 16 March 1940, doubtless with the intention of damaging as many British vessels as possible before the invasion of Norway, German aircraft made a determined attack on Scapa Flow. In this attack, bombs which fell on the island of Hoy caused the first fatal casualties among British civilians.

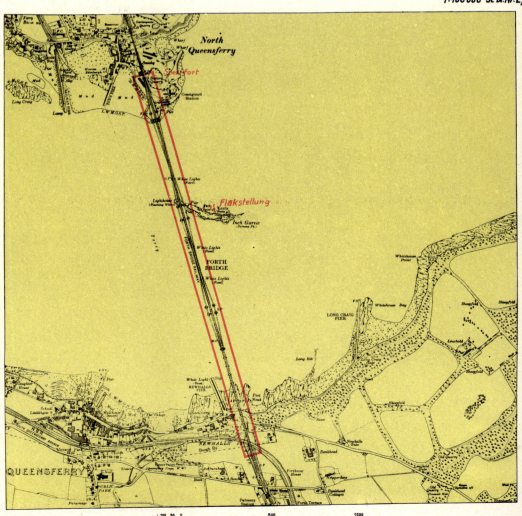

286

German aircraft making these early raids often fought with determination, and several dog-fights took place among the Scottish hills and down in the glens, the latter being a favourite refuge for Heinkels trying to shake off resolute RAF fighters. On one occasion, after a gallant fight at low level, a Heinkel He 111 passed over North Berwick and Dunbar, flying on one engine and heading for the sea. Others, however, gave up the contest more easily and presented the RAF with one or two early intact Heinkels. On 10 February 1940, after raiding shipping in the Firth of Forth, Heinkel 111 1H+EH of KG26 (Löwen-Geschwader) made a forced landing at North Berwick. It landed intact, ran parallel with a small hedge, and after bursting both tyres tipped gently on to its nose. This Heinkel, minus its wings, was towed away and later test-flown.

In the Scottish United Services Museum in The Castle, Edinburgh, there are several relics and trophies associated with 602 and 603 Squadrons. Among them is a German cigarette tin, with charred contents, presented to the museum in 1952 by No 602 Squadron. It came from the Coldingham Heinkel whose crew, in the best possible spirit, helped their victor when his Spitfire tipped up before their astonished eyes.

Opposite page, top: Target photograph of the Firth of Forth, dated October 1939. Warships at anchor can be seen clearly, as can the bridge, emphasised by the sun's shadow

Bottom: Plan of the Forth bridge, dated September 1939. Attention is drawn to an anti-aircraft gun emplacement (flakstellung) defending the area

This page, below: Luftwaffe yellow target brief for the Firth of Forth, dated September 1939

Top: Only slightly damaged, this Heinkel He 111 was brought down on 10 February 1940

Right: German bank note of 1922 for 5,000 Deutschmarks taken from a crew member of the Heinkel brought down on 28 October 1939. As it then had no value, it is assumed to have been some kind of souvenir or keepsake

Geheim!

Zielstammkarte (L)

Land: Großbritannien (N)
Schottland
(Fitcshire-West-Lothian).

Ort: Queensferry (Firth of Forth)
(Nähere Lage)

Geogr. Werte:
56° 00′ 00″ N.
3° 23′ 20″ W.

Ziel-Nr.   G. B. 41 6

Kartenbl.-Nr.   Sch. 27/1:100 000

E. B. Nr.   Sch. 68/1:63 360

Bezeichnung des Zieles: Eisenbahnbrücke über den Firth of Forth.

gl. mit Ziel-Nr.

Bedeutung: Wichtige Nord-Süd-Verbindung.

Beschreibung des Zieles:

Verkehrsanschlüsse: Zweigleisige Eisenbahnstrecke Aberdeen—Edinburgh der London und N. E.-Railway.

Ausdehnung insgesamt: 2·5 km   Bebaute Fläche:

Art der Anlagen und Einrichtungen,
Bauweise, Bauausführung, Luftempfindlichkeit, Brandgefahr:

2 große Stahlbrückenbogen für die Durchfahrt mit 520 m Spannweite ruhen auf 3 Hauptpfeilern in je 4 massiven Fundamentblöcken verankert.
Durchfahrtshöhe bei M.-Hochwasser 45 m.
Höhe der Pfeiler 110 m über M.-Hochwasser.
Viadukte verbinden die stählerne Durchfahrtsbrücke im N. und S. mit dem Festland.
Mittelpfeiler der Brücke ruht auf Insel Inch Garvie.
Baugrund felsig.
Einsturzgefahr.

Erzeugnisse:

Erzeugungsmenge im Monat:
Maximal und normal.
Bei wieviel Schichten und Arbeitern?

Belegschaft:
Männer, Frauen, Volkszugehörigkeit,
politische Einstellung, Unterbringung.

g) Lebenswichtige Teile, Wasser- und Kraftversorgung, Sabotage:
Die Stahlbrückenbogen.

h) Rohstoffversorgung:

i) Lagerung: ca. 125 000 t.

k) Sonstiges: 4 km im N.O. liegen die Fliegerhorste Donibristle (Land und See). (G. B. 10 62 und 10 63)
5 km im S.S.O. liegt Fliegerhorst Turnhouse. (G. B. 10 231)

4. Aktiver und passiver Luftschutz, örtl. Bewachung:
Nördlich und südlich der Brücke schwere und leichte Flakstellungen.
Auf der Insel Inch Garvie, am Mittelpfeiler der Brücke, Befestigungen und Flakbatterie mit Scheinwerfern.
An der O.-Seite des nördlichsten Brückenpfeilers ein kleines Sperrfort.

5. Orientierungspunkte zur Zielerkennung:
Die Verengung des Firth of Forth westl. von Edinburgh bei Queensferry.

6. Bild- und Kartenunterlagen vom Ziel und vom Zielraum:

a) Anliegend: b) Außerdem vom Zielraum vorhanden:

G. B. 41 6 a: Kartenausschnitt.   Z. K. 18
bg. Bildauswertg.
G. B. 41 6 b: Lichtbild.

G. B. 41 6 c: Lageplan.

7. Zielunterlagen hat: September 1939

287

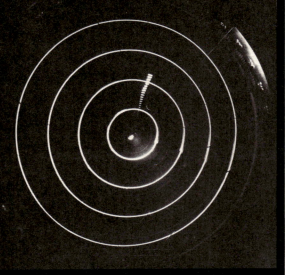

RADAR

Above: A modern secondary radar display at London Airport. The early types of warning radar used during the second World War were often 'cluttered' with many extraneous signals

Right: A Wellington XIII of RAF Coastal Command, festooned with the aerials of wartime ASV (air-to-surface vessel) radar

Above: The first radar for night fighters to go into large-scale service was the British AI (Airborne Interception) Mark IV, seen here fitted to a Beaufighter VI. The arrow-shaped aerial on the nose belonged to the transmitter. The pairs of aerials on the wings belonged to the receiver; when the signals picked up by each of the wing aerials were equal in strength, the target was dead ahead. Range was about $3\frac{1}{2}$ miles (5.5 km) at 18,000 ft (5,500 m)

Left: By 1941 it was possible to pack airborne radar into a 'thimble' nose installation as shown on this YP-61 Black Widow night fighter

Opposite page, top: First radar to be used operationally was the British Chain Home system. The transmitter aerials were suspended between the three 350-ft (107-m) high towers to the left of the picture. The receiver aerials were suspended between the four 240-ft (73-m) towers on the right. Maximum range was about 110 miles (177 km)

Centre: Head of the British research team which perfected radar pre-war was Sir Robert Watson Watt (centre)

Bottom left: Aerials of the German Lichtenstein radar, on the nose of a Junkers Ju 88 night fighter

Bottom right: Electronic countermeasures have always gone hand-in-hand with radar. This picture of the RAF's wartime Operation Corona in action shows the 'ghost voice' microphone over which false messages were passed to enemy night fighters, as if from German radar controllers. Also visible are receivers tuned to German transmissions and a gramophone for jumbled-voice jamming

NOWADAYS RADAR PLAYS a vitally important role in every aspect of air warfare. Using it, fighters are able to hunt down their prey by day or night in all but the very worst weather. Bombers are able to investigate precisely, and aim their deadly loads at targets unseen by their crews. Maritime aircraft are able to detect submarines which expose any part of their structure above the surface of the sea. The list of applications of radar in modern warfare is almost endless.

It was not always so. Prior to 1936 the only means of locating aircraft beyond visual range was with the sound locator. This massive device had a maximum range of about eight miles (13 km) if all went well—but it rarely did. Even against the old biplane bombers this was barely adequate, for eight miles meant a warning time of only about four minutes. The 1930s saw a revolution in aircraft design, during which the speeds of bombers

doubled. Clearly, the defenders needed something much better than the sound locator if they were to get their fighters into position in time to intercept the raiding bombers.

The answer was radar, a device which beamed out high-powered pulses of radio energy and received, amplified and displayed the feeble echo signals bounced back from any aircraft in the path of the beam. Even in 1936 such ideas were not new: as early as 1904 a German inventor named Christian Hülsmeyer had patented a design for a crude radar set. But it was not until the 1930s that the science of electronics had progressed sufficiently for a radar to be built which was able to detect aircraft at ranges beyond those possible with sound locators.

Once the know-how necessary for radar existed, development was rapid. In June 1936 the first experimental radar built by a British research team under Robert Watson Watt was able to detect an aircraft flying 17 miles (27 km) away. The following month an improved set detected an

aircraft at 40 miles (65 km). By the end of September ranges in excess of 55 miles (88 km) were commonplace.

As the war clouds gathered over Europe, men of the Royal Air Force struggled to erect a chain of twenty early-warning radar ground stations along the east coast of Britain. When war broke out in September 1939 the initial chain was complete, and able to detect aircraft flying at 15,000 ft (4,570 m) approaching from the east or south almost anywhere between the northern tip of Scotland and Portsmouth; by this time the radars used had a maximum range of about 110 miles (177 km). When the real test came, during the Battle of Britain in the summer of 1940, these so-called Chain Home radars proved their value time and time again, by providing information which enabled the hard-pressed squadrons of RAF Fighter Command to be used to maximum effect.

The Chain Home radar was a very large piece of equipment: the installation weighed several tons, with three 350-ft (107 m) high towers to carry the trans-

mitter aerials and four 240-ft (73 m) high towers to carry the separate receiver aerials. With this in mind it was, therefore, with some trepidation that Dr Edward Bowen and his team had begun work before the war on a radar set small enough to fit into an aircraft. But it was done, and late in 1937 the first crude airborne radar, occupying most of the cabin of a twin-engined Anson, was able to detect ships out to ranges of about 10 miles (16 km). A refinement of this device, able to detect other aircraft and code-named AI (for Airborne Interception), entered service in Fighter Command in the summer of 1940. During the early morning darkness of 23 July 1940, Flying Officer G Ashfield and his radar operator, Sergeant R Leyland, in a Blenheim fighter, made history when they used AI radar for the first time to assist in shooting down an enemy bomber.

As the war expanded, so did the uses of radar. Coastal Command aircraft operating far out over the Atlantic carried ASV (Air-to-Surface-Vessel) radar to hunt down submarines running on the surface; during the Battle of the Atlantic aircraft sank more than 250 submarines, and assisted surface vessels to destroy more than 40 others. In the early hours of 8 June 1944, Flying Officer K Moore and his crew, flying an ASV-equipped Liberator, made skilful use of radar when they destroyed two German submarines in a space of only twenty minutes.

RAF Bomber Command made use of the Gee device to navigate to and from targets, while aircraft of the Pathfinder Force carried the precision-bombing Oboe and H2S radars to enable them to mark out the targets for the main-force bombers following behind. When the American daylight bombing offensive got under way, the bombers carried a radar similar to H2S, so that attacks could be made through overcast.

During the large-scale paratroop assault which preceded the invasion of Normandy in June 1944, it was the low-powered Eureka radar beacons which marked out the dropping zones for the many hundreds of transport aircraft.

The development of radar in Germany began, quite independently, at about the same time as that in Britain. Initially the rate of development was much slower. However, the Allied bomber attacks on the German homeland forced the Luftwaffe to devote considerable effort to building up its own chain of defensive radar stations in occupied Europe and Germany itself, and for the German night fighters there was a lightweight airborne radar, code-named Lichtenstein. The battle between the German defences and the British night bombers reached its climax during the night of 30 March 1944, when the defenders shot down 94 out of a total of 795 bombers attacking Nuremburg; the great majority fell to radar-equipped night fighters.

During the years between 1936 and 1945, in the forcing-house of war, threatened or actual, radar blossomed from a dream in a scientist's mind into a vast family of devices which revolutionised air warfare. Since the end of the war, development work has continued without pause, for today victory in air combat will go—other things being equal—to the man flying the aircraft with the best radar and weapons system, rather than the man flying the machine with the best performance.

Bottom left: The cupola under the rear fuselage of this Lancaster bomber housed the rotating scanner of the H2S ground mapping radar. The 'H' shaped aerial immediately behind the nose gun turret belonged to the Rebecca device; used in conjunction with a Eureka ground beacon, this enabled the crew to home on their base airfield from more than 60 miles (96 km) away

Above, top to bottom:
By the end of the second World War radar sets were becoming very small indeed. The transmitter and aerial system of the AN/APS 6 radar fitted to these Grumman F6F Hellcat night fighters was so small and light that it could be mounted far along the starboard wing without creating problems due to its asymmetric position

Lichtenstein SN2 radar aerials on the nose of a Messerschmitt Bf 110G-4/R7 night fighter

The aerial of the AI Mark VIII radar was only 5 cm long; it was mounted at the focus of a reflector disc and could be aimed at objects in the same way as a spotlight. It could locate targets with much greater precision than the earlier AI Mark IV; maximum range was 4½ miles (7.25 km) even if the night fighter was only 5,000 ft (1,525 m) above the ground. The aircraft is a Beaufighter, with nose fairing removed

The USAAF's tandem-cockpit radar-equipped P-38 Night Lightning of 1944 could be used both to search for enemy night bombers and as a nocturnal prowler armed with guns, rockets and bombs

Battle of Britain

NAMED WITH HIS PRACTISED eye for the dramatic by Prime Minister Winston Churchill, who took office on 10 May 1940 as the war leader against Germany, the Battle of Britain was the inevitable outcome of confrontation with Europe's aggressor. Ever since the Kaiser's war, in which a mild foretaste of air attack against British civil life had been administered, the Royal Air Force had been husbanding and deploying its strength against a repetition of such an assault—at first from France and later, in the 'thirties, from Germany herself. Despite the clouded intentions of Hitler's real ambitions, the British air defences grew rapidly during the last months of peace; yet not even the most sanguine prophet could foretell the magnitude of disaster that would bring the loss of France and the Low Countries in May and June 1940. Within those two months the most powerful air force in the world arrived on the northern coast of Europe, flushed with scarcely-disputed victory over a half-dozen nations.

Against almost 3,000 Junkers, Heinkels, Dorniers and Messerschmitts, deployed from Norway to the coast of Spain, Britain's Fighter Command mustered at the beginning of July barely 50 squadrons of Hurricanes, Spitfires, Blenheims and Defiants, many of which had suffered crippling losses

in the retreat from France and in the skies over Dunkirk. Nevertheless the structures of defence had been well founded; the nation had nurtured a prolific aircraft industry in the years of peace and now the flow of new fighters did not falter. Fighter Command's chief, Air Marshal Dowding, had been the brilliant architect of a scientific defence—close-knit, with well-deployed airfields interlaced with tight systems of raid reporting and control of fighters. Most vital of these systems was the radar chain, far advanced beyond any in the world, and already an integrated link that permitted economy of effort by the weakened fighter squadrons.

Reichsmarschall Hermann Göring paused only briefly before launching his attack on Britain with Luftflotten (Air Fleets) 2 and 3 from France and the Low Countries. His attacks were mounted as a means of drawing Fighter Command into the air where, as an opening gambit to the invasion of Britain, it would be destroyed as surely as had been the air forces of Poland, Norway, Holland, Belgium and France.

July wore on as the German attacks increased in weight, with numerous raids mounted against convoys sailing in the English Channel and along the east coast. While the German High Command finalised

Top: No picture could symbolise better the preparation within Fighter Command for the inevitable battle to come than this line-up of new Mk I Spitfires

Centre: Partner of the Spitfire in the summer of 1940 was Sydney Camm's Hurricane. The lower aircraft bears a chequerboard badge signifying that its pilot was Polish

Bottom: Three Junkers Ju 88 day bombers of the Luftwaffe. Experience in the Battle of Britain led to later versions having more powerful engines, more armour protection, heavier defensive armament and a bigger bomb-load

Above left: A Spitfire pilot warms up his Merlin engine for take-off

Left: Although outnumbered by Hurricanes the Battle of Britain Spitfires caught the imagination of the public, as even the least technically-minded housewife could recognise easily their 'pointed' wings

Top: The Operations Room at Fighter Command HQ, Bentley Priory, in 1940. The officers on the dais look down on WAAF plotters who display the progress of raids and interceptions with symbols on a map table

Above: Wearing their 'Mae West' lifejackets, pilots of a Spitfire squadron wait tensely for the next call to 'scramble'

Below: Enthusiasts will argue forever the relative merits of the Hurricane and Spitfire. In fact, without either type the Battle of Britain would have been lost

plans for the coming invasion and Hitler called on Britain to surrender, the stabbing attacks against shipping attained their aim —the sapping of defence energy and the grinding of nerves through enforced patrols. Little damage was done among the merchant vessels, but the attrition suffered by Dowding's pilots threatened disaster even before the main attack was met.

The attacks on coastal shipping were accompanied by air raids on the ports and naval bases of Portland, Portsmouth and Dover. This enabled the Luftwaffe to achieve one of its first objectives during July, for its depredations forced the Admiralty to withdraw most British naval forces from the Channel to bases further afield, with the result that scarcely a single convoy could pass through the Dover Straits during the first week in August. Nevertheless, this in turn deprived the Luftwaffe of its favoured targets and thereby gave respite to the weary pilots of No 11 Group who were defending the all-important south-east under the energetic leadership of Air Marshal Keith Park.

No-one in Britain during that lull dared believe other than that Göring was flexing his muscles for the great attack. And so it transpired. From 8 August the avalanche gained momentum. Enemy formations which had hitherto comprised little more than a Staffel of bombers (about eight aircraft) now appeared as a mass of 50 or more with a like number of escorting fighters. At first it seemed that the British

must be overwhelmed; but as Dowding's commanders recognised the German strength, more fighters were scrambled and successively fed into the fight. Radar gave these commanders eyes in the sky and by their tactics the enemy's determination was eroded as raid after raid was turned back.

Already strengths and weaknesses were being exploited. The much-vaunted Junkers Ju 87—the screaming personification of the 'Stuka' dive-bomber—was seen to be easy prey to Spitfires and Hurricanes, for in its dive it was a steady target while its escort was powerless to save it. Diving Stukas fell with flaming trails to litter the summer fields of southern England. Göring's favourite fighter, the Messerschmitt Bf 110 Zerstörer (destroyer) was cumbersome as a bomber escort and losses among Zerstörergeschwadern soon forced the Germans to provide escorts for the escort!

Climax of the planned German air assault (Adlerangriff) was scheduled for 13 August, but bad weather brought delay until Thursday the 15th. On that day Göring launched his 'eagles' from all flanks of his command, from Luftflotte 5 in Norway and Denmark, and from Luftflotten 2 and 3 in Holland, Belgium and France. From mid-morning until late evening the great raids came and went, huge armadas of fighters and bombers feinting and striking, probing and thrusting, carpeting the British airfields with bombs and bullets. But try though they might they found scarcely a flaw in the air defences. Pilots of the British fighters flew and flew again, sweating and straining, turning and

weaving their white patterns against the blue sky. Many fell, others struggled home on tattered wings to find a fresh fighter. From Yorkshire to Dorset was heard the crash of bomb, the rattle of gunfire high above.

The battle died with the sun that day. Almost every enemy tactic failed and Fighter Command held firm. This had been Dowding's sternest test. For the loss of 28 fighters destroyed and 13 damaged, from which all but 12 pilots escaped, the Royal Air Force and anti-aircraft guns destroyed 75 enemy aircraft. More significant, the Luftwaffe, through extraordinarily inept intelligence, failed to destroy a single airfield vital to the defence. Furthermore, so roughly treated were the formations flying from Scandinavia that Göring never again launched Luftflotte 5 in any concerted strength against Britain.

Scarcely daunted by its losses elsewhere on this 'Black Thursday', the Luftwaffe was now committed to all-out attack, believing as it did that crippling losses had been inflicted on Dowding's fighters. The Germans returned day after day throughout the remainder of August. By skilful 'rotation' of squadrons to and from the relative quiet of the north, Dowding strove to bolster his defences round London and the south-east.

But the strain began to show. The battle-trained ranks of squadron and section leaders thinned from combat strain and casualties. Young men became veterans at nineteen. Ground-crews dropped from the sheer fatigue of sleepless nights spent repair-

ing the damaged fighters. Yet this was the glorious time of Churchill's 'Few'; great names like Stanford Tuck, Douglas Bader, 'Ginger' Lacey, Brian Kingcome, Peter Townsend, Don Kingaby, Johnnie Kent, Colin Gray, 'Sailor' Malan and 'Sawn-off' Lock were engraved bright on the tablets of British history to reflect the drama of those heroic days. Men had come from many countries to fly among the ranks of Fighter Command; indeed, it was a Czech, Josef Frantisek, who topped the Allied score of enemy aircraft destroyed before he met his death after one month in action.

As Fighter Command's ordeal approached its climax of terrible exhaustion, there emerged within the echelons of Göring's airmen, too, all the signs of strain, frustration and discouragement, of demoralisation and disenchantment—all the signs of spent determination. For two months the German crews had fought with elan and courage, had met the shock of successive combats, had seen their friends fall in blazing bombers and—too often— simply lost comrades without trace or knowledge of their fate. The fighter pilots, seldom able to penetrate far over the British mainland or divest themselves of their responsibilities of escort to the bombers, fought the constant threat of fuel shortage, often falling not to the guns of British fighters but to the grey waves of a hostile Channel.

This frustration permeated to the fractious Reichsmarschall who, breaking all the rules of war and perpetrating one of

history's classic blunders, suddenly shifted the aim of his attack on 7 September. While Dowding's pilots waited all day for the coming attack, Göring himself arrived on the Channel coast to watch his great armadas pass. Not the British airfields, nor the coastal towns in daylight . . but London at dusk and in darkness. This was to be his point of aim: to break the spirit of the Briton at home. To smash his capital, to lay waste his homes. To destroy his will to make war.

That night a new era of warfare was born, with the ravages of Junkers, Heinkel and the rest. Hundreds of black-crossed bombers droned their way along the Thames to London. Time and again the great shoals of Dorniers shuddered as swift stabs by Spitfires pierced the hostile ranks. But as darkness fell the bombs crashed down, on the sprawling dockland of London, on the close-packed homes of the poor, on the food stores of Britain's capital: on the greatest target on earth.

This was London's ordeal by fire. In streets aflame with incendiary, in blasted brick and cruel shards of driven glass, the ordinary man and woman faced the terror of the new air age, the terror that had come a little earlier to Warsaw and Rotterdam. This was to be the new ordeal—the raid that would last for fifty nights.

Yet it was this raid, in all its horror, that was to spell salvation to the island race; for in that moment of deflected aim Dowding's men gained strength anew, and when, with one final fling, the Luftwaffe turned

again on Britain by day on 15 September, the Hurricanes and Spitfires—which had been too often 'destroyed' in German propaganda—dealt so severely with the raiders that the attack faltered and broke, never again to return in like strength by day.

True, the battle waxed and waned for six more weeks, but the attack had failed. Hitler abandoned his plans for invasion of the British islands, for winter was upon him. Henceforth his gaze turned towards the East. Had he but known, the shift of Göring's aim against British cities had sown the seeds of an ill wind. In time the German nation would reap the whirlwind of great raids by bombers based in the islands it had failed to conquer from the skies of that fateful summer.

At the time, with all the uncertainties of war unresolved, victory and defeat in the Battle of Britain represented not so much the blunting of the Nazi weapon of aggression as the survival of the British will to stand and defend the free world. The fact that Göring's Luftwaffe also survived as a force in being must blur the traditional concept of clear-cut victor and vanquished. Yet not even the passage of years has dimmed the feat of arms gained by those few men of the RAF. No academic analysis by theorists can ever cloud the fact that between that September and Armageddon stood and flew and fought just 3,080 men —the equivalent of an infantry brigade or a warship's crew—and the world lived to fight another day.

Opposite page, top: The harvest fields of southern England bore a strange crop in the summer of 1940. This Bf 109 was crash-landed by its wounded pilot in a cornfield at Berwick, near Eastbourne. When captured he commented: 'That's what we get for coming to England'

Upper left: Before—a Heinkel He 111H-6 waiting to take off

Lower left: After—the remains of an He 111 dominate one of the many graveyards of the Luftwaffe created by the air battles of the second World War

Centre, top to bottom:
When this Bf 110 crash-landed on the south-east coast, other German aircraft tried to destroy it with their bombs. They missed by 20 yards (18 m)

Wolf in sheep's clothing: this Bf 109E was captured intact and test flown by RAF pilots to learn its capabilities and weaknesses

Driven from the daylight skies, the Luftwaffe was forced to seek the cover of darkness for its raids from September 1940. So began the grim testing time of the 'night blitz' for the people of London

HAWKER HURRICANE I

Powered by: One 1,030 hp Rolls-Royce Merlin III twelve-cylinder Vee-type engine, driving a 10 ft 9 in (3.28 m) diameter three-blade propeller
Wing span: 40 ft 0 in (12.19 m)
Length: 31 ft 4 in (9.55 m)
Wing area: 257.5 sq ft (23.92 m²)
Gross weight: 6,447 lb (2,924 kg)
Max speed: 328 mph (528 km/h) at 20,000 ft (6,100 m)
Max range: 505 miles (813 km)
Armament: Four 0.303 in Browning machine-guns in each wing
Accommodation: Crew of 1

First flight: 6 November 1935
Three months before it received an official order for Hurricane fighters, the Hawker company began to make preparations to build 1,000 of these aircraft for the RAF. But for that initiative, the RAF would certainly have had even less than the 300 or so which were in first-line service upon the outbreak of the second World War. Hawker's faith in Sydney Camm's eight-gun monoplane was well justified, for production of the Mk I (to which the data apply) alone reached 3,954 in Britain and Canada, and altogether 14,533 Hurricanes of all models were built.

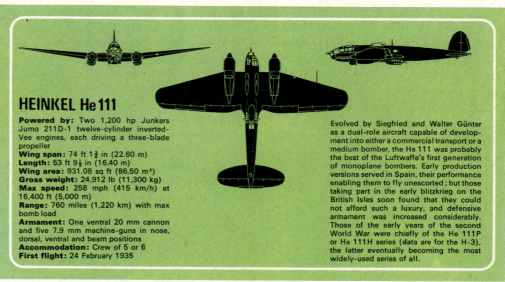

HEINKEL He 111

Powered by: Two 1,200 hp Junkers Jumo 211D-1 twelve-cylinder inverted-Vee engines, each driving a three-blade propeller
Wing span: 74 ft 1¾ in (22.60 m)
Length: 53 ft 9½ in (16.40 m)
Wing area: 931.08 sq ft (86.50 m²)
Gross weight: 24,912 lb (11,300 kg)
Max speed: 258 mph (415 km/h) at 16,400 ft (5,000 m)
Range: 760 miles (1,220 km) with max bomb load
Armament: One ventral 20 mm cannon and five 7.9 mm machine-guns in nose, dorsal, ventral and beam positions
Accommodation: Crew of 5 or 6
First flight: 24 February 1935

Evolved by Siegfried and Walter Günter as a dual-role aircraft capable of development into either a commercial transport or a medium bomber, the He 111 was probably the best of the Luftwaffe's first generation of monoplane bombers. Early production versions served in Spain, their performance enabling them to fly unescorted; but those taking part in the early blitzkrieg on the British Isles soon found that they could not afford such a luxury, and defensive armament was increased considerably. Those of the early years of the second World War were chiefly of the He 111P or He 111H series (data are for the H-3), the latter eventually becoming the most widely-used series of all.

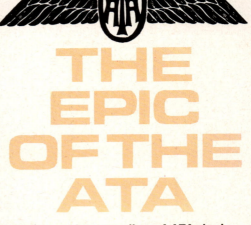

THE EPIC OF THE ATA

Left: Men and women pilots of ATA check the day's orders, involving delivery of anything from a Tiger Moth to a four-engined bomber. 'Pilot's notes' compiled by colleagues warn them what to expect from unfamiliar types

Bottom: Commodore Gerard d'Erlanger, whose pre-war suggestion led to the formation of Air Transport Auxiliary

THE HISTORY OF AVIATION HAS recorded many strange incidents and examples of enthusiasm and courage, but the story of the Air Transport Auxiliary is surely one of the strangest—and the most satisfying. This statement is borne out by two items taken at random. When a young girl not only delivers four-engined bombers but teaches RAF pilots how to fly them —and a one-armed, one-eyed, middle-aged amateur pilot delivers 1,300 combat aircraft to their squadrons in wartime, one may be excused for using the word strange.

After the disquieting events in Munich in 1938 a young banker, Gerard d'Erlanger (later Sir Gerard), who was a private pilot and a director of British Airways, felt strongly that the private pilots in Britain could be used in some effective way if, in spite of the 'peace in our time' optimism of Prime Minister Neville Chamberlain, war should come after all. He visualised the possibility of using the privately-owned light aircraft dotted around the country for the carriage of urgent mail or VIPs to remote spots; and he put his thoughts on paper to the Parliamentary Under-Secretary for Air, Harold Balfour.

In consequence, just before war started in September 1939, the Air Transport Auxiliary came into being—on paper— and d'Erlanger got replies from about 100 of the 1,000 or so civilian pilots to whom he had written. A selection board was created at Whitchurch Aerodrome, near Bristol, and 30 applicants went along to be air-tested. They included publicans, farmers, journalists, first World War pilots and 'Uncle Tom Cobley and all'. Few aircraft were yet available, and the organisation was still in its rather chaotic infancy.

Within a few days some of these pilots, whose experience had been limited to Gipsy Moths or their equivalent, found themselves delivering Harvards, a type

which had a vicious stall, a remarkable ability to spin and an equal inability to stop spinning before it landed—vertically. ATA started the hard way.

From Harvards they moved on to Blenheims, using Anson 'taxis' to collect the pilots after they had delivered their military aircraft and return them to one of their bases. Several of these bases had sprung up, notably at de Havilland's plant at Hatfield and at White Waltham, the latter eventually becoming the central base of ATA.

The organisation grew at phenomenal speed, as did the demands upon it; but the most striking event occurred in January 1940, when Miss Pauline Gower, a highly experienced pilot with several thousand hours' flying, was asked to recruit eight women to ferry Tiger Moth trainers from the de Havilland factory to RAF flying schools. Of those first eight, four continued to the end of the war; they included little Joan Hughes, who at 17 was the youngest woman pilot in Britain and who later flew Lancasters, to the surprise of the squadrons to which she delivered them. Another of the first group, the Hon Mrs Margaret Fairweather, was the first woman to fly a Spitfire; she reached the rank of Flight-Captain and

was killed while flying for ATA.

One of the early recruits to ATA was Amy Mollison (née Amy Johnson). This great woman pilot met her death ferrying an Airspeed Oxford in January 1941. The weather was foul and she undoubtedly got off course. The next thing that was heard of her after take-off from Prestwick was when HMS *Hazlemere,* patrolling off Herne Bay, spotted a parachute coming out of the clouds. The flyer, soon seen to be a woman, dropped into the sea; the Commanding Officer dived overboard but failed to reach her. Both were drowned, and Amy Mollison's body was never recovered. According to her husband, the late Jim Mollison (who also served in ATA), gunfire had been reported overhead, and he was firmly convinced to the end of his life that she was shot down.

In the beginning ATA, though disciplined so far as its actual flying was concerned, was inevitably a little happy-go-lucky, with everyone wanting to do 36 hours work in every period of 24. Gradually, however, a more orderly atmosphere developed, which was just as well, because the organisation was less than a year old when the Battle of Britain started. This was indeed a test of its courage and competence.

Suddenly a demand arose—on the most urgent scale—for the delivery of replacement Spitfires and Hurricanes to the fighter fields in the south of England, already under intense daylight attack from the Luftwaffe.

ATA pilots who, only a year earlier, had limited their flying to joyous weekends, in good weather, in pipsqueak aeroplanes, found themselves handed an eight-gun, 350 mph (563 km/h) fighter which, to the nation, was worth a lot more than the civilian detailed to fly it. The airfield to which they were to fly might be just recovering from an attack which had pot-holed the field with craters and left the operations centre a heap of rubble; it might be the target for a formation only a few miles away or, as it seemed to many of those dedicated airmen and women, more often the attack was going nicely when they arrived. But, somehow, they nearly always delivered the aircraft, even if they had to dive straight into a slit trench from the cockpit.

As the variety of aircraft increased, so did the work of ATA. By 1944 the organisation had no fewer than 22 bases in the United Kingdom, and in that year the number of flying personnel reached its peak, with 551 male pilots, 108 women pilots (in the following year this went up to 110), and 109 flight engineers, this last total also including women, one of whom was killed on a flight.

What had started in 1939 with 30 men, all drawn from Britain, also expanded in scope as the years went on. By the time ATA was disbanded the aircrew included nationals of 22 countries other than Britain. Lists do not always make interesting reading, but this one shows how ATA was a cross-section of the United Nations —with a more common purpose, perhaps —as it included persons from Australia, Austria (this raises some questions), Belgium, Canada, Ceylon, Chile, China, Czechoslovakia, Denmark, Estonia, Ethiopia, France, Holland, India, Ireland, Mauritius, New Zealand, Poland, South Africa, Switzerland, Thailand and the USA. It is not, perhaps, surprising that the last-named country provided a considerable number of aircrew.

With the growth of the system it became necessary for the ATA to run its own flying school, to convert pilots to the immense number of different types they were called upon to fly. Men and women were drawn from the ranks of pilots to act as instructors, and it is noteworthy that Joan Hughes was the only one of either sex to qualify as an instructor on *all* types.

In the pre-Dunkirk period some of the men pilots delivered aircraft to France, and sometimes had to fly the gauntlet of hostile machines. None of the women was involved in this operation, but their turn was to come later.

The first delivery to France after D-day was on 6 September 1944, when Hugh Burgel and Maurice Harlé, a Frenchman, delivered two Spitfires to an airfield with the anonymous designation of B.35. Harlé, with full justice, was allowed to land first and thus brought ATA back to France.

For the next three months ATA pilots were regularly delivering aircraft to France —even though it was not until the end of the year that official permission was given for the operation !

As the Allies moved eastwards, so ATA followed. Ever deeper into France, Belgium, Holland, then into Germany, these civilian pilots took the aircraft still needed so urgently by the RAF. The greatest distance covered on one of these flights was by Stewart Keith-Jopp (the one-armed, one-eyed journalist) when he took a Typhoon almost to the borders of Russia. Women were not allowed to go to the continent until January 1945, when the first over were Diana Ramsay and Betty Hayman, who went to Tilburg in Holland to collect two Mosquitos for overhaul back home.

Among others, Jim Mollison got as far as Pilsen. So, in short, ATA was flying everywhere in Europe, to the limits of Allied occupied territory, and doing so in aircraft which were among the fastest and heaviest in production.

To list all the aircraft flown by these pilots would be impossible in the space available, but they ranged from light trainers to heavy bombers, from fighters to flying-boats, and from single- to four-engined aircraft.

At its peak, the entire staff of ATA totalled 3,555 people, including aircrew, ground staff and RAF attached personnel. It is hard to credit just what they achieved. In their own school they ran no fewer than 6,013 conversion courses in less than five years, and this was only a tiny part of the work. In the period 1944-45 they were ferrying 99 different types of aircraft.

As civilians they were not eligible for the Victoria Cross or the Distinguished Flying Cross. Even the Air Force Cross was denied them, and the George Cross had not then been introduced. So, throughout the whole war, only Commodore d'Erlanger and Senior Commander P A Wills (one of the original 30) received the top award, the CBE. Much later, a George Medal went to Second Officer J Gulson. The women were shabbily treated. Six of them, including Pauline Gower and Joan Hughes, received the MBE; four got the British Empire Medal and three others received commendations of one kind or another.

Enemy action was an ever-present danger for much of the time that ATA was in existence, but a far more potent enemy was the weather. The aircraft had to get through if it was humanly possible, often when it was apparently impossible. Almost all the fatal and other accidents were due to this hazard. In all, 154 ATA personnel were killed on duty, some in the taxi aircraft which collected or delivered pilots after or before their ferry task. The hours flown on this aspect of the work were staggering: a total of almost 200,000, representing some 20 million miles (32,187,000 km), yet the highest average number of taxi aircraft in service in any one of ATA's five years was only just over 200.

As the number of bases (or pools, as they were called later) rose, the distances

Above: Joan Hughes gets a receipt for the Stirling bomber she has just delivered to an RAF station. Squadron pilots found it difficult to believe that such aircraft could be handled without difficulty by a girl so petite that she was overshadowed on the ground by the bomber's wheels

Below: From a mobile 'tower' the Field Control Officer flashes a take-off signal to an ATA pilot

to be flown became a little more manageable, but throughout the war it was normal for a pilot to complete a gruelling flight in an unfamiliar aeroplane from, say, Bristol to Aberdeen, and then have to fight his or her way back on an overcrowded train that crawled through the night— only to be ordered to repeat the trip with a fresh aircraft. The taxi aircraft and their crews did a great job, but their limited numbers often left ferry pilots to their own devices in making the homeward trip.

On 30 November 1945, ATA's work was at last considered to be done. At sunset the last Anson landed at White Waltham, and the flag—ATA had at least been granted the right to fly one—was hauled down for the last time.

The work of ATA can be summarised in two statistics:

309,011 aircraft ferried,
414,984 hours flown.

Winston Churchill's words about the RAF fighter pilots in the Battle of Britain must have been echoed many times by RAF pilots themselves, who relied on ATA to bring them the tools with which to finish the job.

THIS BATTLE, LASTING from 3 September 1939 until 8 May 1945, can fairly be regarded as the only one to continue from the first minute of the war in Europe until the last.

Primarily, of course, it was a naval battle, in which the Royal Navy bore the brunt from beginning to end. The Allied objective was to maintain free passage of men and munitions across the ocean, while that of the Axis was to prevent such passage and force Britain and her allies to submit. But even the most avid naval protagonist would admit that the Fleet Air Arm, Royal Air Force, RCAF and United States flying services, aided by contingents from overrun countries such as France, Poland and Norway, played a vital role in helping the surface forces to combat the underwater menace. Equally, the long-range Focke-Wulf Condor aircraft of the Luftwaffe were a perpetual thorn in the flesh of Allied commanders, and without them the U-boat force's total successes would have been far fewer.

At the start of the second World War long-range aircraft were few and far between. The Sunderlands were the only other major type which came into that category, but at the start of the war Coastal Command had only three squadrons equipped with these flying-boats.

German naval strategy was to use the submarine in ever-increasing quantity. The task of the Allies was to break up the attacks before they developed, if possible. Naval patrols were in short supply, and could not as a rule be spared for general search work. They were needed too badly for escort of convoys, and so general patrol fell to the lot of the air forces. In theory this was a good idea, but submarines a few hundred miles out in the Atlantic were virtually beyond the range of the available aircraft. Also, although the Schnorkel device had not been invented at that time, the U-boats normally surfaced only at night and could not be detected from the air. (Air-to-surface radar was still in the laboratory stage and the Leigh light, an airborne searchlight fitted to Wellington bombers, could be used only near the coast.)

Allied air power was not very formidable in those early days. The aircraft carriers of the Royal Navy were too few in number to give adequate support to the convoys and, although there were successes by the aircraft operating from shore bases, it was not until the *Bismarck* broke out into the Atlantic that the first hint of the value of air power was given. On 26 May 1941, the battleship was spotted by a Catalina of No 209 squadron, RAF, and Swordfish torpedo-bombers of HMS *Ark Royal* attacked, damaging her steering gear. Slowed down, the *Bismarck* was shadowed and brought to battle with

THE BATT
THE ATLA

LE OF
TIC

Above: Known as 'Stringbag' because of its profusion of struts and wires, the Fairey Swordfish torpedo-bomber played an immense role in the war at sea. This one is fitted with underwing rocket rails for attacks on shipping

Left: An inferno of burning oil spells the aftermath of strikes by German U-boats against a convoy in the North Atlantic. There were few survivors from this torpedoed tanker

Bottom left: First American-built aircraft used operationally by the RAF in the second World War, Lockheed Hudsons gave superb service on anti-submarine and reconnaissance duties from bases all round the British coastline

Below: Bombing up an Albacore on a British aircraft carrier, with the pilot already in his cockpit ready to take off

Bottom: The 'wedding ring Wimpey' was a Vickers Wellington bomber fitted with a 48 ft (14.63 m) diameter dural hoop through which a high-voltage electric current was passed to explode magnetic mines from the air. Its main task was to clear ports and harbours of enemy mines

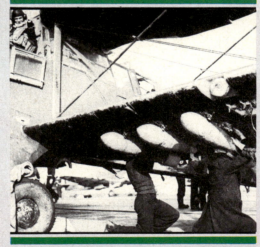

HMS King George V, Rodney, and other ships. She was sunk the following day. Thus did the greatest battleship ever built, the flagship of the German Navy's fleet of commerce raiders and acclaimed as 'unsinkable', succumb to an attack initiated by one of the most 'old-fashioned' aeroplanes to serve in the second World War.

The take-over of Iceland gave the Allies much-needed land bases far to the west and the arrival of Hudson aircraft provided by the USA under the Lend-Lease agreement added teeth to Coastal Command. From Newfoundland the Royal Canadian Air Force provided convoy cover for some distance eastward but, even so, there was a wide area in mid-Atlantic where convoys had no air protection. Aircraft carriers were seldom available, and the U-boat wolf packs wrought terrible destruction in the 'Black Gap', as the Navy called this space. Something had to be done until supplies of longer-range 'killer' aircraft could be produced.

Merchant ships were modified by stripping out all the upperworks and replacing them with a short flight deck. Others were fitted hastily with improvised catapult structures as the so-called 'CAM-Ships', or Catapult-Aircraft Merchantmen. From these vessels modified Hurricane fighters could be launched to observe or tackle the Focke-Wulf Condors if they came within range. The fighters could not, however, land on a 'CAM-ship' again and their pilots had to ditch with the hope that they could be recovered. In typical Atlantic weather these pilots had an unenviable job. It was, indeed, as near as the Allied air forces ever came to the Kamikaze suicide operations of the Japanese, and if the convoys operated up in the Arctic—as they often did—the pilot was usually frozen to death before he could be picked up.

For a long time the U-boats had matters very much their own way, and almost brought Britain to her knees. Then America began to supply Coastal Command with Liberators, which had the range to cover the Black Gap and keep the submarines submerged. When America entered the war her own naval aircraft were added to the protective force. More escort carriers became available, improved air cover made the Condors more vulnerable and thus the U-boats were deprived of vital information. In addition, Allied aircraft began to be fitted with air-to-surface radar and this forced the submarines to remain submerged at night. Only the advent of the Schnorkel enabled them to stay at sea and in action.

However, the Battle of the Atlantic was by no means over yet. The German sub-

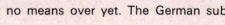

marine service never lacked for brave men, and attacks were repeatedly pressed home, with devastating results to the convoys, despite the increasing U-boat losses.

Fairly early in the battle, Coastal Command was placed under the overall command of the Royal Navy. This state of affairs did not entirely please the airmen, but was a common-sense move. Because of it, air cover could be fully co-ordinated and the resources, always less than were needed, were put to the most valuable use.

In the end the Allies won the Battle of the Atlantic, but the price they paid was immense. Over the whole globe 2,717 Allied merchant ships were sunk during the war, and of these the Atlantic claimed 2,353. U-boats destroyed totalled 782, of which more than two-thirds were lost on Atlantic convoy patrol. This gives some small idea of the immensity of the six-year battle.

No-one can ever take away the credit due to the Royal and Allied Navies, who between them sank 249 of the U-boats destroyed in the Atlantic. But the airmen

did even better. Shore-based and ship-borne aircraft destroyed 289 submarines and combined air-sea action a further 47.

By the time the war in Europe ended there were few aircraft types that had not taken some part in the battle. A variety of British and American carrier-based fighters was used; the old Swordfish played a significant part; Sunderlands and Catalinas flew fantastically long patrols (and, incidentally, picked up a huge number of torpedoed sailors); Liberators gave long-range cover; and Hudsons, despite their shorter range, also accounted for many U-boats. The full list of types is much longer.

In addition, German submarines operated as far west as the US coast, and many convoys running coastwise were escorted by non-rigid airships, or 'blimps', of the US Navy. As in the first World War, when no troopship in the English Channel was ever sunk while escorted by a blimp, so it was in the second, and the 'Poopy Bags', as they are still affectionately known by American sailors, again had an unblemished record.

Top: A Hawker Hurricane 'catafighter' on a CAM-Ship. Unable to land on board after a sortie, the pilot had to ditch in the sea and hope to be picked up by a passing ship

Above: The acceleration provided by the rocket catapult was so high that early trials and training could be carried out with the ship at anchor, followed by a landing ashore

Below: Coastal Command Wellingtons fitted with ASV Mk II radar were distinguished by a line of masts above the fuselage and other antennae under their wings. Some versions were fitted with searchlights, known as Leigh Lights, to illuminate submarines located on the surface, and carried two 18 in (46 cm) torpedoes

Bottom: The 'big bad Wulf'—a Focke-Wulf Fw 200C Condor of the kind which directed German submarines in search of convoys and could make heavy attacks themselves

SHORT SUNDERLAND III

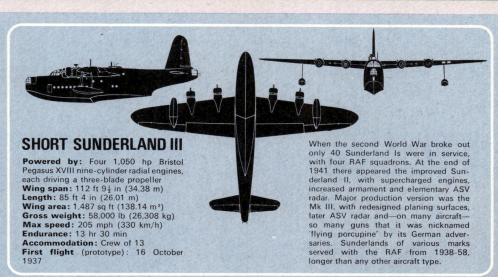

Powered by: Four 1,050 hp Bristol Pegasus XVIII nine-cylinder radial engines, each driving a three-blade propeller
Wing span: 112 ft 9½ in (34.38 m)
Length: 85 ft 4 in (26.01 m)
Wing area: 1,487 sq ft (138.14 m²)
Gross weight: 58,000 lb (26,308 kg)
Max speed: 205 mph (330 km/h)
Endurance: 13 hr 30 min
Accommodation: Crew of 13
First flight (prototype): 16 October 1937

When the second World War broke out only 40 Sunderland Is were in service, with four RAF squadrons. At the end of 1941 there appeared the improved Sunderland II, with supercharged engines, increased armament and elementary ASV radar. Major production version was the Mk III, with redesigned planing surfaces, later ASV radar and—on many aircraft—so many guns that it was nicknamed 'flying porcupine' by its German adversaries. Sunderlands of various marks served with the RAF from 1938-58, longer than any other aircraft type.

Above left: This photograph, taken from the German warship *Prinz Eugen* as it escaped northward through the English Channel on 13 February 1942, shows part of its escort of Bf 110 fighters and E-boats. Continuous attack on German capital ships seeking refuge at Brest had necessitated the famous 'Channel dash' to what seemed like safer waters

Above: A Sunderland of Coastal Command keeping a watchful eye open for U-boats near an Atlantic convoy

Left: When the hunter became the quarry, the Sunderland could take care of itself very well. Multi-gun turrets earned it the nickname 'Flying Porcupine' among Luftwaffe pilots. One Sunderland, attacked by six Junkers Ju 88 twin-engined fighters, shot one down, forced another to land and drove off the other four. Another destroyed three out of eight Ju 88s which attacked it

This page, top left: After early operations had revealed serious deficiencies in their defensive armament, the Handley Page Hampdens of Bomber Command were fitted with twin Vickers guns in their dorsal and ventral positions, armour plate and flame-damping exhausts. After that they took part successfully in many night raids, including the first attack on Berlin and the thousand-bomber raid on Cologne

Top right: Sgt John Hannah, a wireless operator/air gunner of No 83 Squadron, was awarded the Victoria Cross for putting out fires that would have destroyed his Hampden on the night of 15/16 September 1940. The aircraft was hit over Antwerp while engaged in an attack on German barges assembled for the invasion of England

Centre: The industry that made the RAF bomber offensive possible is typified by this photograph of girl workers with Merlin engines, used in aircraft such as the Lancaster and Mosquito

Opposite page, top left: Wartime Lancaster sorties totalled about 156,000, during which 608,612 tons of bombs were dropped. This is how the raids were often chronicled on individual aircraft, together with decorations gained by crew members

Centre left: First used in action in March 1942, the Lancaster spearheaded the night bomber offensive and went on to serve Bomber Command for more than ten years. It was the only wartime aircraft to carry Barnes Wallis's 22,000-lb (9,980-kg) Grand Slam bomb

Right: First of the RAF four-engined 'heavies' of the second World War to be used in action, the Short Stirling had a sufficiently heavy armament to operate over France by day as well as night throughout 1941

One of two Lancasters which survive in an airworthy condition in the UK, this B Mk 1 (PA474) would have joined 'Tiger Force' for an offensive against Japan had the war continued. Instead it was used for six years by No 82 (Photo Reconnaissance) Squadron before switching to research work. Refurbished in wartime colours, it flies regularly from RAF Waddington

THE ALLIED BOMBER OFFENSIVE

DURING THE FIRST World War there were several visionaries who saw in the bombing aeroplane a more potent weapon than those being used for battlefield and tactical activity. Few were better placed than Hugh Trenchard, one of the earliest Army aviators, who had been in military aviation in Britain from its inception. He put forward ideas for the strategic use of aircraft for bombing and, before the war was over, had been asked to form and command the Independent Force, an organisation within the newly-established Royal Air Force with the specific task of employing aircraft in a strategic role.

After the war the Royal Air Force, under Trenchard's guidance, grew up with a strong traditional belief that 'the best form of defence is attack' and that this attack should pre-eminently be strategic bombing. Bomber Command was formed for this primary purpose in the 1930s, when the RAF expanded to meet the threat of the Luftwaffe, and when the second World War started it was anxious to put its theories into practice. The Command was divided into five groups, two with light/medium bombers (Battles and Blenheims) and three with medium/heavy bombers (Whitleys, Hampdens and Wellingtons). A sizeable portion of the light bomber force was hived off straight away to form part of the RAF's forces in France, committed to tactical support of the armies.

Bomber Command opened its offensive with unbounded confidence, but was hedged in by restrictions which impeded the flexibility of its operation. To avoid incurring a full blitzkrieg on this country it was decided that bombers would not fly over Germany nor drop bombs on any but strictly military installations. Within this limitation Bomber Command immediately went on to the offensive, remaining true to the tenet of attack, by sending aircraft out over the North Sea against German Navy installations. A force of Blenheims, sent off for a late afternoon attack on ships in Heligoland Bight, met atrocious weather conditions and the mission was ineffective. Fourteen Wellingtons, attempting the same task in the Wilhelmshafen area, lost two of their number for little result. On the bigger bombers, the Air Ministry practice of arming the aircraft with several gun positions and/or turrets was soon found to be insufficient for daylight operations, and these tentative raids were abandoned.

The next move was to send Whitley squadrons roaming over Germany during the long winter nights, dropping nothing more fearsome than leaflets. They met little opposition: in fact the bombers' fiercest opponent was the winter weather; but little was accomplished apart from the training value to the crews of getting to know their way about Germany at night. This kid-glove approach was maintained all through the 'Phoney War', partly for political reasons and partly because Bomber Command had not yet acquired sufficient resources to mount a sustained offensive. But after the invasion of the Low Countries and France, Bomber Command was im-

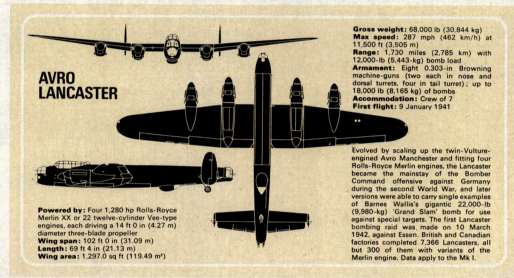

AVRO LANCASTER

Gross weight: 68,000 lb (30,844 kg)
Max speed: 287 mph (462 km/h) at 11,500 ft (3,505 m)
Range: 1,730 miles (2,785 km) with 12,000-lb (5,443-kg) bomb load
Armament: Eight 0.303-in Browning machine-guns (two each in nose and dorsal turrets, four in tail turret); up to 18,000 lb (8,165 kg) of bombs
Accommodation: Crew of 7
First flight: 9 January 1941

Powered by: Four 1,280 hp Rolls-Royce Merlin XX or 22 twelve-cylinder Vee-type engines, each driving a 14 ft 0 in (4.27 m) diameter three-blade propeller
Wing span: 102 ft 0 in (31.09 m)
Length: 69 ft 4 in (21.13 m)
Wing area: 1,297.0 sq ft (119.49 m²)

Evolved by scaling up the twin-Vulture-engined Avro Manchester and fitting four Rolls-Royce Merlin engines, the Lancaster became the mainstay of the Bomber Command offensive against Germany during the second World War, and later versions were able to carry single examples of Barnes Wallis's gigantic 22,000-lb (9,980-kg) 'Grand Slam' bomb for use against special targets. The first Lancaster bombing raid was made on 10 March 1942, against Essen. British and Canadian factories completed 7,366 Lancasters, all but 300 of them with variants of the Merlin engine. Data apply to the Mk I.

Above: 'Bombing up' a Stirling. Because its bomb-bay was divided into sections, the largest weapon this bomber could carry was a 4,000-pounder. More often it carried a heavy load of smaller bombs, as illustrated

Opposite page, top left: One of the biggest problems faced by Germany's night fighter force was to try to intercept the Mosquito light bomber. Able to outfly the opposition, even when carrying a 4,000-lb (1,814-kg) bomb, de Havilland's 'Wooden Wonder' had sufficient range to attack Berlin night after night

Centre left: 'Your vegetables will be planted here.' Bomber Command Stirling crews being briefed for a minelaying mission, known as 'gardening'. Mines laid by the RAF sank 759 German-controlled ships, totalling 721,977 tons, in north-west European waters

Top right: Some of the 800 craters left by a Bomber Command raid on Volkel airfield in Holland on 3 September 1944

Bottom: The railway viaduct at Bielefeld, which carried the main line between Hamm and Hannover, photographed three days after an attack with 22,000-lb (9,980-kg) and 12,000-lb (5,443-kg) bombs by Lancasters of No 617 ('Dam-busters') Squadron on 14 March 1945. The structure remains wrecked to this day

This page, top: Halifax tugs, Horsa and Hamilcar gliders, on the eve of the D-Day invasion of Europe, 6 June 1944. The bombers used for this task retained their full attack capability

mediately thrown into action tactically, bombing behind the enemy lines to relieve pressure on the battlefield.

Even after the fall of France, during which the Command's contingent on the continent was virtually wiped out, bombers from the UK maintained what offensive they could against the enemy air forces and the build-up of invasion forces. Blenheims by day and 'heavies' by night mounted small-scale raids over the nearer Continental airfields and ports. The Command also attacked some strategic targets, principally oil installations. When the immediate danger to Britain ended at the close of September 1940, the Air Staff lost no time in organising a proper strategic bombing policy.

There was a strong and natural desire on the part of Londoners to 'have a crack' at Berlin, but the Air Staff wisely decided that all attacks were to be against precise objectives rather than degenerate into area bombing. The two techniques were combined on the night of 24/25 September 1940, when a force of 119 bombers was mustered to attack gas-works and power stations in Berlin. From then on, the night offensive slowly developed, with oil plants at top priority. Even so, forces were time and again diverted to fulfil more immediate needs, particularly at the behest of the Admiralty, whose own situation was becoming increasingly fraught. This continued into 1941, the ports on the French west coast becoming particularly familiar to Bomber Command crews. In 1941

Stirling four-engined bombers—the first of the real 'heavies'—began to take their effective place in Bomber Command's armoury. They were tried out initially by day but proved no better suited to such operations than the Hampdens, Whitleys and Wellingtons before them, and before long were used solely at night.

During 1941 the move towards area bombing made itself felt. It had many protagonists in Bomber Command, for it was realised increasingly that many of the attacks being made against precision targets were wasteful, in that a high proportion of the bombs were falling outside—some well outside—the target area, resulting in negligible damage. So targets were chosen more and more on the basis of being within an environment which was worth attacking anyway. Targets within an industrial town, for example, would be more favoured than isolated pinpoint targets elsewhere. By this means many towns in Germany were attacked regularly, as well as the particular targets within them.

In the summer of 1941 the bomber offensive strode ahead. Pressure was off the Command to waste its energy on keeping ships in port at Brest, and help from the boffins had arrived to assist the bomber crews with navigational accuracy. This took the form of 'Gee', a radio navigational aid which was the forerunner of a whole series of radio and radar devices that put the bomber offensive ahead of its German opposition. The force, now consisting of nearly 1,000 bombers, was redirected in

July 1941 against the main rail centres of the Reich, with the intention of so dislocating the transportation system as to afford maximum assistance to the Russians. Secondary (on paper at least) was the attack against large centres of industrial population in order to disrupt production of essential means of waging war. More and more, however, this became the real motive behind the offensive, with the intention of wearing down the German population as a whole, not simply by mass murder, but rather by the wholesale destruction of their amenities and services.

The Ruhr valley figured prominently in this offensive, and became the battleground over which bombers fought their fiercest and bloodiest battles—for the defences of the Ruhr were soon so built-up that the area became an almost impregnable fortress. The results were reflected by an increase in Bomber Command's casualties, and as 1941 drew to a close its activities tailed off in order to conserve energies for a spring offensive.

This was officially implemented in February 1942, and was to make use of increasing numbers of aircraft equipped with Gee, before a counter to it was found by the Luftwaffe. To relieve the Russians as much as possible and to pave a way for a second front, the objective was to destroy the morale of the civilian population, particularly the industrial workers. The views of Bomber Command's new Commander-in-Chief, Air Marshal A T Harris, on strategic bomber operation coincided with this directive. His total force then consisted of approximately 600 aircraft and, though this number remained fairly constant throughout the year, 1942 saw the steady replacement of old twin-engined bombers by the new generation of heavies, and the introduction of Bomber Command's two finest bombers, the Avro Lancaster and D.H. Mosquito. Two other factors which added to the power and effectiveness of the bomber offensive appeared in 1942, although their full import was really not effective until the following year. These were the formation of the Pathfinder Force within Bomber Command and the arrival of the first elements of the US Eighth Air Force at bases in Britain.

It was also a year for learning. Bomber Command was adept at analysing its results, and particularly its failures, in order to learn from them. More and more reliance was placed on incendiary bombs, particularly against towns known to be high fire risks—such as Lubeck, which was devastated at the end of March. With the Lancaster another attempt was made at daylight raiding in force with a daring attack on Augsburg in April; but it was a relatively unsuccessful operation and gave no promise of an easy opening to a round-the-clock offensive. Against this gloomy prognostication came the fresh young Americans and their Flying Fortresses during the summer of 1942, eager to show what they could do with bombers armed to the teeth and carrying the Norden bombsight with which they claimed they could

'drop bombs into a pickle barrel from four miles up'. They were trained for daylight operations only, and came in for an awful savaging from German fighters, as sage old heads at the Air Ministry had forecast. But, to their credit, with immense courage they and their successors stuck at it until they had forged a mighty daylight force which, with the RAF's night offensive, produced the desired round-the-clock offensive which eventually helped to force Germany to surrender.

In 1943 the plan began to come true. The previous year had seen the start of Harris's great thousand-bomber raids, the first on Cologne on 30 May, but these were procured by extraordinary means, using many trainee crews; the normal level of operation had been about 200 aircraft. Now the New Year saw the British and US bomber forces working on complementary lines under terms agreed at the Casablanca conference. The highest-priority target for both forces was the German aircraft industry, with the Eighth Air Force attempting precision raids by daylight and the RAF making area attacks by night on towns concerned with the ancillary industries. Beyond these priorities were a host of other targets worked out at lower levels. At last Bomber Command felt ready and equipped for the task at hand. Its face was set resolutely at that toughest of targets, the Ruhr, and all its energies were bent towards destruction

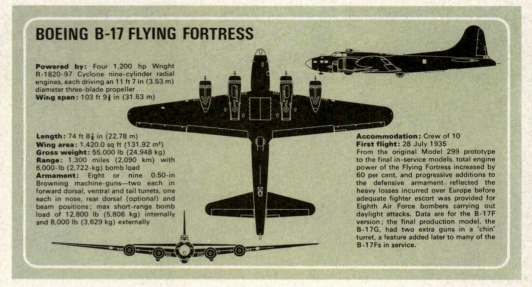

BOEING B-17 FLYING FORTRESS

Powered by: Four 1,200 hp Wright R-1820-97 Cyclone nine-cylinder radial engines, each driving an 11 ft 7 in (3.53 m) diameter three-blade propeller
Wing span: 103 ft 9⅜ in (31.63 m)

Length: 74 ft 8⅞ in (22.78 m)
Wing area: 1,420.0 sq ft (131.92 m²)
Gross weight: 55,000 lb (24,948 kg)
Range: 1,300 miles (2,090 km) with 6,000-lb (2,722-kg) bomb load
Armament: Eight or nine 0.50-in Browning machine-guns—two each in forward dorsal, ventral and tail turrets, one each in nose, rear dorsal (optional) and beam positions; max short-range bomb load of 12,800 lb (5,806 kg) internally and 8,000 lb (3,629 kg) externally

Accommodation: Crew of 10
First flight: 28 July 1935
From the original Model 299 prototype to the final in-service models, total engine power of the Flying Fortress increased by 60 per cent, and progressive additions to the defensive armament reflected the heavy losses incurred over Europe before adequate fighter escort was provided for Eighth Air Force bombers carrying out daylight attacks. Data are for the B-17F version; the final production model, the B-17G, had two extra guns in a 'chin' turret, a feature added later to many of the B-17Fs in service.

Top right: While Bomber Command hammered Europe at night, with its four-engined 'heavies', the US Eighth Air Force completed the 'round-the-clock' offensive in daylight. Staggering losses were incurred initially, until defensive armament and armouring were improved, and escort fighters with sufficient range to accompany the bombers all the way to the target and back were introduced into service. Mainstay of the American bomber force was the Boeing B-17G Flying Fortress; 8,680 of this version were produced by Douglas, Lockheed and Boeing themselves, with 16 coming off the assembly lines at Boeing's Seattle plant every 24 hours

Right: The scale of B-17 production at Seattle is well illustrated in this picture released in 1942, just after America entered the war. Altogether, 12,731 Flying Fortresses were built, a 'big bomber' production total exceeded only by the Convair B-24 Liberator

Far right: At least 49 Flying Fortresses are known to survive world-wide, including this one at the US Air Force Museum, Wright-Patterson Air Force Base, Dayton, Ohio

Centre right: The B-17G had no fewer than thirteen 50-calibre guns to ensure a hail of cross-fire when a formation of Fortresses came under attack. Their positions are indicated in this diagram, which shows the new chin turret introduced on the 'G'. In an attempt to produce a really heavily-armed escort aircraft, 21 Fortresses were modified into B-40s, carrying up to 30 machine-guns and cannon; but these were not successful

Bottom right: Part of the wonderful mosaic ceiling by Francis Scott Bradford at the memorial to men of the US armed forces who died in the second World War, at Madingley, near Cambridge. Dedicated to men of the USAAF, the ceiling shows their aircraft, each type clearly recognisable. The parts of the mosaic in deep blue denote the depth of infinity; the lighter colours reflect the light of Heaven breaking through the earthly layers of the sky, with a lighter nimbus surrounding each aircraft to separate it from earthly forces as it makes its final flight

of the area. But first it had to dispose of an old distraction—the U-boat ports on the French west coast, which were again causing the Navy great trouble. By now further aids were forthcoming: 'Oboe' was first used in March 1943, and the Pathfinder Force was becoming a really economical and devastating means of leading an attack.

This was the year, too, in which the Americans' great bombing fleet was blooded in only too literal a way. Pursuing their intention of massed daylight assaults on Germany brought to the Fortress and Liberator crews a succession of distressing and costly enterprises and they were obliged to fly under the protection of a fighter umbrella. But when they were so escorted

the American raids became far more effective and casualties were reduced to an acceptable level. At first British Spitfires were used as escort, but these had barely enough range for the task; later the American bombers had an escort force comprising their own P-38 Lightnings, P-47 Thunderbolts and (later) P-51 Mustangs. From that moment, the Eighth Air Force was truly in business, and by early 1944 exceeded Bomber Command in numbers.

The pattern was now set, and it remained only for the two forces, side by side, to step up their fearsome offensive until the Reich was defeated. In the process, several other refinements were introduced. Many of these were of a 'black box' nature, not only

providing the bombers with better navigation and bombing aids but helping them to dislocate the German night-fighter and other defensive organisations. A whole Group was built up within Bomber Command whose express purpose was the complete dislocation of the German defensive machine by radio and radar devices. Very effective it was, too, operating 'spoof' raids and sending alternative transmissions on the German control frequencies, with bogus orders to the night-fighter crews, who could never be sure whether they were hearing friend or foe.

In 1944 the attention of both day and night bomber forces was turned increasingly towards the installations which had sprung up across the Channel, from which the German Vergeltungswaffen (reprisal weapons) were to be launched against the UK. But by April a more vital task had dawned, and for some months the whole vast weight of the two forces was put at the disposal of the Supreme Allied Commander in Europe for support of the invasion of Europe. By then such ascendancy had been gained over the Luftwaffe that Allied losses by day were on the wane, and henceforth Bomber Command's heavies came out increasingly by day, providing their own 24-hour offensive. Their well-tried methods of attack underwent increasing sophistication, and outsize bombs like the 'Tallboy' and 'Grand Slam' began to appear on specially-modified Lancasters.

When the invasion forces were established so firmly on Continental soil as to need no further backing from the heavies, Bomber Command and the Eighth Air Force returned to the attack on Germany itself. Again the principal target was oil: if Germany's oil plants could be severely hit, the Luftwaffe would be rendered impotent and the Wehrmacht made immobile. Backing this up were attacks on other transportation systems; 'Bomber' Harris made sure that the RAF's contribution was flown in terms of area attacks where they would most demoralise, and specialised squadrons, using principally Mosquitos, were trained for raids on pinpoint targets.

The stranglehold which this final devastating offensive had on Germany began to make itself felt early in 1945. The writing was on the wall, and it was only a matter of time before the heavy blows which American and British forces alike were raining on Germany took their full effect. Never before had such a huge force of men and machines been built up, skilled in experience and terrible in execution. The protagonists of aerial bombardment had been vindicated in awful fashion.

BARNES WALLIS

This page, top: The airship R100 on its mooring mast at Cardington, Bedfordshire. It was for this huge aircraft that Barnes Wallis devised his unique geodetic form of structure

Above: Inside the control cabin of the R100

Left: Sir Barnes Wallis in his office at Weybridge, Surrey. On the wall is a painting of the R100. On his drawing board is an aircraft that could fly non-stop across the world, from London to Sydney, in three hours

Opposite page, top: Wallis's geodetic 'basket-work' structure made the Wellington bomber so strong that it could absorb tremendous damage in World War 2 and still get home safely

Centre left: A 12,000 lb (5,443 kg) Tallboy bomb immediately after release from a Lancaster bomber

Centre right: A Wellington bomber in flight. The geodetic form of structure is plainly visible under the fabric covering of the wings and tailplane

Bottom: The Moehne dam in Germany, after the raid by 617 Squadron Lancasters using Wallis's 'skipping bomb'

For the average person the name of Barnes Neville Wallis will almost certainly be associated with inventions which contributed to Allied victory in World War 2: the geodetic construction of the Wellington bomber, the skip-bombs which breached the Moehne, Eder and Sorpe dams, and the Grand Slam and Tallboy 'earthquake' bombs—these latter weapons weighing around ten and five tons respectively. From such a record one could easily assume that he is a scientist who has made a life study of warlike instruments and the art of destruction.

No assumption could be further from the truth for, above all, Barnes Wallis is a pacifist. In the Autumn of 1939 his prime concern was to decide how he, as an aircraft engineer, could make a contribution that would hasten the war's end, before too many valuable lives had been sacrificed.

Nothing portrayed this more vividly than his ceaseless pacing of the operations room at No 5 (Bomber) Group headquarters, at Grantham, throughout the period of 617 Squadron's attack on the Ruhr dams. To Wallis each minute seemed an hour, each hour a lifetime of suspense and misery that aircrew whom he had come to know as individuals might, at that very moment, be dying or dead—and that, were the attack successful, many thousands of German civilians might also be drowned.

Success of the attack and the vindication of his theories brought only a temporary elation. He soon faced the bitter realisation that 53 men of the RAF had died to achieve this success and, in a broken voice, exclaimed: 'If I'd only known, I'd never have started this!'

There is a lighter postscript to the skip-bomb saga. The spectacular destruction of the German dams made higher authority wonder if other targets—railway viaducts, for example—might prove vulnerable to the technique. Tests were laid on, and 617 Squadron was detailed to launch dummies of Wallis's bomb against Boscombe Down's 'home security target'—a massive reinforced concrete structure some 20 ft (6.10 m) in height. Official observers were Air Commodore D D'Arcy Greig—best remembered as a Schneider Trophy pilot in inter-war years—and Group Captain Wynter-Morgan. Greig decided that the best observation point was from the top of the target building. The first Lancaster released its bomb most accurately, so that it bounded along and duly impacted on the target. Lancaster number two was fractionally high and late at the moment of release, and as the bomb came hurtling towards them Greig decided it was 'evens' that the final bounce would drop it neatly on top of the building. For once he chose discretion and leapt from the roof. Wynter-Morgan lay prone as the bomb skimmed

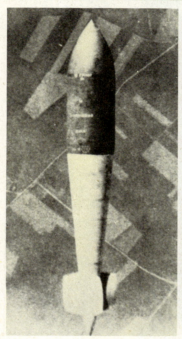

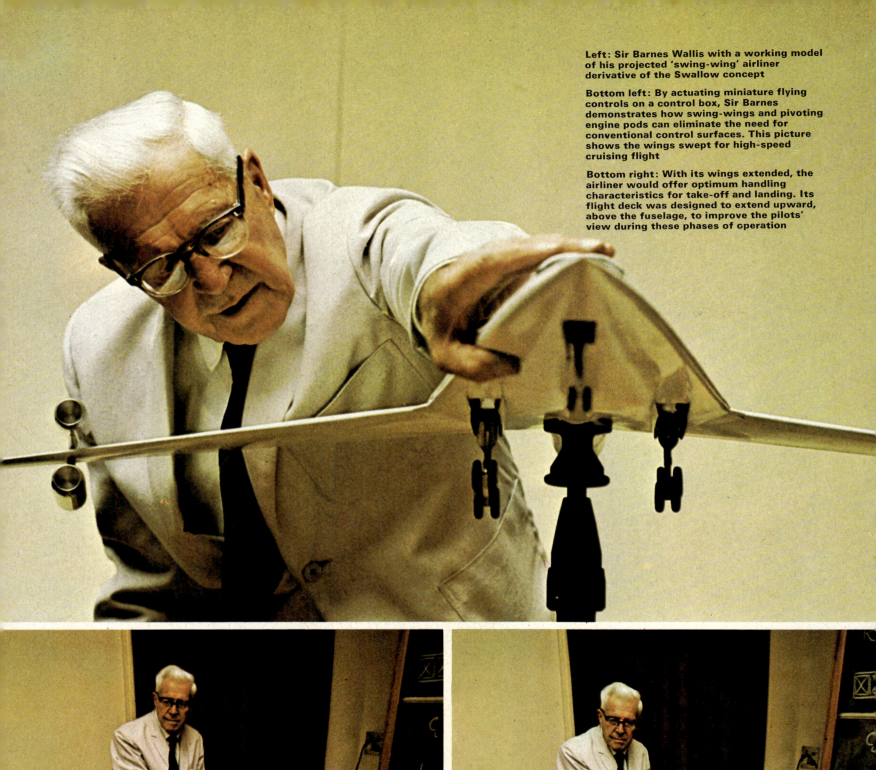

Left: Sir Barnes Wallis with a working model of his projected 'swing-wing' airliner derivative of the Swallow concept

Bottom left: By actuating miniature flying controls on a control box, Sir Barnes demonstrates how swing-wings and pivoting engine pods can eliminate the need for conventional control surfaces. This picture shows the wings swept for high-speed cruising flight

Bottom right: With its wings extended, the airliner would offer optimum handling characteristics for take-off and landing. Its flight deck was designed to extend upward, above the fuselage, to improve the pilots' view during these phases of operation

the parapet, spattering him with mud and debris. When he cleared his eyes, Greig was no longer with him. 'My God', he shouted, 'they've got Greig!' Happily, they hadn't: a winded, wiser and dishevelled Air Commodore was lying safely on the ground.

Barnes Wallis had been connected with aviation long before this—in fact since 1913, when in conjunction with H B Pratt he designed Britain's second rigid airship, the R9, which was completed by Vickers in 1917. Wallis was no run-of-the-mill aviation designer like those, typical of the period, who tended to build by rule-of-thumb and then see whether their creations would fly. His was a painstaking and academic approach—mentally sifting details, scrapping this, improving that and, whenever possible, testing his ideas before passing the final design for construction.

When World War 1 ended, Wallis felt that governmental attitudes to aviation left little scope for his advanced ideas for aircraft capable of establishing long-range routes; and, sadly, he turned his back temporarily on the aviation scene. Then, in 1924, Vickers established the Airship Guarantee Company, and he returned to become its Chief Engineer, entrusted with the design of the airship which became known as the R100, a unique and successful vehicle in which he utilised for the first time the principle of geodetic construction. This form of lightweight, robust and seemingly-complex lattice structure later made the Wellington bomber of World War 2 capable of standing up to severe punishment without its structural integrity being destroyed.

The Wellington was preceded by the two-seat Wellesley bomber, in which Wallis used geodetic construction for the first time in a heavier-than-air craft. The

Wellesley demonstrated clearly the excellent weight/strength ratio of such structures when, in November 1938, it set a new world long-distance record of 7,157.7 miles (11,519 km).

In World War 2 Wallis became involved deeply with the design of bombs, a subject about which he knew practically nothing at the start. With characteristic application he contrived, in a remarkably short time, to master the complex problems involved in the design and construction of contemporary weapons and then, again typically, set out to design 'tomorrow's bombs today'. The skip-bombs and earthquake bombs were evolved from this period, and made their resounding contribution to Allied victory in the war.

Peace enabled Barnes Wallis, once again, to return to what he considered the most important aspect of British aviation: long-range high-speed commercial aircraft to shorten Britain's links with the rest of the world. As leader of Vickers' Research and Development Department—today a part of the British Aircraft Corporation—he was able to concentrate his thoughts on a new configuration that had been exercising his mind for some time. This was the variable-geometry or 'swing-wing' aircraft, which he had explored initially during the closing stages of the war.

Under the code-name 'Wild Goose', development had been financed by the Ministry of Supply and was, of course, a military project. Construction spread over several aircraft in model form, ranging from small hand-launched versions to larger radio-controlled examples that were accelerated to flying speed on a launching trolley. With a slender laminar-flow fuselage, variable-sweep wings set well back, and a swept tail fin, control about the three axes was achieved by co-ordinated and differential degrees of wing sweep-back. It was, in fact, a most advanced project for its time.

Wallis soon became disenchanted with the warlike Wild Goose, and concentrated on the even more advanced 'Swallow' that was taking shape at Vickers. Intended as

the basic design for a large civil transport aircraft, it had a fuselage that was virtually a lifting-body, blending into the wing and contributing its share of lift. The most revolutionary feature involved elimination of all conventional flying control surfaces, offering the potential of considerable reduction in drag. Instead, he intended that the four turbine engines, mounted one above and one below each wing, adjacent to the wingtip, should be able to pivot about all three axes, thus eliminating rudder, ailerons and elevators.

Subsonic and supersonic test flights made by models of the Swallow were entirely successful and proved, within the bounds of model testing, that the swing-wing principle and simplicity of control augured well for the future. Unfortunately, Britain's economic state deprived the project of government support and Vickers, unable to 'go it alone' on such an advanced aircraft, passed the swing-wing principle over to the American aviation industry. In due course a development of this new technique of variable-geometry became incorporated in the General Dynamics F-111 series of aircraft, the first prototype utilising full wing sweep on its second flight on 6 June 1965.

Almost exactly three years later, on 8 June 1968, at the age of 81, Barnes Wallis received a knighthood for his services to British aviation. This would seem to be a fitting end to the career of a successful and brilliant man: except that it was not the end.

Today, Sir Barnes Wallis continues to exercise his mind on advanced projects concerned with long-range high-speed intercontinental transport, believing that a STOL (Short Take-Off and Landing) hypersonic airliner, able to link London and Sydney within three hours, would be more economic than either the now-developing Concorde SST or the subsonic 'Jumbo jets'.

Such plans may seem too far in advance of the state of the art: but it would be prudent to remember how many times before Barnes Wallis has proved to be right.

Below: These photographs of one of the first USAF/General Dynamics F-111E tactical fighter-bombers deployed to the UK show how the 'swing-wing' concept has been utilised in this 1,600 mph (2,575 km/h) combat aircraft

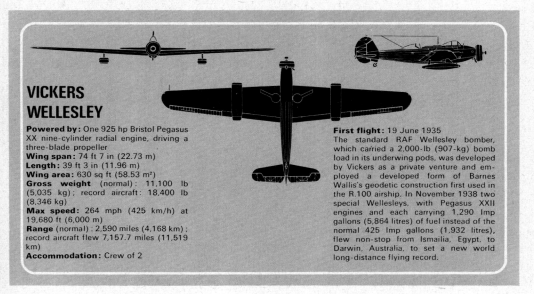

VICKERS WELLESLEY

Powered by: One 925 hp Bristol Pegasus XX nine-cylinder radial engine, driving a three-blade propeller
Wing span: 74 ft 7 in (22.73 m)
Length: 39 ft 3 in (11.96 m)
Wing area: 630 sq ft (58.53 m²)
Gross weight (normal): 11,100 lb (5,035 kg); record aircraft: 18,400 lb (8,346 kg)
Max speed: 264 mph (425 km/h) at 19,680 ft (6,000 m)
Range (normal): 2,590 miles (4,168 km); record aircraft flew 7,157.7 miles (11,519 km)
Accommodation: Crew of 2

First flight: 19 June 1935
The standard RAF Wellesley bomber, which carried a 2,000-lb (907-kg) bomb load in its underwing pods, was developed by Vickers as a private venture and employed a developed form of Barnes Wallis's geodetic construction first used in the R.100 airship. In November 1938 two special Wellesleys, with Pegasus XXII engines and each carrying 1,290 Imp gallons (5,864 litres) of fuel instead of the normal 425 Imp gallons (1,932 litres), flew non-stop from Ismailia, Egypt, to Darwin, Australia, to set a new world long-distance flying record.

AIR WAR OVER AFRICA

THE ENTRY OF ITALY into the second World War found the British in the Middle East dangerously weak both in the air and on the ground. A few squadrons of Gladiator fighter biplanes and Blenheim twin-engined bombers faced a much larger force of the Italian Regia Aeronautica, equipped with aircraft of similar vintage—Fiat C.R.42 fighter biplanes and Savoia-Marchetti S.M.79 tri-motor bombers. The RAF took the offensive early, attacking Italian air-fields in Libya during the first days of the war; but although Italian troops finally advanced over the frontier into Egypt in September 1940, they stopped after a few miles and a stalemate ensued until December. Then, with a far smaller but very efficient mobile force, and with his air strength reinforced by a few Hurricane fighters, General Wavell launched a limited offensive which quickly grew to an all-out push as the vastly larger Italian army retreated across Cyrencaica to the borders of Tripolitania.

Here the British had to halt, due to the shortage of supplies and the long lines of communication; but by this time the RAF had virtually driven the Regia Aeronautica from the skies, and the Hurricanes ruled supreme. Unfortunately, it was at this juncture that the RAF was greatly weakened by the despatch of a number of squadrons to the aid of the Greeks, while at the same time Rommel's Afrika Korps began arriving in Tripoli, bringing with it elements of the Luftwaffe straight from the Battle of Britain and equipped with modern Messerschmitt Bf 109 and 110 fighters, and Junkers Ju 87 dive-bombers.

Late in March 1941 Rommel launched a probing attack on the critically-weakened British positions, and in a few weeks had sent the Imperial forces reeling back right across the Egyptian frontier, the Luftwaffe gaining a considerable ascendancy at this time. While this was happening, apart from the squadrons sent to Greece, RAF and South African units were also fighting the Italians over East Africa; but by May the fighting there was almost over, and the evacuation of Greece and Crete had been completed. The arrival of some reinforcements allowed a small offensive—Operation 'Brevity'—to be undertaken, but this was an immediate failure. Following some fighting with insurrectionists in Iraq, the Vichy French colony of Syria was occupied in July, but not without hard fighting with the garrison forces both on the ground and in the air. By this time, too, the arrival of units released from East Africa and the receipt of such American aircraft as the Curtiss Tomahawk fighter and Martin Maryland bomber provided the opportunity for a further limited offensive, launched in June and known as Operation 'Battleaxe'; this had no more success than 'Brevity'.

A period of consolidation followed, during which time the Western Desert Air Force, as it was now known, was greatly reinforced. This period lasted until November 1941 when an all-out offensive, code-named 'Crusader', was mounted to drive the Axis out of Cyrenaica and to relieve the port of Tobruk, which had been under siege since April. Blenheims, Marylands, Hurricanes and Tomahawks by day, and

Wellingtons by night, hammered at the German and Italian forces and fought the Luftwaffe and Regia Aeronautica in the air as General Auchinleck's troops advanced once more to the borders of Tripolitania in a long, hard-fought battle. The WDAF won a degree of superiority in the air which it never again lost, and which increased with every month that passed. Ju 87s, Bf 110s and Italian aircraft were shot from the skies in furious air battles, though the relatively small number of Bf 109s remained superior to anything the British could put into the air. Too small in numbers now to challenge seriously the growing strength of the WDAF, they kept up a series of sniping attacks on its formations which maintained a rate of loss far higher than the RAF was to suffer in any of its other tactical air forces. It was in attacks of this nature that the legendary German fighter pilot, Hans-Joachim Marseille, was to shoot down the greatest number of British aircraft claimed by any pilot of either war—151 in eighteen months!

At the turn of the year the forces in the Middle East were again weakened when units were withdrawn and reinforcements re-routed to the Far East, where the Japanese had just attacked. Rommel picked this moment to repeat his probing attack of the previous year; catching the Imperial forces off balance, he sent them back across Cyrenaica once more. This time the retreat stopped about half-way to the Egyptian frontier on the Gazala Line, and here stalemate was again the order of the day for several months.

FIAT C.R.42

Powered by: One 840 hp Fiat A.74R.1C 38 fourteen-cylinder radial engine, driving a 9 ft 2¼ in (2.80 m) diameter three-blade propeller
Wing span: 31 ft 10 in (9.70 m)
Length: 27 ft 1¼ in (8.26 m)
Wing area: 241.1 sq ft (22.40 m²)
Gross weight: 5,033 lb (2,283 kg)
Max speed: 267 mph (430 km/h) at 17,490 ft (5,330 m)
Normal range: 482 miles (775 km)
Armament: Two 12.7-mm machine-guns in upper front fuselage; two similar guns or two 220-lb (100-kg) bombs beneath lower wings

Accommodation: Crew of 1
First flight: early 1939
The Falco, as the C.R.42 was known to the Italian Air Force; was the last of a long line of *Caccia* (fighter) *Rosatelli* biplane fighters produced by the Fiat company during the inter-war years. Although the C.R.42 was an excellent example of its genre, the combat value of the fighter biplane in a monoplane age was dramatically highlighted by the Falco's record: Italy entered the war with 143 of these aircraft, a total of 1,781 was eventually built, yet by the time of the Italian surrender in September 1943 only 113 survived.

1940-43

New bombers such as the Boston and Baltimore now reached the front, with a new fighter, the Kittyhawk. Fighter sweeps and bombing attacks over Axis territory were maintained while Auchinleck prepared his army for a new offensive. In the event, Rommel just beat him to the punch in May. The fierce and costly Battle of Gazala ensued, in which the British armour in the Knightsbridge area was decimated. Forced into retreat again, the British forces withdrew across the Egyptian frontier, this time losing Tobruk, and the Afrika Korps reached its high water mark when the 8th Army finally stopped on a prepared line at El Alamein. Throughout July the army held on while the air force threw everything into stopping the Axis advance, including the first Spitfires to arrive in the desert, Hurricane 'tank-busters' with anti-tank guns beneath their wings, Kittyhawks carrying 250-lb (113-kg) and 500-lb (227-kg) bombs, and Beaufighters. Between army and air force, the line was held.

At this time the first American air units arrived to support the British, and P-40 Warhawks, B-24 Liberators and B-25 Mitchells were soon flying alongside the Australian, British and South African squadrons of the WDAF. In early September Rommel again tried to breach the Allied line, but his attack was swiftly beaten off, mainly by air power. By the following month the WDAF had reached its zenith, and though its fighters and fighter-bombers continued to suffer grievous losses to the marauding Messerschmitts, the bombers always got through to destroy stores and supply

dumps, shatter aircraft on the ground and generally demoralise the enemy.

Late in October General Bernard Montgomery, who had taken over command of the 8th Army after the retreat from Gazala, launched his great Alamein offensive, and after a week of slogging, the Axis forces broke and fled westwards, their packed columns the target of continual air attack. As the opposing armies flowed once more to the west, across the Cyrenaican desert, British and American forces, supported by carriers of both the US and Royal Navies, landed in Morocco and Algeria, far in Rommel's rear. Little resistance was met on the ground, but a short, savage battle was fought with the Vichy French in the air. Units of the RAF with Spitfires, Hurricanes and Bisleys, and of the USAAF, also with Spitfires, and with P-40s, P-38 Lightnings and A-20 Havocs, quickly moved in, and the Allies pushed eastwards towards Tunisia. The Axis high command in the Mediterranean acted with commendable speed, flying both ground and air forces into Tunisia just in time to hold the British 1st Army in the mountains west of Bizerta as the winter set in.

At first, with good bases close to the front, the Axis enjoyed air superiority over Tunisia, but the Allies were steadily reinforced throughout late 1942/early 1943 with B-17 Flying Fortresses, B-25 and B-26 medium bombers, and new Spitfire IXs, and many hard-fought actions took place. To the south the 8th Army took Tripoli in January and moved up to the Tunisian border. In February, feeling momentarily safe behind the Mareth Line, which blocked entry into southern Tunisia, Rommel struck north-westwards against the American and French troops in his rear at the Battle of Kasserine Pass, inflicting heavy losses both in the air and on the ground, and nearly succeeded in breaking the Allied front completely. His thrust was finally held, and in March Montgomery attacked his now-weakened forces at Mareth, outflanking the line and sending the Afrika Korps once more into retreat.

By early April the Allied armies had linked, and began compressing the Axis into northern Tunisia. During this month frantic efforts were made to supply the Axis troops by great fleets of transport aircraft from Sicily. Allied fighters patrolled their flight paths and shot them down literally in hundreds. Against the first American daylight raids by four-engined bombers, escorted by long-range fighters, and the ever-growing Allied air power over every corner of their territory, some of the best fighter pilots of the Luftwaffe from both Eastern and Western fronts fought desperately, but in vain; by early May they had to withdraw to Sicily, their bases in Africa no longer tenable. By this time the Allies had begun a final thrust all along the front. In overwhelming numerical superiority, with Allied air power now absolutely supreme, they steadily eliminated the Axis forces, the last resistance ending on the Cap Bon peninsula on 13 May 1943, just under three years since the war in Africa had begun.

The power and vigilance of the RAF and USAAF prevented the possibility of any evacuation to Sicily, and nearly a quarter of a million prisoners were taken, together with quantities of weapons, supplies, etc. In three years the Allied air forces had grown from a tiny contingent to a mighty weapon on which the army had come to rely greatly. Many lessons had been learnt in co-operation, and the Western Desert Air Force was to be the model on which the Allied tactical air forces were based for the rest of the war. Against heat, all-enveloping dust, flies, shortage of water and supplies, and against great odds, the men of the Commonwealth air forces, and later of the USAAF, had carried on and had won. The airmen of the Luftwaffe and Regia Aeronautica had fought bravely and well, and had gained many tactical successes; but they had failed, despite their opportunities, to forge their air forces into a compact whole with a common objective as the British and Americans had done.

Opposite page, top to bottom: On 11 June 1940, the first day of the East African campaign, Vickers Wellesleys destroyed 350,000 gallons (1,591,000 litres) of petrol on the Eritrean airfield of Massawa. They carried bombs in underwing canisters

One of ten Junkers Ju 87 dive-bombers, manned by Italians, which force-landed on or near the British side of the front line in North Africa, to the amazement of the local troops

Fresh from its victory in the Battle of Britain, the Spitfire followed its partner, the Hurricane, to new successes as Rommel's Afrika Korps was driven out of Cyrenaica, then Tripolitania and finally Tunisia

Returning from a low-level attack on enemy tanks, a Hurricane pilot gets a friendly wave from British anti-aircraft gunners

The wreckage of a Fiat G.50 fighter reflects the sad ending of Mussolini's grandiose plan to ride into Alexandria in triumph after clearing the British from North Africa

This page, left: First American bombers used by the RAF in North Africa were Martin Marylands. Their most famous operation was a reconnaissance of the Italian fleet at Taranto before the devastating Fleet Air Arm attack with Swordfish biplanes on 11 November 1940

Below: North American B-25 bombers of the USAAF were among the types which helped to end enemy air superiority over Tunisia in the Winter of 1942/43

For film-makers producing epics of the second World War, finding genuine—and airworthy—examples of some of the aircraft concerned can often be quite a problem. One recent exception involved the use of North American Mitchell bombers, some two dozen of which are still in existence. This one, a B-25J with some typical American 'artwork' of the period on its nose, makes a fine picture as it flies over the Gulf of California during filming for the movie *Catch 22*

the moon men

AS LONG AGO AS 1916 British secret agents were parachuted into enemy territory, often from boxes fixed to an aircraft's wings. These were opened by the pilot as he climbed, allowing the agent's body to slide out as a trapdoor opened. In August 1940, unbeknown to all but a few, Winston Churchill gave orders that volunteers were again to be sent to Occupied Europe, this time to set up resistance groups. At RAF North Weald, Essex, in the thick of fighter operations, No 419 Flight was established in a corner of the airfield, initially with a Whitley bomber coded NF. Later a few Lysander IIIs were added. Early operations were to drop agents and supplies, the first parachuted agent landing in France on 14 November 1940.

The Special Duties Flight moved to Newmarket for a time, continuing the parachuting of agents and their wireless sets (still mainly from Whitleys), and on 10 December began to operate also from RAF Stradishall. Flt Lt Keast flew the first of many successful drops which gained him the DSO. He failed to return in Whitley T4264 on 17 February 1941 after being promoted for his magnificent work for SOE (the Special Operations Executive). In August the Special Duties Flight became No 138 Squadron, and Sqn Ldr Murphy, who had flown many Lysander sorties, putting down agents, was shot as he was about to leave the cockpit—the landing field having been taken over by the enemy. With one hand held to his wound, he immediately took off again and brought his aircraft safely back to England. On another occasion, Sqn Ldr 'Whippy' Nesbitt-Dufort, who flew the first Lysander pick-up on 4/5 September 1941, landed at Tangmere, Sussex, with yards of French telephone wire around his undercarriage.

In February 1942, Nesbitt-Dufort had to abandon his aircraft after a return to

France with two agents he had picked up—flying for no less than seven hours in the Lysander in appalling weather. All three men were picked up weeks later by the first Avro Anson to land in enemy territory—piloted by the newly-promoted Sqn Ldr Murphy. Another brilliant pilot, Flt Lt Bridger, on one occasion hit power cables as he was landing in an improvised field, writing off one tyre. As the incoming and returning agents exchanged places in the rear cockpit Bridger calmly took out his revolver, burst the good tyre to even things up, and lurched into the air, just clearing the cables before setting course for base.

In 1942 a move was made to Tempsford, Bedfordshire, so that SOE could have its own field with the necessary links to London for the speedy and secret moves of agents. No 161 Squadron, under Wg Cdr C E H 'Mouse' Fielden, His Majesty's

personal pilot, was formed from The King's Flight, using Lysanders, Whitleys and (later) Wellingtons, Hudsons and a Halifax coded MA. One of the most brilliant of the pilots—who were nicknamed 'Pimpernels of the Air'—was Sqn Ldr Lewis Hodges, DFC, an experienced bomber captain with No 49 Squadron, who was to succeed as CO of No 161, gaining the DSO and a bar to his DFC for drops and pick-ups. One of his passengers, M Vincent Auriol, became President of France after the war and in 1945 Hodges received the Légion d'Honneur for this pick-up. Today, as Air Chief Marshal Sir Lewis Hodges, KCB, CBE, DSO, DFC, he is a Member of the Air Board, and is remembered also as CO of No 357 Squadron (Dakotas/Liberators) which parachuted Resistance groups into Japanese-held territory, and for his post-war flying in Canberras and Valiants.

Sqn Ldr John Affleck, a post-war BEA captain, also flew exciting sorties in Hudsons, on one occasion landing in a badly-chosen field in which the aircraft slowly sank beyond the wheels—with German troops nearby. All through the night, under Affleck's directions, Resistance workers dug trenches to try and free the machine as an alternative to setting it alight. At last Affleck decided to attempt a take-off with his passengers (who included a pregnant woman). He opened the throttles to full boost and, thanks to a providential bump in the ground, just cleared the trees at the end of the field. A few hours after landing in England a baby was born to the passenger and a code message was radioed to the father, still working under the noses of the Gestapo to set his country free.

Sqn Ldr Lockhart was another great pilot, who outwitted and outflew three Fw 190 fighters, despite searchlights which were co-operating with the Luftwaffe. Wg Cdr ('F for Freddy') Pickard, who commanded No 161 Squadron during 1943, on one occasion was so determined to put his agent down and pick up two others facing execution, if caught, that he circled an enemy-occupied area for almost two hours before going in. On his return he had to land in Cornwall, his fuel tanks virtually empty. He was killed in February 1944 leading the famous 'Operation Jericho' attack on Amiens Jail, where some of those he had taken to France were being tortured.

Lysanders on SOE tasks normally carried 150 extra gallons (682 litres) of fuel between the undercarriage struts and had a metal ladder fixed to the side to expedite the disembarking and embarking of 'Joes', as the agents were called. One passenger only was usual on outward flights, because of the extra fuel; but as many as four were sometimes brought back in emergencies when the Gestapo were closing in. Three Lysanders operated on occasions in 'formation', one going down first and bringing in the others by torch signals if all went smoothly. Sqn Ldr Verity and Flt Lts Fowler and McCairns flew as such a trio; McCairns was a remarkable pilot who, shot down flying a Spitfire, escaped from a German POW camp, and begged to be allowed to fly over Europe again to repay those who had helped him on his solo trek to freedom. Rising from Sergeant Pilot (with the Military Medal for his escape) to Squadron Leader, with a DFC and two bars for his SOE flights, he lost his life post-war, flying a 616 Squadron Mosquito.

With the approach of D-Day, more and more aircraft were added to the squadrons, thanks mainly to Wg Cdr Yeo-Thomas, GC, MC, who had twice been taken to France by 138 Squadron and who pleaded personally with Churchill for additional machines. As a result the Halifax was added to SOE operations and Wg Cdr C G S Rowan-Robinson, DSO, DFC and bar, one-time CO of No 158 (B) Squadron, volunteered to fly in 138's operations, with his complete crew. After making some splendid drops his Halifax was shot down in mid-May 1943 over Holland; he was taken prisoner and became a real thorn in the side of the enemy by continually changing identities in POW camps with others—once masquerading as a Russian to confuse the records.

Fourteen Tempsford machines are known to have been lost over Holland; DG405 'Y' of 161 Squadron, a Halifax Mk V lost on 22/23 June 1943, was one of them, though it is known that its agents had already dropped to safety. Many courageous aircrew lost their lives trying to ensure the accurate release of their 'Joes' and other precious cargoes despite heavy flak and night-fighter opposition above the Dutch fields. Some crews, as well as

Top: A Lysander IIIA equipped for 'Moon Squadron' operations, with under-fuselage long-range fuel tank and a ladder to enable 'Joes' to clamber quickly in and out of the rear cockpit. Such aircraft were usually painted black in service

Above: Aided only by the glimpse of lamps held by members of the 'underground' a Lysander takes off for England from a field in enemy-occupied France. Any reasonably flat area, about 600 yards (550 m) long and 400 yards (365 m) wide, was a potential landing strip for the slow-flying Lysander. Loyal Frenchmen became adept at filling in trenches cut across such fields by the Germans

Left: Wing Cdr C G S Rowan-Robinson, DSO, DFC and bar, who not only flew on 'Moon Squadron' operations but continued to be a thorn in the flesh of the Germans after he had been taken prisoner

agents, joined the Resistance when plans went wrong, and fought bravely until the Allies liberated the country.

Although some 138 and 161 Squadron crews inevitably lost their lives, others performed near-miracles, one such being Norwegian Lt Hysin-Dahl in July 1944, when flak forced him to ditch his Lysander in the Channel. Surfacing to inflate his dinghy, he looked for the three agents and rescued them one by one, only to find that one had died and a second was badly wounded. An American motor torpedo boat picked up the pilot and agents some hours later, but the second agent also died.

Long before D-Day two Canadians, Sgt (now Lt-Col) Raymond LaBrosse and Sgt-Major (later Captain) Lucien Dumais, flew out by Lysander to organise the return to England of servicemen already in hiding and those known to be on the run after the invasion. LaBrosse had parachuted into enemy territory months earlier to organise 'Oaktree', which had sent back 175 Allied airmen by sea from pre-arranged beaches. Dumais, captured during the Dieppe raid of 1942, escaped and returned to England to join LaBrosse in this new plan, code-named 'Shelburne'. In all, 307 Allied airmen owed their safe return to this pair, some coming back by special motor torpedo boats, others via the Pyrenees. Both received a well-earned Military Cross as well as French and American decorations.

Black-painted Halifaxes flew out to Algeria, picking up arms and other supplies and delivering them to Corsican and Sardinian patriots, despite strong Luftwaffe forces in Italy. Other aircraft went as far as the USSR and Yugoslavia. In 1943, 138 Squadron made 2,556 sorties, taking or dropping 1,000 agents; in 1944 mail was even snatched from poles held by Maquis members, requesting more arms and other help. Nine aircraft were lost by 138 Squadron in 1942, 30 in 1943, 27 in 1944 and four in 1945, though many crew-members were assisted by the patriots to get back home and fly again. Both squadrons operated with the Norwegian Resistance, which not only smuggled many RAF crews into Sweden but also boasted that no German ship could sail from Norway without the British Air Ministry or Admiralty knowing within 40 minutes. A silver model of a Viking ship was presented by 'The Spiders', as the Norwegian patriots were known, to No 138 Squadron after the war as a 'thank you' for its gallant contributions to their work.

In 1945, their 'Moon Squadron' tasks no longer needed and re-equipped with Lancasters and Stirlings, the two squadrons flew bomber sorties before helping to bring back prisoners of war.

Air War in the Pacific 1941-45

ON 7 DECEMBER 1941 a powerful force of Japanese carrier aircraft struck at Pearl Harbor, the American naval base in the Hawaiian Islands, and in a devastating surprise attack destroyed or damaged a large part of the US fleet. On the other side of the International Date Line, on 8 December, but in fact at the same time, the Japanese army invaded Malaya, while land-based naval aircraft raided American airfields in the Philippines. Japan had entered the second World War with a rush!

At once the western Allies were made painfully aware that the previously-derided Japanese technology had turned out warplanes which were in many ways superior to anything they possessed. It had also produced a powerful fleet, built around the fast aircraft carrier, and Japanese personnel were both highly trained and, to a large extent, already blooded in four years of fighting over China. The Americans were unprepared, the British Empire forces were already fully committed against the Germans and Italians in Europe and the Middle East. Such forces as were available were poorly-equipped and had little proper training for the task now on hand.

The greatest hope for the Allies lay in the fact that all US aircraft carriers were absent from Pearl Harbor at the time of the attack. The British had a small but powerful fleet at Singapore, formed around the modern capital ships *Prince of Wales* and *Repulse*. However, the latter had no adequate air cover, a factor which was to cost them their existence when they sortied to attack Japanese invasion forces landing in eastern Malaya. A force of JNAF twin-engined torpedo-bombers flew unescorted from French Indo-China to attack at maximum range and succeeded in sinking both British warships.

The brightest star in the Japanese arsenal was the Navy's Mitsubishi Zero fighter, and this, together with the Army's Nakajima fighters, quickly cut a swathe through the Brewster Buffalos, Seversky P-35s, Curtiss Hawks and P-40s of the defending British, Australian, New Zealand, Dutch and American air forces. Reinforcements of British Hurricanes and later-model American P-40s were rushed out, but could do little, and in rapid succession Malaya, Singapore, Borneo, the Dutch East Indies and the Philippines fell to the invaders.

Only in Burma was the picture marginally brighter; here the RAF defenders were joined by the Tomahawks of the American Volunteer Group—the 'Flying Tigers'— experienced pilots trained by Colonel Claire Chennault, air adviser to the Chinese Nationalists, in special tactics devised by him from experience of fighting the Japanese over the previous three years. Early raids on Rangoon were decimated, and for a while brought to a halt, by these fighters. With the fall of Malaya, however, an invasion of Burma began and the British were driven inexorably back into India. The Allied air units put up a splendid fight before losing most of their remaining aircraft on the ground in March 1942, and by the end of that month Burma also was in Japanese hands.

The Japanese carrier fleet, fresh from its triumph at Pearl Harbor, had rampaged through the East Indies, and had launched an attack on the north-west Australian port of Darwin. Then, early in April, it pushed into the Indian Ocean and, unable to bring the British Eastern Fleet to battle, struck at Colombo and Trincomalee on the island of Ceylon. At both ports determined RAF fighter opposition was met, and little damage was done; but out to sea the small aircraft carrier HMS *Hermes* was spotted and sunk, as were two cruisers. This was the first time a carrier had been sunk by carrier-based aircraft, and the Japanese were understandably jubilant.

By May 1942 the Japanese advance was reaching its high-water mark. In the south forces had landed in northern New Guinea; an effort was next made to land a further force on the south-east coast of the island, and a section of the carrier fleet sped to the Coral Sea to support this. American carriers were in the area, spotted the Japanese first, and the first naval battle fought entirely by aircraft ensued. It ended virtually in a draw, each side losing one carrier, with a second badly damaged. However, the Japanese ships were forced to withdraw and the invasion of south-east New Guinea was then repulsed by Australian troops and Kittyhawk fighters.

A month later almost the whole of the Japanese fleet set sail to capture the island of Midway, which was defended by a small force of US Marine Corps aircraft. They attacked the island, decimating the defending Marine Buffalos, and then cut to pieces attacks launched by USMC and USAAF bombers against the massive concentration of shipping. An American force of only three carriers (all that were available) was rushed to the area, and by luck the Japanese

Right: The Republic P-47 Thunderbolt was another US fighter which was flown very successfully by the British services. These Thunderbolts of No 135 Squadron were photographed at an airstrip on the Arakan front in Burma, in November 1944

Far right, top: The sharply cranked wing of the Corsair enabled the undercarriage to be kept quite short despite the large diameter of the propeller

Far right, bottom: Despite troubles with its 1,900 hp Homare Ha-45 engine, the Nakajima Ki-84-Ia Hayate (Gale) was one of the few Japanese fighters able to hold their own against US Hellcats, Mustangs and Thunderbolts in the last year of the war. Instead of the former Japanese emphasis on manoeuvrability at all costs, it introduced better armour protection for the pilot and self-sealing fuel tanks

Opposite page: Mitsubishi Ki-21s were the standard heavy bombers of the Japanese Army Air Force at the time of the attack on Pearl Harbor, having served earlier in the war against China. These Ki-21-IIs could carry a 2,200-lb (1,000 kg) bomb-load

Left: Among other operational types produced by Mitsubishi was the Ki-46-III reconnaissance aircraft. Known to the Allies as 'Dinah' it was one of the most elegant aeroplanes of the second World War

Below: Chance Vought's F4U Corsair was considered by the US Navy to be too fast for carrier operations, until the Royal Navy had taken it to sea and proved its outstanding qualities as a deck fighter. As a result, America used it initially to equip hard-hitting Marine squadrons land-based in places like Bougainville

Left: Kawasaki's Ki-61 Hien (Flying Swallow) fighter had rather Germanic lines as a result of the installation of a licence-built Daimler-Benz DB 601 engine. Although one of the most effective weapons used against high-flying US Superfortress bombers, such attacks often cost the lives of Japanese pilots who rammed their targets rather than relying on guns. This Ki-61-Ic was pressed into post-war service by the Chinese Air Force

Right: Japan's first jet aircraft, the Nakajima J8N1 Kikka (Sacred Blossom), flew for the first time on 7 August 1945, one day after the first atomic bomb had dropped on Hiroshima

Far right: One of the finest fighters of the Pacific War, the Kawanishi N1K2-J Shiden (Violet Lightning) was evolved from the N1K1 Kyofu floatplane. This one survives in the USAF Museum at Wright-Patterson Air Force Base

Below: Firefighters busy on board HMS *Formidable* after a Japanese *Kamikaze* suicide aircraft crashed into the flight deck. Such attacks caused only temporary damage to steel-decked British carriers, but sank several wooden-decked US ships

Bottom: Most suicide attacks by Japanese pilots were made in standard types of combat aircraft. Exceptions were those carried out in specially-designed rocket-powered Yokosuka MXY-7 Ohka (Cherry Blossom) piloted bombs, like this captured example. The Ohka was air-launched from a Mitsubishi G4M2e mother-plane

were again spotted first. Strikes were launched and a force of Douglas Devastator torpedo-planes bored in at low level. They were attacked by fighters and the guns of every vessel in the fleet, and were massacred to the last aircraft—but they were the undoing of the Japanese. As every element of the defence was concentrating on the torpedo-bombers, flying just above the waves, Douglas Dauntless dive-bombers appeared from the clouds directly overhead and plummeted on to the unsuspecting carriers, inflicting terrible damage. The Japanese later got off a retaliatory strike which sank the American carrier *Yorktown;* but at the end of the day no fewer than four Japanese carriers had gone down. It was the turning point of the war in the Pacific.

A period of recoupment on both sides now took place, the USAAF and Royal Australian Air Force settling down to the start of a long war of attrition over New Guinea against JAAF and JNAF air units based on the other side of the island. In October it was noticed that the Japanese had constructed an airstrip on Guadalcanal island in the Central Solomons. This appeared to presage further expansion, and in consequence the first American counter-invasion was launched by Marines to take the island.

This led to heavy activity in the air, as the Japanese fought fanatically to hold on to the island. US Marine Wildcats and Army Airacobras fought off repeated raids by counter-attacking enemy aircraft, operating in appalling conditions in a siege every bit as epic as that on Malta. Violent naval actions around the Solomons erupted in October into the Battle of Santa Cruz, where the Americans came off worst, losing the carrier *Hornet;* but gradually the hold on the island was consolidated and the last flames of resistance were finally quenched.

The only year of the Pacific War which was near to being static was 1943. In the Solomons, Marine Corsairs, Army P-40s and P-38s and New Zealand Kittyhawks arrived to join in a long battle with the garrisons of Japanese air bases in the area. Army Liberators and Marine Dauntlesses struck at targets in New Britain and on other islands. Over New Guinea, too, the fight went on—the Americans sending more modern aircraft, albeit in small numbers, to oppose the highly-manoeuvrable Japanese fighters. The most successful of the US newcomers proved to be the P-38 Lightnings, twin-engined single-seaters.

Japanese bombers had maintained a steady series of raids on the Darwin area of Australia, but early in 1943 a wing of defending Spitfires from England went into action and managed to inflict sufficiently heavy losses to discourage further attacks. Meanwhile the vast industrial power of the United States was finally getting into its stride. New carriers were beginning to roll off the stocks in increasing numbers, while new aircraft such as the Grumman Hellcat fighter, designed in the light of experience with the Zero, the Avenger torpedo-bomber and the Helldiver dive-bomber, were also appearing. The first action by the earliest of the new carriers and Hellcat fighters occurred in August, when they struck at installations on Japanese-held Marcus Island.

Meanwhile, in Burma a British offensive on the Mayu Peninsula had failed early in the year, and in China the Sino-American air forces were not strong enough to do more than hold on. By autumn, however, the RAF and USAAF were able to launch a limited offensive against the Rangoon area; when the Japanese reciprocated they were met by newly-arrived Spitfires and repulsed in a series of fierce battles which extended over the next four months.

By early 1944 the new American fast carrier task forces which made up the 7th Fleet began operations on a really large scale, opening with a strike on the Marshall Islands during February. The USAAF was also preparing to launch a deadly new weapon—the giant B-29 Superfortress bomber. First bases for the B-29 were built in India, and raids began from there in June. They were the first attacks to be made on

the Japanese mainland since a force of B-25 Mitchells, led by Lt-Col 'Jimmy' Doolittle, had taken off from the carrier *Hornet* in 1942, bombed various targets, and then attempted to fly on to China.

The bases in India were far from ideal, as they confronted the bombers with a long flight over the 'Hump', the range of mountains between Assam and China. To provide bases on islands within striking range of Japan, it was decided to invade Saipan in the Marianas in June 1944. The landings were supported by the 7th Fleet's carrier task force, which hit the area first. The Japanese Navy reacted violently as the invasion went in, enemy carriers approaching and launching a number of large strikes on 19 June. The defending Hellcats intercepted each raid, and in a day known subsequently as the 'Marianas Turkey Shoot', shot down 220 of the 328 aircraft opposing them for minimal losses in return. Next day the Americans hit the Japanese carriers, sinking one and damaging four more, as well as a battleship.

Following the Marianas operations, the US carriers struck at bases in the Philippines in September, inflicting further heavy losses, and then repeated the process against Formosa early in October. Meantime the forces in the south and south-west Pacific, supported by the USAAF, USMC, RAAF and RNZAF, had reconquered New Guinea and either invaded, or by-passed and neutralised from the air, islands in the Solomons chain—a process christened 'island-hopping'.

At last these forces under General Douglas MacArthur were ready to return to the Philippines, and a bold stroke was

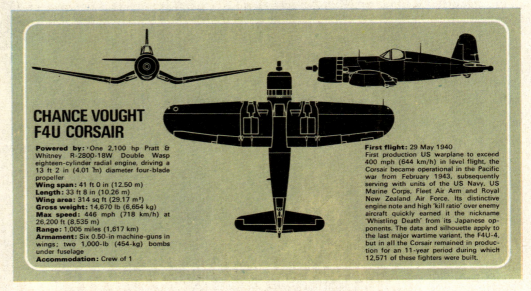

CHANCE VOUGHT F4U CORSAIR

Powered by: One 2,100 hp Pratt & Whitney R-2800-18W Double Wasp eighteen-cylinder radial engine, driving a 13 ft 2 in (4.01 m) diameter four-blade propeller
Wing span: 41 ft 0 in (12.50 m)
Length: 33 ft 8 in (10.26 m)
Wing area: 314 sq ft (29.17 m²)
Gross weight: 14,670 lb (6,654 kg)
Max speed: 446 mph (718 km/h) at 26,200 ft (8,535 m)
Range: 1,005 miles (1,617 km)
Armament: Six 0.50-in machine-guns in wings; two 1,000-lb (454-kg) bombs under fuselage
Accommodation: Crew of 1

First flight: 29 May 1940
First production US warplane to exceed 400 mph (644 km/h) in level flight, the Corsair became operational in the Pacific war from February 1943, subsequently serving with units of the US Navy, US Marine Corps, Fleet Air Arm and Royal New Zealand Air Force. Its distinctive engine note and high 'kill ratio' over enemy aircraft quickly earned it the nickname 'Whistling Death' from its Japanese opponents. The data and silhouette apply to the last major wartime variant, the F4U-4, but in all the Corsair remained in production for an 11-year period during which 12,571 of these fighters were built.

323

Left, top to bottom:
The Aichi M6A Seiran (Mountain Haze) was intended to be launched from the I-400 class of ultra-long-range submarines for an attack on the Panama Canal. In fact it was too late to be used operationally

First and most famous of all American 'sharkmouth' units were the 'Flying Tigers' of the American Volunteer Group who supported the Chinese armies against Japanese invaders. This is one of their Curtiss P-40s

Leading US Marine Corps Corsair 'ace' was Colonel Gregory M 'Pappy' Boyington, who claimed 28 Japanese aircraft destroyed. The flags painted under his cockpit indicate that his 'kills' totalled 20 when this photograph was taken

planned to land direct on Luzon, the northern of the main islands. Supported by the fast carriers, by a force of escort carriers, and by the USAAF's 5th and 13th Air Forces to the south, the invasion took place in mid-October. Again the Japanese Navy reacted, sending strong strike forces which surprised the escort carriers supporting the landings in Leyte Gulf and came near to eliminating them. However, the tables were turned and a number of enemy carriers and battleships were sunk, many more aircraft also being shot down.

It was at this time that the first 'Kamikaze' suicide attacks were launched against the US carriers—a form of attack which was to inflict much damage in coming months, and to prove most difficult to combat.

In Burma the Japanese Army had launched its last offensive early in 1944, British forces being isolated in the Arakan, and then at Imphal and Kohima as the Japanese crossed the frontier into India. Supplied, reinforced and supported entirely from the air, the British forces held out while the Japanese exhausted themselves, and then drove them back towards central Burma. Air transport also supplied Chindit columns operating behind the Japanese lines. Following the 1944 monsoon, the British 14th Army began a strong push southwards, again supported and supplied by air. Spitfires, Thunderbolts, Hurricanes, Beaufighters and Mosquitos provided the support, while Dakotas and Commandos carried the supplies, and Liberators struck further afield. By early May 1945 Rangoon had fallen, and only mopping-up remained to be done in Burma.

In January 1945 a British fast carrier task force made a number of strikes on oil targets in the East Indies, taking a heavy toll of the JAAF's defending interceptors, before passing into the Pacific to join the US Navy in operations around the Japanese home islands. The American carriers meantime had pressed into the South China Sea at the start of 1945, striking again at Formosa, and then at targets along the coast of China.

With the availability of the Marianas bases, B-29s had stepped up the raids on Japan from October 1944, creating new problems for the Japanese. The high-flying and powerfully-armed bombers were difficult to intercept, and ever-larger numbers of fighters had to be recalled from overseas to oppose them. The increasing Japanese resistance to the bombers' regular attacks

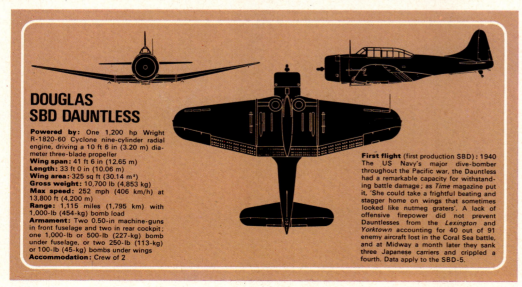

DOUGLAS SBD DAUNTLESS

Powered by: One 1,200 hp Wright R-1820-60 Cyclone nine-cylinder radial engine, driving a 10 ft 6 in (3.20 m) diameter three-blade propeller
Wing span: 41 ft 6 in (12.65 m)
Length: 33 ft 0 in (10.06 m)
Wing area: 325 sq ft (30.14 m²)
Gross weight: 10,700 lb (4,853 kg)
Max speed: 252 mph (406 km/h) at 13,800 ft (4,200 m)
Range: 1,115 miles (1,795 km) with 1,000-lb (454-kg) bomb load
Armament: Two 0.50-in machine-guns in front fuselage and two in rear cockpit; one 1,000-lb or 500-lb (227-kg) bomb under fuselage, or two 250-lb (113-kg) or 100-lb (45-kg) bombs under wings
Accommodation: Crew of 2

First flight (first production SBD): 1940
The US Navy's major dive-bomber throughout the Pacific war, the Dauntless had a remarkable capacity for withstanding battle damage; as *Time* magazine put it, 'She could take a frightful beating and stagger home on wings that sometimes looked like nutmeg graters'. A lack of offensive firepower did not prevent Dauntlesses from the *Lexington* and *Yorktown* accounting for 40 out of 91 enemy aircraft lost in the Coral Sea battle, and at Midway a month later they sank three Japanese carriers and crippled a fourth. Data apply to the SBD-5.

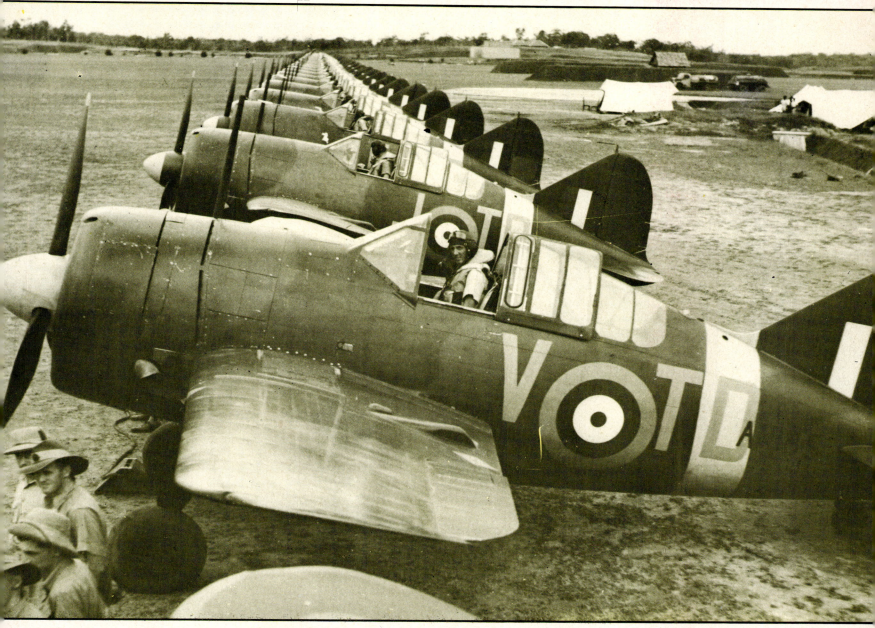

Top left: In their first clash with Japanese aircraft in New Guinea, pilots of USAAF Lockheed P-38 Lightnings claimed the destruction of 14 'Zeros' without the loss of a single US pilot. One of the 12 P-38s was disabled but the pilot returned to his base

Top right: With special markings painted on its side, a Mitsubishi Ki-57 arrives at Mingaladon Airfield, Rangoon, carrying envoys to sign the Japanese surrender in August 1945

Above: Brewster F2A Buffalo fighters, bought from America, were considered quite suitable for RAF squadrons in the Far East in 1940-41, enabling more potent home-produced fighters to be retained for use against the Germans and Italians. Early experience in combat against the 'Zero' quickly disproved the adequacy of the Buffalo and it was withdrawn from service

Left: Carrying two 1,000-lb bombs and armed with eight 0.50-in machine-guns, a Thunderbolt belonging to the USAAF's 'Burma Banshees' prepares to take off for an attack on Japanese positions

Right: Flight crew members turn the propeller of a C-46 transport at Chenyi in China, prior to a routine operation over the 'Burma Hump'. Flying over high mountain ranges, often in terrible weather, USAAF aircrew kept open this vital supply route from India to their Chinese allies

Far right: The Nakajima B6N1 Tenzan torpedo-bomber was superior in many respects to its Allied counterparts and might have inflicted disastrous blows on US and British naval units in 1944-45 had the Japanese still possessed a large carrier fleet and sufficient skilled pilots

Below: The Martlet fighters and Swordfish torpedo-bombers massed on the flight deck of this British carrier would have formed a tempting target for Japanese *Kamikaze* attack at a later stage of the Pacific War

Bottom: The bomber which brought the Pacific War to an end—the Boeing B-29 Superfortress. Although remembered mainly as the vehicle for America's atomic bombs, the B-29 earlier caused terrible destruction in conventional bombing raids on the Japanese home islands

Left: An RAF Blenheim bomber dives to machine-gun shipping in the harbour at Akyab, a vital Japanese supply centre in Burma

Below: Most successful US Navy dive-bomber of the second World War, the Douglas Dauntless inflicted crippling damage on the Japanese fleet in actions such as the Battle of the Coral Sea, Midway and the Solomons campaign

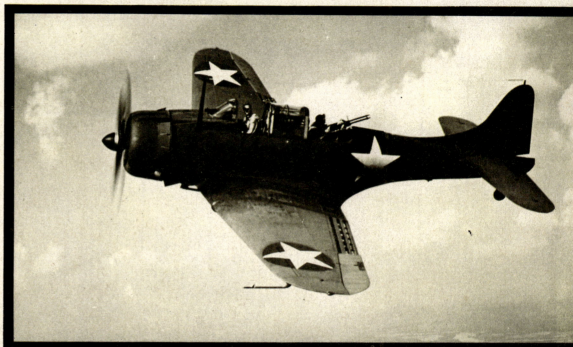

on their industrial capacity made the provision of long-range fighter escort desirable. So, in February 1945, carrier forces supported the invasion of the island of Iwo Jima, to provide a base for P-51 Mustang fighters for this purpose, as well as a useful emergency landing ground for damaged bombers returning from their targets. In support of the landings the carriers also launched a series of attacks on the Japanese home islands.

Iwo Jima fell after a hard fight. In April the operation was repeated against the island of Okinawa, still closer to Japan, and it was here that the British Pacific Fleet joined the US 7th Fleet. The B-29s meantime had switched in March to night attacks, against which the Japanese had practically no defence. Using area bombing techniques perfected by RAF Bomber Command in Europe, which proved particularly effective against the flimsy structure of most of Japan's buildings, they burned out large areas of the country's major industrial cities in a very short time.

With the Philippines well on the way to being secured, the American and British carriers now operated all around Japan, picking off the remaining vessels of the Japanese Navy and striking at any worthwhile targets remaining on the mainland. Everywhere reconquest was approaching completion, except in China where little progress had been made. All supplies had had to be flown in from India over the 'Hump' route, until the liberation of central Burma reopened the land route, and this prevented a really great concentration of strength ever being achieved—particularly as opportunities elsewhere offered better results for the effort expended.

Much has been made of air power in the European theatre, but it was in the Pacific that its exercise was paramount and decisive in all areas. Now it was to provide the final stroke. Japan's ability to continue the war had been virtually destroyed by July 1945, but still she fought on fanatically. An invasion would clearly be costly in Allied lives, but only one other alternative seemed likely to produce the desired unconditional surrender. On 6 August a B-29 dropped the first atomic bomb on Hiroshima. Two days later the Soviet Union declared war, attacking the Japanese forces based in Manchuria, and next day the second atomic bomb was exploded over Nagasaki. Japan, an outstanding exponent and victim of air power, surrendered on the 14th.

Above and left: Among exhibits at the USAF Museum is the B-29 Superfortress *Bockscar* from which the second atomic bomb was dropped on Nagasaki, on 9 August 1945, ending the Pacific War

LIEUTENANT GENERAL J.

Never was a man so paradoxically named: yet perhaps this surname and the natural pugnacity of a man of small stature provided the spur that has driven 'Jimmy' Doolittle to tot up a mass of achievements sufficient for half-a-dozen ordinary men.

As a youth he was well-known in the amateur boxing ring, where flailing fists and indomitable spirit made him the bantam-weight champion of the Pacific coast. It was boxing skill that earned the money to buy a motor-cycle engine to power his first home-built aircraft. Fate decreed that he should not fly this rather dubious machine, when a gale force wind lifted it from the Doolittles' backyard and deposited it as a heap of wreckage some distance away.

In 1917 'Jimmy' enlisted as a cadet in the Aviation Section of the Signals Reserve Corps of the US Army. Height proved his greatest problem—he could hardly see over the side of the 'Jenny' in which he made his first dual flights—but he demonstrated quickly that he was a natural pilot and flew solo after only six hours of instruction. Commissioned on 11 March 1918, Doolittle waited impatiently to join the battle that was raging in Europe: but the only battle he fought in World War 1 was with his own temperament, for his exceptional skill as a pilot earmarked him as a flying instructor. He proved to be exceptional at that, too. . . .

When the war in Europe ended Doolittle stayed on in the Air Service, and in 1921 was posted to Langley Field, Virginia, to take part in experiments being conducted by General 'Billy' Mitchell. Engineer officer and flight leader of a D.H.4 squadron, 'Jimmy' served during the controversial bombing tests against naval vessels, becoming in the process one of Mitchell's disciples.

In the following year came the exploit that, for the first time, inked Doolittle's name across the newsprint of America's national dailies: on 4 September 1922 he became a national hero by making the first transcontinental crossing of the United States in a single day. To achieve this he flew a D.H.4B the 2,163 miles (3,481 km) from Pablo Beach, Florida, to San Diego, California, in 21 hours 19 minutes.

In 1925 the name Doolittle hit the headlines again when, flying a Curtiss R3C-2 racing seaplane at Baltimore, he won the Schneider Trophy race for America at an average speed of 232.57 mph (374.28 km/h), beating the 1923 contest record by more than 55 mph (88.5 km/h). Three days later, in the same aircraft, he set a world speed record for seaplanes at an average of 247.17 mph (397.78 km/h).

Following this success, Doolittle was appointed Chief of the Flight Section at Wright Field, with responsibility for supervising and taking part in flight tests. Once again he adapted quickly to a new challenge. The theoretical training gained in a graduate aeronautical engineering course at the Massachusetts Institute of Technology now paid off, for allied to his superb skill as a pilot this combination produced one of the most professional test pilots of that era.

A spell of sheer delight followed when the Army 'loaned' him to the Curtiss company to take their P-1 fighter on a demonstration tour of South America. 'Jimmy' has a droll reminiscence of this tour: it seems that on one occasion, en route to Rio de Janeiro, he emerged from a fog bank with no idea of his position. He spotted a railway track and followed it to a station that had 'Mictorio' written on its only small building. Curiously, he could not find the name on his map, and was more than disconcerted to find that the next two stations were named identically. He thereupon abandoned 'Bradshaw' navigation in disgust. When he found Rio eventually he grumbled to the welcoming officer: 'I would have been here sooner but for a place called Mictorio which has three railroad stations'. The set, official gaze creased into a grin: 'The name is on every railway station in our country', said the officer. 'It means Men's Room'.

Following this tour came a serious attempt to combat the menace of fog. Henry Guggenheim, president of a fund for the promotion of aeronautics, persuaded the Army to release Doolittle to head their Full Flight Laboratory, established in 1928. Doolittle lost no time in getting down to the problems of flight in poor visibility: prime needs were an accurate altimeter, a compass more reliable than the conventional magnetic type, an instrument to depict the aircraft's attitude relative to the ground, and special radio aids.

First discovery was a young man named Paul Kollsmann who had perfected an extremely sensitive barometric altimeter. Tests showed Doolittle that he could rely upon it to tell him when his aircraft's wheels were a few feet from the runway. The other instruments came from Dr Sperry, then nearly 70 years of age. Imagine Doolittle's surprise to learn that the basic gyro compass he needed had been used by Sperry's son in 1915. It was not long before 'Jimmy' had a directional gyro—replacing the compass—and a second gyro which showed the aircraft's attitude, and which they called an artificial horizon. In conjunction with newly-developed radio aids this instrumentation proved adequate for Doolittle, with a check pilot in the front cockpit, to make a successful take-off, extended circuit and landing, in pretty dense fog on 24 September 1929.

MES H. DOOLITTLE

Above, left to right:
Jimmy Doolittle with the Laird Super Solution in which he won the 1931 Bendix Trophy race at a record 223 mph (359 km/h). This photograph shows the aircraft as it came off the assembly line. By the date of the contest, the wire-braced interplane struts had been replaced by 'I' struts, and the wheel fairings had been painted the same medium green as the fuselage. The wings and horizontal tail surfaces were bright yellow

Doolittle, at the age of 29, in the cockpit of an Army Curtiss R3C-1 racing biplane of 1925

A Curtiss JN-4D 'Jenny'—most-produced version of the aircraft on which the young James H Doolittle, and 95 per cent of all other American and Canadian pilots of the time, were trained. Powered by a 90 hp Curtiss OX-5 engine, it had a take-off weight of 2,130 lb (966 kg), spanned 43 ft 7$\frac{1}{2}$ in (13.29 m) and had a maximum speed of 75 mph (121 km/h). A total of 2,664 were built

Left: After the second World War, Doolittle returned to private business, but has continued to serve on advisory boards and commissions concerned with many aspects of aviation. This photograph shows him (right) with Frank Coffyn at the Hiller Aircraft plant in 1956. Coffyn visited the factory to take his first ride in a helicopter. He had soloed his first aeroplane back in 1910, after two and a half hours of instruction by the Wright brothers. In 1912 he fitted the first aluminium floats to his Wright Model B and made many notable flights around New York Harbour. During one of them he startled New Yorkers by flying under both the Manhattan and Brooklyn bridges. The meeting between two such men must have produced some remarkable reminiscing

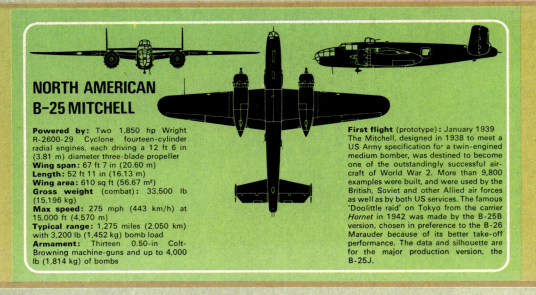

NORTH AMERICAN B-25 MITCHELL

Powered by: Two 1,850 hp Wright R-2600-29 Cyclone fourteen-cylinder radial engines, each driving a 12 ft 6 in (3.81 m) diameter three-blade propeller
Wing span: 67 ft 7 in (20.60 m)
Length: 52 ft 11 in (16.13 m)
Wing area: 610 sq ft (56.67 m²)
Gross weight (combat): 33,500 lb (15,196 kg)
Max speed: 275 mph (443 km/h) at 15,000 ft (4,570 m)
Typical range: 1,275 miles (2,050 km) with 3,200 lb (1,452 kg) bomb load
Armament: Thirteen 0.50-in Colt-Browning machine-guns and up to 4,000 lb (1,814 kg) of bombs

First flight (prototype): January 1939
The Mitchell, designed in 1938 to meet a US Army specification for a twin-engined medium bomber, was destined to become one of the outstandingly successful aircraft of World War 2. More than 9,800 examples were built, and were used by the British, Soviet and other Allied air forces as well as by both US services. The famous 'Doolittle raid' on Tokyo from the carrier *Hornet* in 1942 was made by the B-25B version, chosen in preference to the B-26 Marauder because of its better take-off performance. The data and silhouette are for the major production version, the B-25J.

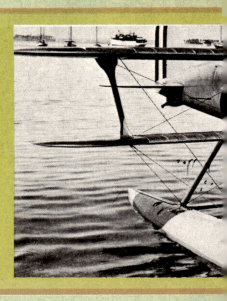

The next day, banner headlines in the *New York Times* announced triumphantly: 'Blind plane flies 15 miles and lands; fog peril overcome'. History has shown this statement to be a little premature: but for Doolittle it was a great achievement, as well as an important step in the development of instrument flight. Yet again the name 'Doolittle' was in the public eye and mind—a constantly recurring event that, by its very repetition, did much to make the people of America air-minded.

Despite his fame in America, 'Jimmy' Doolittle was little known to men and women throughout the rest of the world. It took an exploit in World War 2 to rectify this, for millions of people thrilled at the audacity of the 'Doolittle Raid' in April 1942. Sixteen specially-prepared North American B-25 Mitchell medium bombers, with volunteer crews, were loaded on board the carrier USS *Hornet*. The intention was to approach within 400 miles (644 km) of the Japanese coastline, at which point the B-25s would have adequate range to find their target and fly on to landing fields in China, to refuel there and rendezvous at Chunking.

When Japan was still 800 miles (1,287 km) away, an enemy patrol vessel came within visual contact. Take-off could be delayed no longer without grave risk, and the B-25s and their crews were readied as quickly as possible. It was a dramatic moment and, as so often before, it all depended upon Doolittle. Never before had a fully-loaded B-25 taken off from the deck of a carrier at sea: 'Jimmy's' take-off had to serve as object lesson and morale booster. In fact, his skill made it look incredibly easy, as he took off with 100 ft (30 m) to spare, and all 16 aircraft got away safely.

Complete surprise was achieved and the Mitchells attacked Tokyo without any serious opposition; but with the attack behind them their real problems started. It had been intended that Doolittle's force should be 'homed' by Chinese radio, and that flares would pinpoint landing fields. By a chapter of accidents there was no guidance of any sort, and the crews had

either to bale out or 'ditch' their aircraft just off the shoreline. Most of the crews eventually rejoined their units, but eight men were captured by the Japanese, and three of their number were executed. One aircraft and its crew, which landed at Vladivostock, were interned by the Russians.

The 'Doolittle Raid', which caused little material damage, achieved important results in other ways. It was responsible for the Japanese retaining four fighter groups in the home islands—groups that would have been invaluable for deployment in the south Pacific: in attempting to prevent a repetition of the attack the Japanese over-extended their perimeter of defence, creating even longer and more vulnerable lines of supply and communication. Most important of all, it proved to the American nation, in their darkest hour, that the Japanese were neither unreachable nor invincible.

Once again Doolittle had done an exceptional job exceptionally well—and he has gone on doing so ever since!

Top centre: The Curtiss R3C-2 seaplane in which Doolittle won the 1925 contest for the Schneider Trophy at Bay Shore Park, Maryland. The smooth streamlined fuselage made possible by the Curtiss water-cooled engines of the early 'twenties inspired British manufacturer C R Fairey to acquire the licence to build them. His Curtiss-powered Fox advanced the speed of RAF day bombers by nearly 50 per cent in 1926

Top right: Another racer flown by Doolittle was this Travel Air Mystery, owned by the Shell Oil Company. Powered by a 400 hp Wright J-6-9 engine, it could average just on 200 mph (322 km/h) around the pylons

Centre: This North American B-25B Mitchell, displayed in the US Air Force Museum, has been modified to the configuration of aircraft used in the 'Doolittle Raid' on Tokyo on 18 April 1942. The exploit earned its leader the Congressional Medal of Honor, America's highest award for military achievement

Bottom: One of Doolittle's small force of Mitchells taking off from the carrier *Hornet*, bound for the Japanese capital. Although they caused little destruction, they did much to raise American morale after a period when all the successes had seemed to go to the Japanese

Sir Frank **Whittle**

PIONEER OF JET PROPULSION

Above: Sir Frank Whittle, the former Cranwell cadet whose ideas on jet propulsion for aircraft were realised on 15 May 1941, when Britain's first jet aeroplane took to the air—appropriately, at Cranwell

Above right: One of the first pictures which wartime security allowed to be published of Britain's first jet-propelled aircraft, the Whittle-engined Gloster E.28/39

Below right: Displayed in the Science Museum, London, the Whittle W.1 engine which powered the Gloster E.28/39 had a centrifugal compressor and in its original form developed a thrust of 860 lb (390 kg)

Over a century ago the names of Britain's great engineers were known to all. Rennie, Trevethick, Brunel, Stephenson, Whitworth and Watt were household words. How many British engineers can you name today? Unless you are an engineer yourself you will probably know none at all—with perhaps one exception. Sir Frank Whittle is still familiar to most of us as 'the man who invented the jet'. And the fact that he has been totally out of the public limelight for 25 years, yet is still a well-known name, adds emphasis to the magnitude of his achievement.

Whittle was born at Coventry on 1 June 1907. As a boy he watched the fighters and bombers of World War 1, and by 1923 had enlisted in the RAF as a boy apprentice. He wanted keenly to become one of the six apprentices who were selected each year for officer training at the RAF College at Cranwell. Imagine his feelings when, on passing out of the Apprentice School, he found himself in seventh place! But destiny intended Whittle to have the thorough engineering training that he sought: the cadet in sixth place failed the eyesight test, and young Frank accordingly became Flight Cadet Whittle in September 1926.

Then, as now, a cadet at Cranwell received broad theoretical as well as practical education. Whittle soon learned that a piston-engine driving a screw propeller suffered from limitations which no amount of painstaking development could overcome. He learned that a piston-engine is restricted by the amount of air it can 'breathe', and that this limitation is made progressively worse as the aircraft climbs, due to the falling density of the air.

The propeller, too, suffered from inherent limitations. The angle at which its blades are set to the air (the pitch) has to be very large if the aircraft is to fly at high speed, because if the blades were set to a fine pitch the propeller would turn at an excessive speed without driving the aircraft very fast; yet a very fine pitch is needed at take-off and landing to enable the engine

to develop full power with the aircraft moving slowly.

There was a more basic limitation still: if the aircraft was intended to fly very fast indeed (which in the late 1920s meant about 400 mph = 645 km/h), the propeller became extremely inefficient. But the official view at Cranwell in Whittle's day was that no RAF aircraft would ever be likely to fly at 400 mph, nor to climb to a height much above 25,000 ft (7,620 m).

While almost everyone else either knew nothing of these limitations or accepted them as inviolable laws of nature, Whittle looked for a way round them. In his final term at Cranwell he wrote an essay in which he considered how an aircraft might be propelled by a jet, produced by some form of engine which drew in air, heated it and expelled it at high speed through a nozzle. In the RAF College Journal for 1928 he published a short piece called *Speculation*, in which he set forth the basic equations of thermodynamics for such a propulsion system—taking as his cruising height the unheard-of altitude of 115,000 ft (35,000 m)!

As Pilot Officer Whittle, he was posted from Cranwell to the Central Flying School for training as an instructor. He already had a reputation as an amateur 'boffin', but the CFS Commanding Officer became so certain that Whittle's idea of jet propulsion was sound that he arranged a meeting at the Air Ministry so that the whole proposal could be examined officially. That Whittle's ideas were sound is now common knowledge, but in 1929 they sounded as practical as sending a man to the Moon. Whittle was treated to the often-heard reasons for inaction: it would prove difficult, it would cost a lot of money, it had not been shown to work, and it was too far advanced in its concept.

Whittle approached various industrial firms, but again received polite expressions of disinterest. So he took out a patent on his idea in January 1930 and then got on with his RAF career.

In 1935, things suddenly began to move at last. Another former Cranwell cadet, R D Williams, arranged for a firm of bankers to help finance a new company called Power Jets Ltd to develop Whittle's invention. In June Whittle began to design a real jet engine. Starting completely from scratch, he would have preferred to develop his engine piece by piece, so that he could finally assemble it from proven components. But time and money did not allow this. With the help of the former BTH company, Whittle and his handful of Power Jets colleagues finally completed their first engine, the U Type, and started up the first turbojet in the world on 12 April 1937.

Whittle was by no means the first man to make a gas-turbine, but he *was* the first to make one for the sole purpose of propelling an aircraft by reaction to the hot gas jet emitted from the exhaust pipe. When Air Ministry officials saw his first engine actually working, they decided reluctantly that perhaps they ought to give Whittle financial support; but they still regarded this revolutionary new form of engine as a long-term idea that need not be hurried.

In March 1938 the Air Ministry placed a contract for a revised engine, intended to power an aircraft. A second contract went to Gloster Aircraft for the E.28/39 experimental aircraft, and on 15 May 1941, at dusk on a remarkably bitter day, Flt Lt P E G Sayer took off from Cranwell in the first British jet. By the summer of 1944 squadrons of Meteor twin-jet fighters were forming, and effectively catching and destroying flying bombs in the first all-jet encounters in history. Shortly after the war, the Vampire entered RAF service and the American Lockheed Shooting Star was in production with a Whittle-derived engine. In May 1952 a BOAC Comet inaugurated the jet age for fare-paying passengers, and in April 1953 the Viscount brought in the era of turboprop travel,

giving Britain for the first time in history a world-wide best-selling civil transport.

By this time Whittle, now knighted and retired from the RAF as an Air Commodore, was no longer engaged in the daily development of aero-engines, although his experience and advice continued to be invaluable. Today he lives in a remote and rugged part of Britain and has for years been developing a new type of drill for oil or natural gas prospecting. As one of Whittle's colleagues in his drilling company (a branch of Rolls-Royce) has pointed out, his former RAF motto *Per Ardua ad Astra* has now been replaced by *Per Ardua ad Antipodes* !

GLOSTER E.28/39

Powered by: One 860 lb (390 kg) st Power Jets (Whittle) W.1 centrifugal-flow turbojet engine
Wing span: 29 ft 0 in (8.84 m)
Length: 25 ft 3¾ in (7.72 m)
Wing area: 146.5 sq ft (13.6 m²)
Gross weight: 3,700 lb (1,678 kg)
Max speed: 338 mph (544 km/h) at 15,000 ft (4,570 m)
Accommodation: Crew of 1

First flight: 15 May 1941
The data above apply to the first E.28/39 prototype with original engine. Later, with a 1,700 lb (770 kg) st Power Jets W.2/500 engine, it flew at approx 450 mph (724 km/h). The second prototype, fitted with a Rover W.2B engine of 1,200 lb (544 kg) st, reached a speed of 466 mph (750 km/h) during tests.

Above left: First of the two E.28/39 prototypes, now in the Science Museum in London, photographed during a take-off from the Royal Aircraft Establishment's airfield at Farnborough in January 1945

Below left: One of the most remarkable and attractive aeronautical collections in the world is that in the Deutsches Museum in Munich. This corner of one of its galleries provides an interesting link between the subjects of this article and the one which follows, for in the foreground is one of the world's first operational jet aircraft, the Messerschmitt Me 262. Above it is suspended a replica of the Wright *Flyer*

Above: A typical wartime pose for Frank Whittle, then a Group Captain at the RAF Staff College

Right: Copy of 'Jerry' Sayers' test report after the first flight of the E.28/39 at Cranwell on 15 May 1941. Earlier, during taxying tests at Brockworth in April, the aircraft had reached take-off speed after a run of 600-700 yards (549-640 m) and had left the ground for 100-200 yards (91-183 m) at a height of a few feet

A

GLOSTER AIRCRAFT CO. LTD.

TEST FLIGHT REPORT No.: 1

PILOT P.E.G.Sayer.

Type of Test : 1st Flight. General experience of the type.

Date and Time of Start 15.5.41. 1940 hrs. Duration 17 mins.

AIRCRAFT : Type and No. E.28/39. W.4041.
Type of Undercarriage Dowty nose wheel type. All retractable.
Other Features Main wheel lever suspension type. Nose wheel strut type.
AIRSCREW : Type and No. No airscrew fitted with this method of propulsion.
Dia. :
Pitch Setting Fine   Coarse
Ground Clearance Flying Position   Tail on Ground
ENGINE : Type and No. Whittle Supercharger Type W.1.
Reduction Gear
R.P.M. O.G. Fine Pitch 16500 Take-off.   Coarse Pitch
Boost O.G.   "   "   "   "   ..
Type of Air Intake
Radiator Stbd radiator blanked off. Port radiator in circuit.
Other Features

WEIGHTS CARRIED : ~~Petrol~~ Paraffin 50 galls.   Oil 1 gall.
Cooling Liquid 3.5 galls water.
Total Weight 3441 lb. estimated from Tare C.G.
C.G. Position .284 A.M.C. U/C Down. .297 A.M.C. U/C Up calculated from
Loading Sht. No. 142   Date 7.5.41.   (Tare C.G.

REMARKS :
Exhaust System
Cooling System
Oil System
Guns and Mountings
Bombs and Racks
Sights
Nav. and Ident. Lamps
Aerial
Fairing
Type of Cockpit Heating
Pilot Position & Type

Nose wheel leg total travel 12" as against 10" on original nose wheel leg fitted for taxying trials at Brockworth. Static travel 6" instead of 7" on the first leg. Nose wheel strut pressure reduced from 140 lbsq.in. to 115 lbsq.in. Tyre pressure reduced from 35 lbsq.in. to 20 lbsq.in. Steering on nose wheel 11° either side of the centre line Brakes on all three wheels.

TEST INSTRUMENTS :
Ican. Altimeter No. :   Calibrated
A.S.I. Instrument No. :   "
R.P.M.   "   "   "
Boost Gauge ..   "   "
Air Temp. ..   "   "

Signature of Pilot

PROFESSOR ERNST HEINKEL

PIONEER DESIGNER FOR SPEED

Opposite page, top left: Prof Dr Ernst Heinkel (1888-1958)

Top right: One of Ernst Heinkel's first major successes was the W 12 seaplane designed for the Hansa Brandenburg company. By mounting the rudder beneath the tailplane, he left a clear field of fire for the rear gunner

Left: One of the C-series He 111s operated by Luft Hansa in the late 'thirties. Little different from the bomber versions, these aircraft were too uneconomical to be popular with the airline, but at least two carried cameras for reconnaissance while on 'route proving' flights over Britain, France and the Soviet Union

Above, top to bottom: The 22 He 8 seaplanes bought by the Royal Danish Navy were so efficient for northern-latitude reconnaissance and survey that more than half of them remained in service until the German occupation in 1940, thirteen years after the first one flew

First fighter of the resurrected German air force in the mid-thirties, the He 51 had a 750 hp BMW engine and speed of 205 mph (330 km/h). It pioneered ground attack in Spain and 38 were built as He 51B-2 seaplanes for catapult launching from naval vessels

The He 70 transport of 1932 set such an unrivalled standard of clean modern design that Rolls-Royce bought this one as a flying test-bed for their Kestrel V engine

TO-DAY'S FAST, STREAMLINED turbine aircraft owe a great deal more than is generally appreciated to that aristocrat of the heyday of Germany's aircraft industry, Professor Ernst Heinkel, who combined exceptional foresight with immense tenacity of purpose. Notable 'firsts' to his credit include the first jet aircraft to fly, and a streamlined, high-performance landplane with retractable undercarriage which ushered in a new era of modern aircraft design.

Born in January 1888 in the small village of Grunbach, South Germany, Ernst Heinkel was the son of a local plumber. His first significant aeronautical inspiration came just 20 years later when, as a mechanical engineering student, he watched the LZ4 Zeppelin airship burn to cinders after being struck by lightning. Reflecting on this dramatic spectacle, he saw that the real future of aviation lay in the more robust heavier-than-air aeroplane, then still something of a curiosity and the object of more ridicule than faith.

Heinkel spent the next $2\frac{1}{2}$ years finding out all he could about such aircraft and their design, and completed his first aeroplane in the summer of 1911. Following closely the style of the Wright brothers' biplanes, this contraption had one of the most powerful aero-engines then built, a 50-hp Daimler, and made about ten successful flights before crashing. Its designer was hurt in the accident, but within two months was on the road in search of his first job with an aircraft company. He joined the Luftverkehrs Gesellschaft, a small concern directed by the Swiss industrialist Jacques Schneider, who is still remembered for the design advances inspired by the seaplane races for the Trophy which he awarded.

A first breakthrough for Heinkel came in 1913, when he accepted an invitation to join the Albatros company as chief designer. There he was soon able to demonstrate the advantages of the then-radical monoplane, without the wires, struts and other impedimenta of the conventional 'flying boxkite' biplane. One of Heinkel's early Albatros designs created a sensation by climbing to 1,500 ft (455 m) in just 11 minutes 6 seconds! Thus the young designer made such a name for himself that, in 1914, he was asked to head the design team of the large, newly-founded Brandenburgische Flugzeugwerke.

Within a few months, the Austrian millionaire and entrepreneur Camillo Castiglioni was anxious to secure Heinkel as chief designer of an aircraft company he proposed to establish. Heinkel felt he could not leave his existing position; so the indefatigable Castiglioni secured him by purchasing the Brandenburg concern outright, and this became the Hansa and

Brandenburg aircraft company. A succession of Heinkel-designed military seaplane types followed, of which the most successful were the Brandenburg W 12, W 19 and W 29. These all saw active service during the first World War, becoming the terror of the English Channel on their over-water reconnaissance tasks. Most notable was the W 29, a two-seat monoplane capable of 109 mph (175 km/h), of which 78 were built.

In anticipation of the restrictions that would be placed on Germany's aircraft industry following the country's defeat, Castiglioni closed down his Hansa Brandenburg firm; but in 1921, after more than two years in the doldrums, Heinkel found a new niche in the small aircraft concern established by Carl Caspar—designing and building seaplanes for the United States and Swedish Navies. At this time, he took on Karl Schwarzler, who was to become one of his leading designers. When Sweden announced a competition to enable the Swedish Air Force to select new aircraft, Heinkel saw this as a cue to set up his own aircraft manufacturing company, which he did on 1 December 1922. The Ernst Heinkel Flugzeugwerke AG was formed on a lakeside site at Warnemünde, near the north coast of Germany.

The success of the new company was immediate. Its first design, the He 3 (two earlier Caspar types became known as the He 1 and He 2), was the best in its class at the 1923 Gothenburg seaplane competition. Like many early Heinkel types, it had a low-set cantilever monoplane wing. This breed of aircraft proved robust and gave a respectable performance, many serving with the Swedish and Danish Navies. In the mid-1920s they were followed by a series of biplanes designed specially for shipboard use, to take off from a rail-mounted trolley. Among them, the He 25 and He 26 both served with the Japanese Navy and led to the catapult-launched He 12 and He 58, which pioneered air mail operations from merchant ships.

By 1925 much of Heinkel's work had become experimental, and his obsession with speed was soon able to bear fruit. Stimulated by the 1929 Schneider races, he worked out a way of beating even the record-breaking Supermarine seaplanes—by opting for ultra-streamlined landplanes, with moderate landing speeds. In 1930 Heinkel sent for Siegfried Günter, the designer of a small sporting monoplane which had reached 150 mph (241 km/h) on only 60 hp. With his identical twin Walter, Siegfried joined the Heinkel company and was soon able to evolve the aerodynamic shape which Heinkel had been seeking. Combining technical efficiency with aesthetic beauty, they

produced in 1932 a revolutionary sports monoplane featuring the ultimate in streamlined design, with a slender fuselage and elliptical wing. This aeroplane was remarkable enough; but, with the addition of much more power, Heinkel produced as a sequel an aircraft which set the trend in high-speed aircraft design for the next 15 years. First flown in December 1932, the He 70 four-passenger transport had a metal fuselage with countersunk riveting, wooden elliptical wings and a retractable undercarriage. It could fly at over 220 mph (355 km/h). Following in the same vein, the much larger He 111 twin-engined airliner and bomber subsequently became —first in Spain and then for much of the second World War—the backbone of the Luftwaffe's bombing force. Other Heinkel designs, including the He 51 biplane fighter, played a major role in the build-up of the Luftwaffe from 1933.

Above all, however, Ernst Heinkel will always be remembered for his pioneering accomplishments in the field of jet and rocket propulsion. In 1935 he met Dr Wernher von Braun, now famous for his post-war work in the USA, who was then studying rocket power plants suitable for installation in a conventional aeroplane. Heinkel entered into a close association with von Braun, affording him research facilities and eventually designing an aircraft specially for the novel powerplant. This, the He 176, was a potent little beast, with a wing area of only 58 sq ft (5.40 m²) and a fuselage barely 24 in (61 cm) wide. It made a successful initial flight in June 1939, and subsequently reached more than 500 mph (805 km/h).

A parallel and even more significant development was that of gas-turbine power. In 1936 Heinkel had engaged Pabst von Ohain, then working on gas-turbine engines for aircraft, and sponsored his engine development work entirely as a private venture. The first such engine, burning hydrogen, ran initially in September 1937. Two years later, on 27 August 1939, the He 178 monoplane took to the air for the first time, powered by an 838 lb (380 kg) thrust Heinkel-built HeS 3B turbojet developed by von Ohain. With this flight, the first of its kind in the world, the jet age began. Further development of the concept was hampered by Luftwaffe and government vacillations and obstinacy; so, although Heinkel went on to produce the He 280, the world's first jet fighter (and first-ever twin-jet aircraft), this did not enter military service.

Other significant second World War designs, which were technically ambitious but suffered through the Luftwaffe's misplaced priorities or unrealistic demands on the aircraft, included the He 177 four-engined bomber, the He 219 high-altitude night fighter (intended to combat the RAF's Mosquito), and the extra-ordinary He 162 Volksjäger (People's Fighter) turbojet aircraft. Had the war lasted longer, even more revolutionary designs would have been built. As it was, the Heinkel enterprise, much of it in East Germany, swiftly vanished beyond all trace in 1945, and the Günter brothers eventually went to the USSR.

Ernst Heinkel lived long enough to restore his name in German aviation by re-establishing his aircraft company in 1955. It now forms a part of one of that country's largest aircraft manufacturing concerns, Vereinigte Flugtechnische Werke (VFW)—in turn a partner of the famous Dutch Fokker company. The great pioneer died almost exactly on his 70th birthday, on 30 January 1958.

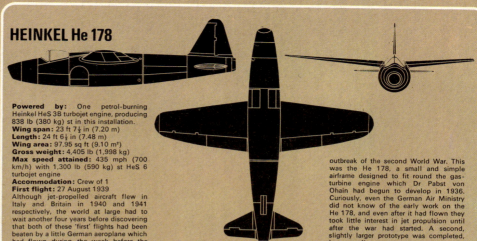

HEINKEL He 178

Powered by: One petrol-burning Heinkel HeS 3B turbojet engine, producing 838 lb (380 kg) st in this installation.
Wing span: 23 ft 7½ in (7.20 m)
Length: 24 ft 6½ in (7.48 m)
Wing area: 97.95 sq ft (9.10 m²)
Gross weight: 4,405 lb (1,998 kg)
Max speed attained: 435 mph (700 km/h) with 1,300 lb (590 kg) st HeS 6 turbojet engine
Accommodation: Crew of 1
First flight: 27 August 1939

Although jet-propelled aircraft flew in Italy and Britain in 1940 and 1941 respectively, the world at large had to wait another four years before discovering that both of these 'first' flights had been beaten by a little German aeroplane which had flown during the week before the outbreak of the second World War. This was the He 178, a small and simple airframe designed to fit round the gas-turbine engine which Dr Pabst von Ohain had begun to develop in 1936. Curiously, even the German Air Ministry did not know of the early work on the He 178, and even after it had flown they took little interest in jet propulsion until after the war had started. A second, slightly larger prototype was completed, but never flown.

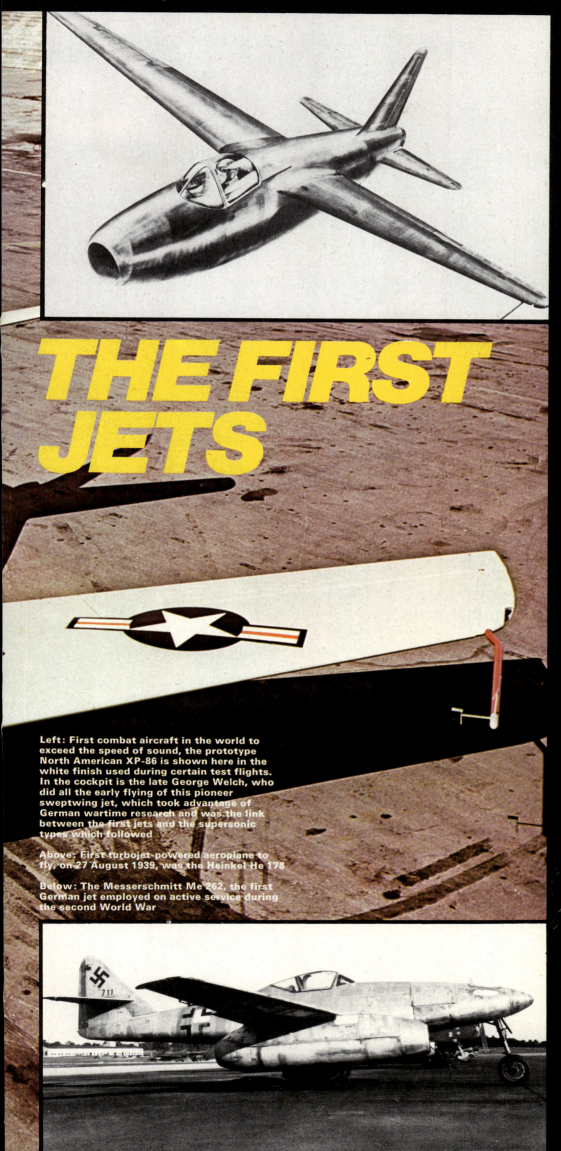

THE FIRST JETS

Left: First combat aircraft in the world to exceed the speed of sound, the prototype North American XP-86 is shown here in the white finish used during certain test flights. In the cockpit is the late George Welch, who did all the early flying of this pioneer sweptwing jet, which took advantage of German wartime research and was the link between the first jets and the supersonic types which followed

Above: First turbojet-powered aeroplane to fly, on 27 August 1939, was the Heinkel He 178

Below: The Messerschmitt Me 262, the first German jet employed on active service during the second World War

DISCOUNTING PILOTLESS models and the rocket-boosted glider of Fritz von Opel in 1929, the first 'jet' aircraft was one of which hardly anyone today has heard. We do not even know the day on which it first flew, but Ernst Heinkel believed from memory, after the second World War, that it was 15 June 1939. The aircraft was the He 176 rocket-plane, one of the smallest aircraft ever built and planned for an attempt on the world speed record. The He 176 was flown by Flugkapitän Erich Warsitz in the hot summer of 1939, a few weeks before he flew the somewhat larger He 178, the first aircraft ever powered by a turbojet. And on 5 April 1941 Heinkel's twin-jet fighter, the He 280, started its programme of flight trials. All three of these remarkable jet aircraft flew before any other jet in the world, except for an odd Italian machine which really was nothing more than a diversion.

In 1939 Ing Secondo Campini had managed to persuade Caproni, one of the most renowned Italian aircraft constructors, to build a prototype to test his idea of jet propulsion. An ordinary piston-engine was used to drive a three-stage variable-pitch fan, which blew air out of a variable-area propelling nozzle at the rear of a jet-pipe in which fuel could be burned to increase thrust. The idea was sound but uninspired, and the CC.2 (or N.1, as it was officially called) was a big, lumbering machine which could barely stagger off the ground when it was taken up for its first flight by Mario de Bernardi on 28 August 1940. The test authorities at Guidonia, the great Italian research establishment, did not try to conceal their ridicule; nevertheless, the Caproni-Campini gained a good world press because it looked outwardly like a jet.

Despite his early lead, Ernst Heinkel was overtaken in both engines and airframes by his rivals—especially by Messerschmitt, Junkers and Arado. By far the most important German jet in the second World War was the Me 262, powered by two Jumo 004 engines—eventually rated at 1,984 lb (900 kg) thrust each—slung under its sweptback low wings and intended as a 525-mph (850-km/h) single-seat fighter. By the end of 1943 the first version of the Me 262 was in initial production, and as it carried the formidable armament of four 30-mm guns and was approximately 100 mph (160 km/h) faster than any Allied fighter it could at that time almost have won the air war for Germany single-handed. Fortunately, Hitler himself ordered its conversion into a fighter-bomber, and it was not until September 1944 that one aircraft in every 13 was permitted to be used as a fighter. By the end of the war some 1,400 Me 262s had been completed, more than all other jets combined. They were formidable, but not aircraft for novices, and many inexperienced pilots were killed in Me 262 crashes in the final months of the war.

Among other significant German jets flown before 1945, two that could have proved a great thorn in the Allies' side were the Arado 234 and Heinkel 162. The Ar 234 was a high-wing bomber and high-altitude

reconnaissance machine, of which over 200 were built as single-seaters with two Jumo 004 engines before production switched to various bomber and fighter versions, with four BMW 003 jets and often with two seats. The He 162 'Volksjäger' was a last-ditch effort to fend off the mighty onslaught of the RAF and USAAF. A diminutive single-seat fighter, it had a high wing and twin fins between which blasted a BMW 003 turbojet mounted above the finely-streamlined fuselage.

Victorious allies can easily disregard the accomplishments of a defeated enemy, and in 1945 there was a general tendency to dismiss the incredible profusion of German jet and rocket aircraft as futuristic, impractical and merely of cursory technical interest.

This was a great mistake because, while there is no law laying down the rate of technical progress men should seek to attain, it is folly to ignore progress that is real and visible. In 1945 the German jets included prototypes with delta wings, reheat, ramjets, swept wings and even variable-geometry. Britain, in contrast, was to have nothing but conventional straight-wing fighters in service for a further ten years (apart from the American Sabre).

Yet in many ways the Allied jet technology, which for practical purposes was founded solely on the work of Sir Frank Whittle, was superior to the German. British airframe development may have seemed to range from the modest to the pathetic; and, measured against what was done under infinitely more trying conditions in Germany, British jet aircraft got off to an almost unbelievably slow start. But British jet engines were world-beaters.

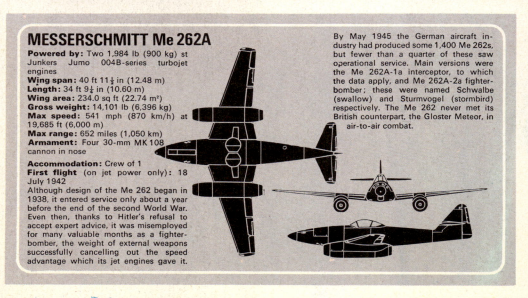

MESSERSCHMITT Me 262A

Powered by: Two 1,984 lb (900 kg) st Junkers Jumo 004B-series turbojet engines
Wing span: 40 ft 11½ in (12.48 m)
Length: 34 ft 9¼ in (10.60 m)
Wing area: 234.0 sq ft (22.74 m²)
Gross weight: 14,101 lb (6,396 kg)
Max speed: 541 mph (870 km/h) at 19,685 ft (6,000 m)
Max range: 652 miles (1,050 km)
Armament: Four 30-mm MK 108 cannon in nose

Accommodation: Crew of 1
First flight (on jet power only): 18 July 1942
Although design of the Me 262 began in 1938, it entered service only about a year before the end of the second World War. Even then, thanks to Hitler's refusal to accept expert advice, it was misemployed for many valuable months as a fighter-bomber, the weight of external weapons successfully cancelling out the speed advantage which its jet engines gave it.

By May 1945 the German aircraft industry had produced some 1,400 Me 262s, but fewer than a quarter of these saw operational service. Main versions were the Me 262A-1a interceptor, to which the data apply, and Me 262A-2a fighter-bomber; these were named Schwalbe (swallow) and Sturmvogel (stormbird) respectively. The Me 262 never met its British counterpart, the Gloster Meteor, in air-to-air combat.

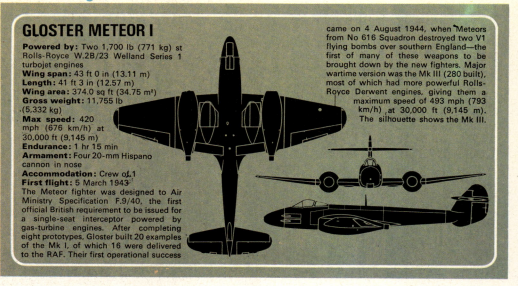

GLOSTER METEOR I

Powered by: Two 1,700 lb (771 kg) st Rolls-Royce W.2B/23 Welland Series 1 turbojet engines
Wing span: 43 ft 0 in (13.11 m)
Length: 41 ft 3 in (12.57 m)
Wing area: 374.0 sq ft (34.75 m²)
Gross weight: 11,755 lb (5,332 kg)
Max speed: 420 mph (676 km/h) at 30,000 ft (9,145 m)
Endurance: 1 hr 15 min
Armament: Four 20-mm Hispano cannon in nose
Accommodation: Crew of 1
First flight: 5 March 1943
The Meteor fighter was designed to Air Ministry Specification F.9/40, the first official British requirement to be issued for a single-seat interceptor powered by gas-turbine engines. After completing eight prototypes, Gloster built 20 examples of the Mk I, of which 16 were delivered to the RAF. Their first operational success

came on 4 August 1944, when Meteors from No 616 Squadron destroyed two V1 flying bombs over southern England—the first of many of these weapons to be brought down by the new fighters. Major wartime version was the Mk III (280 built), most of which had more powerful Rolls-Royce Derwent engines, giving them a maximum speed of 493 mph (793 km/h) at 30,000 ft (9,145 m). The silhouette shows the Mk III.

Top left: Running the engine of the Caproni-Campini N.1 with the tail section removed

Far left: Known originally as the Spider-Crab, the prototype Vampire flew in September 1943

Far left below: Prototype Gloster E.1/44 fighter of 1948, which was outdated in a sweptwing era

Left: Like the first Vampire, the prototype Lockheed XP-80 Shooting Star flew with a (D.H.) Halford H.1 turbojet

Above right: From the Shooting Star fighter was evolved the two-seat T-33A advanced trainer, which continues in service with many air forces in the early 'seventies

Right: The MiG-15 sweptwing fighter of Mikoyan and Gurevich was the first modern Soviet aircraft to challenge western leadership in the air. It was to offer tough opposition for USAF squadrons in the later war in Korea by combining German wartime sweptwing technology with the unrivalled power of Britain's Rolls-Royce Nene turbojet

It could easily have turned out differently. Pabst von Ohain ran his first engine at much the same time as did Whittle, and at that time the climate in Germany was much more favourable to the jet and other forms of aircraft gas-turbine that it was in Britain. But some essence of sheer quality in the British engineers led swiftly to better jet engines. Stanley Hooker and J P Herriot at Rolls-Royce and Major Frank B Halford and Eric S Moult at de Havilland had by 1943 created the first of a long line of British aircraft engines which, have more than made up for pedestrian British aircraft and given Britain a major place in the first 30 years of the jet age.

Britain's original jet research aircraft was the Gloster E.28/39, an eminently straightforward barrel-like machine which flew on 15 May 1941 and can today be seen in the Science Museum, London. Not including this, nor its German He 178 counterpart, while the Germans evolved 22 jet aircraft types by 1945, backed up by countless projects, Britain produced two. The Gloster Meteor and de Havilland Vampire are too well-known to call for a description, but both demonstrated qualities of tractability, safety and fitness for operational service that were less in evidence in most of the more-futuristic German machines. Both British fighters enjoyed a long period of development and a world-wide market, and a few examples of each were still in use in 1971.

In the United States jet propulsion research was very active by 1941. The Durand Committee sifted through a wide range of possible ideas and issued contracts to three firms: Westinghouse for a small axial jet, General Electric for a turboprop and Allis-Chalmers for a turbofan. In the same year Pratt & Whitney were funding their own gas-turbine research, while Lockheed, Menasco and Northrop were busy with turbojet engine and aircraft projects, and the NACA and several small firms were also active. Into this bubbling cauldron dropped the Whittle turbojet, imported from Britain at the personal urge of General 'Hap' Arnold, Chief of Staff of the Army Air Force. General Electric swiftly 'Americanised' the Whittle unit and ran its own engine after only 28 weeks, in March 1942. Two of these engines took the first Bell XP-59A Airacomet into the air on 1 October that year, but the P-59 was hardly an advance on the piston-engined Mustang. Lockheed, however, teamed up with de Havilland's Goblin engine—the turbojet used in the Vampire—and created the XP-80 Shooting Star. This was a world-beater, a trim, flashing fighter which could outmanoeuvre and in most respects outperform every other aircraft in the world when it flew in January 1944. Powered in its production form by the more powerful General Electric I-40 (later called the Allison J33), the F-80 bore the brunt of early combat in Korea and still serves in minor air forces. Later it was joined by the F-84 Thunderjet and the remarkable sweptwing F-86 Sabre, and it was the Sabre that led the way to the supersonic fighters of today.

In the Soviet Union a great deal of work had been done on rocket-powered aircraft, and a possible prototype of a rocket fighter was flown in 1942; but turbojet development had to wait for German and British technology to become available in 1945. The BMW, Junkers and Heinkel-Hirth engines were all studied carefully and the first two were actually used in hasty but successful conversions of existing piston-engined fighters. But Soviet fighter design was suddenly put on the map by the MiG-15, first flown in the summer of 1947 with a Rolls-Royce Nene which the British government shipped at just the right time. Klimov soon had similar and improved versions of the Nene in massive production, making possible the production versions of both the MiG-15 and the Il-28 bomber.

Many other nations were eager to share in the new form of propulsion. In Japan a simple, underpowered twin-engined jet fighter just managed to log 11 minutes in the air in the final days of the war. In France a jet research aircraft, together with various jet and turboprop engines, was schemed during the German occupation, and the SO.6000 Triton flew with a Jumo 004 in November 1946. The Swedes found to their delight that the excellent British Goblin turbojet fitted like a glove into the engine bay of the twin-boom pusher J 21 fighter, and lost no time in installing one of these engines in place of the original Daimler-Benz DB 605 piston-engine. The resulting J 21R began its very successful career in March 1947. Five months later a jet fighter designed and built wholly in Argentina began its flight trials: the Pulqúi (Arrow), powered by a Rolls-Royce Derwent.

Jet propulsion rapidly became international. It was only natural that all the first jets should have been fighters. Today most nations are more concerned with air transport. It is no exaggeration to claim that it was the jet, especially in the form of the turbofan, that turned air transport into the efficient giant it is today.

A NEST OF VIPERS

AS THE ALLIED TANKS menaced Stuttgart in April 1945 a group of ten curious vertical open-work structures might have been seen in the vicinity of that city. Their purpose was the launching of some of the most remarkable aircraft ever built; so remarkable in fact that they were utterly destroyed to prevent their capture by the forces which a few days later were to link with the Russians.

The aircraft concerned were tiny, vertically-launched rocket-propelled single-seat fighters, measuring only about 13 ft (4 m) in span and fittingly named Natter (Viper), for they would have struck at the massed Allied bomber formations swiftly, venomously and wholly unexpectedly.

The vertical launching of fighters had been proposed as early as the summer of 1939 by Dr Wernher von Braun, in later life to figure eminently in the American space programme; but the Natter in the form in which it materialised was built to the ideas of an engineer named Erich Bachem. Although itself rocket-propelled, the aircraft was to be boosted from its launching tower by additional rockets, burning for ten seconds and then jettisoned. An automatic pilot would be controlled from the ground by radio to position the Natter within one or two miles from a bomber formation, when the pilot would take over control, jettison the tip of the fuselage nose, thus exposing a battery of rocket projectiles, and fire them in salvo. The attack having been made, he would release connections by which the entire forward portion of the fuselage was attached; simultaneously a parachute would be deployed from the rear section. The sharp deceleration would throw the pilot forward and separate him from the nose section, enabling him to descend with his own parachute. Thus both the pilot and the rear part of the fuselage, containing

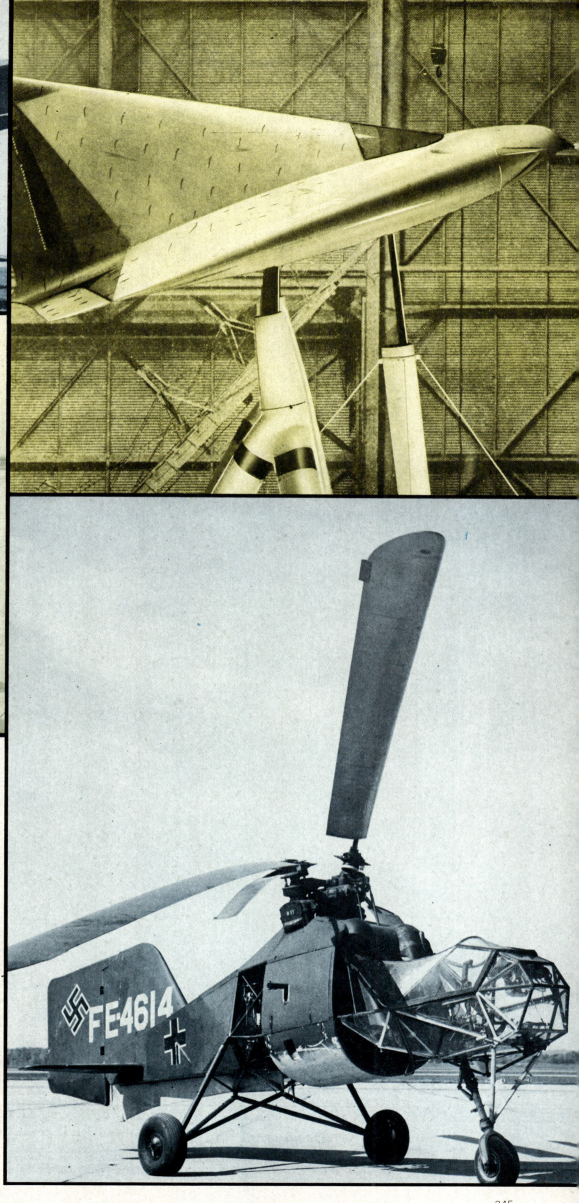

Opposite page, top: To save weight and overcome stowage problems, the Arado 234 reconnaissance-bomber was designed as an undercarriageless aircraft. It took off from the wheeled trolley shown in this picture of a four-engined Ar 234C prototype, and landed on skids

This page, top: Known as the 'flying aquarium' because of its extensively-glazed fuselage, the Arado Ar 198 was tested in 1938 as a reconnaissance aircraft for the Luftwaffe. It proved less successful than its unorthodox competitors, the asymmetrical BV 141 and twin-boomed Fw 189

Above: The fantastic little interceptor which suggested the title of this article—Bachem's Ba 349 Natter (Viper). Vertically launched from a ramp, it carried a battery of 24 Hs 217 Föhn rockets in its nose

Top right: Lippisch delta-wing design under test in a wind-tunnel. Perhaps the most advanced of all German wartime projects, this family of deltas included two fighters powered by ramjet engines burning coal granules as fuel

Left: Six examples of the little Arado Ar 231 reconnaissance aircraft were flight tested in 1941. Intended for operation from U-boats, they dismantled for stowage in a tube only 6 ft 7 in (2 m) in diameter for carriage by the submarines when submerged

Right: Plans to build 1,000 Flettner Fl 282 light anti-submarine helicopters did not materialise, and only 26 experimental models had been produced when the war ended. They were one- or two-seaters, with a seven-cylinder radial engine driving two two-blade intermeshing rotors

MINIATURE FIGHTER

B & V P179

B & V P202

Go P60 C

Ju 8-635

Top: The Luftwaffe's Mistel composite aircraft was an extension of the pilotless 'flying bomb' concept. In this case the pilot of the Fw 190 fighter was intended to take off on the combined power of his own aircraft and the explosive-laden crewless Ju 88 on which it was mounted. Over the target the Ju 88 was to be released to glide on into its target

Above: Central engine of the Heinkel He 111Z Zwilling glider tug, produced by joining together a pair of otherwise-standard He 111H-6s by a rectangular centre-section replacing the port outer wing panel of one and the starboard outer wing panel of the other. The additional engine was mid-set on the centre-section. An attempt to use Zwillings to tow Me 321 gliders packed with supplies for the beleaguered German garrison at Stalingrad failed in 1943

Left: Five of the more incredible German projects of the second World War: the Arado miniature fighter spanned only 16 ft 5 in (5 m), carried a prone pilot and a single large cannon, and was to be carried beneath the fuselage of an Ar 234C mother-plane; the Blohm & Voss P179 dive-bomber had an offset cabin for the pilot; the same company's P202 fighter was designed with a pivoting wing to offer the same advantages as a swing-wing without alteration of the centre of lift; the Gotha P60C was a projected twin-jet tailless all-weather fighter; the Junkers 8-635 was a long-range reconnaissance project produced by joining together two modified Do 335 'push-and-pull' fighters

Upper right: The asymmetrical layout of the Blohm & Voss BV 141 reconnaissance aircraft was intended to give the crew of this single-engined machine the best possible view. Plans to put it into large-scale production were abandoned

Lower right: Heinkel's He 162 'People's Fighter' was designed, built and flown in 90 days, as a 'last-ditch' interceptor that could be mass-produced by slave labour

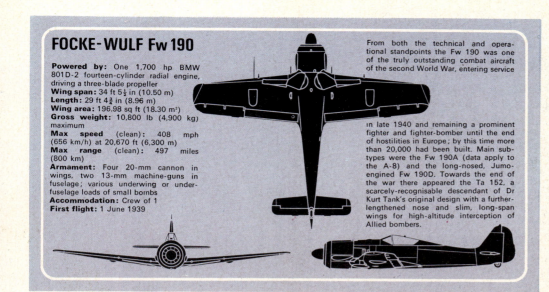

FOCKE-WULF Fw 190

Powered by: One 1,700 hp BMW 801D-2 fourteen-cylinder radial engine, driving a three-blade propeller
Wing span: 34 ft 5½ in (10.50 m)
Length: 29 ft 4¾ in (8.96 m)
Wing area: 196.98 sq ft (18.30 m²)
Gross weight: 10,800 lb (4,900 kg) maximum
Max speed (clean): 408 mph (656 km/h) at 20,670 ft (6,300 m)
Max range (clean): 497 miles (800 km)
Armament: Four 20-mm cannon in wings, two 13-mm machine-guns in fuselage; various underwing or under-fuselage loads of small bombs
Accommodation: Crew of 1
First flight: 1 June 1939

From both the technical and operational standpoints the Fw 190 was one of the truly outstanding combat aircraft of the second World War, entering service in late 1940 and remaining a prominent fighter and fighter-bomber until the end of hostilities in Europe; by this time more than 20,000 had been built. Main subtypes were the Fw 190A (data apply to the A-8) and the long-nosed, Jumo-engined Fw 190D. Towards the end of the war there appeared the Ta 152, a scarcely-recognisable descendant of Dr Kurt Tank's original design with a further-lengthened nose and slim, long-span wings for high-altitude interception of Allied bombers.

BACHEM Ba 349 NATTER

Powered by: One 4,409 lb (2,000 kg) st Walter HWK 509C-1 bi-fuel rocket motor, plus (for take-off) four 1,102 lb (500 kg) or two 2,205 lb (1,000 kg) solid-fuel rockets
Wing span: 13 ft 1½ in (4.00 m)
Length: 19 ft 9 in (6.02 m)
Wing area: 50.59 sq ft (4.70 m²)
Gross weight: 4,920 lb (2,232 kg)
Max speed: 620 mph (1,000 km/h) at 16,400 ft (5,000 m)
Max endurance: approx 4¼ min
Accommodation: Crew of 1
First flight (powered, unmanned): 22 December 1944

The first powered flight of a Natter followed trials, in November 1944, of the aircraft in unpowered form; on 28 February 1945, when the first attempt was made at a piloted flight, the pilot, Oberleutnant Lothar Siebert, lost his life. The Natter had its origins in a proposal by Dr Wernher von Braun for an interceptor which could reach the operating altitude of Allied bombers—about 26,250 ft (8,000 m)—in less than one minute. Fortunately for the Allies it never became operational; only two-thirds of the 36 built were actually test-flown before VE-day, seven of them with pilots. Data apply to the intended production version, the Ba 349B-1.

the rocket engine, would be recovered.

That, at least, was the intention. The first attempt to launch a Natter with a pilot proved fatal, apparently because the cockpit enclosure was not securely locked and the pilot was stunned. Although seven piloted launches were accomplished later, in the circumstances already described the Natter never had an opportunity to utilise in combat its phenomenal rate of climb—initially over 37,000 ft (11,280 m) per minute.

Such unorthodox aircraft were by no means the prerogative of lesser-known constructors such as Bachem: the great names of the German aircraft industry were all associated with extremely advanced, or ambitious, projects. Messerschmitt, it might be supposed, should have been sufficiently occupied with developing and producing the Me 163, the world's first rocket-propelled fighter, and the Me 262, the finest turbojet fighter of the war; but this was far from the truth. Flights were actually made with a little single-seater, the Me 328, which was intended to be used as an expendable piloted missile for attacking heavily defended targets, the pilot baling out before impact. This machine was powered with pulse-jets, of the kind fitted to the V1 flying bomb, and two prototypes were lost because of structural failures associated with the (literally) shattering pulsations.

Another little-known Messerschmitt was the Me 264 long-range reconnaissance bomber, prototypes of which were built with piston-engines. One Me 264, however, was set aside for the testing of a massive steam turbine, fed by four boilers and driving one of two forms of propeller—the first, of 17½ ft (5.4 m) diameter, revolving at 400-500 rpm, the second, measuring only 6½ ft (2.0 m), turning at the unprecedented speed of 6,000 rpm. The Me 264 so allocated was destroyed in an air raid.

Although the Heinkel company is best known for its bombers, it pioneered the development of jet fighters. The He 280 was, indeed, the first fighter in the world to have jet propulsion, and set a new pattern also in having an ejection seat. Although this type was not ordered in quantity, very large production was intended for the He 162 Volksjäger (the 'People's Fighter') in the design of which simplicity was emphasised. The standard He 162 was remarkable in having its single turbojet engine mounted on top of the fuselage, and studies were made of two other versions having unusual power plants. In one of these a rocket unit was combined with the turbojet, whereas the other depended for propulsion on one large, or two smaller, ramjets. Other Heinkel fighter projects included jet-propelled flying wings; a piston-engined type with pusher propellers; one designed to have a ramjet over 16 ft (5 m) long and to land on a retractable skid; and yet another, of the class known to the Germans as 'target-defence interceptors', in which the pilot lay prone.

But bombers were by no means neglected by this famous company, though the He 177

—a type which went into service and which appeared to have only two engines, though in fact it had four, in coupled pairs—was not a success. One projected development was to have had no fewer than six separate engines, and, following the destruction of the Me 264 allocated for the steam-turbine experiments, an He 177 was intended for the continuance of these.

Curious Heinkels were not wholly paper projects, for the He 111Z five-engined glider tug consisted essentially of two He 111 bombers joined together. Following its experience with this remarkable aircraft, Heinkel embarked on a project for a four-engined twin-fuselage development of the Dornier Do 335, which may now be named as a very unusual aircraft in its own right.

Like Heinkel, the Dornier concern is best known for its bombers, but as the war approached its end Do 335 twin-engined fighters and fighter-bombers were in production, and a few of the latter were delivered to the Luftwaffe. The most unusual feature of these aircraft was the mounting of an engine amidships in the fuselage and driving a pusher propeller through a shaft, in addition to a conventional tractor engine/propeller combination in the nose. The distinctive appearance thus presented was further accentuated when a second cockpit, for a pupil or radio/radar operator, was added behind and considerably above that for the pilot.

Like Heinkel, Dornier had plans for a 'twin' development of this aircraft, but nevertheless undertook extensive design work on jet-propelled fighters, one of which was based on the Do 335 itself. Dornier was famous also for its flying-boats, and one projected type, the Do 214, was to have been used for the refuelling and re-arming of U-boats. For stowage on board, and operation from, these underwater craft the Germans built the Arado Ar 231, the major components of which could be dismantled and stowed in a cylindrical container.

Although a relatively little-known company, Arado also built the world's first jet-propelled bomber, the Ar 234, some versions of which had two turbojets and some four. Early examples took off on a trolley and landed on skids, but wheels were standardised. Many developments were projected, one of which was to tow a V1 flying bomb and another to carry one of these weapons on its back. Yet another scheme provided for the carrying of a miniature fighter, the pilot of which lay prone, under the fuselage.

Another German scheme was to tow a 'glide fighter', for attacking bomber formations, behind a Bf 109. In this instance also the pilot lay prone, and the glider was to take off on a wheeled bogie and land on a skid. The idea was that the combined aircraft should approach a formation head-on and at a higher altitude. The glider would then be released, enter a 20-degree dive, and make a frontal attack.

This was but one of many projects under study by the Blohm und Voss concern. Some of the others were of asymmetrical layout, following the pattern set by the BV 141 reconnaissance aircraft, which caused the raising of many eyes and eyebrows by reason of the fact that the pilot and gunner sat in a fuselage, or nacelle, on the starboard wing, whereas the engine was mounted in the nose of a second, unmanned, fuselage, offset to port and carrying the tail. In another design the pilot and gunner were to be seated in a nacelle at the extreme tip of the port wing, additional guns being mounted in a corresponding structure to starboard. Perhaps the most astonishing Blohm und Voss project of all was a fighter having a wing which could be swivelled in flight about its vertical axis. By this means it was hoped to achieve the same effect as afforded by variable sweepback. Compared with such a scheme a proposal to convert the huge BV 222 flying-boat into a landplane seemed a shade conservative!

Far from conservative was a project by the Focke-Wulf company for a fighter with three rotating wings, each having a ramjet mounted at the tip. For take-off this fighter was to sit on its tail, and the wings were to be rotated initially by rockets. This was but one of numerous Focke-Wulf schemes, which included the towing or carrying of an explosive-laden Ta 154 (a pale German shadow of the de Havilland Mosquito) for detonation in the middle of a bomber formation. The same company was studying a fighter propelled by two ramjets nearly nine feet (2.7 m) long but with an undercarriage track of only about 2½ feet (0.7 m).

Famed for its pioneering of metal construction, the Junkers company, among others, was contemplating the use of wood. A twin-jet flying bomb, planned as the lower component of a 'Mistel' composite aircraft, was to be of this material, and a wooden wing was a feature of a single-jet fighter measuring only about 30 ft (9 m) in span but having an armament of four 30-mm cannon. These aircraft never materialised, but hardly less remarkable was the Ju 287, two prototypes of which were completed. This jet-propelled bomber had a forward-swept wing, and two of its four turbojets were attached to the sides of the fuselage. Although having abundant projects of its own, the Junkers company was yet another which was planning a twin combination of Do 335s.

By no means all the remarkable German projects were in respect of structural and aerodynamic design. A Lippisch fighter, for instance, would not only have had the pilot seated in the tail-fin but would have used a solid fuel in the form of coal, carried in a circular rotating basket, or, alternatively, granules made from coal dust. The range of ideas, like the nature of them, was in truth fantastic, and Germany's ultimate defeat could certainly not be laid to the charge of her aircraft and power plant designers. Such was the breadth of their vision and ingenuity that the V1 flying bomb—built originally as a revolutionary robot weapon —was not only designed, but actually built and flown, with a human pilot.

Opposite page, top two photographs:
The He 111Z-3 was intended as a long-range reconnaissance version of the Zwilling with sufficient fuel internally and in four external tanks to fly 2,670 miles (4,300 km)

An Ar 234 prototype of the world's first jet reconnaissance-bomber taking off on its launch trolley. The production versions had a normal wheeled undercarriage

Opposite page, bottom two photographs:
The Junkers 287 four-jet heavy bomber prototype was unique in having sweptforward wings—a configuration resurrected on the current German Hansa business jet

Another view of the Ju 287, with a Walter 501 jettisonable assisted take-off rocket under each turbojet nacelle. The fixed undercarriage was acceptable on a 'test-bed' prototype

Above: In-flight photograph of the Dornier Do 335 V1 prototype fighter, which had propellers at the nose and tail. This was one of the most unorthodox German designs to enter series production, but was just too late to be used operationally.

Left: Tandem two-seat version of the Do 335 in the Dornier assembly and repair plant at Oberpfaffenhofen, near Munich. Five heavy attacks by the US Eighth Air Force had put the factory out of action before it fell into Allied hands

Below: Although it was not ordered into production, the Heinkel He 280 is remembered as the first jet fighter to fly anywhere in the world. It did so on 2 April 1941, with its HeS 8A turbojets uncowled as shown

Overleaf:
Several first-generation tactical missiles in the US armoury had configurations like conventional jet-powered aircraft. Chance Vought's RGM-6B Regulus 1 served with the US Navy for more than a decade; the improved Regulus 2 (illustrated), which had a J65 jet engine, was not ordered into production for operational purposes, but many were used as target drones

BUZZ-BOMBS & BALLISTIC MISSILES

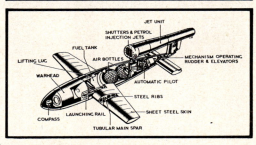

Top: One of the piloted V1 'flying bombs'. Flight tested successfully, they were to be dropped from He 111 bombers, their pilots subsequently baling out after aiming them at their target

Above, centre: German troops wheeling an operational Fieseler FZG 76A (V1) to the launch ramp

Above: Cutaway drawing of a V1. Produced during the early stages of the attack on England, this diagram is not quite accurate. The wings, for example, had a constant chord; but it is correct in most essentials

Below: To avoid having to fly through the cloud of debris resulting from the blowing up of a V1 by gunfire, RAF Spitfire pilots sometimes tipped them over into a spin, with their wingtip, as shown in this camera-gun shot from another aircraft. Such tactics were possible only over un inhabited areas

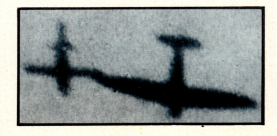

DESPITE EARLY ACHIEVEMENTS in the USA, Britain and Russia (described elsewhere in *History of Aviation*), it was Germany which perfected the flying bomb. This was the V1, used in large numbers during the second World War against south-east England and various Continental targets. Englishmen called it the 'doodle-bug' or 'buzz-bomb'.

The 26 ft (7.90 m) long mid-wing mono-plane, powered by a simple pulse-jet engine, was designed by a team under Dipl-Ing Robert Lüsser of the Gerhard Fieseler Werke GmbH in Kassel. It was ramp-launched and had a pre-set guidance system which steered it roughly in the required direction. The launch weight of some 4,806 lb (2,180 kg) included 1,874 lb (850 kg) of Amatol high explosive.

Mounted above the fuselage in a simple 'stove-pipe' installation was the Argus propulsion unit, which gave a thrust of 660 lb (300 kg). This drew in air at the front through a system of flap valves behind which petrol was injected intermittently, air being sucked in through the valves after each combustion cycle.

The first V1 test-firing—an air launch from an Fw 200 Condor patrol bomber—took place over Peenemünde in December 1942. More than 8,600 were subsequently launched towards London and the Home Counties, between 13 June and 4 September 1944, many from ramps established in the Calais district. Of these, 1,847 fell victim to Allied fighters, 1,866 to anti-aircraft fire and 232 to the balloon barrage. Nearly 12,000 more were launched by the German Army against targets in Europe between 1 September 1944 and 30 March 1945.

Under the code name 'Reichenberg', some 175 V1 missiles were converted to carry a human pilot. They were to have

been carried aloft and launched from under Heinkel He 111 bombers, their pilots baling out after aiming them at their target; but, although test and training flights were undertaken, no piloted V1s were used operationally. Air-launching of *pilotless* V1s did, however, continue until early January 1945, raising to some 10,500 the total number of these weapons despatched against targets in Britain.

An entirely new form of long-range weapon was born with the V2 rocket, which the Germans began to fire on London in the autumn of 1944. Developed under Dr Wernher von Braun at the Peenemünde research establishment, V2 was the first large rocket missile and, unlike the V1, could not be intercepted once it had been launched, because of its great speed and the fact that it travelled to its destination by leaving the Earth's atmosphere. The only defence was to seek out and destroy the launch sites.

Despite the fact that the German rocket was liquid fuelled and had to be supported by tankers and other vehicles, it was designed from the beginning as a mobile launch system. Rockets were brought to the launch area—which could be any reasonably flat surface—on tractor-drawn trailers. A trailer could also raise the rocket into a vertical position for firing from a simple launch platform, and great attention was paid to concealment from air attack. Some of the rockets which fell on London, for example, were set up between avenues of trees in the Dutch town of Wassenaar, near the Hague, which provided excellent natural cover.

After the 46-ft (14-m) rocket had been fuelled with ethyl alcohol and liquid oxygen and checked out, the battery commander fired it via an interconnecting cable from

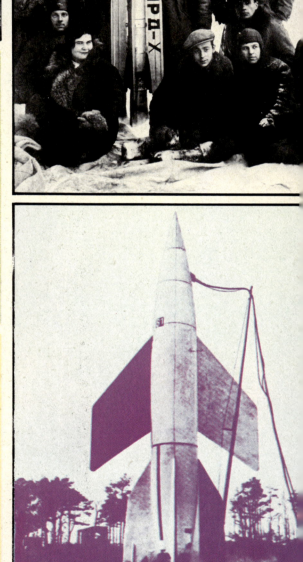

FIESELER Fi 103

Powered by: One 660 lb (300 kg) st Argus As 014 pulse-jet engine
Wing span: 17 ft 4½ in (5.30 m)
Length: 25 ft 11 in (7.90 m)
Wing area: approx 51 sq ft (4.7 m²)
Launch weight: 4,806 lb (2,180 kg)
Warhead: 1,874 lb (850 kg) of high explosive
Max speed: 408 mph (656 km/h) at 9,845 ft (3,000 m)
Range: approx 205 miles (330 km)
First flight: early December 1942 (air launch); 24 December 1942 (ground launch)
The original proposals which led to the V1 guided missile were made in 1939 by the Argus Motorenwerke. Go-ahead for the project was given in 1942, with Gerhard Fieseler's company allocated high priority and overall responsibility for the programme. The device was called FZG 76 (Flak Ziel Gerät = anti-aircraft target apparatus) by the Luftwaffe in a hopeful but vain attempt at a security cover for its true function. At the end of a pre-set range the V1 was thrown into a dive, halting the flow of fuel and causing the engine to cut out; this brief 'early warning' gave people in the vicinity a few seconds in which to take cover.

HENSCHEL Hs 293

Powered by: One 1,320 lb (600 kg) st Walter 109-507 rocket engine, suspended below body of the missile
Wing span: 9 ft 6¼ in (2.90 m)
Length: 11 ft 9 in (3.58 m)
Max diameter: 1 ft 7 in (0.48 m)
Launch weight: 1,989 lb (902 kg)
Warhead: 1,102 lb (500 kg) of high explosive
Max speed: 373 mph (600 km/h)
Max range: 10 miles (16 km) from launch height of 19,685 ft (6,000 m)
First flight: 16 December 1940
Soon after the outbreak of the second World War, proposals by the Henschel Flugzeug Werke for a radio-controlled bomb were awarded a development contract, and in January 1940 Dr Herbert Wagner joined the company from Junkers to lead the project team. One of the first operational 'stand-off' weapons, the Hs 293 was air-launched from beneath Do 217, He 177 or Ju 290 aircraft; it was fitted with ailerons and elevators and could be controlled by radio from the parent aircraft. Its first success was with II/KG 100 on 27 August 1943, when the British corvette *Egret* was sunk in the Bay of Biscay. Used by day and night in the Mediterranean and Atlantic, the Hs 293s' successes were not widespread, and Allied jamming of their radio controls and lack of trained German bomber crews led eventually to their eclipse. Some 1,700 were built, and several developed versions were projected.

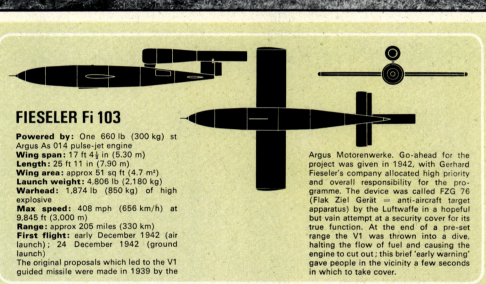

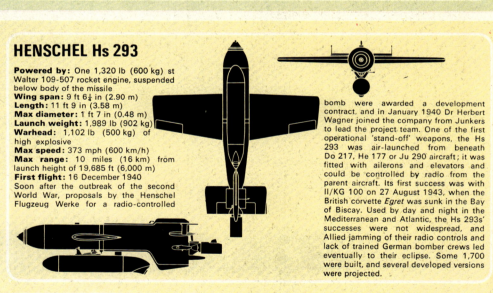

Top to bottom:
The robot that surrendered! One of the V1s that failed to cross the Channel was discovered by Canadian soldiers near its launch site in the Pas de Calais

Led by Sergei Korolyev, members of GIRD (Group for studying jet propulsion) built and tested successfully this first Soviet liquid-propellant rocket on 17 August 1933

A winged V2 rocket under test at Peenemünde in 1945. The possibility of attacking New York by using such rockets as the second stage of the A-9/A-10 weapon was under consideration as early as June 1940

This captured example of the piloted V1 was included in an exhibition of German aircraft at the RAE, Farnborough, shortly after the end of the war in Europe

an armoured vehicle resembling a tank.

The V2, first test-fired successfully on 3 October 1942, was steered by a three-axis gyro-pilot acting through steerable exhaust vanes and aerodynamic surfaces on the fins. A successful missile could travel nearly 200 miles (320 km), reaching a height of 60 miles (96.5 km) halfway to its target. The rocket engine burned out when the speed was about 3,500 mph (5,630 km/h), and people at the receiving end heard both a sonic bang *and* an explosion. Even without an explosive warhead, V2s on test left a crater about 45 ft (13.7 m) deep and 120 ft (36.6 m) across!

Altogether some 4,320 V2s were fired between 6 September 1944 and 27 March 1945, 1,120 of them against London and 2,500 against Continental targets. The rest were used for training and test purposes in Germany. Civil Defence records show that 1,050 actually fell on England, the first on 8 September. Two aimed at Paris on 6 September, before the London campaign started, were misdirected.

Apart from the rocket itself, many of the techniques developed for V2 were to set the standard in the post-war years. The idea of a mobile transporter-erector for large rockets has been freely adopted by both east and west. The Soviet Union, for example, has devised a whole family of highly-mobile missile carriers which can be deployed along the entire frontier with the west, and on the border with China.

The larger intercontinental ballistic missiles (ICBMs) which today hold the balance between east and west also owe much to the influence of the Peenemünde design team. Years before V2s were launched against England, von Braun and his team were preparing designs for a two-stage rocket known as the A-9/A-10 (the V2 had been the A-4). A drawing dated 10 June 1940 shows a 191,000-lb (86,600-kg) missile, about 80 ft (24.4 m) long, with a winged V2 as its second stage. The idea was that the winged rocket, having separated from its booster, should extend its range by gliding in the thin upper air, to reach the Atlantic seaboard of the United States. Possible launch sites were in western France or Portugal, but there is no evidence that the A-9/A-10 was ever considered seriously for development. In the pre-atomic age, its one-ton warhead of chemical explosive was plainly inadequate. Nevertheless, the concept of the ICBM owes much to the early Peenemünde design.

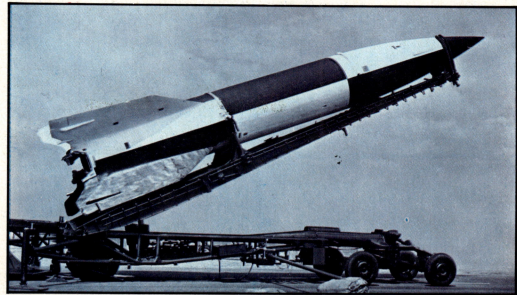

Below left: Dr Wernher von Braun, former designer of the V2 war rocket and now one of the leading figures in America's space programmes

Top: A V2 rocket on its transporter/erector trolley. The chequerboard markings identify it as a test round

Above: RAF personnel recovering the remains of a V2 rocket motor after the missile had fallen and exploded in a field in Belgium in November 1944

Right, top to bottom:
The German V2 test firing site at Blizna, in Poland, photographed by the RAF in June 1944. The railway wagons carry camouflaged rockets. 'A' indicates rocket cradles

The solid-propellant two-stage Rheintochter R-1 was one of four surface-to-air missiles tested in Germany during the second World War. None reached operational status

The caption to this official photograph from Moscow states simply 'Soviet ballistic missile'. In fact it is a captured V2. Such rockets were test fired extensively by the Russians post-war, and improved versions made up the first generation of the Soviet Union's ballistic missile force

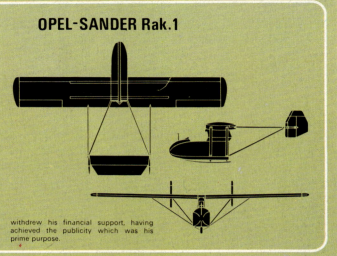

Powered by: Sixteen Sander solid-fuel (powder) rockets, each of 55 lb (25 kg) thrust, mounted in four banks of four and fired in stages
Attained speed: 95 mph (153 km/h)
Distance flown: approx 5,000 ft (1,525 m)
Accommodation: Crew of 1
First flight: 30 September 1929
This and a number of other freakish designs were built with money provided to the VfR (Society for Space Travel) in Germany in the late 1920s by the publicity-seeking automobile tycoon Fritz von Opel. First to fly was the tail-first *Ente* (duck) designed by Prof A M Lippisch; piloted by Fritz Stamer, it made a rocket-propelled flight of about 4,000 ft (1,220 m), lasting some 70 seconds, on 11 June 1928. However, it was virtually uncontrollable and made only two further tests. The *Rak.1*, designed by an engineer named Hatry and flown by von Opel, did somewhat better a year or so later; it took off from a raised track and covered a greater distance, though it was still extremely difficult to control. On a later flight, with more powerful rockets, it was severely damaged in a heavy landing. Von Opel subsequently withdrew his financial support, having achieved the publicity which was his prime purpose.

OPEL-SANDER Rak.1

FIRST PIONEERS OF THE SPACE AGE

MOST OF THE developments upon which our present technology is based were introduced to a sceptical world by a select band of pioneers. Astronautics is no exception, and in the period of intense and rapid progress between the turn of the century and the second World War, four significant names stand out. These pioneers of the space age were Konstantin E Tsiolkovsky of Russia, Robert Esnault-Pelterie of France, Robert H Goddard of the United States and Hermann Oberth of Austria.

Of these, the most remarkable was undoubtedly Tsiolkovsky. Born on 5 September 1857 at Izhevsk, he is as indisputably the 'father of astronautics' as Britain's Sir George Cayley is the 'father of aeronautics'.

Tsiolkovsky was deeply interested in physics and mathematics, and at the age of thirty published a theoretical study of an all-metal dirigible. In 1890 he presented the results of his work in aeronautics to the Imperial Technical Society. From that time on, however, he concentrated his research and theories on rocket propulsion. In 1898 he suggested, for the first time, the use of liquid propellants, demonstrating convincingly the advantages these had over solid fuels. He recommended the use of hydrogen and oxygen for rockets, as well as hydrocarbons.

Tsiolkovsky's first technical paper on rocket motion was published in 1903—the year of the Wright brothers' first historic aeroplane flight. In this paper he expounded the principle of reaction and proved theoretically that a rocket could work in a vacuum. He also indicated the fundamental law that the final speed of a rocket depends directly upon the ejection speed of the exhaust. The manuscript describing this last discovery was lodged with Moscow's *Technical Review* in 1903, but was not published until 1923.

To Tsiolkovsky also goes the credit for the first serious calculations concerning the possibility of interplanetary travel and for placing artificial satellites in orbit. In 1911 he suggested that the undesirable effects of protracted weightlessness could be overcome by providing artificial gravity on board spacecraft.

At first Tsiolkovsky's ideas were received with indifference. He was left in obscurity until the time of the Russian Revolution, but was then greatly encouraged by the new regime. Continuing his work on liquid propellants, he put forward various projects for staged and multiple rockets in order to reach the greatest possible altitudes.

An often-displayed model of a manned spacecraft based upon the works of Tsiolkovsky shows a long-nozzled liquid-propellant rocket engine extending from the base of a pear-shaped craft to Skylab-sized living quarters which include, of all things, a cast-iron bath for the convenience of the cosmonauts. Tsiolkovsky died, at the age of 78, on 19 September 1935.

* * *

The second astronautical pioneer, Robert Esnault-Pelterie, was born in Paris on 8 November 1881. He is remembered as one of the first engineers to give a scientific foundation to aviation. He himself, however, considered this part of his work as transitional, and early in his career decided to devote the majority of his activities to astronautics.

In 1907 he began a mathematical investigation into the possibilities of flight through space. The work was expanded and in November 1912 was delivered as a lecture before the French Physical Society. It created some commotion, and was received generally with scepticism, but is today regarded as marking an important development in the history of space navigation.

Esnault-Pelterie resumed his work after the first World War, and as early as 1920 concluded that the gas-ejection velocities achievable at that time made the mass ratio data almost acceptable. On 8 June 1927 he gave a second lecture, to the French Astronomical Society, entitled *The Exploration by Rockets of the Upper Atmosphere and the Possibility of Interplanetary Travel*. This time the paper had world-wide repercussions.

In 1928 he published *L'Astronautique*, which assessed the position of research at that time. It was his most important work and is regarded today as one of the classic studies of the subject.

Esnault-Pelterie's work also included several jet-engine designs of various types, and experiments with combinations of liquid propellants. In the course of one such experiment, he was seriously injured in an explosion. He was, together with General Ferrie, one of the first to foresee the application of nuclear energy to rocket propulsion.

This great pioneer died, in Paris, on

HEINKEL He 176

Powered by: One Walter HWK R I-203 liquid-fuel rocket engine, designed to produce 1,323 lb (600 kg) of thrust
Wing span: 16 ft 4¾ in (5.00 m)
Length: 17 ft 0¾ in (5.20 m)
Wing area: 58.12 sq ft (5.40 m²)
Gross weight: approx 3,530 lb (1,600 kg)
Attained speed: approx 171 mph (275 km/h)
Endurance: 50 seconds
Accommodation: Crew of 1
First flight: 20 June 1939
Following ground and air tests of early Walter liquid-fuel rocket engines in Junkers A 50 and Heinkel He 112 airframes in the mid-1930s, Ernst Heinkel initiated as a private venture the He 176, which was designed by Siegfried and Walter Günter specifically for rocket propulsion. The span and area apply to the open-cockpit, fixed-undercarriage first prototype as originally designed; larger wings were fitted before the first flight. The speed and endurance are those achieved on this flight, although much better performances were achieved later. The He 176 was demonstrated before Hitler, Goering and other senior German military officials early in July 1939. They remained unconvinced of the potential of rockets for aircraft propulsion, firmly believing that the imminent war could be won with the more conventional aircraft already in service. The more advanced second prototype, with enclosed cockpit and retractable landing gear, is shown by the silhouette, but this aircraft was never built.

6 December 1957, having lived long enough to witness the launching of Sputniks 1 and 2 by Russia.

*   *   *

Robert H Goddard was born in Worcester, Massachusetts, on 5 October 1882. In 1899, at the age of 17, he began to speculate about conditions in the upper atmosphere and in interplanetary space. In one of his notebooks an entry dated 19 October 1899 includes a comment about the possibility of using rockets as a means of carrying instruments.

In 1907 he prepared a paper suggesting that the heat from radioactive materials could be used to expel substances at high velocities, through a rocket motor, to provide the power required for travel through interplanetary space. He was, however, half a century ahead of his time, for the article was firmly rejected in turn by the *Scientific American, Popular Science Monthly* and *Popular Astronomy.*

Goddard realised that high velocities would be needed for interplanetary flight. In 1909 he advocated the use of high-energy propellants such as liquid oxygen and liquid hydrogen, and drew attention to the necessity of employing a rocket constructed on the step principle. For the next ten years he investigated the possible use of rockets for the exploration of very high altitudes, and in 1919 the Smithsonian Institution, which had provided financial support for his work, published his first paper, entitled *A Method of Reaching Extreme Altitudes.* This little book of less than 100 pages opened the modern era of rocket research, for it

showed conclusively that rockets could be used to carry scientific instruments to heights never before imagined.

The book contains calculations showing that a rocket with a take-off weight of 8 to 10 tons would be capable of reaching the Moon, carrying sufficient magnesium powder for the impact flash to be visible from the Earth through telescopes exceeding 12 in (30.5 cm) in diameter. The Appendix includes a survey of the probability of a rocket in space being hit by a meteor, and calculations showing that the use of oxygen and hydrogen as propellants would give considerably improved performance.

A point of interest is that recent research has shown that this well-known paper of 1919 was, in fact, a watered-down version of the original drafted in 1914 with the title *The Problem of Raising a Body to a Great Altitude above the Surface of the Earth.* Dr Goddard felt that *real* space exploration would be derided, and so toned down the 1914 version to mention only the Moon as the goal. This discovery enhances further the remarkable foresight of a gifted pioneer.

In 1917, when the United States declared war on Germany, Dr Goddard turned his energies to investigating the military possibilities of rockets, and developed a number of promising applications. One involved a long-range bombardment missile fed by successive cordite charges; others were short-range projectiles for use by infantry. One was intended to be fired from a launching tube steadied by two short legs—a device similar to the American 'Bazooka' weapon

of the second World War and the Russian Katucha rockets currently seeing deadly service in Vietnam and the Middle East.

A number of these weapons were demonstrated successfully, but with the signing of the Armistice the US Army lost interest in rockets and Goddard returned to his private studies.

By 1921 he realised that the future of high-performance rockets lay not with solid propellants but with higher-energy liquids, and decided to concentrate on static tests with liquid-propellant motors. By 1923 a small rocket engine had been constructed and fired, in a proving stand, with a fair degree of success. After a considerable number of experiments a second rocket, this time employing a nitrogen pressure-feed system for the petrol and liquid oxygen propellants, was also fired in a proving stand. In 1925 a similar rocket was constructed, employing oxygen pressure feed. It was a spindly contraption some 10 ft (3.05 m) high, with the 2 ft (0.6 m) long rocket motor at the top; the 'in-line' propellant tanks, directly below, were protected by a conical shield.

After testing this rocket in a proving stand at the Clark University Physics Laboratories in December 1925 and January 1926, it was tested statically out of doors for the first time on 8 March. Then, on 16 March 1926, it was launched from a site on a farm at Auburn, Massachusetts. It was airborne for only 2½ seconds, covering a distance of 184 ft (56 m) at an average speed of 60 mph (96 km/h). It was, nevertheless, the first successful

Opposite page: On a launching tower near Roswell, New Mexico, in 1940, two assistants work on one of Dr Goddard's liquid-fuel rockets. This rocket was more advanced in design than the German V2s used against the Allies four years later. The tower still survives, and is now an exhibit in the grounds of the Goddard Rocket and Space Museum at Roswell

This page, top: The 1940 Goddard rocket on its assembly frame, showing combustion chamber (left) and oxygen and gasoline tanks (right). Dr Goddard is on the left of the picture, with assistants N T Ljungquist, A W Kisk and C W Mansur

Above: Robert Goddard standing beside the liquid-fuel rocket at Auburn, Massachusetts, which on 16 March 1926 became the first of its type to be launched successfully and paved the way for today's adventures in space. In 1960 the launch site was marked by a memorial sponsored by the American Rocket Society

launching of the type of rocket which has since carried men to the Moon, and instruments to the planets Venus and Mars.

This successful flight was followed by many others over the next eleven years. A significant development was that Goddard stabilised some of his missiles by means of gyroscopes and control surfaces fitted in the exhaust efflux. Such rockets represented a positive advance over the types then being constructed in Germany.

During the second World War, Goddard developed Jet Assist Take-Off (JATO) units for the US Navy. Before he died on 10 August 1945, he had seen many of the principles that he had formulated put into practice.

* * *

The last pioneer of the quartet is Hermann Oberth, born on 25 June 1894 at Harmannstadt in Transylvania. It was as a student that he became absorbed in the theory of rockets and the problems of interplanetary navigation, and in 1923 published, at his own expense, a thesis entitled *Die rakete zu den planetenraumen* (*The rocket into interplanetary space*). The thesis went into the requirements of interplanetary rocket flight in considerable detail, and provoked bitter criticisms, although it sold well. Six years later Oberth expanded his thesis and republished it under the title *The way to space travel*. This time he dealt in detail with all the fundamental problems of spaceflight, not only from the mathematical, but also from the engineering aspect. Perspective is given to his advanced thinking if one remembers that at the time the largest rocket ever built weighed only a few pounds. Deservedly, the book is today regarded as a 'bible' of astronautics.

Oberth collaborated in the pre-war science-fiction film *Girl in the Moon*. To publicise the film, he designed a large, high - altitude liquid - propellant rocket, which was to have been fired on the day of the film première. Unfortunately, it was not completed owing to a lack of time and money.

During the war Oberth worked on rocket developments at Peenemünde in Germany. He arrived at Peenemünde when design work on the A4, or V2, was virtually complete, and was amazed by the progress that had been made in the decade since his own early experiments with small rockets. Later in the war Oberth was transferred to Reinsdorf, Germany's best powder-rocket factory, to work on anti-aircraft missiles.

After the war Oberth returned to his country of birth, and continued with his astronautical studies, the importance of which was now becoming genuinely recognised. These studies included numerous ideas for rockets and spacecraft, in addition to research into propellants and their composition. Thus, with his contemporaries, Tsiolkovsky, Esnault-Pelterie and Goddard, Oberth laid the theoretical basis for spaceflight, the practical achievement of which is being witnessed by the world in our time.

Above and above right: Boeing's Stratocruiser, more than any other airliner, was the type which set the standard for long-range operations in the late 'forties. Only 55 were built, with a new two-deck pressurised fuselage married to the wings, engines, landing gear and other components of the wartime Superfortress bomber. Their most popular feature was a lower-deck lounge and cocktail bar

Far left and centre: Like the DC-3, the Curtiss C-46 transport aircraft which had served so well in wartime was snapped up by airlines hungry for new equipment. Many schemes for improving and updating it were evolved, and C-46s remained in service through the 'sixties, mainly on charter operations with smaller companies such as Austral of the Argentine and Andes of Ecuador

Below, left: Most widely-used commercial long-haul transports in the immediate post-war era were Douglas DC-4s, usually surplus C-54s that had been built for wartime service with the USAAF. Among other achievements, they re-opened trans-Atlantic operations in the insignia of major international airlines

Right: Passengers boarding the DC-4 *Tatana* of Australian National Airways

POST-WAR AIRLINERS
The First Generation

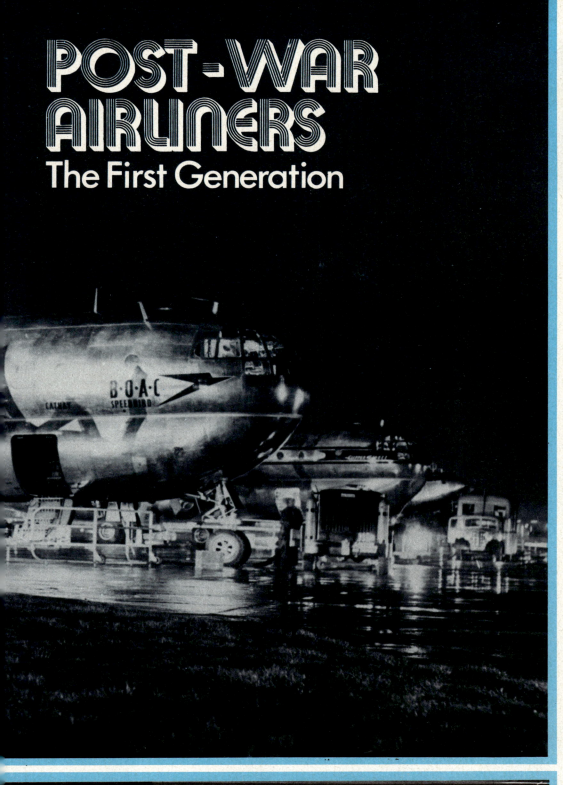

WITH THE END of the second World War the airlines began their return to peacetime operation, re-established their route networks, provided essential communication and set about the task of developing commercial aviation to become an accepted form of public mass transport.

Initially Germany, Italy and Japan were barred from participation in such operations, although subsequently these countries' airlines were to record some of the most remarkable growth figures.

Most widely-used transport aeroplane in the immediate post-war period was the Douglas DC-3, many of those in use being military versions modified, in varying degrees, to civil standards. But on the longer routes, and where traffic was heavier, two remarkable aeroplanes were soon to make their appearance—the Douglas DC-4 and Lockheed Constellation.

The DC-4 traced its origins back to the mid-1935 requirement of five major United States airlines for a four-engined trunk route aeroplane. A prototype appeared in June 1938 as the DC-4E; but it was unsuccessful and the type was drastically redesigned. The new DC-4 flew in February 1942, but the war caused it to enter service as a military transport under the designation C-54 Skymaster. A total of 1,163 were built, and after the war 79 purely civil DC-4s were constructed. The DC-4s and many converted Skymasters went into airline service all over the world, beginning operation in October 1945 with American Overseas Airlines across the North Atlantic.

The DC-4 was an all-metal low-wing monoplane with single fin and rudder, nose-wheel undercarriage and four 1,450 hp Pratt & Whitney R-2000 engines. Original accommodation was for 44 passengers, but eventually this figure was nearly doubled in high-density configurations. The cruising speed was about 220 mph (354 km/h) and maximum range more than 4,000 miles (6,440 km). This aeroplane played a major part in the development of air transport, but had one serious shortcoming: it was unpressurised.

The Constellation, although designed to a 1939 specification and first flown in January 1943, was not only pressurised but about 100 mph (160 km/h) faster than the DC-4. It was these aspects of the Constellation which were directly responsible for Douglas developing the DC-4 into the DC-6 and DC-7 series.

The Constellation had a magnificently efficient 123-ft (37.49-m) wing, a beautifully-streamlined fuselage and triple fins and rudders. Like the DC-4, it first entered service as a military aeroplane (the C-69),

LOCKHEED CONSTELLATION

Powered by: Four 2,200 hp Wright R-3350-C18-BA3 eighteen-cylinder radial engines, each driving a 15 ft 2 in (4.62 m) diameter three-blade propeller
Wing span: 123 ft 0 in (37.49 m)
Length: 95 ft 2 in (29.00 m)
Wing area: 1,650 sq ft (153.28 m²)
Gross weight: 98,000 lb (44,452 kg)
Typical cruising speed: 313 mph (504 km/h) at 20,000 ft (6,100 m)
Range: 2,260 miles (3,635 km) with max payload of 18,423 lb (8,257 kg)
First flight: 9 January 1943

Unlike the DC-4, which received an extensive work-out on military transport duties during the second World War, the Constellation did not make its mark in the field of air transportation until the war was over. It quickly showed a great potential for development following its entry into service early in 1946, and eventually more than 500 members of the Constellation/ Super Constellation/Starliner family were built for civil customers, as well as many hundreds more for military duties of various kinds. Data apply to the Model 049; the silhouette illustrates the longer-range Model 749, which entered production in 1947.

The four-engined Lockheed Constellation had been conceived before the war as a commercial airliner and then taken over as a transport for the USAAF. Larger, faster, and more sophisticated than the Douglas aircraft, it offered the advantages of a pressurised cabin and more adequate range for trans-Atlantic operation. In consequence, it became standard equipment with major airlines, being 'stretched' to carry more passengers in the Super Constellation versions with more powerful engines. Some models, such as the Royal Air Maroc 'Connie' illustrated below, carried extra baggage and freight in a detachable under-belly Speedpak. Others, like the L-1049D/H Super Constellations, were equipped as specialised freighters. On retirement from airline service, a few former Air France (below left) and Air-India machines were converted for air-sea rescue duties. Last of the 'family' were the 45 L-1649A Starliners (above) which had a new wing and increased fuel capacity

and civil operation began in February 1946 when Pan American Airways introduced Constellations on their New York-Bermuda route. Soon it was to be operating round-the-world services. There were a number of versions of the 'Connie', and 233 were built; accommodation ranged from 44 to 81 seats.

In order to compete with the early Constellations, Douglas built the pressurised DC-6 with 2,400 hp Pratt & Whitney R-2800 engines. Initially this had seating for 50 passengers, and entered service in April 1946 with American Airlines and United Air Lines. More than 170 DC-6s were built; developments were the lengthened DC-6A cargo transport and passenger DC-6B.

The DC-6B ranks with the DC-3 as one of the world's truly great transport aeroplanes. It was reliable, comfortable and economic, and was introduced by American Airlines on US transcontinental services in April 1951, originally with 54 seats. Douglas built a total of 288, and the DC-6B remained in production until 1958.

Meanwhile, Lockheed had developed the Constellation into the Super Constellation, with an 18 ft (5.49 m) longer fuselage and 2,700 hp Cyclones; and this new version entered service with Eastern Air Lines, as the L-1049, at the end of 1951. Beginning with the improved L-1049C model, the Super Constellation was fitted with 3,400 hp Wright Turbo-Compound engines and a total of more than 600 were produced, ending with the L-1049G passenger and L-1049H passenger/cargo versions. Initially there were 66 first class (then standard class) seats, but later high-density configurations carried as many as 102 passengers.

The Douglas equivalent of the Super Constellation was the DC-7. This had Turbo-Compound engines, 60/95 seats, and was capable of providing non-stop US transcontinental service. It was introduced on New York-Los Angeles services in November 1953 by American Airlines. The DC-7 worked to an 8 hr schedule eastbound and 8 hr 45 min westbound. The DC-7B was a longer-range version, and then came the 60/105-passenger very-long-range DC-7C Seven Seas, with increased wing span and North Atlantic non-stop capability. The DC-7C was introduced on non-stop North Atlantic services by Pan American World Airways on 1 June 1956. Altogether Douglas built 343 of the DC-7 series, its last family of piston-engined airliners.

The last of the piston-engined Lockheed family was the L-1649A Starliner. This was a further-developed Super Constellation, with an entirely new one-piece 150-ft (45.72 m) wing. The Starliner could carry up to 99 passengers and had a maximum-fuel range of more than 6,000 miles (9,660 km). It entered service exactly a year after the DC-7C, when TWA introduced it on non-stop New York-London services. Although an excellent aeroplane, the Starliner appeared too late and only 43 were sold.

These Douglas and Lockheed families of four-engined airliners carried the bulk of

VICKERS VIKING

Powered by: Two 1,690 hp Bristol Hercules 634 fourteen-cylinder radial engines, each driving a 13 ft 3 in (4.04 m) diameter four-blade propeller
Wing span: 89 ft 3 in (27.20 m)
Length: 65 ft 4 in (19.91 m)
Wing area: 882 sq ft (81.94 m²)
Gross weight: 34,000 lb (15,422 kg)
Max cruising speed: 210 mph (338 km/h) at 6,000 ft (1,830 m)
Range: 520 miles (837 km) with max payload of 7,240 lb (3,284 kg)
Accommodation: Crew of 2 and up to 38 passengers
First flight: 22 June 1945
Flying for the first time only some six weeks after the end of hostilities in Europe, the Vickers VC1 Viking was the first new civil transport aircraft to enter post-war production and service in Britain. Prototypes and early production Viking 1As made use of the engine nacelles, landing gear and geodetic outer wings of the wartime Wellington bomber, but a more conventional stressed-skin construction was introduced on later aircraft. Less than 200 were built altogether, yet as late as 1960 there were still about 100 of these on scheduled or charter services. One Viking, fitted experimentally with two Rolls-Royce Nene turbojet engines, became on 6 April 1948 the first British transport aeroplane to fly entirely on jet power. Data and silhouette apply to the Viking 1B.

Top left: In retrospect, the first generation of post-war piston-engined airliners often seem unexciting, yet they did a superb job in re-establishing commercial aviation and paving the way for the tremendous growth of airline flying in the 'fifties and 'sixties. One of the lesser-known types of this period was the 32-passenger Swedish-built Saab Scandia

Centre left: Like many of the other 'bread-and-butter' types, the DC-4 embodied a tremendous capacity for development. It was stretched successively into the DC-6 and DC-7 series, with pressurised cabin, more seats and more powerful engines. This DC-6B is in the insignia of Civil Air Transport of Nationalist China

Below: Here shown in the markings of Faucett of Peru, the DC-3 could be illustrated in the colours of most of the world's airlines, big and small

Bottom: Russia's first 'DC-3 replacement' was the 27/32-passenger Ilyushin Il-12, with 1,775 hp engines

Above: The Vickers Viking was the airliner with which BEA built up its fine reputation for service and safety after the war. Subsequently, Vikings served the 'independents' equally well, equipped usually to carry 24-27 passengers

Left: An aircraft that proved as difficult to replace as the DC-3 was the de Havilland Rapide. Carrying six to eight passengers, the veteran biplanes served for many post-war years on BEA routes, notably in Scotland and to the Isles of Scilly

Below: To tide over a shortage of aircraft until the turboprop Viscount and jet Comet were ready for service, Britain's aircraft industry built first passenger versions of wartime bombers and then a series of interim piston-engined designs. The Viking used many Wellington bomber components; the York, shown here in Skyways markings, was based on the Lancaster

the world's medium- and long-range traffic until the wide-scale introduction of jet transports in the period 1958-60. Also playing an important role, with BOAC and the major Canadian airlines, were Canadair Fours, which were basically pressurised DC-4s with Rolls-Royce Merlin liquid-cooled engines.

Mention must also be made of the four-engined Boeing Stratocruiser, which was developed from the Superfortress bomber. The Stratocruiser was a large (55/100-passenger) aeroplane, with a lower-deck lounge. It entered service on North Atlantic routes with Pan American in 1949 and 55 were built.

Just as the Douglas and Lockheed four-engined aircraft were vital for the successful operation of profitable long-distance services, the twin-engined Convair-liner was the most important tool for the short-stage operator. First of the family was the Convair 240, which began service with American Airlines in June 1948. It was powered by two 2,400 hp Pratt & Whitney R-2800 engines and had pressurised accommodation for 40 passengers. The lengthened and improved 44-seat Convair 340 appeared in service in 1952, and in February 1956 the 56-seat Convair 440 Metropolitan was introduced.

The Convair-liners saw world-wide service; more than a thousand were built for civil and military use, and over 200 of these

were eventually refitted with turboprop engines.

Far less successful than the Convairs were the somewhat similar Martin 2-0-2s and 4-0-4s. The 42-passenger 2-0-2 entered service late in 1947 with Northwest Airlines in the United States and LAN in Chile; the 4-0-4, which entered service in October 1951, was used mainly by TWA and Eastern Air Lines.

France produced two important piston-engined transports which played a role in developing post-war air transport. These were the four-engined 33/44-passenger Languedoc, of which 100 were built, and the double-deck Breguet Deux-Ponts. Air France had the biggest Languedoc fleet, but the type was used also by a number of other airlines including Misrair, Air Liban, Tunis Air and Polish Air Lines (LOT). The Deux-Ponts entered service on Air France's trans-Mediterranean routes in March 1953 and after a period as a freighter was withdrawn in March 1971. Twelve were built.

Also deserving mention is the Saab Scandia, a Swedish twin-engined 24/36-passenger transport which was built in Sweden and the Netherlands. The Scandia entered service with SAS in 1950 and also saw service in Brazil.

The two most important British post-war piston-engined landplane transports were the Vickers-Armstrongs Viking and the Airspeed Ambassador. The Viking was roughly equivalent to a DC-3, carried 21/36 passengers, was powered by two Bristol Hercules engines, and entered service with BEA in September 1946. This type formed the main fleet of BEA for several years and was used by many other airlines in various parts of the world; 163 were built.

The Ambassador, a beautiful high-wing monoplane with accommodation for 47/55 passengers, was powered by two 2,700 hp Bristol Centaurus engines and entered service with BEA in 1952 under the class name 'Elizabethan'. BEA's fleet of 20 flew 31 million miles and carried 2,430,000 passengers before being withdrawn in July 1958; even after that, the Ambassador continued in service with various independent airlines, one being used to carry racehorses.

This page, top to bottom:
A DC-4 of AREA of Ecuador. The circular cabin windows distinguish this type from the later DC-6 and DC-7 series, which had rectangular windows

A DC-6 of Aerovias Condor de Colombia, which was formed in 1955 to operate scheduled internal and international services

This DC-6B of Hawaiian Airlines reflects the way in which airline markings have become steadily more colourful since the war. Simple 'cheat lines' along the fuselage were supplemented first by a white top, to lower temperatures in hot climates. Noses and tails began to sport more daring designs. Overall pinks, greens and orange finish were to be pioneered much later by Braniff

Unusual markings carried by this Convair 240 are those of Central Air Transport of China

Left: The Martin company made a brief bid to enter the commercial air transport field after the war with the Model 2-0-2 and its refined successor, the 4-0-4 shown here

Below: The Canadair Four was a bold attempt to combine the basic DC-4 with a pressurised cabin and war-proven Merlin engines. It served BOAC well as the 'Argonaut' class

Bottom: A DC-6 of Canadian Pacific Airlines

Left: Converted Handley Page Halifax bombers, with a freight pannier built on to their bomb-bay, were used by many of Britain's post-war 'independents'. This Halifax 8, *Red Eagle,* is the aircraft with which Harold Bamberg founded Eagle Aviation

Right: Another former RAF wartime type which gave fine service to struggling peacetime operators was the Avro York. The wings, Merlin engines and undercarriage of the Lancaster bomber were fitted to a new fuselage for passengers or freight

POST-WAR AI

WHEN THE EUROPEAN WAR of 1939-45 ended, in a splendid, sunny May, there were countless men whose prime thought was to carry on flying in any way possible in the years ahead. For many of them, this was fairly easy; the war had been the means of teaching them to fly, in the RAF or some similar Service, and all they had to do was to 'sign on' to continue as a Service pilot. For others the international airlines held promise; and in Britain the state airline BOAC, which had its origins in the pre-war Imperial Airways, was an obvious choice, for this required pilots of strong experience —as would other airlines as they began to expand. The choice was widened somewhat further in Britain in 1946 when British European Airways was formed, as a sister company to BOAC.

But for many young men the confines of further Service life were quite unacceptable after they had endured five or six years of it; equally, they had no desire to join the state airlines. They simply wanted to be their own bosses and, confident of their skill, experience and aggressiveness, they launched out on their own. Many of them started airlines or air operating companies in the immediate post-war period, and many failed; but a number stayed the course, and their efforts laid the foundations for the big business that constitutes international air transport today.

In Britain, at least, the climate for starting a new airline was mixed. No great amounts of capital were required of ex-Servicemen, and there were certainly no shortages of ideas or enthusiasm. In the immediate post-war period about 70 small airlines were registered. The stumbling-block was the political situation presented by the existence of first one and then a second state airline. Both, quite rightly, had to be protected in a number of ways, for they were the designated flag-carriers of the nation for which international route operating authority had to be bargained for by the government.

Many pioneers soon found their enthusiasm dampened by the regulations, for the Air Corporations Act of 1939 laid down that all international air transport activity in the United Kingdom was to be run by the state. By law, therefore, it was out of

Above: G-ANAJ *City of Funchal* and G-AKNU *Sydney,* **Short Solent 3s of Aquila Airways, were equipped to carry 39 passengers in a high degree of comfort. They linked Britain with the holiday island of Madeira which then had no airstrip ashore**

Centre: In eight years of service with BEA, Vickers Vikings flew 65 million miles, carried 2,748,000 passengers and earned £35 million revenue. They were then taken over by independent operators and continued to make money carrying passengers and, later, freight

Left: One of the brightest 'stars' of Britain's post-war independent operators has been Freddie Laker, who founded Air Charter Ltd and now heads Laker Airways

TRAMPS

The three lower illustrations on this page illustrate the activities of Silver City Airways. Perhaps the most inspired of all Britain's post-war 'independents' it pioneered vehicle ferry services by taking advantage of the speedy nose-loading facility offered by the Bristol Freighter. Hundreds of thousands of cars and passengers were ferried between Britain and airports on the European coastline. Unfortunately the Freighter has had no economical replacement for such low-cost services and has been succeeded largely by Hovercraft. The illustration on the right shows the first scheduled air cargo service for flowers from Guernsey

The DC-3 with which American Airlines inaugurated the first scheduled air freight service in the USA in October 1944

the question for any private operator to start an airline to Europe, for example. The Labour government of 1945 confirmed and extended the laws so that all air services were nationalised; and when BEA came into being officially on 1 August 1946 it took over all the airlines in the United Kingdom, together with the European routes of BOAC.

It seemed a gloomy time for the free-enterprise merchants of air commerce; but for those who were really tenacious, work was still available and ways of flying were to be found. The overseas world had become very air-minded, and if the price was right there was no shortage of interested partici-pators in the post-war air transport busi-ness. Manufacturers, too, were turning their attentions to producing aeroplanes specific-ally for airline work, and this made a welcome change from the kind of death-dispensing craft they had been obliged to maintain for so long.

On to the scene came people like Squad-ron Leader Jack Jones, who founded East Anglian Flying Services, and who later became famous for his creation of Channel Airways. Others included F A ('Freddie') Laker, Harold Bamberg, Eric Rylands, Air Commodore Powell, Don Everall and Barry Aikman. They wanted to fly and to bring the benefits of air transport to an eager world. Harold Bamberg was fairly typical. He was young (25), had little capital (£100), but was ready to undertake any work. In April 1948 he founded Eagle Aviation Ltd, and his first aeroplane was a converted Halifax bomber, fitted with a freight pannier beneath the fuselage to deepen and make more capacious the volume of the original bomb-bays.

In June of that year Bamberg and his contemporaries were suddenly called upon to increase their air freighting efforts in a remarkable way—paradoxically by the British and American governments. For no apparently valid reason the Soviet authori-ties in Germany had closed all railways, canals and roads from the western zones of Germany into Berlin, which lies in the eastern sector, and thus effectively cut off Berlin from the other zones except by air. Under the Quadripartite Agreement signed by Britain, the USA, France and the Soviet

Union in 1945, access to Berlin had been provided for all four powers, and air 'corridors' into the city were arranged so that aircraft from each nation could reach Berlin from its own sector of occupied Germany. There were four of these corri-dors (one led to Warsaw) each 20 miles (32 km) wide.

With the surface routes closed, the only way into the city was by air, and on 26 June 1948 the United States Air Force organised a freight service into Berlin from Frankfurt. The city had to be maintained and its people fed and cared for, so the RAF, too, intro-duced a freight service for that purpose from Wunstorf on 28 June.

The Berlin Air Lift, as it came to be called, gathered momentum, and became one of the major aerial operations of the day. Down the Frankfurt, Hamburg and Hanover corridors British and American aircraft of all sizes and descriptions carried food, coal, fuel oil, clothing, mail, heavy machinery and other kinds of cargo. At the height of the operation 55 per cent of the total delivery was of coal, and 26 per cent was food. At the start the RAF aimed at carrying into Berlin 750 tons of freight a day; but so massive an operation did the Air Lift become that, on Good Friday of 1949, 12,940 tons of cargo of all kinds were landed in Berlin. By the time the Air Lift ended, a year after it had begun, 1,952,660 short tons of cargo of all descrip-tions had been flown into the besieged city.

The aircraft used on the Air Lift ranged from the ubiquitous DC-3 to the Avro York, Hastings, C-54 Skymaster and even the Sunderland flying-boat. The Sunder-lands, which carried 5½ short tons each, were operated by the RAF and the British charter company Aquila Airways, and were landed at Klare Lanke on the north shore of the Havelsee. Among the other fleets of 'suc-couring angels' were Harold Bamberg's three Halifax Mark 8s (otherwise known as Haltons) and the Avro Tudors of Air Vice-Marshal Don Bennett's charter company Fairflight. The Tudors carried ten tons each, specialising in liquid fuel delivery.

When the Air Lift ended abruptly, opera-tors such as Bamberg and Don Bennett were equipped with even more experience than previously, but had to look around

hard for further—and regular—work. For-tunately, the climate was easier, and the Civil Aviation Act of 1949 provided a break for British operators, if a small one. It permitted the licensing of independent com-panies to operate as 'associates' of the state airlines BOAC and BEA, and a host of operators saw in this mild thawing of the freeze an omen for a slightly better future: if the independent operators were not allowed to operate scheduled services directly competitive to the national carriers, at least they were to be given a chance.

A further change for the better for the 'independents' came in 1952, for the new Conservative government put a much more liberal interpretation upon the 1949 Act, and allowed private airlines to apply for permission to operate subsidiary scheduled services lying outside the sphere of activity of BOAC and BEA. Over the previous five years Britain's private airlines had been growing in number, and now they began to make an impression. Famous names were soon put upon the map. Eagle Airways followed Eagle Aviation, and Harold Bam-berg replaced his original aircraft fleet with Yorks and then Vickers Vikings.

Morton Air Services began regular sched-uled services from Bristol, and Cambrian Airways from Cardiff, both to the Channel Isles. Sivewright Airways started a Man-chester-Isle of Man service, and Flightways a service between Bournemouth and Jersey. Manx Air Charter tried their hand, and Lancashire Aircraft Corporation. Transair started carrying mail as well as newspapers on its London-Paris route with a small fleet of Avro Ansons.

Aquila Airways put on a regular, concen-trated basis its flying-boat services to such places as Madeira and Genoa, and then, using Hythe flying-boats, to Mediterranean resorts like Capri. Notable among the 'aerial work' type of operations was that started by Silver City Airways on 14 July 1948. Silver City Airways was founded (in 1946) by an Australian mining group based at Broken Hill (the 'Silver City'), and the entire shareholding was purchased by Air Commodore G. J. Powell and the British Aviation Services Group in 1948. Operating on a charter basis, using a Bristol Freighter leased from the manufacturers, the airline

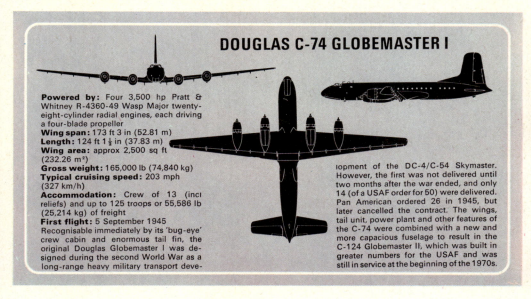

DOUGLAS C-74 GLOBEMASTER I

Powered by: Four 3,500 hp Pratt & Whitney R-4360-49 Wasp Major twenty-eight-cylinder radial engines, each driving a four-blade propeller
Wing span: 173 ft 3 in (52.81 m)
Length: 124 ft 1½ in (37.83 m)
Wing area: approx 2,500 sq ft (232.26 m²)
Gross weight: 165,000 lb (74,840 kg)
Typical cruising speed: 203 mph (327 km/h)
Accommodation: Crew of 13 (incl reliefs) and up to 125 troops or 55,586 lb (25,214 kg) of freight
First flight: 5 September 1945
Recognisable immediately by its 'bug-eye' crew cabin and enormous tail fin, the original Douglas Globemaster I was designed during the second World War as a long-range heavy military transport deve-

lopment of the DC-4/C-54 Skymaster. However, the first was not delivered until two months after the war ended, and only 14 (of a USAF order for 50) were delivered. Pan American ordered 26 in 1945, but later cancelled the contract. The wings, tail unit, power plant and other features of the C-74 were combined with a new and more capacious fuselage to result in the C-124 Globemaster II, which was built in greater numbers for the USAF and was still in service at the beginning of the 1970s.

This page, top right: The Douglas C-74 Globemaster was designed for the USAF as a heavy freighter, with a lift under the rear fuselage for loading bulky items. It was taken over eventually by charter operators and used for transporting both freight and livestock such as cows. HP-379 is shown here in the markings of Aeronaves de Panama

Top centre: With a huge new fuselage replacing the original circular type, the C-74 was evolved into the C-124 Globemaster II and became a standard USAF nose-loading transport

Below: After re-establishing post-war long-haul passenger services, the DC-4 became a mainstay of many cargo carriers. This one, in the insignia of Ace Freighters, was photographed at Biggin Hill as late as May 1965

Left: Another of the post-war leaders of Britain's independent airlines has been Harold Bamberg, founder of British Eagle. For a period he linked with the great Cunard shipping company, and the DC-6A (above) was operated under the Cunard Eagle Airways banner. Capital injected by the shipping lines was of equal help to other operators and even BOAC aircraft appeared for a time with the name 'Cunard' on their noses

The Miles Aerovan of 1945 represented a bold attempt to market a small but capacious and easy-to-load aerial freighter. The rear of the cabin pod hinged to one side, opening up the full cross-section and enabling cars to be driven in quickly via a ramp. Modern inheritor of the Aerovan concept is Short's fine little Skyvan

started the world's first car ferry service, from Lympne to Le Touquet, the most convenient Channel crossing. During the following year, 2,600 cars and 7,900 passengers were carried, on a scheduled basis. From then the traffic grew each year, and so successful was the operation that Silver City built its own airport further down the coast, at Lydd, and named it, appropriately, Ferryfield. This terminal offered specialised car handling facilities and a paved runway, which Lympne had not, and there were obvious advantages to Silver City in owning its own airport. The service went from strength to strength, and by 1957 Silver City had transported 230,000 vehicles and 612,000 passengers to the Continent and back.

In 1956, a rival came upon the scene in the shape of Freddie Laker's company, Air Charter, which operated from Southend to Rotterdam and Ostend using the same type of aircraft. Air Charter operated what it called the 'Channel Air Bridge', and was similarly successful from the outset. Air Charter was eventually to become a member of the British United Airways group, and its founder and managing director, Freddie Laker, subsequently left BUA to form his own holiday charter airline, Laker Airways.

Meanwhile, other companies were trying their hand with varying degrees of success at aerial work operations, transporting a fantastic variety of cargoes. Dan-Air Services began operations from Blackbushe in 1955. BKS, Derby Airways, Don Everall Aviation and Skyways introduced DC-3s, Yorks and other types, and Airwork (formed in 1928) joined with Hunting Air Transport to operate cargo services to Africa and elsewhere. Hunting-Clan Air Transport, as the latter airline became, developed into a specialist in the carriage of livestock—pigs in particular, for it carried 50 pigs regularly in York aircraft to Vienna and other destinations for breeding purposes. Racehorses, machinery, aircraft engines and parts, flowers, newspapers, dresses, animals for zoos, mail, tropical fish, motor cars—including racing cars—and military stores on special charter to the Army were all airlifted; not always at a profit, but it was believed that one contract would lead to another.

After many years of superb service with Air Canada, this turboprop Vanguard 952, photographed at Dusseldorf, is used on the freight operations of Invicta Air Cargo

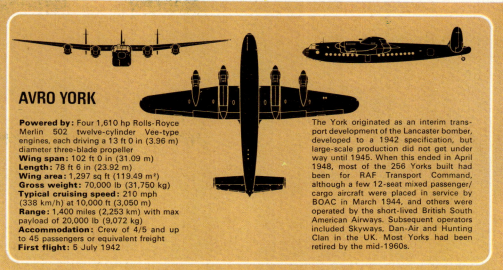

AVRO YORK

Powered by: Four 1,610 hp Rolls-Royce Merlin 502 twelve-cylinder Vee-type engines, each driving a 13 ft 0 in (3.96 m) diameter three-blade propeller
Wing span: 102 ft 0 in (31.09 m)
Length: 78 ft 6 in (23.92 m)
Wing area: 1,297 sq ft (119.49 m²)
Gross weight: 70,000 lb (31,750 kg)
Typical cruising speed: 210 mph (338 km/h) at 10,000 ft (3,050 m)
Range: 1,400 miles (2,253 km) with max payload of 20,000 lb (9,072 kg)
Accommodation: Crew of 4/5 and up to 45 passengers or equivalent freight
First flight: 5 July 1942

The York originated as an interim transport development of the Lancaster bomber, developed to a 1942 specification, but large-scale production did not get under way until 1945. When this ended in April 1948, most of the 256 Yorks built had been for RAF Transport Command, although a few 12-seat mixed passenger/cargo aircraft were placed in service by BOAC in March 1944, and others were operated by the short-lived British South American Airways. Subsequent operators included Skyways, Dan-Air and Hunting Clan in the UK. Most Yorks had been retired by the mid-1960s.

Left: Companies still flying the irreplaceable Bristol Freighter include Safe Air Ltd of New Zealand, whose eleven-strong fleet provides an aerial conveyor belt between the North and South Islands

Right: Another freighter of the early post-war years, only recently retired by Air France, was the two-deck Breguet Deux-Ponts, known to Air France first as the Provence and then as the Universel Freighter.

Below right: Although less familiar than the slightly smaller DC-3/C-47, the wartime Curtiss-Wright C-46 Commando is also still in service with a number of freight carriers

The aircraft employed by these operators for their multifarious duties began as a hotch-potch of types and evolved only gradually into fleets really suitable for the tasks allotted them. The supremely adaptable DC-3, a war-surplus aircraft with a three-ton loading capability, would apparently go anywhere—and often had to. It was only in 1949 that its Douglas-built successor, the DC-6, entered the lists as a worthy newcomer. The DC-6A, which flew in September 1949, was a cargo version able to carry over 14,000 lb (6,350 kg) of payload; on one occasion a DC-6A carried the largest single piece of freight airlifted up to that time, a 23,000-lb (10,430-kg) extrusion press.

The Halifax, in its 'civilianised' version, and the Lancastrian, with its maximum payload of 4,845 lb (2,195 kg) or nine passengers, had always been uneconomic for their peacetime roles; but they were at least improved upon by aircraft such as the Avro York, with its seven-ton payload, and the Bristol Type 170 Freighter, which brought a new dimension to air cargo work with its capacity for three saloon cars and 14 passengers. The Freighter is still in service today with a few operators such as Safe Air Ltd in New Zealand, which operates a fleet of eleven across the Cook Strait.

Even more of an anachronism in the immediate post-war years, apparently, were the D.H.89 Rapides and Junkers Ju 52/3ms operated by BEA, although they did valuable work. As many as 45 D.H.89s were operated by BEA at one time, and a fleet of

ex-German Ju 52s was reconditioned by Short Bros & Harland at Belfast for the airline and impressed into service in Scotland and across the Irish Sea. The Ju 52/3m 'Jupiters' carried a payload of 3,500 lb (1,587 kg).

In the early post-war years a number of interesting new types were produced, some of them to have surprisingly long lives, others soon to disappear from the scene. Among the former was the Breguet 763 Deux Ponts, a French type which flew for the first time in February 1949. Although it was a fairly large passenger and cargo aircraft, Breguet had decided when designing it that the only practicable way of achieving the required floor area was by using two decks. The first prototype was followed by three pre-series 761S aircraft, and one of these was awarded a Certificate of Airworthiness for a maximum take-off weight of 99,208 lb (45,000 kg), exceeding even the 93,000 lb (42,184 kg) of the DC-6. The maximum take-off weight of the Breguet 763 Deux Ponts was eventually to become 113,760 lb (51,600 kg). Air Algérie used the Model 761, and in 1953, still with a French registration, the aircraft flew for 240 hours on Berlin-Hamburg cargo services for Silver City Airways. In 1965 Air France re-introduced the Breguet 763 as the Universel freighter on the Paris-London route, and in January 1966 between Paris and Bristol.

Less noteworthy, perhaps, but nonetheless important for their time, were the Aerovan and the Merchantman, produced in 1946-48 by the well-known firm of Miles

Aircraft, which had built hundreds of training aircraft for the RAF during the war. The Aerovan was a high-wing, twin-engined aircraft of composite wood and metal construction, powered by two Cirrus Major engines. It had a capacity for nine passengers or a single motor car, and had a special rear-loading door so that the car could be driven straight in. Its range was 400 miles (645 km).

Its larger successor, the Miles Merchantman, was a four-engined development along the same basic lines, with 250 hp Gipsy Queen engines and a capacity for 20 passengers or two tons of freight. The whole rear fuselage consisted of a streamlined door which could be swung open, as on the Aerovan, to admit its cargo load. The Aerovan was offered as a freighter, air ambulance, operating theatre, mobile workshop, flying classroom, horse-box or general feeder-line aircraft, and its maximum range was 850 miles (1,370 km).

Like the Aerovan, the Merchantman had a short and not particularly memorable life, but this is less important than the fact that both types made their strong contribution to the post-war development of the air freighting business and helped aspiring operators on their ways. Both can be put firmly on record as having pointed the way for the later development of aircraft such as the Skyvan, a product of the 1960s; and the name Merchantman is perpetuated today by British European Airways, which has named its Vanguard freighter conversions after the trailblazer of 20 years earlier.

Above: Mightiest military transport ever flown, the USAF's Lockheed C-5A Galaxy can carry a payload of nearly 120 tons. Its lower deck alone is 144 ft 7 in (44.07 m) long, 19 ft (5.79 m) wide and 13 ft 6 in (4.11 m) high

Left: Earlier double-deck transport giant from Lockheed was the 92-ton Constitution of 1946, which could carry 180 passengers. Spiral staircases linked the two cabins. Man-size tunnels inside the wings gave access to the engines in flight

Right: The size of Boeing's eight-jet B-52 Stratofortress prototype was emphasised by photographing it with a B-17 'heavy bomber' of the second World War

Post War Giants

EVER SINCE MAN FIRST conquered the air, designers have devoted a large amount of their creative talent to the problems of producing larger and larger aircraft. Indeed, for many years it seemed that each generation of transport and bomber aircraft was destined to outstrip the one before it in size.

While the size of any one category of aircraft is purely relative to what has gone before, what can now justifiably be labelled 'aerial giants' have ceased to be a novelty. The Boeing 747, with its cavernous interior and potential 490-passenger capacity, is already a familiar sight at airports around the world. The Lockheed C-5A Galaxy military freighter, which boasts equally large proportions, is also well known.

Even these two mammoths could be eclipsed in the size league table if some of the projects now on the drawing board were translated into actual hardware, for aviation's crystal-ball gazers are predicting that in the 1980s transports of 1,000-passenger capacity will be feasible.

This desire to build outsize aircraft was already apparent in the years immediately following the second World War. It was not simply a matter of building a giant as an exercise in technological skills. Aircraft like the Bristol Brabazon and the Saunders-Roe Princess flying-boat were conceived as sound commercial projects, intended to capitalise on the booming world market in long-range air travel. In the USA, bomber aircraft such as the Convair B-36 and Boeing B-52 were built to extend the long arm of Strategic Air Command and to maximise its efficiency.

The Brabazon and Princess proved to be white elephants for the British aircraft industry. Both fell victim to the need for national economy, although such were the complexities of the technical problems surrounding the aircraft that it is doubtful if either type could have lived up to the bright commercial future initially forecast for it.

The Brabazon, Bristol Type 167, took its name from that of Lord Brabazon of Tara, the pioneer airman who headed a government-sponsored committee that was given the wartime task of advising on Britain's civil aircraft building policy after the war. Although it did not fly until September 1949, its concept dated back to 1943, when the Bristol Aeroplane Co had been authorised to proceed with two prototypes and up to 10 production aircraft, provided that the work did not interfere with war production.

Bristol's concept, readily agreed by the British government, was for an aircraft with what was then a large carrying capacity, able to fly the Atlantic non-stop at high speed. The basic design was settled late in 1944 and work on the first aircraft began about a year later.

When the finished product ultimately emerged, the world was startled by its prodigious size. The wing span was 230 ft (70.10 m), the overall length 177 ft (53.95 m), and from ground level to the top of the fin measured 50 ft (15.24 m). Bristol had

The photographs on these two pages give some indication of the spaciousness and high standard of comfort that the Bristol Brabazon would have offered trans-Atlantic passengers had it entered airline service. It represented the end of an era of gracious first class air travel in the tradition of the flying-boats that preceded it. The post-war mass transportation business demanded instead higher speed and as many seats as possible, packed sardine-like into smaller cabins, to make air travel cheap enough for millions who had never flown before. The old tree over which the Brabazon is landing at Farnborough (left) is that to which 'Colonel' S F Cody tethered his great 'Cathedral' biplanes when testing their engines forty years earlier

to build a special hangar at Filton for final assembly, and before the Brabazon could be flown the airfield runway had to be extended—at no little cost, for houses had to be demolished and a road diverted—and strengthened considerably.

The Brabazon introduced a whole host of technical innovations, many of which were adopted later for other British transport aircraft. It also had an unusual power plant arrangement. Eight Centaurus radial piston-engines were coupled in pairs to drive contra-rotating propellers. The aircraft weighed a maximum 290,000 lb (131,540 kg) for take-off, could cruise at 250 mph (402 km/h) and had a potential 5,500-mile (8,850-km) range with full fuel.

Initially it was never intended that this version should go into production, although when BOAC showed keen interest a specification was written for a 72/80-seat variant capable of undertaking the airline's North Atlantic operations. As a follow-on an updated design was proposed, with four Coupled Proteus turboprops and seating 100 passengers, but this was abandoned in 1952.

Because of its sheer size and technical innovations, the Brabazon was costing huge sums and this finally proved to be its undoing. The politicians who had backed the programme in its early stages had an attack of cold feet and the one and only Brabazon to fly—it spent only 400 hours in the air in four years—ultimately went to the scrap heap.

A similar fate befell the Princess—a project that was intended to continue Britain's supremacy in flying-boat design. But a combination of factors—notably development costs far outstripping budget, a bad dose of engine problems and BOAC's diminished interest in big commercial flying-boats—all contributed to its demise.

As in the case of the Brabazon, the idea for such an aircraft had germinated during the war years but took a long time to reach fruition. In 1946 BOAC's interest in the project was strong enough to warrant the ordering of three prototypes by the Ministry of Supply. All three of these 145-ton giants were built, but only one of them ever flew.

The Princess was more than 10 tons heavier than the Brabazon, and shared with its contemporary the idea of having coupled engines to drive contra-rotating propellers. Ten Proteus turboprops powered the aircraft, all but the two outboard engine positions having doubled-up units.

The massive 219 ft 6 in (66.90 m) span wing of the Princess incorporated retractable wing-tip floats and housed 14,500

gallons (65,915 litres) of fuel, to give a 5,270-mile (8,480-km) still-air range—ample for BOAC's intended Southampton-New York operations when carrying the full 105-passenger payload.

Even before its eventual cancellation, the writing was on the wall for the Princess. BOAC ended flying-boat operations in November 1950 and thus downgraded its interest. The Princess did not fly until August 1952, although the sight of it flying over Farnborough at the SBAC Show in the following month is never likely to be forgotten. Then, when flight testing showed a serious mechanical fault in the gearboxes connecting the four inboard engine pairs, rectification of which would have cost much in time and money, the whole programme ground to a halt.

Ultimately the three Princesses were beached at Calshot and Cocooned, awaiting an ignominious fate. There they stayed for several years as a memorial to the glorious past—but indefinite future—of the flying-boat.

In the USA the accent on large aircraft development was primarily on strategic bombers, although these projects did provide some spin-off for unsuccessful transport ventures. An exception was the huge wooden flying-boat built by multi-millionaire Howard Hughes. Reportedly the Hughes aircraft remains in existence today in California, and its enigmatic sponsor still pays a small technical team to watch over its upkeep. But it flew only once.

Convair and Boeing were the two primary US manufacturers of giant aircraft of the 'forties and early 'fifties. The Convair XB-36, prototype for America's first intercontinental bomber, weighed 100 tons, and when it first flew on 8 August 1946 was the world's largest and heaviest aircraft. Within its 162 ft 1 in (49.40 m) fuselage was a trolley on rails, on which crewmen propelled themselves between the flight deck and the rear defensive armament and crew rest positions.

The B-36 was something of a flying arsenal: although never called upon to drop a bomb in anger, it had the capability of lifting more than 80,000 lb (36,290 kg) of bombs and bristled with sixteen 20-mm guns, in eight paired positions. Missions of up to 30 hours duration were possible. The type remained in service with the USAF's Strategic Air Command until May 1958. It was produced in several versions, one of the major improvements being to supplement the six original 'pusher' piston-engines with four auxiliary jets, one pair under each wing, to boost performance.

Opposite page, top: Largest land-based aeroplane in the world in 1955 was the Convair XC-99 cargo transport, which combined the 230 ft (70.1 m) wing and six 3,500-hp engines of the B-36 bomber with a new double-deck fuselage big enough to carry 400 fully-equipped troops

Above: Unlike the XC-99, the B-36 itself was built in quantity, spearheading the USAF's nuclear deterrent force for many years. It was so large that even Convair's huge assembly works could accommodate a line of B-36s only by angling them across the 'shop floor

Upper left: The NB-36H version of the B-36 is the only aeroplane that has yet flown with an operating nuclear reactor on board. It enabled the effects of radiation upon the airframe and equipment to be measured in flight, and methods of shielding the crew and electronics to be tested. The nuclear reactor did not power the aircraft

Lower left: Jet successor to the B-36 was Boeing's big B-52 Stratofortress. Its size was dictated by the need to carry a heavy load of nuclear weapons over many thousands of miles to potential targets from bases in the USA

Right: First flown on 18 April 1952, the YB-60 represented Convair's attempt to develop from the B-36 a long-range bomber that would keep their factories busy in the jet age. The USAF preferred the all-new B-52

The B-36 thus became a 10-engined bomber.

The final version to see production was the B-36J, which had a possible overload weight of 205 tons—more than double that of the XB-36 prototype. The main piston-engines were each of 3,800 hp, compared with the 3.000 hp of the prototype, with four J47 turbojets each providing 5,200 lb (2,358 kg) of extra thrust.

Special versions of the aircraft included the NB-36H, which flew in September 1955 to flight test the world's first airborne nuclear reactor, and the GRB-36J, designed to act as 'mother ship' to an RF-84F reconnaissance fighter. A jet derivative of the B-36, the YB-60, was designed as a replacement, and the first of two prototypes flew in April 1952, powered by eight Pratt & Whitney turbojets. No production contracts were placed, however, the Boeing B-52 being selected instead to replace the B-36 in the heavy bomber role.

The B-52 was chosen to be the spearhead of the USAF's H-bomber force and still remained in use in 1971 as a conventional bomber in Vietnam. Although of more compact dimensions than the B-36—the last production version, the B-52H, has a span of 185 ft (56.39 m) and a length of 157 ft 6 in (48.10 m)—it nevertheless qualifies as a 'giant'.

The first B-52 Stratofortress flew in August 1952, and the last B-52H model was completed in June 1962. In between, a programme of progressive improvement

saw different variants of the aircraft appear with more powerful engines, improved performance and bomb-load carrying capability, with only minor changes in the basic design.

Other large aircraft of US design which appeared in the late 1940s and early 1950s included the Lockheed Constitution, an unsuccessful transport project for the US Navy which featured a 'double-bubble' fuselage, and the Convair XC-99, a cargo transport version of the B-36. The XC-99 had the 230 ft (70.10 m) span wing of the bomber and its basic power plant of six piston-engines, the sole example built serving with the USAF's Air Materiel Command from 1950-57. Within its 183 ft (55.78 m) fuselage there was space for 50 tons of cargo.

Nowadays giant aircraft such as the Boeing 747, McDonnell Douglas DC-10, Lockheed TriStar and others of similar ilk have the wide-body, 'well-fed' look, and modern technology has done away with those ultra-long-span wings. The 747, for example, has a span of only 195 ft (59.44 m) compared with the B-36's 230 ft, and the DC-10 Series 10 measures only 155 ft (47.24 m) from wing-tip to wing-tip.

So no more, it seems, will we see those elongated, pencil-slim shapes gracing the skies. The Brabazon and its colleagues belong to a bygone era—an era that had more failures than successes, but nevertheless provided the basis for the creation of the 'jumbos' of today.

Opposite page, top to bottom:
The huge, graceful Saunders-Roe Princess was 'the flying-boat after the last'. By the time it flew for the first time, on 22 August 1952, the world's major airlines had switched irrevocably to landplanes

For years the three Princesses lay Cocooned and engine-less by the waters from which they might have linked Britain with countries overseas. Finally, they were taken away and broken up

Even bigger than the Princess was the Hughes Hercules, which remains the largest aeroplane ever flown. A firm of house movers had to be called in to move the hull from Culver City, California, where it was built, to Terminal Island in June 1946

From a tower, Howard Hughes looks down on the Hercules, the wooden giant that he piloted on the one, brief hop that it made before being stored away in a huge hangar

This page, above: The Princess graced the skies over Britain for two years, its passengers including Sir Alliott Verdon-Roe, greatest of all British pioneers and one of the founders of the company that built it. Had it gone into service, it would have been able to carry 200 passengers for 5,270 miles (8,480 km) at 360 mph (579 km/h)

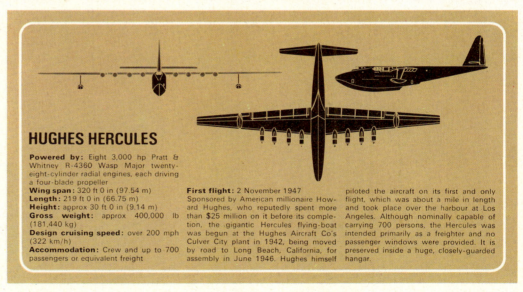

HUGHES HERCULES

Powered by: Eight 3,000 hp Pratt & Whitney R-4360 Wasp Major twenty-eight-cylinder radial engines, each driving a four-blade propeller
Wing span: 320 ft 0 in (97.54 m)
Length: 219 ft 0 in (66.75 m)
Height: approx 30 ft 0 in (9.14 m)
Gross weight: approx 400,000 lb (181,440 kg)
Design cruising speed: over 200 mph (322 km/h)
Accommodation: Crew and up to 700 passengers or equivalent freight

First flight: 2 November 1947
Sponsored by American millionaire Howard Hughes, who reputedly spent more than $25 million on it before its completion, the gigantic Hercules flying-boat was begun at the Hughes Aircraft Co's Culver City plant in 1942, being moved by road to Long Beach, California, for assembly in June 1946. Hughes himself piloted the aircraft on its first and only flight, which was about a mile in length and took place over the harbour at Los Angeles. Although nominally capable of carrying 700 persons, the Hercules was intended primarily as a freighter and no passenger windows were provided. It is preserved inside a huge, closely-guarded hangar.

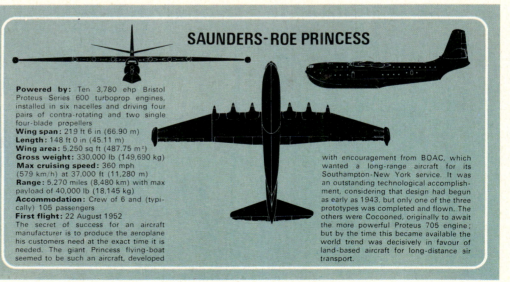

SAUNDERS-ROE PRINCESS

Powered by: Ten 3,780 ehp Bristol Proteus Series 600 turboprop engines, installed in six nacelles and driving four pairs of contra-rotating and two single four-blade propellers
Wing span: 219 ft 6 in (66.90 m)
Length: 148 ft 0 in (45.11 m)
Wing area: 5,250 sq ft (487.75 m²)
Gross weight: 330,000 lb (149,690 kg)
Max cruising speed: 360 mph (579 km/h) at 37,000 ft (11,280 m)
Range: 5,270 miles (8,480 km) with max payload of 40,000 lb (18,145 kg)
Accommodation: Crew of 6 and (typically) 105 passengers
First flight: 22 August 1952
The secret of success for an aircraft manufacturer is to produce the aeroplane his customers need at the exact time it is needed. The giant Princess flying-boat seemed to be such an aircraft, developed with encouragement from BOAC, which wanted a long-range aircraft for its Southampton-New York service. It was an outstanding technological accomplishment, considering that design had begun as early as 1943, but only one of the three prototypes was completed and flown. The others were Cocooned, originally to await the more powerful Proteus 705 engine; but by the time this became available the world trend was decisively in favour of land-based aircraft for long-distance air transport.

BROKEN BARRIERS

Opposite page, top: First aeroplane to exceed the speed of sound was the Bell X-1. Later versions of the same design were the X-1A and X-1B, shown here. Although comparatively simple and straight-winged, the X-1A had logged a speed of no less than Mach 2.42 by June 1954

Bottom: Most US high-speed research aircraft have been designed for air-launching from 'mother-planes', to conserve their rocket propellants for brief dashes at maximum speed. This photograph shows the swept-wing Bell X-2 cradled under the cutaway bomb-bay of a B-50 Superfortress

Above: The X-1B in flight, after release from its B-29 'mother-plane'. This aircraft was specially equipped to investigate the thermal problems of high-speed flying

Below: Starting the rocket engine of the X-2 after release from a B-50. As always, an F-86 'chase-plane' is in attendance, its pilot watching closely to check that all is well and ready to offer help in an emergency. On more than one occasion 'chase' pilots have guided other aircraft to a safe landing when their pilots have run into difficulties

Bottom: The swept-wing X-2 did not enjoy the success of the X-1 family, both examples being destroyed in accidents. On its fatal last flight, one of them reached a speed of Mach 3.2, setting a record which was unbeaten for five years

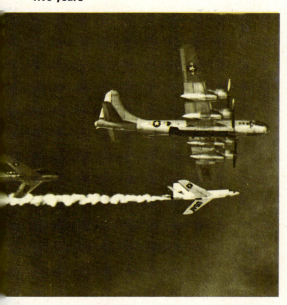

FOR RESIDENTS IN the Worthing and Portsmouth areas of England's South Coast, Saturday 10 March 1956 was unusually noisy. What the London evening newspapers described as 'particularly heavy' sonic booms on that day disturbed residents enjoying the early Spring sunshine. Sonic booms were a manifestation of a flying phenomenon which had received wide publicity in the years following the second World War—the phenomenon of the 'sound barrier'. However, not only the sound barrier was being broken on that sunny March day; the '1,000 mph' barrier was also being broken as the Fairey Delta 2 research aircraft outpaced the sun to set a four-figure (in mph) World Air Speed Record for the first time.

Both of these 'barriers' exist more in the minds of journalists than in fact. No physical barriers exist to impede the passage of aeroplanes through the air, and today supersonic flight—ie, flight at speeds greater than the speed of sound, or beyond the 'sound barrier'—is a commonplace, experienced not only by highly-trained professionals but by passengers in the new generation of supersonic transports like the Concorde. For a time, it is true, the 'sound barrier' did seem to represent a hazard, causing aircraft to behave strangely as their speed approached that of sound. [The speed of sound is usually referred to as Mach 1, and it varies from about 760 mph (1,223 km/h) at sea level to 660 mph (1,062 km/h) at 36,000 ft (11,000 m), above which height it remains constant. In the same way, Mach 2 means twice the speed of sound at any given altitude, and so on.]

At Mach 1, the behaviour of the airflow around an aircraft changes, giving rise to a shock wave and other effects which could cause control of the aircraft to be lost, or could create such a high drag that Mach 1 could not actually be surpassed at all. Once these phenomena were fully understood, it became relatively simple to design aeroplanes in such a way that the so-called 'barrier' could be surmounted smoothly, with virtually no effects noticeable within the aircraft.

The possibility that some kind of barrier to high-speed flight might exist was first realised during the second World War, when the effects of compressibility (that is, the air becoming compressed ahead of a fast-travelling aeroplane) were first experienced with such aeroplanes as the Supermarine Spitfire and Lockheed Lightning. In a maximum power dive, the Spitfire could reach speeds equivalent to about 9/10ths the speed of sound—fast enough for compressibility to be experienced. At about the same time, it became clear that the advent of the jet engine would make even higher speeds possible, and serious research into the so-called sound barrier began.

Credit for the design of Britain's first supersonic aeroplane goes to the Miles company, which was officially commissioned in 1943 to design and produce a jet-plane capable of flying at 1,000 mph (1,609 km/h) at 36,000 ft (11,000 m)—more than double

the speed of the fastest aeroplane then in service. The Miles design, known as the M.52, was well advanced by 1946, when the whole programme was officially cancelled on the flimsy pretext that manned flight at such a speed was too dangerous. No such trivial excuses were allowed to stand in the way of the parallel American research programme which, started a year after the M.52, led to the construction of the world's first supersonic aeroplane, the Bell X-1.

The design of the X-1, which was conceived originally to fly at only a little above the speed of sound, was similar in many general respects to that of the M.52. It had a very thin-section wing, without any sweepback, but a major difference was that the X-1 was rocket-powered, and therefore had to be air-launched after being carried aloft beneath the fuselage of a B-29 Superfortress. The first air-launch of the X-1 was made on 19 January 1946, but powered flights were not attempted until 9 December of that year, using the second prototype. Nearly another year passed before supersonic flight was achieved, this milestone being reached by Captain Charles 'Chuck' Yeager on 14 October 1947.

The speed reached by the X-1 on that historic occasion was 670 mph (1,078 km/h) at a height of 42,000 ft (12,800 m), and therefore equivalent to a Mach number of 1.015. In all, six members of the X-1 'family' were built; in one of them, the X-1A, Yeager reached a speed of Mach 2.42 on 4 June 1954. This achievement emphasised that, whatever impediment might have existed to flight at Mach 1, once that point had been surpassed no further aerodynamic 'barrier' remained. An aeroplane designed to overcome compressibility effects at the speed of sound could be accelerated beyond Mach 1 to the limits imposed by the available engine thrust or until a much more cogent barrier was encountered—the 'heat barrier'.

Heat becomes a problem at very high speeds because of the friction between the surface of the aeroplane and the molecules of air in contact with it. This friction causes the skin, and therefore the inside of the aeroplane, to heat up; and for flight at speeds much above Mach 2 special precautions have to be taken. The temperatures that can be reached not only degrade the strength of the metal structure but can also cause such unpleasant effects as boiling in the fuel tanks.

For the next research step beyond the X-1, therefore, Bell elected to use a stainless steel airframe, together with sweptback wings. The resultant X-2 appeared in 1952, but the two prototypes of this design were dogged by misfortune, both being destroyed in accidents. Before the second X-2 crashed in 1956, however, it reached a speed of Mach 3.2 (2,094 mph; 3,370 km/h), and this remained the highest speed at which man had flown until 1961.

The X-2, it will be noted, exceeded Mach 3 only a few months after the Fairey Delta 2 set the first 'over 1,000 mph' speed record. As the X-1 and X-2 were air-launched, they could not set records under the terms laid

down by the FAI, but ever since 1946 the USA has had a clear lead over other nations in 'barrier-breaking' research aeroplanes. The first British aeroplane capable of bettering Mach 1 in level flight was the English Electric P.1A, which first exceeded the speed of sound on 11 August 1954 and provided the basis for the RAF's first truly supersonic fighter, the Lightning. The first British supersonic flight (in a dive) had been made on 9 September 1948 by John Derry in the D.H.108.

In France, supersonic flight research began somewhat later than in Britain, the first aeroplane capable of exceeding Mach 1 being the Sud-Ouest S.O. 9000 Trident, first flown on 2 March 1953. Straight-winged like the Bell X-1, the Trident had two turbojet engines and a rocket unit to boost it to a maximum speed of Mach 1.6. French experience of supersonic flight was then extended by the delta-winged SFECMAS Gerfaut which, on 3 August 1954, became the first aeroplane in Europe to exceed Mach 1 in level flight on the power of a turbojet alone, without rocket or afterburner. Further development of the design by Nord led to the Nord 1500 Griffon, which was powered by a ramjet and achieved Mach 1.85 in 1957.

Whilst the work in France and Britain provided a basis for the design of operational aircraft with supersonic performance, following the American lead, a further research programme was put in hand in the USA which led to production of the most remarkable research aeroplane flown to date. This programme evolved from discussions that started in mid-1954, between representatives of the USAF, USN and NACA, with the aim of defining new objectives for flight research beyond the X-1 and X-2. By the end of the year, it was agreed that the objective would be an aeroplane capable of flying at 4,500 mph (7,240 km/h; nearly Mach 7) and reaching an altitude of 250,000 ft (76,200 m). The primary structure would be required to withstand temperatures as high as 1,200°F, with heating rates of 30 BTU per sq ft of surface area per second.

In every respect, the requirement was far ahead of the state of the art in 1955, but the programme went ahead rapidly and with remarkably few setbacks, considering its radical nature. North American Aviation won the design contest and was awarded a development contract on 30 September 1955. The aircraft was designated X-15 and was designed around an XLR99 liquid-fuel rocket engine capable of delivering a thrust of more than 60,000 lb (27,215 kg) for a period of several minutes. Like the X-1, the X-15 was to be air-launched, since precious fuel could not be expended in getting the X-15 off the ground and up to operating altitudes. Two Boeing B-52s were therefore modified as carriers for the X-15s, three of which were ordered. With a span of only 22 ft (6.70 m) for the slightly swept-back trapezoidal wings (again reminiscent of the Miles M.52 design) the X-15 had a gross weight at launch of over 31,000 lb (14,060 kg), of which more than 18,000 lb (8,165 kg) was accounted for by the liquid

Opposite page: The North American X-15 rocket-powered research aircraft in its original form. Before it completed its test programme, this remarkable aeroplane attained a speed of 4,534 mph (7,297 km/h)—the fastest man has yet travelled in anything but a spacecraft

This page, top to bottom:
The X-15 was fitted with a conventional nose-wheel unit. In this picture the tail is supported on a ground trolley. The aircraft landed on two retractable steel tail-skids

The stubby Fairey F.D.1 research aircraft spanned a mere 19 ft 6½ in (5.95 m), which gave it a fantastic rate of roll

The French SFECMAS Gerfaut was the first aeroplane in Europe to exceed Mach 1 on the power of a turbojet engine alone in level flight, on 3 August 1954

Even more spectacular was the Nord Griffon, the whole body of which formed the outer casing of a huge ramjet engine. A turbojet mounted in the centre of the ramjet provided power for take-off and low-speed flying, and a means of igniting the ramjet itself

oxygen and anhydrous ammonia rocket propellants.

When the first X-15 free flight was made on 8 June 1959 the aircraft was fitted with lower-powered engines, as the XLR99 was not then ready. With two XLR11-RM-5s, giving a combined thrust of about 33,000 lb (15,000 kg), the first powered flight was made by the second X-15 prototype on 17 September 1959, a speed of Mach 2.3 being achieved. From that point on, both the speed and the altitude reached by the X-15s climbed steadily, with Mach 3 being reached in November 1961 after the XLR99 engine had been fitted in the second prototype. By December 1963 the X-15s had reached a speed of Mach 6.06, had encountered a skin temperature of 1,320°F and reached an altitude of 314,750 ft (95,936 m).

Following a landing accident with the No 2 X-15 in 1962, this aircraft was rebuilt as the X-15A-2, with a number of modifications to permit an even higher performance, and first flew in this guise on 28 June 1964. In October 1967, this X-15 reached a speed of 4,534 mph (7,297 km/h), equivalent to Mach 6.72 and matching the original design requirement. This is the highest recorded speed yet achieved by man in an aeroplane capable of being controlled in normal flight.

Higher speeds than those mentioned above have been experienced by astronauts in space capsules orbiting the Earth or in a lunar trajectory. Whether there is any practical use for such speeds in travelling between two points on the Earth's surface remains to be proved. Limits there certainly are, so far as everyday travel is concerned; but they are limits imposed by the habits and requirements of the traveller rather than by any physical limitations on the aeroplane. The barriers, such as they were, have been broken and the high speed research conducted during the past 25 years has provided all the information needed to design and build the fastest aeroplanes likely to be required for military or commercial purposes for many decades to come. When the destination is the stars, other unknown barriers may still await discovery—but that is another story, another day.

MILES M.52

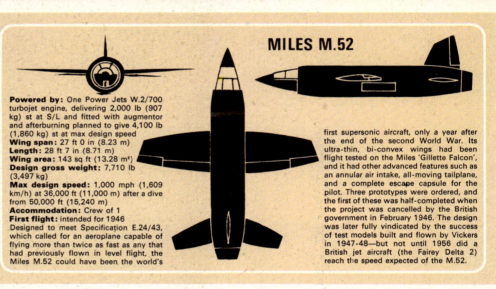

Powered by: One Power Jets W.2/700 turbojet engine, delivering 2,000 lb (907 kg) st at S/L and fitted with augmentor and afterburning planned to give 4,100 lb (1,860 kg) st at max design speed
Wing span: 27 ft 0 in (8.23 m)
Length: 28 ft 7 in (8.71 m)
Wing area: 143 sq ft (13.28 m²)
Design gross weight: 7,710 lb (3,497 kg)
Max design speed: 1,000 mph (1,609 km/h) at 36,000 ft (11,000 m) after a dive from 50,000 ft (15,240 m)
Accommodation: Crew of 1
First flight: intended for 1946
Designed to meet Specification E.24/43, which called for an aeroplane capable of flying more than twice as fast as any that had previously flown in level flight, the Miles M.52 could have been the world's

first supersonic aircraft, only a year after the end of the second World War. Its ultra-thin, bi-convex wings had been flight tested on the Miles 'Gillette Falcon', and it had other advanced features such as an annular air intake, an all-moving tailplane, and a complete escape capsule for the pilot. Three prototypes were ordered, and the first of these was half-completed when the project was cancelled by the British government in February 1946. The design was later fully vindicated by the success of test models built and flown by Vickers in 1947-48—but not until 1956 did a British jet aircraft (the Fairey Delta 2) reach the speed expected of the M.52.

DE HAVILLAND D.H.108

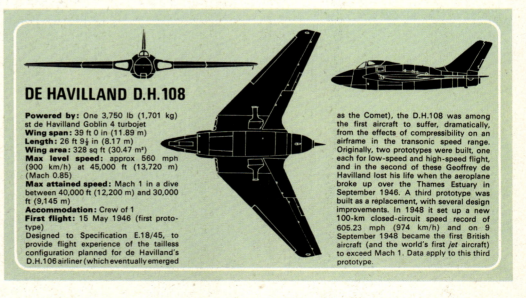

Powered by: One 3,750 lb (1,701 kg) st de Havilland Goblin 4 turbojet
Wing span: 39 ft 0 in (11.89 m)
Length: 26 ft 9½ in (8.17 m)
Wing area: 328 sq ft (30.47 m²)
Max level speed: approx 560 mph (900 km/h) at 45,000 ft (13,720 m) (Mach 0.85)
Max attained speed: Mach 1 in a dive between 40,000 ft (12,200 m) and 30,000 ft (9,145 m)
Accommodation: Crew of 1
First flight: 15 May 1946 (first prototype)
Designed to Specification E.18/45, to provide flight experience of the tailless configuration planned for de Havilland's D.H.106 airliner (which eventually emerged

as the Comet), the D.H.108 was among the first aircraft to suffer, dramatically, from the effects of compressibility on an airframe in the transonic speed range. Originally, two prototypes were built, one each for low-speed and high-speed flight, and in the second of these Geoffrey de Havilland lost his life when the aeroplane broke up over the Thames Estuary in September 1946. A third prototype was built as a replacement, with several design improvements. In 1948 it set up a new 100-km closed-circuit speed record of 605.23 mph (974 km/h) and on 9 September 1948 became the first British aircraft (and the world's first jet aircraft) to exceed Mach 1. Data apply to this third prototype.

Opposite page, top: The Fairey Delta 2, first aeroplane to set up an 'over-1,000 mph' speed record, in 1956. It also pioneered the type of drooping nose now fitted to the Concorde and Tu-144 supersonic airliners

Bottom: First flown on 16 May 1957, the Saunders-Roe S-R.53 was an experimental 'mixed-power' interceptor, powered by a Viper turbojet and a de Havilland Spectre variable-thrust rocket engine for rapid climb and combat boost. It was intended to be armed with two wingtip-mounted Firestreak missiles. Its production development, the P.177, was cancelled under one of a series of government economy measures

This page, top: Another mixed-power experimental fighter design was the French S.O.9000 Trident, which pioneered supersonic flight research in France

Centre: This rear view of the Trident shows well the three chambers of its SEPR 25 rocket engine, in the tail, and the wingtip-mounted turbojets. The designed top speed was Mach 1.6 for a duration of 4½ minutes

Bottom: End product of years of supersonic research in Britain was the superb Lightning interceptor. In this view, the Lightning has underwing bombs and two overwing jettisonable auxiliary fuel tanks for ferrying

ENTER THE COMET

The history of the de Havilland Comet 1, the world's first jet airliner, is summed up in the seven illustrations on this page and opposite. The prototype (G-ALVG, above and top left) flew first with a single large wheel on each main landing gear leg; by the time it entered service the Comet 1 (centre left) had multi-wheel bogies. In general, development had gone smoothly and rapidly, and the Ministry of Civil Aviation had no hesitation in awarding a Certificate of Airworthiness (below). Then came tragic accidents over the Mediterranean. Parts of the wrecked 'Yoke Peter' were recovered (bottom left), the cause of the accidents was established, and all jet airliners were made safer as a result

M.C.A. Form No. 9

UNITED KINGDOM

MINISTRY OF CIVIL AVIATION

CERTIFICATE OF AIRWORTHINESS

No. A.3215

NATIONALITY AND REGISTRATION MARKS	CONSTRUCTOR AND CONSTRUCTOR'S DESIGNATION OF AIRCRAFT	AIRCRAFT SERIAL No. (CONSTRUCTOR'S No
G-ALYS	The de Havilland Aircraft Co. Ltd. Comet D.H.106 Series 1.	06005

CATEGORY : Normal

SUBDIVISION : (a) Public transport for passengers
(b) Public transport for mails
(c) Public transport for goods
(d) Private (e) Aerial work
(h) Demonstration (1) Crew familiarisation

This Certificate of Airworthiness is issued pursuant to the Convention on International Civil Aviation dated 7th December, 1944, and the Air Navigation Order, 1949, the Air Navigation (General) Regulations, 1949, and the Air Navigation (Radio) Regulations, 1949, in respect of the above-mentioned aircraft, which is considered to be airworthy when maintained and operated in accordance with the requirements of the above-mentioned Order and Regulations, and the pertinent Flight Manual.

John S Maclay

Minister of Civil Aviation

Date 22nd January, 1952.

This certificate is valid for the period(s) shewn below

From	22nd January, 1952	to	21st January, 1953.
From		to	
From		to	
From		to	
From		to	

Signature, Official Stamp and Date

No entries or endorsements may be made on this Certificate except in the manner and by the persons authorised for the purpose by the Minister of Civil Aviation.

If this Certificate is lost, the Secretary, Ministry of Civil Aviation (R.L.2) should be informed at once, the Certificate Number being quoted.

Any person finding this Certificate should forward it immediately to the Secretary, Ministry of Civil Aviation (R.L.2), Ariel House, Strand, London, W.C.2.

A BRITAIN DEEPLY EMBROILED in all-out war would not seem to be the likely starting point for one of the most far-reaching innovations in commercial air transport since Douglas built the DC-3. Yet it was the deliberations of an official body during 1943, and the actions which flowed from those deliberations, that led to construction of the Comet and its use to launch the world's first passenger jet services nine years later.

As early as December 1942, the British Minister of Aircraft Production set up a committee, under the chairmanship of Lord Brabazon, to outline requirements for the civil transport aircraft which Britain should be ready to produce after the war had ended. This step was in itself a dramatic gesture of faith in the future; even more dramatic were the recommendations of this committee, made in February 1943, for among the

types that it proposed was a trans-Atlantic *jet-propelled* mailplane capable of carrying a one-ton load at 400 mph (645 km/h) and having a pressurised cabin for the crew. The boldness of this concept can be realised when it is recalled that at the time of the report, only one jet aeroplane had flown in Britain—the first of two prototypes of the Gloster E.28/39—and that pressurised cabins were yet to become an operational feature of military aircraft.

The de Havilland Aircraft Company began a series of design studies before the end of 1943 for so-called 'Brabazon Type 4' aircraft. Several of the initial designs featured three jet engines grouped in the rear fuselage—two side-by-side and one above and further aft, in an arrangement strikingly prophetic of that used in the same design office 15 years later for the Trident. However, the Brabazon 4 design evolved

along different lines, for by late 1944, with the needs of BOAC fed into the equation, it was becoming clear that something rather larger than a one-ton mail carrier was wanted—in fact, it should be a passenger-carrier for regular service across the Atlantic. Four engines, rather than three, would be needed for the size of aircraft now envisaged, and a wing-root 'buried' installation was eventually chosen.

When prototypes of the D.H.106 design were ordered in May 1946, the aircraft had evolved as a low-wing monoplane with 40° of wing sweepback and a sweptback tail unit, with a fuselage to seat 24 passengers, but by the time the first aircraft flew on 27 July 1949 the sweepback had been halved to 20°, unswept tail surfaces had been substituted, and the accommodation increased to 32. The name Comet had been bestowed on the D.H.106 some 18 months before the first flight. Power was provided by four 4,450 lb (2,018 kg) st de Havilland Ghost centrifugal turbojet engines.

Throughout the design and development period of the Comet, BOAC played a key role, showing unwavering faith in the new concept at a time when no other airline in the world had ordered either a turbojet or even a turboprop airliner. As early as October 1946 BOAC undertook to buy eight production Comets, and eventually bought nine, providing the fleet which operated the world's first passenger jet services in May 1952. North Atlantic operations proved to be beyond the range of the Comet 1, but it was ideally suited to the so-called Empire routes eastward from Britain, the inaugural route being from London to Johannesburg. Cruising at 490 mph (788 km/h), the Comet was able to halve the flying time of its contemporaries on any route, but its attraction lay not only in its speed, but also in the unprecedented smoothness of jet travel at 'over-the-weather' altitudes in pressurised comfort.

The success which attended the introduction of the 36-seat Comet was as spectacular as it was short-lived. While BOAC was busy pioneering, other airlines began to form a queue at Hatfield, among them Pan American, Air France, Canadian Pacific, Air-India and UAT. But between May 1953 and April 1954 three of the nine Comets in service broke up in the air, and with the third accident the career of the Comet 1 was over. One of the three accidents may have been attributable to extreme turbulence in the monsoons off Calcutta, but the other two, which occurred over the Mediterranean, were caused by fatigue failures of the pressure cabin structure. This was established only after one of the most remarkable accident investigations in the history of aviation, which revealed for the first time the fatiguing effect on metal of constantly increasing and decreasing the pressure, as occurred every time the Comet climbed and descended.

Meanwhile, however, Britain had made another notable contribution to the changing post-war pattern of commercial aviation, in the form of the four-turboprop Vickers Viscount. This, too, had been backed by a

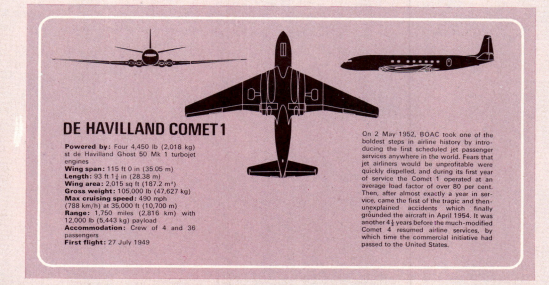

DE HAVILLAND COMET 1

Powered by: Four 4,450 lb (2,018 kg) st de Havilland Ghost 50 Mk 1 turbojet engines
Wing span: 115 ft 0 in (35.05 m)
Length: 93 ft 1¼ in (28.38 m)
Wing area: 2,015 sq ft (187.2 m²)
Gross weight: 105,000 lb (47,627 kg)
Max cruising speed: 490 mph (788 km/h) at 35,000 ft (10,700 m)
Range: 1,750 miles (2,816 km) with 12,000 lb (5,443 kg) payload
Accommodation: Crew of 4 and 36 passengers
First flight: 27 July 1949

On 2 May 1952, BOAC took one of the boldest steps in airline history by introducing the first scheduled jet passenger services anywhere in the world. Fears that jet airliners would be unprofitable were quickly dispelled, and during its first year of service the Comet 1 operated at an average load factor of over 80 per cent. Then, after almost exactly a year in service, came the first of the tragic and then-unexplained accidents which finally grounded the aircraft in April 1954. It was another 4½ years before the much-modified Comet 4 resumed airline services, by which time the commercial initiative had passed to the United States.

Above: When the Comet taxied past piston-engined Stratocruiser, DC-3 and Convair-liner transports at London Airport, it made them look like relics of a by-gone age. On BOAC's London-Tokyo route in 1953, it cut flying times by half and operated at an 89 per cent load factor (only one seat in ten empty)

Right: The neatness of the Comet's flight deck was matched by the far greater smoothness of high-altitude cruise and the unprecedented quietness in flight of its turbojet engines so far as crew and passengers were concerned

Brabazon Committee recommendation, following proposals put forward by Vickers for a successor to the twin piston-engined Viking, and the 32-seat Dart-engined Type 630 prototype, G-AHRF, was flown for the first time on 16 July 1948. At government instigation, BEA cancelled its original Viscount order in favour of the piston-engined Ambassador, but renewed interest was shown in a 53-seat stretched version, and when, in the Summer of 1950, BEA borrowed the 630 prototype for four weeks' operation there was no doubt about passenger reaction to the new type. By the end of the year the airline had ordered 26 of the larger Viscount 701s, and the snowball had begun to roll. It ended some ten years later, by which time 444 Viscounts had been built for a worldwide market, a success story surpassed in the turboprop field only by the Fokker/Fairchild Hiller Friendship, which first flew in November 1955 and was still in production in 1971, with orders having passed the 560 mark.

These two types apart, the turboprop-driven airliner has not enjoyed a success comparable with that of the jet airliner. America, still squeezing the last ounce of power out of the piston-type engine in the mid-1950s, in the form of the Turbo-Compound installed in the DC-7 and Super

Constellation, did not put its first turboprop design, the Lockheed Electra, into service until three months later than the Boeing 707, and most of the 170 built were for domestic customers. The other best-selling turboprop types over the years have been the Hawker Siddeley 748 and Japan's YS-11A, though in both cases sales have been steady rather than spectacular. Elsewhere, only Russia can be said to have pursued the development of turboprop engines with any intensity, its range of types including the twin-engined An-24, four-engined An-10, An-12 and Il-18 and the gigantic An-22 and Tu-114. This last pair are powered by the Kuznetsov NK-12, which at around 15,000 shp is the most powerful turboprop engine in the world today.

However, it was the jet rather than the turboprop which was really to change the post-war face of air travel. The Comet was a step into the unknown, and de Havilland, BOAC—and, indeed, Britain—paid a high price for the imaginative pioneering of commercial jet travel. That the decision to develop this type of aircraft was right is shown by the pattern of air transport today, when non-jet transports are regarded as positively old-fashioned.

Although the weakness in the Comet's original structural design made it impossible for de Havilland to maintain the leading position in jet transport production that it so richly deserved, the type did achieve

Opposite page, top to bottom:
Delivered in June 1953, G-AMOC was one of BEA's pioneer fleet of Viscount 701 turboprop airliners. It was still giving good service with Cambrian Airways in 1971

Another great airline which took delivery of Viscount 803s in 1957 was KLM. The first of its fleet, PH-VIA, was named after Sir Sefton Brancker, who had done so much to encourage Britain's pioneer airlines in the 'twenties, before being killed in the crash of the airship R.101

Designed as an enlarged, second-generation replacement for the Viscount, the turboprop Vanguard quickly found itself outmoded in a jet age. Nonetheless, it gave many years of fine service with BEA and Air Canada

What is often forgotten is that this Avro Tudor 8, its Merlin piston-engines replaced by four Rolls-Royce Nene turbojets, first flew on 6 September 1948, many months before the Comet. But it was not intended for use as an airliner

Below: Two very significant aircraft 'met' at Seattle when Peter Bowers, well-known as a design engineer, historian and veteran 'plane enthusiast, landed his 1912 Curtiss replica near the prototype Boeing 707

Right, top to bottom: The Herald represented Handley Page's attempt to capture the promising turboprop short-haul market. But for overwhelming competition from other types such as the Fokker Friendship—with the same Dart engines—it might have succeeded and staved off the eventual collapse of this great company

Boeing converted two B-47B Stratojet bombers into XB-47Ds to flight test Wright's 9,710 hp YT49 engine. By flying at 597 mph (960 km/h), an XB-47D reached the highest speed ever recorded by a propeller-driven aircraft in level flight

Most successful of Britain's twin-Dart feederliners is the Hawker Siddeley 748, with sales now past the 250-mark. This one helped to operate Skyways' cheap-fare coach-air services between London and Paris, from the famous old aerodrome at Lympne in Kent

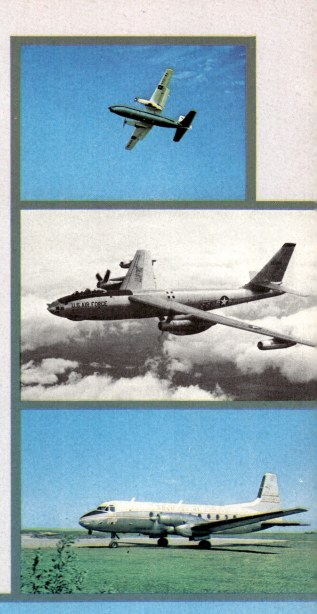

Below: When the Comet re-entered service in 1958, in its Mk 4 version, it made history for the second time by operating the first trans-Atlantic jet airline flights. By 1960 BEA, too, was operating these Comet 4Bs

Right: With sales totalling 568, from 125 customers in 48 countries, by the beginning of 1971, the Fokker Friendship (built also in the USA by Fairchild) is one of the major successes of the post-war aircraft industry

Centre: The Antonov An-12 is a rear-loading freighter version of Aeroflot's An-10 turboprop airliner. Enormous numbers serve with the Soviet Air Force for transport and paratroop dropping. Others, like the Egyptian SU-AOJ (illustrated), have been supplied to Russia's friends and allies

Above: This Soviet-built Ilyushin Il-18 turboprop airliner was delivered to CAAC, the state airline of China, before relations between the two nations became strained

TUPOLEV Tu-104

Powered by: Two 21,385 lb (9,700 kg) st Mikulin AM-3M-500 turbojet engines
Wing span: 113 ft 4 in (34.54 m)
Length: 127 ft 5½ in (38.85 m)
Wing area: 1,877 sq ft (174.4 m²)
Gross weight: 156,525 lb (71,000 kg)
Max cruising speed: 560 mph (900 km/h) at 32,800 ft (10,000 m)
Max range: 1,645 miles (2,650 km)
Accommodation: Crew of 5 and 50 passengers
First flight: 17 June 1955

The Tu-104, which appeared during the temporary eclipse of the Comet and more than two years before the entry into service of the Boeing 707, was of more than usual interest to western nations. Not only did the existence of a Soviet jet airliner take them by surprise, but its obvious ancestry gave a more than useful clue to the size and probable performance of the Tu-16 'Badger' medium bomber from which it was developed. The first Aeroflot passenger service with the Tu-104 began between Moscow and Irkutsk on 15 September 1956; later models seated up to 100 passengers, and the design also formed the basis for the smaller Tu-124, which was the USSR's first turbofan-engined commercial transport to enter service.

further modest success after being thoroughly redesigned and 'stretched' into the Comet 4 series. By the time the new Comet was ready, its lead had been lost to the Boeing 707, but one brief moment of glory remained as, on 4 October 1958, two BOAC Comet 4s flew the world's first trans-Atlantic jet services for fare-paying passengers, thus at last fulfilling the vision of the Brabazon committee 15 years earlier. A non-stop North Atlantic crossing was really still beyond the Comet's range, and the 75 Comet 4s built have served mostly as regional or short-haul transports.

As already noted, the Comet's lead was forfeited to the Boeing 707—the first in a line of Boeing jet transport designs of which more than 2,000 examples had been sold by mid-1971. The Boeing 707 was not, however, the first jet transport on the American continent, honours for this achievement going instead to the Avro Canada company. This highly innovative concern—an associate of the British Avro company and part of the Hawker Siddeley Group—began work on a jet transport in 1946, making use of the test results obtained by its British parent company with the Tudor 8 testbed. The Avro C-102 Jetliner was powered by

four Rolls-Royce Derwent 5s in paired nacelles on each wing, and had a circular-section fuselage to accommodate up to 50 passengers.

The first flight was made on 10 August 1949, only two weeks after the Comet, and test flying continued for more than a year, in the course of which a mail-carrying flight was made to New York, giving America her first sight and sound of the future. However, the C-102 attracted no customers, partly because the design had failed to break away from piston-engined convention and was therefore unable to derive the best economics from the new form of propulsion, and partly because airlines were waiting to see how the Comet progressed before committing themselves to jet transports.

With the decision to stop development of the C-102, Avro Canada left the North American field open to manufacturers on the US west coast; but before Boeing, Douglas and Convair (in that order) could gear up for production, one more jet transport was to appear in Europe—and that, to the surprise of one and all, emerged from the Soviet Union.

Recognising that the development of civil aeroplanes provided a means of updating

her technology and improving her overseas status, Russia embarked during 1953 on an ambitious programme to modernise the Aeroflot fleet. One of the first fruits of this programme emerged as the Tupolev Tu-104, first flown on 17 June 1955 but unknown outside Russia until the prototype flew into London Airport on 22 March 1956. The aircraft was then seen to be based on the Tu-16 bomber, with virtually identical wings, power plant and tail unit, but a new fuselage with room for 50 passengers.

By western standards, the Tu-104 was crude and uneconomic. Nevertheless, it entered service with Aeroflot in September 1956 to become the world's second jet transport and, as the Comet 1s were then grounded, it was the only jet in commercial service until October 1958, when the Comet 4 entered service and the Boeing 707 also started to fly passengers commercially, launching America into the jet airliner age. Since these early types a dozen more have gone into service, and during 1971 still others are nearing completion, with the first supersonic transports already in production. Nearly 4,000 pure-jet transports now fly the world's air routes, following in the trail of the Comet.

British Overseas Airways Corporation operated the world's first passenger services by jet in 1952 with the original de Havilland Comet 1, and introduced the new, long-bodied Comet 4 into its fleet in 1958. By the end of the 'sixties it had replaced its Comets with VC10s and Boeing 707s; in 1971 the only Comet 4 still 'operating' in BOAC colours was G-APDT, used at the airline's Heathrow headquarters as an instructional aircraft for the training of apprentices

The Gas Turbine Revolution

Intake of one of the four CJ805-23B turbofan
engines of a Swissair Coronado

Above: Compared with the bristling cylinders of the piston-engines that preceded them, modern turbojets often look unimpressive at first glance; yet an engine like this General Electric turbojet has no difficulty in thrusting an aircraft to twice the speed of sound

Left: The RB.163 Spey is one of Rolls-Royce's by-pass or turbofan engines. Power plant of the Trident and BAC One-Eleven airliners, it also equips the American Gulfstream II, Dutch F.28 Fellowship and versions of the military Buccaneer, Phantom and Corsair II

Bottom left: The Hawker Siddeley Trident took its name from the 'three-pronged' arrangement of its rear-mounted Spey turbofans. A similar layout was adopted subsequently for other jetliners such as the Boeing 727 and Tupolev Tu-154

Right: Those who remember the work involved in replacing a wartime piston-engine will appreciate the relative ease with which most jet-engines can be removed and re-installed. Typical is this into-tail installation of the Corsair II's Allison TF41 (Rolls-Royce Spey). On some other types the complete rear fuselage detaches quickly and easily for access to the engine

Far right: A Rolls-Royce RB.162-86 turbojet on the test-bed. This engine is mounted in the tail of the latest BEA Trident 3B airliners to give added boost for take-off with a heavy load at 'hot and high' airports

EVERYONE KNOWS THAT A JET engine is 'something like a giant vacuum cleaner: it sucks air in at the front and blows it out at the back.' This description, put forward by a young RAF officer in 1941, really does hold good. But there is a bit more to it than this. The aircraft jet engine is a gas turbine, a type of engine first built at the turn of the present century and considered for aircraft use since 1916 or earlier. Indeed, devices which could be called gas turbines figure in aerial patents from the mid-19th century. It is also a jet-propulsion engine, and various forms of jet propulsion have been considered for aerial locomotion for about two centuries. But nobody before Flight Cadet Frank Whittle, in 1928, ever thought of combining the two: to use a gas turbine solely in order to provide jet propulsion. This was one of those supremely obvious notions which nobody thought of; and when Whittle did suggest it there were plenty of experts to argue why it could not be done.

A gas turbine has three basic parts. At the intake end is a compressor, which induces a steady flow of air and compresses it. In the middle is a combustion chamber, where fuel is mixed with the air and burned steadily, just like the flame of a blowlamp or gas cooker. At the outlet end is a gas turbine, a bladed wheel spun at high speed by the flow of hot gas escaping from the combustion chamber. All that is needed to complete the engine is a shaft to join the gas turbine to the compressor. Hopefully, the engine will now run as long as the fuel is kept turned on. Indeed, the gas turbine should be able to provide useful work. If the turbine wheel takes out only just enough energy to drive the compressor, the residual energy in the flow of hot gas should be great enough for it to be expanded out to the atmosphere through a constricting nozzle at a very high velocity, providing a large and sustained forward

thrust by reaction. Such an engine is called a turbojet. Alternatively, the turbine can be made to extract a great deal more energy from the gas stream than is needed merely to drive the compressor. In this case the surplus energy is available at the end of a rotating shaft. This can be used to drive a speed-reducing gearbox coupled to a propeller. Such an engine is a turboprop.

Twenty years ago the whole future of aircraft propulsion appeared to lie with either the turbojet or the turboprop. The turbojet was simple, light, compact and cheap. It gave adequate thrust for take-off, very good thrust at high speeds and seemed ideal for robust, mass-produced military aircraft. Its drawbacks were that it had a high fuel consumption and was very noisy; but these characteristics seemed a small price to pay for the immense advantage offered by the new engine in breaking through the barrier to flight performance which had hitherto been imposed by the piston-engine. Suddenly, instead of a fight to gain two or three miles per hour at the upper limit of the aircraft speed range, at around 470 miles per hour (756 km/h)—which seemed the best that could be done with a practical and useful piston-engined aircraft—the jet opened up vistas of 600 mph (965 km/h) and above, with the early promise of realising the dream of supersonic flight.

In contrast, the turboprop was aimed not so much at opening up new and unexplored realms of flight performance but with improving the efficiency, and especially the smoothness and passenger appeal, of aircraft in the 250-400 mph (400-645 km/h) class.

All gas turbines burn fuel at a rate which varies with the temperature and density of the surrounding air. For best fuel economy a gas turbine should be operated in the thin, cold air of the stratosphere at a height of at least 35,000 ft (10,670 m). On short

flights it is obviously not practical to fly so high, but the basic influence of all gas turbines on cruising height has been a strong upward trend. So the new generation of turboprop aircraft in the period after 1947 offered their occupants a ride that was not only faster and smoother but also higher and much less affected by bad weather and cloud.

In general, the turboprop gave excellent take-off performance, a climb better than that of most piston-engined aircraft of comparable design, and a level speed generally 25 to 80 mph (40-130 km/h) faster. But the turboprop was prone to the mechanical and aerodynamic problems of the propeller, and in particular to the same general limit on flight speed of the order of 500 mph (800 km/h)—although eventually the big Tupolev swept-wing Tu-95 bomber and Tu-114 transport flew considerably faster than this on turboprops, and the Americans even tried to make supersonic propellers.

Since the early 1930s Whittle had realised that there could be an intermediate form of engine, which he called a ducted fan. The company formed to exploit his ideas, Power Jets, took out patents for various forms of fan engine, but official interest was lukewarm. The established view was that the ducted fan would be heavy and complicated and would have most of the drawbacks of the turbojet and turboprop without the main advantages of either. Nobody bothered to devote very much time to seeing how such an engine could best be designed and constructed.

It can be done in various ways. One is to build what is essentially a turboprop but to use the surplus shaft power to drive a large-diameter fan at the front of the engine, rather like a many-bladed propeller. This fan can be driven directly by the turbine or it may be geared down to rotate at a lower speed, and it can be either shrouded by a

short fan duct or placed at the intake to a long by-pass duct surrounding the whole 'core engine' and discharging at the rear into a common jet-pipe where the cool fan air mixes with the hot jet from the core. A quite different arrangement is to use a turbojet to provide a stream of hot gas to drive an additional turbine wheel added at the rear. Surrounding the turbine blades are much larger fan blades, operating in the air flowing past the basic engine. Such an arrangement is known as an aft-fan, and has the advantage that the basic unit can be an existing turbojet, with virtually no modification.

Various kinds of turbofan were constructed in Germany, the United States and Britain between 1941 and 1950, but the first such engine ever to fly was a little French design by the Turboméca company. This engine, the Aspin, was a major modification of the Piméné turbojet, the first of the company's prolific family of small gas turbines to fly. Rated at 440 lb (200 kg) thrust, the Aspin powered the twin-fuselage Fouga Gemeaux in January 1952, and was later flown in the same aircraft in a modified form giving 794 lb (360 kg) thrust.

By this time, in mid-1952, Rolls-Royce was running on the bench the first prototype of what it called a by-pass turbojet, an engine named the Conway. Effectively, this was a two-spool, or split-compressor, turbojet in which the blades of the front (low-pressure) spool were lengthened to deliver excess air through a by-pass duct in the way previously described. First run at about 9,000 lb (4,080 kg) thrust, the Conway was developed to give 13,000 lb (5,900 kg) thrust and was chosen at this stage to power the Vickers V1000 military transport. Although this was cancelled in 1956, the Conway was continued, and eventually powered some early versions of the Boeing 707 and DC-8 at 17,500 lb (7,940 kg) thrust, the Handley Page Victor B.2 bomber at 20,600 lb (9,345 kg) thrust and the BAC VC10 and Super VC10 at ratings up to 22,500 lb (10,205 kg).

But the modern turbofan stemmed at least as much from the bold decision in 1958 of Pratt & Whitney to rebuild the well-proven JT3 (J57) two-spool turbojet and turn it into a front-fan engine. The change was made available to existing airline users of the JT3C turbojet in the form of a kit of parts which they could incorporate themselves. The intake and first three stages of the low-pressure compressor were removed, and in their place was added a large two-stage fan, secured to the front of the remainder of the LP spool and rotating with it, but of much greater diameter. To provide the additional shaft power to drive the big fan, a third stage was added to the LP turbine. The result

was an engine only a little longer and slightly heavier than the original turbojet, and with an intake having more than twice as great an area. Despite its large diameter, the drag of the installed engine was only slightly more than that of the JT3 turbojet. Fuel consumption was very nearly the same, for the fuel system and combustion chamber were hardly altered. But thrust rose from round about 12,000 lb (5,440 kg) to 17,000 lb (7,710 kg), and the noise level was sharply reduced.

This apparent 'lash-up' had the most profound effect throughout the world of

Opposite page, top: Turbofan engines have superseded turbojets in transport aircraft of all sizes. Typical of the current and next generation are a JT3D-engined Boeing 707-323C freighter of American Airlines, and a mock-up of the forthcoming 24/28-passenger Falcon 20T version of the Dassault Mystère 20 business jet with rear-mounted CF700s

Centre left: Pioneer of the now generally accepted turbofan principle was Rolls-Royce's Conway 'by-pass' engine. Among aircraft it made possible was the superb BAC VC10 rear-engined airliner (below)

This page, below: With two Pratt & Whitney JT15D-4 turbofans, the Aérospatiale Corvette will carry 12 passengers at up to 497 mph (800 km/h)

Below, centre: The version of the Fokker-VFW F.28 Fellowship in current service carries up to 65 passengers on the power of two lightened and simplified Spey 555-15 turbofans

Bottom left: Most widely used of all the twin-turbofan short/medium-range jetliners is the McDonnell Douglas DC-9. This Series 30 aircraft of JAT (Yugoslavia) has 14,000 lb (6,350 kg) st Pratt & Whitney JT8D-7 engines

Bottom right: DC-8s of CP Air and Atlantis at Athens International terminal. The advent of more powerful and economical turbofans enabled McDonnell Douglas to give the DC-8 a new lease of life, by stretching the hitherto one-size fuselage almost to 'Jumbo' proportions in the 259-passenger Super 61 and 63 models

subsonic aviation. Without the JT3D, turbofans would still have come sweeping in, but it was this engine more than any other which demonstrated beyond argument the massive advances that such power plants make possible. The effect on the airline industry was startling. American Airlines, one of the earliest operators of the Boeing 707 and 720 jetliners, decided in 1959 to convert every turbojet in its Boeing fleet into the JT3D, and introduced the term 'fanjet' as a trademark for its improved equipment. Almost every other operator later did likewise, and today there are comparatively few 'straight' jet airliners of any type still in service.

Only one major type of aft-fan engine ever went into airline service. In the late 1950s General Dynamics was putting a lot of money into the short- to medium-haul jet built by its Convair division that eventually became the Model 880. This was succeeded by a slightly larger and considerably heavier machine, the Model 990 Coronado, which was powered by an aft-fan conversion of the 880's engine. For the 880, General Electric had produced the CJ805, a civilianised form of the J79 supersonic military turbojet. For the 990, GEC added a large free-wheeling aft fan equipped with double-deck 'bluckets' (a word coined from 'blade' and 'bucket'), the inner part comprising a turbine blade ('bucket') worked upon by the hot gas stream and the outer part being a fan blade acting in the surrounding airflow. By 1962 a much smaller conversion along the same lines, the CF700-2B, rated at 4,000 lb (1,814 kg) thrust (a quarter as much as that of the aft-fan CJ805) was flying in the French Dassault Mystère 20 business jet, which was promptly re-christened by PanAm's Business Jets Division as the Fan Jet Falcon.

Today there are not many new turbojets.

Even in the smallest sizes the turbofan is the preferred engine, on the scores of better economy, better propulsive efficiency (because its mean jet velocity is less) and reduced noise. Jet velocity is one of the most profound factors affecting the performance of all aircraft propulsion systems. The propeller has the lowest jet velocity. The result is that it gives the highest take-off thrust and highest propulsive efficiency, and can in theory have the lowest noise level. On the other hand its performance falls away rapidly as aircraft speed increases, until at about 400 mph (645 km/h) it has about reached its limit in practical commercial service.

The turbofan fills in the whole spectrum of engines from the propeller right across to the turbojet. A high ratio turbofan of the mid-1970s will have a by-pass ratio of about 10; in other words, ten times as much air will pass through the fan as through the core engine. Such an engine is not far short of a shrouded turboprop. It would give slightly lower take-off thrust, for a given level of fuel consumption, but the performance would fall less rapidly than that of the turboprop and would suffice amply for a speed of 500 mph (800 km/h). Noise would in theory be slightly greater than that of the propeller engine, because the fan and jet effluxes would have a mean speed rather higher than the propeller slipstream; but in practice the vibration of propeller blades, sonic flow at the tips, gearbox noise and other factors could well make the turboprop noisier than an equivalent turbofan.

For the fastest current airliners, such as the 620 mph (1,000 km/h) Boeing 747, a by-pass ratio of about 5 is common. This ratio, which a few years ago would have been thought extraordinarily high, still results in a quiet engine provided that great attention is also paid to the details of

DASSAULT FAN JET FALCON

Powered by: Two 4,315 lb (1,957 kg) st General Electric CF700-2D-2 turbofan engines
Wing span: 53 ft 6 in (16.30 m)
Length: 56 ft 3 in (17.15 m)
Wing area: 441.3 sq ft (41.00 m²)
Gross weight: 28,660 lb (13,000 kg)
Max cruising speed: 536 mph (862 km/h) at 25,000 ft (7,620 m)
Typical range: 2,190 miles (3,520 km) with 8 passengers
Accommodation: Crew of 2 and 8-10 passengers
First flight: 4 May 1963

Known by the dual names of Mystère 20 and Falcon 20, this attractive twin rear-engined executive transport is one of the most successful yet to appear, more than 260 having been sold by mid-1971. The prototype was powered by turbojet engines for its first flight, but just over a year later was refitted with turbofans, which are standard on production aircraft, and have resulted in the name 'Fan Jet Falcon' bestowed by Pan American's Business Jets Division, the sales agency for the western hemisphere. About three-quarters of the total sales have been in this area. Data apply to the Falcon Series F, which was introduced in 1969 and has additional high-lift devices to improve airfield performance.

Top: If Boeing's supersonic airliner had not been cancelled early in 1971, this is one of the mighty General Electric GE4 afterburning turbojet engines that would have powered it. Most powerful aero-engine in the world, the GE4 was tested at a thrust of 68,600 lb (31,100 kg)

Above: At the other extreme were the two baby Turboméca Piméné turbofans fitted to the strange-looking twin-fuselage two-seat Fouga Gemeaux lightplane in the early 'fifties. The Aspin was the first turbofan to fly

Below: Few commercial transports have had to overcome such desperate financial problems as those which plagued the Rolls-Royce RB.211-engined TriStar in 1971. With its Douglas counterpart, the DC-10, this airliner should dominate the 'airbus' market for the next ten to twenty years

its mechanical design. The jet velocity from a 5:1 by-pass ratio engine is well matched to very high subsonic cruising speeds, but would be quite incapable of propelling a supersonic fighter. The very large fans fitted to the biggest of these engines are of the order of 8 ft (2.44 m) in diameter, and the tips of the blades are invariably supersonic at take-off rotational speed. Most of the fan air is discharged straight back to atmosphere through a short fan duct; only the central portion goes through the core engine. For thrust reversal it is possible, with such engines, to achieve the desired reverse from the fan airflow alone, and merely to provide blocker doors to 'spoil' the core jet. But in some big turbofans full reversal is possible on both the fan and core flows without undue mechanical complexity or weight.

Mention has been made already of turbofans with a by-pass ratio of 10. Such engines normally need a step-down gearbox between the turbine and the fan, because the small-diameter turbine should ideally spin considerably faster than the large-diameter fan. The original Aspin had a geared fan, and modern units of this kind include the TFE 731 fan engine for business jets, produced by the US Garrett-AiResearch company.

An even later development than the high-ratio geared fan engine is the fan with variable-pitch blades. This is only to be expected, because it follows the principle established over the past 40 years with propellers. Such fan blades can be set to any angle between full ahead and full astern. For the first time in history this will give the pilot immediate and powerful control of forward or reverse thrust, both for landing and in the air. This is particularly important in the case of STOL (short take-off and landing) aircraft. Until now, fixed-wing STOL machines have been un-

able to land at maximum landing weight in the same restricted space as that from which they could take off. This is due partly to the fact that jet reverse is ineffectual below about 60 mph (95 km/h) and has operational drawbacks at low speeds, while wheel brakes may be ineffective on slippery surfaces. But the reverse-pitch fan provides very powerful braking right down to a dead stop, and the high by-pass ratio engine matches this by providing extremely powerful take-off thrust in addition. By 1973 such engines should lead to a new family of quiet, efficient STOL machines with a cruising speed raised from the 200 mph (322 km/h) of today's STOLs to 400 mph (645 km/h).

There remain to be discussed some of the basic design characteristics and mechanical details of turbojet and turbofan engines. Today's large engines use only the axial type of compressor, in which the duty of compressing the airflow is carried out by a succession of discs each carrying blades like miniature wings projecting radially around its edge. But the earliest gas turbines used centrifugal compressors, in which the air is flung outwards across a spinning disc with radial blades, and such compressors are still used in small engines—often as the final compression stage after several axial fan and compressor stages.

The axial compressor is more efficient and has a smaller frontal area for a given airflow, but the centrifugal type is generally cheaper and more robust. Turbines are virtually always axial, although in one or two very small engines the radial in-flow type is used. In more advanced engines the turbine rotor blades are made with numerous fine axial passages through which high-pressure air bled from the compressor can be blown to cool the blade. Air-cooled turbine rotor blades, a

technique pioneered by Rolls-Royce, can hold the metal of the blade everywhere below 750°C in a gas stream at 1,150°C and extend the life of the blade from a matter of minutes to 10,000 hours or longer.

Throughout the engine the closest attention is paid to the design of the rotating assemblies, the compressor and turbine discs and blades, the shafting and the bearings in which the shafts rotate. Air at different pressures is bled off and piped to front and rear faces of turbine discs and other items, both to provide cooling and to balance out the end loads; the end load on a big axial compressor may be many tons, due to the aerodynamic forces on the blades, and whatever cannot be balanced out by the opposite force on the turbine blades or discs has to be carried by one or more sets of ball-bearings. Maintenance of very close gaps between fixed and whirling blades is no easy matter in a big engine subjected to severe flight loads, to extremes of heat and cold and to such sudden impacts as bird strikes and collision with hailstones. Altogether the design of a modern aero-engine is one of man's greatest challenges: little wonder that a big fan engine can cost well over £300,000.

Below left: The huge single-stage fan at the front of the RB.211 engine is typical of that fitted to the current generation of turbofans. In its initial form, this engine gives 40,600 lb (18,416 kg) of thrust

Below: By far the most successful of commercial turboprop engines, the Rolls-Royce Dart was used for the first-ever turboprop airline operations in 1953 and continues in production for a variety of British and foreign aircraft. The 3,025 hp Dart RDa.10, produced for the Japanese YS-11 airliner, gives double the power of the Darts used in the first Viscounts, with only a 35 per cent increase in weight and no increase in overall dimensions

Bottom right: Among many veteran aircraft that have been given a 'face-lift' by conversion to turboprop power is the Grumman Goose amphibian. As the Turbo-Goose, with Pratt & Whitney PT6A engines, it gains both payload and performance by comparison with standard piston-engined models

RUSSIAN AVIATION AFTER 1945

UNTIL THE SECOND WORLD WAR the Soviet aircraft industry had never been regarded as equal in design quality to the famous companies in the western nations, although there was never any doubt about its ability to produce in quantity. During the 'great patriotic war' of 1941-45 the Russians concentrated on a small number of fairly pedestrian yet effective aircraft which could be built economically in vast numbers. But 1945 was seen at the time as a watershed. What should the exhausted Russians do to meet the competition of peace? What should they do to meet the unexpected challenge of the jet?

By a mixture of political adroitness, good luck and considerable skill, they not only met both challenges in a remarkably effective way but even built up a design expertise that within 15 years had no rival outside the United States. Many would claim that by 1965 the Soviet Union was a world leader in the design and manufacture of advanced military aircraft, and a good second to the US in civil transports. But at the start there had to be some short cuts, and these were staggeringly effective.

For example, in 1945 the standard Soviet heavy bomber was the Tupolev TB-7, a B-17-style aircraft of pre-war design developed by Petlyakov into the Pe-8. It was not in the same class as the formidable Boeing B-29, four of which had force-landed in Manchuria and eastern Siberia in 1944-45 after operating for the 20th Air Force against Japan. Although the B-29 was by far the most complicated and advanced aircraft in service in the world, a special task group under Tupolev dissected its design, worked out all the part and material specifications, designed their own jigging and tooling and, with almost impossible speed, had the B-29 in production as the Tu-4 by 1947. By 1948 the first squadron was operational.

Thus did the Russians overtake bomber development in Britain. While Tu-4s poured from the Russian assembly line, RAF Bomber Command soldiered on with the Avro Lancaster and Lincoln. Not until 1952 did the RAF get the B-29, and then only because a special arrangement with the USAF made some freely available, together with spares and provision for training crews and ground staff—by which time the RAF, denuded of skilled men, was hard pressed to man and

The Soviet Union was alone among the major combatants in not producing a jet-engined combat aircraft in the second World War. By April 1946, Yakovlev completed the prototype of his Yak-15 fighter—a development of the piston-engined Yak-3 with a German Jumo 004B turbojet mounted in the forward fuselage. From this was evolved the improved Yak-17 and the Yak-17UTI tandem two-seat trainer (illustrated)

Opposite page, top: A combination of wartime German research into swept wings and the fortuitous gift of Rolls-Royce engine technology made possible Russia's first truly modern combat aircraft, the MiG-15 fighter, and its successor the MiG-17 (illustrated)

Centre: There is nothing very handsome about the Yak-18, which has been Russia's standard military and civil primary trainer since 1946; but superb flying qualities have made it a consistent winner of international aerobatic competitions

Bottom: Similar in general layout to the American Sikorsky S-55, the Mi-4 has been Russia's most-used and most-exported piston-engined helicopter. In Aeroflot service it carries 8-11 passengers

This page, above: Referred to sometimes as Il-20s, a number of demilitarised Il-28 bombers were used by Aeroflot to gain jet experience before the Tu-104 was ready for service. They carried newspaper matrices over the Moscow-Sverdlovsk-Novosibirsk route from February 1956

Below left: Drawing by a *Flight International* artist of the MiG-15 cockpit

Below: The Rolls-Royce Nene turbojet helped to establish the aircraft jet-engine industries of a number of countries, including France (Hispano-Suiza version illustrated), the USA (as the Pratt & Whitney J42) and the Soviet Union (as the MiG's RD-45 and VK-1)

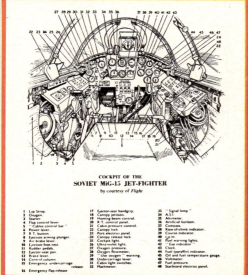

COCKPIT OF THE
SOVIET MiG-15 JET-FIGHTER
by courtesy of *Flight*

maintain such complex aircraft. The Soviets did it all for themselves, and five years earlier. They even made a transport version.

This 'unholy alliance' of Tupolev and an unwilling Boeing had far-reaching effects. Much of the technology of the B-29 was transplanted into the Tu-16 and then into the Tu-104. The former was a classically-simple twin-jet bomber, made possible by the ability of a design team (that of A A Mikulin, previously known mainly for a small 125 hp piston-engine) to design, qualify and go into production in 1953 with a turbojet which began life at 15,000 lb (6,800 kg) thrust and soon rose to 20,000 lb (9,070 kg). At that time no other nation had found use for such a powerful jet, although General Electric in America and de Havilland in Britain both had equivalent prototypes. This valuable engine helped the twin-engined Tu-16 to be built for less than half the cost of the broadly-comparable four-engined Valiant and six-engined Boeing B-47. Today many hundreds of these cost-effective aircraft are still in world-wide service in many versions.

Converting the Tu-16 to a civil transport was simple. The main problem was the need to redesign the centre wing to fit a completely new and much bigger, pressurised fuselage between and above the giant engines. The job took less than a year, and by the end of 1955 the Tu-104A had almost completed its flight development programme. Again it was a case of cost-effectiveness. Although in some ways inferior to the later Comets, and not in the same class as the Boeing 707 and Douglas DC-8 then rapidly taking shape, the Tu-104 proved to be extremely effective, trouble-free and economical to buy and maintain. Even more important, it provided a basis of experience on which the Soviet design staffs have capitalised to the utmost degree, with the result that, backed up by engines of increasing excellence, modern Soviet civil transports are swiftly becoming a highly competitive and very worrying threat to western industry which never existed before.

In the field of fighters the little wartime piston-engined machines appeared far removed from the jet age, yet in nine months Aleksandir Yakovlev had converted his Yak-9 to take a German Jumo 004B and put it through a flight test programme. The resulting Yak-15—surely the only piston-to-jet conversion to rival the Swedish J 21 for simplicity—was in service in 1946, by which time

the improved nosewheel-equipped Yak-17 was in production and the already famous MiG team of Mikoyan and Gurevich had flown the twin-Jumo 004 MiG-9. But all these faded into insignificance before a completely new design planned by the MiG bureau: the MiG-15.

Far quicker off the mark than the British, Soviet designers had read all they could about earlier German research on sweepback as a -means of delaying 'compressibility drag rise' at high subsonic Mach numbers, and considered that they could develop quickly an all-swept fighter that would reach well over 1,000 km/h (621 mph). The MiG-15 was planned to use an axial engine of about 4,000 lb (1,814 kg) thrust which was being derived urgently from the 1,984 lb (900 kg) Jumo 004B, using the maximum number of available German workers with experience of turbojet engineering. But the British government naïvely agreed to supply the Soviet Union with examples and drawings of the two latest and most powerful British jet engines, the Rolls-Royce Derwent 5 and Nene. When the first Nene was uncrated eagerly early in 1947 the Russians took the swift and fateful decision to go straight into production with it —not bothering about such a nicety as a licence—and to use it in the MiG-15. By the end of the year the new fighter was in the air.

Nobody in the west knew of this until 1951, when American fighter pilots operating over Korea found speedy fighters, looking like silver arrows, confronting them. Generally, the MiG-15 was badly flown by inexperienced pilots in that conflict, but it soon showed itself to have an edge in performance over all Allied fighters except the F-86 Sabre, and even the Sabre could not climb or manoeuvre so well. Britain had nothing in the same class—merely a few prototypes and promises. Nor did the MiG bureau stop there. Just as improved Sabres and Grumman Cougars were beginning to acquire an edge, the MiG-17 appeared. Soon after the end of the Korean war there followed the MiG-19 which, like the American F-100, was capable of supersonic speed in level flight.

From then the Russians have never looked back. Since the mid-1950s they have flown more revolutionary and world-beating aircraft than any other country. Variable sweep, jet VTOL, giant heavy-lift helicopters, STOLs, all come alike to the remarkable Russians. Today the F-14 and F-15 are being developed urgently in the United States to meet the challenge of the MiG-23 of the early 1960s, while the F-5E is hurriedly being planned to beat the latest MiG-21 of even earlier vintage. Which in turn poses the question: what are the Russians doing *now*?

MIKOYAN/GUREVICH MiG-15

Powered by: One 5,004 lb (2,270 kg) st Klimov RD-45F turbojet engine
Wing span: 33 ft 0⅜ in (10.08 m)
Length: 33 ft 1⅞ in (10.10 m)
Wing area: 221.7 sq ft (20.6 m²)
Gross weight: 12,756 lb (5,786 kg)
Max speed: 665 mph (1,070 km/h) at S/L
Range: 882 miles (1,420 km) with under-wing drop-tanks
Accommodation: Crew of 1
First flight: 30 December 1947

The MiG-15, one of the most extensively used jet aircraft ever built, was a remarkable combination of German wartime aerodynamic research, British jet-engine technology and Soviet design ingenuity. When one was encountered in combat over Korea in 1951 by a Lockheed F-80 Shooting Star—to the detriment of the American fighter—this was the first occasion on which jet fighters had met one another in an air-to-air engagement. The American Sabre, flown by more thoroughly-trained pilots, eventually established a superiority over the MiG-15, despite the appearance of the improved MiG-15bis at a later date. A developed version, the MiG-17, entered production in 1953 but was too late for service in the Korean War.

Above: Unfamiliar in USAF markings, a MiG-15 is taxied out to take-off position by an American pilot in Okinawa in October 1953. The fighter had been presented to the USAF by a defecting North Korean Air Force pilot

Left: First Soviet fighter to exceed the speed of sound in level flight, the MiG-19 entered service in 1955. Unlike the MiG-15/17 series, it was twin-engined

Top right: In the summer of 1956 many Soviet military forces staged their official withdrawal from East Germany. These Il-28 twin-jet bombers of the 221st Air Force Division are shown leaving Oranienburg airfield

Centre right: With a wing span of only 23 ft 6 in (7.16 m) and Mach 2 performance, the MiG-21 is very much a 'pilot's aeroplane'. The early MiG-21F version, shown here in Czechoslovakian Air Force service, was rather deficient in range, armament and radar by western standards

Bottom right: These Soviet Air Force fighters are of the MiG-21PF type, with uprated engine, improved radar and other changes. Continued development has produced several later versions for both interception and ground attack duties, as well as the MiG-21UTI two-seat trainer

The First 'Post-War' Wars

Top: Korea marked the operational swan-song of the F-51 Mustang in USAF service. In a jet age it gave fine service as a ground-attack aircraft

Centre, left to right:
While marking targets for attack in Korea, Harvards often attracted considerable ground fire, but even this one got home safely

As a change from 'ghost' attacks on terrorists in the jungle, men of the RAAF's No 1 Squadron take some of their gallant Gurkha allies for a 'flip' in a Lincoln bomber

Meteor F.8 jet-fighters of No 77 Squadron, RAAF, which gave good service alongside the USAF in Korea, although outclassed by Chinese MiG-15s

Right: The helicopter was, perhaps, the greatest discovery of the Korean War. This Marine Sikorsky H05S (S-52), evacuating wounded from a front-line area, was able to carry the men straight to base hospital in relative comfort, over almost impossible terrain. The percentage of casualties who died was the lowest in military history thanks to the 'choppers'

Above: As well as evacuating casualties, helicopters like this Sikorsky HRS (S-55) ferried ammunition and supplies to hilltop positions that no other vehicle could have reached

Top right: One of the strangest aspects of the Korean War was that combat aircraft of both sides often took off from bases in countries that were never subjected to enemy attack. It was quite safe for Captain Johnnie Gosnell's family to wave him farewell as he took off from Japan in his Twin Mustang for a sortie over the war zone

Right: F-80 Shooting Stars of the USAF's 51st Fighter Interceptor Wing used JATO rockets to help them lift heavy loads from short Korean runways

THE OLD ADAGE that necessity is the mother of invention is never more true than in wartime. In the two great wars since aviation began, the pace of military aircraft development was dramatically increased over that which has occurred in times of comparative peace.

But one must stress the 'comparative', for since the end of the second World War there has never been, for the major powers, real peace. While the strategic nuclear balance—the balance of terror—has involved the two 'super-powers' in rapid development of aircraft, missiles and other weaponry, there has been a rash of confined 'brushfire' wars and counter-insurgency campaigns which have also affected aircraft development.

The profusion of these wars until about the mid-1960s was one outcome of the balance of terror. Locked as they were in a nuclear stalemate, with Armageddon as the inevitable outcome of open conflict, the two big power blocs grappled and probed each other's weaknesses, each seeking an advantage, often on the territory of the uncommitted nations of the 'third world', or of puppet states and colonial territories.

First and biggest of these wars was that which began in 1950 in partitioned Korea. A Chinese-inspired Communist North Korea invaded and largely overran the US-supported South Korea. Many nations sent forces to fight under the United Nations banner—in fact this Korean campaign is the largest conflict to have involved the UN collectively—while opposing Chinese forces entered the fray on a massive scale.

Effectively, only the United States forces and the RAAF fought for the south in the Korean air war, with RAF Sunderlands flying maritime reconnaissance against sea-borne incursions and movement around the Korean peninsula.

For the US forces, it was the first com-

mitment in combat of jet aircraft, though that magnificent piston-engined fighter of the second World War, the F-51 Mustang, was heavily engaged as a ground-attack aircraft. Following the overt entry of Communist China into the war, many were the dog-fights in the skies above North Korea which engaged, principally, China's Soviet-supplied MiG-15s and the USAF's F-86 Sabres, together with carrier-borne USN jet fighters operating from flat-tops in the South China Sea.

Technically, the MiG-15 and the F-86 were closely matched, though the superior training and tactics of the US pilots gave them a clear margin in combat—still, at that time, fought with guns rather than air-to-air missiles. But this was hardly surprising—Communist China as an undivided mainland state was only two years old when the war began and the massive build-up of her air forces, even with Russian advisers, resulted in tyro pilots meeting in combat experienced veterans of the second World War.

US President Harry S Truman forbade his forces (the UN contingents were effectively under US command) from taking the war beyond the Yalu River, the border between North Korea and Communist China, and even aerial hot pursuit was forbidden. The Chinese airmen, therefore, had a safe sanctuary in operating from Chinese bases and they confined their incursions only to a relatively narrow band of North Korean airspace beyond the river. Elsewhere, Allied supremacy in the air was total.

The RAAF's unit was 77 Squadron, sent originally in the air fighting role with Meteor F.8s but found to be outclassed in combat by the more manoeuvrable MiG-15, even when flown by less experienced pilots. The unit was therefore switched to ground attack, in which it fought alongside USAF

units equipped primarily with the F-84C Thunderjet and USN Skyraiders from carriers offshore. Light bombers dating from the second World War, particularly the Douglas Invader, were also heavily engaged.

Korea saw the first use of that horrifying air-dropped weapon, napalm; but, technically, the war's main outcome was the rapid development of helicopters and methods of their deployment. When the war began helicopters were still none-too numerous military novelties; by the cease-fire in 1953 they were standard tools of military forces with a vast accumulation of operational experience behind them.

It was in casualty evacuation and combat rescue that they were most used. The feats of the combat rescue helicopters, in particular, drew the world's admiration. Frequently making long incursions into enemy-held territory under aerial top-cover, they rescued downed pilots from beneath 'rescue caps' of ground-strafing aircraft which kept enemy forces away from the men being rescued. The technique has since been standard in Vietnam, and if Korea has a place in aviation history it is for its demonstration of the military potential of the helicopter.

Concurrently with Korea, British Commonwealth forces were engaged in their own lower-key, immensely-drawn-out brushfire war against Communist guerillas operating in the dense jungle country of Malaya. This campaign lasted more than 10 years and was always one of punching at shadows; eventually it was won by the success of the 'hearts and minds' campaign in which the guerillas were denied the support and succour of the local populace and, quite literally, starved into defeat.

But it was a war in which air power was used to a limited extent, for reconnaissance and for blasting hard-to-find terrorist jungle ide-outs. Principally, piston-engined aircraft of second World War vintage were used, the RAAF making a big contribution with its Lincoln bombers and the main RAF types during the earlier years being Mosquitos, Hornets and Brigands. Ultimately a technique was evolved under which well-developed ground intelligence networks, native trackers and radio monitoring were used to track Communist movement, after which air strikes were called in. The successful conclusion of the campaign was followed only a few years later by the opening of another Malaysian chapter—confrontation with Indonesia, whose regime objected to the creation of the Malaysian Federation. In this three-year war the same techniques, and many more helicopters, were used.

Throughout the 'fifties there were numerous conflicts involving other colonial territories. While decolonisation of many French territories went smoothly, very bitter and complex guerilla wars were fought in Indochina (where the conflict was no more than a prelude to the current Vietnam war and was merely one phase in 30 years of continuous warfare there) and in Algeria. The French made heavy use of paratroops in both theatres, but their air support was always less than adequate.

Helicopters were employed more heavily with the passing of the years and were soon seen, as in other brushfire wars, to be extremely vulnerable to small-arms sharp-shooting from the ground, a problem which even now leads to a high rate of attrition in hot-war situations. France fought these wars with a miscellany of equipment, much of it retired from the second World War, and the Algerian conflict will be remembered as the last operational use for the 'Jug'—that great fighter-bomber, the F-47 Thunderbolt.

In Kenya in the early 'fifties Britain was faced with an infinitely bizarre war, if one can call it that—the Mau-Mau campaign. This was more the uprising of a particular tribal faction, an emergency of blood-chilling if comparatively small-scale atrocities. Again, the air power task was to hit jungle hide-outs and keep terrorists on the move by air strikes against their lairs with an ad hoc collection of equipment. Lincolns were used, as were armed Harvard

This page, top to bottom:
Noratlas transport aircraft of the French Air Force were used very effectively to drop parachute troops during the brief Suez campaign of 1956

The 'invasion' stripes around the rear fuselage of these French Mystere IV-A fighters identify them as aircraft deployed for use at Suez

This Hunter F.Mk 5 of No 34 Squadron was one of the newest types equipping the 34 RAF Squadrons based in Malta and Cyprus for action during the Suez fighting

French counterpart of the Hunter was this F-84F Thunderstreak of the 3e Escadre, photographed at Akrotiri, Cyprus

Piston-engined aircraft like this rocket-armed Brigand were ideal for the wearisome job of trying to track down and attack terrorists in the jungles of Malaya

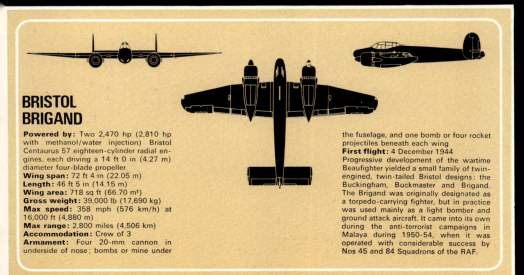

BRISTOL BRIGAND

Powered by: Two 2,470 hp (2,810 hp with methanol/water injection) Bristol Centaurus 57 eighteen-cylinder radial engines, each driving a 14 ft 0 in (4.27 m) diameter four-blade propeller.
Wing span: 72 ft 4 in (22.05 m)
Length: 46 ft 5 in (14.15 m)
Wing area: 718 sq ft (66.70 m²)
Gross weight: 39,000 lb (17,690 kg)
Max speed: 358 mph (576 km/h) at 16,000 ft (4,880 m)
Max range: 2,800 miles (4,506 km)
Accommodation: Crew of 3
Armament: Four 20-mm cannon in underside of nose; bombs or mine under

the fuselage, and one bomb or four rocket projectiles beneath each wing
First flight: 4 December 1944
Progressive development of the wartime Beaufighter yielded a small family of twin-engined, twin-tailed Bristol designs: the Buckingham, Buckmaster and Brigand. The Brigand was originally designated as a torpedo-carrying fighter, but in practice was used mainly as a light bomber and ground attack aircraft. It came into its own during the anti-terrorist campaigns in Malaya during 1950-54, when it was operated with considerable success by Nos 45 and 84 Squadrons of the RAF.

trainers, and in this campaign much valuable work was performed by reservist fliers and light aircraft pilots.

The 'brushfire' era saw, in 1956, a week-long 'war' quite unlike any of the others. This was the Anglo-French invasion of the Suez Canal Zone, in company with Israel, following the Egyptian government's decision to nationalise the Suez Canal. The seaborne assault was in the classic second World War pattern, with a substantial invasion fleet assembled off Port Said. Air strikes against Canal Zone air bases were flown by both British and French fighter-bombers from carriers and from bases in Cyprus, while longer-range attacks on targets around Cairo were mounted from Malta by Canberras and Valiants, the latter then newly in service and operating not in their nuclear design role but with the high-altitude high-explosive precision-bombing techniques of the second World War.

But though classical in concept, the operation was not a classic in execution. It was badly bungled and it ended on a note of political farce when strong United Nations disapproval and in particular the outspoken condemnation of the United States caused the Anglo-French forces to withdraw before advancing along the full length of the Canal. Meteors, Venoms and Vampires were the strike aircraft used by the RAF, while Fleet Air Arm Wyverns and Sea Venoms also took part. Again, the only significant feature of the Suez operation, so far as aviation history is concerned, was the use made of helicopters in the assault landing, in which to a large extent they replaced the highly-vulnerable inshore landing craft used in similar assaults during the second World War.

By 1956 neither the French nor the British forces were well enough endowed with helicopters able to lift significant payloads (the biggest in British service were Westland S-55s), and the small number assembled were drawn from naval anti-submarine units and a joint RAF/Army experimental helicopter trials unit. They performed well—against virtually no opposition—and set a pattern from which helicopter tactical assault squadrons, and the Royal Navy's commando carriers, evolved naturally.

Above: Five squadrons of Royal Navy Sea Venoms from the carriers *Albion* **and** *Eagle* **flew side-by-side with four RAF Venom squadrons from Cyprus in devastating ground-attack operations which helped to eliminate the Egyptian Air Force. Most of the 120 MiGs and 50 Il-28 jet bombers that had been supplied by Russia were wiped out on the ground; only eight were lost in air combat over Suez**

Right: Skyraider attack aircraft of the US Navy first displayed their great versatility and hitting power in Korea. But they were to add immeasurably to their 'battle honours' in a later, even tougher war in Vietnam

Private flying is as varied as the types of aircraft it employs. The busy executive wants a vehicle that will save him hours of precious time. The farmer needs a sturdy implement that will spray his crops from a height of a few feet without trampling them like tractor-towed equipment. Just a few of the most highly-skilled and adventurous pilots eschew modern looks and monoplane efficiency and choose biplanes like the Stampe for thrilling, precise aerobatic displays of the kind that have chilled the spines of onlookers since Nesterov and Pégoud performed the first loops before the 1914-18 War

The Post-War Growth of Private Flying

Above: Morane-Saulnier Rallyes, here seen with Finnish and German markings, are among the finest present-day training and glider-towing lightplanes. More than 1,800 have been sold, in 57 countries, to swell impressive French aviation exports

Top left: Chipmunks, many of them RAF-surplus, have formed a mainstay of British club flying and training for years. This one embodies a number of refinements, including a one-piece blown canopy

Left: Another of the great British club aircraft—a Tiger Moth, final open-cockpit variant of the family of Moth biplanes which started it all

PRIVATE FLYING really began in 1925, with the de Havilland Moth, for although most early efforts to fly were essentially 'private' in terms of enterprise, the numbers of individuals involved were very small. The Moth and its originators, however, can accept most of the credit for the build-up of a large and active movement throughout the 'thirties, for although this came to an abrupt halt on the outbreak of war in 1939, the Royal Air Force absorbed hundreds of club pilots who held A licences (the predecessor of today's Private Pilot's Licence) and trained them for Service flying duties. Many others, men and women, joined the civilian Air Transport Auxiliary and ferried almost every type of military aircraft then in use.

With no private flying between 1939 and 1945, and with all aircraft production facilities geared to the needs of war, the light aviation movement was unable to make a rapid return to health and activity. New aeroplanes were virtually unobtainable, and clubs had no accrued funds with which to re-start operations, but the Air Ministry was persuaded to part with small numbers of suitable training types for sale exclusively to club operators. Two main batches were released. Most of these, understandably, were Tiger Moths, but smaller numbers of Miles Magisters and an assorted bag of Auster variants were included in the disposal. Most of these machines were sold at nominal prices—in the region of £50 each —but some had been stored and all needed conversion to standards laid down by the Air Registration Board, the body that governs British civil airworthiness requirements. It was—and at times remains—ironical that aircraft capable of withstanding harsh Service flying lives should need to

start afresh before being allowed to operate in private hands.

Neither flying clubs nor private ownership burst very rapidly into new life during the first few years of peace. A successful three-seat civil version of the Auster, known as the Autocrat and powered by the economical if not wholly reliable Cirrus Minor engine, first flew in 1946 and production specimens flowed from the firm's Rearsby (Leicester) works almost immediately, selling initially at the very practical price of just under £1,000, but soon beginning to rise. From Woodley, near Reading, came a flow of Miles Messenger four-seaters and a twin-engined counterpart, the Gemini, while more Service machines were disposed of at surplus sales. Among them were several Percival Proctors. These, being comparatively fast and comfortable four-seaters, formed the basis of several 'mushroom' organisations run by former Service pilots. Unfortunately, their owners had had neither business nor civil aviation experience, and most of these firms lasted little more than a year or two; the great British travelling public just did not wish to get into the air on light charter flights.

The Association of British Aero Clubs and Centres came into being to co-ordinate the activities and interests of the operators of flying clubs. Again the Air Ministry moved to the forefront and negotiated a contract under which 17-year-old cadets of the Air Training Corps could be trained at clubs on a Flying Scholarship Scheme. The original aim of this plan was as much to help a struggling civil flying movement as to provide air-minded recruits for the Royal Air Force, for when the scheme started very few new Service entrants were needed. The

scholarship scheme still exists today, but it is geared wholly and solely to the requirements of the RAF and certainly is not intended to boost either the morale or the funds of the flying club movement.

Another move agreed by the government to help the general public to fly for recreational purposes and at economical prices was the introduction of petrol tax rebate. This was allowable only on flights carried out by flying clubs and genuine co-ownership groups; it was not granted to purely private aircraft owners, who might well be using their aeroplanes for personal commercial gain. As a result, many dozens of new groups were formed all over the country. This hastened the birth of the current group movement, whereby five or more pilots join forces and operate a light aeroplane on a self-help co-ownership basis to provide a relatively inexpensive way of getting into the air. This rebate scheme (computed on an agreed allowance for each recorded hour flown and not on petrol consumed, so removing the possibility of people running their cars on tax-free petrol) was withdrawn in the early 1960s.

The private and club fleets consisted of Austers (still the most numerous, and available in a range of variants seating two, three or four occupants and having a choice of several engine ratings), smaller numbers of Messengers and Geminis and ever-dwindling numbers of Tiger Moths, Proctors and Magisters. Of the three ex-Service stalwarts, only two Proctors remained in use in 1971 and only one preserved Magister was still flying, but the Tiger Moth is far from dead and no fewer than 86 were then on the current British Register of Civil Aircraft. In 1954 a few Chipmunks were released from the RAF; these boosted the numbers with an aeroplane that proved delightful to fly but expensive to operate. Now, 21 years after it first went into military use, it is again one of the RAF's primary trainers and the Service is drastically short of sound specimens.

The British aircraft industry, which before the war had led the world in light aircraft design, development and production, seemed disinterested or unable to produce a post-war winner. The Miles factory ceased production through financial insolvency and only the Auster lines remained in business. Austers had—and still have—much to commend them, for they were built to be strong and reliable and have proved that they pass the test of time; unfortunately, they are noisy, not particularly comfortable and too difficult to fly for the type of aviator who seeks car-type ease of handling. So the numbers of British private pilots remained few.

In the early 'sixties, however, the scene began to change. Since the war the government had refused to allow foreign-built light aircraft to be imported to the UK, but throughout this period of 'make-do-and-mend' on the British light aviation front other countries had developed a new approach to private aviation and a new style of pilot had been born to match. Not surprisingly, the change took place more in the United States than elsewhere, for there aircraft were produced to suit the needs of the man with no sporting tendencies whose main aim was to fly from A to B with the minimum of flying skill. Tricycle undercarriages went far towards easing the pilot's load on take-off or landing, and stall-warning devices (both visual and aural) helped to prevent him from falling out of the sky. Comfortable, sound-proofed cabins completed the modern picture, and radio aids replaced the traditional topographical map as the major method of navigating. Ashtrays, built-in cigar lighters and other trappings of modern society all gained and held their places in the new scheme of things.

When Britain lifted her import embargo, American aircraft at first entered the country more slowly than many had anticipated, but this was logical, for before a demand could really exist, hundreds more people needed to learn to fly. Piper Tri-Pacers and Colts (a later and smaller two-seat development) and Cessna 150s soon formed the fleets of flying clubs and schools, and the new pattern had arrived on the British doorstep. More pilots led to more need for mounts, so Piper and Cessna agents stepped up their sales campaigns and American manufacturers such as Beech, Mooney and others saw to it that they too were represented on English soil. So far, however, only Piper and Cessna have really got to grips with UK sales, acquiring and steadily maintaining first and second places respectively.

The new range of private aircraft has, however, divided the movement into several groups. Advertising, and the resulting publicity associated with sales of new aeroplanes, have combined to create an impression that the American style of aviation is the only kind that exists. Certainly, when we visit airports and the larger aerodromes—especially those in or near areas of controlled airspace—we find US machines filling the hangars and parking aprons, but we should not overlook the more rural scene, where the change has made less of an inroad. Dozens of amateur constructors are busy in their garages, and even their drawing-rooms, building ultra-light do-it-yourself aeroplanes just as in the 'thirties; in some cases the home-builts now being constructed are similar in design to those of nearly 40 years ago, for the requirements of this brand of individual have not changed. He seeks an inexpensive, easy-to-build, cheap-to-operate and *enjoyable* mount, and possibly intends to house and fly it from his own or a neighbouring farmer's field. Fortunately the driving force of the amateur constructor is still there in strength, and personal enterprise in this area is alive and healthy.

Many of these small machines, since they are meant only to be operated for purely private purposes, do not conform to the full design requirements necessary in a machine to be operated for public transport. Their airworthiness needs are handled on a delegated basis by the Popular Flying Association.

Apart from those who 'roll their own' are many who own or share ready-made profes-

Left: In the early post-war era of 'RAF-surplus' lightplanes, it was possible to obtain a Tiger Moth for as little as £50. Today these veteran biplanes are highly cherished by sporting pilots and cost more than a top-quality sports car when they can be bought at all

Opposite page, top: By importing American aircraft, and building others to US or British designs, companies in the UK are helping to introduce an exciting new kind of round-the-pylons air racing in Europe. Typical of American Formula One designs is this Owl Racer, which was lost in an accident in 1971 before it had time to show its paces properly

Centre, left to right: Italy has re-entered the private flying market in a big way through the products of the SIAI-Marchetti company. This S.205-22/R, with 220 hp Franklin engine and retractable undercarriage, is one of a family of lightplanes which share many common components

Switzerland's Pilatus Porter is typical of the kind of sturdy STOL aircraft that must live among tall mountains and take off from tiny strips in valleys. This version carries up to ten people on the power of a 500 hp turbocharged Lycoming piston-engine

Another Tiger. Distinguishing features include vertical interplane struts, as those of the otherwise-similar Stampe are splayed-out. The fin and rudder shape is also characteristically 'DH'

Bottom: Changes of a different kind have affected the Piper Cherokee through the years since it first flew. Conceived originally as a low-cost, easy-to-fly tourer/trainer for up to four people, it will now carry seven in the Cherokee Six version illustrated. Engine power is 260 or 300 hp and the electronics almost up to airline standards in some aircraft

BEECHCRAFT BONANZA

Powered by: One 285 hp Continental IO-520-B six-cylinder horizontally-opposed engine, driving a 7 ft 0 in (2.13 m) diameter two-blade metal propeller
Wing span: 33 ft 5½ in (10.20 m)
Length: 26 ft 4½ in (8.04 m)
Wing area: 181.0 sq ft (16.80 m²)
Gross weight: 3,400 lb (1,542 kg)
Max cruising speed: 203 mph (327 km/h) at 6,500 ft (1,980 m)
Typical range: 600 miles (965 km)
Accommodation: Crew of 1 and up to 5 passengers
First flight: 22 December 1945

In continuous production since 1947, the little Beechcraft Bonanza, with its distinctive 'butterfly' Vee tail, is one of the longest-lived private aircraft still being sold; in 1971 total sales were close to the 10,000 mark and showed little sign of abating: ample evidence that its name was well chosen! Engine power has been steadily advanced from the 165 hp of the original prototype, and interior furnishings, baggage capacity and other features have been improved to keep the Bonanza competitive against the almost bewildering variety of rival aircraft that have appeared during its more than 20 years of production life. In addition to this prodigious production, the Bonanza also provided the foundation for the design of the conventional-tailed T-34 Mentor, for many years a primary trainer for the US and foreign services.

Right: Aircraft designed in Italy by Ing Stelio Frati have the sleek, racey look of a thoroughbred sports car. Typical is the 235 mph (375 km/h) SIAI-Marchetti SF.260, which several air forces and airlines use for pilot training

Below: this photograph illustrates well the great variety of light aircraft to be seen at most airfields. From under the wings of a modern all-metal lightplane is caught a glimpse of a pre-war Hornet Moth biplane and a single-seat Tipsy Nipper, designed post-war by Ernest Tips in Belgium as a 'modern Blériot monoplane' that almost anyone could build at home

sionally-produced aeroplanes for the pleasure that goes with them. Here, the Tiger Moths, Austers and others still have important parts to play. There are others who indulge in the sports of aerobatics and air racing, both of which, though appealing to and within reach only of minorities, are showing signs of sustained health.

The term 'private flying' has tended to give way progressively to the more broad-based name of 'general aviation', for the latter includes nearly all activities other than those of the Services or the airlines. Executive aircraft, including jets, dozens of light twins and some of the more sophisticated singles, must increase in quantity and scope as business markets become less localised. Many an aeroplane falls between the bounds of private and commercial ownership, for just as many a man uses his car for both business and pleasure, so an aeroplane that qualifies for a company tax concession also takes the family and friends on holiday.

Until 1 April 1971, light aeroplanes were classified into a number of airworthiness groups and could be certificated in any one of five categories—with the main proviso that any aircraft used for hire and reward (including charter, flying training or merely hiring from one individual to another) must be maintained in the Public Transport category on a basis comparable with that of an airliner. However, long-term discussions within, and representations from, the movement have brought about a much simpler system and most aircraft weighing 6,000 lb (2,720 kg) or less have since been transferred to a new General Purpose Schedule. Under this scheme an owner may undertake certain well-defined items of maintenance on his own aeroplane, and a foreign licensed engineer may sign for work carried out on a British-registered machine, thus reducing the problems of a pilot who experiences technical troubles in or over another country.

Personal aviation is expanding not only in terms of numbers of aircraft and pilots but also in scope. Many people tend to consider those who fly their own or hire other people's aircraft to be the small and weak relation of the truly commercial sector, but in practice the situation is quite the reverse. There are four general aviation aircraft for every airliner on the British Register, and the numbers of pilots and airfields from which they operate swamp the heavier brigade to an extent that is enabling them to have their weight felt. The representative body that looks after these many interests is the British Light Aviation Centre which, through Corporate, Pilot and Aerodrome Operator membership, caters for all needs. About 15,000 people in Britain hold Private Pilots' Licences, and although this is a very small percentage of all those who live in our over-populated island, the growth *rate* is the important factor. In the mid-1950s only 5,000 private pilots were licensed in Britain, and if their numbers continue to increase at the pace of recent expansion the airspace planners will need to think very seriously about the needs of the person who flies his own aeroplane—whether he does so for business or as a pleasurable pastime.

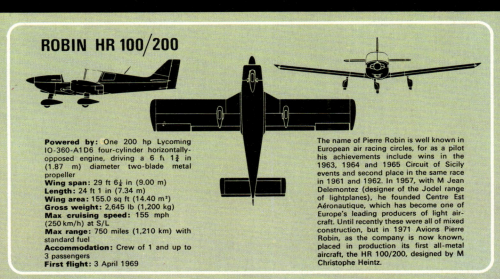

ROBIN HR 100/200

Powered by: One 200 hp Lycoming IO-360-A1D6 four-cylinder horizontally-opposed engine, driving a 6 ft 1½ in (1.87 m) diameter two-blade metal propeller
Wing span: 29 ft 6½ in (9.00 m)
Length: 24 ft 1 in (7.34 m)
Wing area: 155.0 sq ft (14.40 m²)
Gross weight: 2,645 lb (1,200 kg)
Max cruising speed: 155 mph (250 km/h) at S/L
Max range: 750 miles (1,210 km) with standard fuel
Accommodation: Crew of 1 and up to 3 passengers
First flight: 3 April 1969

The name of Pierre Robin is well known in European air racing circles, for as a pilot his achievements include wins in the 1963, 1964 and 1965 Circuit of Sicily events and second place in the same race in 1961 and 1962. In 1957, with M Jean Delemontez (designer of the Jodel range of lightplanes), he founded Centre Est Aéronautique, which has become one of Europe's leading producers of light aircraft. Until recently these were all of mixed construction, but in 1971 Avions Pierre Robin, as the company is now known, placed in production its first all-metal aircraft, the HR 100/200, designed by M Christophe Heintz.

Above: The family of Zlin lightplanes produced in Czechoslovakia has few equals for training and aerobatic flying. More than 1,400 of the various versions have been produced since 1947, and have won between them most of the worthwhile international aerobatic competitions, not once but repeatedly. This is a two-seat Z 526F Trener-Master, with a 180 hp Avia M 137 engine

Right: Despite its fairly recent civil registration, G-AYDW is an Auster built many years ago for military duties and updated subsequently to Beagle Terrier standard as a two/three-seat club and private aircraft

Below right: The similarity of this little single-seat 'home-built' to the speedy Hawker Fury fighters of the 'thirties is no coincidence. Its designer/builder, John Isaacs, evolved it as a 7/10th scale all-wood replica of the pre-war type

Left: One of many 'oldies' still to be seen flying in the UK, G-AFGE is a British Aircraft Swallow evolved from the German Klemm L.25 of 1927. As in the motoring world, much love and care are lavished on such veteran and vintage types by keen private owners

The Famous & the Few

Above: The Caravelle is now produced by Aérospatiale, France's great state-owned consortium which absorbed the former Sud-Aviation. Sud itself had absorbed the Caravelle's former manufacturer; but this was only one more of a long chain of events. The aircraft's designation SE 210 reflects the fact that it was produced originally by the Sud-Est company, which could trace its ancestry, via pre-war nationalisation, to such famous pioneer private manufacturers as Dewoitine and Lioré-Olivier

THE HISTORY OF AVIATION—as these pages have shown regularly—is sprinkled with the names of famous aircraft companies; names which in their day have been household words and which, even now, have the power to evoke vivid memories of adventure and achievement in the field of aeronautics. A glance at any aviation reference book more than a dozen or so years old will show, for example, that the British aircraft industry boasted companies with such proud names as Armstrong Whitworth, Avro, Blackburn, Boulton Paul, Bristol, Cierva, de Havilland, English Electric, Fairey, Folland, Gloster, Handley Page, Hawker, Hunting, Miles, Percival, Saro, Supermarine and Vickers.

Today, hardly one of those company names survives as that of an aircraft manufacturer.

Or go back to pre-war and wartime years to recall the great names of French and German companies: names like Amiot, Blériot, Bloch, Caudron, Farman, Latécoère, Lioré-et-Olivier, Morane-Saulnier, Potez; Arado, Blohm und Voss, Bücker, Fieseler, Focke-Wulf, Heinkel, Henschel.

These, too, have all departed.

The airframe manufacturing industry in Britain today comprises a mere handful of companies. The two largest—the British Aircraft Corporation and the Hawker Siddeley Group—are amalgamations, respectively, of several of the companies listed in the first paragraph above; among the smaller companies, the name of Short, associated with aircraft manufacture in Britain since 1900, still proudly survives;

so too does that of the 15-years-younger Westland, though now it is known exclusively for its helicopters. Britten-Norman and Scottish Aviation, currently among the few successful smaller British companies, have relatively short histories as aircraft builders.

Similarly, in France and Germany only a handful of companies survive with still-famous names—Dornier and Messerschmitt in Germany (and even the latter is part of a large group); Breguet in France (merged now with Dassault, the post-war successor to the original Bloch company). Others among the great names of the past have been swept into the large company groups—Aérospatiale, VFW, MBB, MTU—and their previous identities have been lost.

Famous aero-engine names have disappeared in similar fashion.

In any line of business, there are naturally failures as well as successes. Bankruptcy has taken its toll in the aerospace business throughout the world, as would be expected; but the companies that have failed have generally been (with one or two notable exceptions) smaller organisations that never really made the 'big time'. The disappearance of the larger companies already mentioned is attributable mainly to economic pressures, not bankruptcy. Rather, it is through amalgamation and merging that so many company names have passed into the history books.

Although, in Britain, the Hawker Siddeley Group had become the parent company of Armstrong Whitworth, Avro, Gloster and Hawker before the second World War, the individual companies retained their identity within the Group. It was not until the late 1950s that a major trend towards amalgamation began to appear. In this period, the scale of individual new aircraft programmes was escalating rapidly and the resources of the existing British aircraft companies were such that it was increasingly difficult to compete with larger American companies. Mergers offered

Above: The designation BO 105 for this five/six-seat light helicopter signifies that it was developed by the Bölkow company, now one of the constituent parts of the largest German aerospace concern, Messerschmitt-Bölkow-Blohm GmbH

Below: Nationalisation and amalgamation, allied to continued support for gifted private companies like Dassault, has brought prosperity and success to the French aircraft industry. These are just a few of the 2,000-plus Alouette helicopters delivered by the Marignane plant of Aérospatiale

Bottom: The Westland Sea King is based on the airframe of the American Sikorsky SH-3D. Sikorsky itself, like Pratt & Whitney and others, is part of United Aircraft Corporation. Westland took over Saunders-Roe and absorbed the helicopter activities of Fairey and Bristol to become the only major helicopter manufacturer in Britain

Below: The Skyliner STOL transport is produced by Short Brothers and Harland Ltd. Although the British government now holds the controlling interest in this company, the name recalls the very earliest days of British flying. The brothers Eustace, Oswald, and Horace Short made their first balloons after visiting the Paris Exhibition in 1900 and switched to aeroplanes in 1908. Among their first products were licence-built Wright biplanes

obvious theoretical advantages; helping to turn theory into practice was the pressure of the government of the time, exercised through the Minister of Supply, Duncan Sandys. This, in effect, denied future government contracts for military or civil aircraft development to companies that did not join forces. The eventual result of this policy was the creation of the British Aircraft Corporation (from Vickers, Supermarine, Bristol, English Electric and Hunting) and Hawker Siddeley (adding de Havilland, Blackburn and Folland, and submerging all these well-known names in the single HS identity); while Westland acquired Saro, Fairey and the helicopter interests of Bristol.

Similar economic pressures have led to similar groupings in Germany, where today only three major companies survive; and in France where, apart from the Dassault-Breguet group, almost all the remaining industry has gradually been drawn into the monolithic, state-owned Aérospatiale. In America, too, the same process has gone on, if for slightly different reasons. McDonnell and Douglas merged, Convair became a part of General Dynamics, Fairchild acquired Republic and Hiller; and several other well-known companies, Bell among them, became subsidiaries of larger, non-aviation corporations.

During the 'sixties a further trend emerged. The same politico-economic pressures that encouraged the formation of large national groups led to the forging of *international* links between companies and groups of companies. At first, these international arrangements were built around the manufacture of existing aircraft designs, such as the Lockheed F-104 and Breguet Atlantic, but the process was quickly taken a stage further with the linking of companies to collaborate in both design and manufacture. One of the first examples of this practice was the Transall C-160 transport, shared by France and Germany, whose name is a contraction of *Trans*porter *Alli*anz.

More striking in its scope was the agreement between France and Britain to launch a supersonic transport, the Concorde. This brought together two large national groups —BAC and Sud (now Aérospatiale).

From being a novelty in the 'sixties, collaboration such as that which produced the Concorde is now a commonplace in Europe. Other Anglo-French projects followed: the Jaguar; the Gazelle, Puma and Lynx helicopters; the engines for these and other projects; and similar bi-national links were formed between other countries. A further stage was to bring together companies in three or more countries on a single project, such as France, Germany and Britain on the A 300 Airbus; or France, Belgium, Spain, Italy and Switzerland on the Dassault Mercure.

In these projects, however, the contributing companies retain their identities, even though the product is a joint one. The merging of companies across national boundaries now appears to be a likely continuation of the trend, as European airframe makers seek to stay in business in the face of escalating development and production costs, diminishing markets and intensifying competition from across the Atlantic.

An interesting step towards formation of an international company was taken by Fokker in the Netherlands and VFW in Germany, when the two companies merged as equal subsidiaries of a new jointly-owned parent. An alternative approach, and perhaps the most significant pointer for the future, is the formation by companies in Britain, Germany and Italy of a single company, Panavia, to design, develop and produce the MRCA combat aircraft for all three countries. It may not be unreasonable to suppose that multi-national companies like Panavia will one day swallow up their constituents (BAC, MBB and Aeritalia), just as each of the constituents has absorbed, in the last decade or two, the companies which bore the names of the pioneers.

Above: Britain's uniquely wonderful Hawker Siddeley Harrier V/STOL combat aircraft at least retains in its name a link with the old Hawker company. This enables it to trace its ancestry back to Hawker's predecessor, the Sopwith Aviation Company, which produced many of the greatest fighters of the first World War

Below: The British Aircraft Corporation, maker of the One-Eleven jet-liner, hides under its anonymous title such great antecedents as Vickers, Supermarine, Bristol, English Electric and Hunting. Nor are the operators more enduring, for British United is now a part of British Caledonian

Bottom: One of the greatest shocks to date came when Douglas Aircraft Company, best-known of all the world's manufacturers of transport aircraft, was bought up by McDonnell, to become a Division of McDonnell Douglas Corporation. It was not entirely a surprise to those who had long admired the quality of McDonnell fighters such as the Phantom II, shown here

Top left: The Anglo-French Jaguar has been developed by an international company known as SEPECAT. This merely represents the two prime airframe contractors, BAC and Breguet. In mid-1971, Breguet merged into the new Marcel Dassault-Breguet Aviation Company

Left: The C-160 transport is produced by Arbeitsgemeinschaft Transall—an abbreviation of Transporter Allianz. The name represents a group formed by companies which have since become units of Messerschmitt-Bölkow-Blohm, Aérospatiale and VFW-Fokker of Germany

Top right: Most companies have managed to remain alive, even under other names, by merging. One of the 'truly-greats' that disappeared altogether was Handley Page, liquidated in 1970. Its final product, the Jetstream turboprop transport, did not die with it; instead, a new company named Jetstream Aircraft Ltd has been formed by the pilot who won the great England-Australia Air Race of 1969-70, Captain W J Bright, to put the aircraft back into production

Above: The type flown in the England-Australia Air Race by Captain Bright was a Britten-Norman Islander. Its manufacturers are two young men who have proved that it is still possible to create a new and profitable aircraft company provided one has sufficient faith, drive, and a superb product to put on the market

Above: First supersonic bomber operated by the USAF, the B-58 Hustler, was built by General Dynamics Corporation. Having discovered that its own name meant less than that of the former Convair company, which had become one of its operating divisions, GD may decide to designate all its future aeroplanes as Convair types

McDONNELL DOUGLAS PHANTOM

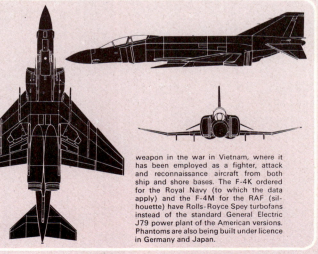

Powered by: Two 12,500 lb (5,670 kg) st Rolls-Royce Spey RB.168-25R Mk 201 turbofan engines (21,250 lb; 9,638 kg st with afterburning)
Wing span: 38 ft 5 in (11.70 m)
Length: 57 ft 11 in (17.65 m)
Wing area: 530.0 sq ft (49.24 m²)
Gross weight: 58,000 lb (26.308 kg)
Max speed: 1,386 mph (2,230 km/h) at 36,000 ft (11,000 m)
Typical tactical radius: 550 miles (885 km)
Accommodation: Crew of 2
First flights: 27 May 1958 (XF4H-1 prototype); 27 June 1966 (F-4K)

Subject of one of the most massive military aircraft programmes since the second World War, the F-4 Phantom II has been in production for more than a decade, several thousand having been built up to mid-1971 for all three US services and the air forces of a number of America's allies. It has been a major weapon in the war in Vietnam, where it has been employed as a fighter, attack and reconnaissance aircraft from both ship and shore bases. The F-4K ordered for the Royal Navy (to which the data apply) and the F-4M for the RAF (silhouette) have Rolls-Royce Spey turbofans instead of the standard General Electric J79 power plant of the American versions. Phantoms are also being built under licence in Germany and Japan.

Starting to look at Space

EARLY RESEARCH ROCKETS

THIRTY YEARS AGO the world's major centre of rocket activity was in neither the United States nor the Soviet Union, but at Peenemünde on the Baltic coast of Germany. It was here, from 1937-44, that a major breakthrough in rocket engineering—the V2—was to light the way for spectacular advances at the frontier of space.

No sooner had the second World War ended than Russia and America began a race to round up as many of the German rocket scientists as they could find. The star prize was Dr Wernher von Braun, the brilliant young technical director at Peenemünde. With more than 100 others, he was given the opportunity to work for the US Army.

The German group, based at Fort Bliss, Texas, began by assembling V2s and firing them from the White Sands Proving Ground in New Mexico. The first example was launched on 16 April 1946—well ahead, as it transpired, of similar launchings in the Soviet Union. Although the trials were mainly for military purposes, many of the rockets were fitted with instruments to probe the upper atmosphere.

Before the rocket era the highest altitude achieved by any man-made object—a sounding balloon—was about 25 miles (40 km). A man-carrying balloon had ascended 13.8 miles (22.2 km) in 1935 and an aeroplane 10.6 miles (17 km) in 1938. Other information about the Earth's atmosphere had been obtained by indirect methods including the reflection of radio waves from the ionosphere.

The White Sands V2s began to increase rapidly the scope of these investigations and by the time the programme ended in 1952 scientists had studied atmospheric composition, pressure, temperature, micrometeoroids, solar radiation and cosmic rays more than 100 miles (160 km) above the Earth.

Opportunity was also taken to carry out some unique biological experiments. The first launch for this purpose was made on 17 December 1946 when a V2 reached a height of 116 miles (187 km). Scientists wanted to find out if space flight had any unusual effect on the growth and mutation of fungus spores. Spores having a short life cycle were placed in five cylinders, four being flown in the rocket and one kept on the ground as a control sample. Unfortunately, none of the specimens was recovered.

Next to go aloft were fruit flies, which travelled in a pressurised container aboard a V2 which achieved 106 miles (170 km) in 1947. A mortar charge ejected the container as the rocket fell back to Earth, at the same time releasing a small ribbon parachute. At 100,000 ft (30,480 m) altitude a larger parachute opened to complete the recovery. The flies remained alive, seemingly none the worse for their experience.

After this, four rhesus and cebus monkeys were sealed in pressurised capsules aboard a V2 and were shot to a height of 80 miles (129 km). The 'passengers' were each given a morphine injection to make them uncon-

scious before take-off, and secured by nylon nettings on sponge rubber beds. Oxygen was supplied by means of face masks.

In true astronaut style, instruments attached to each animal gave measurements of heart rate, pulse and respiration. However, although the capsules were ejected successfully from the rocket, only one reached the Earth intact because of parachute failures. Even the one monkey that did soft-land died of heat exposure in the desert before it was located by the recovery team.

In 1952, not long after these experiments were made, the US Air Force made its own animal tests aboard American-developed Aerobee rockets launched from Holloman Air Force Base. The Aerobee nose-cone, which contained two monkeys and two mice, was separated from the rocket for recovery by ribbon-type parachutes.

After an initial failure a payload was recovered successfully from a height of 37 miles (59.5 km). The animals apparently suffered no adverse effects from the flight, despite a brief initial acceleration of about 5 *g*, lasting less than a second as the booster fired, and a longer force of 3 to 4 *g* lasting 45 seconds from the Aerobee sustainer.

The anaesthetised monkeys showed remarkable freedom from disturbance when their bio-medical flight records were analysed; and the mice, which travelled without anaesthetic, were photographed by an automatic cine camera to see how they stood up to both acceleration and weightlessness. One mouse had part of the balance mechanism of its inner ears removed to find out how it reacted. Inside their transparent chamber the mice had complete freedom. The film showed that they moved with some difficulty under acceleration, but after the rocket engine had cut out they floated from 'floor' to 'ceiling' making vigorous but ineffective leg movements. The mouse which had been deprived of its balance mechanism remained curled up in a corner, apparently unaware that it was weightless.

Meanwhile, on 24 February 1949 at Cape Canaveral (now Cape Kennedy), another major step on the road to space travel had been taken. A WAC-Corporal rocket, launched from the nose of a V2, attained a record height of 244 miles (392 km) and a top speed of 5,150 mph (8,288 km/h). Al-

Opposite page, top: In 1954, pictures of this kind gave a glimpse of the cloud-covered land masses that would one day be photographed by satellites and astronauts. It is made up of 310 separate prints from a 16mm colour film shot from an Aerobee research rocket at a height of about 100 miles (160 km) above the Earth. Prominent at top left is the first-ever picture of a complete hurricane, about 1,000 miles (1,600 km) in diameter

Bottom: Launch of an Aerobee. Rockets of this 'family', manufactured by Aerojet-General Corporation, have been standard upper atmosphere sounding vehicles in both military and civilian use for many years. They can carry scientific payloads to heights of up to 350 miles (560 km)

This page, top, left to right:
Early post-war research in both America and the Soviet Union centred around the use of captured German V2 liquid-fuel rockets. When US scientists fired the two-stage WAC-Corporal from Cape Canaveral on 24 February 1949 (first three pictures) it represented a major step on the road to space travel. The fourth picture shows the remains of the afterbody of a V2 in the New Mexico desert. After travelling to a height of nearly 100 miles (160 km), the afterbody was separated from the rocket's heavy nose-cone by an explosive charge. It then tumbled to Earth much more slowly, making possible the safe recovery of photographs taken by cameras inside it

Right: Engineers run through the pre-launch check-list for the US Navy's Martin Viking No 7 rocket, which climbed subsequently to a height of 135 miles (217 km)—a record for single-stage rockets in 1951

Below: No 7's record was equalled by Viking No 9, launched from White Sands Proving Ground, New Mexico, on 15 December 1952. These rockets made possible early studies of the upper atmosphere, the ionosphere, solar and terrestrial radiation, and cosmic rays during brief 'up-and-down' flights

though this was still a long way short of the nearly 18,000 mph (28,968 km/h) required to achieve orbit close to the Earth, it was the first practical demonstration of a large liquid-fuel step rocket.

Now it was the turn of the US Navy, which sponsored a further advance in rocket technology with the single-stage Viking. This had a much lighter structure than the V2, and could reach greater altitudes. Whereas only 67 per cent of the German rocket comprised propellants (liquid oxygen and ethyl alcohol), the extensive use of aluminium in Viking increased the figure to around 80 per cent. On 24 May 1954, an improved Viking—number 10 of the series—lifted research instruments to an altitude of 158 miles (254 km).

While these research activities were in progress, von Braun's group had been transferred to Redstone Arsenal in Huntsville, Alabama, with the object of developing a military successor to the V2. The Army rocket, to be known as Redstone, would have battlefield mobility and be capable of launching a heavy warhead 200 miles (322 km). After 36 development firings between 1953 and 1958 the rocket entered service with the US Army in Germany. It was a development of this rocket—Jupiter C—fitted with solid-fuel upper stages, that enabled von Braun's group to launch America's first artificial satellite, Explorer 1, on 1 February 1958.

Soviet rocketry in the early post-war period had taken a broadly similar path, though the German contribution was less significant. V2 launchings began from a site 125 miles (201 km) east of Stalingrad (now Volgograd) on 30 October 1947, when a rocket travelled a distance of 185 miles (298 km).

Russia's 'von Braun' turned out to be Sergei Pavlovich Korolyev, who died in January 1966. A pioneer of pre-war Soviet rocketry, he was appointed head of a design bureau in 1947 to develop long-range ballistic rockets. His team, still in being as the Koroylev Institute is responsible for all major Soviet space launchers.

Improved V2s built by Soviet engineers were launched from Kapustin Yar (48.6°N, 45.8°E) near the east bank of the Volga downstream of Stalingrad. The US Air Force had the site under surveillance from

HANDLEY PAGE W8b

Powered by: Two 360 hp Rolls-Royce Eagle VIII twelve-cylinder Vee-type engines, each driving a 10 ft 6 in (3.20 m) diameter four-blade propeller
Wing span: 75 ft 0 in (22.86 m)
Length: 60 ft 1 in (18.31 m)
Wing area: 1,456 sq ft (135.26 m²)
Gross weight: 12,500 lb (5,670 kg)
Max speed: 104 mph (167 km/h)
Range: approx 500 miles (800 km)
Accommodation: Crew of 2 and 12 passengers
First flight: 4 December 1919 (W 8)
Following its initial services into Europe with modified O/400 bombers shortly after the first World War, Handley Page Transport operated a series of two- and three-engined developments of the bomber, designated W 8, W 9 and W 10. Best known of these were the trio of W 8bs named *Princess Mary*, *Prince George* and *Prince Henry*, with which a London-Paris service was started in May 1922. The W 8b can also claim to have been among the first aircraft used to increase man's knowledge of other 'worlds' in space, for one of these aircraft was sent up in June 1927 carrying a photographer to take pictures of an eclipse of the Sun from above the clouds.

a radar station in Turkey and was able to keep a watch on its progress. At first, trials concentrated on directing rockets at remote target areas; but by 1949 vertical launchings were being carried out, signifying interest in upper-air research.

More powerful rockets (NATO code name 'Shyster') made their appearance and throughout the 1950s military and 'geo-physical' rockets continued to be launched in large numbers at Kapustin Yar. Unknown to the west, an extensive series of animal experiments had begun, as a first step in the development of manned spacecraft. The key to this bold step was a huge liquid-fuel ICBM, which Korolyev's group was building in great secrecy.

Both the Russian version of the V2 and the new geophysical rockets contributed to this programme, making possible bio-medical studies of animals on sub-orbital paths high in the upper atmosphere.

Dogs clad in made-to-measure pressure suits, with transparent 'fish-bowl' helmets, were installed in special carriages which could be catapulted from the rocket for parachute recovery.

The animals experienced the effects of noise, vibration and acceleration simultaneously while the engine was running, their weight increasing no more than five times. As in the case of the American experiments, weightlessness set in after the engine cut off and the rocket rose under momentum to the peak of its trajectory, continuing during the free drop of the rocket's nose-cone. Partial or total weightlessness during these flights lasted 220 seconds.

The carriage with the first dog was ejected at an altitude of 49.7 to 46.6 miles (80 to 75 km), the second at 21.7 miles (35 km).

Then, small pressure cabins were installed in detachable rocket nose-cones which reached heights of 130 miles (210 km) and eventually 280 miles (450 km). A typical load comprised scientific research instruments, animal test chambers, chemical batteries and recovery parachutes.

After falling back into the atmosphere, petal-shaped drag brakes opened both to stabilise the nose-cone and to reduce its speed ready for the deployment of landing parachutes.

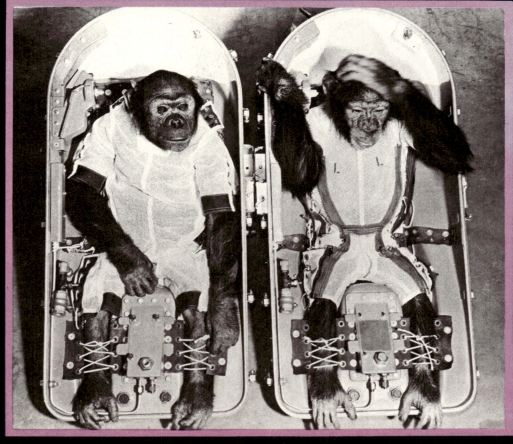

Important data were obtained from these experiments. Physiological studies showed no essential heart irregularities; blood pressure deviations were insignificant, and respiration was rhythmic. Film cameras in the rockets recorded that the animals attached to special trays had tolerated weightlessness fairly well. It warranted the conclusion that weightlessness lasting from 5 to 10 minutes did not threaten survival.

By the mid-1950s the scene was nearly set for the big spectacular. At the northern end of the Aral Sea in central Asia, a few miles to the east (45.63°N, 63.27°E), a major new launch site was under construction. In August 1957 Korolyev's huge ICBM was taken out of its preparation building, placed on the launch pad, fuelled and fired. *Tass* recorded that '. . . a super long-distance intercontinental multi-stage ballistic rocket flew at . . . unprecedented altitude . . . and landed in the target area'.

Two months later Russia was to astound the world by launching the first artificial satellite; and one month after that the dog Laika was placed in orbit.

Opposite page, top: Soviet research rockets in the Cosmos Pavilion at the Exhibition of Economic Achievement in Moscow. The V2 ancestry of the rocket in the foreground is very apparent; its nose-cone and the packages on each side were all recoverable by parachute. The single-stage V-5V rocket in the background carries a spherical instrument package inside jettisonable nose fairings

Bottom: In pre-rocket days, Britain helped to set the pace in space research. In June 1927 an eclipse of the Sun was photographed from the open cockpit of a Handley Page W.8 airliner, above clouds that might have obscured it from cameras on the ground

This page, top: The chimpanzees Enos and Ham on couches of the kind on which they travelled into space in advance of US astronauts. Ham flew 420 miles (675 km) down the Atlantic Missile Range inside a Mercury capsule on 31 January 1961, showing that it would be safe to send men on similar trips

Bottom left: This Soviet ground tracking station is typical of those used to monitor the flights of the first spacecraft

Bottom right: Early tests of Mercury manned spacecraft included 'up-and-down' flights with the aid of Little Joe boosters. This rhesus monkey travelled on board one of the capsules used in this phase of the programme

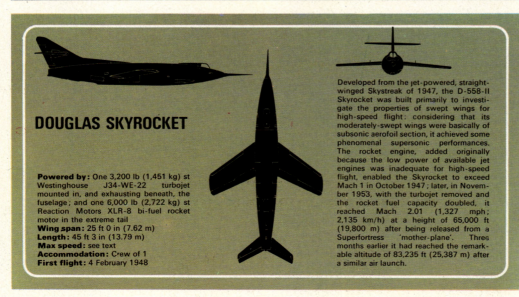

DOUGLAS SKYROCKET

Powered by: One 3,200 lb (1,451 kg) st Westinghouse J34-WE-22 turbojet mounted in, and exhausting beneath, the fuselage; and one 6,000 lb (2,722 kg) st Reaction Motors XLR-8 bi-fuel rocket motor in the extreme tail
Wing span: 25 ft 0 in (7.62 m)
Length: 45 ft 3 in (13.79 m)
Max speed: see text
Accommodation: Crew of 1
First flight: 4 February 1948

Developed from the jet-powered, straight-winged Skystreak of 1947, the D-558-II Skyrocket was built primarily to investigate the properties of swept wings for high-speed flight; considering that its moderately-swept wings were basically of subsonic aerofoil section, it achieved some phenomenal supersonic performances. The rocket engine, added originally because the low power of available jet engines was inadequate for high-speed flight, enabled the Skyrocket to exceed Mach 1 in October 1947; later, in November 1953, with the turbojet removed and the rocket fuel capacity doubled, it reached Mach 2.01 (1,327 mph; 2,135 km/h) at a height of 65,000 ft (19,800 m) after being released from a Superfortress 'mother-plane'. Three months earlier it had reached the remarkable altitude of 83,235 ft (25,387 m) after a similar air launch.

The men most responsible for putting America's first satellite, Explorer 1, into orbit hold aloft a replica of it at a Washington news conference in January 1958. Left to right are Dr William H Pickering of California Institute of Technology, Dr James Van Allen of the University of Iowa and Dr Wernher von Braun, designer of the Jupiter C launch rocket

Far left: Long years of work on military rockets, in wartime Germany and post-war America, preceded the achievement of von Braun's dream of spaceflight. This is one of his Redstone intermediate-range ballistic missiles, which formed the basis of the Jupiter C launch vehicle for Explorer satellites

Left: Before long-range military missiles or manned spacecraft could be launched successfully, methods had to be worked out for recovering objects from space without their being burned up on re-entry. First to be recovered were missile nose-cones like this conical re-entry vehicle from a Jupiter IRBM, designed under the leadership of Wernher von Braun. The cone had travelled 1,500 miles (2,400 km) through space in May 1958

One Man's DREAM

WHEN THE FULL HISTORY of the 20th century comes to be written, one man will stand head and shoulders above all others in space-age achievement. He is Dr Wernher von Braun, the rocket engineer most directly responsible for putting the first men on the Moon.

Born a member of the Prussian aristocracy on 23 March 1912, his father was Minister of Agriculture in the last pre-Hitler government. The young Baron von Braun was a talented and cultured man. He spoke five languages, was a keen pianist, and was passionately interested in astronomy, rockets and space travel.

After leaving school in 1930, he spent a short period at the Borsig AG locomotive and turbine factory and later continued his academic studies at the Technical High Schools of Berlin and Zurich. He obtained his first engineering degree in 1932, and in the same year was granted a pilot's

licence to fly gliders and sailplanes. A licence for powered aircraft followed in 1933.

By this time von Braun was already taking his first steps in rocket engineering. As a youth of 18 he had joined a group of rocket enthusiasts at the Verein für Raumschiffahrt (VfR), the famous German Society for Space Travel. At the VfR he participated with Professor Hermann Oberth and others in some of the first experiments with liquid-fuel rockets at the Society's Raketenflugplatz (rocket flying field) in a Berlin suburb, and by the age of 21 was a member of the group's board of directors.

When shortage of funds led to collapse of the VfR in the early 'thirties, von Braun—now even more imbued with the idea of space travel—saw that the only hope of continuing his researches was within a military budget. He took his ideas to the

German Army, and with the help of Captain (later General) Walter Dornberger, a small experimental rocket station was set up near Berlin by the Army Ordnance Department in 1932. A thesis entitled *Theoretical and experimental contributions to the problem of the liquid-propellant rocket* gained him a PhD in physics from the University of Berlin two years later.

By 1937, the Army proving grounds at Kummersdorf had six test stands and a staff of about 80 people. And a mark of the seriousness with which the German authorities viewed von Braun's ideas was the 11,000,000 Reichmarks (nearly one million pounds) voted in 1935 for work to begin on a much larger rocket establishment at Peenemünde on Germany's Baltic coast. Dr von Braun was installed as technical director of the new, secret, base in 1937.

Developments between 1933 and 1941 began with the small experimental rockets A1, A2, A3 and A5—then rocket motors for the Ju 50, He 112 and He 176 aircraft, and jettisonable assisted take-off units (types B2 and B8) for heavy bombers. All these motors burned alcohol and liquid oxygen.

Meanwhile, work was moving forward on the big rocket—the A4—with which Germany was to bombard London and south-east England near the end of the second World War.

It must be stated clearly that this use

SUD-OUEST TRIDENT

4 September 1954 (with rocket fitted)
One approach to interceptor fighter design which enjoyed a certain vogue in the first half of the 1950s was that of the mixed-power aircraft using both jet and rocket power: the former for take-off, cruise and landing, the latter for acceleration and combat. First such type was the S.O.9000 Trident I, whose design was begun in 1949 by the French engineer Lucien Servanty. For its early flights it had 880 lb (400 kg) st Marboré II turbojets at the wingtips, the more powerful Vipers being substituted in 1955; the data apply to it in the latter form. An improved version, the S.O.9050, was fitted with 2,425 lb (1,100 kg) st Turboméca Gabizo wingtip jets and a 6,614 lb (3,000 kg) SEPR 631 rocket motor, and could carry a 330 lb (150 kg) Matra self-homing missile under the fuselage. This aircraft reached a speed of Mach 1.8 (1,188 mph; 1,912 km/h) during test flights.

Powered by: One 9,920 lb (4,500 kg) st SEPR 481 three-chamber liquid-fuel rocket motor in rear fuselage and two 1,640 lb (744 kg) st Dassault-built Armstrong Siddeley Viper 5 turbojet engines in wingtip pods
Wing span: 26 ft 8¾ in (8.15 m)
Length: 45 ft 11¼ in (14.00 m)
Wing area: 99.03 sq ft (9.20 m²)
Gross weight: 12,125 lb (5,500 kg)
Max speed: 1,056 mph (1,700 km/h) at 36,000 ft (11,000 m)
Accommodation: Crew of 1
First flights: 2 March 1953 (jets only);

Opposite page, left: The space age began for America when this Jupiter C, carrying the Explorer 1 satellite, blasted off its launch-pad at Cape Canaveral (now Cape Kennedy) on 31 January 1958

This page, far left: Progress was rapid. Little more than two years after Explorer went into orbit, von Braun was able to report to a US Senate Space Sub-committee that the booster engines for the projected Saturn rocket had been test-fired successfully. Shown here (right) with Sub-committee Chairman John Stennis, von Braun could hardly have guessed that Saturn would put men on the Moon before the decade ended

Left: Dr James Van Allen, whose name will be associated forever with the radiation belts around the Earth discovered by Explorer satellites. In this picture, he traces on a map the orbital path followed by Explorer 4

of the weapon was not any part of von Braun's plan. The A4, or V2 as it became known, was designed originally for use by Army units in the field. Its size and range were limited by its ability, on flat wagons, to pass through railway tunnels. It became Hitler's 'revenge weapon' only after Allied bombing raids had taken their toll of German cities, at a period when the Luftwaffe was no longer capable of mounting a worthwhile counter-attack.

By the time the war ended some 4,450 men and women worked at Peenemünde, including about 900 scientists and engineers. Under von Braun's direction they had developed the rocket from a spluttering toy to the stage where rockets, at last, could be launched to the fringe of the Earth's atmosphere.

There were other developments, too. Design studies had been made for the A9/A10 project—meant to carry a payload across the Atlantic. A winged V2 made a successful vertical flight in 1945; but these projects had little practical value for the war and reflected von Braun's primary interest in rocket travel.

All this became clear after von Braun and other leading rocket scientists surrendered to the western allies in 1945. In his interrogation report, the former Peenemünde chief even spoke of the coming utility of orbital rockets and space platforms.

Not long afterwards von Braun was again at the helm of rocket activity—this time under contract to the US Army. He directed high-altitude firings of the V2 at White Sands, New Mexico, and later became director of guided missile development at Fort Bliss, Texas, with 120 of his former associates from Peenemünde.

In 1950 this group moved to Huntsville, Alabama, to form the Army Ballistic Missile Agency which produced the Redstone and Jupiter ballistic rockets. It was a modification of Redstone—fitted with solid-propellant upper stages—that von Braun evolved to test ballistic nose-cones under the searing conditions of atmospheric re-entry at 15,000 mph (24,140 km/h). From this—Jupiter C—came the opportunity to launch America's first artificial satellite, Explorer 1.

Long before the first satellites were placed in orbit, von Braun had astonished readers of *Colliers Magazine* with proposals for a three-stage rocket for transporting men and supplies to a wheel-shaped space station 250 ft (76.2 m) in diameter which spun slowly on its axis to provide artificial gravity. The proposed rocket had a lift-off weight of 7,000 tons and a 36-ton payload. The orbiter stage had wings for recovery and the two boosters were assumed to have wire-mesh parachutes.

Meanwhile, as an outcome of the cold war between Russia and America in the 'fifties—and the prestige blow to the United States in being second into space, following the orbiting of Sputnik 1—the stage

was set for a truly mammoth enterprise. On 25 May 1961 President Kennedy announced that America would aim to land men on the Moon by 1970.

Already in 1960 von Braun's Army group had been reorganised as the Marshall Space Flight Center under NASA. The team worked night and day to develop the huge rockets that would be necessary to achieve this goal—first, Saturn IB, to test basic hardware in Earth orbit, and then the mighty Saturn V for the actual Moon-landing mission. The Apollo man-on-the-Moon programme was to reach its climax with the landing of Neil Armstrong and Edwin Aldrin in the Sea of Tranquillity on 20 July 1969—well within Kennedy's target. A measure of the achievement is that not a single launch vehicle failed throughout the entire development period.

Yet still the immense talents of the former Peenemünde engineer are far from expended. In 1970 von Braun was appointed NASA's Deputy Associate Administrator for Planning, with responsibility for selecting new space ventures.

High on his list of priorities is the reusable space shuttle, the two-stage winged launch system which promises big reductions in the cost of spaceflight. The orbiter stage is being designed for a crew of two and up to 10 passengers. This, he believes, will open the way to major space station projects, of the kind of which he has dreamed since boyhood.

The First Man-made Satellites

Top: Symbol of America's early frustration, this tiny Vanguard satellite was still 'bleeping' when recovered from the wreckage of its launch rocket which had exploded in December 1957

Above: Determined to reverse early setbacks, America's rocket teams worked day and night to perfect launch vehicles that would be capable of putting spacecraft—and even men—into orbit. This photograph shows giant liquid-rocket engines under test at the Santa Susana Mountains site of Rocketdyne Propulsion Field Laboratory in the early evening darkness

WHEN THE SECOND World War ended in 1945, rockets had come of age. The German V2 had been an enormous technical triumph; but if further progress was to be made in the direction of spaceflight, engines and structures had to be made more efficient. It would also be necessary to develop more precise guidance systems, based on gyroscopes and inertial references.

One obvious method of increasing performance was to design lighter structures. Another was to build multi-stage launch vehicles with two or more rockets mounted in tandem. The bottom rocket accelerates all the upper stages, separating when its propellants are used up. The next rocket

then ignites, burns and falls away, building up still more speed, and so on.

Design studies for small multi-stage rockets capable of reaching orbital velocity —nearly 18,000 mph (28,968 km/h) close to the Earth—were made in the United States and Europe. A three-stage rocket proposed in 1951 by three engineer-members of the British Interplanetary Society, for example, had a launch weight of about 16 tons and a thrust of 30 tons. The American physicist Professor S F Singer made this the basis of his 1953 proposal for a 100 lb (45.4 kg) satellite which he called MOUSE (the acronym of 'Minimum Orbital Unmanned Satellite, Earth'). The chosen orbit was

circular at 200 miles (322 km).

It was not long afterwards that world scientists began to develop ideas for the International Geophysical Year—actually an 18-month period between 1 July 1957 and 31 December 1958. This had as its overall objective the exploration and measurement of all large-scale aspects of the Earth, its major land and sea areas, its crust and core, the deep ocean currents, the tides, weather and climate, the high atmosphere and surrounding space.

President Eisenhower announced that part of the United States' contribution would be an artificial satellite. It would be launched by a rocket developed for purely peaceful purposes.

The vehicle that emerged was the three-stage Vanguard. The first stage was developed from the successful Viking sounding rocket which in May 1954 carried an 825-lb (374-kg) payload to a height of 158 miles (254 km). Stage two was a new liquid-fuel rocket and stage three a new spin-stabilised solid motor. The satellite was to be a 20-in (50.8 cm) diameter sphere weighing 21.5 lb (9.75 kg), containing a radio transmitter, chemical batteries and scientific instruments.

While the Vanguard project gathered momentum, Soviet scientists at a space conference in Copenhagen also spoke of putting satellites into orbit. Little heed was paid to this prospect until, on 4 October 1957, Moscow Radio made the triumphant announcement that the world's first artificial satellite was orbiting the Earth every 96 minutes. Tass gave its weight as 184 lb (83.5 kg)—more than eight times that of the Vanguard payload.

What the Russians had done was to adapt their huge intercontinental ballistic missile as the launcher. At night its big central core, fully 80 ft (24.4 m) long, could be observed as it tumbled in space, catching sunlight from beyond the horizon.

A Soviet witness at the Baikonur cosmodrome recalled the dramatic scenes before the launching. When the rocket had been set up on 3 October, final systems checks were made in conjunction with the blockhouse command centre. In the evening special wagons arrived on parallel tracks to pump propellants into the tanks. The launch pad was cleared and only Korolyev—the chief designer—silent and concentrated, remained near the rocket with his closest associates.

Then, recalled the anonymous witness, a bugler appeared on the launch apron and 'the sharp sounds of the bugle cut through the night, as though to herald the new era of space exploration'.

The lift-off, early on 4 October, was seen from an observation point near the radio station. 'Finally came the reflection of the

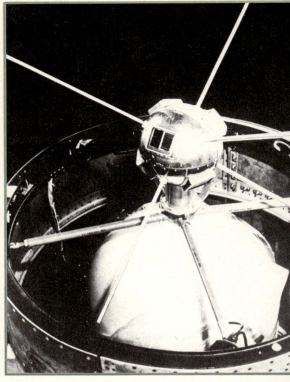
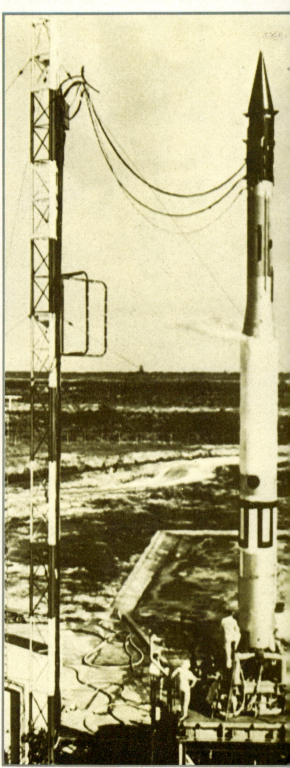

Opposite page, left: Launch of a US Navy Viking research rocket from Cape Canaveral in May 1957. The Vanguard launch vehicle was evolved from the highly successful Viking

Top right: The first Vanguard on the nose of its launch vehicle. Although it never reached orbit, later Vanguards gave ample proof of the US technological brilliance, particularly in the miniaturisation of equipment

Bottom right: The unfortunate Vanguard rocket which exploded on its launch pad in December 1957. Up to this moment, America had hoped, vainly, to disassociate its first step into space from any links with military rocketry

This page, top left: Another replica of Sputnik 1, with its long antennae extended. Scientists in the west were astounded by its weight of 184 lb (83.5 kg)

Top right: The huge ball of fire which engulfed the Vanguard rocket lost in December 1957. America's space programme emerged phoenix-like from the ashes to put Explorer 1 into the wake of Sputnik 1 just 80 days later

Left: Russia had no qualms about using variants of its ICBMs to put into orbit satellites like Sputnik 1, launched on 4 October 1957. Beyond this replica of the satellite in a dummy nose-cone, a portrait of Konstantin Tsiolkovsky, pioneer of space-flight, looks on approvingly

Below: Cutaway drawing of Explorer 1. About 80 in (203 cm) long and 6 in (15 cm) in diameter, the satellite carried 18 lb (8.2 kg) of instruments

exhaust flame as the engines came alive, followed by a low rumble. At first the rocket was shrouded by smoke, rising higher and higher. And then suddenly came a bright splash of light. Flames burst from the launch pedestal, breaking the darkness. And slowly and confidently the white body of the rocket moved upwards.'

America, outpaced unexpectedly by a nation that it still considered technically inferior, was stung into activity. Within two months Vanguard was brought to the launch pad at Cape Canaveral (now Cape Kennedy), though not with its full payload. In its nose was a highly-miniaturised test satellite weighing just 3.25 lb (1.47 kg) which Premier Krushchev was later to call America's 'grapefruit satellite'.

The world's press gathered for the launch in December 1957—and America suffered a second blow to her flagging prestige. Instead of blasting off into space, Vanguard lifted barely an inch, then slowly toppled over to explode in a sea of flames. Its tiny satellite, still 'bleeping', lay at the fringe of the inferno.

A rescue operation was immediately ordered and, with the help of a team of scientists, von Braun's Jupiter C rocket—used for testing nose-cone re-entry vehicles—was made ready as a satellite launcher. The designer himself had previously made urgent requests to launch an Army satellite with this multi-stage rocket, but had been refused because of the military connection.

However, with the plan finally approved, it took only 80 days after the Vanguard disaster to launch America's first satellite, Explorer 1. The 18-lb (8.16-kg) scientific package, attached to the rocket's solid-fuel fourth stage, contained micrometeoroid detectors, temperature gauges and cosmic ray instruments. Its orbit ranged from 224 to 1,584 miles (360 to 2,549 km) inclined at 33.24° to the equator.

Soon the scientific world was buzzing with excitement. When Explorer 1 was furthest from Earth its cosmic ray counter became unexpectedly saturated by radiation. This, the first major discovery of the space age, led Dr James A Van Allen—the chief experimenter—to conclude that our planet is girdled by a belt of radiation trapped by its magnetic field. Would this make the manned exploration of space impossible?

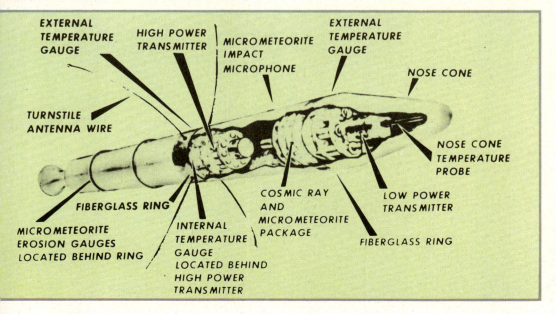

EXTERNAL TEMPERATURE GAUGE

HIGH POWER TRANSMITTER

MICROMETEORITE IMPACT MICROPHONE

EXTERNAL TEMPERATURE GAUGE

NOSE CONE

TURNSTILE ANTENNA WIRE

NOSE CONE TEMPERATURE PROBE

FIBERGLASS RING

COSMIC RAY AND MICROMETEORITE PACKAGE

LOW POWER TRANSMITTER

FIBERGLASS RING

MICROMETEORITE EROSION GAUGES LOCATED BEHIND RING

INTERNAL TEMPERATURE GAUGE LOCATED BEHIND HIGH POWER TRANSMITTER

first men in space

Flight Major Yury Gagarin, pilot-navigator of the satellite-spaceship Vostok and citizen of the USSR, will be remembered with Columbus and Cabot as one of the great explorers of history. He was the first man to slip the shackles of Earth's gravity and venture into the weightless world of space

Below: The glories of space can be described only by those who have seen them personally. This photograph of a sunset, seen over Earth's rim, was taken by Gherman Titov from Vostok 2 on 6 August 1961

Opposite page, top: Yury Gagarin in the spherical cabin of the first Vostok. Ingenious and extremely simple design ensured that it re-entered the atmosphere 'right way up' without any need for steering rockets

Первый человек, проникший в космос,— гражданин Союза Советских Социалистических Республик Герой Советского Союза летчик-космонавт СССР Юрий Алексеевич ГАГАРИН.

'THE WORLD'S FIRST spaceship, Vostok (East), with a man on board, was launched into orbit from the Soviet Union on 12 April 1961. The pilot-navigator of the satellite-spaceship Vostok is a citizen of the USSR, Flight Major Yury Gagarin.'

So began one of the most dramatic announcements in human history, broadcast by Moscow Radio. The craft was moving round the Earth at a height ranging between 105 and 195 miles (169 and 314 km). Its path, inclined at 64.95° to the equator, took it over most of the inhabited world.

Gagarin described sights never before seen by man: 'I could clearly discern the outlines of continents, islands, rivers and water reservoirs, and geological relief. When I flew over my country I distinctly saw the large squares of collective-farm fields and could easily tell ploughed land from meadows. . . . I saw the Earth's spherical form for the first time with my own eyes. The horizon presents a sight of unusual beauty. A delicate blue halo surrounds the Earth, merging with the blackness of space in which the stars are b ght and clear cut. But when I emerged from the night side of the Earth the horizon had changed to a bright orange strip which changed to blue and then to deep black again. . . .'

Gagarin's epic journey had begun at the Baikonur cosmodrome at 0907 hours local time; and just 108 minutes later—having circled the globe—he was back on Soviet soil. The landing was made near the village of Smelovaka, not far from Saratov in the Ternov district of the USSR. Villagers who ran to greet him were astonished by the strangely-garbed figure from the skies. With his white space helmet and orange coverall concealing a bulky pressure suit, he must have seemed like someone from another planet.

In the light of today's flights to the Moon and space station activity, it is easy to forget the doubts that still existed, even as recently as the early 'sixties, about man's ability to survive in space. Although animals had been sent aloft in rockets and satellites, it took supreme courage for a man to allow himself to be rocketed into orbit for the first time.

Launch failures, ending in a rocket's destruction, were not unknown. In May 1960 a dummy cosmonaut had been lost in space when the retro-rocket of Sputnik 4 —a Vostok prototype—fired in the wrong direction. The following December two dogs, Pchelka and Mushka, had perished when their re-entry capsule hit an incorrect trajectory and burned up in the atmosphere.

As it was, Gagarin's flight went without a hitch, proving beyond all doubt man's ability to adapt to the strange environment of weightlessness, at least for a limited period. However, it was four years before details of the spacecraft were revealed by the Soviet authorities.

When at last a replica was put on display in Moscow it was seen to have two basic components. The cabin was a metal sphere, of about 7.5 ft (2.29 m) diameter, protected from the searing temperatures of re-entry by an all-embracing ablative heat shield. The cosmonaut lay on an ejection seat in which he could be catapulted clear of the rocket in the event of a launch mishap after the explosive removal of a circular hatch.

Attached to this ball-shaped re-entry capsule was an equipment module with a retro-rocket. The total weight—without the final stage of the launch vehicle—was 10,417 lb (4,725 kg).

Air was supplied to the cabin at normal atmospheric pressure from oxygen and

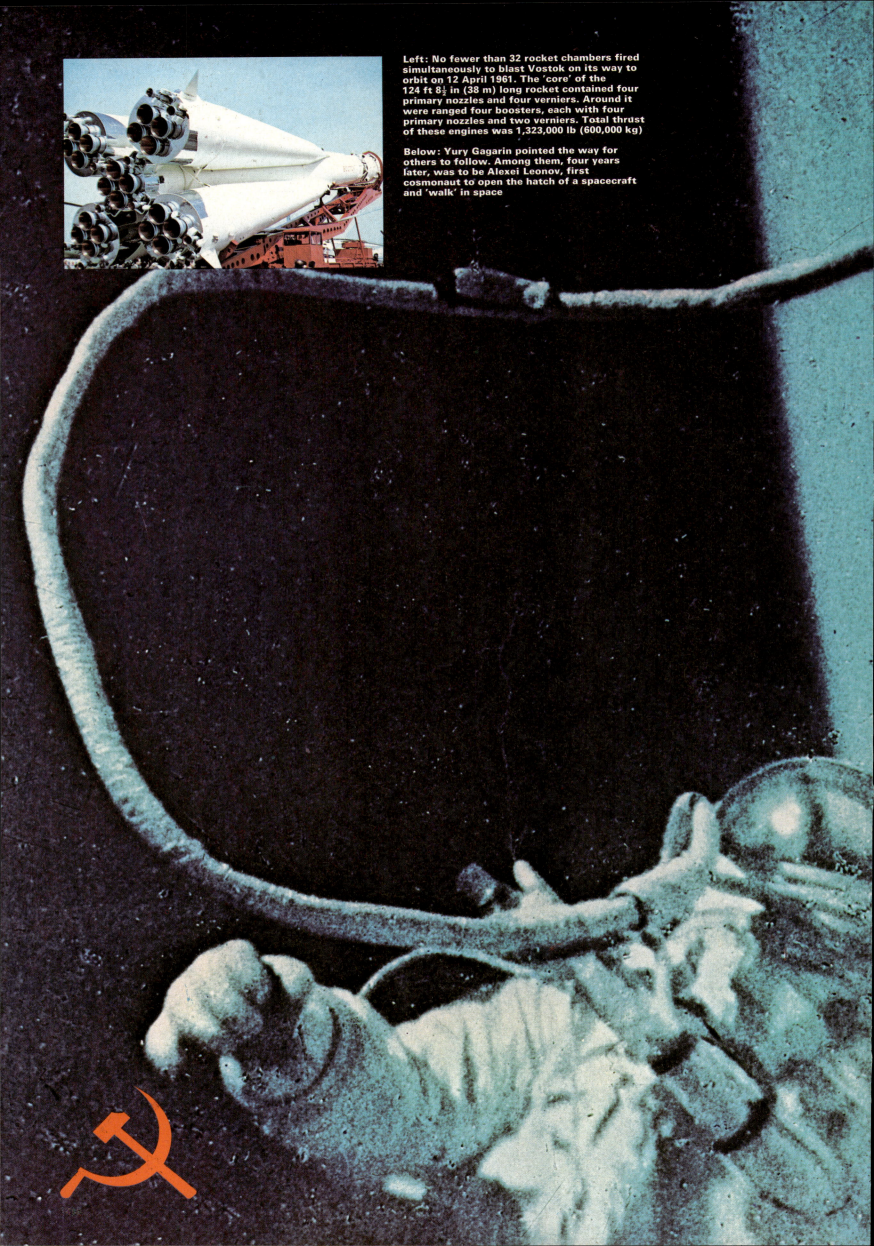

Left: No fewer than 32 rocket chambers fired simultaneously to blast Vostok on its way to orbit on 12 April 1961. The 'core' of the 124 ft 8½ in (38 m) long rocket contained four primary nozzles and four verniers. Around it were ranged four boosters, each with four primary nozzles and two verniers. Total thrust of these engines was 1,323,000 lb (600,000 kg)

Below: Yury Gagarin pointed the way for others to follow. Among them, four years later, was to be Alexei Leonov, first cosmonaut to open the hatch of a spacecraft and 'walk' in space

nitrogen bottles arranged in a ring on the equipment module. For additional protection Gagarin wore a pressure suit with the helmet visor open. If for any reason the cabin lost pressure, he could close the visor and pressurise the suit.

When it was desired to return to Earth the spacecraft was turned into a backward attitude by gas-jet controls. The retro-rocket fired at the appropriate moment to reduce speed and bring the craft out of orbit. Almost immediately the equipment module was jettisoned, leaving the ball-like re-entry module to enter the atmosphere. Remarkably, it had no gas-jets to keep it stable. Weighted forward of the centre like a heavy-bottomed toy, it assumed the correct re-entry attitude automatically as it encountered the atmosphere, presenting the thickest portion of its heat shield to the relative airflow.

After air-drag had reduced the capsule's speed below that of sound, Gagarin could have used the ejection seat for separate parachute recovery. Instead, he elected to land in the capsule. Sadly, Gagarin was killed on 27 March 1968, in a routine flying accident.

The five Vostok cosmonauts who came after Gagarin—including Valentina Tereshkova, the first woman to travel in space—all used the ejection seat because of the relatively fast descent rate of the capsule beneath its parachute.

Vostok spacecraft were launched by a modification of the same type of rocket that placed the first Sputnik into orbit in October 1957, fitted with a new top stage. Total thrust of all stages was 1,323,000 lb (600,000 kg).

When Gagarin went into orbit, America was close to launching a man into space, though not into orbit. A Mercury capsule had been installed on a modified Redstone medium-range rocket developed by von Braun's Army team at Huntsville. The bell-shaped craft, weighing about two tons at lift-off, incorporated an automatic gas-jet orientation system which the astronaut could override and operate manually by means of a hand control. At the blunt end was a heat shield which protected the capsule during re-entry.

On 5 May 1961 America's first astronaut, Cdr Alan B Shepard jr (who later went to the Moon with Apollo 14), made an historic flight of 302 miles (486 km) down-range from Cape Canaveral, reaching a peak altitude of 115 miles (185 km).

Ten weeks later Capt Virgil Grissom made a similar sub-orbital lob over the Atlantic. However, after the capsule landed, the escape hatch blew out inexplicably and it quickly filled with water. With the help of 'Scuba' divers from a rescue helicopter, the astronaut escaped but the capsule was lost in deep water. (Grissom was later to lose his life, with Ed White and Roger Chaffee, in the Apollo launch-pad fire at Cape Kennedy in January 1967.)

It was not until 20 February 1962 that America was ready to launch a man into orbit. The astronaut was John Glenn, a Lieutenant-Colonel of the US Marine Corps,

Left: Not until ten months after Gagarin's orbit was America ready to send John Glenn in his wake. But less than a month after Vostok's blast-off this Redstone rocket projected Alan Shepard on an 'up and down' ballistic trajectory along the Atlantic missile range

Below: America's first astronaut, Alan Shepard, inside the Mercury capsule Freedom 7 prior to launch. Ten years later Shepard was to bring his career in space to a triumphant climax by leading the Apollo 14 expedition to the Moon

Bottom: After splashdown in the Atlantic, Alan Shepard is winched up into a recovery helicopter from his floating spacecraft (bottom left)

USSR Spacecraft	Date	Orbits	Cosmonaut
Vostok 1	12 April 1961	1	Yury Gagarin
Vostok 2	6 August 1961	17	Gherman Titov
Vostok 3	11-15 August 1962	64	Andrian Nikolayev
Vostok 4	12-15 August 1962	48	Pavel Popovich
Vostok 5	14-19 June 1963	81	Valery Bykovsky
Vostok 6	16-19 June 1963	48	Valentina Tereshkova*

*first woman into space

USA Spacecraft	Date	Orbits	Astronaut
Mercury:			
Freedom 7	5 May 1961	Sub-orbital	Alan Shepard
Liberty Bell 7	21 July 1961	Sub-orbital	Virgil Grissom
Friendship 7	20 February 1962	3	John Glenn
Aurora 7	24 May 1962	3	Scott Carpenter
Sigma 7	3 October 1962	6	Walter Schirra
Faith 7	15-16 May 1963	22	Gordon Cooper

Above: John Glenn was the first American astronaut to make an Earth orbital flight, in the Mercury capsule Friendship 7 on 20 February 1962. All Mercury spacecraft had names ending with '7' to mark the fact that seven men had been chosen as the astronaut team for their country's first manned space programme

Right: Redstone was replaced by a man-rated version of the Atlas ICBM for Mercury orbital launchings. This photograph shows the start of John Glenn's three-orbit mission. Atop the dark-painted capsule, shaped rather like a TV tube, is the rocket escape tower that would have pulled it free of the Atlas in the event of an emergency before or during blast-off

Below: Hoisting Walter Schirra's Sigma 7 spacecraft into position above the Atlas launch vehicle at Cape Canaveral (now Cape Kennedy) on 26 September 1962. Later a faulty fuel valve caused it to be removed again; but the actual launching and flight were completed successfully in the following month

Opposite page, bottom: America's first three men in space: left to right, Alan Shepard of the US Navy, Virgil Grissom of the USAF and John Glenn of the US Marine Corps. It was suggested that the choice of a Marine for the first orbital flight would prevent an inter-Service 'war' between the Navy and Air Force in competition for the honour

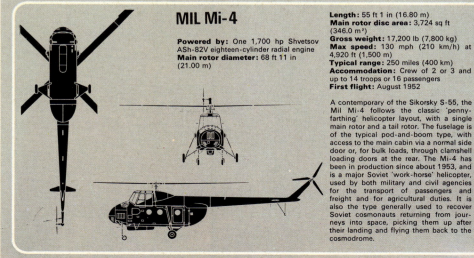

MIL Mi-4

Powered by: One 1,700 hp Shvetsov ASh-82V eighteen-cylinder radial engine
Main rotor diameter: 68 ft 11 in (21.00 m)

Length: 55 ft 1 in (16.80 m)
Main rotor disc area: 3,724 sq ft (346.0 m²)
Gross weight: 17,200 lb (7,800 kg)
Max speed: 130 mph (210 km/h) at 4,920 ft (1,500 m)
Typical range: 250 miles (400 km)
Accommodation: Crew of 2 or 3 and up to 14 troops or 16 passengers
First flight: August 1952

A contemporary of the Sikorsky S-55, the Mil Mi-4 follows the classic 'penny-farthing' helicopter layout, with a single main rotor and a tail rotor. The fuselage is of the typical pod-and-boom type, with access to the main cabin via a normal side door or, for bulk loads, through clamshell loading doors at the rear. The Mi-4 has been in production since about 1953, and is a major Soviet 'work-horse' helicopter, used by both military and civil agencies for the transport of passengers and freight and for agricultural duties. It is also the type generally used to recover Soviet cosmonauts returning from journeys into space, picking them up after their landing and flying them back to the cosmodrome.

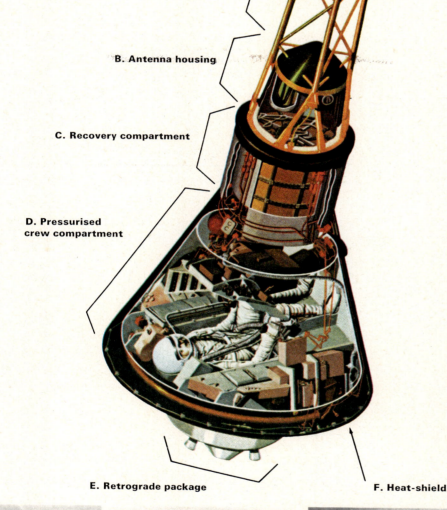

MERCURY CAPSULE

A. Escape rockets, tower jettison rockets, and escape tower provide safe recovery of vehicle in case of booster malfunction

B. Antenna housing for ground command, telemetry and voice antennae; 6 ft (1.83 m) drogue parachute; and infra-red horizon scanners for attitude reference

C. Recovery compartment contains the 63 ft (19.2 m) diameter main and reserve parachutes; recovery beacon antennae; flashing recovery-aid light

D. Crew compartment contains major spacecraft systems, including communications, electrical power, environmental control, instrumentation, navigation aids, stabilisation and control

E. Retrograde package contains three retro-rockets for initiating the spacecraft's return from orbit; and three rockets for separating the spacecraft from the booster after orbital velocity is reached

F. Ablative (burn-away) heat-shield provides protection for the astronaut from the extreme temperatures experienced during re-entry

A. Escape tower

B. Antenna housing

C. Recovery compartment

D. Pressurised crew compartment

E. Retrograde package

F. Heat-shield

and his three-orbit mission did not go without difficulty. First a series of 'technical holds' kept Glenn sealed up on the launch pad in his Mercury capsule for 3 hr 44 min. He finally lifted off under the thrust of an Atlas-D booster at 0947 hours local time.

At the end of the first orbit Glenn reported trouble with the capsule's attitude control system, which forced him to take over manual control. Then, as the craft came round for the third and last time, the Muchea ground station in Australia picked up a telemetry signal which indicated possible detachment of the capsule's heat shield due to a faulty switch.

Mercury's heat shield was designed to drop down 4 ft (1.22 m) with a perforated air bag to cushion touchdown in the sea during the final stages of parachute recovery. If it became detached in space, there was nothing to prevent the capsule from burning up during the plunge through the atmosphere. Glenn was therefore instructed to keep the retro-rocket pack attached, in the hope that it would hold the shield in place long enough for air pressure to act.

The retro-rockets fired on cue some 600 miles (965 km) west of Los Angeles, starting the capsule's descent. As air friction began to take its effect Glenn felt a sudden 'bump' and concluded that the retro-pack had jettisoned. In fact it was only one of the steel retaining straps breaking under the heat. As temperature increased an orange glow appeared outside the cabin and flaming chunks of debris began to stream past the window. In a moment of anguish Glenn thought the heat shield was breaking up; but in fact it was the retro-pack.

Happily, there was no disaster. His capsule made a copybook landing in the Atlantic about 210 miles (338 km) north-west of San Juan, Puerto Rico. Later it was found that the warning had been false; the heat shield was attached all the time.

Despite three more one-man flights (see table), America was far behind Russia in man-hours spent in space when the Mercury and Vostok programmes ended in 1963. Russia's cosmonauts had logged no fewer than 382 hours compared with America's 53. Valentina Tereshkova alone had spent 17 hours longer in space than all the Mercury astronauts put together.

It took America two more years to turn the tables with the highly-successful series of two-man Gemini spacecraft. Astronauts not only set new endurance records (330 hr 35 min 17 sec in the case of Gemini 7) but began the first experiments to dock spacecraft together in orbit—an essential step to Apollo and the triumph of a Moon landing.

Few aircraft in recent times can have been named so aptly as Lockheed's Model 382 Hercules, which has airlifted every conceivable kind of military load and has been in continuous production since 1952 for air forces all over the world. Apart from their more powerful engines and some internal equipment the sixty-six Hercules C. Mk 1s operated by Air Support Command of the RAF are basically similar to the major USAF version, the C-130E

Left: Not all the tasks undertaken by aircraft in support of manned and unmanned space flights are glamorous and exciting. This Lockheed C-130 Hercules was used simply to carry the Discoverer 13 capsule—first payload recovered from Earth orbit—from Honolulu to Washington in 1960

Lower left: After its arrival at Andrews Air Force Base, the Discoverer 13 instrument capsule was taken to the White House for presentation to President Eisenhower

Below: Triumphant homecoming to Moscow's Vnukovo Airport of Yuri Gagarin, the first spaceman, whose Il-18 airliner was escorted by MiG fighters. Sadly, he was to be killed later in the crash of a two-seat MiG-15

Bottom: This Mi-4 helicopter scattered leaflets over Moscow's streets, welcoming Gagarin to his nation's capital—surely one of the most unusual ways in which aircraft have 'supported' man's venture into space

AIRCRAFT & ASTRONAUTICS

TO SUPPORT THE flight of John Glenn, the first US astronaut to go into Earth orbit, the Department of Defense used no fewer than 126 aircraft, 24 ships and 26,000 people. This impressive force was deployed around the world as an essential part of Project Mercury.

For stage two of the US manned space programme, Project Gemini, improved recovery techniques and equipment permitted a reduction in the support required, although the two-man flights were of longer duration. Even so, 96 aircraft were allocated to a typical mission, plus 18 ships and 9,665 people.

Project Apollo, the third step of the space programme, benefited from further increased efficiency. But to support a typical Apollo mission the Department of Defense still needed 52 aircraft, 7 ships and nearly 6,000 people.

These impressive figures provide a graphic indication of the scale of effort required to support a manned space flight. Almost certainly many more aircraft, in a wider variety, are used than is generally realised.

Best known of the aircraft involved are the helicopters utilised by both Russia and America to recover their astronauts when they have returned from a mission. No 'live' pictures have been televised of a Russian recovery operation, mainly because the cosmonauts so far have all landed on Russian soil and, once the touch-down point has been pin-pointed by radar, it is obviously a simple matter of getting a helicopter to the spot to pick up the crew. There is little point in delaying

the recovery until a TV crew can be flown out as well. However, even if it were possible, pictures might not be shown right away, as the Russian authorities usually like to be sure that everything can be seen to have gone 'according to pre-arranged plans' before releasing details of events of this nature.

By contrast, America's spacecraft have been designed to land in the sea, and most readers will have seen the exciting scenes of a recovery when these have been televised live from the Pacific Ocean, using communications satellites, to viewers all over the world. The high skill of the pilots usually makes such operations look deceptively simple, but this is the result of many hours of practice.

The helicopters used are Sea Kings made by the Sikorsky Aircraft Division of United Aircraft Corporation. Specially designed for anti-submarine-warfare duties, the Sea King has extensive equipment and instrumentation for all-weather ship- and shore-based operations to detect, track, identify and, if necessary, destroy enemy submarines. Its equipment includes standard radio and navigational aids, and a dead-reckoning tracer which receives its guidance information from a Doppler radar. It is thus well equipped and ideally suited for making pick-ups at sea.

Five Sea Kings are used during a typical recovery of an Apollo crew. Two, each with a team of swimmers, are deployed 10 miles (16 km) up-range and 10 miles down-range of the target point; both are 15 miles (24 km) north of the ground track of the command module. A third is

deployed 10 miles nearer the target point. For 'quarantine-type missions' (as were the original missions involving contact with the Moon) this third aircraft, designated the Astronaut Retrieval Helicopter and having the call sign 'Recovery 1', has been used for the actual recovery of the astronauts. It carries biological isolation garments for the swimmers and astronauts, protective garments for the hoist operator, two seven-man life-rafts, decontamination dispensers and additional Scuba tanks for the swim team. A NASA physician is also aboard, and because of the important role of Recovery 1 a second, back-up machine has always been available on the prime recovery ship.

A fifth helicopter is charged with photographing all stages of the recovery operation. This provides visual records of the command module, should it sink, and also leads to improvements in recovery technique. It is from this helicopter also that television pictures are transmitted to all parts of the world.

Four fixed-wing aircraft work in conjunction with the helicopters. Two of these are Grumman E-1B Tracers, flown from the deck of the prime recovery ship. The Tracer is a modification of the well-established S-2 Tracker. Using its 20 ft x 30 ft (6.1 m x 9.1 m) radome, one E-1B acts as the on-scene commander of the recovery operation while flying above the prime recovery ship; appropriately, the call sign of this aircraft is 'Air Boss'. The second E-1B, with the call sign 'Relay', is used for communications relay duties.

The other pair of fixed-wing aircraft are Lockheed HC-130H Hercules, stationed 165 miles (265 km) up-range and 165 miles down-range of the target point. These aircraft carry ARD-17 Cook Tracker automatic direction equipment for location of the command module during re-entry, and a surface-to-air-retrieval system (STARS). This comprises a two-pronged fork on the nose of the aircraft to snare a cable which is attached to the object to be recovered and hoisted aloft by a balloon. In addition to the flight crew, these Hercules carry three para-rescue men, and would go into action should a spacecraft land unduly wide of the target point and require assistance before the recovery helicopters could arrive.

Yet another aircraft which plays an important part in general recovery operations is an EC-135N ARIA (Apollo range instrumented aircraft) which is on station in the vicinity of the primary landing area prior to the command module re-entry, for network support.

NASA uses eight of these EC-135N ARIA craft. They are special versions of the USAF's Boeing C-135 four-jet transport aircraft, modified to provide a communications link between Apollo astronauts and NASA's Manned Space Flight Center at Houston, particularly while the Apollo spacecraft are in 'parking' orbit around the Earth. Outbound, they provide coverage of the critical translunar injection burn; inbound, they support re-entry from the moment of command and service module separation, through the period of blackout just after re-entry, to splashdown, and receive and record telemetry from the command module.

ARIA aircraft communicate with the spacecraft through a 7 ft (2.1 m) diameter parabolic S-band antenna housed in a distinctive 10 ft (3.05 m) long drooping nose radome. The antenna scans for the Apollo spacecraft and then locks on to it

for voice and telemetry communications. An HF antenna, similar to that on the tail fin, is installed above each wingtip. Inside its cabin, the EC-135N contains 15 tons of communications and telemetry equipment.

Four of the ARIA aircraft are adapted to carry ALOTS (airborne lightweight optical tracking system). This is an integrated automatic tracking and photographic system, housed in an externally-mounted pod. The pod contains two rate gyros, two vidicon tracking sensors and a 70-mm high-resolution camera, all attached to a 200-in (508 cm) telescope housing. The system provides precision photographic coverage of missiles and spacecraft during the early launch, stage separation and re-entry phases of a flight. The ALOTS-ARIA aircraft also virtually eliminate weather as a cause of a missile or satellite launch delay, as they operate at an altitude of 40,000 ft (12,200 m), above normal cloud cover.

When an Apollo spacecraft leaves Earth orbit and is injected into a lunar path over the Atlantic, three EC-135Ns cover the range, with a fourth in the area as a reserve. Injection over the Pacific requires the availability of six aircraft, plus two reserves, to cover all possible points of injection.

Other aircraft are utilised to support an Apollo mission once the astronauts have been taken to the safety of the prime recovery ship. For example, a surface-to-air-retrieval (STAR) pick-up may be required about two hours after the astronauts have been recovered, involving the use of a C-130H Hercules to collect a container of news film from the prime recovery ship. A small balloon is launched and attached to the container by a nylon cord. The Hercules, with STAR retrieval gear installed, flies under the balloon and traps the nylon line in its nose recovery yoke. The balloon breaks away at a weak link in the line, and the container is pulled off the deck, trailing back beneath the aircraft's fuselage to be gently winched in. The gear, which can also be used to retrieve people, is so designed that the load snatched is prevented from striking the aircraft. Teflon lines from the aircraft's nose to each wingtip deflect the nylon line past the airframe if it misses the yoke.

Meanwhile, below decks, the three Apollo astronauts will have left the retrieval helicopter and entered the small caravan-like container known as the Mobile Quarantine Facility. Upon reaching port, the MQF is off-loaded from the ship, taken to a waiting Lockheed C-141 StarLifter aircraft, and flown to Ellington Air Force Base, near the NASA Manned Space Flight Center at Houston, where it is transferred to the Lunar Receiving Laboratory. Aircraft are also used to transfer from the port to Houston the precious load of

lunar samples and data collected so expensively by the astronauts. The load is divided and carried in separate aircraft to prevent total loss in the event of an accident.

Aircraft are utilised during many other stages of a manned spaceflight mission. In fact, they begin playing a vital part long before the countdown begins.

Using great skill and much money, it has become possible to reproduce or simulate many of the forces and the general environment experienced in space. Centrifuges, for example, can give astronauts an idea of the 'g' forces to which they will be subjected during both lift-off and re-entry into the atmosphere. One important facet of space travel, however, cannot be duplicated in laboratories on the ground—the simulation of 'weightlessness', to which astronauts are subjected continually whenever they are coasting through space, which in practice means the greater part of a mission.

This sensation is so totally different to anything experienced in normal everyday living that it has been the cause of some of the major medical upsets experienced during manned missions, particularly by Russian cosmonauts. It is thus imperative for astronauts to acquire experience of the sensation during their training, to minimise the risk of someone going into space who cannot withstand it, becoming ill, and thereby jeopardising the success of a mission and, possibly, the lives of his colleagues.

Fortunately, scientists have devised a clever but simple manoeuvre that reproduces the sensation of weightlessness. An aircraft is first dived to gain speed and then put into a gentle coasting 'zoom climb', during which it follows what is known as a parabolic trajectory. This means that it follows a ballistic path, similar to that taken by a shell when it is fired. During the manoeuvre the aircraft—and its occupants—are weightless. The period of weightlessness (about half a minute) is much shorter than the ideal, but the great advantage of this method is that astronauts under training can experience a large number of such periods during the course of a single flight.

Most astronauts conduct tentative weightlessness zoom climbs early in their careers, either in training aircraft or in US Air Force or Navy fighters. The bulk of the official NASA training, however, is carried out by the use of specially modified KC-135 aircraft. These are virtually standard Air Force machines, but with the cabin well padded on the inside to prevent astronauts from injuring themselves and equipment from getting damaged during training sessions. During the weightless training flights, astronauts practise activities such as eating and drinking, free float

Most famous of all aircraft serving America's space programmes is 'old 66', the Sikorsky Sea King helicopter which has been used to retrieve many astronauts from the sea at the end of their missions. It is shown below hauling up one of the Apollo 10 astronauts who had orbited the Moon in May 1969. The same retrieval 'net' is shown in use above from a Coast Guard HH-52A helicopter during training of the Apollo 9 crew

SIKORSKY SH-3A SEA KING

Powered by: Two 1,250 shp General Electric T58-GE-8B turboshaft engines, driving a five-blade main rotor and five-blade tail rotor
Main rotor diameter: 62 ft 0 in (18.90 m)
Length: 72 ft 8 in (22.15 m)
Main rotor disc area: 3,019 sq ft (280.5 m²)
Gross weight: 20,500 lb (9,300 kg)
Cruising speed: 136 mph (219 km/h)
Max range: 625 miles (1,005 km)
Accommodation: Crew of 4 in ASW role; varies in astronaut recovery aircraft according to individual mission
First flight: 11 March 1959
Known to television viewers in all parts of the world as the type of helicopter which stands by to carry out, and to photograph, the recovery of astronauts returning from missions in space, the SH-3A is but one of many variants of Sikorsky's basic S-61 design which first appeared a dozen years ago. These are used by all three US services, and also by the armed forces of Britain, Brazil, Canada, Denmark, Germany, Japan and Italy. Primary function is that of anti-submarine patrol, but other variants are employed for search and rescue or mine countermeasures duties.

manoeuvring, self-rotation and tumble-and-spin recovery.

These flights have also been used to enable astronauts to gain experience in handling equipment. For example, Alan Shepard and Edgar Mitchell, of Apollo 14, made flights in which the trajectories were calculated to reproduce one-sixth 'g' conditions, so that they could try out the portable workshop, known officially as the Modular Equipment Transporter, used on this mission to the Moon. One-sixth 'g' flights were also used to evaluate operation of the Lunar Roving Vehicle first carried on the Apollo 15 mission.

Spacecraft flight readiness is maintained by means of a flight programme utilising high - performance jet aircraft. These aircraft, supersonic Northrop T-38 Talons, are assigned to the Manned Space Flight Center and based at Ellington Air Force Base. In addition to local flights, they are used by astronauts for cross-country flights in support of engineering and training activities. They permit greater flexibility in travelling, as well as maintenance of the crew members' flying skills. In addition, a continuing programme of helicopter flying provides the astronauts with an opportunity to familiarise themselves with lunar landing trajectories.

Apart from playing an important part in recovery operations, fixed-wing aircraft and helicopters also perform vital tasks during launch preparations. Aircraft fly meteorological missions, and patrol the coastal areas off Cape Kennedy to warn ships approaching the region. To provide medical aid and retrieval of the crew in the event of an abort shortly after lift-off, three Sikorsky HH-3E helicopters of the USAF Aerospace Rescue and Recovery Service proceed down the ground track until the impact prediction point for an abort exceeds their maximum operating radius of 160 miles (257 km).

Also on station at this time is at least one Sikorsky HH-53C, carrying a fire suppression kit suspended beneath it to combat either hypergolic or brush fires should one be started by a command module impact on land. The kit is modified to carry 83 gallons of water in place of the foam usually carried. Hypergolic fires cannot be extinguished until the fuels have been expended, but the water in the fire suppression kits would be able to lower the temperature of a hypergolic fire so that firemen could work in the area.

Aircraft are also used extensively to support many unmanned missions, or missions by 'automatic interplanetary devices' as the Russians call them. For example, it is often necessary to recover spacecraft that have been brought out of orbit, such as a satellite carrying animals or plant seeds. It is often vital to examine such payloads on Earth to determine the

Above: Four of the eight ARIA (Apollo Range Instrumented Aircraft) EC-135Ns, converted by Douglas Aircraft Company from standard Boeing C-135s. Each aircraft carries inside its bulbous nose a dish-shaped radar antenna to track spacecraft and lock on to them for the transmission and reception of radio messages and data telemetry

Opposite page, bottom: Watched by a TV camera in the Sea King hovering in the background, Apollo 12 lunar module pilot Alan Bean leaves the command module after splash-down in the Pacific on 24 November 1969. His companions, Charles Conrad and Richard Gordon, are already in the life-raft

Centre left: The Earth Observation Division of NASA uses for its photographic missions aircraft like this RB-57F, a much-modified development of the Canberra bomber with huge new wings for high-altitude flying

Bottom left: On board a KC-135, Astronaut Gerald Carr tests methods of getting on and off a mock-up of the Lunar Roving Vehicle under one-sixth gravity conditions

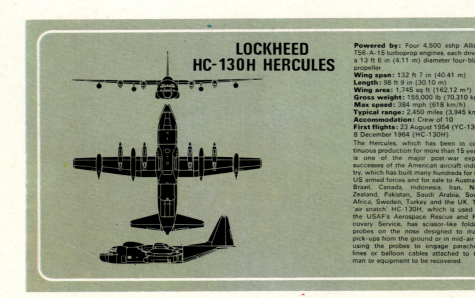

LOCKHEED
HC-130H HERCULES

Powered by: Four 4,500 eshp Allison T56-A-15 turboprop engines, each driving a 13 ft 6 in (4.11 m) diameter four-blade propeller
Wing span: 132 ft 7 in (40.41 m)
Length: 98 ft 9 in (30.10 m)
Wing area: 1,745 sq ft (162.12 m²)
Gross weight: 155,000 lb (70,310 kg)
Max speed: 384 mph (618 km/h)
Typical range: 2,450 miles (3,945 km)
Accommodation: Crew of 10
First flights: 23 August 1954 (YC-130); 8 December 1964 (HC-130H)
The Hercules, which has been in continuous production for more than 15 years, is one of the major post-war export successes of the American aircraft industry, which has built many hundreds for the US armed forces and for sale to Australia, Brazil, Canada, Indonesia, Iran, New Zealand, Pakistan, Saudi Arabia, South Africa, Sweden, Turkey and the UK. The 'air snatch' HC-130H, which is used by the USAF's Aerospace Rescue and Recovery Service, has scissor-like folding probes on the nose designed to make pick-ups from the ground or in mid-air by using the probes to engage parachute lines or balloon cables attached to the man or equipment to be recovered.

Below, top to bottom: A Lockheed HC-130H of the USAF's Aerospace Rescue and Recovery Service with one of the balloons that form part of its retrieval system. The balloon carries aloft a nylon cable, which is snared by the yoke on the nose of the HC-130H in flight. The balloon is then cut free of the cable, which is hauled up into the rear of the aircraft's cabin together with whatever load is attached to its lower end

An HC-130H in flight with its nose-yoke extended. The recovery gear can be used to pick up personnel awaiting rescue or packages for urgent collection from places where there are no airstrips

10 August 1960: the launch of Discoverer 14, the first payload from space that was recovered by mid-air 'snatch'

detailed effects of the weightlessness and radiation to which they have been subjected. Similarly, it may be necessary to recover cameras carried into orbit by satellite, or at least the photographs they have taken. Although America's Lunar Orbiter spacecraft sent back remarkably detailed pictures of the Moon, and weather satellites send back adequate pictures of clouds, more detailed results are needed for some purposes. Military reconnaissance photographs, for example, obviously need to be as detailed as possible; so do those needed for map-making.

Russia recovers most of her satellite payloads within the confines of the Soviet Union itself, for which a relatively simple parachute recovery system is sufficient, the payload being tracked by radar to the ground impact point, from where it is normally recovered by aircraft. America, on the other hand, recovers most of her satellite payloads over the sea, and for this a most remarkable technique of mid-air recovery has been evolved.

Basically, the technique entails snatching the payload as it descends on its parachute, using a trapeze-like apparatus trailed behind specially-adapted aircraft. If the

trapeze snares the parachute shrouds, the capsule is winched into the aircraft. If the trapeze misses, there is often time to go round again for a second attempt.

Although basically simple, the technique calls for a high degree of piloting skill. In fact, when the Americans first announced their intention to attempt the mid-air recovery technique, many experts derided the proposal, declaring that it was quite impractical. Most important, the technique requires the re-entry path of the capsule to be determined accurately. This is not easy, since a delay of a fraction of a second in firing the retro-rockets can alter the impact point by many miles. It is thus not surprising that the technique went through a long and discouraging development period.

Satellites in the Discoverer series served as test vehicles for spacecraft stabilisation, capsule ejection, and perfection of the air-snatch technique. The first Discoverer was launched on 28 February 1959, a little over a year after Sputnik 1 ushered in the space age. This Discoverer was the first satellite to achieve a polar orbit, and technicians were overjoyed, especially when Discoverer 2, launched on 13 April

Left: Recovery from the sea of a dummy Apollo command module by a Sikorsky CH-53A Sea Stallion in 1967. Purpose of the operation was to test the stability of the helicopter/spacecraft combination

Bottom left: Four of the fleet of Northrop T-38 Talon two-seat jets used by NASA as spaceflight readiness trainers for its astronauts

Top: As part of his training for an Apollo mission, Astronaut Eugene Cernan builds up his helicopter flying proficiency in one of NASA's Bell 47s over the Gulf of Mexico. During the Apollo 10 mission, Cernan piloted the lunar module to within about 9 miles (14 km) of the Moon, as a prelude to Apollo 11's landing on the surface

Above: No aircraft but this Aero Spacelines Super Guppy is large enough to transport the S-IVB third stage of the Saturn V/Apollo launch rocket from factory to space centre. It is a much-modified turboprop conversion of a C-97 airframe, with parts from four other Stratocruisers

1959, successfully ejected its capsule. Unfortunately, it was ejected at the wrong moment, came down in the far north of Norway and has never been found.

Discoverers 3 and 4 failed to go into orbit; No 6 ejected its capsule, but this was not recovered. The capsule of Discoverer 7 was also ejected successfully, but failed to re-enter correctly because of inaccuracies in the spacecraft's attitude. Three of the next five Discoverers failed to go into orbit; on the other two the capsules were ejected, but were not recovered.

On 10 August 1960 Discoverer 13 was launched. This went into orbit successfully, and ejected its capsule on the 17th orbit. As the capsule floated down it was spotted by aircraft which attempted to catch it. The attempts failed, but this time the capsule was located and recovered from the Pacific Ocean by frogmen. It was the first time a payload had been brought back to Earth safely from orbit and represented a significant step forward in the exploration of space.

It looked as if the critics of the air-recovery technique were being proved right. But eight days later, on 18 August

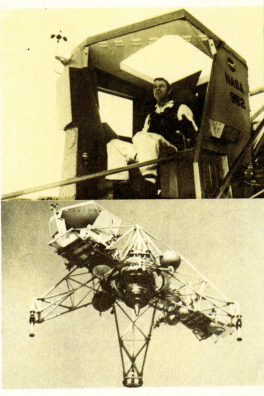

Top: Apollo 14 commander Alan Shepard in the pilot's seat of a Bell Aerospace Lunar Landing Training Vehicle (LLTV) at Ellington Air Force Base on 14 December 1970

Above: The LLTV in flight. Downward-pointing jets cancel out five-sixths of the vehicle's weight, enabling it to simulate the effect of landing a lunar module in the low-gravity environment of the Moon

Right: Alan Shepard waits patiently for recovery from a life-raft while fellow-Astronaut Stuart Roosa is hoisted up in a 'Billy Pugh' net after returning from the Moon

Bottom right: The streamlined ALOTS package on the side of this C-135 contains equipment to track and photograph spacecraft after launch and during re-entry

1960, success was achieved at last with Discoverer 14, the air snatch being made by a Fairchild C-119 transport aircraft; Lockheed Hercules are now used for this work.

An initial success did not mean that the air-snatch technique had been perfected. The capsule of Discoverer 15, launched on 13 September, was lost in the ocean, and the second success did not come until Discoverer 17 was launched on 7 December 1960, the capsule being recovered in mid-air.

When the Discoverer programme ended in February 1962, 38 satellites had been launched, of which 26 had gone into orbit. Of the 23 attempted capsule recoveries, eight air-snatches were made and four capsules were recovered from the ocean.

The air-snatch technique is now the basic method used by the US for recovery of film from her strategic reconnaissance satellites. For obvious reasons, no figures have been released giving the tally of successful air-snatches of these 'spy capsules'; but it is thought that the great majority are recovered successfully, the photographs keeping America informed of Russia's tremendous build-up of strategic missiles.

The Space Shuttle craft promises greater economy in future missions by employing reusable vehicles to carry men, equipment and supplies to orbiting space stations. As a first step, the Grumman company proposes that only the second-stage orbiter should be recoverable; it would be launched by a Saturn booster of the kind used for Apollo missions, as shown at right. The smaller illustration shows a typical orbiter docked under a 250,000 lb (113,400 kg) space station. An extended-arm manipulator has removed one of the reaction control system modules from the station, so that it can be ferried back to Earth in the orbiter for servicing

The First Space-Walkers

Below: As this superb picture testifies, not the least of Gemini 12's achievements was to secure some of the best photographs taken in space up to that time. During the course of the four-day mission astronaut Edwin 'Buzz' Aldrin, the EVA pilot, 'walked' and worked in space for a total of 5 hr 30 min, including one continuous period of 2 hr 29 min 25 sec

Opposite page, left to right: In March 1965, twenty months before the flight of Gemini 12, Soviet cosmonauts Pavel Belyaev and Alexei Leonov had been launched into Earth orbit in the two-man spacecraft Voskhod 2. Leonov (centre) became the first man ever to walk in space, remaining outside the spacecraft for 10 minutes. Television pictures received on Earth (right) showed him performing a somersault and other manoeuvres

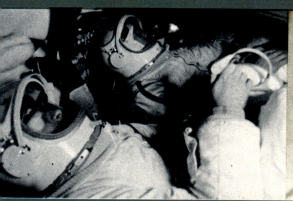

RUSSIA WAS WELL to the fore in manned space travel when the Vostok series ended in 1963. From intelligence reports reaching the west, it was already clear that plans were well advanced for a multi-man spacecraft. Yury Gagarin himself spoke of scientists and engineers going into space alongside cosmonauts in order to make direct observations of the space environment. Even then, Soviet interest seemed more intent on establishing a space station in Earth orbit than in racing America to landing men on the Moon.

The world did not have long to wait for the new programme to begin. On 12 October 1964 the first multi-man spacecraft, Voskhod 1, blasted off from the Baikonur cosmodrome to achieve an orbit, inclined at 65°54′ to the equator, which ranged between 100 and 255 miles (161 and 410 km) altitude. Aboard were cosmonaut Vladimir Komarov, doctor Boris Yegorov and scientist Konstantin Feoktistov.

The 11,730-lb (5,320-kg) craft completed 16 orbits of the Earth in a flight lasting 24 hr 17 min 3 sec. Having a qualified doctor aboard gave new insight into the medical problems of weightlessness and the subsequent return to gravity conditions.

Several innovations were introduced on this mission. The crew dispensed with space-suits in an oxygen-nitrogen environment maintained throughout at normal atmospheric pressure. Ejection seats were omitted and they remained inside the capsule during its parachute recovery. The actual touchdown was cushioned by solid-fuel retro-rockets which fired automatically when the capsule was 1 m (3.3 ft) from the ground.

Voskhod 2 brought still more surprises. This time there were only two cosmonauts, Pavel Belyaev and Alexei Leonov, and both wore space-suits.

After being launched from Baikonur into an orbit ranging between 107 and 308 miles (172 and 495 km), at 65° inclination, an expandable airlock was extended from the left-hand side of the spacecraft. Leonov entered the airlock and the cabin hatch was closed behind him. Then, with the cosmonaut secure in his space-suit, air was pumped out of the airlock chamber. When vacuum-equivalent conditions were obtained, the outer hatch was opened and Leonov climbed out to become the world's first space walker.

The spacecraft was then on its second orbit, and Leonov remained outside for about 10 minutes, tethered by a safety line. The cosmonaut himself fixed a television camera to a bracket on the edge of the open airlock, and ground observers could see a

ghostly figure performing 'space gymnastics', turning slowly over and over and controlling its actions by arm movements some 15 ft (4.6 m) from the ship. The experiment gave renewed confidence that man would be able to work effectively in space. (Leonov received oxygen from a back-pack, and the safety line merely carried cables for voice communication and bio-medical data).

With the space-walker safely back in his seat, preparations were made for the spacecraft to land, with retro-fire scheduled at the end of the 16th orbit. It was then realised that the solar sensor of the automatic control system had failed to align the craft at the correct backward angle for firing the braking engine, and the cosmonauts were forced to make another orbit.

During re-entry, which was controlled manually by Belyaev, not only was the return path displaced westward by the Earth's rotation but there was an 'overshoot': the cosmonauts made a perilous landing in a snow-clad forest near Perm, in the Urals, and it was 2½ hr before a rescue helicopter arrived to pick them up. The flight had lasted 26 hr 2 min 17 sec.

No further Voskhod flights were made. It does not seem to have come up to expectations, and the extensible airlock system was abandoned. Instead, the experience was carried forward to the Soyuz-class spacecraft with which Soviet cosmonauts began to develop space station techniques some years later.

Meanwhile, America was steadily developing her own series of two-man Gemini spacecraft, which were destined to set new records of space achievement. The launch vehicle was a modified Titan 2 ICBM and, depending on the mission, Gemini's launch weight varied between 7,100 and 8,350 lb (3,220 and 3,787 kg).

Only two unmanned launches were required to qualify Gemini for human experiments. The first, carried out on 8 April 1964, was to test the compatibility of launcher and spacecraft. There was no attempt at separation. The Gemini and Titan second stage orbited together between 100 and 204 miles (161 and 328 km) altitude at 33° to the equator.

The second unmanned test was suborbital. The spacecraft separated as planned at an altitude of nearly 100 miles and parachuted down into the Atlantic on 19 January 1965.

Details of subsequent manned missions are given in the Table. Gemini 3 sent Virgil Grissom and John Young on a three-orbit mission during which they performed ex-

tensive power manoeuvres. Grissom became the first man to go into space for a second time.

Gemini 4 set another milestone when Ed White became the first American to 'walk' in space. As Gemini had no airlock, the entire cabin had to be depressurised with both astronauts wearing pressure suits. Three minutes after the hatch was opened, White launched himself into space on the end of a 25 ft (7.6 m) umbilical cable. Through the line he received oxygen supply from the ship and established communication with his companion James McDivitt and ground control. Until its fuel was expended, White used a gas-gun to help him manoeuvre in space. Altogether he was outside for about 21 minutes.

Gemini 5 scored in other ways. Apart from being the first spacecraft to employ fuel cells instead of chemical batteries for electrical power, its eight-day mission exceeded by a handsome margin the flight duration of any previous manned spacecraft, Russian or American.

Next was to be a first attempt to dock two spacecraft together in orbit. The target —an unmanned Agena spacecraft—failed to achieve orbit after a successful launch on 25 October 1965. Astronauts Schirra and Stafford, who were to have followed it into orbit some 90 minutes later aboard Gemini 6, were immediately stood down.

As another Agena was not available, it was decided to put Geminis 6 and 7 up at the same time, to see if the craft could be manoeuvred close together as they moved round the Earth.

Gemini 7, which aimed to keep astronauts aloft for 14 days, was launched first, on 4 December 1965. A technical fault delayed the lift-off of Gemini 6 from 12 to 15 December, and then it was off to a spectacular success. Some 5 hr 47 min after rising from the pad at Cape Kennedy, Schirra and Stafford manoeuvred their spacecraft within 100 ft (30.5 m) of Gemini 7 as it held a circular course 185 miles (298 km) above the Earth. The two craft continued in formation for more than 20 hours, sometimes coming within a few feet of each other in controlled manoeuvres. The astronauts could see and signal to each other through their windows.

Still to be achieved was the physical joining of two craft in space. Perfection of this technique was the key to landing men on the Moon and achieving their safe return.

Another Agena target was launched on 16 March 1966—this time with complete success. Astronauts Neil Armstrong and

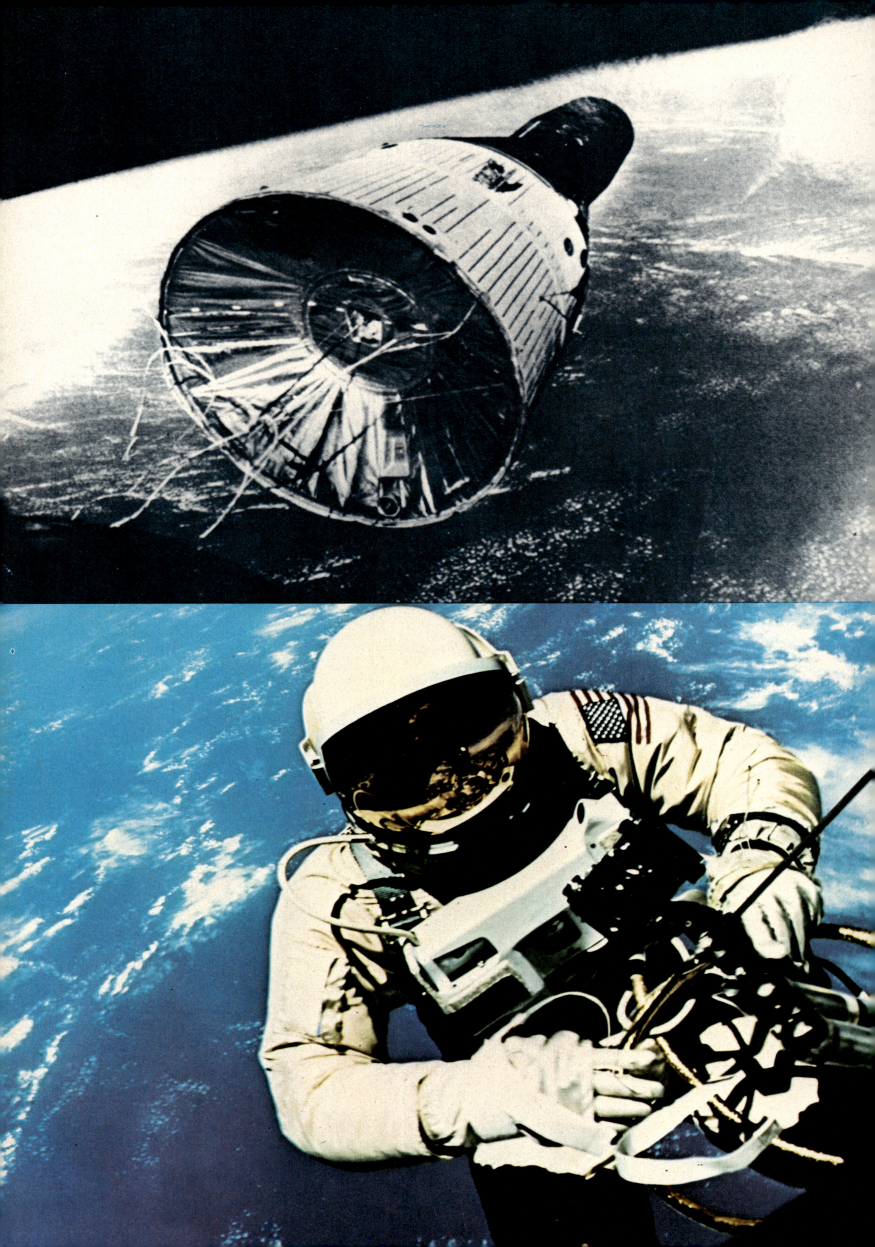

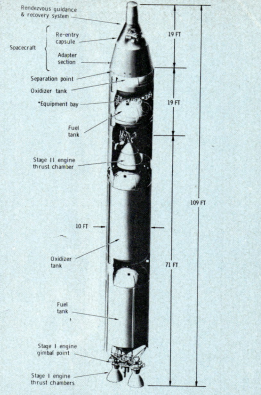

This semi-cutaway drawing shows the main elements of the Titan 2 Gemini launch vehicle

THE GEMINI SERIES*

Astronauts	Spacecraft	Launch Date	Flight Duration
Virgil Grissom/ John Young	Gemini GT-3	23 Mar 1965	4 hr 53 min
James McDivitt/ Edward White	GT-4	3 June 1965	97 hr 56 min
Gordon Cooper/ Charles Conrad	GT-5	21 Aug 1965	190 hr 56 min
Frank Borman/ James Lovell	GT-7	4 Dec 1965	330 hr 35 min
Walter Schirra/ Thomas Stafford	GT-6	15 Dec 1965	25 hr 51 min
Neil Armstrong/ David Scott	GT-8	16 Mar 1966	10 hr 42 min
Thomas Stafford/ Eugene Cernan	GT-9	3 June 1966	72 hr 21 min
John Young/ Michael Collins	GT-10	18 July 1966	70 hr 46 min
Charles Conrad/ Richard Gordon	GT-11	12 Sept 1966	71 hr 17 min
James Lovell/ Edwin Aldrin	GT-12	11 Nov 1966	94 hr 34 min

*All data used in this article are taken from *Manned Spacecraft* by K W Gatland (Blandford Press Ltd, London)

David Scott took off in pursuit in Gemini 8, and 6 hr 34 min later they had introduced the small end of Gemini into the docking collar of the Agena.

The action of docking automatically linked the propulsion system of Agena with Gemini's control system, and Armstrong had completed successfully a yaw manoeuvre using this engine when the combined vehicles began to yaw and tumble uncontrollably. Armstrong quickly separated Gemini 8 from the Agena, only to find that the trouble was a stuck valve in one of Gemini's roll thrusters.

When at length the spacecraft was brought under control, it was found that nearly 75 per cent of the re-entry system's fuel supply had been lost; and ground control immediately ordered the astronauts' return. They splashed down safely in the Pacific some 690 miles (1,110 km) south-east of Okinawa after a flight of 10 hr 42 min 6 sec instead of the planned three days.

After another Agena target was lost on 17 May 1966, an Augmented Target Docking Adapter (ATDA) was hastily improvised for experiments with Gemini 9. Although it had a docking collar there was no propulsion system, and it could not be used for power manoeuvres.

As soon as the astronauts came close to it in orbit they could see that the split nose cap had failed to jettison. The two halves hung open like the jaws of an alligator, shrouding the docking collar which Gemini was meant to engage. Although this part of the mission had to be abandoned, astronaut Cernan made a record 2 hr 9 min space-walk.

Gemini 10 brought a docking bonus in the astronauts' ability first to link with their own Agena target at 185 miles (298 km) altitude and then with the Agena of Gemini 8 which had been repositioned into a higher orbit by ground control after the curtailed mission.

Without actually docking, Gemini 10 was brought within a few feet of it and held in this position while astronaut Collins space-walked across to the target vehicle. He succeeded in removing from it a micrometeoroid detector pack which astronaut Scott had meant to retrieve before Gemini 8 ran into trouble four months earlier.

New records were set by Gemini 11, which achieved the first rendezvous within the first orbit, some 94 minutes after lift-off. After docking, Agena's restartable engine was used to boost the combined space vehicles into an elliptical orbit with a high point (apogee) of 850 miles (1,368 km). Upon returning to a lower, circular orbit, astronaut Gordon space-walked to the attached Agena to hitch a 100 ft (30.5 m) Dacron tether between the two craft. After he returned and the cabin was repressurised, the Agena was released and the two vehicles were allowed to drift around the Earth with the tether keeping them together.

As space-walkers Cernan and Gordon had shown signs of fatigue—including suit overheating and misting-up of the helmet visor—the last Gemini mission was devoted largely to clearing up outstanding problems. Again a docking was made with an Agena target, and astronaut Aldrin made a record space-walk of 2 hr 29 min 25 sec, taking care to rest after each period of work outside the spacecraft. Once again the two space vehicles were tied together with a 100 ft (30.5 m) tether. Aldrin made use of handrails on the outside of the craft, used foot restraints, and worked at a test board on which he loosened and tightened bolts and plugged and unplugged sockets.

Despite his exertions the suit did not overheat. It was the final test before America could move on with confidence to the larger effort of Project Apollo and the Moon landing.

AIR POWER IN THE MIDDLE EAST AND IN VIETNAM

The so-called periods 'between the wars' and 'after the war' have in fact hardly ever been free of national or international conflict somewhere in the world, often resulting in changes in concepts of aerial warfare. In Vietnam, where conditions do not favour use of complex supersonic aircraft, Vought's subsonic A-7 Corsair II has proved highly effective as an attack aircraft, and the jungle terrain has necessitated a widespread return to the camouflage techniques of earlier days

SINCE THE MID-1960s there have been two wars quite unlike any others in history, and both have had profound effects on the development of military aviation, on technology and on strategies.

One, the June 1967 clash between Israel and neighbouring Arab states, lasted six days. The other, in Vietnam, began in earnest in 1965, is running still and is merely the latest phase in almost 30 years of continuous warfare in the area.

The 'six-day war' was one of history's shortest and most brilliant against-the-odds campaigns. It was a conflict won entirely by the inspired use of airpower, and is the outstanding example of the pre-emptive strike—hitting the enemy so hard, so early, before he is able to bring into play his numerically superior forces, that victory is almost inevitable.

It began shortly after dawn on 5 June. In flights of four, Israeli fighter-bombers swept in very low over the Sinai desert and the Nile delta. They attacked 19 Egyptian air bases—one flight to each airfield. Lined up in serried ranks, and sometimes in revetments, was Egypt's massive Soviet-supplied air fleet—more than a hundred MiG-21s, squadrons of Tu-16 and Il-28 bombers, MiG-17, MiG-19 and Su-7 strike fighters, and hosts of transports and helicopters.

On their first strike, the Israelis ignored all these. Flying low, avoiding radar detection, catching the Egyptian anti-aircraft defences unawares and below the altitudes at which their SAM 2 missiles could be used, they flew straight down the runways after pulling up to a height of about 300 ft (90 m).

They were flying fast—about 575 mph (927 km/h)—and they dropped an entirely new type of bomb. It had to be new, for any conventional bomb dropped at this combination of speed and height would bounce and skitter to the horizon, if it did not explode on first impact and destroy the aircraft that dropped it.

These bombs were different. Developed in Israel, they had four powerful retro-rockets to slow them after separation from the aircraft. After a fraction of a second a drogue mounted in the tail deployed, slowing them further. The drag also rotated the bomb nose downwards. After an angle of 60°-80° to the horizontal was reached, four booster rockets ignited to blast the bomb downwards, into the runway, without bounce. By this time the aircraft that dropped it was safely—about four seconds—away. And then it exploded, with quite a modest bang, blowing a crater in the runway.

Two or three such craters, neatly stitched along or across a runway, rendered it useless. The Egyptian Air Force was grounded and, when the second and third waves of Israeli aircraft came in, its aircraft were sitting-duck targets for conventional rocket and cannon strafing. Literally in their hundreds they went up in flames, their columns of smoke appearing as funeral pyres against the desert sky.

Later in the day it was the turn of the Jordanian and Syrian air forces to receive

Above, top to bottom: The element of surprise, and the pin-point accuracy with which its 'concrete dibber' bombs were dropped on Egyptian runways, enabled the Israeli Air Force to achieve almost complete sovereignty of the air on the first day of the 'six-day war'. From then onwards Arab aircraft, like this burnt-out Egyptian MiG-17, were sitting-duck targets for later air strikes

Used to increasing advantage in Vietnam is the FAC (forward air control) aircraft, which acts as a pathfinder to mark strike targets and can also loiter long enough to observe the results. Aircraft like this O-2A, military counterpart of the Cessna Super Skymaster, can carry rocket pods and other ordnance to conduct light strikes of their own if necessary

Part of the US policy in South Vietnam is to build up the strength of the country's own air force—providing yet another livery for the ubiquitous Douglas C-47 to wear

Opposite page, top: Specially developed to the particular needs of the war in Vietnam, the Bell AH-1G HueyCobra was the first of the new class of helicopter 'gunships', combining a 219 mph (352 km/h) top speed with a powerful armament and a fuselage only about 4 ft (1.22 m) wide which makes it difficult for enemy gunners to hit

Centre: Part of the assembly line at Fort Worth, Texas, which up to mid-1971 had received orders for more than 1,000 HueyCobras for the US forces. The extremely slim profile is particularly evident from this angle

Bottom: One of the least cost-effective aspects of the war in Vietnam was the carpet-bombing of relatively small areas of jungle using huge B-52 Stratofortresses. Flying these eight-engined, global-range giants more than 5,000 miles (8,050 km) to a target, often to little or no effect, savoured of using the proverbial steam-hammer to crack a nut

the same treatment. Then, on the Tuesday, the nearer Iraqi bases got it. In one hammer blow, the IAF had established total air command which enabled the Israeli ground forces to achieve all their objectives—to reach the Suez Canal, conquer the Syrian Golan Heights, thrust south to Sharm el Sheik, push the Jordanians east of the River Jordan, and seize the old city of Jerusalem—all by 6 pm on Saturday, when a cease-fire was declared. The war was over, though the insoluble political situation is with us still.

The Israelis had appreciated and exploited the greatest weakness of modern jet warplanes, with their high-pressure tyres, their long field distances (lengthened still more by reduced power in high desert temperatures) and their engines' inability to withstand the ingestion of stones. The aircraft were unable to take off from the hot, sharp gravel of the Sinai, or soft delta soil, without 8,000-10,000 ft (2,440-3,050 m) of ribbon-smooth concrete beneath them. Without it they were useless—and without it, they were destroyed.

All else that followed was mere detail against this one essential strike. As an example of the Israelis' precise planning, and the accuracy of their bombing, some Egyptian runways in Sinai were bombed to a specific length. Though the strikes grounded the resident MiGs, sufficient length was left undamaged to accept Israeli transports a few days later when the bases were over-run—a requirement which was met by putting two or three craters across a jet runway about one-third of the way along it.

Other aspects of the Israelis' air war would be farcical had they not been effective. Armed Magister trainers, flown by reservists, were used in the heavy fighting for East Jerusalem. And not only by day, for by night a massive searchlight set up on a tall trade union building in the Israeli part of the city served to illuminate the adjacent Jordanian slopes for the merciless onslaught to continue.

Great confusion was caused among the airborne remnants of the Arab air forces by Arabic-speaking Israelis broadcasting on their frequencies, giving false orders, countermanding others—an extension of an RAF Bomber Command technique used over Germany in the second World War, when RAF bombers carried native German speakers for the same purpose.

As for improvisation—if you have no anti-submarine aircraft then a rear-loading transport, like the Noratlas, makes a good alternative. Load up with depth charges, fly with the rear doors open and then, if one of your naval craft radios you a suspected contact, slip the lashings, push the throttles forward, pull up the nose and over the sill they roll. . . .

* * *

For the Americans it has been not six days but more than six years of frustrating agony since their unequivocal entry into Vietnam in 1965, following nine years' involvement as numerically limited and ostensibly non-combatant 'advisers'.

For 2½ years they hammered away in a

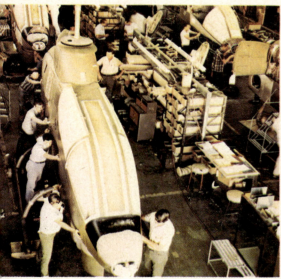

REPUBLIC F-105 THUNDERCHIEF

Powered by: One 26,500 lb (12,030 kg) st Pratt & Whitney J75-P-19W afterburning turbojet engine
Wing span: 34 ft 11¼ in (10.65 m)
Length: 67 ft 0½ in (20.43 m)
Wing area: 385 sq ft (35.77 m²)
Gross weight: 52,545 lb (23,814 kg)
Max speed: 1,485 mph (2,390 km/h) at 36,000 ft (11,000 m)
Typical combat radius: 920 miles (1,480 km)
Armament: One 20-mm General Electric Vulcan multi-barrel cannon in fuselage; more than 14,000 lb (6,350 kg) of bombs, rockets, napalm containers or drop-tanks under wings and fuselage.

Accommodation: Crew of 1
First flights: 22 October 1955 (YF-105); 9 June 1959 (F-105D)
One of the most sophisticated aircraft to be thrown into the struggle in Vietnam, the Thunderchief has been called by publicists a 'one-man air force'; to its crews it is known affectionately as the 'Thud'. Major version is the all-weather F-105D (data and silhouette), which entered USAF service in 1960; more than 600 of this model were built. In August 1969 the first example was flown of a modified F-105D, distinguishable by its 'saddleback' dorsal fairing which contains the electronics for a new T-Stick II integral bombing system; about 30 other Thunderchiefs were similarly modernised in 1970.

BELL AH-1 HUEYCOBRA

Powered by: One 1,400 shp Lycoming T53-L-13 turboshaft engine, derated to 1,100 shp
Main rotor diameter: 44 ft 0 in (13.41 m)
Fuselage length: 44 ft 5 in (13.54 m)
Main rotor disc area: 1,520.4 sq ft (141.2 m²)
Gross weight: 9,500 lb (4,309 kg)
Max speed: 219 mph (352 km/h)
Max range: 387 miles (622 km)
Armament: XM-28 'chin' turret, mounting either two 7.62-mm six-barrel Miniguns, two 40-mm grenade launchers, or one Minigun and one grenade launcher; racks under stub-wings for four rocket packs, two Minigun pods or two TOW missile pods

Accommodation: Crew of 2
First flight: 7 September 1965
Developed privately by Bell as a small, agile, well-armed 'gunship' helicopter, the HueyCobra was adopted by the US Army in 1966 and entered service in Vietnam in mid-1967 as the AH-1G. The Miniguns can carry out 'search' firing at 1,600 rounds per minute, increasing this to 4,000 rounds per minute in an attack. More than 1,000 HueyCobras have already been ordered for the US Army, and a twin-engined AH-1J SeaCobra version is being built for the US Marine Corps. The AH-1's small size and slim profile make it easy to conceal on the ground and difficult to hit in the air.

bombing offensive at North Vietnam which, in tonnage, surpassed their efforts against Germany in the second World War. They learned the impossibility of bombing a subsistence economy to a halt. They learned—at vast cost—the absurdity of risking a five-million-dollar Phantom against a five-hundred-dollar bamboo bridge. A Phantom lost was a Phantom lost, often with two valuable crewmen; a buckled bridge could be, and would be, rebuilt in a night, or at most in a week.

In their attempts to halt the southward flow of material into South Vietnam, along the winding Ho Chi Minh jungle trail, they sometimes had only trucks to hit. Often they were committing their multi-million-dollar F-4s and F-105s against 15-dollar bicycles. Cheap Chinese bikes, with special panniers to accommodate about 250 lb (113 kg) of stores were, and still are, pushed on their way south, unloaded and ridden north again along the trail. Small wonder that the Americans were reduced to desperate frustration, for how do you accomplish successful aerial interdiction against bicycles?

The bombing of North Vietnam eventually was stopped—the political odium, and the vast cost, were simply not offset by the manifest lack of success of it all. US air effort returned to 'in-country' operations— within South Vietnam's borders—and some-times in neighbouring Cambodia and Laos. Air support for ground forces was the task.

Pre-eminently, this has involved helicopters, operated (and lost) in their thousands and salvaged in their hundreds. Helicopters are the standard means of assault movement all over South Vietnam, and 'air cavalry' divisions have been formed around their own organic helicopter fleets. With the assault helicopters, themselves carrying light sideways-firing guns to return often-deadly small-arms fire from the ground, went more-heavily-armed 'gunships' to prepare the way for airborne assaults. Initially the gunships were no more than the same types of helicopter mounting more armament, including grenade launchers and rocket pods, and from them evolved the attack helicopter, designed from the start as an actual weapon platform.

The first true gunship to enter service was the AH-1 HueyCobra, which itself used the dynamic components and power plant of the established UH-1 'Huey' series, married to a new, ultra-slim, two-seat fuselage of minimal frontal area. This, combined with higher speed, made it a more difficult target for the ground-based marksman to hit than the standard wide-body troop-carrying 'choppers'. The AH-1, and similar developments using existing power, transmission and rotor systems, were intended as interim measures until the true AAFSS

(advanced airborne fire suppression system) helicopter was available. This concept, resulting in the very fast, radical Lockheed Cheyenne, has unfortunately been plagued with development troubles and, up to the autumn of 1971, had not reached operational service.

The US air role in South Vietnam is essentially that of providing airlift and firepower for troops on the ground, and hitting constantly-shifting, small targets in dense jungle country, or in rice paddy and marshland. Other simple firing platforms have been evolved to avoid committing sophisticated, supersonic jets to the fray. One was the 'Dragonship' or 'Spooky'—a ferociously-armed C-47 Dakota with three 6,000-rounds-a-minute Miniguns bristling through its port-side windows and aimed by the captain through a special left-seat sight. Similarly-armed AC-119 and AC-130 dragonship conversions followed, mounting heavier firepower for use against ground targets.

Other veteran types were in great demand as the intensity of the Vietnam war increased. The Douglas Skyraider, last operational piston-engined fighter-bomber with the USN, was valued highly for its ability to absorb tremendous anti-aircraft punishment (in marked contrast to modern jets) and still return safely home. The world was scoured for Skyraiders previously sold

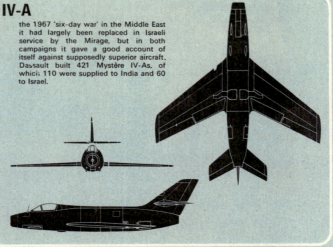

DASSAULT MYSTÈRE IV-A

Powered by: One 7,716 lb (3,500 kg) st Hispano-Suiza Verdon 350 turbojet engine
Wing span: 36 ft 5¾ in (11.12 m)
Length: 42 ft 1⅛ in (12.84 m)
Wing area: 344.4 sq ft (32.00 m²)
Gross weight: 18,700 lb (8,482 kg)
Max speed: 696 mph (1,120 km/h) at S/L
Range: 820 miles (1,320 km) with two underwing drop-tanks
Armament: Two 30-mm DEFA cannon (with 150 rpg) and pack of 55 unguided air-to-air rockets in fuselage; two 1,000-lb or four 500-lb bombs, two air-to-air or air-to-surface rocket packs or two napalm containers under the wings
Accommodation: Crew of 1
First flight: 28 September 1952
Developed from France's first production jet fighter, the straight-winged Ouragan, via the interim Mystère II-C, the Mystère IV-A entered service with the French Air Force in 1955. It first fired its guns in anger during the 1956 Suez crisis, both with French squadrons and with the Israeli Air Force, with which it was just beginning to enter service. By the time of the 1967 'six-day war' in the Middle East it had largely been replaced in Israeli service by the Mirage, but in both campaigns it gave a good account of itself against supposedly superior aircraft. Dassault built 421 Mystère IV-As, of which 110 were supplied to India and 60 to Israel.

Above left: The adage 'simplify, and add lightness' is one which the US forces have learned in Vietnam only at tremendous cost. In March 1968 six of the USAF's new swing-wing F-111A fighters arrived in Thailand; in the first week of operations two of them were lost, adding another unhappy chapter to the story of this ill-starred warplane

Top: More successful has been the 'Thud', or F-105D Thunderchief, although in general the use of such advanced and expensive aircraft has not been justified by the results achieved

Above: Code-named 'Stinger', the Fairchild Hiller AC-119K is one of two gunship versions of this large transport aircraft operating in Vietnam. It has underwing jet pods to improve performance, and carries side-firing Miniguns and equipment for night operations

or given away to other nations as part of military aid, and they were much used as escort aircraft for rescue helicopters, the exploits of which form one of the more creditable chapters in the American story in Vietnam.

The 'in-country' war has been one of ceaseless conflict against elusive, ever-moving guerilla forces, and it needs to be one of constant surveillance, or quiet reconnaissance. Much radio monitoring and fixing of Vietcong transmissions has been done by aircraft as small as O-1 Bird Dogs, skimming the matted jungle treetops with two enormous whip aerials on their wing-tips. The same type, now succeeded by the O-2 and the OV-10A, has been the mainstay of ceaseless visual searching by the USAF's skilled forward air controllers—daily roaming the jungle, highly vulnerable to small-arms fire from below—watching for signs of enemy encampments, movements and stores. When they find them, they stay close in over the target while calling in and directing air strikes against them; and they linger still—to make an assessment of the damage wrought.

The early in-country combination of tiny piston-engined O-1 and supersonic F-100 Super Sabre fighter-bomber has given way, first to lighter jet aircraft such as the F-5 and the A-37, and latterly to a new class of aircraft doing both jobs. With total air superiority the speed, the high ceiling, the complexity and cost of the modern jet fighter are not required for such action against guerilla forces, however able. So again, the attack helicopter has prospered, together with such combined FAC/attack aircraft as the twin-turboprop OV-10A. Now, after several years of project studies, there are other relatively-low-cost attack aircraft and 'bomb trucks' on the stocks to meet the USAF's AX air support requirement.

In this catch-as-catch-can war there has been much emphasis on quiet aircraft for the electronic monitoring, for 24 hours a day, of forces infiltrating over borders and along jungle paths. The quiet-aircraft programmes started from a quiet and logical point—gliders—and have resulted in trials with powered adaptations of production gliders, packed with electronics, including such sensors as 'people sniffers' which can detect the presence of human beings by sensing the exuding of sweat from quite incredible heights and distances. Climbing high and gliding for long periods with power off, or cruising under power from muffled engines fitted with 'whispering' low-speed paddle-bladed propellers, these almost silent listeners have already had some success and further developments, including unmanned drone versions, are in hand.

Conventional medium- and high-level heavy bombing has been used, too, with big formations of the USAF's B-52 strategic bombers attacking over 5,000 miles (8,050 km) from Okinawa and Guam and carpet-bombing areas of jungle designated as Vietcong war zones. Again, the measured success has been minimal in proportion to the immense cost involved.

Another costly lesson learned has been 'Operation Ranch-hand'—the systematic defoliation of jungle to deprive the enemy of cover and, incidentally, the destruction of crops when they are likely to sustain the enemy. Fairchild C-123 Providers, fitted with big tanks and spray bars, have been the instrument for this—and unenvied has been the job of the aircrew flying these bulky transports on low, slow, pre-determined paths, in neat echelon formations, immediately over jungle covering hostile forces. Happy has been the enemy gunner presented with such a target—four or five big, slow aircraft in a steady, undeviating cruise not far overhead. Even if he missed one, he was almost certain to get the one behind.

If there are lessons to be learned from the Vietnam war it is that absolute military might is no answer to determined indigenous guerillas enjoying a substantial measure of local support, when the strategic balance of the world—the balance of terror—is such that the fear of nuclear retribution prevents the exercise of that might. Heavy bombers, supersonic fighters and even clattering gunships have only a limited effect against highly-mobile, ever-moving jungle forces. And such disasters as Operation Ranch-hand, such political hot potatoes as defoliation, 'destroy and burn', free-fire zones and widespread napalm attacks, lose more international and local support than their military objectives justify.

Aviation technology can help to gain 'intelligence' in this kind of war; it is essential for mobility; and, at quite modest levels, exemplified by the gunship, it can bring into play the firepower that may, on occasions, be needed. But it can be no substitute—as, tragically, the Americans for too long thought it could—for determined, well-trained forces sweating, stalking, hitting and pacifying on the ground.

As far as the technology is concerned, Vietnam brings one back to the old adage: 'simplify, and add lightness'. One feels that it is a lesson the Israelis would have understood, instinctively, all the time.

Above: The Douglas Skyraider was on the verge of being retired from service when the Korean War broke out in 1950. Instead, it has stayed to become one of the greatest work-horses not only of that conflict but of the even more demanding war in Vietnam. This picture shows an A-1E of the USAF armed with eight 250-lb (113-kg) general-purpose bombs and four 20-mm guns

Left: American troops in Vietnam signal 'all clear' for incoming helicopters to land in a jungle clearing. These four are Bell UH-1 Iroquois, one of the most widely-used of all 'choppers' in this theatre of operations

Below left: One of the USAF's largest helicopters is the Sikorsky HH-3E. Built for the Aerospace Rescue and Recovery Service, it has armour plating, jettisonable fuel tanks, a rescue hoist and a gigantic refuelling probe

GENERAL AVIATION

THERE IS A persistent belief that the world of flying is made up almost entirely of airliners, fighters and bombers, with a sprinkling of light aircraft belonging to privileged private owners. Far from it: the majority of aircraft are engaged in branches of flying known collectively as 'general aviation', and embracing not only private ownership for pleasure, but flying in the pursuit of business; charter flying with passengers and freight; survey and mapping; the spraying and dusting of crops and the seeding and fertilisation of soil; pipeline, forestry and fishery patrol; firefighting; mineral prospecting; rescue and ambulance work; training; racing and other forms of sporting flying; press, broadcasting, advertising and exhibition flying; and even traffic control.

Activities such as these have been increasing in scale and scope since the end of the first World War; and by the 1960s some sixty per cent of all the world's aeroplanes were engaged in general aviation. True, by the early 'seventies the production of aircraft suited to these applications had been cut back somewhat by the closure of certain production facilities, and plans for a number of new and improved types had been laid aside or abandoned; but this situation was expected to be temporary. In any case, general aviation continues to grow rapidly: in five years from 1965 more than 53,000 aircraft in this category were built, and in 1970 nearly half a million people (excluding those in the USSR) held private pilot's licences.

In enumerating above some of the principal functions of aircraft in general aviation, a distinction has been made between privately-owned examples for pleasure flying and those for business use, though frequently private owners also use their cherished little aeroplanes for trips connected with their work. It is usual, however, to make some differentiation between the fields of activity known as private and executive flying, the latter category being concerned with aircraft operated or chartered by companies for the use of senior staff and key personnel.

Not surprisingly, business flying in general has been nurtured to its present high standards of efficiency and dependability, not to mention its impressive extent, in the USA, and much specialised designing and adaptation of aircraft has been done in this regard. Nevertheless, even there close affinities exist between aircraft for business and personal use, particularly in respect of the lower-priced 'utility' types. Perhaps the most outstanding of these is the Cessna 172 single-engined high-wing monoplane, normally seating four. This model was first marketed in 1955, and by 1968 over 14,000 had been sold. Of these 58 per cent were for personal or business use; 16 per cent were owned by companies primarily for business

Above: Trout fishing—the modern way. Pictures such as this emphasise how the aeroplane can contribute to man's enjoyment of his leisure hours. This group is making the most of a fishing trip in the delightful setting of Lake Mavora, New Zealand

Left: Delivery line of one of the most successful types of business jet, the Hawker Siddeley 125. Having sold more than 200 on its own account, Hawker Siddeley now has a sales partnership with Beech Aircraft Corporation in the US, where the aircraft is marketed as the Beechcraft Hawker 125

Opposite page: New Zealand is also the setting for this Cessna 150, baby of the Cessna range of lightplanes and ideal for learning to fly as well as for joy-riding

GRUMMAN AG-CAT

Powered by: One 220 hp Continental R-670-4 seven-cylinder radial engine, driving a two-blade propeller
Wing span: 35 ft 11 in (10.95 m)
Length: 24 ft 4 in (7.42 m)
Wing area: 328.0 sq ft (30.47 m²)
Gross weight: 3,600 lb (1,633 kg)
Working speed: 75-85 mph (121-137 km/h)
Range: 300 miles (483 km) with 1,420 lb (644 kg) payload
Accommodation: Crew of 1
First flight: 22 May 1957

As its name implies, the Ag-Cat was designed primarily for agricultural work, for which its biplane layout gives it ideal slow-flying characteristics. It was certificated for such work in January 1959; by the end of 1967 Ag-Cats in more than 20 countries had flown some 1½ million hours without a single fatal accident, and well over 500 have been built. The original Ag-Cat has appeared with a variety of engines ranging from 220-275 hp; from the 401st aircraft there appeared the Super Ag-Cat, with engines ranging up to 600 hp and corresponding increases in payload and operating weights. Since 1962 the aircraft has also been cleared for operation on patrol and survey duties.

Top left: Combining the grace of a sailplane with the basic reliability and economy of the Volkswagen engine, the Sportavia/Fournier RF4D (background) can give up to 3¾ hours of flying on only 8.4 gallons (38 litres) of fuel. The RF5, nearest the camera, is slightly larger, has a 63 hp engine, and can carry two persons for up to 4 hours

Top right: Aircraft are an essential form of communication in large, lightly-populated areas. In Australia, most large sheep and cattle stations, like this one in Queensland, have their own airstrip and depend on aviation to provide a link with the nearest townships

Above: Japan is fast becoming one of the world's major producers of light utility and club aircraft. Fuji, present-day successor to the famous Nakajima company, employs more than 3,200 persons in its aircraft factory at Utsunomiya City, where one of the chief products is the four-seat FA-200 Aero Subaru. Production of this aircraft was running at eight per month in 1971

Above: Training, club flying, agricultural work, glider towing or ambulance duty—all come easily to the Rallye series, originated by the famous Morane-Saulnier company and still in production by the Socata division of Aérospatiale

Above right: Developed from the Colonial Skimmer of 1946, the four-seat Lake LA-4 is an improved version still in production a quarter of a century later. Equipment and performance belie its somewhat utilitarian lines, and it has a gross take-off weight of only 2,400 lb (1,089 kg) with four people on board

Right: Large tyres and a wide-track landing gear simplify grass-field and cross-wind landings with the Beechcraft Musketeer, one of this manufacturer's most popular 'singles'

purposes ('corporate flying', as it is widely known in the USA); 14 per cent were engaged in training; 6 per cent were classed as air taxis, or engaged in charter flying; and one per cent were modified for special applications, notably agricultural work.

The types of aeroplane now available off-the-shelf for private and executive flying are far too numerous to identify individually. They are classed in general as 'light' aircraft, weighing in flying trim from well under 1,000 lb (454 kg) to some 6,000 lb (2,720 kg). Smallest and lightest are the single-seaters and two-seaters, including home-builts. Commercially available are such types as the American Aviation Yankee; the Swedish Andreasson; the Anglo-French Rollasons; and the German (formerly French) Sportavia/Fournier powered sailplanes of a mere 40 hp. Far more prolific and versatile are models having up to four seats, and powered in the 100-150 hp range, notably the smaller members of the Beechcraft Musketeer range (together with Cessna and Piper this US manufacturer builds the majority of aircraft sold for general-aviation purposes); three Bellancas; the same number of Cessnas; the Australasian Airtourers—also sold in the UK; three of the German Messerschmitt-Bölkow-Blohm range; a pair of Pipers; French Robins (fittingly named after their manufacturer); the Anglo-French Rollason Condor; two French Socatas; two Italian

SIAI-Marchettis; a Fuji from Japan; and, to round out the range, the American Thurston Teal, an amphibian seating two side-by-side, having a flying-boat hull and retractable undercarriage, and with its engine mounted above the cabin.

Prominent among types seating up to five, and having from 150 to 210 hp available, are the principal Beechcraft Musketeers; more of the immensely popular Cessnas; another amphibian, in this instance made by the American Lake company and seating four; the attractive little Aerostar Ranger and Executive; two more Pipers and three more Robins, additional to other French types by Socata and Wassmer and four more SIAI-Marchettis. One step further up the size and cost scale are the types seating up to six and having from 210 to 300 hp— a most impressive proliferation of Beech-crafts, Cessnas and Pipers, having names as colourful as their 'paint jobs'; the Helio Courier and Super Courier, remarkable for their short take-off and landing runs; three more SIAI-Marchettis, and a pair of Wassmers.

At length we arrive at the swift and luxurious twin-engined models, for the more affluent private owners and the more demanding business companies: the Beech-craft Barons; Cessna Super Skymaster, 310Q and Turbo-system 310Q; Helio Twin Couriers and Piper Twin Comanche C, Aztec E and Turbo Aztec E. (These types mark the transition from the predominantly-

personal to the predominantly-executive class; they also afford an opportunity to explain that the word 'turbo' denotes not turboprops, turbojets or turbofans but turbocharged piston-engines, for improved high-altitude performance).

The more sophisticated forms of power plant are reserved for the largest and most luxurious commercially-available types: Britain's turboprop Jetstream and turbojet Hawker Siddeley 125; America's turboprop Beechcraft King Air and Swearingen Merlin, and the faster turbojet- or turbofan-powered Cessna Citation, Grumman Gulf-stream II, Gates Learjet, Lockheed JetStar and North American Rockwell Sabreliner, together with Italy's Piaggio-Douglas PD-808 and France's Aérospatiale Corvette and Dassault Mystère/Falcon 10 and 20. Yet in this same category gas-turbine power by no means dominates, as witness the success of the North American Rockwell piston-engined Commanders and the sleek Beechcraft Queen Air and Duke.

Such a list of currently-available private and business aircraft at least begins to dispel the impression, noted at the outset, that airliners and military types are pre-eminent in the aeronautical scene; yet the picture is by no means complete; for air-liners and bombers, new and old, have been converted for business use, while a great number of commercially-obsolete light aircraft remain in private hands, and will long continue to do so, such is the

Above: The promise that was never fulfilled. British Executive and General Aviation Ltd (Beagle) was created for the purpose of fostering light and general aviation in the UK. To follow its Husky and Airedale, which were single-engined Auster developments, it produced the twin-engined B.206 to compete with comparable American twins; but, though the quality was there, the price was far from competitive and commercial sales were poor. As a result, Beagle went out of business in 1970, just as sales of the single-engined Pup and Bulldog military trainer seemed likely to give the company its first major success

Left: Meanwhile, the American giants of general aviation continue to offer a huge range of models. Cessna's 401A, seen here, is a six/eight-seat executive transport, offering twin-engined safety, nine different interior layouts and a wide range of equipment and 'trimmings' at a competitive price

Below left: The Piper Aztec, which appeared in 1959, was developed from Piper's first business twin, the Apache. Successive improvements in furnishing, power plant and other features have ensured that it is still one of the leaders in its class

Opposite page, top· At the upper end of the 'biz-jet' price range is North American Rockwell's six/ten-seat Sabreliner, produced originally to meet a military requirement and now available in three commercial versions

Bottom: Only four-engined executive jet in current production, Lockheed's JetStar was powered originally by Bristol Siddeley Orpheus engines, but those in service have an all-American power plant

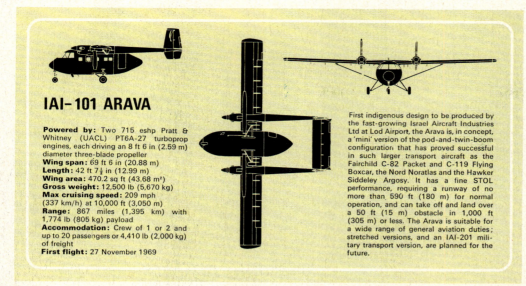

IAI-101 ARAVA

Powered by: Two 715 eshp Pratt & Whitney (UACL) PT6A-27 turboprop engines, each driving an 8 ft 6 in (2.59 m) diameter three-blade propeller
Wing span: 69 ft 6 in (20.88 m)
Length: 42 ft 7½ in (12.99 m)
Wing area: 470.2 sq ft (43.68 m²)
Gross weight: 12,500 lb (5,670 kg)
Max cruising speed: 209 mph (337 km/h) at 10,000 ft (3,050 m)
Range: 867 miles (1,395 km) with 1,774 lb (805 kg) payload
Accommodation: Crew of 1 or 2 and up to 20 passengers or 4,410 lb (2,000 kg) of freight
First flight: 27 November 1969

First indigenous design to be produced by the fast-growing Israel Aircraft Industries Ltd at Lod Airport, the Arava is, in concept, a 'mini' version of the pod-and-twin-boom configuration that has proved successful in such larger transport aircraft as the Fairchild C-82 Packet and C-119 Flying Boxcar, the Nord Noratlas and the Hawker Siddeley Argosy. It has a fine STOL performance, requiring a runway of no more than 590 ft (180 m) for normal operation, and can take off and land over a 50 ft (15 m) obstacle in 1,000 ft (305 m) or less. The Arava is suitable for a wide range of general aviation duties; stretched versions, and an IAI-201 military transport version, are planned for the future.

affection in which they are held. In the late 'sixties, before the recession mentioned earlier had taken effect, it was stated that America's fleet of aircraft engaged in all forms of general aviation embraced over 300 makes and models: and whereas the airliner fleet numbered rather more than 3,000, general aviation in 1970 accounted for some *one hundred and sixty-six thousand* active aircraft. Of these, 141,000 were single-engined, 19,000 were piston-engined twins and 4,000 were helicopters.

The pleasures of private ownership (not forgetting that in North America seaplane flying adds greatly to the joy), and the convenience and comfort afforded by executive flying, need hardly be stressed again here; though the point may be made that business today is not merely facilitated by, but actually conducted during the course of, air travel. Nor is it the executive aircraft alone which serve the businessman where the bigger airlines fail, for commuter flying, increasingly using new and specialised eye-catching (and fare-catching) types such as the Beechcraft 99A Airliner, is making its own expanding contribution to the sociological benefits of air travel. Charter flying and air-taxi operations are supplemented by diversifying air freight operations, similarly demanding, and receiving, specialised aircraft as well as adaptations of older types. Contrasting examples—both with significant contributions to make to general aviation—are the little Short Skyvan, designed specifically for its task, and one of the most astonishing aeronautical adaptations of all time, the Aero Spacelines Guppy. It is gratifying to observe that, although developed initially for the transport of missile components, the Guppy is finding an application also in transferring to the assembly point similarly large components for airliners. Surprisingly, no new types have yet emerged to replace the Carvair or Bristol Freighter in the aerial car ferry role.

With continuing expansion and diversification, the manifold problems of crowded airspace mount formidably as aircraft of every description make their particular demands. Yet numerous types engaged in general aviation find employment over tranquil lands, though in the case of agricultural flying occupational hazards are by no means absent. This class of flying, and others allied with it in sustaining and enriching the peoples of the world, dates from the period immediately following the first World War, initially in respect of forestry protection, next in the patrolling of shoals of fish.

Experiments in the dusting of crops with chemical preparations began in 1921-22 at the Ohio Agricultural Experimental Station, using war-surplus Curtiss 'Jennies', and by about 1925 a fleet of specially-constructed crop-dusting aircraft was applying calcium arsenate for boll weevil control in Louisiana and neighbouring states. In the interests of economy many aircraft used today in agricultural applications (often by farmers themselves) are adaptations of standard types, though highly-original specialised types exist, and the Agrinautics company in the USA has even adapted the ubiquitous Douglas Dakota to take one of its many 'aerial dispersal systems'.

The mapping of large regions of the Earth's surface is a continuing task for the aeroplane, using special photographic equipment, while the camera finds expanding applications in the service of industry, broadcasting and the press. Prospecting for minerals makes its own invaluable contribution to economic growth, and, sometimes following upon this activity, the aeroplane is called upon in the service of the civil engineer. The world's great oil companies are, perhaps, the most ardent advocates and users of air transport, and the helicopter is today regarded as an inseparable companion to the multiplying off-shore oil rigs. Rotary-wing aircraft, indeed, have already brought new dimensions to civil operations, and not least in alleviating suffering and need, while expanding applications of fixed-wing aircraft, as exemplified by the water-bombing of forest fires, sustain the hope for ever-increasing utilisation of aircraft in the service of society.

This page: The term 'general aviation' includes working aircraft of all kinds, as well as those used for pleasure or corporate flying

Top: Perhaps the most exciting combination of work and play is the performance of aerobatic display teams in many parts of the world. This picture shows one of the Stampe biplanes which make up the Rothmans team

Above: The Agusta-Bell 206A JetRanger is one of many types of helicopter used by police and other agencies for highway patrol and similar duties

Right: A steadily-increasing job, tailored perfectly to the capabilities of the helicopter, is that of providing communications and supply links with the many offshore oil drilling rigs that have sprung up in recent years

Right: A display aircraft of a rather different kind: this Rapide is used by members of the Free Fall Club of the Army's Parachute Regiment

Below right: Fire control in heavily-forested areas being demonstrated by a Canadair CL-215 water-bomber, an aircraft specially designed for this extremely important task

Bottom of page: This Twin Pioneer operated 'scheduled' services for an oil company for several years in the mid-'sixties, its STOL performance enabling it to use 400-yard (365 m) landing strips in the area of the Niger Delta

Unique as the only high-wing member of Piper's current huge family of lightplanes, the PA-18 Super Cub has been flying since 1949 in a variety of steadily-improved forms, and in the early 'seventies was still being built at the rate of one every two days. This typical scene shows a PA-18S seaplane version at rest on the Uganik River on Kodiak Island, southern Alaska

LIGHTPLANES
BY THE THOUSAND

Avions Pierre Robin has been one of Europe's most consistently successful lightplane manufacturers since 1957. Known originally as Centre Est Aéronautique, it employs fewer than 100 people in its small works at Dijon yet produces about 150 aircraft a year, of seven different types. Until recently all were based on Jodel designs and made of wood. The four/five-seat DR 253 Regent, illustrated on this page, was the first Robin type to switch from tail-wheel to tricycle landing gear in 1967. Two years later the first all-metal Robin HR 100 flew for the first time, marking the next stage in the company's progress

'LIGHTPLANES BY THE THOUSAND' is a reality today, despite the 'softening trend' of worldwide economy. Fourteen thousand and eight general-aviation aircraft were built in the United States in 1969; 13,400 were listed in an FAA forecast for 1970, and an annual production total of 30,800 aircraft by 1980 is predicted for the United States alone.

In mid-1971, the writer* visited Wichita, Kansas, the heart of the lightplane industry in America, where Cessna and Beechcraft between them produce more aircraft than anyone else. After the heavy redundancies of recent years, both factories were re-hiring 'furloughed' employees—and one production test pilot was working as a local bellhop in the faith that 'things are on the upswing and I don't want to move out of the area'.

During this visit to Wichita, Cessna alone had rehired 400 employees within a month and more jobs were anticipated.

Perhaps the most significant sign of that upswing was the near-zero inventory of general aviation aircraft awaiting customers. It was only with the greatest good fortune that we were able to find a Cessna Aerobat needing delivery to the west coast.

Much of the success in general aviation production has come from economies in manufacture. Cessna, for example, points out that 'savings in time occur most frequently through tooling improvement and machine application. The production of 3,000 Model 150s in 1966 was made possible largely through these two factors'.

Other factors resulting in time savings, according to Cessna's production specialists, 'include the use of new materials like ABS sheet stock. This is a plastic material which comes in various thicknesses and can be shaped — most commonly by vacuum-forming—to conform to a variety of uses. You'll find it in such areas as throttle/fuel-selector centre consoles, window mouldings, instrument panel covers, glove-box doors, back-of-the-seat magazine pockets, etc. The material is virtually unaffected by temperature and is highly resistant to warping; it is pre-textured and colour-fast. It is able to be formed smoothly into very complex bends, instead of corrugating as aluminium sometimes does.'

Cessna uses matched dies for glass-fibre nose-caps, in place of the former method of painstakingly applying layer after layer of material.

Rolled aluminium sheet is used rather than the older 4 x 12 ft (1.2 x 3.7 m) sheets. By buying the aluminium coiled, there is virtually no end (you can get it as long as you want) and no 'cutback' worry after you've cut your part. It is less expensive from the mill and easier to handle.

Some manufacturers are abandoning

*American pilot-journalist Don Downie.

Above, top to bottom:
No company in the world has built more aeroplanes than Cessna, which delivered its 95,000th machine in December 1970. Of these, 80,863 had been single-engined. Production at Wichita is supplemented by licence manufacture in Europe, by Reims Aviation, who sold this FR-172F Reims Rocket to a Spanish club

There is considerable commonality of components between the high-wing monoplanes of the Cessna range, which cuts costs. This four-seater is an Austrian-registered Model 182H with 230 hp Continental engine. The Model 172 is very similar, but has a 150 hp engine. The Skylane and Skyhawk are de luxe versions of the 182 and 172 respectively

When the Model 177 appeared in 1967, it broke tradition by having a cantilever wing instead of the familiar strut-bracing. It is a four-seater with a 180 hp Lycoming engine. This one was photographed at Bankstown, Australia

Another Cessna pace-setter was the Model 336 Skymaster, a 4/6-seat light twin with a 'push-and-pull' engine layout which avoided asymmetrical handling problems for the pilot if he suffered an engine failure in flight. This Super Skymaster, registered in Tanzania, is an improved Model 337 with retractable landing gear and an under-fuselage cargo pack for 300 lb (136 kg) of baggage or freight

Right: This photograph, taken a few years ago, is the kind that must fill European manufacturers with envy and dismay. It shows just part of the parking area for new lightplanes straight off the assembly lines at Cessna's Wichita plant

During 1970, which was a rather poor 'recession' year for the aircraft industry, Cessna still managed to sell 3,730 aircraft. This picture shows some of them awaiting collection from the company's Commercial Delivery Centre

Baby of the current Cessna range is the Model 150, introduced in 1958 when Cessna decided to re-enter the two-seat market. The wisdom of the move is reflected in the fact that sales totalled 15,189 by the end of 1970

glass-fibre for the new ABS sheet stock, which is used by Cessna, for example, for wheel fairings, wingtips, tailplane and elevator tips and seat backs. Approximately 12 per cent of the parts of a Cessna are now made with some kind of plastic rather than aluminium.

Riveting is also on the decline, for metal-bonding techniques are increasing in use, both in Wichita and other parts of the USA.

Beechcraft has embarked on a dual programme of 'commonality' and 'value engineering' to keep costs from joining other inflationary trends. The commonality concept has cut the number of parts on three Beechcraft Baron models and three versions of the Bonanza from 195 to 65; the number of tools required has been reduced from 379 to 194, the number of full assemblies from 7 to 3, and the number of sub-assemblies from 64 to 18. This reduction was accomplished on wing-spar assembly, where spin-off economies included reductions in inventory, records and tooling.

Piper, America's other lightplane 'giant', reports that at least 90 non-metallic components, primarily thermoplastics and glass-fibre, can be found on each of its 18 production models. The largest single part produced by Piper's glass-fibre operation is the chemical hopper for the Pawnee agricultural aircraft; the smallest is an electric trim-tab button.

Thermoplastic parts include interior trim, panel knobs, air vents and cable guides. The entire instrument panel and windows are fabricated from plastics at Piper.

North American Rockwell's new four-seat Model 112, undergoing FAA certification flights in 1971, stresses a 'technology transfer of design, engineering, tooling, jigging and production skills from North American's "brain bank",' according to Richard N Robinson, President of the company's General Aviation Division.

'Unique circumstances allowed our technology team to move up, from lightplanes as a career starter through exotic research aircraft such as the XB-70 and X-15, into the missile age and Moon landings, Now, as such projects recede, these leaders in aerospace advancement can move back to lightplanes. . . . This cycle in the development of general aviation advancement will probably never be repeated. . . .'

The new Aero Commander 112 has reduced the basic number of parts by use of beaded wing skins. The wing panel aft of the single spar, for example, has only four ribs: one on each side of the walkway, one at the outboard end of the flap and one at the tip rib. Skins on the aft fuselage and tail-cone come all the way up to join at the top. A long dorsal fin along the top seam is a structural member, in addition to housing the cabin air intake so that the airflow is quietened before reaching the

Top: Another of America's 'big three' of the lightplane industry is Piper. Its number-one profit-maker is the Cherokee, which comes in a wide range of models with various engines, seating arrangements and landing gears. This photograph shows some of the plastic and glass-fibre components that go into every Cherokee

Above: To provide a low-cost two-seat trainer for their 400 Flite Centres, Piper introduced early in 1971 a simplified version of the Cherokee 140 known as the Flite Liner. Like all Cherokees, it is manufactured at Vero Beach, Florida, where the Dodgers baseball team have their training camp—and their private Boeing 707

Right: Next size up from the 140 is the Cherokee 180, a full four-seater with a 180 hp Lycoming engine and plenty of room for luggage on holiday or business trips

Below: All over the USA, hotel keepers and owners of 'dude' ranches maintain landing strips where week-enders can drop in, at minimum cost in travelling time

Bottom left: World's largest turntable, in the Piper plant at Vero Beach, positions Cherokees rapidly for transfer to one of three paint rooms. The turntable can carry nine Cherokees and makes a complete turn in 4½ minutes. It has cut total finishing time from 2½ days to 6 hours

Bottom right: One of the most famous Pipers is G-ATOY, the Comanche 260 used by Sheila Scott for many of her record-breaking flights to all corners of the world

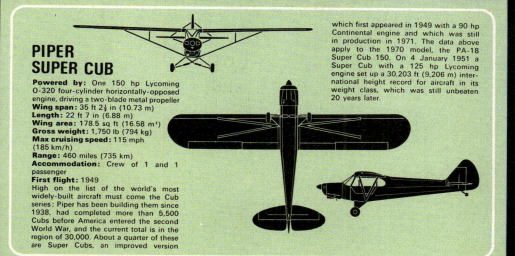

PIPER SUPER CUB

Powered by: One 150 hp Lycoming O-320 four-cylinder horizontally-opposed engine, driving a two-blade metal propeller
Wing span: 35 ft 2½ in (10.73 m)
Length: 22 ft 7 in (6.88 m)
Wing area: 178.5 sq ft (16.58 m²)
Gross weight: 1,750 lb (794 kg)
Max cruising speed: 115 mph (185 km/h)
Range: 460 miles (735 km)
Accommodation: Crew of 1 and 1 passenger
First flight: 1949

which first appeared in 1949 with a 90 hp Continental engine and which was still in production in 1971. The data above apply to the 1970 model, the PA-18 Super Cub 150. On 4 January 1951 a Super Cub with a 125 hp Lycoming engine set up a 30,203 ft (9,206 m) international height record for aircraft in its weight class, which was still unbeaten 20 years later.

High on the list of the world's most widely-built aircraft must come the Cub series: Piper has been building them since 1938, had completed more than 5,500 Cubs before America entered the second World War, and the current total is in the region of 30,000. About a quarter of these are Super Cubs, an improved version

Above: Cessna and Piper both do good business in marketing agricultural aircraft; so do North American Rockwell, who bought up the former Snow and IMCO companies and their ag-planes. The Quail Commander, ferried here by Don Downie, author of this article, is a North American Rockwell product with 290 hp Lycoming engine and 1,600 lb (726 kg) chemical payload

Opposite page, top right: A low-altitude 'beat-up' of the airstrip before leaving for home with a new Quail Commander presents no hazards. Agricultural aircraft spend most of their life just above the ground and are designed to give the pilot the best possible all-round view

Below: No better proof of the sturdy reliability of modern lightplanes is possible than the round-the-world flight made by Cliff Tait in this New Zealand-built two-seat Airtourer. It was the smallest aircraft ever to complete such a circumnavigation

Below right: Despite the name 'Waco Minerva 220' painted on its cowling, this little four-seater is a variant of the French Socata Rallye Commodore. Assembled for a time in the USA, the Minerva has a 220 hp Franklin engine instead of the more usual Lycoming or Rolls-Royce/Continental power plants of other Rallyes

PZL-104 WILGA 35

Powered by: One 260 hp Ivchenko AI-14R nine-cylinder radial engine, driving an 8 ft 8 in (2.65 m) diameter two-blade wooden propeller
Wing span: 36 ft 4¾ in (11.14 m)
Length: 26 ft 6¾ in (8.10 m)
Wing area: 166.8 sq ft (15.50 m²)
Gross weight: 2,711 lb (1,230 kg)
Max cruising speed: 120 mph (193 km/h)
Max range: 410 miles (660 km)
Accommodation: Crew of 1 and up to 3 passengers
First flights: 24 April 1962 (Wilga 1 prototype) ; 28 July 1967 (Wilga 35)
The state-owned aircraft industries of eastern European countries have, in the past quarter of a century, been noted for a range of maid-of-all-work, general-utility aircraft, such as the L-60 Brigadyr from Czechoslovakia and the PZL-101A Gawron and PZL-104 Wilga (thrush) from Poland. The later of the two Polish designs has been built in considerable numbers since the early 1960s, and is used for passenger- or light cargo-carrying, ambulance, glider-towing, flying-club, liaison, paratroop training and many other duties. The roomy 4-seat cabin offers a good all-round view, high-lift devices on the wings give an excellent STOL performance, and wheel, ski or float landing gear can be fitted. The latest versions have automatic wing leading-edge slats, an all-moving tailplane and a detachable under-fuselage cargo container.

cabin. The rear cabin bulkhead is recessed for hanging clothes, and has an opening so that long items—skis, fishing rods and the like—can extend into the tail-cone.

The design of the 112 was 'frozen' for production, with the first five aircraft built from production parts to accelerate both FAA certification and service testing.

Another pace-setter in the USA is veteran lightplane designer John Thorp of Burbank, California, who assembled his first design in 1933 and has been in the business ever since. He designed the 'Little Dipper' for Lockheed as 'every-infantryman's airplane' during the second World War, and certificated and produced his two-place 'Sky Skooter' before surplus military aircraft became available and caused a slump in lightplane production. Thorp was the preliminary designer of the outstandingly successful Piper Cherokee series, and has been consulting engineer for many other modern lightplanes.

Thorp feels that some strides can be made in 'design integration' by getting one part to do a number of jobs. He quotes the transmission system of Henry Ford's old Model T car as a classic example of one assembly which served as a transmission, clutch, brake and for other functions. He points out that substantial savings can be made by keeping the total number of parts as low as possible, since it takes almost as many man-hours to build a small part as it does a big one.

Breakthroughs can be expected in power plants, according to Thorp. He looks at the new two-cylinder 60-hp Franklin used on the reborn Aeronca Champ as being only 60 per cent as complex as a similar four-cylinder engine. One of Thorp's early flight experiences involved a two-cylinder Aeronca C-3 'bathtub' that began to run rough over Lake Merritt near Oakland, California. When he looked out to see one spark-plug lead dangling in the slipstream, he was faced with the option of landing in the lake or reaching out and taking the electrical shocks while he re-installed the lead. (A pilot could reach the engine on the C-3.) He took the shocks and re-installed the plug lead.

Thorp sees a future in the ever-expanding line of Volkswagen engines, now from 1,000 to 2,187 cc, as relatively inexpensive power plants for light aircraft. 'Making a double ignition out of the VW isn't difficult once you make up your mind you have to do it,' comments Thorp, who believes that the FAA is probably correct in requiring twin ignition on factory-built aircraft. 'A four-cylinder engine running on three

doesn't give you much power to work with'.

Thorp emphasises that airframe refinements are not the key to lower-cost aircraft, since the airframe itself is only 12 per cent of the total selling price of an aeroplane. A 1969 NASA report listed the following breakdown:

Dealer mark-up	25 %
Engine	14 %
Hardware and instruments	10 %
Burden, including engineering, taxes, etc	29.5 %
Manufacturing mark-up	6.8 %
Raw materials ($4\frac{1}{2}$%) and direct airframe labour (8%)	12.5 %
Flight line delivery cost	2.3 %
	100.0 %

'This has been the basic fallacy of my life,' explains Thorp. 'I've been working on the $12\frac{1}{2}$ per cent and not doing anything about the really important percentages. When a complete wing panel costs $500, an engine costs $3,500 and electronics can go to $10,000, everything is out of perspective'.

Thorp predicts that existing aircraft will remain more or less as they are now. 'We've had the Bonanza for 24 years and we'll probably have it for another 24. However,

the next big step forward will be the avail-ability of cheap, simple fan-jet engines. We already have such power plants flying in target drones. I have a design on my drawing-board for a four-passenger twin-fanjet that will cruise at 300 mph (483 km/h) on 60 US gallons (227 litres) of jet fuel. It would be no more difficult to fly than a Bonanza. With these new power plants, we'll have a completely new ball game'.

When you're producing lightplanes by the thousand, deliveries become some-thing of a chore. At the end of the second World War the first J-3 Cubs, Aeroncas and Taylorcrafts were delivered by railroad and assembled at local airports. Ferry flights soon became popular, and now everything except some single-engined overseas deliveries are FAF (Fly Away Factory). Most pilots on these ferry flights are airline engineers or co-pilots, who get free or low-cost one-way travel and can thus show a small profit on each delivery.

However, more and more new owners go to the factory to pick up their own air-craft, particularly those who purchase larger, faster equipment. The ferry services usually deliver the slower trainers.

In the course of many years of aviation reporting, the writer has had the oppor-tunity to ferry more than the normal share of new aircraft from factories in the mid-west and east coast to southern California. There have been some 20 Cessnas of various ages, shapes and sizes. Piper has released nearly a dozen, ranging all the way from a J-3 Cub (40 flying hours in 5 days!) to an Aztec twin. There were a Quail Commander from Albany, Georgia, and two Citabrias from Osceola, Minnesota. Even as this report was being printed, he was scheduled to bring out the first production 60-hp 'cheap Champ' that has a list price of $4,995 without accessories.

Most ferry flights are made without radios, since each flying school wants to keep the radios it has. So it's strictly VFR (Visual Flight Rules) down the highway for a wonderful view of the United States. Once you programme your mind to the mile-and-a-half-a-minute for ground speed against headwinds, you can relax and enjoy it.

After several of these cross-country delivery flights, you find that, for the private flyer, there's still plenty of unused airspace just 'over the hill' from every busy metrop-olis; in town, it's another story.

ANDREI NIKO

Above: Andrei Tupolev's ANT-25, which had just failed to set a new distance record at its first attempt, dominated the Russian stand at the 1936 Paris Air Show. Beneath its red-painted wings in this picture stand the 10-seat ANT-35 transport and Polikarpov's prototype TsKB-19 (I-17) fighter

Left, top to bottom:
The three-seat ANT-2 of 1923 derived its 'Junkers' appearance from its skin of Kolchugalumin corrugated light alloy

Used by the Soviet air force for reconnaissance, the two-seat ANT-3 was the first production aeroplane designed by Tupolev at TsAGI

Proof of the growing capability of Russia's industry was given in 1934 when more than 250 TB-3 (ANT-6) four-engined bombers of this type flew over Red Square on May Day

An ANT-9 (three 365 hp Wright Whirlwinds) of the pre-war Soviet-German airline Deruluft. Most of the 70 or so aircraft of similar type used by Dobrolet and Aeroflot were twin-engined, with 680 hp M-17s

Largest landplane of its day was the eight-engined ANT-20 *Maxim Gorki*

ANDREI NIKOLAEVICH TUPOLEV has been well described as the 'Father of Soviet Aviation', for his career is virtually a summary of Soviet aviation history, from his first aircraft completed in 1923 to the world's first supersonic transport aircraft, which flew in December 1968. It also epitomises the Russian predilection for giant aircraft, no fewer than four of the world's largest landplanes having been designed by Tupolev or a team under his direction.

Born in 1888, A N Tupolev was an early pupil, at the Moscow Technical High School, of the internationally famous aerodynamicist, Professor N E Zhukovski. His studies and early gliding experiments were, however, interrupted in 1911 when he was arrested for revolutionary activities. During part of the first World War, Tupolev worked in the Duks aircraft factory in Moscow, then the largest in Russia.

After the Bolshevik Revolution, Tupolev became one of Zhukovski's leading assistants in setting up the Central Aero- and Hydro-dynamics Institute (TsAGI). This brought together pre-war Russian research establishments with other, newly-created bodies, and in 1920 Tupolev became head of its design department (AGO).

Before the first World War Russia was deficient in high-quality metals; home production of aluminium and duralumin did not start until 1922, and not until the end of 1931 did a type of chrome molybdenum appear.

In 1920, Tupolev was appointed chairman of a committee set up to evolve all-

LAEVICH TUPOLEV

metal aircraft. In his dual capacities as committee chairman and head of AGO, he designed the first such aircraft to be built in Russia.

The ANT-2, completed in 1923, was a single-engined, three-seat monoplane, with cabin accommodation for two passengers. It had a thick multi-spar wing, triangular-section fuselage and thin corrugated-duralumin covering, called Kolchugalumin after the village where it was produced. The overall design was not unlike that of the Junkers K 16 of 1922, and indeed a close study of Junkers design and practice had been made at TsAGI since the first Junkers C.I was captured during the civil war. Negotiations by the new Soviet government for the production of Junkers aircraft in Russia were started in 1919; they resulted in German production in Russia of the A 20, H 21 and H 22 single-engined military aircraft between 1923-25, and assembly of the F 13 transport from German-manufactured parts.

Other experimental craft produced under Tupolev's supervision at that time, to try out the new metal, were the ANT-III aerosleigh and ANT-1 hydroplane boat.

The first production aircraft designed and built by Tupolev at TsAGI was the ANT-3 two-seat biplane, which made propaganda flights abroad in 1926 and 1927 and was used by the air force for reconnaissance until about 1932.

Design work on Tupolev's first large aircraft, the twin-engined ANT-4, began before the first flight of the ANT-3. It owed

much to the three-engined Junkers G 23 transport, and was built on the second floor of a former Moscow merchant's house which formed part of the TsAGI premises. The walls had to be knocked down and the components taken to the Central Aerodrome for assembly before the seven-minute first flight on 26 November 1925.

In its production form, as the TB-1 heavy bomber, the ANT-4 was armed with three pairs of 7.62-mm DA machine-guns, in the nose and two dorsal positions. Two hundred and sixteen were produced at the former Junkers concessionary factory at Fili, Moscow, which had been taken over by the Soviet authorities in July 1926. In 1929 an unarmed ANT-4, named *Strana Sovetov* and registered URSS-300, flew from Moscow to New York via Siberia and the west coast of the USA.

The TB-1 was used for a number of duties (torpedo-bomber, freight-plane) and experiments (in-flight refuelling, rocket-assisted take-off), and was the first Tupolev component of the 'Zveno' series of composite aircraft, devised by V S Vakhmistrov at the Soviet equivalent of Britain's Boscombe Down to extend the radius of action of fighter aircraft. Two I-4 (ANT-5) single-seat fighters were to be carried into action on the wings of a TB-1 motherplane. The Zveno-1, as it was known, was first—and successfully—tested on 3 December 1931.

The TB-1 was replaced in 1932 by the TB-3 (ANT-6), a four-engined bomber designed by scaling up the TB-1. First

flown by M M Gromov on 22 December 1930, it was Tupolev's first stake to the claim of having built the world's largest landplane.

The first TB-3s closely resembled the TB-1, and carried the same bomb-load, but were more powerful and more heavily armed. The 1936 version, powered by M-34FRN engines, established a number of weight-lifting records for the USSR in that year, and in May 1937 four unarmed TB-3s airlifted the Schmidt Polar Expedition to the North Pole. Over 800 TB-3s were produced between 1932-37.

The TB-3 was also used as a mother plane for fighters, carrying five in one experiment, and a squadron of six TB-3s, each carrying two I-16 fighter-bombers, was used against the advancing Germans in 1941.

In May 1933 Tupolev's TB-6 (ANT-16) six-engined bomber succeeded the TB-3 as the world's largest landplane. It did not go into production, but served as the prototype of the even larger eight-engined ANT-20 *Maxim Gorki*, built to commemorate the great Soviet writer's fortieth anniversary.

This aircraft—monstrous for 1934, when it was completed—was built as a propaganda machine and was equipped with a printing press, cinematograph equipment and darkroom, and 'sky-shouting' apparatus as well as passenger cabins and sleeping berths. Its history was brief and dramatic. The first flight took place on 19 June 1934, and on 18 May 1935 the ANT-20 was destroyed in a mid-air col-

TUPOLEV Tu-114

Powered by: Four 14,795 eshp Kuznetsov NK-12MV turboprop engines, each driving 18 ft 4½ in (5.60 m) diameter eight-blade contra-rotating propellers
Wing span: 167 ft 8 in (51.10 m)
Length: 177 ft 6 in (54.10 m)
Wing area: 3,349 sq ft (311.10 m²)
Gross weight: 376,990 lb (171,000 kg)
Max cruising speed: 478 mph (770 km/h) at 29,500 ft (9,000 m)
Range: 3,850 miles (6,200 km) with max payload of 66,140 lb (30,000 kg)
Accommodation: Crew of 10-15 (incl cabin staff) and 120-220 passengers according to range
First flight: 1957

Just as Russia's first jet airliner, the Tu-104, was evolved by giving the Tu-16 'Badger' bomber a new, passenger-carrying fuselage, so the Tu-114 was achieved by a similar process, using the wings, power plant and tail assembly of the Tu-95 'Bear' long-range bomber. The prototype Tu-114, named *Rossiya* (Russia) to celebrate the 40th anniversary of the 1917 Revolution, established a large number of speed, height and distance records with payloads of up to 66,216 lb (30,035 kg), and the production version has been in Aeroflot service since 1961. Military versions include an airborne warning and control version code-named 'Moss'.

Top: Largest and heaviest commercial airliner designed by the mid-fifties, the Tu-114 was completed in time to mark the 40th anniversary of the Russian Revolution, in the autumn of 1957. Its wings, tail unit, landing gear and turboprop engines were similar to those of the Tu-95 bomber

Above: Next stage in the post-war evolution of Tupolev's jet transports was the switch to a rear-engined layout for the twin-turbofan 64/72-seat Tu-134. This one, climbing out of Heathrow Airport, London, is operated by Balkan Bulgarian Airlines

Opposite page, centre: Soviet counterpart to the Trident and Boeing 727 is the Tu-154. It carries up to 158 passengers at 528-605 mph (850-975 km/h) on the power of three Kuznetsov NK-8-2 turbofans

Right: The old master: Andrei Tupolev was an honoured guest at the first public showing of the Tu-144 supersonic airliner, designed under the leadership of his son Alexei, at Sheremetyevo Airport, Moscow, on 21 May 1969

Left: Derived by a similar process to that which produced the Tu-114, Russia's pioneer Tu-104 jet airliner embodied many components of the Tu-16 bomber. This one was exported to Czechoslovakia

Below left: Scaled down to carry 44-56 passengers, the same basic design became the Tu-124, here seen on display outside the Exhibition of Economic Achievement in Moscow

A Tu-16 maritime reconnaissance bomber, in Egyptian Air Force insignia, is escorted by an American F-8 Crusader fighter as it flies near NATO warships in the Mediterranean

lision with an aerobatting fighter. A replacement aircraft, with only six engines but the same dimensions and an even-greater all-up weight, was built as the PS-124 or ANT-20*bis*. A twelve-engined, 70-tonne development was planned, but was never built.

In 1935 Tupolev initiated work on a smooth-skinned, four-engined high-altitude bomber which, while developed from the TB-3, was much more modern in conception, with an oval-section fuselage, retractable undercarriage and enclosed positions for the crew. Designated TB-7 (ANT-42), it is better known as the Pe-8 after V M Petlyakov, who undertook its further development.

Design teams, headed by P O Sukhoi and A A Arkhangelski but under Tupolev's general direction, were responsible before the second World War for a series of high-speed and long-range bombers, including the ANT-25 (RD) which captured the world long-distance record for the USSR in 1937 with a flight from Moscow to San Jacinto, California, via the North Pole. Sukhoi also designed the first Soviet single-seat fighter with an enclosed cockpit and retractable undercarriage.

In 1936 Tupolev, who since about 1931 had also been Chief Engineer to the Chief Administration of the Aviation Industry,

was arrested and imprisoned. Few heads of the aviation industry escaped the prewar purges. Some, like K A Kalinin, were never heard of again; others, including Professor B S Stechkin, head of the Central Aero-engine Institute, were later released and awarded Stalin Prizes. Tupolev himself was released in about 1942 and awarded a Stalin Prize for his Tu-2 medium bomber, the only wholly-new Soviet wartime aircraft to go into production.

Since the second World War, Andrei Tupolev's design bureau has been responsible for the Tu-4 copy of the Boeing B-29 Superfortress, produced as a stop-gap following the abandonment of heavy bomber production during the war; and for the Tu-14, a straight-winged jet bomber produced for the Soviet naval air force, the Tu-16 twin-jet swept-wing medium bomber, the Tu-95 turboprop-engined heavy bomber (which at the time of construction was the world's largest land-plane), its Tu-114 transport counterpart, the Tu-104 series of jet transports, the Tu-22 supersonic bomber and the Tu-144, the world's first SST to fly.

The Tu-104 jet airliner created a sensation when the prototype flew into London Airport on 22 March 1956. Until then, the Soviet airline (Aeroflot) had been dependent on the unpressurised Il-12/Il-14 medium-haul airliners and the Li-2 (licence-built DC-3) for its passenger services. The Tu-104 was the first aircraft in Aeroflot's turbojet/turboprop re-equipment programme, and from 15 September 1956 until the de Havilland Comet re-entered airline service in October 1958 it was the only turbojet transport in regular airline service anywhere in the world.

However, its military engines, with their high fuel consumption, were uneconomic, and so the scaled-down turbofan-engined Tu-124 was developed. This in turn was superseded by the rear-engined Tu-134. The 158-seat, tri-jet Tu-154, due to enter scheduled service in the autumn of 1971, has been scaled up from the Tu-134.

Tupolev's son, Alexei A Tupolev, was primarily responsible for the design of the Tu-144 supersonic transport, which has been flying since 31 December 1968 and is the first airliner to have exceeded Mach 2. In May 1971 it made its first appearance outside the USSR, at the Paris Air Show.

By that time Andrei Tupolev, then aged 83, was believed to have retired from active design work; Alexei appears to have assumed general responsibility for his father's design bureau. Among the many awards that have been made to A N Tupolev are several Lenin and State (ie Stalin) Prizes, and the FAI Gold Medal (1959). He is twice Hero of Socialist Labour, an Academician and General of the Engineering Service, and an Honorary Fellow of the Royal Aeronautical Society.

Show-stealer at the 1971 *Salon de
l'Aéronautique et de l'Espace* in Paris was the
Soviet Union, which presented the western
public with its first glimpse of several
modern Russian commercial aircraft. Major
interest centred around the Tupolev Tu-144
supersonic transport, the first SST to fly
anywhere in the world. It should go into
regular service in 1973-74; the prototype
shown had already reached Mach 2.3
(1,518 mph; 2,443 km/h) during test flying

SUPERSONIC TRANSPORTS

Before the Concorde enters airline service, this fuselage—similar to the flight test aircraft in every respect—will have undergone countless hours of fatigue testing. In this way BAC of Britain and Aérospatiale of France will be able to assure customers that the Concorde will withstand the stresses and strains of many years of passenger service at supersonic speed

WHEN THE ANGLO-FRENCH Concorde and the Russian Tu-144 supersonic airliners enter airline service in the mid-seventies, flying times on the world's intercontinental routes will be halved. The effect of this on travel habits and airline operations will be profound: for the first time no one person in the world need be more than a day's journey from any other person. Indeed, if the two people live in major centres such as London and Sydney then only twelve hours will separate them.

Many more cities—notably those separated by the already-busy North Atlantic routes—will be brought within reasonable day-return distance. Travel records, from stage-coaches onwards, have shown that whenever a day-return becomes possible between two points then traffic on those routes increases significantly. The supersonic transport, or SST, will, therefore, engender even more air travel and could provide the boost which world airlines currently need.

No aircraft type has ever offered such an increase in performance in a single step. It will be even greater than that offered initially by jet aircraft over piston-engined machines.

It is very easy to go on dramatising the effect of supersonic transports on the world scene, but drama is not enough to sell aircraft to airlines or aircraft seats to the travelling public. Ever since work started on the Concorde, it, and subsequent designs in Russia and the USA, have existed in an atmosphere of bubbling controversy. If SSTs are, indeed, to take their place on the air routes in the future they will have to provide answers to some very pertinent questions:

● Will the admittedly high cost of development and production, and subsequent high selling price, prevent economic operations by the airlines?

● Will the travelling public want to travel at such speeds?

● Will the side effects of supersonic aircraft be such that their effect on world pollution will lead to their banishment in many parts of the world?

● Is there a need for the SST anyway?

These are just some of the questions which require answering if we are to accept that supersonic transports will be viable.

Why So Fast?

When we can already travel through the air at ten times the speed of the average car on a motorway, there may seem to be little point in travelling even faster. But this point of view ignores the fact that the only commodity which the airlines have to sell is speed.

A look at airline advertising may give the impression that it is wide-screen films with stereo sound, the standard of cuisine or even the comeliness of the air hostesses which sells seats. This is because subsonic airlines have reached a performance plateau and the airlines have to cast around for some extra service or gimmick to try to persuade travellers to use *their* particular services. But if any one airline should be in a position to state that it runs the fastest service between, say, London and New York, then the frills will be forgotten. It is speed which sells air travel, and the supersonic airliner will double that speed.

There is, therefore, a very large and ready market waiting for an acceptable—in all senses of the word—supersonic transport.

It was this reasoning which, in the late 'fifties, led companies in Britain and France to apply the art of supersonic design to the commercial aircraft scene. Two completely independent programmes went ahead at The Bristol Aeroplane Company (which, in 1960, became part of British Aircraft Corporation) and Sud-Aviation (now Aérospatiale, France). By the early 'sixties both companies had reached very similar conclusions; slim, delta-winged aircraft carrying around 100 passengers could be designed to fly at supersonic speeds. The two separate programmes also came up with one other important discovery: the cost of developing the aircraft was going to be very high indeed, and it was unlikely that either the French or the British governments would, by themselves, find the necessary money.

Fortunately for the Concorde, this occurred at a time when there was already a realisation in Europe that international collaboration could help to overcome problems caused by the increasing cost and complexity of new aerospace projects. So it came about that, on 29 November 1962, two important agreements were signed, one between the British and French governments who would provide development money, and the other between the four companies which would collaborate on airframe and engine design and production — British Aircraft Corporation and Rolls-Royce in the United Kingdom and Sud-Aviation and Société Nationale d'Étude et de Construction de Moteurs d'Aviation in France.

Thus was conceived the aircraft which was later to become known as the Concorde. At that time, so far as was known,

Concorde 001 photographed during a demonstration flight at the 1969 Paris Air Show. By the time production versions are completed, the smoke trails left behind by the aircraft's four Olympus turbojets will be things of the past

Opposite page, left to right:
Inside the Concorde. This photograph, taken in the cabin mock-up at BAC Filton, shows a galley unit and toilet in the foreground, and one of the two main passenger cabins. The second cabin is through the rear doorway

A scene from 1966, when fuselage section 12 of the first Concorde prototype was being lowered into position for assembly at Aérospatiale's Toulouse Blagnac works

The original design for the Concorde flight deck, shown in mock-up form at the 1967 Paris Air Show

Below: From the start the Concorde project was undertaken with confidence that the end product would be a fully-viable airliner that operators would be eager to put into service. Work was started on production planning, as well as the construction of two prototypes, two pre-production aircraft and other airframes for ground structural testing. In contrast, a single prototype of the Russian Tu-144—the only other supersonic transport in the world—had flown by the summer of 1971

it was the world's first supersonic passenger transport.

One of the most important decisions taken between the signing of the agreements and February 1965, when prototype aircraft construction began in Britain and France, concerned the design cruising speed of the new aircraft. This was pegged at Mach 2.2, or around 1,400 mph (2,250 km/h) at the 63,000 ft (19,200 m) cruising altitude. If this speed had to be exceeded for long periods, the accompanying aerodynamic heating would prohibit use of the aluminium alloys which have been employed for basic aircraft structures for many years. The manufacturers would then have to work large areas of the aircraft in titanium or stainless steel which would, inevitably, increase both design and construction problems, and the price. So the decision to limit the Concorde's speed to Mach 2.2 was taken for the soundest possible reasons.

America and Russia

The supersonic airliner activity in Europe did not go unnoticed in the USA, which was quick to realise the sales potential of such an aircraft. A design competition organised by the Federal Aviation Administration was won by The Boeing Company, which received a contract for two prototypes of its 2707 design in May 1967.

At this late stage there was no question of America beating the Concorde to the market; so the US entry had to be superior in both size and performance if it was to start selling some years after the Concorde was available for service. The Boeing 2707 was, indeed, an ambitious design: it was more than twice the size of the Concorde and was designed to carry up to 350 passengers at a cruising speed of Mach 2.7 (1,800 mph; 2,900 km/h). This meant that large areas of the aircraft would have to be machined in titanium, and its complexity was further compounded by the need for variable geometry or 'swing-wings'.

Structural problems with the 2707 led to weight problems and, unfortunately, this design had to be abandoned. It was replaced by the more conventional 2707-300—a fixed, gull-wing design which retained the Mach 2.7 cruising speed and its associated manufacturing problems.

Such problems required the spending of a great deal of money, and the Boeing 2707-300's supply of cash was finally cut off by a narrow government decision in March 1971. There are, however, few people in the aerospace industry, anywhere, who believe that this is anything more than a temporary decision by the United States. Manufacturers on that side of the Atlantic will be back in the race either when the Concorde's success forces them to build SSTs, or in the unlikely event that the Concorde is cancelled and the

market becomes wide open once again.

Meanwhile, the Russians have taken up the western challenge with their Tupolev Tu-144, the existence of which was first revealed by a model shown at the 1965 Paris Salon de l'Aéronautique.

The Tu-144 is designed to fly at a slightly higher speed than the Concorde—Mach 2.35 compared with Mach 2.2—and to accommodate about the same number of passengers, although initially it will carry fewer. Its overall performance is close enough to that of the Concorde for there to be a marked similarity in appearance. There are few alternatives available to designers when working on aircraft with such advanced performance, so this similarity is by no means remarkable.

The Tu-144 made its maiden flight on 31 December 1968, to steal the thunder from the Concorde by becoming the world's first flying supersonic passenger transport. Two Concorde prototypes, 001 in France and 002 in Britain, followed in March and April 1969 respectively.

Few reliable details of Tu-144 flight testing have been revealed by Russia and it is difficult to gauge its progress. The evidence, however, is that the Anglo-French Concordes, which have covered their complete speed spectrum in a flight test programme remarkably free from major problems, are at a much more advanced stage than the Russian aircraft. Both BAC and Aérospatiale have stated publicly that they can now guarantee the performance which had been promised to airlines, and that the Concorde will enter airline service with the ability to carry a payload of 20,000 lb (9,070 kg) non-stop between Paris and New York.

Sales Prospects

Sixteen major airlines took out options on a total of 74 Concorde aircraft when the project was started, and during 1971 the Anglo-French sales team was engaged in a series of discussions with customers to convert these options to firm orders. The attraction of speed has already been explained, and whether or not the Concorde will be sold depends entirely on whether the airlines will be able to operate it profitably. This is not a question which can be answered simply.

There is little doubt that, despite the fact that its initial price and high performance will make its operating costs high, the Concorde could be operated profitably even at 1971-72 fares. If passengers were offered the choice of a trans-Atlantic journey taking seven hours at a cost of, say, £100, and the same journey taking only three-and-a-half hours at the self-same price, there is little doubt which the majority would choose. The 120/130-seat Concorde would thus operate continually with a full passenger payload and make a profit. Unfortunately, airline economics

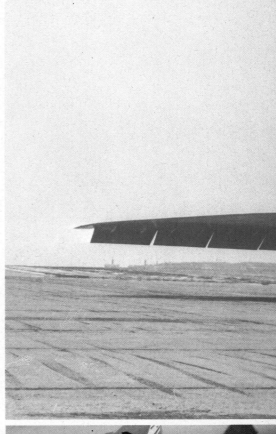

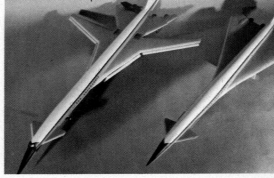

are not based on 100 per cent seat load factors but on something nearer 50 per cent. If the Concorde were to operate continually with a full load, this could only be done at the expense of the large numbers of subsonic aircraft owned by all airlines and which must be operated alongside the Concorde for a number of years.

Much of the discussion taking place between the Concorde's manufacturers and the airlines in 1971-72 concerns this very point. One answer to the problem suggested by BAC and Aérospatiale is to operate the Concorde as a single-class aircraft and charge slightly less than current first class fares. This would offer full first class conditions plus a dramatic saving in journey time. Subsonic aircraft could also be operated in a single class (all-tourist) and the ability to accommodate more people in the slower aircraft could, in turn, lead to a reduction in tourist fares.

BAC-Aérospatiale claim that a 60 per cent load factor in the Concorde would give a return on investment of more than 13 per cent. At a 70 per cent load factor, the return would be near to 16 per cent.

Backed by much computerised research, the manufacturers state confidently that sufficient passengers will be found to make the Concorde viable, despite the higher

Like the Concorde, the Tu-144 has a drooping nose which can be lowered to improve the view from the flight deck during take-off and landing

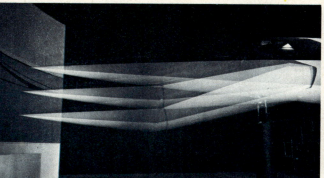
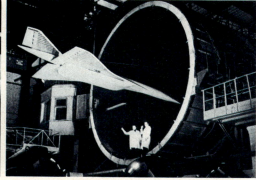

fares. These people will come from those who travel first class already, plus a healthy proportion of the businessmen for whom time is money. These men, and women, currently travel tourist class because they would not save any time by paying more money.

Once such passengers were given the chance to 'buy time', many of them would change to the 'first class' Concorde and, together with the other first class passengers, would make up a reasonable Concorde load.

The Environmental Question

Powerful as all the arguments in favour of supersonic transports are, they would be of little avail if the side effects of the aircraft were such that they would be socially unacceptable in many areas of the world. Criticisms directed at the SST over the years have ranged from accusations that sonic booms would cause wide-scale collapse of buildings, to dire warnings that upper-atmosphere pollution would cause a rise in Earth's temperature, a melting of the ice-caps and subsequent floods.

In some ways it is strange that aircraft should have attracted so much attention from the 'environmentalists' when all forms of transport account for only a tiny percentage of pollution caused by man.

Aircraft produce less pollutants than any other type of transport, and the supersonic aircraft is cleanest of all.

A lot of the pollution argument centres around a report by Professor Harold Johnstone of the University of California. This states that, because SSTs will operate at heights of around 60,000 ft (18,300 m), oxides of nitrogen contained in their exhausts will erode the Earth's protective layer of ozone and allow harmful radiation to reach ground level. This theory has been discounted by leading scientists in the United Kingdom and, indeed, by a report commissioned by the British government which concluded:

'Our studies indicate that the effect of operating even a large fleet of Concorde aircraft will be less than the normal range of changes from natural variations and will not lead to the harmful effects suggested by Dr Johnstone.'

No serious-minded person is suggesting that all fears concerning the SST's effect upon the environment should be summarily dismissed. Obviously the position will have to be watched closely. Even so, none of the evidence now available—and hundreds of thousands of hours at SST heights and speeds have been flown by military aircraft—indicates any cause for alarm. But noise is also a very real form

of pollution. Over the years aircraft have been getting steadily noisier, and there is now general agreement that this trend must be halted. Brief evidence at the Paris Air Show in 1971 indicated that the Tu-144 is not unduly noisy in airport operations. The Concorde prototypes on the other hand do produce slightly more sideline noise than current jets. New developments and refinements in the production-standard engines which will power

later models have led the manufacturers to state with confidence that, when it enters service, the Concorde's noise level will be in every respect on the same overall level as that of Boeing 707s, VC10s and DC-8s.

Thus, threats that some American airports may ban Concorde, because its noise level is too high, miss the point that the majority of other aircraft using the airport would also have to be banned.

The sonic boom is a different matter. Flight tests have shown that the supersonic boom—the noise made when the shock wave caused by the Concorde at supersonic speeds reaches the ground—is nowhere near as great as some prophets had forecast. It is not likely to damage property which is in a reasonable state of repair, nor will it cause physical harm. It is, however, an intrusion to which some countries have already reacted by declaring a ban on supersonic operations over their territory. This fact has been taken into account by both manufacturers and airlines in planning operations. The majority of the world's long-distance routes are over water, and simple re-routing can avoid even more land areas. The Concorde can, in fact, be flown almost as far at subsonic speed as at Mach 2.0 in terms of fuel consumption; a short period spent at slower speed, if necessary, will have a negligible effect on both journey times and economics.

As these words were being written, two Concorde prototypes had already flown for more than 500 hours. A third aircraft— pre-production Concorde 01—was about to join the programme.

All the experience so far has underlined the fact that the Concorde is pleasant and easy for airline pilots to fly, that it is very acceptable to passengers, and that its economics will be right for the airlines. Consequently, there seems every justification for the confidence exuded by both BAC and Aérospatiale, that Concorde is not just a technological miracle, not just a masterpiece in engineering, but a completely operable, profit-making and acceptable working airliner which will be the first of a new breed that will make the twelve-hour world a reality.

One of the most remarkable features of the Concorde programme has been the smooth progress of flight testing and the comparatively few major changes that will be embodied in the design of production aircraft. While the prototypes (001 above) complete their flight development, major components of later aircraft (right) are already being assembled at factories in Britain and France

TUPOLEV Tu-144

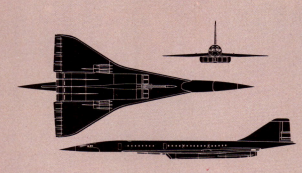

Powered by: Four 38,580 lb (17,500 kg) st Kuznetsov NK-144 afterburning turbo-fan engines
Wing span: 90 ft 8½ in (27.65 m)
Length: 190 ft 3¼ in (58.00 m)
Height: approx 43 ft 3 in (13.20 m)
Gross weight: 395,000 lb (179,150 kg)
Max cruising speed: 1,550 mph (2,500 km/h) at 65,000 ft (20,000 m)
Range: 4,040 miles (6,500 km) with 121 passengers
Accommodation: Crew of 3 and up to 130 passengers
First flight: 31 December 1968
Often nicknamed 'Concordski' by the western press, implying that it is a copy of the Anglo-French design, the Tu-144 was in fact the world's first supersonic transport aircraft to fly, preceding the first prototype Concorde by some two months. It flew at Mach 1 four months before the Concorde and at Mach 2 six months before its western rival; moreover, the entire test programme up to the autumn of 1971 had been carried out by a single prototype. A second and third aircraft were due to fly before the end of 1971, with deliveries of production Tu-144s starting in 1973 or 1974.

AÉROSPATIALE/BAC CONCORDE

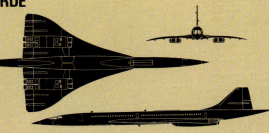

Powered by: Four 38,050 lb (17,260 kg) st Rolls-Royce/SNECMA Olympus 593 Mk 602 afterburning turbojet engines
Wing span: 84 ft 0 in (25.60 m)
Length: 203 ft 11½ in (62.17 m)
Wing area: 3,856 sq ft (358.25 m²)
Gross weight: 385,000 lb (174,640 kg)
Max cruising speed: 1,450 mph (2,333 km/h) at 54,500 ft (16,600 m)
Range: 4,020 miles (6,470 km) at Mach 2.05 cruise/climb with payload of 28,000 lb (12,700 kg)
Accommodation: Crew of 3 and 128-144 passengers
First flight: 2 March 1969
As the comparative data show, the Concorde and the Soviet Tu-144 supersonic transports are broadly comparable in terms of size, payload, engine power and performance. Main differences are the choice of turbofan engines to power the Soviet aircraft, which is designed for a slightly higher cruising Mach number with a slightly lower maximum passenger capacity. The Concorde first exceeded Mach 1 on 1 October 1969, and Mach 2 was passed during a test flight on 4 November 1970. Airline options on the Concorde totalled 74 aircraft by 1971, with deliveries due to begin in 1974. From the 41st aircraft onwards, Mk 612 engines of 39,940 lb (18,116 kg) st will be fitted.

Below: Night scene at America's Western Test Range, as final preparations are made to put an ITOS (Improved Tiros Operational Satellite) spacecraft into orbit on 11 December 1970. The vehicle used to launch this 681 lb (308 kg) meteorological satellite was a Delta Super Six, more than 106 ft (32.37 m) tall, with a launch weight of 230,000 lb (104,500 kg)

Right: Russia's Cosmos programme includes everything from small, peaceful, research satellites like this to FOBS 'space bombs' and interceptor satellites designed to destroy other orbiting spacecraft

SATELLITES AT WORK TODAY

A QUESTION ASKED frequently is: 'What are the benefits of aerospace research and development to the man in the street?'

When ordinary people hear of the vast sums of money expended on space research, this is, perhaps, a natural question. From the technical viewpoint, the first essential up to the present has been to develop techniques and equipment, and overcome problems. There has been little time to spare for 'benefits'.

Another point to remember is that the space age is, after all, only 14 years old and still very much in its infancy. When asked about 'benefits', space technicians must be tempted to repeat the classic reply 'Of what use is a new-born baby?'

The remarkable thing is that there have been any everyday benefits at all so far. Fourteen years after the Wright brothers made their first aeroplane flights, the only 'benefits' of that great technical innovation had been the development of faster and more heavily armed fighters, and bigger and better bombers—for war. We should be thankful that man's venture into space has not produced that kind of mixed blessing.

In fact, the very first satellite, Russia's historic Sputnik 1, indicated a use to which satellites could be put. While listening to the signals transmitted from Sputnik 1, a pair of young American scientists at the Johns Hopkins University experimented with tracking it by means of the Doppler effect. This is the phenomenon by which sound waves from a moving object increase in frequency as the source of the sound approaches the ear, and decrease as it moves away. A popular example is the siren of a diesel locomotive which seems to rise and fall in pitch as the train goes by.

The scientists noticed that the signals from Sputnik 1 increased in frequency as it approached them, and then decreased as it receded. They managed to track the satellite with remarkable accuracy and also, 'working backwards', to determine their position relative to the satellite. As the path of the satellite itself could be computed and forecast, then the position of any receiver picking up its signals could also be determined, wherever it was. Such a satellite functions as an 'all-weather' star, to which clouds mean nothing, and is thus ideal for navigational purposes.

Transit 1B, launched by the US Navy in April 1960, was the first of a series of proper navigational satellites. Although this initial system was developed primarily for military purposes, merchant ships of all nations can now avail themselves of the developed Transit service if they so desire: all they need is a whip aerial and a low-cost computer. In the not-too-distant future, it is also likely that a new navigational aid using a Transit-type satellite will be developed for use by civil airliners.

Most readers of *History of Aviation* will have experienced the annoyance of an incorrect weather forecast. It may have spoilt an afternoon's sport or part of a holiday. To many people, however, a wrong forecast can mean economic disaster; to some, perhaps, even death.

In spite of the importance of weather forecasting, regular measurements are taken over only a tiny proportion of the Earth's surface. This is because the cost of establishing stations on all the land areas would be prohibitive, and as far as the sea is concerned—which covers about 70 per cent of the surface—utterly out of the question.

It was thus with considerable excitement that American technicians prepared the Thor booster rocket carrying Tiros 1, America's first weather satellite. Launched

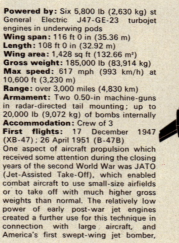

Powered by: Six 5,800 lb (2,630 kg) st General Electric J47-GE-23 turbojet engines in underwing pods
Wing span: 116 ft 0 in (35.36 m)
Length: 108 ft 0 in (32.92 m)
Wing area: 1,428 sq ft (132.66 m²)
Gross weight: 185,000 lb (83,914 kg)
Max speed: 617 mph (993 km/h) at 10,600 ft (3,230 m)
Range: over 3,000 miles (4,830 km)
Armament: Two 0.50-in machine-guns in radar-directed tail mounting; up to 20,000 lb (9,072 kg) of bombs internally
Accommodation: Crew of 3
First flights: 17 December 1947 (XB-47); 26 April 1951 (B-47B)
One aspect of aircraft propulsion which received some attention during the closing years of the second World War was JATO (Jet-Assisted Take-Off), which enabled combat aircraft to use small-size airfields or to take off with much higher gross weights than normal. The relatively low power of early post-war jet engines created a further use for this technique in connection with large aircraft, and America's first swept-wing jet bomber,

BOEING STRATOJET

the B-47 Stratojet, was among those to incorporate built-in JATO units in its early versions. The B-47B, to which the data and silhouette apply, was fitted with eighteen 1,000 lb (454 kg) st rocket units mounted in the fuselage aft of the wings.

British first stage of the Europa 1 launch vehicle on the firing pad at Woomera Rocket Range, Australia. This satellite launch vehicle has a British Blue Streak first stage, French second stage and German third stage

Tiros 1 was followed by nine others in the series, and by the more advanced ESSA (Environmental Survey Satellites) and Nimbus weather satellites. Nimbus, in addition to carrying better cameras, was stabilised in orbit so that it always pointed towards the Earth; the Tiros satellites were spin-stabilised, like a top, and thus only pointed towards the Earth for part of each orbit. In addition, Nimbus carried what is known as an APT, or Automatic Picture Transmission system. This enabled anyone, anywhere on the Earth in the path of the satellite, to receive on relatively inexpensive equipment pictures of the local cloud coverage within a radius of about 1,000 miles (1,610 km). Similar equipment is installed in the current series of ITOS, or Improved Tiros Operational Satellites, information from which is used regularly by 500 APT stations in 50 countries to help compile daily weather forecasts. This second-generation operational spacecraft is not only doubling the daily weather coverage possible with the earlier ESSA satellites, but at less cost, more effectively and during a longer lifetime.

Russia too has orbited her own series of weather satellites. Known as the Meteor system, this comprises three satellites in orbital planes at 90° and 180° to each other, so that they pass over a given area of the Earth on the northbound pass at intervals of about 6 and 12 hours, and again during the southbound pass. Information received from the Meteor satellites is transmitted to Washington, Geneva, Tokyo, Sydney and other foreign weather services.

Early warnings from weather satellites are credited with saving thousands of acres of crops and thousands of lives. In 1968 satellite information on Hurricane Carla led to 300,000 people being evacuated; and when Hurricane Camille hit the Gulf coast in August 1969, it is estimated that 50,000 people would have perished if they had not been evacuated.

Another field in which satellites are already producing benefits for the man in the street is that of communications. Rapid and reliable communications are a bedrock of our present civilised world, and in the early nineteen-sixties the submarine telephone cables used normally for long-distance calls were nearing saturation point; radio services, relying as they did upon the reflection of signals from the ever-changing and unpredictable Heaviside layer in the upper atmosphere, were as unreliable as ever. As for television, its signals could not readily be carried by submarine cables, nor could they be reflected off the Heaviside layer—they went right through it and out into space.

The possibilities of reflecting radio waves from something reliable, such as a satellite, were foreseen as early as 1946 by a British

successfully in April 1960, it was an immediate success. From a near-circular orbit some 450 miles (725 km) above the surface the satellite, equipped with two television cameras, began to send back hundreds and thousands of photographs of cloud formations. One camera photographed an area 800 miles (1,290 km) square and the other an area of 80 miles (129 km) square in greater detail. The pictures showed that cloud systems are much more highly systematic than was previously supposed; some cloud formations, thousands of miles apart, were in fact connected by wisps of cloud. Some pictures showed great spiral-shaped formations whose existence was previously unknown.

One set of photos depicted a gigantic cyclonic formation 2,000 miles (3,220 km) across, much bigger than any previously recorded. Others indicated the presence of jet-streams, regions of moist air, thunderstorm fronts and other meteorological phenomena. The value of being able to see enormous stretches of 'weather' at once was obvious, and copies of the photographs were sent all over the world so that meteorologists could begin to learn how the new knowledge could help them in making more accurate forecasts. Before its batteries gave out, after seventy-eight days, the satellite had transmitted the incredible total of 22,952 photographs.

Above: All spacecraft need complex ground equipment to support them in flight and to 'interpret' the vast streams of data that they transmit. One of the tasks of this antenna array at a Soviet manned spacecraft control centre is to 'listen' to signals relayed back to Earth from Venus and Mars

Below: Satellite Earth Station aerial No 1 at Goonhilly, Cornwall, was the first to transmit, via a satellite, a live television programme from Europe to America. Weighing over 1,000 tons, this 85 ft (25.9 m) diameter aerial is fully steerable, with an accuracy of 2 minutes of arc. About 40 per cent of all trans-Atlantic communications are now handled by satellites. Goonhilly alone deals with more than 4,000 'calls' a day

engineer, A C Clarke, who also predicted their use for the transmission of television signals. Thus, when satellites became a reality, it was not long before experiments were made to see if they could be used for this purpose.

Initial experiments involved Echo 1, launched in August 1960—a 100-ft (30.5-m) diameter balloon covered with a thin layer of aluminium to permit the reflection of radio waves. This simple 'passive' satellite was used for hundreds of experiments involving the relay of teletype messages, photographs, speech and music.

This was followed in October 1960 by Courier 1B, an 'active' satellite carrying no fewer than five tape devices, capable of transmitting and receiving 68,000 words a minute, or a total of nearly three and a half million words a day.

The results obtained with Echo and Courier were so promising that several large US companies began to develop experimental communications satellites for the commercial relay of telephone calls and television programmes. The outcome was the now-historic Telstar satellite and the lesser-known but equally important Relay spacecraft.

Launched in July 1962—less than five years after Sputnik 1—Telstar was used for a series of dramatic trial television programmes between America and Europe, across the Atlantic. In the long record of man's scientific successes, this triumph of the space age ranked with Morse's first telegraphed message—'What hath God wrought'—and Bell's first telephoned sentence—'Mr Watson, come here, I want you'.

Telstar, for once, represented an experiment in which millions of ordinary people could take part, not just a handful of scientists, and those who did will never forget the excitement.

The first picture transmitted via Telstar was, appropriately, a view of the American flag waving near the ground tracking facilities. Technicians had expected the satellite to transmit only across America during its first experimental and 'settling down' orbits, but viewers in Britain—still up after midnight—glimpsed a brief wavering picture of the Vice-President before the picture was lost. In France, reception had been excellent.

The next night France reciprocated by transmitting a programme of music to excited viewers in the United States, telling people they were 'in Paris' and inviting them to spend a few pleasant moments 'in France'.

Telstar had one major drawback. Because television signals travel in straight lines, it could be used only when it was in the line of sight simultaneously to both the transmitting and receiving stations in the US and Europe. It was in a relatively low, elongated orbit, varying in height from 3,503 miles (5,638 km) to 593 miles (954 km). When it went below the horizon of a station on one side of the Atlantic or the other, transmissions ceased.

It had long been known that if a satellite were placed 22,300 miles (35,890 km) above the Earth, it would take exactly one day to complete each orbit, and would thus keep pace with the Earth's rotation and stay above the same spot on the map.

Above: Technicians at the US Naval Research Laboratory, Washington, check one of the tiny 3½ lb (1.5 kg) test satellites which were the best that the Vanguard rocket could put into orbit initially in 1958. Although hardly inspiring, the little Vanguard 1 'grapefruit' satellite continued transmitting for years and will still be in orbit a thousand years from now unless somebody eventually 'sweeps up' all the debris in space

Below: A full-scale test version of the Skylab orbital workshop which America hopes to put into Earth orbit in 1973, for manned research in space. Separated from Vanguard 1 by a mere 14 years, Skylab is 50 ft (15.25 m) long and 21 ft 8½ in (6.6 m) in diameter; it will provide living and working quarters for a team of astronauts for periods of up to 56 days

Bottom: Another of America's early satellites, launched in 1960, was Echo 1. Used as a 'passive' communications relay station, it was a 100 ft (30.5 m) diameter balloon, covered with a thin coating of aluminium to reflect radio waves

Since such satellites are 'synchronised' with the Earth, they are often known as synchronous satellites, and their orbits as synchronous, geostationary or twenty-four-hour orbits. Three such satellites, equally spaced above the equator, could cover almost all of the civilised and inhabited areas of the world.

Three experimental synchronous satellites, appropriately named Syncom, were placed in orbit. The insertion of a satellite into a synchronous orbit requires extremely complex guidance and intricate space manoeuvres and precise thrust control. Even so, commendably near-synchronous orbits were achieved. Syncom I, although launched successfully, failed to go on the air; but Syncom II, launched in July 1963, worked well, as did Syncom III, launched in August 1964. It was Syncom III which played a major part in the world-wide TV transmissions of the Olympic Games from Tokyo.

Syncom III was followed, in April 1965, by the commercial satellite Early Bird, which was put into public service in June 1965. Providing up to 240 two-way telephone channels, it more than doubled the number of telephone circuits between Britain and the United States.

Since that time an entire industry has grown out of research and development in communications satellites. Early Bird was followed by the 'second-generation' Intelsat 2 satellites which, in their turn, were followed by the series of third-generation Intelsat 3s. Stationed above the Atlantic, Pacific and Indian Oceans, these are now in full operational service.

The latest of the series announced by 1971 was Intelsat 4, four of which have been ordered. The largest communications satellite yet designed, Intelsat 4 offers facilities 25 times greater than earlier satellites. It can carry over 5,000 two-way telephone calls and transmit 12 colour television broadcasts simultaneously.

All these Intelsat satellites have been ordered by the Communications Satellites Corporation (Comsat) on behalf of the International Telecommunications Satellite Consortium (Intelsat).

Many of the world's long-distance business telephone calls are now made via communications satellites. Furthermore, progress in the field of satellite communications has reduced the cost of a single telephone channel across the ocean from more than £7,000 to about £250. These spacecraft also enable the man in the street to see many exciting major sporting events —the World Cup football series, for example—as they take place on the other side of the world.

In addition to the uses to which satellites have been put in the fields of navigation, meteorology and communications, there have been many instances of other and

This page, top: Full-scale exhibition model of one of Russia's 2,200 lb (998 kg) Molniya communications satellites. Like its US counterparts, Molniya handles both TV and radio-telephone communications, drawing its power from panels of solar cells. These are deployed on extending arms, whereas the US satellites are usually drum-shaped, with the solar cells covering their cylindrical outer shell

Upper right: Full-scale structural model of the US Applications Technology Satellite. Built by Hughes Aircraft Company, ATS was able to contribute to a variety of meteorological, communications, navigational and stabilisation projects

Lower right: When launched in 1965, Pegasus was the largest 'solid' structure that had been put into orbit up to that time. Spanning 96 ft (29.25 m), its 'wings' were made of thin sheets of aluminium separated by Mylar plastic. They were charged with electricity in such a way that, when hit by a tiny meteoroid particle, the hole made in the panel was filled with metal vapour and a pulse of electricity passed through the panel from one side to the other. Data on each 'hit' was then transmitted to Earth

Opposite page, top: On 5 August 1970, after 15½ months in orbit, the Nimbus 3 weather satellite sent back this panoramic view of the United States, taken from an altitude of 700 miles (1,125 km). The area extends from Florida in the South, beyond the Great Lakes in the North, into Canada. Cloud cover is much less than normal

Bottom: This remarkable photograph of Hurricane Gladys, about 150 miles (240 km) south-west of Tampa, Florida, was taken during the Apollo 7 manned Earth-orbital flight in October 1968, at a height of 112 miles (180 km)

BOEING EC-135

Powered by: Four 13,750 lb (6,237 kg) st Pratt & Whitney J57-P-59W turbojet engines in underwing pods
Wing span: 130 ft 10 in (39.88 m)
Length: 136 ft 3 in (41.53 m)
Wing area: 2,433 sq ft (226.04 m²)
Gross weight: 297,000 lb (134,715 kg)
Typical cruising speed: 532 mph (856 km/h) at 45,000 ft (13,700 m)
Endurance: 5 hr 30 min
First flight: 31 August 1956 (KC-135A) Military counterpart to the well-known Boeing 707 passenger transport, the Boeing C-135 Stratolifter and KC-135 Stratotanker have served with the US Air Force for many years in transport and flight-refuelling tanker roles; the data apply to the standard KC-135A tanker version. In 1967 eight aircraft were

modified to EC-135Ns (as shown in the silhouette) for the special duty of providing an airborne radio link between the NASA Manned Space Flight Center at Houston, Texas, and the astronauts taking part in the Apollo man-on-the-Moon programme. These flying relay stations are known generally as ARIA (Apollo Range Instrumented Aircraft); some are equipped to provide an airborne lightweight optical tracking system (ALOTS) which monitors photographically the spacecraft (and other missiles) during the initial launch, separation and re-entry periods of a mission.

more down-to-earth applications growing out of the research and development undertaken to develop these spacecraft.

For example, many recent dramatic developments in the medical field have had their origins in aerospace research. A NASA scientist, conducting basic research into the interfering effects of ionising space radiations on normal cell division in the body, has discovered intercellular linkages, a discovery which has increased our understanding of the behaviour of certain types of cancer.

Doctors can now watch film of the beating of patients' diseased hearts, identifying dead spots or scar tissue in the heart wall, aneurisms and other malfunctions, using a computer technique devised by a NASA-Stanford University team. A small analogue computer that can continuously monitor changes in a patient's blood pressure and cardiac output has been developed at NASA's Lewis Research Center, Cleveland. A brain sensor and radio transmitter system developed for space medical research with test pilots appears to allow major improvements in the diagnosis and treatment of schizophrenic mental patients.

The computer used to enhance pictures radioed back by American spacecraft from the Moon and Mars has been used successfully to analyse pictures of human chromosomes. Chromosomes in a human blood cell have been so analysed in three minutes, about one-tenth of the time required previously.

An astronaut's pressure suit was used to save the life of a young woman whose internal bleeding could not be stopped by established procedures.

Techniques developed in the space programme to separate chemical fuels in NASA boosters are now being adapted to separate oil from natural waters to reduce pollution. Work done in developing high-performance rocket engines has been adapted for use in reducing industrial pollution.

In the United States the computer industry, stimulated and accelerated by space research requirements, has grown to a £3,000 million-plus-per-year business, employing 800,000 people.

It is not suggested that either the direct benefits being obtained from navigational, meteorological and communications satellites or the side benefits of the associated research, or even both taken together, balance exactly the immense sums of money that have been expended on space research—any more than the aviation industry has earned, commercially, all the money spent on its associated research and development. But even this short account is enough to show the average person that he is getting quite a lot for 'his' money.

PROBES TO VENUS

AND A GAME OF INTERPLANETARY BILLIARDS

EVEN BEFORE MEN landed on the Moon, robot spacecraft were being launched to investigate the nearer planets. This meant keeping vehicles in working order for months on end, compared with the few days or weeks of the early Moon probes.

Getting a space probe into the correct departure trajectory means releasing the craft entirely from the Earth-Moon system. In effect, it becomes an artificial planet of the Sun.

Such missions cannot be flown at any time: it is necessary to wait until Earth and the target planet are in the correct relationship in their respective orbits. Opportunities to launch to Venus, for example, occur only at intervals of about 19 months, and to Mars at intervals of about 26 months.

In the case of Mars the probe must first be accelerated by the launch vehicle to a speed of more than 25,000 mph (40,234 km/h). Then, if correctly aimed, it will 'free-wheel' across space without further propulsion, taking up its own curved path around the Sun but moving outwards to intercept Mars in its orbit some months later.

A probe sent to Venus, which orbits closer to the Sun, must *reduce* speed relative to the Earth after achieving escape velocity. The Earth orbits the Sun at an average speed of about 66,000 mph (106,220 km/h). Therefore the probe is aimed against the direction of the Earth's motion, making it swing nearer the Sun to intercept Venus.

At first it seemed that Russia would win early success in its bid to reach Venus. The Venera 2 spacecraft passed within 14,900 miles (23,980 km) of the planet on 27 February 1966, and on 1 March Venera 3 made a direct hit. But the Soviet deep-space tracking station in the Crimea failed to pick up signals from either craft, even though both had been active up to the point of arrival. Venera 3 was meant to deliver an instrument capsule to the surface of Venus by parachute.

Venera 4 was more successful. On 18 October 1967 its 3 ft 3¼ in (1.0 m) diameter

capsule entered the atmosphere of Venus, and after a period of aerodynamic braking released a high-temperature parachute. As it floated down through the thick carbon-dioxide atmosphere, instrument signals were sent to Earth giving pressure and temperature readings; but they stopped long before the capsule could soft-land. (Radar soundings from Earth, in fact, suggest that beneath its thick cloud mantle Venus has a solid surface with mountainous features.)

Venera 5 and 6 arrived on 16 and 17 May 1969 respectively, but again transmissions stopped abruptly above the surface. Pressure was about 27 atmospheres (27 times the sea level pressure on Earth) and the temperature 320°C.

It was left to Venera 7, on 15 December 1970, to make the full descent. At first it was thought that this too had failed, but further study of the taped record disclosed faint signals which could only have come from the surface of Venus. They lasted about 23 minutes, indicating a temperature of 475°C ($\pm$ 20°) and a crushing pressure of 90 atmospheres ($\pm$ 15).

Soviet scientists concluded that previous capsules must have had the lids of their radio compartments pushed in by the sheer weight of the Venerian atmosphere. The capsule of Venera 7 had been specially strengthened and its parachute reduced in area to increase the rate of descent.

While the Americans did not attempt to land instruments, they flew Mariner 2 within 21,594 miles (34,750 km) of the planet in 1962 and in October 1967 Mariner 5 passed within 2,480 miles (3,990 km). During the fly-by, Venus was scanned with an array of sensing instruments.

The Russian and American experiments confirmed that the atmosphere was mainly carbon dioxide and that its outer extremities did not extend far into space. The upper atomic hydrogen cloud measured by Mariner's ultra-violet photometer faded out some 12,000 miles (19,312 km) up. Earth's cloud reaches five times as far. The magnetic field strength was also much weaker than Earth's and there was no detectable radiation belt.

In September 1973 (see table) America plans to launch another Mariner close to Venus, using the planet's gravitational field to 'whip' it on towards Mercury which it should reach in March 1974. The principle of gravitational acceleration is the same one that the 'Grand Tour' spacecraft will employ later in the decade.

Whereas Russia scored heavily in the early exploration of Venus, it was America that triumphed with Mars.

A planet only a little more than half the size of Earth, Mars has a mythology all its own. The Romans named it after their god of War, and some late 19th-century astro-

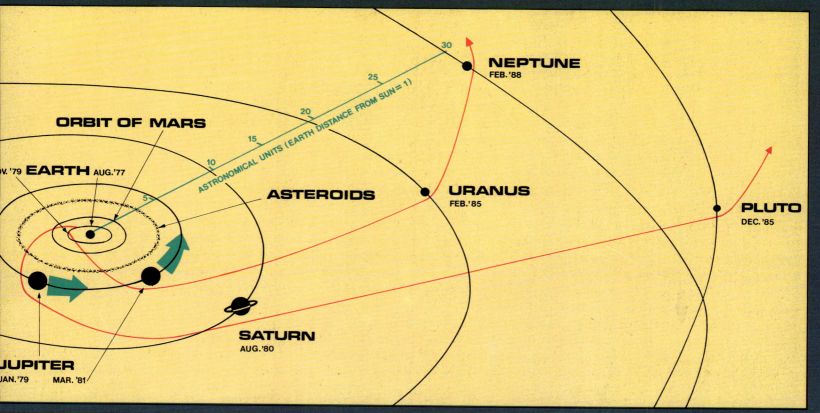

ORBIT OF MARS

EARTH AUG.'77

'79

ASTRONOMICAL UNITS (EARTH DISTANCE FROM SUN = 1)

ASTEROIDS

NEPTUNE
FEB. '88

URANUS
FEB. '85

PLUTO
DEC. '85

SATURN
AUG. '80

JUPITER
JAN. '79   MAR. '81

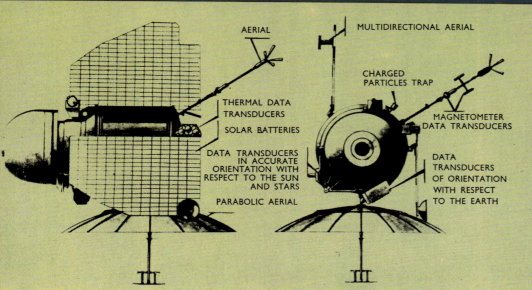

AERIAL

MULTIDIRECTIONAL AERIAL

CHARGED
PARTICLES TRAP

THERMAL DATA
TRANSDUCERS

SOLAR BATTERIES

MAGNETOMETER
DATA TRANSDUCERS

DATA TRANSDUCERS
IN ACCURATE
ORIENTATION WITH
RESPECT TO THE SUN
AND STARS

DATA
TRANSDUCERS
OF ORIENTATION
WITH RESPECT
TO THE EARTH

PARABOLIC AERIAL

Above: Two of the 'Grand Tour' trajectories projected by NASA. On the first mission the spacecraft would swing around Jupiter in January 1979, travel on to Saturn by August 1980 and eventually pass Pluto in December 1985. The second probe, launched in November 1979, would journey via Jupiter to Uranus and Neptune by February 1988.

Left: Venera 1 was the first Soviet space probe to depart for Venus, on 12 February 1961. Radio contact with it was lost after only 15 days

Below: Diagram issued by NASA at a February 1963 conference. Press representatives were told what had been learned from instruments on board Mariner 2 during its 42-minute fly-by of the planet Venus

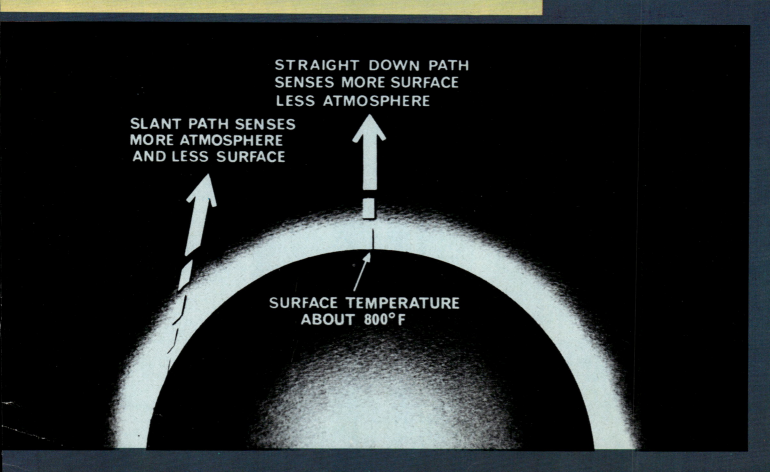

STRAIGHT DOWN PATH
SENSES MORE SURFACE
LESS ATMOSPHERE

SLANT PATH SENSES
MORE ATMOSPHERE
AND LESS SURFACE

SURFACE TEMPERATURE
ABOUT 800°F

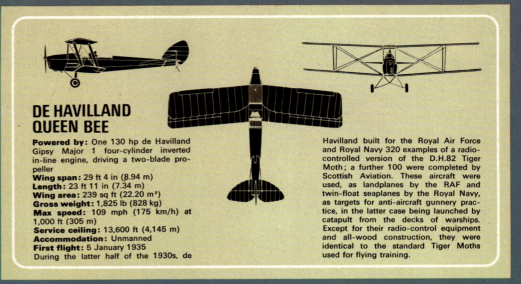

DE HAVILLAND QUEEN BEE

Powered by: One 130 hp de Havilland Gipsy Major 1 four-cylinder inverted in-line engine, driving a two-blade propeller
Wing span: 29 ft 4 in (8.94 m)
Length: 23 ft 11 in (7.34 m)
Wing area: 239 sq ft (22.20 m²)
Gross weight: 1,825 lb (828 kg)
Max speed: 109 mph (175 km/h) at 1,000 ft (305 m)
Service ceiling: 13,600 ft (4,145 m)
Accommodation: Unmanned
First flight: 5 January 1935
During the latter half of the 1930s, de

Havilland built for the Royal Air Force and Royal Navy 320 examples of a radio-controlled version of the D.H.82 Tiger Moth; a further 100 were completed by Scottish Aviation. These aircraft were used, as landplanes by the RAF and twin-float seaplanes by the Royal Navy, as targets for anti-aircraft gunnery practice, in the latter case being launched by catapult from the decks of warships. Except for their radio-control equipment and all-wood construction, they were identical to the standard Tiger Moths used for flying training.

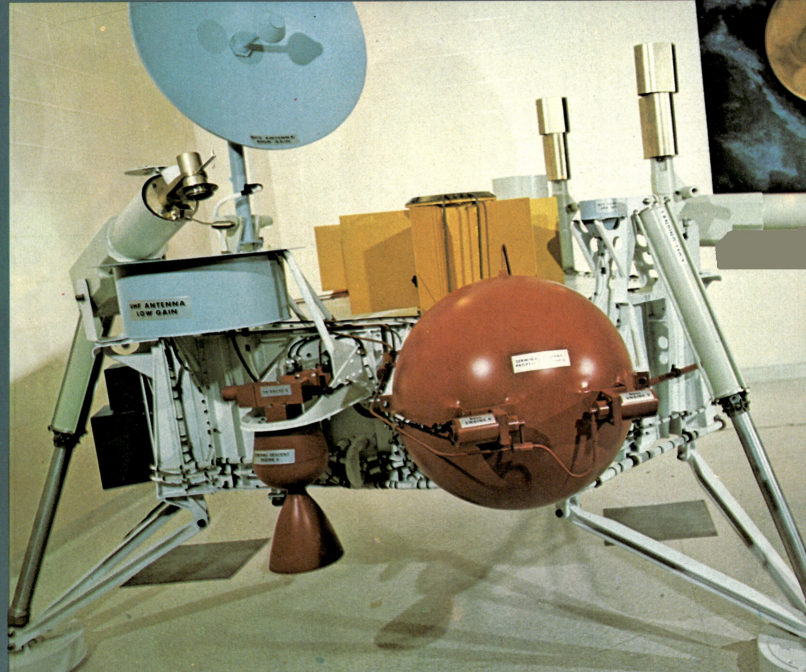

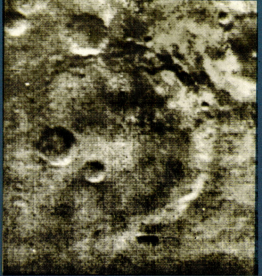

nomers even thought it was inhabited. In 1877 the Italian astronomer Giovanni Schiaparelli described faint markings which he called *canali* (Italian for channels). And as late as 1910 astronomer Percival Lowell of Flagstaff, Arizona, was still propagating the idea of intelligent beings who had constructed immense waterways to irrigate their dying world.

Science long ago disposed of the Martians. The so-called canals were recognised to be irregular surface markings which, at the distance of Mars, the human eye tends to join up into straight lines. And even before space probes made close contact, Mars was shown to be extremely hostile to life. Two-thirds of its surface is covered by immense arid deserts of a distinctly orange hue. It is bleak, cold and has a very thin atmosphere lacking in oxygen and nitrogen.

There are thin polar caps which recede with the onset of spring, when dark areas begin to spread from pole to equator. Some astronomers thought this was evidence of vegetation but it could equally be due to wind-borne dust or chemical changes in the soil.

It was Russia that began the assault on Mars from space, though initially with little success. As early as 10 and 14 October 1960, American tracking stations bordering Soviet territory detected the launching of two Mars probes, both of which failed, from the Baikonur cosmodrome in Kazakhstan.

A third attempt, on 24 October 1962, also failed. Instead of being ejected from parking orbit round the Earth, the probe burst into pieces. At least 24 large fragments were tracked by the Americans.

However, on 1 November 1962 a sister craft got away successfully. Its payload included a television camera and various instruments for probing the Martian environment as it passed by. The Russians announced it as Mars 1, only to lose contact with it four months later. Yet another Soviet Mars probe had been lost in Earth-orbit on 4 November 1962.

Russia's next try came on 30 November 1964, with a vehicle called Zond 2. Though it departed from orbit it developed a communications fault and was lost in space.

Now it was the Americans' turn, and they too started badly. Mariner 3, launched from Cape Kennedy on 5 November 1964, was destroyed when the nose shroud broke up soon after the rocket rose into the air. But then came a most spectacular success.

Mariner 4, which passed within 6,200 miles (9,978 km) of Mars on 14 July 1965, sent 21 photographs of the surface by television, revealing a Moon-like landscape with many large craters. As it left the neighbourhood of the planet its radio signals passed through the Martian atmosphere, causing attenuation of the signals. This allowed scientists to estimate the atmospheric pressure.

Pre-Mariner pressure values were anything from 85 to 10 millibars. Mariner 4 and subsequent spacecraft indicated a surface pressure in the region of 6 to 7 millibars, compared to Earth's 1,000 millibars. This is about equal to the pressure over 20 miles (32 km) above the Earth's surface.

Mariners 6 and 7 in July 1969 did even better.

With a gap of only four days between them, the 'space twins' flew past Mars, coming as close as 2,130 miles (3,428 km). Clear pictures were obtained of large areas of the planet, confirming that craters were widespread. Little water vapour was found in the thin atmosphere, which was almost entirely carbon dioxide. Instruments working at ultra-violet and infra-red wavelengths probed the south polar cap. It gave off infra-red radiation consistent with solid carbon dioxide (dry ice). Photographs showed clearly the snow along the edge of the cap, in drifts from a few inches to a few feet thick.

Mariner 9, due to go into orbit round Mars on 13 November 1971, was designed to photograph details on the surface as small as a football field. Its two TV cameras, one with a telephoto lens, infra-red sensors and spectrometers were expected to give two or three times as much information about the 'Red Planet' as was known before. It was hoped to photograph nearly 70 per cent of the surface and, on command from Earth, to direct Mariner 9's cameras on 'transient events' such as clouds, dust storms and the planet's seasonal 'darkening'.

After Mariner 9's orbital reconnaissance in 1971, NASA plans to send two 7,440 lb (3,375 kg) Viking spacecraft in 1975. When they arrive in Martian orbit, they will first examine the surface with TV cameras, then release 'clamshell' entry vehicles into the atmosphere.

After a period of aerodynamic braking, they will deploy parachutes and then break open to release small, three-legged landing vehicles which will descend to the surface using braking rockets.

Each Viking lander, weighing about 1,200 lb (544 kg), will operate on the surface for at least 90 days, sending television pictures and scientific data to Earth stations. Remarkable instruments have been devised to probe for life. One is a boom sampler that unrolls itself, curling in the process like a steel tape measure pulling in soil samples for analysis from a distance of 10 ft (3.05 m). The soil is passed to a robot chemical laboratory inside the craft which checks it for microorganisms, signalling Earth automatically if any are found.

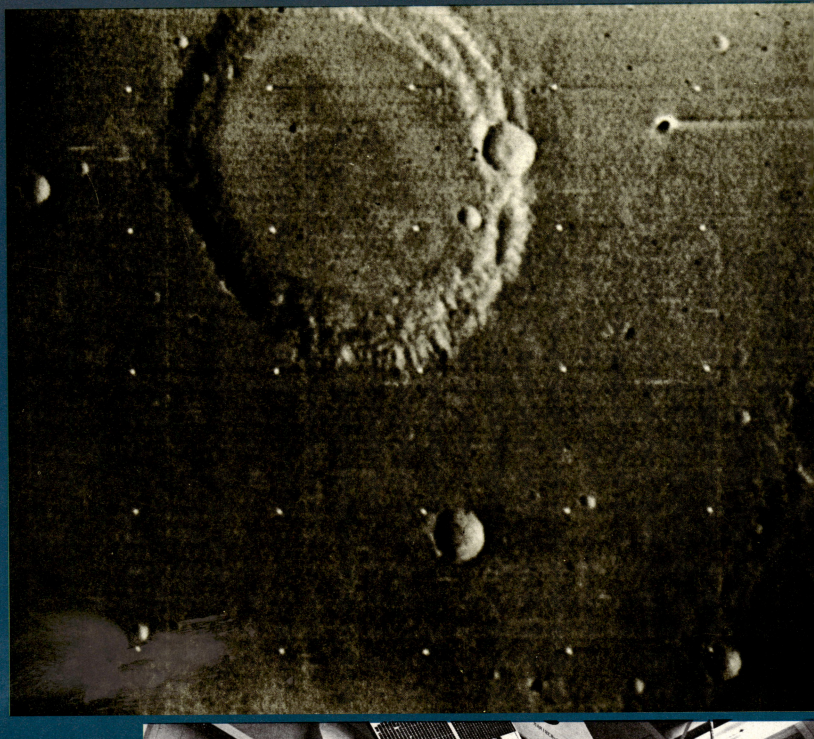

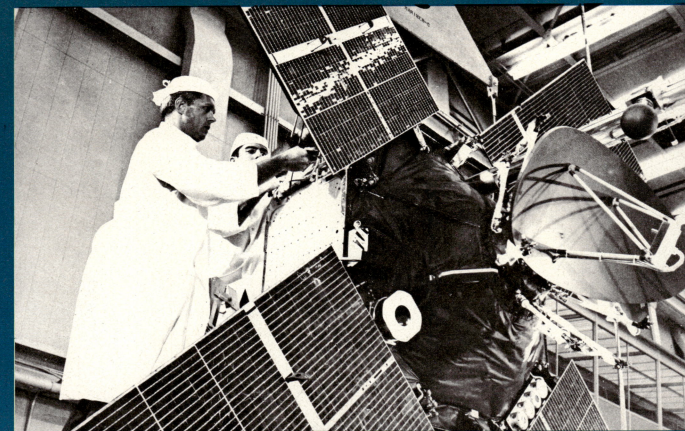

Future Probes to the Planets (NASA)

Spacecraft	Launch Date	Target Planet	Arrival Date
Pioneer F	March 1972	Jupiter	December 1973
Pioneer G	April 1973	Jupiter	October 1974
Mariner-Mercury	September 1973	Venus	February 1974
		with 'gravity assist' to	
		Mercury	March 1974
Viking A	October 1975	Mars	April 1976
Viking B	October 1975	Mars	April 1976
Grand Tour (1)	August 1977	Jupiter	January 1979
		with 'gravity assist' to	
		Saturn	August 1980
		with 'gravity assist' to	
		Pluto	December 1985
Grand Tour (2)	November 1979	Jupiter	March 1981
		with 'gravity assist' to	
		Uranus	February 1985
		with 'gravity assist' to	
		Neptune	February 1988

It is assumed that similiar missions will be flown by the USSR Academy of Sciences.

Above left: One of the truly striking and inspiring space pictures of the 'sixties, this photograph was taken from only 2,300 miles (3,700 km) above the surface of Mars by a camera on the US spacecraft Mariner 6, on 30 July 1969. The area shown measures 63 miles (101 km) from east to west, 48 miles (77 km) north to south

Below left: Engineers of the Jet Propulsion Laboratory in Pasadena, California, preparing an early Mariner spacecraft for shipment to Cape Kennedy. Solar cells, mounted on four large panels, provide spacecraft power during the 8½-month journey to the planet

This page, top to bottom: A mock-up of Viking lander photographed in the sort of environment scientists expect to see on TV pictures from Mars in the mid-seventies

This early NASA diagram of Mariner/Viking shows the lander inside the circular package that protects it during the long journey through space. A soft landing should be ensured by parachute and retro-rockets

Another of the Mariner 6 photographs which left no doubt of the cratered appearance of Mars. The area shown, measuring about 560 by 430 miles (900 by 690 km) in size, reveals at least 100 craters, the largest of them about 160 miles (257 km) in diameter

Meanwhile, the orbiters will serve as data links with Earth and independently observe changing conditions on the planet.

Beyond lies the still greater challenge of exploring the outer planets. In 1972 NASA expects to send the first of two Pioneer space probes on a 21-month fly-by mission to the giant planet Jupiter. To achieve its objective it must cross the asteroid belt of rocky debris which orbits between Mars and Jupiter. Each craft will carry 12 experiments, including a TV system which, at the distance of Jupiter, will send pictures at the rate of one per hour.

The flights—the second is to start in April 1973—besides giving us a close-up of Jupiter will give scientists vital experience for the Grand Tour spacecraft which, later in the decade, NASA plans to send close to several planets in turn to the very edge of the solar system.

In effect, space scientists will be playing 'interplanetary billiards' by making space probes 'bounce' from the gravitational field of one planet to the next, and so on.

Such missions are made possible by a rare alignment of the outer planets which will not occur again for more than 170 years.

What happens is that a spacecraft is directed first to Jupiter, which orbits the Sun at an average speed of about 29,200 mph (46,990 km/h) and exerts a gravitational pull more than 2½ times as great as that of our own planet. As the probe approaches Jupiter its gravity both accelerates the vehicle and turns its flight path towards the next planet, whose gravity whips it on again. As a result a journey to Neptune, which theoretically could take 30.7 years, can be achieved in about nine years.

A tour of Jupiter, Saturn and Pluto could begin in August 1977 and one to Jupiter, Uranus and Neptune in November 1979. Needless to say, the spacecraft that make the Grand Tour must be highly reliable. Scientists at NASA's Jet Propulsion Laboratory in Pasadena, California, are developing a Self Testing and Repairing (STAR) computer which will monitor on-board functions automatically throughout the flight. It is the first step towards a really efficient, highly-miniaturised electronic brain.

Keeping track of Grand Tour spacecraft will be three 210 ft (64 m) steerable dishes of NASA's Deep Space Network situated at Goldstone, California; near Madrid, Spain; and at Tidbinbilla, near Canberra, Australia.

It seems quite possible that the spacecraft will be accelerated beyond the outer limits of the solar system. If they remain in working order, these big dishes should be able to follow them—and receive their data—for several hundred millions of miles into space.

Overleaf:
US astronaut Edwin Aldrin, one of the first men to walk on the Moon on 21 July 1969, approaches one of the foil-covered legs of the Apollo lunar module spacecraft *Eagle.*

Men and Robots Explore the Moon

WHEN NASA BEGAN to look at the problem of sending men to the Moon in the early 1960s, a number of techniques were considered in detail. One group of engineers, which included Maxime Faget, a principal designer of the Mercury space-craft, favoured a rocket that would boost a spacecraft directly to the Moon. A vehicle with a lift-off thrust of at least 12 million lb (5.44 million kg) would have been needed to achieve this. To avoid this scale of engineering, a second design group, including Dr Wernher von Braun, suggested refuelling the spacecraft in Earth orbit before it departed for the Moon. An early scheme proposed launching the Mooncraft and its crew in one vehicle and sending up to it five orbiting tankers, each launched by rockets of 2 million lb (0.9 million kg) thrust.

A third group, led by scientists at the Jet Propulsion Laboratory, who were developing the unmanned Ranger Moon

probes, proposed that extra propellant and supplies might be landed in advance of a manned expedition. Astronauts would then use the supplies during their exploration and the propellant for returning to Earth. Although ingenious, this involved the risk that the astronauts might land too far from the supplies to retrieve them.

It was Dr John C Houbolt, a NASA engineer, who supplied the final solution in what has become known as Lunar Orbit Rendezvous. This entailed sending a two-part spacecraft into lunar orbit. One part—a small Mooncraft equipped with a pressure cabin, rocket motors and landing legs—would then separate with astronauts and descend to the surface. The other part, containing all the propellant for the return journey, would remain in lunar orbit awaiting its return.

This scheme had the advantage that fuel and bulky equipment needed only for the return flight did not have to be carried down

to the Moon and re-launched. There was, therefore, a large saving in the overall performance requirements of the mission, and it was possible to 'scale down' the launch vehicle to the size of Saturn V.

The idea of a Moon-landing ferry, detachable from the main spacecraft, failed at first to raise enthusiasm within NASA. Not least of the problems was that of re-launching the craft from the Moon and ensuring its docking with the orbiting parent. If the vital link-up was missed the landing party would be stranded beyond recall, for only the main vehicle could return to Earth.

It was the series of rendezvous and docking experiments brilliantly executed by Gemini astronauts which proved beyond doubt that the technique would work. But in passing, it should be recorded that many of the techniques adopted for project Apollo—including landing a Mooncraft on legs, using a rocket motor for braking

against lunar gravity[1], as well as lunar orbit rendezvous[2]—had been investigated by the British Interplanetary Society long before the Apollo programme was established.

Although based originally on the use of solid propellants, the BIS Mooncraft design was re-evaluated after the second World War in the light of liquid-propellant technology derived from the German V2. In the archives of the Society are detailed drawings by the late R A Smith dated 1946 and 1947. They show a vehicle, remarkably similar to the Apollo lunar module, designed to lift off from the Moon using the leg-supported base section as a launch platform. Included are liquid-propellant rocket motors for main propulsion and vernier control of direction and velocity; a double-walled pressure cabin for good thermal insulation and protection against micro-meteorites; inertial instruments for navigation; and contour couches for a crew of three.

* * * * *

Was Russia never in a race with America to land the first men on the Moon? There seems little doubt that similar objectives were investigated thoroughly in the Soviet Union in the early 1960s. At the 1963 Congress of the International Astronautical Federation in Paris, the late Yury Gagarin drew attention to the lack of a large rocket

capable of launching a Mooncraft weighing 'several tens of tonnes'. The alternative, being studied in his country, was to assemble a Mooncraft from separate components delivered into Earth orbit. Gagarin went on to say that such techniques involved very complicated systems of communications and radar and optical observation.

However, in 1965-66, it was America's Gemini astronauts who set the pace in proving the feasibility of docking spacecraft in Earth orbit. By then Russia had decided that, if manned spaceflight was to proceed in safety, each stage of the operation would have to have overriding automatic control. Thus, the first rendezvous and docking experiments performed by the Soviet Union were between two unmanned vehicles, Cosmos 186 and 188, in October 1967. By then, however, the technique was related not to a Moon landing but to the development of manned Earth-orbiting laboratories within the Soyuz programme.

At the same time it was recognised that a suitably modified Soyuz, launched by the more powerful Proton booster, could carry two or three men on a circumlunar flight.

Zond 5, in September 1968, was the dummy run. After passing around the Moon, it returned a capsule into the Indian Ocean. Its passengers were turtles and other biological subjects, but Jodrell Bank picked up taped voice messages from the craft suggesting that communications were being tested for a subsequent manned mission.

When Zond 6 followed two months later, after looping the Moon its capsule made an aerodynamic 'skip' in the Earth's atmosphere and landed in the Soviet Union. This had every indication of being the final unmanned test.

The imminent possibility that Russia would steal some of Apollo's thunder by sending the first men around the Moon must have weighed heavily in NASA's decision to send Apollo 8, with astronauts Frank Borman, James Lovell and William Anders, into lunar orbit at Christmas 1968. Until then, Apollo test flights had been restricted to Earth orbit and NASA was criticised for rushing its fences.

The huge success of Apollo 8, including 10 lunar orbits, is now recognised as a landmark in the conquest of the Moon. Although another circumlunar flight was being prepared by the Russians, no challenge came. The craft was flown later as a third unmanned mission in August 1969.

It was already apparent that Russia could not compete with America in landing men on the Moon. There were rumours of a Soviet super-booster bigger than Saturn V; but such a vehicle clearly needed years of testing before it could carry men. In any case, it seemed more related to Russia's long-term goal of establishing a manned space station in Earth orbit.

Russia's last chance lay with her unmanned programme of Moon exploration. We know now that while NASA concentrated on Apollo and its Saturn V launcher,

[1]'Lunar Space-Vessel', by R A Smith, *Flight*, 12 February 1942
[2]'Rockets in Circular Orbits', by K W Gatland, *Journal* of the British Interplanetary Society, March 1949

Left: St George's crater darkens the hillside behind astronaut James B Irwin and the Boeing-built Lunar Roving Vehicle (LRV) which the lunar module *Falcon* ferried down to the Moon on 30 July 1971. The mountains near Hadley Base appear deceptively low in many photographs; in fact the lunar Apennines rise some 7,000 ft (2,100 m) above the plain

Above: The superb success of the Apollo 15 mission made this LRV one of the crowd-catching showpieces of London's 1971 Motor Show. Would-be owners were impressed to learn that it was developed under a NASA contract valued at approximately $19 million!

Above right: The crew of Apollo 15 comprised (left to right) James B Irwin, lunar module pilot; David R Scott, commander; and Alfred M Worden, command module pilot. Ninth manned Apollo crew, theirs was the fourth successful lunar landing mission and the first to utilise an LRV

Right: Near-vertical view of the Hadley Rille/Apennine area of the Moon shows the Apollo 15 landing site (arrow). The picture was taken from lunar orbit with a 75 mm mapping camera soon after the *Falcon* had touched down

Soviet engineers were secretly putting together robot Mooncraft capable of extracting Moon samples automatically.

The challenge began with Luna 15, which was in lunar orbit as Apollo 11 astronauts Neil Armstrong and Edwin Aldrin were preparing to make their historic touchdown in the Sea of Tranquillity in July 1969. After making 52 orbits of the Moon, during which it performed several manoeuvres, Luna 15 crashed in the Sea of Crises about two hours before the Americans lifted off on their return journey.

Russia's triumph, therefore, had to wait until Luna 16. After going into lunar orbit, this soft-landed in the Sea of Fertility (0°41′S/56°18′E) on 20 September 1970. The landing technique—virtually sub-scale Apollo—required the craft to enter first a circular orbit of 68 miles (110 km) inclined at 70° to the equator. Corrective manoeuvres were made on 18-19 September, during which the station's orbit was made elliptical, 66 to 9.3 miles (106 to 15 km), inclined at 71° to the lunar equator.

After further trajectory measurements had been obtained by Soviet ground control, and the craft had been orientated for descent, the main braking engine was switched on at a predetermined point and the craft began to fall towards the Moon.

At 1,970 ft (600 metres) altitude, the thrust of the rocket motor was modulated according to a set programme and incoming data on descent speed and altitude. When the robot Mooncraft was down to 65 ft (20

metres), its main engine cut off and vernier rocket motors completed the landing, being switched off about 6.5 ft (2 metres) above the ground.

Luna 16 carried a ground-sampling device capable of drilling holes in the Moon's surface and taking a 'core' of loose soil and rocks as hard as basalt to a depth of 13.8 in (35 cm). An electric drill, which could move vertically and horizontally, delivered the samples to a container which transferred them to a returnable capsule, in which they were hermetically sealed. All operations were carried out by Earth command, and after completing each task the sampler stopped automatically.

After 26 hr 25 min the command was given for the lunar escape rocket to relaunch the capsule from the Moon into a direct trans-Earth trajectory. Left behind on the Moon was the leg-supported descent stage, which continued to telemeter radiation and temperature measurements to Earth.

The capsule, with its 100 gramme (nearly 4 oz) core sample, parachuted on to Soviet territory, south-east of Dzhezkazgan, in Kazakhstan, at 08.26 hr Moscow time on 24 September.

Immediately, Soviet scientists began to stress the advantages of making preliminary investigations of different sites on the Moon by robot vehicles, at a cost which, they suggested, might be 20 to 50 per cent below that of a manned expedition. There were also places on the Moon where it would be

dangerous for men to go, they remarked—for example into deep craters and rilles. It might even be possible to land robot vehicles on the Moon's far side, using artificial Moon satellites to complete the communications link with Earth.

In unspoken reply, the Apollo team demonstrated that, where astronauts can be landed, the ability of a man to leave the Mooncraft on foot or by roving vehicle not only makes the exploration more comprehensive but allows carefully-documented samples to be taken from different places en route; the recovered samples are thus far more valuable scientifically. It will be some time before a robot—or 'telepuppet'—rivals the achievement of Apollo 15 astronauts David R Scott and James B Irwin, who made three separate excursions in their Lunar Roving Vehicle at Hadley Rille, set out a third ALSEP scientific station and brought home more than 170 lb (77 kg) of rock and soil samples.

Meanwhile, continuing her programme of unmanned lunar exploration, Russia had already landed the first self-propelled 'Moon buggy', Lunokhod 1, in the Sea of Rains on 17 November 1970. It arrived aboard Luna 17, which employed the same type of descent stage as the earlier soil sampler, and emerged on to the lunar surface down ramps which had extended automatically.

The electrically - powered, eight - wheeled robot was steered by radio control by a team of five engineers seated comfortably before TV consoles in the Soviet Union,

nearly a quarter of a million miles from the scene. TV 'eyes' on the Moon buggy gave the controllers a forward view of craters and rocky obstructions, enabling them to steer a safe course.

At stopping points, on-board instruments examined the mechanical properties and chemical composition of Moon soil. An X-ray telescope scanned the heavens, and laser signals sent from Earth were reflected back from the vehicle to measure the Earth-Moon distance, the Moon's libration (rocking motion), and variations in the Earth's axial spin. During each successive lunar night, lasting nearly 14 Earth days, Lunokhod was 'rested' with its solar cell panel closed to conserve heat.

By 15 September 1971 the vehicle had completed its 11th lunar day of exploration, having travelled a total distance of about 6.5 miles (10.5 km). The reliability achieved by this tiny vehicle astonished western scientists, and already there is talk of using more sophisticated robot equipment. For example, Soviet astronomers are keen to land a robot observatory on the Moon for obtaining X-ray, ultra-violet and infra-red spectra of stars, galaxies and other celestial objects. Such observations cannot be made from Earth because of the scattering and absorbing effects of the atmosphere.

With America's Apollo man-on-the-Moon programme due to end in December 1972, the way will be open for robots to expand their activities. The lessons being learned on the Moon will certainly be applied to the exploration of Mars and other planets, moons and asteroids of our solar system.

Top: Russia's pioneer automatic lunar exploration vehicle, Lunokhod 1, has been described variously as a mechanical bug-eyed monster and a Victorian bath-tub on wheels. In fact, its sustained operation through eleven lunar days represents a major triumph of space science

Above left: Another pointer to the kind of robot exploration that must follow the end of the Apollo programme was given by Russia's Luna 16. After soft-landing on the Moon, it obtained a core sample of the lunar crust and flew it back to Earth for analysis

Above: This picture, taken by an automatic 16 mm colour camera mounted on the Modularised Equipment Transporter (MET) cart, shows Apollo 14 astronaut Alan Shepard during the mission's first EVA (extra-vehicular activity). The EVA check-list is attached to Shepard's left wrist. In the background, Edgar Mitchell sets out parts of the Apollo Lunar Surface Experiments Package (ALSEP)

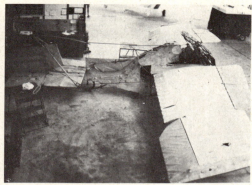

This, almost, is where we came in...

The pictures at the top of this page show Richard Pearse's second aircraft at the Museum of Transport & Technology in Auckland, New Zealand. When received (right) it was in a damaged state, with distorted rear fuselage structure and badly bent tail rotor drive. Advanced features of this design included proper ailerons, leading-edge flaps, a variable-pitch propeller, a tilting engine/propeller assembly for STOL take-off and hovering, a shaft-driven tail rotor to offset torque while hovering, and folding rear fuselage to simplify storage

Left: Richard Pearse

WITH THIS ARTICLE we come to the end of *History of Aviation*—though by no means to the end of the history of aviation, for today's events are tomorrow's history. Fortunately, a flourishing market in aviation literature ensures nowadays that virtually everything important that happens is recorded for the benefit of future generations. The recording of history is, however, a continuing process, and although aviation is still a comparatively young subject new aspects of its beginnings are still being discovered, investigated and allocated their appropriate place in the overall picture. Two recent examples show how this may come about, and how careful the historian must be in his appraisal of new discoveries.

In 1953 there died in New Zealand a farmer and brilliant engineer named Richard William Pearse. Some years later a New Zealand newspaper published an article suggesting that Pearse might have designed, built and flown a powered aeroplane earlier than the historic 17 December 1903 flights by Orville and Wilbur Wright. The article also suggested that Pearse had invented the aileron and had been the first to use it on an aeroplane.

The possibility was taken up by George Bolt, himself one of New Zealand's early aviators, to see whether the claim was valid. He was given access to family papers. He talked to Pearse's brother, to other members of the family, and to people associated with Pearse during his early working life. The remains were found of an aircraft (the second) and an engine built by Pearse. Bolt collected accounts from many who had witnessed Pearse's first attempts to fly and believed firmly that these occurred at the end of March 1903. And Pearse was found to have taken out, in 1906, a patent for his first aeroplane and its control system. Even allowing for some natural family bias and the dimming of memories after nearly 60 years, it began to look as though there was some claim to be made for Pearse.

But the dedicated investigator leaves no stone unturned. In Britain another eminent aviation historian, Charles Gibbs-Smith—personifying E M Forster's dictum that 'the historian must have some conception of how men who are not historians behave' —was able to discount the dating of some of the 'facts' half-remembered by contemporaries of Pearse. He also spotted, in the

PEARSE 1904 MONOPLANE

Richard Pearse, like the Wright brothers, designed not only his own aircraft but the engines to power them. A New Zealander, he carried out his first aviation experiments in the early years of this century, and for a time it appeared possible that he had predated the Wrights in making the first powered, man-carrying aeroplane flights in history. The silhouette is provisional, depicting the machine in which his first attempts were made. Numerous eye-witnesses of these attempts believed firmly that Pearse had flown in this machine in March 1903; but further research revealed Pearse's own admission that his first attempt was made in the spring of 1904, and that it was unsuccessful. He also acknowledged that the Wrights were the first to make a successful flight in a powered aeroplane. Pearse did claim, though wrongly, to have been the first aviator to fit ailerons to an aeroplane. In fact he had not appreciated the true function of such devices, and the movable over-wing surfaces fitted to his 1904

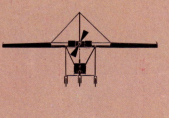

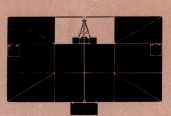

monoplane may well have been one reason why it became uncontrollable immediately after leaving the ground, crashing into a nearby hedge.

Nevertheless, Pearse was an able and gifted engineer. His 1904 monoplane featured a tricycle landing gear, with a steerable nose-wheel, and a direct-drive propeller. His second aircraft, now in the Museum of Transport and Technology in Auckland, was even more ingenious. It forecast, almost uncannily, some of the techniques being applied in STOL aircraft of the 'seventies, including a tilting engine, with a variable-pitch propeller, and a shaft-driven anti-torque rotor at the tail, combined with such other now-commonplace items as true ailerons, leading-edge flaps and wheel brakes.

1906 patent, what Bolt had missed: that Pearse's own description of his aileron system showed a fundamental misconception of the function of such surfaces, which would, in Gibbs-Smith's words, 'have been positively lethal if applied to an aircraft'. The invalidity of the 'first flight' claim was clinched when Bolt, during further research, came upon articles written by Pearse himself in which he (a) dated his own earliest attempts as February or March 1904, (b) admitted that they were not real flights, and that the aircraft was uncontrollable, and (c) acknowledged that the Wrights had been the first men to make a powered flight.

The second example is more recent and has, for the subject of the discovery, a happier outcome. A hint of it was given on page 19 of *History of Aviation,* in the reference to the hot-air balloon demonstrated in August 1709 by Bartolomeu de Gusmão (born Bartolomeu Laurenço). Charles Gibbs-Smith played a part in this story too, for further investigation was prompted by references to Gusmão's *Passarola* and model balloon in his standard work *Aviation: an Historical Survey from its Origins to the end of World War II.* If a glider model of the *Passarola* did fly, it was the first aeroplane in history, predating Cayley's model glider by 95 years; if the balloon story was true, Gusmão was 74 years ahead of the Montgolfier brothers, although theirs was still the first entirely successful man-carrying balloon.

The challenge was taken up by *Air BP,* the journal of the International Aviation Service of the BP Group. Through BP's organisation in Portugal, one of that country's most eminent air historians, Col Edgar Pereira da Costa Cardoso, was asked to study original documents, in 18th-century Portuguese, relating to Gusmão's early studies and his achievements in 1709. His report, published in *Air BP* in 1971, shows clearly that Gusmão was a brilliant student of physics and mathematics, and was inspired with the idea of aerostation (lighter-than-air flight) almost immediately after entering the Coimbra University in 1708. With royal patronage and funds, he evidently tried out many designs during the spring and summer of 1709.

After an unsuccessful indoor demonstration, on 3 August, of a small paper balloon which caught fire before it could rise, Gusmão repeated the experiment more successfully five days later. Before an audience which included the King and Queen of Portugal, a future Pope, princes of the Court and noblemen, his little balloon rose about 12 ft (3.6 m) into the air before, like its predecessor, it caught alight. In a later, outdoor test, the balloon climbed 'to some height before falling to the ground'. Before such an assembly of unassailable witnesses there can be little doubt that Gusmão did, successfully, demonstrate the first hot-air balloon in history.

Of the *Passarola* the picture is less clear; but one thing that does now seem virtually certain is that the illustration reproduced—

on page 17 of *History of Aviation* is a fanciful and therefore unreliable artist's impression, probably drawn from hearsay evidence of a 'flying machine'. Documents consulted recently suggest a more reasonable explanation—that this drawing represented only a man-carrying nacelle, the complete *Passarola* design including a roughly spherical hot-air balloon from which this carriage was to be suspended.

Is it mere coincidence that the man-carrying hull of Sir George Cayley's convertiplane (page 35), conceived more than a century later, resembles so closely the shape of the *Passarola*? Cayley's biographers have shown, albeit reluctantly, that the great pioneer 'borrowed' the convertiplane's rotor/wings from an inspired project by the almost-unknown Robert B Taylor of Liverpool. Did Cayley realise that the *Passarola* shown in drawings was no more than part of a 'flying machine' and decide to make use of this, too, in his old age, when the days must have been all too short for what he longed to do?

The museum of the city of São Paulo, Brazil, contains this fine painting by Bernardino de Sousa Pereira of *Bartolomeu de Gusmão's first experiment.* The Luso-Brazilian pioneer is shown releasing his model hot-air balloon in the presence of King John V, Queen Maria Anna, the papal nuncio Cardinal Conti, Infante Francisco of Portugal, and noblemen and ladies of the Court. We are able to illustrate this historic scene in *History of Aviation* through the kindly interest of Dr José Manuel Fragoso, Portuguese Ambassador in Brazil, who supplied a colour transparency to *Air BP* magazine during its investigation of Gusmão's contributions to the conquest of the air

INDEX

Compiled by Maurice Allward

References in bold figures, thus: **67,** indicate an illustration. References in italic, thus: *262* indicate that the subject is described in a 'data box', with a silhouette. Major civil aviation features are listed under Civil Aviation, and major military features under Military Aviation.

Many of the interesting 'firsts' described in this history are listed under First. It should, however, be borne in mind that a number of these are based on ancient records, and new discoveries may indicate that some of the 'firsts' listed were, in fact, preceded.

508

Vought Corsair (F4U). See Chance Vought.
Vought Corsair (A-7). See LTV.
Vought Regulus. See LTV.
Vuia, T, 56, 88
  No. 1 monoplane, *63*
Walker, T, 10, 11
Wallis, Sir Barnes, 308-11
Warfare, aerial. See Military Aviation.
Warsitz, E, 245
Watt, R Watson, 289
Wayland the Smith, 10, 11
Weather satellites, 488, 489
Weir of Eastwood, Lord, 134
Weiss, José, 224
  Albatross, 85
Wenham, F H, 61, 62
Wellington. See Vickers.
Westland aircraft:
  CL.20, 214
  Dreadnought, 253
  Lysander, 318, *319*
  P.V.3, 209
  Wapiti, 168, 170
  Whirlwind (fighter), 276
  Woodpigeon, 185, **185**
Westland-Hill Pterodactyl, 250, **250**
Weyl, A R, 158
White, E, 449
Whittle, Sir Frank, 332-35, 395
Wilhelm Kress triplane, 92, 93
Williams, Sqn Ldr G, 87
Williams, R D, 334
Willows, E T, 31
Wise, J, 24, **25**
Wladyslaw IV, King, 11
World Wars, first and second. See Military Aviation.
Wright, Orville (1871-1948) and Wilbur (1867-1912), 15, 34, 39, 43, 46, 47, 48-51, **55, 77,** 80, 103, 122, 128, 216, 238
  Flyer I, 46, *46*, **47, 334**
  Flyer II, 50
  Flyer III, 50, *51*
  Gliders, 45, 46, 47, **51**
  Model B, 50, **51,** 57
  Models C to H, 51
  Model L, 50
X-1. See Bell.
X-2. See Bell.
X-15. See North American.
XC-99. See Convair.
Yeager, Capt Charles 'Chuck', 381
Zeppelin, Count Ferdinand von (1838-1917), 30, 83, 109, 110, 111
  Zeppelins, 29, 30, **108, 109, 110,** *111*, 130
  Graf Zeppelin, *150*, 151, 209
  Hindenburg, 151
Ziolkowski. See Tsiolkovsky.
Zlin aircraft, 414
Zond spacecraft, 497

ERRATA

Page No:

161 Para 3 in centre column: This early method of direction finding, using strings and weights, was still being used for emergency fixes by the RAF in the SW Air Traffic Control Centre at Gloucester as late as 1957, when it was superseded by a radar technique

222 Maxim Gorki 'data box': the first flight date should be 19 June 1934. In line 11 of the following paragraph, the last three words should be amended to read 'After less than one . . .'

246 Para 2 in second column: The fourth of the five main control points in the 'MacRobertson' race has been left out. This should be inserted before 'and Charleville' and should read 'Darwin (9,124 miles; 14,684 km)'

History of Aviation was edited jointly by:

John W R Taylor, FRHistS, AFRAeS, FSLAET, whose technical background includes seven years as a member of Sir Sydney Camm's design team at Hawker Aircraft Ltd. He has been Editor and Compiler of *Jane's All the World's Aircraft* since 1959, Consultant Editor of *Air BP* magazine since 1956, and is the author of 160 books on aerospace subjects

Kenneth Munson, who has specialised for many years in aviation journalism and is the author of more than two dozen books. He is an Assistant Compiler of *Jane's All the World's Aircraft* and is author and editor of the *Pocket Encyclopaedia of World Aircraft in Colour* series published by Blandford Press Ltd

They were assisted by:
Ann C Tilbury, Photographic Librarian of *Flight International*, Britain's foremost aviation journal, who was Photographic Editor of *History of Aviation*

Michael J. H. Taylor, who is an Assistant Compiler of *Jane's All the World's Aircraft, Jane's Fighting Ships* and *Jane's Weapon Systems*, and is co-author of *Missiles of the World*

Aircraft Silhouettes
The aircraft silhouettes appearing throughout *History of Aviation* were provided by Dennis Punnett and John W Wood

History of Aviation was designed and produced for New English Library by the Ian Allan Group:
Art Editor Allen J Weston
Designers: Michael D Stride, Jonathan A Bingham, David J Kingston, David J Tarbutt

Contributors to History of Aviation were:
(Figures in italics give the numbers of the pages on which the contributors' articles appear)

Jean Alexander *476-9*
Acknowledged to be one of the most sound historians and students of Russian aviation in the West, Miss Alexander has contributed to several standard reference works on Russian aircraft and airmen. Her comprehensive history of *Russian Aircraft since 1910* is being published in 1972

Roy Allen *366-71*
Formerly on the editorial staff of *Aeronautics* magazine, Roy Allen is now a freelance writer specialising in airport and airline affairs. He is the author of several books on international airports

Maurice Allward *48-51, 190-93, 234-7, 354-7, 439-46, 487-93*
Assistant Manager (Technical Publications) with Hawker Siddeley Aviation, Maurice Allward has also written some 40 books on aerospace subjects. His interests range from special study of the Wright brothers to rocketry and space travel

Ralph Barker *238-41*
After wartime service as an RAF wireless operator/air gunner, Ralph Barker flew in civil aviation as a radio officer. Rejoining the RAF, he served in Forces Broadcasting, at the Air Historical Branch and in Intelligence, but left in 1961 to write full-time. His latest aviation book is on *The Schneider Trophy Races*

Chaz Bowyer *116-27*
Twenty-six years in the RAF, beginning as a 16-year-old 'Trenchard brat' at Halton, underlie Chaz Bowyer's special interests in the first World War generally and the RAF in particular. Editor of the journal of the Cross & Cockade (GB) Society, he is currently writing a book on *The Mosquito at War*

Basil Clarke *17-31, 76-87, 106-11, 152-5, 164-7, 186-9, 216-9, 224-9, 296-301*
As a young engineer, Basil Clarke helped with pioneer work on talking films and television, leading to wartime radar duties. His aviation writings, over 40 years, have included books on Polar flying, Atlantic flying and a history of airships

J B Cynk *278-9*
A quarter-century of meticulous research and exclusive interviews with former Polish aircraft designers and industrial figures made it possible for Jerzy Cynk to write *Polish Aircraft 1893-1939* for Putnam's famous aviation history series. He is today the recognised authority in this field

Don Downie *467-75*
Don Downie began flying Piper Cubs in 1937, the same year that he joined the *Star News* in Pasadena, as their one-man photographic staff and feature writer. Wartime service in the USAAF, including 68 round-trips over the Burma Hump, earned him the Air Medal with cluster and DFC with cluster. Today he ferries aircraft, makes flying films and writes, with more than 6,000 hours in his log-book

Christopher Elliott *284-7*
A journalist since 1948, Christopher Elliott was on the staff of the Air Ministry's aircrew journal *Air Clues* from 1956 to 1958 and Editor of *Fire Protection Review* 1960-64. A proud East Anglian, he is author of *Aeronauts and Aviators*, covering the growth of aviation in that part of the UK between the 1780s and 1930s, with a wartime volume to follow. He has an extensive collection of aviation relics, documents and books

Thomas G Foxworth *194-7*
Tom Foxworth flew with the US Navy for 5½ years, three of them on carrier-based Tracker anti-submarine aircraft, before becoming a commercial pilot. Since 1967 he has been a Pan American training captain and represents IFALPA members on the ICAO airworthiness committee. One of his keen interests is pre-war air racing

Kenneth W Gatland, FRAS, FBIS *202-4, 351-3, 420-37, 447-50, 494-504*
Formerly a member of the design office of Hawker Aircraft Ltd, Kenneth Gatland is now an aerospace consultant and Editor of the magazine *Spaceflight* published by the British Interplanetary Society. He has been a Council member of the BIS since 1945, Vice-President from 1959, and is the author of several books on missiles and space flight

W T Gunston *102-5, 242-5, 332-5, 340-43, 393-403*
'Bill' Gunston was a natural choice to contribute our articles on aero-engines and other technical subjects. As well as being responsible for compiling the 'Aero-engines' section of *Jane's All the World's Aircraft*, he is a former Technical Editor of *Flight International* and, subsequently, of *Science Journal*. Before that he was a pilot in the RAF

Raymond Hankin *220-23, 372-9*
Formerly on the editorial staff of *The Aeroplane* and *Flight*, Raymond Hankin is now with the journal *Travel News*

Clive Hart, BA, PhD *13-15*
Born in Perth, Western Australia, Clive Hart is now Professor of English at the University of Dundee. He has a special interest in the history of kites and in mediaeval aeronautical concepts, and is the author of *Your Book of Kites, Kites: An Historical Survey* and *The Dream of Flight: Aeronautics from Classical Times to the Renaissance*

Leslie Hunt *317-9*
An acknowledged expert on the whereabouts of veteran and vintage aircraft, Leslie Hunt is the author of a standard reference work on the subject. He is also an active worker for several charities, notably the muscular dystrophy campaigns, and has written many articles about Missionary Aviation Fellowship

Roth Jones *173-5*
After wartime service as a flying-boat pilot in the Royal Australian Air Force, Roth Jones is now Public Relations Manager of BP Australia and a gifted journalist whose features on aviation and travel are much in demand

H F King, MBE *32-5, 40-47, 52-9, 61-5, 67-75, 88-97, 100-101, 112-5, 132-5, 157-9, 168-71, 178-85, 208-15, 246-53, 260-61, 270-77, 344-9, 458-65*
'Rex' King joined *Flight* magazine in 1930 and was a passenger on an early flying-boat service to Australia. He saw Dornier production in Germany pre-war, later witnessed 'Cobber' Kain's first combat victory and interviewed Kain. An RAF technical intelligence officer from the Battle of Britain to the V-weapons, he interrogated German designers before rejoining *Flight* and visiting the Korean war. After becoming a much-respected Editor of that journal, he is now a freelance writer and author

H P Macklin *140-43*
Now Deputy Director of Press Services for BOAC, H P Macklin has long experience of British airline operations. He collaborated closely with editor Kenneth Munson in producing the *Pictorial History of BOAC* published in 1970

Francis K Mason *291-5*
Francis Mason brings to his aviation writings the experience gained as a night fighter pilot and fighter controller in the post-war RAF and eight years on the project design team of Hawker Aircraft Ltd. Twelve years of research went into his book on the Battle of Britain, published in 1969

David Mondey *176-7, 205-7, 308-11, 328-31*
A former engineer in the RAF, David Mondey first demonstrated his writing ability in features for *Air BP* magazine. He is an Assistant Compiler of *Jane's All the World's Aircraft;* his first book, a *Pictorial History of the USAF*, was published in 1971

Kenneth Munson (Editor) *9-12, 36-9, 505-6*

Geoffrey Norris *481-6*
After starting his career as a journalist with the *Sphere* illustrated newspaper, Geoffrey Norris became Assistant Editor of *RAF Flying Review* in 1956 and Editor 1960-64. He moved to industrial public relations with Short Brothers & Harland and, since 1968, has been Manager, Press Services, BAC. His publications include *The Wright Brothers, Jet Adventure* and *The RFC—a History*

David F Ogilvy *408-15*
An obvious choice as contributor of the feature on post-war private flying, David Ogilvy served in the RAF 1946-52 and was Director and Principal of the London School of Flying until 1966. He is now General Manager of the famous Shuttleworth Collection of Historic Aircraft and Warden Aviation and Engineering Co; and Member, Board of Management and Chairman, Corporate Members' Committee, British Light Aviation Centre

Alfred Price *288-90*
A serving officer in the Royal Air Force, Flight Lieutenant Price has earned a high reputation for his books on the wartime Luftwaffe and the methods and equipment of electronic warfare

The Rev John D R Rawlings *302-7*
John Rawlings served in the RAF as a pilot during and after the second World War and later entered Holy Orders in the Church of England. He has made a particular study of British military aviation, past and present. His books include the standard reference work on *Fighter Squadrons of the RAF*

Robert R Rodwell *404-7, 452-7*
After RAF service in 1952-5, Bob Rodwell became a staff writer with *Aeronautics* magazine. His lively, informed style was enhanced by a period as press officer with Fokker in Holland, and he joined *Flight* as a military specialist in 1963, combined with editorship of *Air-Cushion Vehicles*. After three years as Public Relations Manager for Short Brothers & Harland, he is now freelancing

Christopher F Shores *312-5, 320-27*
After eight years in the ATC and RAF, Christopher Shores became a chartered surveyor in local government, but began writing in his spare time. His first book, *Aces High*, was published in 1966, followed by *Fighters over the Desert* and *2nd TAF;* others are in preparation

John Stroud *136-9, 144-7, 160-63, 230-33, 256-9, 358-65*
Aviation author, artist and consultant, John Stroud joined Imperial Airways in 1933. Since the war he has concentrated on writing about air transport, in the course of which he has flown nearly a million miles in about 180 types of aircraft. His published books include *Japanese Aircraft, Annals of British and Commonwealth Air Transport 1919-1960, European Transport Aircraft since 1910, Soviet Transport Aircraft since 1945*, and the *BP Books of IATA Airlines*

Gordon Swanborough *128-31, 148-51, 198-201, 254-5, 266-9, 380-91, 416-9*
Since becoming a staff writer on *The Aeroplane* and *The Aeroplane Spotter* in 1943, Gordon Swanborough has had a distinguished career in aviation journalism. He was appointed Editor of *Flying Review International* in 1964 and now holds a similar appointment with *Air Enthusiast* magazine. His books include Putnam histories of US military and naval aircraft and a reference to all aircraft that have appeared on the British Civil Register

P St John Turner *336-9*
Author of five full-length aviation books by the age of 21, Paul St John Turner is now in his final year of a BSc degree course in commerce and accountancy at Southampton University. He intends to make his ultimate career in the airline industry

John Vader *262-5*
John Vader is an Australian who lived in the outback and served in the AIF and RAAF, as a fighter pilot, 1939-45. Now writing and painting in the South of France and England, he is the author of *Spitfire, Pacific Hawk, Anzac, The Fleet without a Friend* and other books

Martin C Windrow *280-83*
In 1964 Martin Windrow left a London daily newspaper to join the staff of *Flying Review International*. Since then he has worked in magazine and book publishing, and collaborated with Francis Mason in the preparation of *Battle over Britain*

Photographs Index and Acknowledgements

More than 1,275 photographs appear in the 512 pages of *History of Aviation*. They have been taken by, or supplied from the collections of, more than 200 individuals, aircraft and aero-engine manufacturers, air forces, airlines, museums, agencies, the aviation trade press and other bodies. The editors and publishers gratefully acknowledge their indebtedness to all of them; they are listed alphabetically below.
[NOTE: Suffix letters following a page number (T=top, C=centre, B=bottom, L=left, R=right) refer to the position of a photograph *on the page*, and not necessarily in relation to other illustrations on the same page.]

AB Aerotransport 161 BL
Acricius Ltd 291 CR, 315 B, 316
"The Aeroplane" 204 T, 244 B, 277 B
Société Nationale Industrielle Aérospatiale 397 CL
"The Age", Melbourne 174 BC, 174/5 T
Costruzioni Aeronautiche Giovanni Agusta SpA 464/5 C
"Air BP" 59 TL, 103 C, 121 CL, 140 CR, 241 BL, 251 C, 308 BL, 310 (all), 333 B, 334 B, 505 B
Air-Britain 48/9, 148/9 T, 201 CL, 241 TR, 280 T, 290 C upper, 323 TR, 339 B, 346 CR, 348 TR upper, 351 CL upper,